WELCOME

Unprecedented challenges

Changing times on the East Coast main line: in December 2019 LNER withdrew its HSTs from service, with the milestone marked by a four-day farewell tour using a set painted into the original livery. At the conclusion of the tour on 21 December, the set stands at King's Cross alongside one of the Azumas which have replaced them. **TONY MILES**

If there has been one word to sum up the year 2020, it would have to be 'unprecedented'. The coronavirus crisis has had a profound impact on all areas of our lives, and the rail industry is no exception.

The year began with the railways in something of a hiatus, awaiting decisions on the future of High Speed Two and the outcome of the Williams review.

On the former, there was good news when the Government backed the project, albeit with elements of Phase 2b under review through an Integrated Rail Plan setting out how the high-speed line will be phased with other enhancements such as Northern Powerhouse Rail and Midlands Engine Rail. Despite the pandemic, the go-ahead for Phase One has enabled HS2 to begin construction work, with Phase 2a onwards from the West Midlands to Crewe planned to follow not far behind. 2021 is set to be an exciting year for HS2 with many major milestones, not least the start of tunnelling through the Chilterns and the announcement of a preferred bidder for the rolling stock contract.

The Williams review was set to have more profound implications for the structure of the industry, but its publication and outcomes seem to be perpetually delayed. An overhaul of the franchise system was one expected output, but the dramatic fall in passenger demand caused by the pandemic delivered a major perturbation, requiring emergency arrangements for franchisees to enable services to keep operating.

By the autumn, the cost of this was becoming clear, and the Emergency Measures Agreements introduced in March morphed into Emergency Recovery Measures Agreements, albeit with a few exceptions, including for devolved franchises. While implying longer-term stability, in fact the ERMAs prompted tough negotiations between the Department for Transport and franchisees on the terms under which pre-existing franchise agreements could be terminated. And with passenger demand unlikely to return to pre-pandemic levels any time soon, those historic franchise agreements will not be sustainable for very long.

Transport Secretary Grant Shapps, in a somewhat contradictory statement, suggested the pandemic had helped accelerate some of the reforms proposed by the Williams review while at the same time continuing to delay the publication of either the review itself or a White Paper setting out its recommendations. The ambition seems to be for Direct Award contracts as a pathway to concession arrangements, but that pathway seems unlikely to be a smooth one.

A bumpy ride for the passenger sector then, but a happier picture for freight. While the sector took a hit at the height of the pandemic, this was not so pronounced as that for passenger operators and the recovery in demand was much stronger, albeit freight operators received none of the support available to franchises. The biggest challenge for freight looks to be decarbonisation, with electric and diesel haulage the only feasible options at the moment for powering heavy freight trains.

The pandemic has perhaps averted some attention from the decarbonisation challenge, but it has also heightened awareness of issues around air quality. The publication of Network Rail's Traction Decarbonisation Network Strategy (TDNS) and the Scottish Government's Rail Services Decarbonisation Action Plan both help advance the case for diesel replacement, and both point to the need for a major programme of electrification. Probably the biggest challenge will be securing funding for this in a world where the pandemic has crippled public sector finances.

A pleasing feature of 2020 was the way the railway industry knuckled down and got on with the job amidst an unprecedented situation. Whether this was keeping services running for key workers and freight deliveries or pressing on with projects, the commitment to overcome the obvious challenges does the industry great credit. Aside from HS2, both development and delivery of infrastructure schemes has made reasonable progress during the year, with much more in the pipeline for 2021.

But despite all these positives, these are uncertain times for the railway. The growing passenger demand on which so many plans for enhancement schemes were built has been obliterated in one fell swoop, and rebuilding passenger confidence and getting passengers back onto trains is a major challenge. With both business and commuting likely to be permanently affected, the railway will need to reorient its focus to a different passenger market.

In this context, a further challenge will be to justify these major projects and enhancements and the investment they require at a time when there will be huge pressure on public finances. Rail will need to fight even harder for every bit of government expenditure, and it seems likely leaner times may be ahead.

Saying all this, the railway has faced tough times before and emerged stronger for it. How the severity of the current situation will compare remains to be seen, but the imperative of forming a united position and presenting a co-ordinated message, both to passengers and politicians, can surely never be greater.

Within these pages we present a snapshot of the industry as it stands towards the end of 2020, in the midst of all this uncertainty. There is much to celebrate and, we hope, much to look forward to, and while the journey may not be a smooth one it is sure to be interesting. ■

PHILIP SHERRATT
Editor, The Modern Railway

CONTENTS

- **3** Welcome from the Editor

SETTING THE AGENDA – INDUSTRY STRUCTURE

- **8** 2021: The year of the rail recovery: Darren Caplan, Chief Executive, Railway Industry Association
- **9** Rail freight faces its challenges: Maggie Simpson, Director General, Rail Freight Group
- **10** Clarity needed in 2021: Elaine Clark, CEO, Rail Forum Midlands
- **11** 2021 – Year of Upheaval: business review by Roger Ford, Industry and Technology Editor of *Modern Railways*
- **16** The rail industry since 1993: a brief history of developments since privatisation
- **18** Coronavirus and the railway: summary of the impact of the pandemic
- **19** Across the Industry: overview of key organisations
    - Government departments
    - Network Rail
    - Industry and regulatory bodies
    - Institutional organisations
    - Campaigning organisations
- **30** Setting the innovation agenda: editorial from BCRRE

FINANCE AND LEASING

- **32** Angel Trains
- **33** Porterbrook
- **34** Eversholt Rail
- **35** Rock Rail
- **36** Britain's rolling stock – who owns it?
- **40** ROSCO fleets

TRAIN FLEET MAINTENANCE AND MANUFACTURE

- **44** Pandemic threatens to reset rolling stock market: review by Roger Ford
- **49** Precision Engineering with the iWFL and ToRFM Systems: editorial from Rowe Hankins
- **50** CAF
- **52** Stadler
- **54** Hitachi
- **56** Bombardier
- **57** Alstom
- **58** Siemens
- **59** Nomad Digital
- **60** Sector specialists

PASSENGER TRAIN OPERATORS

- **64** Emergency measures for franchises and TOC index
- **65** Finances before Covid: review of TOC finances
- **70** Train operator owning groups
- **72** FirstGroup and Trenitalia TOCs: Avanti West Coast, Great Western Railway, South Western Railway, TransPennine Express, Hull Trains, c2c
- **80** Serco, Abellio and Mitsui TOCs: Merseyrail, Caledonian Sleeper, East Midlands Railway, Greater Anglia, ScotRail, West Midlands Trains
- **87** Operator of Last Resort TOCs: LNER, Northern
- **90** Arriva TOCs: Chiltern Railways, CrossCountry, London Overground, Grand Central
- **96** Govia TOCs: Govia Thameslink Railway, Southeastern
- **99** Transport for Wales Rail Services
- **100** MTR Elizabeth line
- **101** Heathrow Express
- **101** Getlink
- **102** Eurostar

FREIGHT AND HAULAGE

- **104** Rail freight's decarbonisation opportunity: *The Modern Railway* freight review
- **111** Rail freight fights back: report on freight operator finances
- **112** DB Cargo

113	GB Railfreight
114	Freightliner
115	Freight and haulage operators

INNOVATION AND ENVIRONMENT

118	The future of Britain's railway depends on people and skills: editorial from Porterbrook
119	Decarbonisation strategy published: review of documents from Network Rail and Transport Scotland
122	Top innovations celebrated: review of *Modern Railways* Fourth Friday Club events
124	Back to basics: *Modern Railways* columnist Alan Williams assesses community rail developments

MAJOR PROJECTS

128	HS2 gets building
132	Crossrail opening slips to 2022
133	East West Rail construction underway
134	Cross-Pennine connectivity in focus

INFRASTRUCTURE ENHANCEMENT AND RENEWAL

136	Resilience – coping with a changing world: analysis by Roger Ford
138	Putting passengers first: Network Rail completes restructure
139	Projects beat the pandemic: review of infrastructure schemes in 2020

SIGNALLING AND CONTROL

| 149 | Signalling schemes press on |
| 151 | Digital railway cost reduction plan |

LIGHT RAIL AND METRO

| 154 | Transport for London |
| 157 | Light rail developments |

INTO EUROPE

| 162 | Europe looks to post-pandemic world: review by *Modern Railways* Europe Editor Keith Fender |

THE MODERN RAILWAY DIRECTORY

| 168 | Compendium of more than 2,800 rail businesses, suppliers and industry bodies |

Skegness HST: 2020 was expected to be the last year in which East Midlands Railway operated HSTs to Skegness on summer Saturdays. No 43257 leads the 12.35 Skegness to Nottingham service at Heckington on 29 August 2020, with No 43296 on the rear. **PHILIP SHERRATT**

The Modern Railway

Editor: Philip Sherratt
Production Editor: David Lane
Contributors: Chris Cheek, Keith Fender, Roger Ford, John Glover, Tony Miles, Alan Williams, Julian Worth
Advertisement Manager: James Farrell
Business Development Manager: Daren Davis
Advertising Production: Rebecca Antoniades
Design: Matt Chapman

Group CEO: Adrian Cox
Chief Content & Commercial Officer: Mark Elliott
Head of Production: Janet Watkins
Head of Design: Steve Donovan
Head of B2B Sales: Tristan Taylor
Head of Distance Selling: Martin Steele
Head of Finance: Nigel Cronin
Head of Content: Hans Seeberg
Head of Content Management: Finbarr O'Reilly
Chief Digital Officer: Vicky Macey

The Modern Railway is published by:
Key Publishing Limited, PO Box 100,
Stamford, Lincolnshire PE9 1XP

Printing:
Printed by Melita Press, Malta

Purchasing additional copies of *The Modern Railway*:
Please contact the Key Publishing mail order team on 01780 480404. Corporate and bulk purchase discounts are available on request.

Thank you!
We are very grateful to the many individuals from businesses in all sectors of the railway who have kindly provided help in compiling *The Modern Railway*. Information contained in *The Modern Railway* was believed correct at the time of going to press in November 2020. We would be glad to receive corrections and updates for the next edition.

© Key Publishing Ltd 2021

All rights reserved. No part of this publication may be reproduced or transmitted in any form by any means, electronic or mechanical, including photocopying, recording or by any information storage and retrieval system, without prior permission in writing from the copyright owner. Multiple copying of the contents of the publication without prior written approval is not permitted.

Cover photo: Greater Anglia Class 745 at Norwich. Keith Fender

ISBN 978-1-913295-68-4

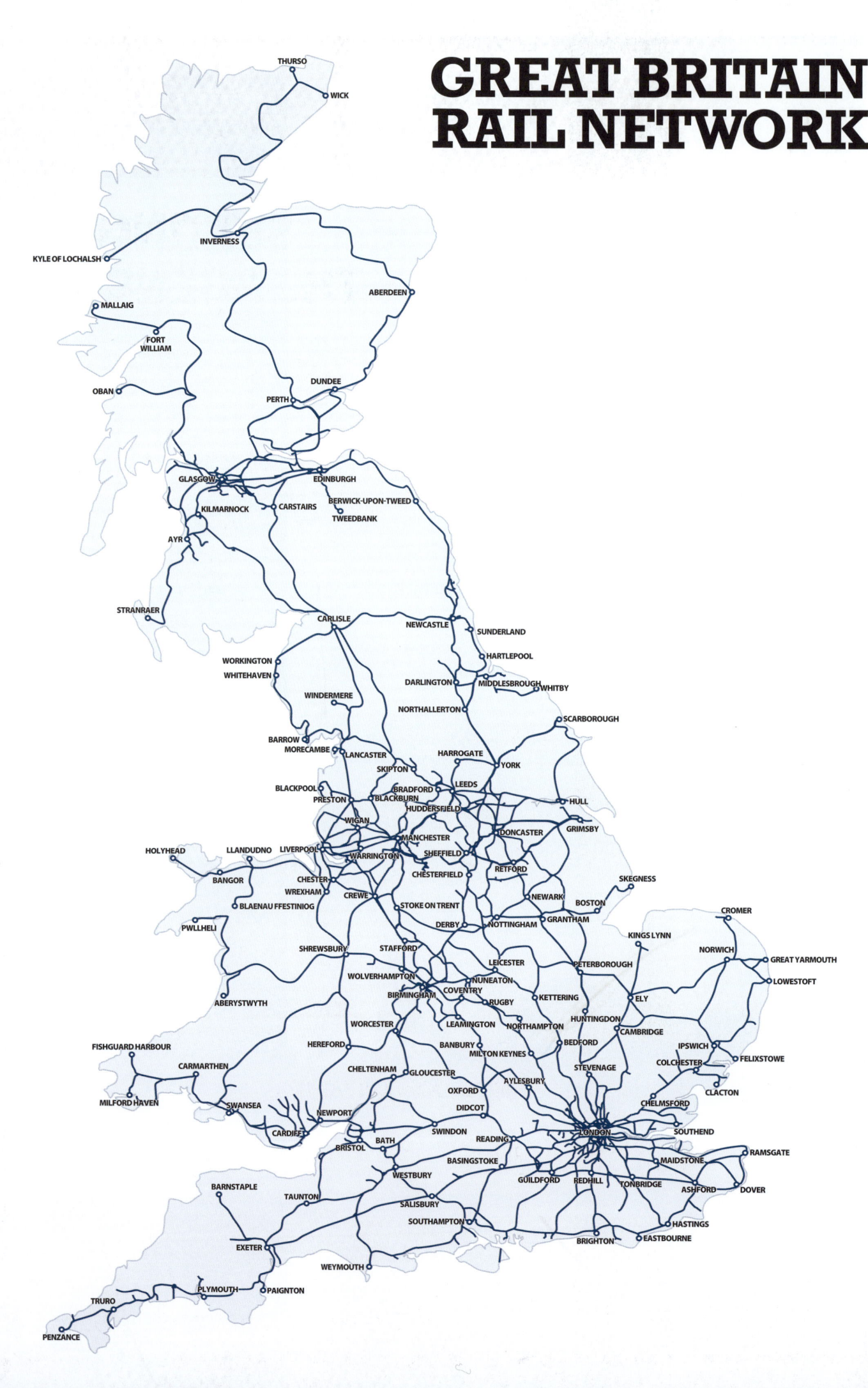

SETTING THE AGENDA

IN ASSOCIATION WITH

UNIVERSITY OF BIRMINGHAM | BCRRE   railalliance   UKRRIN

SETTING THE AGENDA

Projects pressing on: schemes completed in 2020 despite the challenges of coronavirus included the opening of the new platform 5 at Stevenage station as part of the East Coast upgrade. **STUDIO 66 PHOTOGRAPHY**

2021: THE YEAR OF THE RAIL RECOVERY

2020 was set to be the year that the UK rail industry was to finally get some much-needed certainty on its future.

Politically, there was now a Government majority, giving the governing party a concrete foundation and mandate to deliver its manifesto. In the industry, the long-awaited Williams rail review was soon to be published, setting out how the Government would restructure the rail sector, including what financial model would replace the franchise system.

On infrastructure projects, there was a clear commitment from Government on the importance of renewing and enhancing our rail network, and the High Speed 2 Oakervee review, although not yet released, was rumoured to confirm the UK's commitment to HS2, laying to rest the question of whether the project should go ahead.

Internationally, Brexit was going ahead early in the year and the EU withdrawal agreement had been confirmed – with trade negotiations with the EU and other nations getting started, businesses were anticipating a clear sense of the Government's priorities going forward.

THE CORONAVIRUS PANDEMIC

Then coronavirus struck. Instead of the rail industry securing the much-desired certainty it needed, 2020 has turned out to be one of the most uncertain, tumultuous and challenging years in living memory. The pandemic has had implications right across society, and its impact will be felt for many years to come, whether on public health or the economy.

Nevertheless, coronavirus – and the response to it – has also demonstrated rail's worth. In the darkest days of the spring national lockdown, rail workers across the country worked tirelessly to keep services running so key workers and resources could get to where they needed to be. UK rail showed itself to be an essential service, which could be relied on when needed, and everyone in the railway industry should be proud of their work.

The pandemic could lead to a significant change in the way the industry functions and we should look to keep many of the collaborative behaviours developed over the past few months. When it comes to passenger numbers, though, we should be careful about forecasting the future based on 2020 alone – rail is a 30-year plus business.

Most notably, in March the industry saw passenger numbers fall dramatically, with ridership at between 10% to 30% of past levels between March and the time of writing (October). If this continued over the coming years, it would of course pose challenges to the industry. Promoting the benefits of rail will be crucial to coaxing passengers back.

BUILDING BACK RAIL

Yet, whether we think passenger numbers will return in a year, two years, or in a decade, we must not lose sight of the importance of rail to our economy and to society. We need to ensure we have a railway ready for them when they do return. That means ensuring the recommendations of the Williams review are published quickly, so industry has the certainty of what the future holds, whilst investing in and accelerating infrastructure improvements now whilst there is less traffic on the network.

The Government has set out its agenda to 'build back better', investing in infrastructure to spur an economic recovery. Rail is a prime candidate for this investment – our railways are spread across the UK, so any funding will go directly to towns and communities where investment is much needed. Rail investment is green and can help the UK meet its net zero goal. And rail catalyses economic growth, with every £1 spent in rail generating £2.20 in the wider economy.

This will require speeding up rail projects, and to do so the Government must work with the rail supply community. The rail industry will also have to work even harder to show value for money – that it can deliver efficiently, to time and to budget, at a time where the Treasury will be under pressure to make every penny count.

But there is plenty we can do today. Rail enhancements could be accelerated by simplifying and speeding up the Rail Network Enhancements Pipeline. Delivering a consistent profile of electrification, for example, could help deliver a low carbon railway whilst also generating jobs and investment now.

On rolling stock, the sector is ready to invest in low carbon rolling stock, whether new or refurbished. This requires a steer from Government as to its priorities for a clear rolling stock strategy for the years ahead – one that develops a sustainable rolling stock sector without the volatility of previous times.

On digital railway, with 60% of signalling units on the rail network requiring renewal over the next 15 years, there is both a huge challenge and opportunity to develop a new digital network that utilises in-cab signalling to improve capacity and reliability. With a significant amount of work required in Control Period 7 (2024-29), now is the time to bring forward work, so the industry can be 'match fit' for the decade ahead.

As we look to 2021, there are many challenges ahead, whatever the impacts and effects of coronavirus. We must now be ready for a new world where rail will play an increasingly important role, safely and cleanly transporting people and freight around the UK. Rail can also be a catalyst for the country, as it seeks to reboot its economy in the months and years to come. ■

Darren Caplan
Chief Executive, Railway Industry Association

IN ASSOCIATION WITH UNIVERSITY OF BIRMINGHAM | BCRRE | railalliance | UKPRIN

RAIL FREIGHT FACES ITS CHALLENGES

The fortunes of freight transport are dictated by numerous factors, but none so important as the economic health of the country. In downturns, consumer spending falls, construction falters and factory output is suppressed. Imports reduce at ports, and exports can suffer, particularly if the recession is being felt globally.

You might therefore think that the rail freight sector would approach 2021 with some trepidation – and of course you would not be wrong. The twin factors of Covid and the end of the Brexit transition period signal a long period of uncertainty ahead, building on what has already been a disastrous year for the UK. But there are also many reasons for a more positive outlook, and the opportunity to build success over the months ahead.

Rail freight has suffered from the impacts of Covid and the prolonged periods of lockdown. As private sector businesses, freight train operators have not had any direct Government support other than through schemes such as furlough. They have had to be fleet footed to respond to the rapidly changing requirements of their customers, whilst also maintaining financial security.

Meanwhile, customers have seen their demand for rail vary significantly – in some cases services stopped as economic output plummeted, and in others volumes increased as demand for supermarket goods soared. Overall, rail freight volumes dropped to around 50% in April and May 2020, recovering to over 90% of usual levels by the autumn. That recovery outperformed many sectors, and certainly was ahead of passenger rail. So, as we move into 2021, we will all be watching to see whether the recovery can sustain and indeed return to growth.

HS2 has been a particular boost for rail freight with the construction of Phase One now underway. Since the Notice to Proceed was issued in the late spring of 2020, we have seen an increase in construction volumes into terminals in the West Midlands, and the first 'direct' train ran into the Washwood Heath terminal in August. These trains are supplying construction aggregates and cement for the project, and the number of services will increase as the building work ramps up. This will also include removal of construction waste once tunnelling work commences. Other infrastructure, such as the roads programme, is also helping create demand.

In intermodal, new services have been starting across the autumn, including new flows into the East Midlands Gateway terminal, and a new route into Daventry from Teesport. Tesco has also been trialling fresh produce from Spain via the Channel Tunnel and HS1 and into warehouses in Barking. So we are seeing no shortage of appetite in our customers to use more rail freight in their supply chains. The likely changes to our trade after the end of the Brexit transition period may also bring more traffic to rail, particularly if companies look to move away from roll on, roll off (ro-ro) ferries on the Dover Straits to using lift on, lift off services via other ports, or move to direct rail freight services through the Channel Tunnel which have the ability for customs clearance at the inland terminal.

So what are the challenges ahead? The most basic is capacity on the network for those new trains and making sure the paths we have are as efficient as they can be. With fewer passengers travelling, there is a good opportunity to rebalance the service pattern to support freight productivity. This is often about small changes to schedules which can improve the running performance of a train. More structurally, we also need to look at how capacity is shared between modes if there is less demand for more passenger trains.

Secondly, we need to make sure rail reform works for rail freight as well as for passengers. Although the commercial model for franchises has fundamentally changed, that for freight has not, and freight operators remain in the private sector without any direct contract with Government. The framework for the railway therefore needs to give those private sector companies the certainty they need to continue growing, making investments and employing skilled people in their businesses. This means Network Rail must offer fair and equal access for freight, and there will still be a strong role for the Office of Rail and Road.

Finally, we need to continue making progress on decarbonisation. In the last year there has been a great deal of research and development to bring real clarity to the challenges and options ahead. There is a real energy in operators and customers to reduce fuel use and carbon, but we now also need to start making progress on electrification for freight. There are a number of small infill schemes that would enable whole journeys to use electric haulage today (for example, the link to London Gateway port), and we need freight to be included as a core part of any electrification work that is undertaken on the trunk network (such as Trans-Pennine).

We hope the introduction to the 2022 *Modern Railways* yearbook will be able to say that the uncertainty of Brexit and Covid is behind us. Yet whatever happens, the rail freight industry remains in a good place to deliver growth for its customers in the year ahead. ■

Maggie Simpson
**Director General,
Rail Freight Group**

Cornish china clay: DB Cargo's No 66020 alongside the river Fowey at Golant with a Goonbarrow Junction to Fowey Dock Carne Point working on 9 September 2020. **KEN BRUNT**

SETTING THE AGENDA

Clarity needed in 2021

In the last edition of *The Modern Railway* directory, Roger Ford predicted 2020 would be a year of 'turmoil'. I suspect not even Roger could foresee it would turn out to be just as tumultuous as it has been, for the reasons we have all had to come to terms with.

2020 was always set to be a year of change. The long-awaited Williams review was to be published and Network Rail would complete its major restructuring and devolution process. But this time last year, when colleagues were writing their contributions to the directory, no-one had heard of Covid-19 and none of us could have predicted the huge impact it would have on our everyday lives or our industry.

At the start of the pandemic the UK Government made a clear strategic decision to support rail, underwriting passenger franchises following a collapse in passenger numbers and hence fares as people heeded the Government's message to 'stay at home'. Network Rail made a herculean effort to engage with its suppliers and ensure prompt payment flowed down through the supply chain, maintaining much-needed liquidity for many smaller organisations.

Throughout the Covid-19 crisis Rail Forum Midlands (RFM) has kept members aware of evolving Government policies and acted as a conduit for key issues into Westminster. In September Government signalled the end to the current franchising model with the introduction of Emergency Recovery Measures Agreements (ERMAs), which will run for up to 18 months. Whilst these provide much-needed stability compared to the situation in some other industries, it is clear there is additional scrutiny now being applied to previously agreed projects; this is a source of frustration for the supply chain and has had the unfortunate effect of stopping us from delivering the very projects that have been identified as being vital for improving the passenger experience. RFM will continue to work with both members and Government with a view to ensuring the emergence of a robust but pragmatic decision-making process and we will keep members updated on proposed new industry structures so they are best prepared for any new opportunities and challenges.

Despite the pandemic, the industry has achieved a lot in 2020 – be it infrastructure project delivery, the start of HS2 construction work, delivery of more new rolling stock or the next phase of development and testing of new technologies to support decarbonisation. 2020 has seen the publication of the Traction Decarbonisation Network Strategy, a refreshed and simplified Rail Technical Strategy and the commencement of work on a Whole Industry Strategic Plan. The latter is something many have long argued for and it can't come soon enough, but it does need the involvement of the whole industry and the rail supply chain and we will play our part to represent our members' interests.

Tragically, 2020 also saw the derailment of a passenger train at Stonehaven in Scotland and our thoughts and our sympathies remain with all those involved; this extremely sad event served as a sobering reminder that we must never take safety for granted.

At the time of writing, the end of the transition period with the EU will soon be upon us, and with no sign of a deal in place it is a worrying time for many UK companies. As we look forward, it is vital UK Government addresses the concerns of suppliers to ensure not just a level playing field for them to compete on but to address once and for all the issue of 'lowest initial cost' versus 'whole life cost', both on infrastructure and in rolling stock. We owe it to the companies that have kept rail moving during the pandemic to ensure they have those opportunities going forward and we owe it to UK taxpayers that they get value for money from our investment in rail in the broadest economic and social sense.

Only by working together can we restore the confidence of passengers to use public transport and only together can we provide the confidence to Government to continue to invest in the railway as a long-term asset and carbon-friendly mode of transport – for people and freight. Rail has a key role to play in the country's decarbonisation efforts and in the 'levelling up' agenda.

At the 2020 RFM Annual Conference a Government Minister said the 'best days of the industry lie ahead'. I firmly believe that and as we look forward to 2021, whilst there is perhaps much 'turmoil' still to come, I hope the coming year will bring the much needed clarity the industry we exist to serve both needs and deserves. ■

Elaine Clark
CEO, Rail Forum Midlands

Heart of the Midlands: EMR's No 222104 at Derby on 7 February 2020. **PHILIP SHERRATT**

NHS tribute: the coronavirus pandemic saw numerous trains adorned with liveries recognising the efforts of key workers, particularly NHS staff. This striking example was applied to the driving vehicles of GWR IET No 802020, with the words 'The nation says thank you'. The set forms the 13.28 Paddington to Cheltenham Spa service approaching Swindon South Marston Junction on 2 July 2020. **KEN BRUNT**

2021 – YEAR OF UPHEAVAL

Modern Railways Industry and Technology Editor **Roger Ford** sets the scene for an unprecedented year for the railway

Last year, *The Modern Railway* forecast that 2020 would be a 'year of turmoil'. But the emerging uncertainties we identified were soon swept away by the all-consuming turmoil of the coronavirus pandemic, which will dominate policy through 2021 and beyond.

With lockdown came government warnings about reserving train travel for key workers. 'Do not travel by train unless your journey is essential, and even then try to use an alternative form of transport' was the gist of the Government's advice.

This was successful, with train ridership initially falling to 5% of levels before the lockdown. Clearly, train operators taking revenue risk could not survive without farebox income. The Department for Transport responded by providing Emergency Measures Agreements (EMA).

Under an EMA, the train operating companies (TOCs) handed over any income they received and DfT paid their pre-lockdown operating costs. There was also a management fee of 1.5% of the cost base plus a potential 0.5% performance related incentive payment.

LIFE SUPPORT

At the depth of the ridership collapse, EMAs were costing DfT around £700 million per four-weekly reporting period. This reduced slightly as ridership returned and revenue increased. Even so, the Treasury was concerned by what it saw as the 'generosity' of the EMAs and the speed with which they were introduced. The Welsh Assembly Government also expressed its irritation that it was 'bounced' by DfT into accepting the 2% management fee when it had been prepared to drive a harder bargain.

Having put the TOCs on Government life support, DfT found that getting out of the deal was more difficult, particularly with the Treasury looking to cut public spending. A repeated concern voiced by the Treasury was the large number of trains running almost empty. However, DfT had pressured TOCs to restore full timetables to ensure availability of the maximum number of seats within social distancing rules.

Eventually an exit 'glide path' was agreed. On 21 September Transport Secretary Grant Shapps made the historic announcement that, after 24 years, rail franchising had ended.

Emergency Recovery Measures Agreements (ERMAs) would take over from EMAs, 'moving operators onto transitional contracts to prepare the ground for the new railway'. Described as 'the first step in bringing Britain's fragmented network back together', the ERMAs also heralded an early start on key reforms, including, ominously, 'driving down the railways' excessive capital costs'.

ERMAs were expected to morph into new direct award franchise agreements. These would buy time to procure the long-term replacement for franchises – assumed to be the concessions recommended by the (still unpublished) Williams review.

TREASURY GRAB

Behind the bland announcement, the ERMAs contained a major shock for train operators. In addition to the basic management fee being cut to 0.5%, by 13 December 2020 each TOC had to agree the terms for terminating its existing franchise agreement when the ERMA ended. This could include making 'termination payments' to DfT.

Franchise agreements include bonded financial commitments from the owning group. The largest of these

KEEPING THE RAILWAY RUNNING

'Until passenger numbers return, significant taxpayer support will still be needed, including under the transitional contracts announced today. But the reforms will enable substantial medium and longer-term savings for taxpayers.'
DfT announcement, 21 September 2020

SETTING THE AGENDA

King's Cross remodelling: major works are planned in the station throat in 2021, but will the extra capacity be needed post-pandemic? Azuma No 800107 departs with the 10.06 to Newark Northgate on 29 July 2019. **PHILIP SHERRATT**

are the Parent Company Support (PCS) and the Performance Bond.

If the franchise is loss-making, the PCS is drawn down to compensate for the revenue shortfall. This support is capped: when the money runs out the franchise defaults. When Virgin Trains East Coast defaulted, the PCS cost the owners £260 million.

In addition, the Performance Bond is forfeited and the franchise's Net Asset Value also passes to DfT. These assets, typically worth low double figure millions of pounds, are normally sold to the successor franchise operator.

Several loss-making franchises were saved from default by the EMAs. According to DfT's Director General Rail Ruth Hannant, while operators should not be penalised for the effect of the pandemic on their business, they 'absolutely should not be relieved of any losses that they would have suffered if the pandemic had not occurred'.

DOOMSDAY MODEL

DfT commissioned consultant LEK to develop a model which generated a projection of a TOC's financial performance had the pandemic not occurred. This was shared with the nine operators with ERMAs (Table 1). A panel of DfT officials and experts reviewed the responses 'and incorporated them into the model where relevant'.

Had there been no pandemic, and rail travel and the economy had continued as normal, the LEK model calculates how long a loss-making 'zombie' franchise would have continued in business before the PCS ran out. If it would have defaulted before the end of the franchise term, DfT wanted the remaining PCS plus any bonds which would have been forfeited.

These 'transition payments' had to be agreed by 13 December 2020. If agreement could not be reached, the previous franchise agreement would be reinstated from mid-January 2021. With reduced ridership, the franchise would rapidly burn through the PCS and go bust.

Should a TOC agree termination costs, DfT would negotiate a new direct award contract to follow on from the expiry of the ERMA. This would then lead into bidding for the award of a long-term concession.

A significant feature of the ERMA negotiations was that cross-default – a feature of franchise agreements – did not apply. Although never enforced, cross-default meant that if a franchise failed, the owning group also lost any other franchises. With no cross-default, franchise operators were able to choose which TOCs they wanted to keep, although this did not free them from any termination payments due to default.

COST REDUCTION

As a result, 2021 opens with substantial uncertainty surrounding the operation of the passenger railway. As Table 1 also shows, while most ERMAs run for six, 12 or 18 months, some continue to the end of franchises or management agreements. In addition to uncertainty over the nature and terms of the contracts which replace the ERMAs, there is also the question of whether the Operator of Last Resort (OLR) will have added to its stable of defaulted TOCs.

But dominating the year will be the rate at which traffic and revenue

TABLE 1: TRAIN OPERATOR STATUS PRIOR TO 13 DECEMBER 2020

OPERATOR	OWNER	CURRENT STATUS	ERMA TERM ENDS
Direct awards			
LNER	Operator of Last Resort	Direct award to June 2023 plus two-year option	n/a
Northern	Operator of Last Resort		n/a
Southeastern	Govia (Go-Ahead (65%)/Keolis (35%))	Direct award to October 2021 plus six-month option	EMA continues
Great Western Railway	FirstGroup	Direct award to March 2023 plus 12-month option	EMA continues
Concessions			
TfL Rail (Crossrail)	MTR (Hong Kong Mass Transit Railway)	Concession to May 2023	n/a
London Overground	Arriva (Deutsche Bahn)	Concession to November 2024	n/a
Merseyrail	Serco/Abellio (Netherlands Railway)	Concession to July 2028	n/a
Transport for Wales Rail	KeolisAmey/Transport for Wales Rail (2)	Operator and Delivery Partner to October 2033	EMA to February 2021
Franchises			
Caledonian Sleeper	Serco	Franchise to April 2030	January 2021
ScotRail*	Abellio (Netherlands Railways)	Franchise to April 2022	January 2021
South Western Railway*	FirstGroup (70%)/MTR (30%)	Franchise to August 2024	March 2021
c2c*	Trenitalia	Franchise to November 2029	March 2021
TransPennine Express*	FirstGroup	Franchise to April 2023	March 2021 – option to September 2021 (1)
Govia Thameslink Railway	Govia (Go-Ahead (65%)/Keolis (35%))	Management contract to September 2021	September 2021
Greater Anglia*	Abellio (Netherlands Railways, 60%)/Mitsui (40%)	Franchise to October 2025	September 2021
West Midlands Trains	Abellio (Netherlands Railways, 70%)/JR East (15%)/Mitsui (15%)	Franchise to March 2026	September 2021
Chiltern Railways	Arriva (Deutsche Bahn)	Franchise to December 2021	December 2021
East Midlands Railway	Abellio (Netherlands Railways)	Franchise to August 2027	March 2022
West Coast Partnership	FirstGroup (70%)/Trenitalia (30%)	Franchise to March 2026, option on five-year extension	March 2022
CrossCountry	Arriva (Deutsche Bahn)	OCFA to October 2023, plus one-year option	n/a

* has incurred losses or identified onerous contract provision; (1) subject to no default being indicated under termination agreement; (2) takes over operational responsibility from February; EMA = emergency measures agreement; ERMA = emergency recovery measures agreement; OCFA = operating contract franchise agreement

will return. In the first quarter of 2020-21, essentially the first three months of lockdown, revenue for the franchised TOCs was £170 million. In contrast, DfT payments to TOCs under the EMAs were £2 billion.

Subsequently ridership continued to recover, reaching 40% of pre-pandemic levels, before falling back to around 30% as restrictions tightened with the second wave (Figure 1), with a four-week 'firebreak' lockdown in England added during November. In the case of ScotRail, the six months of restrictions had already reduced revenue to around £90 million compared with operating costs, before track access charges of £400 million.

While Government statements referred to the new structures as cutting the railways' 'excessive capital costs', in the short-term the ERMAs incentivise performance rather than reductions in operating costs. Table 2 shows the breakdown of TOC operating costs for 2018-19 with the support required under ERMA. Note that this is in addition to the £3.9 billion paid in direct grant to Network Rail.

With ERMA payments costing an optimistic £500 million per month, this analysis explains the Treasury's demand to recover transition payments, put at around £500 million in total. This was coupled with pressure for operating cost savings in the short term.

POTENTIAL CUTS

At the time of privatisation, a franchise's costs were split roughly equally between staff, rolling stock leases and track access charges. Track access charges paid to Network Rail are a 'wooden dollar' transaction, since Network Rail is an arm of Government. This leaves staff costs and rolling stock leases plus maintenance as the primary targets for cost reduction.

Under the EMAs and ERMAs staff numbers have been protected. When the ERMA replacements come into effect, cost reduction measures are likely to be prioritised.

Source: Department for Transport

Staff cuts are unlikely to affect frontline staff. For example, social distancing has restricted driver training. The driver and conductor age profile means shielding has also reduced numbers available.

However, there is potential for savings in back office staff, where groups owning multiple franchises could consolidate activities, such as social media, ticket sales and accounting, subject to DfT approval.

RATIONALISATION

On several routes, franchised operators provide overlapping services. With traffic, especially commuting, unlikely to return to previous levels, over-capacity, even with social distancing, is likely to be an issue. For example, in the 2019 'summer' timetable, York to Newcastle had four trains an hour: CrossCountry leaving at 10.31; LNER at 10.35 and 10.54; and TransPennine Express at 11.07.

On 8 October 2020, DfT wrote to Network Rail Chief Executive Andrew Haines commissioning 'a review of the way capacity is allocated on the East Coast main line'. DfT emphasised the work would be 'from the perspective of a neutral single guiding mind, not in your capacity as CFO of NR'.

Noting that the May 2022 timetable is already in development, DfT said that starting from a 'blank sheet' and remaining agnostic of operator during timetable development 'may yield a more efficient way to use the network'. Significantly, DfT recognised that starting from a 'blank sheet' 'may lead to recommendations that are not deliverable within the current legislative and regulatory environment'. Mr Haines was prompted to work with the Office of Rail and Road to establish which recommendations could be delivered now and which would require a change to the current system.

Overall, given the lead time on new timetables – over a year – any attempt to match capacity closer to demand and reduce rolling stock costs is unlikely to come into effect before the December 2021 timetable.

INFRASTRUCTURE SAVINGS

Reduced train mileage would result in lower track access charges (TACs) for TOCs. These charges have two components.

A fixed charge represents the notional cost of providing the infrastructure. The Variable Usage Charge (VUC) is a surrogate for the wear and tear caused by train operation and is based on vehicle mileage, with a cost per mile allocated to each vehicle.

Typically, the fixed component represents around 15% of the total. However, while savings for the TOC would result from lower mileage, this would reduce Network Rail's income.

Network Rail's programme of maintenance and renewal work, plus associated line closures, is integrated with the timetable and planned up to 18 months in advance. Thus any reduction in TACs would require further direct funding by DfT until the reduced schedule came into effect. However, Network Rail has already studied contingency plans for reductions in renewals spending of up to £1 billion a year for the remaining years of Control Period 6 (2019-24).

TABLE 2: FRANCHISED TOCs ANNUAL BUDGET AT NOTIONAL 40% RIDERSHIP

	£ MILLION
Costs (less track access charges)	5,642
Track access charges	4,751
Total cost	10,393
Revenue (40% ridership)	3,870
ERMA support	6,523
Less previous subsidy	(400)
Net ERMA support	6,123
ERMA support per month	**510**

Source: ORR and DfT data

TABLE 3: TOC OPERATING COSTS, 2018-19

	£ MILLION
Staff costs	2,960
Fuel costs	359
Rolling stock charges	2,323
Total	**5,642**

Source: ORR

SETTING THE AGENDA

Meanwhile, major capacity and other enhancements projects have continued during the pandemic. They will, of course, come on line at a time when the only constraint on ridership is the number of seats available under social distancing requirements, rather than track capacity.

Network Rail has also been taking advantage of the less busy network to bring maintenance work forward. In the first six periods of 2020-21, expenditure on Operations, Maintenance and Renewals was around £170 million ahead of programme.

On major projects, reduced demand in the commuter market has allowed some recovery of the schedule for the King's Cross capacity works, with the upgraded station opening in June this year, almost a year earlier than originally feared.

Also on the ECML at Werrington, following a nine-day closure in January a further three-day blockade will complete the dive-under project in 'mid-2021'. Further north, Stage 2 of the ECML Power Supply Upgrade (PSU2) between Bawtry and Edinburgh has been authorised. This will provide sufficient power for all electric operations over sections where bi-modes are currently required to run under diesel traction.

These works will provide eight long-distance paths an hour. The new timetable, including the new FirstGroup open access service, is now planned for May 2022. Whether the full capacity will now be required remains uncertain.

FREIGHT

For freight, 2020 was a case of survival. In the first quarter of 2020-21, effectively the first three months of lockdown, at 3.16 billion net tonne kilometres total freight moved was down 26% on Q1 2019-20.

Since the demise of coal traffic, two commodities generate around 70% of freight tonne kilometres. Domestic intermodal now represents around 40% of freight tonne kilometres, with construction at 30%. Domestic intermodal fell 22% in the first quarter of lockdown, with construction traffic suffering a 37% drop.

Investments by the freight operators suggests domestic intermodal traffic is expected to recover in 2021, with new traction and rolling stock on order by GB Railfreight, for example. The switch to online shopping also offers the prospect of new domestic business. Rail Operations (UK) Ltd is launching its new Orion High Speed Logistics service using converted passenger trains to cut road delivery times.

Construction should also see better times in 2021, assuming the Government's 'build back better' slogan transfers into hard projects. To this should be added the growing demand as construction of High Speed 2 gathers pace.

BREXIT

Exit from the European Community will add to the upheaval in 2021. Under the Interoperability Legislation, the use of Technical Specifications for Interoperability (TSIs) for equipment procurement, acceptance and similar activities has ended.

From 1 January 2021, the supply of interoperable equipment to the UK market has been based on a 'UK conformity assessment process'. This requires compliance with 'UK National Technical Specification Notices' (NTSNs).

According to DfT 'the applicable requirements in NTSNs are identical to those contained in EU TSIs'. EC conformity assessment documentation against the relevant TSI requirements will continue to be accepted up to 1 January 2023.

MAJOR PROGRAMMES

Further long-term investment programmes are likely to be put on hold. On 21 October 2020 the Chancellor announced that instead of the expected three-year comprehensive spending review covering spending budgets from 2021-22 to 2023-24, and capital budgets until 2024-25, a one-year spending review for 2021-22 would be published in November. This is likely to delay commitments to major capital expenditure, notably the start of a rolling programme of electrification as recommended by Network Rail's Traction Decarbonisation Network Strategy (TDNS), and could affect the scope of the eastern arm (Phase 2b) of HS2.

NEW WORLD

2021 has been the hardest year to call in the 14 editions of *The Modern Railway*. Clearly, the course of the recovery from the pandemic and its effects on the economy are unpredictable. Whether the Williams report and its recommendations are still relevant is another unknown. Apart from the uncertainty over the transition out of the ERMAs, what succeeds them was unclear as TMR went to press.

According to DfT, the three-year Operating Contract Franchise Agreement (OCFA) awarded to the CrossCountry franchise was unique. The contractual arrangements which will follow the ERMAs 'should termination clauses be successfully agreed' are subject to 'ongoing discussions'. Truly, 2021 is a case of into the unknown. ■

Operating under an OCFA: a new contract for CrossCountry began in October 2020. No 43357 leads the 06.06 Edinburgh to Plymouth service at The Chevin, Milford on 27 May 2020, with No 43301 on the rear. PHILIP SHERRATT

Freight holds up: the sector has fared better than passenger operations through the pandemic. This is Freightliner's No 66556 leading a Southampton to Lawley Street container train at Mortimer on 28 July 2020. KEN BRUNT

We are engineers, innovators and asset managers

At the heart of Britain's railway for over 25 years

London
Lynton House
7-12 Tavistock Square
London, WC1H 9LT
+44 (0) 207 380 4560

Derby
Ivatt House
7 The Point, Pinnacle Way
Pride Park, Derby, DE24 8ZS
+44 (0) 1332 285 050

www.porterbrook.co.uk

porterbrook

SETTING THE AGENDA

The rail industry since 1993

British Rail(ways) was a publicly owned and vertically integrated railway, in which the Board provided the infrastructure, owned the trains and operated the services. Under the Railways Act 1993, those functions were separated into around 100 companies, which notably parted operations from the infrastructure. All were privatised.

Running trains on the national network resulted in a track access regime with a charge payable to the infrastructure company, Railtrack. This included signalling and electrification systems.

The Franchising Director used competitive tendering to let (initially) 26 passenger train operations, nominally for seven-year terms. Awards took into account what the bidders offered for additional services and investment commitments, and whether they would require a subsidy or pay the government a premium.

The independent Rail Regulator plus the Health & Safety Executive undertook the licensing.

Most passenger stations were leased to and then run by the Train Operating Companies (TOCs). Passenger rolling stock was owned by rolling stock companies (ROSCOs), which leased it to the TOCs.

The freight companies (FOCs) owned their locomotives and any wagons not owned by their customers.

The Association of Train Operating Companies (ATOC) provided support services.

NEW GOVERNMENT, NEW IDEAS

The 1997 Labour Government wanted some overall direction and planning, creating the Strategic Rail Authority (SRA). But some franchisees were in financial difficulties and rising traffic levels led to performance problems.

Following the Hatfield derailment of 2000, caused by poor track condition, Railtrack was replaced by Network Rail.

Over time, many franchises were acquired by bus industry groups and/or by overseas companies.

The cost of the railway to the public purse rose fast. Following the Rail Regulator's 2003 ruling, access charges were funded by Government.

The Railways Act 2005 transferred most the SRA's functions to the Department for Transport. Safety policy, regulatory and enforcement functions became the responsibility of the Office of Rail and Road (ORR).

Separately, the Government sets out what Network Rail is expected to deliver for the public money it receives in a High Level Output Statement (HLOS) plus a Statement of Funds Available (SoFA). Control Period 6 covers the years 2019-24.

Political and public faith in the ability of what seemed to be an ever busier railway to contribute to capacity shortfalls, to regional economic growth and the wellbeing of society, was growing. The railway was becoming a solution to problems affecting everybody, rather than being a problem in itself.

DEVOLUTION

Devolution has resulted in Network Rail setting up a Regions and Route structure, while bodies such as Transport for the North are enhancing local decision-making. Transfers of certain powers and budgets to Scotland, Wales and London have also taken place.

What should be determined locally and what centrally? A long-term vision and strategy, together with assured funding, are key requirements.

Operationally, the big challenge will always be to design a timetable that is economical in resource use, makes good use of the available capacity,

Blending the old and the new: visual of Curzon Street HS2 station in Birmingham; on the left is the Old Curzon Street building, which will be incorporated into the design of the high-speed station.

provides connections where needed, and is resilient to problems. It must also meet both passenger and freight traffic needs, if the result is to bring in the revenue. While most passenger traffic is reasonably stable over time, freight flows can alter very quickly.

Is more freedom for TOCs compatible with the aims of public funding and protecting the interests of rail users? How can open access operation be reconciled with the contractual obligations of TOCs?

COPING WITH GROWTH

Growth became a major problem. Platform lengthening and signal repositioning for longer trains is one approach, with the prize being the ability to run (say) 10-car instead of eight-car trains. That raises capacity, but also stock requirements, by 25%.

Advanced signalling systems can allow trains to follow each other more closely, as demonstrated by London Underground on the Victoria Line. With a train every 100 seconds, the time taken to clear the platform of those alighting and refilling it with those wishing to join the next train becomes critical.

The national system challenges are different. Running a stopping service inbetween fast services on the same track will cause nothing but trouble when capacity is at a premium.

Where does the workforce stand? Some TOCs have yet to manage a successful move to Driver Controlled Operation, despite its widespread use on London Underground and elsewhere in Britain. The sad result has been a series of long-running industrial disputes.

The battle to retain passengers: a pair of GWR Intercity Express Trains call at Swindon on a Paddington to Bristol Temple Meads service on 22 November 2018. **TONY MILES**

PASSENGER

What has happened to traffic volumes since privatisation?

Taking the 20 years from 1998-99 to 2018-19, passenger traffic showed sustained growth, as measured in millions of rail passenger kilometres. From a total of 36,300 million, growth was an astonishing 87% in the ensuing two decades, reaching 67,800 million in 2018-19. That was spread over all three business sectors, with regional doing particularly well. Elsewhere, London Underground showed an 81% gain and light rail more than doubled, but that was on a then fast expanding network.

While the start of passenger growth more or less coincided with the mid-1990s privatisation, this was not necessarily the cause. Factors such as employment levels, economic activity generally, population distribution and its age bands are likely to have been rather more important.

So had the new railway age come about? Sadly, it had not. Huge drops in passenger usage occurred in the first half of 2020 as a result of the Covid-19 pandemic (see next page). Suddenly, the train services being provided were vastly in excess of what was needed, even allowing for passengers being spaced out to ensure they were socially distanced. Thus, a two-metre spacing meant only one passenger on each side of a vehicle, with at most only 10 such pairs along its length – and that took no account on the positioning of doors etc. Dealing with heavy commuter traffic (in particular) on such a basis is effectively impossible.

FREIGHT

A similar measure of growth for rail freight showed more of a variation, ending 2018-19 more or less where it started in 1998-99 as measured in millions of net tonne kilometres. This was the result of the almost total loss of its one time staple traffic of coal. This was almost completely offset by vigorous marketing, which resulted in gains, particularly in construction and intermodal traffics.

Since then, Covid-19 effects saw a significant drop in freight traffic, though nothing like as serious as that for passenger. If the construction industry is brought to a halt, so too is the business of those conveying construction materials. By autumn 2020, the rail freight business seemed to have largely recovered.

WHERE NEXT?

Public attitudes towards the railway seem now to be more confused than ever, due in part perhaps to the ever varying messages emanating from ministers. When and where is it safe to travel by train, if indeed it is safe at all? Meanwhile, concerns over fares levels generally, how much people travelling only a few days a week will be asked to pay, and the old favourites of overcrowding and system performance have all been the subject of criticism. Neither, it needs to be said, are such concerns without justification.

Phase One of HS2 to Birmingham now looks secure, with Phase 2a to Crewe also likely to go ahead. Phase 2b on to Manchester and separately via the East Midlands to Leeds is much less certain and is now linked with Northern Powerhouse Rail aspirations based on cross-Pennine developments. Completion before the 2040s now looks unlikely.

Will the result see HS2 as part of a future, vastly superior rail network, or will the overall vision just wither away? That raises questions about the West Coast Partnership, let alone how capacity issues are to be tackled.

The Government's devolution agenda also raises a series of questions. Local services for local people is a worthy goal, but how do the much wider interests of long-distance passengers and, especially, freight operations get taken into account? Are serious improvements to existing routes across the Pennines to be made, including clearance for container traffic, and how does this fit in with a wholly new line? How does any of it relate to the present services, let alone where the funding is coming from?

There is still considerable political uncertainty as to how Brexit issues will be resolved. Other matters concern future sources of traction power if diesel operation is to be eliminated in the next 20 years or so. Should more electrification be part of the answer, and few in the industry doubt it, that work needs to be started as soon as possible. ■

SETTING THE AGENDA

Coronavirus and the railway

The Covid-19 pandemic has had a disastrous effect on the railways in terms of traffic loss. Critically, the Prime Minister announced on 16 March 2020 'Now is the time to stop all unnecessary travel', to ensure public transport was available for use by those termed 'key workers'.

On 23 March, the introduction of six-month Emergency Measures Agreements (EMAs) was announced. These enabled franchise agreements to be superseded. The present operators would continue to run the passenger services, transferring revenue and cost risks to the Government. In exchange, they would be paid a management fee at a maximum of 2% of their cost base for their operation. Broadly similar arrangements with slightly different dates were introduced separately for Wales and Scotland, and for light rail services. See the TfL section for London Underground (p154).

An important element was the introduction of social distancing, whereby people were expected to leave gaps of two metres between themselves and the next person. When applied to trains, in particular, this resulted in the capacity of a vehicle being reduced to perhaps no more than 10% of the total passengers that could normally be carried. Together with strong pressure applied by the Government to avoid rail use and work from home if at all possible, passenger usage continued to fall. Face coverings for passengers became compulsory from 15 June.

JOURNEYS SLUMP

In the last quarter of 2019-20 (to 31 March), passenger journeys fell by 51 million (11.4%) compared with the last quarter of 2018-19. This was the largest fall for any quarter since the time series began in 1994-95. In the first quarter of 2020-21 (April to June) passenger numbers were at their lowest since the mid-19th century.

Passenger numbers rose slowly through the spring and into the summer. On 17 July, the Prime Minister announced: 'anybody may (now) use public transport, while of course encouraging people to consider alternatives…'. Social distancing rules were relaxed slightly and from 1 August working from home ceased to be encouraged.

Face coverings compulsory: passengers at Manchester Piccadilly on 15 June 2020, the day this instruction became a legal requirement. TONY MILES

Passenger journey levels from mid-July continued to rise slowly, reaching 40%-45% of pre-lockdown levels during August, before dropping back to around 35% by the end of September. With renewed calls to work from home as infection levels rose, further rises seemed unlikely.

But how dangerous to health was rail travel? On 20 August RSSB released some encouraging research. This showed the risk of passengers contracting Covid-19 while travelling by train was about 1 in 11,000 journeys, or less than 0.01%.

ERMAs

The EMAs lasted until September 2020 and the Government set out details for their replacements, to last for a period of up to 18 months. These ERMAs (Emergency Recovery Measures Agreements) are another form of management contract. The ERMAs are generally similar to the EMAs they replace, but with higher performance requirements and with lower management fees payable to operators (2.0% down to 1.5%).

The ERMAs will be a prelude to a new system of organisation, based it seems on the report by Keith Williams, which remains unpublished. A White Paper will set out the Government's intentions 'when the course of the pandemic becomes clearer'.

FREIGHT RESILIENT

Rail freight traffic was much less severely affected, with volumes falling significantly at the low point and largely recovering afterwards. Thus the important construction industry traffic relied on the associated construction work continuing, which was only partially the case during lockdown.

LONG-TERM IMPACT

What might the long-term effects on the rail industry be? The key difficulty in coming to any worthwhile conclusion is that the demand for rail transport is derived. With few exceptions, people travel by rail to get to a certain place, whether it is for work, education, shopping, visiting friends and relatives, or another reason. Any enjoyment of the journey itself is only a secondary consideration. Thus travel to or in the course of work is dependent on that work itself existing.

As of autumn 2020, opinions seemed to suggest passenger volumes would not return to more than 50% of pre-Covid levels by the end of 2020. They would then not exceed 80% for the next couple of years or so. Should that prove to be the case, both Government and the industry are likely to be looking to cut costs wherever possible.

The post-Covid situation will need to take into account the levels to which rail traffic has declined, the outlook for its recovery (unlikely to be the same for all sectors), the timescale over which this might take place, and how the industry is to be funded in the interim. Will serious adjustments to the railway services on offer be needed?

This is also a period in which the railway and the products it offers can be reviewed. What is right and what is wrong about the way it has been developed, operated, engineered and managed? Where does more electrification fit in? How important is rail freight in the overall scheme of things and how can it be certain of acquiring suitable infrastructure and train paths? What should the strategic framework be and the place of both private and public organisations? One matter which seems certain to receive attention is fares.

The key questions revolve around the organisation to take charge, the availability of funding and its sources, and who should take what decisions, together with responsibility for their accompanying risks?

Perhaps most importantly, what is the appropriate call the railway should make on public funding, and how compatible is this with the increasingly devolved nature of political control?

Above all, though, the Government needs to stop demonising the railway as an unsafe means of travel, or passenger traffic levels might never recover fully. ■

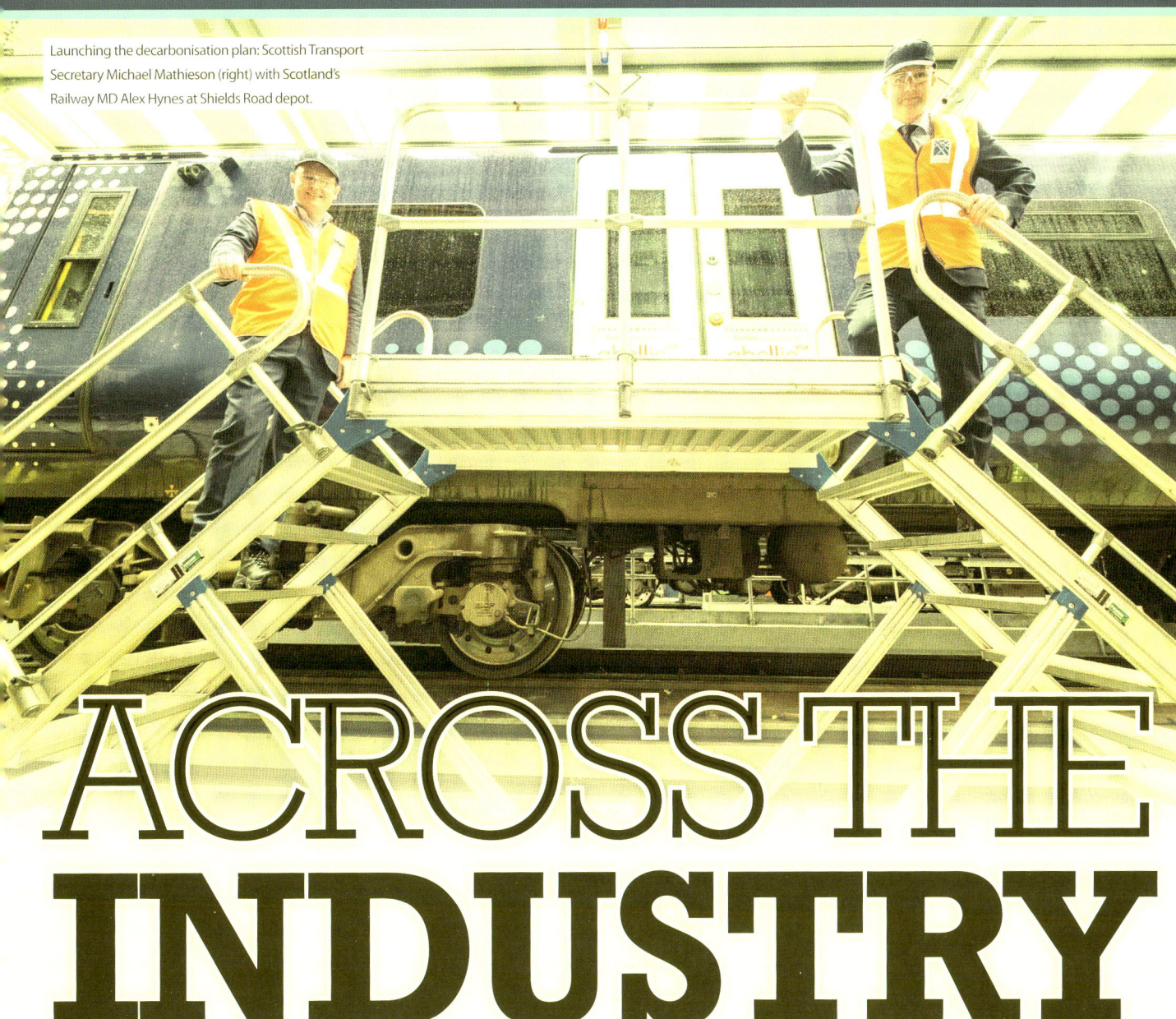

Launching the decarbonisation plan: Scottish Transport Secretary Michael Mathieson (right) with Scotland's Railway MD Alex Hynes at Shields Road depot.

ACROSS THE INDUSTRY

DEPARTMENT FOR TRANSPORT

The Department for Transport (DfT) is the civil service body which delivers the UK Government's objectives for the industry. It sets the strategic direction for rail, funds investment through Network Rail, has awarded and managed rail franchises and regulates rail fares. It encourages the use of new technology and the maintenance of high standards of safety and security.

Priorities include the improvement of the existing network, creating new passenger capacity and influencing how the railway should respond to climate change. The DfT's Office of Rail Passenger Services is responsible for delivery.

With the onset of Covid-19, franchises were in effect suspended from 23 March 2020 when Emergency Measures Agreements were introduced. Operators continued to run services for a pre-determined management fee, with all revenue and costs transferred to the Government.

What might follow is still unclear. The Williams review on possible future arrangements, as seen from before the Covid-19 pandemic, remains unpublished. It was clear that a major rethink of the franchising arrangements was being considered. Are concessions to be preferred? To what extent might or should rail service planning and funding be devolved to more local bodies?

The West Coast Partnership led by First Trenitalia took over the West Coast main line franchise in December 2019. The partnership operates the existing services, but will also be responsible for the planning and execution of Phase One of HS2 operations (London to West Midlands) for a number of years.

However, it is presently unresolved as to how much of the subsequent phases of HS2 will be completed, in their present form or as amended, in what timescale and at what cost. The relationship of HS2 to the Trans-Pennine ambitions of Northern Powerhouse Rail is yet to be resolved.

The parliamentary stages of Phase One of HS2 are complete and Phase 2a to Crewe nearly so. Phase 2b (Manchester/Leeds) remains delayed.

Other matters receiving DfT attention are the much heralded reversing of (some) of the Beeching cuts of more than half a century ago, and the establishment of an Acceleration Unit to speed up transport infrastructure projects. These include some Network Rail projects.

Rail activity at DfT is overseen by a Director General and the franchising programme has a single responsible director.

Secretary of State for Transport Grant Shapps
Minister of State for Rail Chris Heaton-Harris
Director General, Rail Group Polly Payne, Ruth Hannant (job share)
Managing Director, Passenger Services Peter Wilkinson

TRANSPORT SCOTLAND

Transport Scotland is an agency of the Scottish Government, whose purpose is to increase sustainable economic growth through the development of national transport projects and policies. It is accountable through Scottish Ministers.

A total of 93 million passenger journeys are made annually on ScotRail, most of which are entirely within Scotland. The Glasgow area is the largest commuter operation outside London and users account for about 60% of passenger journeys made on Scottish railways. Other Scottish operations are those of Caledonian Sleeper, while Avanti West Coast, CrossCountry, LNER and TransPennine Express provide services originating in England.

SETTING THE AGENDA

Core Valley Lines modernisation: Welsh Transport Minister Ken Skates inaugurates work on the new depot and control centre at Taff's Well in January 2020.

Transport Scotland's Rail Directorate manages the ScotRail and Caledonian Sleeper franchises, the governance of a programme of rail projects, advises ministers on investment priorities and develops future strategies, and liaises with the Office of Rail and Road on Network Rail issues. Safety and the licensing of railway operators remain reserved for Westminster.

Scotland's rail services decarbonisation plan foresees the electrification of an average of 130 single track kilometres of railway every year until 2035. This would extend the wires to Aberdeen, Carlisle via Kilmarnock, Girvan (but not Stranraer), Inverness via Perth, and Tweedbank (on the reinstated part of the Waverley route). Other more minor schemes such as that to East Kilbride would also be implemented. Aberdeen to Inverness might be electrified in a longer timescale. There would also be important effects on freight traffic.

Other lines such as the West Highland line, that to Kyle and the Far North might use 'alternative traction'.

The key strategic outcomes for Network Rail in Transport Scotland's output statement are: improved services, improved capacity, improved value for money for taxpayers, the farepayer and the rail freight customers alike, more effective integration between operations and infrastructure, and economic growth.
Cabinet Secretary for Transport, Infrastructure and Connectivity Michael Matheson
Director of Rail Bill Reeve

TRANSPORT FOR WALES

It is the duty of the Welsh Assembly Government to promote and encourage integrated transport in Wales. Transport for Wales is a wholly-owned, not-for-profit company, established by the Government in 2015.

The network serves a wide range of markets with significant commuting to Cardiff and Swansea. There are important cross-boundary flows to Manchester, Birmingham, Bristol and London, as well as on the borders link between Chester, Shrewsbury, Hereford and Newport. There are also extensive rural services, such as the Central Wales line, services west of Carmarthen, and those to Blaenau Ffestiniog.

The 15-year Operator and Development Partner contract for Wales & Borders was awarded to KeolisAmey, with effect from October 2018. However, in October 2020 the Welsh Government announced day-to-day delivery of rail services would transfer to an agency of Transport for Wales, although KeolisAmey would continue to lead on the upgrade of the Core Valley Lines as part of the South Wales Metro.

The CVL upgrade follows the transfer of infrastructure from Network Rail to TfW in March 2020. £119 million of EU funding has been secured for track doubling, a new depot at Taff's Well and station work for the scheme. This will enable many services to be increased from two to four trains per hour. Cardiff and the Valleys presently account for about half the total number of train services on Network Rail's Wales route.

Orders have been placed with Stadler and CAF for new tram-trains, tri-modes and diesel units to operate most services across the Welsh network. However, the timescale for the Core Valley Lines modernisation has now slipped so badly that some of the promised EU funding will be lost. Some other capital schemes may be paused or cancelled as a result.

A National Development Framework for Wales is due to be adopted formally in 2021.
Minister for Economy, Transport and North Wales Ken Skates
TfW Chief Executive James Price

LOCAL GOVERNMENT IN ENGLAND

Combined Authorities (CAs) are legal bodies set up using national legislation that enables a group of two or more councils in England to collaborate and take collective decisions across council boundaries. They are responsible for economic development as well as general transport policies.

Passenger Transport Executives (PTEs) in the former metropolitan areas are statutory bodies, responsible for setting out policy and expenditure plans for public transport.

They are now responsible to, or have become an executive body of, the Combined Authorities. Some CAs have a considerably greater geographical coverage than the former metropolitan areas. In general, they are not operators, but Tyne and Wear Metro operation is now in house. Merseytravel lets and manages the Merseyrail Electrics concession. The CAs are also information providers.

Elsewhere, but not in London, the Local Transport Authority is either the unitary authority or the county council. They are responsible for transport planning, passenger transport and highways.

The Urban Transport Group is a non-statutory body bringing together and promoting the interests of large urban areas.

Local Enterprise Partnerships are voluntary between local authorities and businesses to help determine local economic priorities. Their Strategic Economic Plans set out priorities for transport investment and bids for funding from the Local Growth Fund.

TRANSPORT FOR THE NORTH

Transport for the North (TfN) was the first sub-national transport body (STB) in England to be accorded statutory status in 2018. The Government's aim is to allow groups such as TfN to advise transport ministers on investment priorities in their own areas and on strategic transport schemes to boost growth. Statutory status will give the groups the permanence they need for the long-term.

TfN represents the combined authorities, unitary authorities, county councils and all 11 Local Enterprise Partnerships from north Lincolnshire and Cheshire to the Scottish border. TfN also works with Highways England, HS2 Ltd and Network Rail.

TfN manages the Northern and TransPennine Express franchises. These are partnership agreements with DfT. However, temporary arrangements to cope with the fallout from the Covid-19 pandemic are in place, and what will follow has yet to be seen.

A Strategic Transport Plan set out an extensive programme and a number of options are being considered, chiefly under the Northern Powerhouse Rail programme:
- faster and more frequent services between Liverpool and Manchester Piccadilly, via Warrington and Manchester Airport;
- a new hub station at Manchester Piccadilly;
- faster links between Manchester and Leeds via a new line also serving Bradford;
- a significant upgrade to the Hope Valley line between Sheffield and Manchester, via Stockport;
- Leeds to Sheffield as delivered by HS2 plus upgrading the present route;
- Leeds to Newcastle via a junction with HS2 and significant East Coast main line upgrading;
- significant upgrading for Leeds to Hull and Sheffield to Hull.

A variety of potential funding sources has been identified.
Chairman John Cridland
Chief Executive Barry White

UNIVERSITY OF BIRMINGHAM

www.birmingham...
+44 (0)...

www.railalliance.co.uk
+44 (0)1789 720 026
@therailalliance

at the **heart** of
the UK Rail Supply Chain

UNIVERSITY OF BIRMINGHAM | DR DIGI-RAIL

European Union
European Regional
Development Fund

www.birmingham.ac.uk/digi-rail
digi-rail@contacts.bham.ac.uk
@digi_rail

UKRRIN
UK RAIL RESEARCH AND
INNOVATION NETWORK

www.ukrrin.org.uk
ukrrin@rssb.co.uk
@UKRRIN

to facilitate
acro...

SETTING THE AGENDA

Interchange: visual of the HS2 station in Solihull, with automated people mover connecting to Birmingham International station, the airport and NEC at bottom right.

TRANSPORT FOR WEST MIDLANDS

The transport arm of the Combined Authority, Transport for West Midlands, was set up to co-ordinate infrastructure investment and create a fully integrated, safe and secure network. It also plans for future needs. The extensive area covered incorporates 10 non-West Midlands local authorities including, for instance, both Herefordshire, on the Welsh border, and Northamptonshire.

The West Midlands Rail Executive has co-managed the West Midlands Railway franchise with the Department for Transport and has planned the strategic future of the rail network. Midlands Connect is a separate and much wider partnership, bringing in the East Midlands as well. This body plans the strategic future of West and East Midlands rail connectivity. It aims to recommend projects which will bring the greatest possible economic and social benefits.

Director of Rail, TfWM Malcolm Holmes
Director, Midlands Connect Maria Machancoses

EUROPEAN UNION (EU)

The Government's approach to negotiations meant the UK will be leaving the EU's Single Market and Customs Union on 31 December 2020. Controls on the movement of goods will be introduced, in both directions, during 2021.

EU decisions which have been incorporated into British law will remain in force, unless or until they are specifically revised or revoked by domestic legislation.

There are four Railway Packages in the common European transport policy. Their objective is to promote the efficiency and competitiveness of railways through gradual liberalisation, and are summarised as follows:

1st Opening the trans-European rail freight market for international services.
2nd Providing a legally and technically integrated European railway.
3rd Revitalising international rail passenger services by extending competition, improving interoperability and growing rail freight.
4th Standards and authorisation for rolling stock, workforce skills, independent management of infrastructure, liberalisation of domestic passenger services.

Given their complexity and the need to consider each case separately, the passing of any new legislation might be long drawn out. In many cases, the need for change might be questioned.

EUROPEAN UNION AGENCY FOR RAILWAYS

The agency contributes to the implementation of the European Union legislation aimed at improving the competitive position of the railways, through interoperability and a common approach to safety. The aim is to make the railway sector work better for society. In its 2020 progress report, the agency notes that:

- the fatality risk for an average train passenger is about 0.05 per billion passenger kilometres, making rail the safest form of EU land transport;
- a weekly average of six fatalities and an additional six serious injuries occur on level crossings in Europe.

The Agency is now the European authorisation and certification body for international railway transport.
Executive Director Josef Doppelbauer

HOUSE OF COMMONS TRANSPORT COMMITTEE

The Transport Committee's purpose is to examine the expenditure, administration and policy of the Department for Transport and associated public bodies.

The committee decides the topics and calls for written evidence from interested parties, who may be called before it. Formal reports are made to the House. These are published, together with a verbatim report of the evidence sessions and the main written submissions.

An inquiry 'Reforming Public Transport after the Pandemic' began on 24 July 2020.
Chair Huw Merriman

NETWORK RAIL

Network Rail (NR) is the infrastructure manager of the national network. The company owns, operates, maintains and develops the national railway infrastructure in Britain. This consists of the track, signalling, bridges, viaducts, tunnels, level crossings and electrification systems, of which it is the monopoly owner (apart from the Core Valley Lines in south Wales, which are now owned by the Welsh Government).

Network Rail also owns and operates 20 large stations. With a few minor exceptions, the others are also owned by Network Rail, but the primary responsibility for day-to-day operations is that of the train operating company to which the station is leased.

Network Rail Ltd is a public sector company, whose task is the delivery of a safe, reliable and efficient railway network. It is licensed by the Secretary of State for Transport and was allocated £53 billion of public funding for Control Period 6 (CP6, 2019-24). Network Rail retains the commercial and operational freedom to manage the railway infrastructure, but borrowings are constrained by the requirements of HM Treasury.

The company is accountable to its operator customers through access contracts and is regulated by the Office of Rail and Road (ORR). Network Rail is held to account by the ORR for delivering what it promises, at the price agreed, while meeting its operational obligations.

The long-term planning process looks at the network up to 30 years into the future, to enable the company to promote the efficient use of its capability and capacity. What future interventions are needed, and what are the strategic issues?

In 2019, Network Rail operations were devolved to five Regions and 14 Routes (see box). Each route has its own managing director and a senior leadership team. The route businesses operate, maintain and carry out minor renewals to the infrastructure. They are responsible for day-to-day performance and liaison with operators. Their objective is to deliver a safe and reliable railway for all concerned.

Central functions include matters such as standards and services, where the economies of scale or specialist expertise make it sensible for them to be provided on a national basis.
Chair Sir Peter Hendy
Chief Executive Andrew Haines

NETWORK RAIL'S REGIONS AND ROUTES

REGIONS	ROUTES
Eastern	Anglia, East Midlands, North & East, East Coast
North West & Central	North West, Central, West Coast main line South
Scotland's Railway	Scotland
Southern	Kent, Sussex, Wessex, Network Rail High Speed
Wales & Western	Wales, Western

nomad-digital.com
Connecting everything

The market leader for your intelligent journey

Nomad Digital is the world's leading provider of passenger and fleet-management solutions.

The integration of Nomad's solutions into the on-train environment improves levels of passenger satisfaction, connectivity, journey information and entertainment, whilst increasing operational efficiency of the fleet.

- Solutions on more than 100 fleets – on over 11,000 vehicles world-wide
- Utilising 38,000 passenger information screens
- Carrying over 7 million WiFi sessions per month
- Serving infotainment to circa 1.7 billion passengers each year

Contact our experts today

E: experts@nomad-digital.com

W: nomad-digital.com

A: Nomad Digital Limited
5th Floor, One Trinity
Broad Chare,
Newcastle upon Tyne,
NE1 2HF

Follow us

@NomadDigital

SETTING THE AGENDA

Riding with Pride: in August 2020 Avanti West Coast launched a Class 390 Pendolino wrapped in an all-over Pride livery, using the colours of the progressive Pride flag; the train was later named *Progress* following a competition. The launch trip featured a Euston to Manchester service staffed by an all-LGBTQ+ crew.

OFFICE OF RAIL AND ROAD

The Office of Rail and Road (ORR) is a non-ministerial Government department, funded by the industry for its rail regulatory role. It operates within the framework set by UK and European legislation and is accountable to Parliament and the public.

ORR is both an economic and safety regulator. Its principal rail functions are in respect of Network Rail's stewardship, the licensing of operators of railway assets, and the approval of access arrangements to track, stations and light maintenance depots.

Passenger Train Operating Companies (TOCs), which are granted franchises or concessions, need to apply to ORR for operating licences, as do freight train operators. TOCs and Network Rail undertake track and station access agreements and these require ORR approval.

Similarly, ORR regulates High Speed 1. It also regulates Channel Tunnel operations, in conjunction with the French rail regulator ARAF.

The ORR has concurrent jurisdiction with the Competition and Markets Authority to investigate anti-competitive practices in relation to railways.

The ORR is the independent health and safety regulator for the railway industry, covering both the travelling public and industry workers. HM Railway Inspectorate (HMRI) is part of ORR and its inspectors and policy advisors develop and deliver the safety strategy.

ORR is the enforcing authority for the Health & Safety at Work Act 1974 and various railway specific legislation. It is led by a board appointed by the Secretary of State for Transport.
Chair Declan Collier
Interim Chief Executive John Larkinson

RAIL DELIVERY GROUP

The Rail Delivery Group (RDG) leads and represents the collective voice of the railway industry on cross-industry issues, develops and issues policies, strategies and plans for the industry, and promotes better alignment of conflicting interests between those concerned.

The purpose of the RDG is to lead a programme of change, particularly in terms of cost reduction, the industry culture, encouraging more integrated whole-system approaches, and improving the speed and effectiveness of the way it works. A safe, efficient and high quality rail service for users and for taxpayers alike is the aim.

With it likely the Government will create some form of 'guiding mind' to bring greater co-ordination to the railway, the Rail Delivery Group has created two distinct pillars to sit, currently, within the present organisation. The first is Service Delivery, which provides functions, such as ticketing systems and online journey planning, that support railway operation. The second, Advocacy & Change, contributes to the development of railway policy while also facilitating cross-industry collaboration.

RDG membership is a licence condition of Network Rail, passenger and freight operators that operate over the main line network.

The RDG acts as a clearing house for passenger train operators through the Rail Settlement Plan and by providing the National Rail Enquiry Services (NRES), promoting the various railcards and administering staff travel.
Chair Steve Montgomery
Chief Executive (leading Service Delivery) Jacqueline Starr
Director General (leading Advocacy & Change) Andy Bagnall

RAIL SUPPLY GROUP

The Rail Supply Group (RSG) is the leadership body for the supply sector. It works in partnership with the Rail Delivery Group to set the direction and guidance to industry and government. Formed in 2014, the RSG comprises railway industry business leaders and senior representatives from the Departments for Transport, Business, Energy & Industrial Strategy and International Trade.

The RSG aims to strengthen capability and competitiveness. Its work focuses on digitalisation, data sharing, sustainability and boosting exports and inward investment, all underpinned by efforts to enhance skills, people and productivity.
Chair Philip Hoare

RAIL FORUM MIDLANDS

Rail Forum Midlands represents some 200 rail supply businesses from across the UK. It is a not for profit organisation, owned and governed by its members. These include infrastructure and rolling stock consultancies, manufacturers and a wide range of service providers.

Rail Forum Midlands supports its members, enabling them to grow, export and innovate. It has strong links to major rail clients, government and key stakeholders and a vast network of supply chain companies.
Chief Executive Elaine Clark

RAILWAY INDUSTRY ASSOCIATION

The Railway Industry Association (RIA) is the trade association for UK-based suppliers, established more than 140 years ago. Its more than 300 member companies include manufacturers, maintainers, contractors, consultants, leasing companies and specialist service providers.

RIA represents members' interests to Government, regulators and Network Rail and offers a forum for member discussions. Key issues are exports, innovation and skills. Information on a wide range of technical, commercial and business issues is circulated.

RIA offers a one-stop advice service for sourcing equipment, services and expertise from the UK.
Chief Executive Darren Caplan

RSSB

RSSB is a not-for-profit company owned by the major industry stakeholders. Its technical strategy is to deliver a railway fit for the future. The RSSB's principal objective is to lead and facilitate the rail industry's work to achieve continuous improvement in the health and safety performance of the railways in Great Britain.

RSSB activities are divided into seven main groups of:
- safety intelligence;
- workforce safety;
- workforce health and wellbeing;
- passenger and public safety;
- rolling stock;
- infrastructure; and
- sustainability.

Key activities include the support of cross-industry working groups, the management of system safety, management of an industry-wide programme of research and development in co-operation with the Department for Transport, Network Rail and others, and developing the content of Railway Group Standards and the Rule Book.

This includes identifying all significant risks, including those from train accidents, and ranking the risks of trains passing signals at danger.

CONNECTING THE FUTURE OF MOBILITY

Hitachi Rail is a fully integrated, global provider of rail solutions across rolling stock, signalling, operation, service & maintenance, digital technology and turnkey solutions. With a presence in 38 countries across six continents and over 12,000 employees, our mission is to contribute to society through the continuous development of superior rail transport solutions.

hitachirail.com

HITACHI
Inspire the Next

SETTING THE AGENDA

Leeds improvement: a new platform 0 on the north side of the station was due to be brought into use by the end of 2020.

Standards may have the force of law through conditions attached to licences granted by ORR, or by a company through its safety management systems and contracts.

RSSB is registered as the Railway Safety & Standards Board.
Chief Executive Mark Phillips

RAIL ACCIDENT INVESTIGATION BRANCH (RAIB)

Established in 2003, the Rail Accident Investigation Branch (RAIB) is a statutory but independent accident investigation body, whose Chief Inspector reports directly to the Secretary of State for Transport.

The RAIB is not a prosecuting body and it does not apportion blame or liability.

RAIB's responsibilities include:
- investigating the causes of railway accidents and incidents where it believes this will bring safety learning to the industry;
- identifying risks which may lead to a similar accident happening again, or make an accident worse;
- making and publishing recommendations, where appropriate, to improve railway safety.

The RAIB's scope covers main line railways (including those of Northern Ireland), London Underground, metros, tramways, heritage railways and the British part of the Channel Tunnel. By law, all must report certain types of accidents or incidents. All reports of investigations undertaken are published.

In general, the UK railway industry's safety record remains among the best in Europe.
Chief Inspector Simon French

NATIONAL INFRASTRUCTURE COMMISSION (NIC)

The Commission's task is to enable long-term strategic decision making by providing a dispassionate and independent assessment of future infrastructure needs. Established as an Executive Agency of HM Treasury in 2017, it aims to be the UK's most credible, forward thinking and influential voice on infrastructure policy and strategy.

A National Infrastructure Strategy needs to meet the following tests:
- a long-term strategy for policy up to 2050;
- clear goals and plans to achieve them with specific deadlines;
- a firm funding commitment, such as 1.2% of GDP for infrastructure; and
- a genuine commitment to change.

The Commission has already reported in favour of substantial investment in Trans-Pennine services, to be integrated with HS2, and the redevelopment of Manchester Piccadilly.

The Government's Integrated Rail Plan for the Midlands and North will be informed by the NIC's work looking at the rail needs of the area, including evidence from Northern Powerhouse Rail, Midlands Rail Hub, HS2 Phase 2b and other proposed Network Rail projects. The plan was to be published by the end of 2020.

The Commission has reported in favour of Crossrail 2, but recognises it is now at best unlikely to open before the late 2030s.
Chair Sir John Armitt

BRITISH TRANSPORT POLICE

British Transport Police (BTP) is the specialised police service for Britain's railways. BTP provides a service to rail operators, staff and passengers on the national network throughout Britain, as well as London Underground, Docklands Light Railway, Glasgow Subway, the Sunderland extension of the Tyne and Wear Metro, West Midlands Metro, London Tramlink and Emirates Air Line.

BTP has three operational divisions covering south east England, the rest of England plus Wales, and Scotland. In 2019-20, there were 3,019 police officers, 300 special officers, 362 PCSOs and 1,689 support staff.

The force's strategic plan for the years 2018-21 aims to protect people from crime, reduce disruption to rail services, invest in a skilled and specialist workforce and offer value for money. Of the £318 million budget for 2019-20, £56 million was for core Underground policing and £262 million for the rest.

The most common crimes were theft of passengers' property and violence against the person.
Chief Constable Paul Crowther

RAIL FREIGHT GROUP

The Rail Freight Group (RFG) includes all the main freight operators, but also ports, terminal operators, property developers, equipment suppliers and support services. Its aim is to increase the volume of goods moved by rail, promoting the benefits of so doing.

Main customers are from the following industries:
- shipping lines, freight forwarders;
- power generation;
- oil and petroleum;
- auto manufacturing;
- construction materials;
- steel manufacture;
- household and industrial waste;
- retailers, especially supermarkets;
- fruit wholesalers;
- whisky producers;
- Network Rail maintenance and upgrading.

The largest freight companies are DB Cargo and Freightliner, with Colas Rail, Direct Rail Services and GB Railfreight accounting for most of the rest. RFG campaigns for a policy environment that supports rail freight, promotes the sector generally and the business growth of members.

The RFG engages with railway organisations, railway authorities and Government at all levels. Its campaigning aims to ensure politicians and key policy makers are well informed on what rail freight can offer.
Director General Maggie Simpson

HIGH SPEED 1

HS1 Ltd is the concession holder for HS1, the 109km high-speed rail line from London St Pancras International to the Eurotunnel boundary. The 30-year contract continues until 2040, when assets revert to the Government.

There are HS1 stations at St Pancras International, Stratford International, Ebbsfleet International and Ashford International. The line is signalled for bi-directional operation and the maximum gradient is a relatively stiff 1 in 40. The traffic, signalling and electrical controls and the communications centre for the whole of HS1 are located at the Ashford Area Signalling Centre.

Maximum train lengths on HS1 are 400 metres for international passenger services, 276 metres for domestic passenger and 750 metres (including locomotive) for freight.

Eurostar services run under an open access agreement and Southeastern domestic operations under its own franchise agreement. Trains on HS1 must be authorised specifically to ensure their compatibility with the route.

HS1 Ltd is regulated by the Office of Rail and Road, whose Control Period 3 runs from 2020 to 2025. The ORR has determined that although the charges paid by operators are higher

STADLER IS BUILDING TRAINS FOR NETWORKS UP AND DOWN THE UK

www.stadlerrail.com

SETTING THE AGENDA

than in CP2, they will be significantly lower than those proposed by HS1. The total charges of £25.9 million per year are levied on a per train kilometre basis for freight, and a combination of per train kilometre and per train minute for passenger services.

The number of revenue earning trains timetabled in 2019-20 was as follows:

Domestic (North Kent)	28,766	39.4%
Domestic (Ashford)	26,324	36.0%
International passenger	17,594	24.1%
Freight	392	0.5%
Total	**73,076**	**100%**

Three-quarters of the total demand of around 200 trains per day was from domestic passenger services, the overall importance of which can hardly be overstated. Eurostar services made up nearly all the rest, with freight traffic very light and accounting for only slightly more than one train per day.

Eurostar has not received government support as a result of the Covid-19 virus. Falling demand meant services were cut drastically and station calls at Ebbsfleet and Ashford have been abandoned until at least 2022.
Chief Executive Dyan Crowther

CHARTERED INSTITUTE OF LOGISTICS AND TRANSPORT

The Chartered Institute of Logistics and Transport (CILT) is the professional body for those involved in all aspects of transport and logistics. It is not a lobbying organisation, so it is able to provide considered and objective responses on transport policy to Government and others. Through a structure of forums and regional groups, it provides a network for professionals to debate issues and disseminate good practice.

There is an active Strategic Rail Policy Group and another on Rail Freight. The Railway Study Forum (formerly the RSA) provides for the exchange of experience, knowledge and opinion on railway industry issues through meetings or otherwise.
Chief Executive Kevin Richardson

RAILWAY CIVIL ENGINEERS ASSOCIATION

Founded in 1921, the Railway Civil Engineers Association (RCEA) is an Associated Society of the Institution of Civil Engineers. It encourages the exchange of knowledge and experience between its members and continuing professional development. Members are involved in the development, design, construction or maintenance of railway infrastructure, including metros and light rail. Activities aim to foster those interests and achieve a broader understanding of the industry.
Chair Stewart Piercy

INSTITUTION OF ENGINEERING AND TECHNOLOGY

The railway network of the Institution of Engineering and Technology (IET) is focused on engineering. This includes the promotion, construction, regulation, operation, safety and maintenance of railways. This also covers metros, tramways and guided transport systems. Activities feature lectures, conferences and training courses.

The IET sees transport as a system, so developments in one area will have impacts elsewhere, and that new technology requires a long-term policy goal and incentives for its use.
Chief Executive & Secretary Nigel Fine

THE INSTITUTION OF MECHANICAL ENGINEERS

The railway division of the Institution of Mechanical Engineers (IMechE) covers research, design, development, procurement, manufacture, operation and maintenance of traction and rolling stock, also infrastructure, plant and their subsystems and components. This is for all forms of rail-borne guided surface transport, including rapid transit.

The Railway Division hosts an annual Railway Challenge, where teams of contestants each design and build a 10¼-inch gauge locomotive to strict specifications and rules. The resulting locomotives are then evaluated on the (private) Stapleford Miniature Railway. This last part of the event had to be cancelled in 2020 as a result of Covid-19.
Chair, Railway Division Felix Schmid

PERMANENT WAY INSTITUTION

The Permanent Way Institution (PWI) promotes technical knowledge, advice and support about the design, construction and maintenance of every type of railed track on an international basis. Membership is open to those actively engaged in the rail industry and anyone with a general interest.

A series of local events is arranged through its various sections, as well as on substantial technical learning occasions. Its textbooks, updated from time to time, have been industry standard works for many years.
Chief Executive Officer Stephen Barber

INSTITUTION OF RAILWAY OPERATORS

The Institution of Railway Operators (IRO) was launched in 2000. It aims to advance and promote the safe and reliable operation of the railways by improving the technical and general skills, knowledge and competence of all those thus engaged.

The educational programme offers varying levels of academic qualifications in the management of railway operations. There are also apprenticeships for those wishing to develop their understanding of the rail industry.

Through its seven area councils, the IRO offers a series of local events.
Chief Executive Fiona Tordoff

INSTITUTION OF RAILWAY SIGNAL ENGINEERS

The Institution of Railway Signal Engineers (IRSE) was formed in 1912. It aims to advance the science and practice of train control and communications engineering within the industry and to maintain high standards of knowledge and competence within the profession. The over-riding purpose is to help ensure the safe and efficient movement by rail of people and freight, for the public benefit.

A licensing scheme provides assurance about the competence of individuals to carry out technical safety-critical or safety-related work on signalling or railway telecommunications equipment and systems.

Half of the IRSE membership comes from outside the UK.
Chief Executive Blane Judd

YOUNG RAIL PROFESSIONALS

The Young Rail Professionals (YRP) was founded in 2009 to promote the railway industry as a great place to work and to inspire and develop the next generation of railway talent. YRP is open to any young rail professional, whether their interests are in asset management, engineering, franchising, human relations, maintenance, marketing, regulation, rolling stock design, strategic planning, or train operations. YRP now has over 14,000 members spread across eight regions.

For those starting out in their careers, YRP offers networking and professional development opportunities to enhance

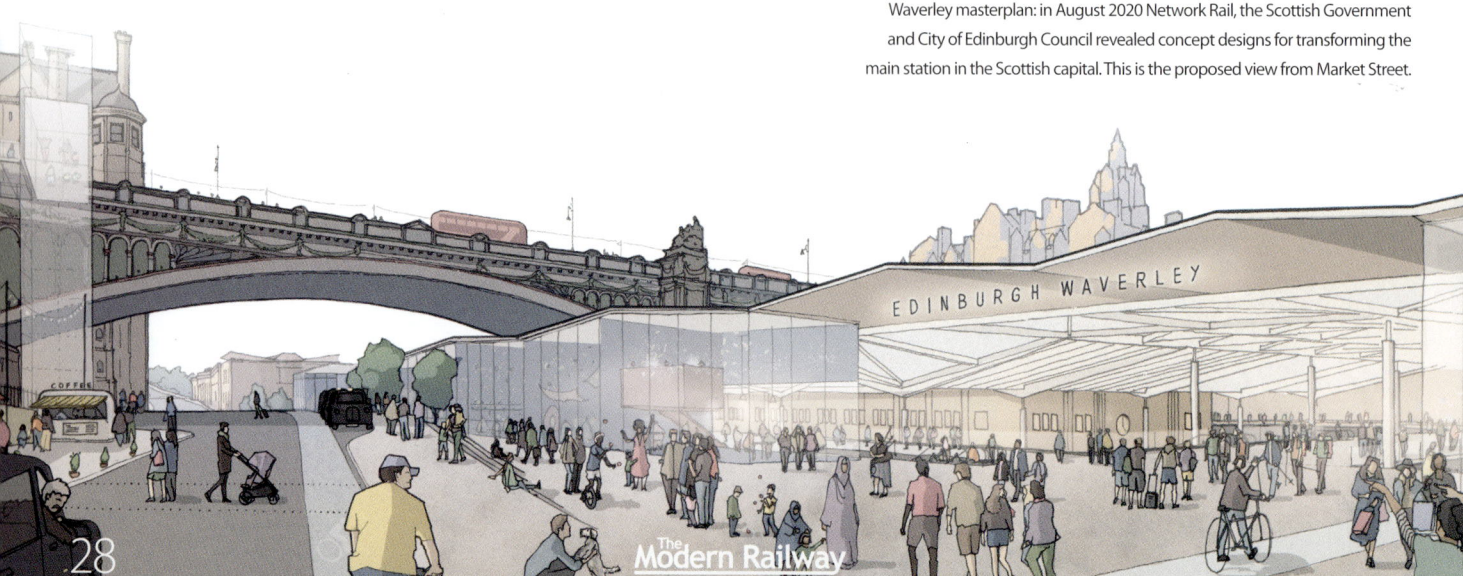

Waverley masterplan: in August 2020 Network Rail, the Scottish Government and City of Edinburgh Council revealed concept designs for transforming the main station in the Scottish capital. This is the proposed view from Market Street.

skills and encourage its members. An ambassadors' programme provides opportunities to visit educational establishments to attract the next generation into the railway.

Membership is free and there is no charge for such events. There is no formal YRP age limit, but activities are aimed at those in their first 10 years in the industry.
Chair George Chilcott

REF
The REF (Railway Engineers' Forum) aims to harmonise the various strengths of the constituent institutions in devising and undertaking activities in support of the railway community. The constituent members represent ICE, IET, IMechE Railway Division, IRO, IRSE, PWI, RCEA and CILT. Associated societies are YRP and the International Council on Systems Engineering (INCOSE).

As a non-political body, the REF can provide a common voice on railway topics from operations to engineering, thus offering a co-ordinated response to requests for professional comment. The REF also produces a regular listing of professional meetings of its member organisations throughout Britain.
Chair Andrew Simmons (IRSE)

NATIONAL SKILLS ACADEMY FOR RAIL (NSAR)
The National Skills Academy for Rail (NSAR) covers the skills needed for engineering, operations, service delivery and the digital railway. The aim is to enable the industry to increase its competitiveness through matching skills and workforce demand to its supply, education and training.

NSAR itself does not deliver training, but works with employers to understand their training needs, with training providers to ensure they are delivering what the industry needs and with others such as sector skills bodies and government to make sure those in the industry have the right qualifications. These are the skills needed to support the maintenance, operation, development and expansion of a cost-effective 21st century railway.

How will the newcomers be recruited? Will there be enough of them? When and where will they be needed? At what level of expertise and in which disciplines? Who will train and accredit them? How will this be funded? Are these general industry requirements, or are they related more to specific large projects such as HS2?

NSAR activities include the accreditation of training organisations, course content standardisation, services for employers and training companies, and promoting railway careers. Training companies also need the appropriate capability and capacity.

For the broad categories of infrastructure and rolling stock, there will always be a need for maintenance, renewal and enhancement.
Chief Executive Neil Robertson

INSTITUTE OF TRANSPORT STUDIES, UNIVERSITY OF LEEDS
A principal interest has been the economics of rail transport. The primary purpose is to advance the understanding of transport activity, operation and use, and to develop skills and best practice among transport professionals and decision makers. Key research topics include demand forecasting and travel behaviour, infrastructure cost modelling, efficiency analysis and pricing, project appraisal methodology, off-track and on-track competition, and transport safety.

UKRRIN
The UK Rail Research and Innovation Network (UKRRIN) has established a network of centres of excellence of key railway technology across the UK. The aim is faster development of new products and technologies in the rail sector, using purpose-built simulation and testing facilities.

The subject groups are digital systems (University of Birmingham, with Lancaster), rolling stock (Huddersfield with Newcastle, Loughborough, Bristol and Cambridge) and infrastructure (Southampton, with Loughborough, Nottingham, Sheffield and Heriot-Watt). Testing is led by Network Rail from a variety of sites.

TRANSPORT FOCUS
Transport Focus is a non-departmental public body sponsored by the Department for Transport. It is the consumer body for Britain's rail passengers. Transport Focus aims to get the best deal possible for them; its independence is guaranteed by Act of Parliament.

Transport Focus uses research to influence decision makers on behalf of users, focusing on a number of key issues. These are:
- performance and disruption;
- fares and tickets;
- quality and level of services;
- investment; and
- information for passengers.

The bi-annual National Rail Passenger Survey measures the overall satisfaction of passengers, by operator and by sector. That for spring 2020 found that 82% were satisfied with their overall journey, while the biggest decline in satisfaction was with punctuality and reliability. The highest overall rating for franchised companies was for LNER at 91%, the lowest South Western Railway at 75%.
Chief Executive Anthony Smith

COMMUNITY RAIL NETWORK
Community Rail Network, formerly ACoRP, is dedicated to supporting community rail groups. There are about 70 rail partnerships and many more station friends groups and other organisations. The aim is to bring people together and help communities get the most from their railways, as well as helping the railways themselves to thrive.

The focus is on practical initiatives to advance the local railway, for which it provides support, advice and information. Community Rail Network tries to ensure the importance of the local railway is fully recognised at all levels of decision-making. It also helps to find solutions for common problems, and disseminates examples of good practice.
Chief Executive Jools Townsend

RAILWAY HERITAGE TRUST
The Railway Heritage Trust is an independent company limited by guarantee, which commenced operations in 1985. Its objectives are:
- to assist operational railway companies in the preservation and upkeep of listed buildings and structures; and
- to facilitate the transfer of non-operational premises and structures to outside bodies willing to undertake their preservation.

The Trust gives both advice and grants. Grants may cover repair, conservation and restoration works. It supports a wide range of projects, with a balance struck between buildings and structures, and between large projects and small. It does not deal with rolling stock or artefacts.
Executive Director Andy Savage

Saying thank you: during the spring lockdown period, many railway stations and structures were lit in blue as a tribute to the efforts of NHS staff fighting the pandemic. This is Charing Cross station on 23 April 2020.

SETTING THE AGENDA

Setting the innovation agenda

2020 was something of a unique year, not only because of the way our world was turned upside down by a virus, but also from projects which were unveiled and brought to fruition.

The Birmingham Centre for Railway Research and Education (BCRRE) at the University of Birmingham opened the doors to its brand new building, which houses collaborative working and research space in the UK Rail Research and Innovation Network (UKRRIN) Centre of Excellence in Digital Systems (CEDS). It's an industry-on-campus environment where academic researchers and industrial collaborators can come together to work on new ideas, developments and innovation for the rail industry, worldwide. It includes space for just a day or a few hours, up to private offices and laboratories available for weeks and months at a time.

Why do all of this? Across all industries it is no secret that innovation is important – but it's also no secret that innovation is a big challenge in the UK rail industry. This is where BCRRE and UKRRIN come in: BCRRE leads UKRRIN's Introducing Innovation theme which responds to the loud request for help in driving ideas through the innovation process, from initial bright idea or fundamental research, through the development stages of proof of concept, validation, demonstration, testing, launching into the market and (hopefully) commercial and operational success.

We should remind ourselves that the purpose of innovation is to generate value through improved products, services or solutions in response to needs. There is no shortage of good ideas and no lack of enthusiasm to turn these into solutions that can provide real, tangible benefits to the railway. The new facilities available in Birmingham, together with our suite of business support initiatives, mean it's easier than ever to take the plunge and innovate our way through the post-Covid and post-Brexit world.

KEY THEMES IN THE INNOVATION AGENDA

What are the headline innovation themes? As we predicted last year, the two big words across our sector are Decarbonisation and Digitalisation.

We have seen decarbonisation strategies worldwide and in early autumn 2020 we made history by delivering the UK's first hydrogen fuel cell train on the main line railway. You can read all about HydroFLEX in Porterbrook's profile on page 33. The success of the project shows that hydrogen fuel cell technology can become a mainstream topic for railway traction – with its associated new products, services and supply chain.

Hydrogen isn't the only decarbonisation opportunity and earlier in 2020 BCRRE launched its Centre of Excellence in Decarbonisation covering six themes:

- low-carbon traction systems;
- power electronics and battery charging technologies;
- resilience and adaptation strategies, including climate change and managing its associated risks;
- aerodynamics and the effects of passing trains on structures and infrastructure;
- sustainable infrastructure and low-carbon materials; and
- asset management and intelligent decision-making systems.

Find out more at www.birmingham.ac.uk/raildecarbonisation.

What about digitalisation? BCRRE leads the CEDS now which includes the University of Lancaster, Imperial College London and Swansea University, with themes across future railway operations and control; data integration and cybersecurity; and smart monitoring and autonomous systems. CEDS is already the go-to place for integration and verification of digital technologies and will be more accessible with the opening of the new facilities in Birmingham.

WHAT'S AVAILABLE FOR THE RAIL INDUSTRY FOR 2021 AND BEYOND?

BCRRE welcomes organisations of all sizes to come and work with us. Funded projects and different-sized packages of academic input are available – all you have to do is choose which is most appropriate for your needs.

- Digi-Rail: BCRRE's technology and business support project for eligible SMEs across the West Midlands offers at least 12 hours' support towards digital product and service development. We recently added the Sheffield City Region LEP and have partnered with the University of Derby's Innovate 4 Rail project, widening the opportunities to yet more companies across these regions. Find out more at www.digirail.co.uk.
- The West Midlands Growth Hub brings extra support to SMEs in the Greater Birmingham & Solihull LEP area. A cross-sector network includes a rail-ready business reckoner, advice and guidance, and support towards business development. Find out more by emailing us at railway@contacts.bham.ac.uk.
- BCRRE's new facilities means companies of any size can take advantage of the ever-widening network of academic and industrial facilities. Joining UKRRIN costs a nominal sum in return for preferential access to facilities and expertise and support for winning funding for your project. The unique feature of UKRRIN is its scalability and opportunities for all partners, large and small. Find out more at www.ukrrin.org.uk.
- Innovation is complemented with skills and BCRRE is home to a suite of undergraduate and postgraduate study, including Degree Apprenticeships, CPD and short courses. Details at www.birmingham.ac.uk/railway.

Last, but by no means least, is the BCRRE Rail Alliance: the UK's largest business-to-business networking organisation for the rail supply chain. It's the go-to organisation for connecting the rail industry together, across the UK, Europe and worldwide. The Rail Alliance offers a wealth of industry information, member news and monthly events where we share timely news, opportunities and provide a forum for networking. Find out more at www.railalliance.co.uk.

Supporting R&D: in November 2020 work was completed on a new building which will be home to the Centre of Excellence for Digital Systems at the University of Birmingham, part of the UK Rail Research and Innovation Network (UKRRIN).

Sustainable Traction Systems

Power Electronics and Energy

Sustainable Infrastructure

Climate Adaptation and Rail Resilience

Aerodynamics

Geotechnical Engineering and Asset Management

Centre of excellence in decarbonisation: launched by BCRRE in 2020, this has a focus on six themes.

FINANCE AND LEASING

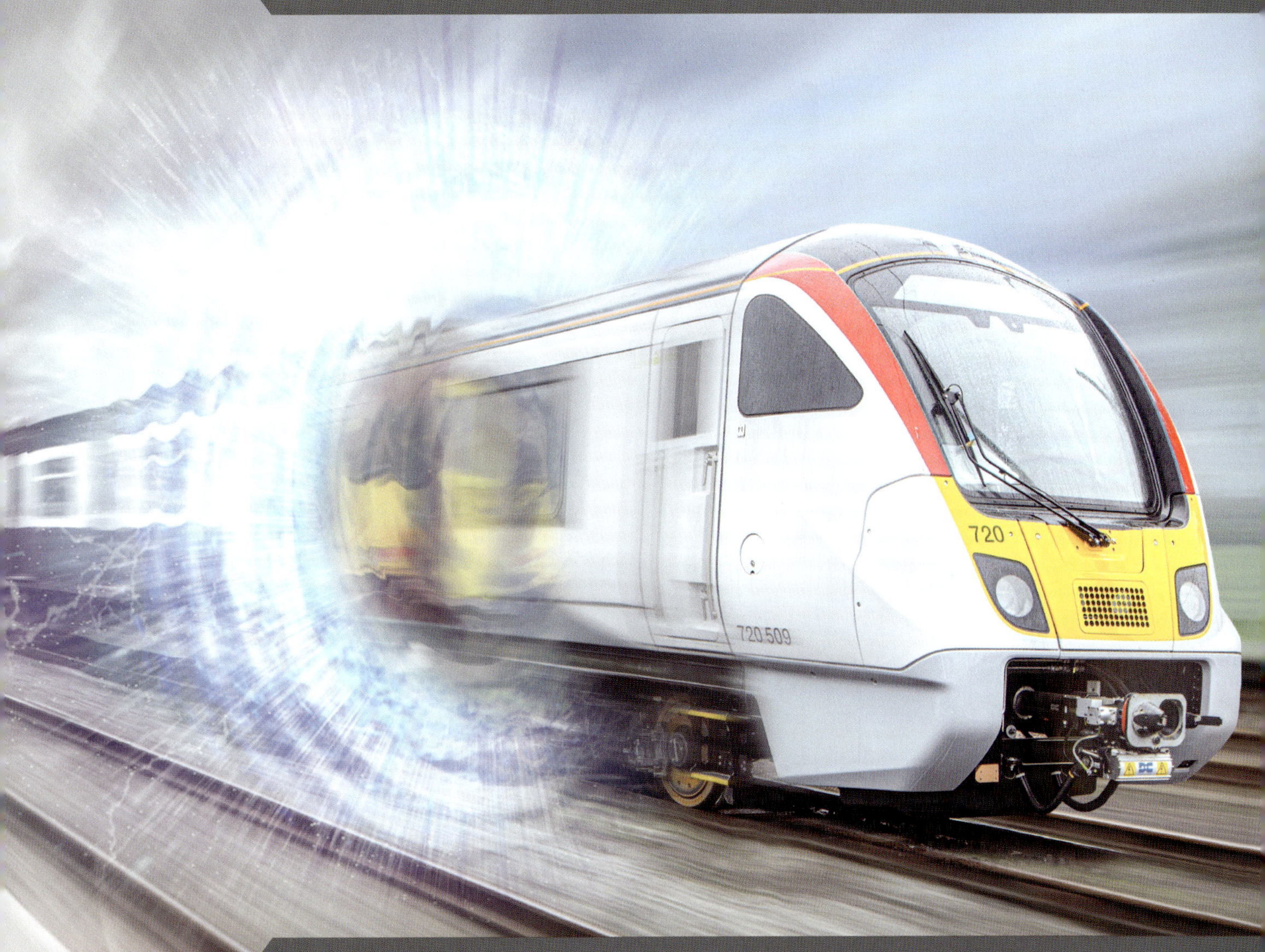

IN ASSOCIATION WITH

angel Trains

Rail People
Real Expertise

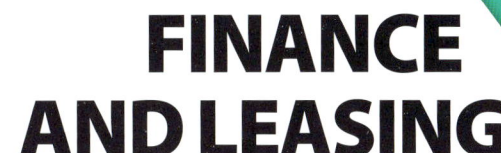

FINANCE AND LEASING

Class 165 hybrid drive: Angel Trains is supporting the conversion of a Class 165 DMU into a self-charging hybrid.

The UK rail industry is facing some of the biggest challenges in its history. As one of Britain's leading train asset managers and biggest investors in rail, we are committed to working together with the government, train operating companies and partners across industries to ensure rail continues to meet the needs of the modern-day passenger.

We understand we have an important part to play in developing and implementing solutions that can make rail travel greener and more efficient, and there are two key sectors in which our teams are making a mark in delivering these objectives: sustainability and innovation.

SUSTAINABILITY AT THE HEART OF RAIL

In light of the climate crisis and the net-zero target of carbon emissions set by the government for 2040, there has been an increased need for solutions that can lower emissions and be adopted quickly to reduce the impact rail has on the environment in the immediate future.

As one of the largest investors in UK rail, and as chair of the rail industry decarbonisation taskforce, we are working in partnership with industry to deliver actionable solutions that deliver positive environmental change, from supporting world-leading solar rail pioneer Riding Sunbeams to creating low carbon rolling stock technologies.

Our conversion of a diesel multiple-unit (DMU) into low-emission, self-charging battery hybrid drive will become an innovative, intermediary solution that bridges the gap between diesel and fully electrified rail. This £4 million project moves us closer towards decarbonisation by providing a 'ride now' solution that is not only a benefit to our customers, but makes rail travel cleaner, quieter and smarter for passengers.

In addition to this, we have declined to buy a diesel-only train for the past decade, instead choosing to focus on investing in new electric multiple-units (EMUs).

OUR APPROACH TO INNOVATION

Innovation is in our DNA and is intwined into every aspect of our business. Through our smart approach to innovation, we have been able to listen to and provide solutions for our customers.

We are harnessing the power of 3D printing to improve the manufacturing process of rolling stock parts, in order to optimise production costs and create better value for our customers.

By collaborating with 3D printing specialists Stratasys, engineering consultancy DB ESG and Chiltern Railways, we have successfully deployed the UK rail industry's first 3D printed parts on an in-service passenger train. We are proud to have collaborated on this industry-first project to deliver technology that reduces whole life rolling stock costs and enables vehicles to remain in passenger service for longer.

Our Product Technology team's industry-leading progress has helped to address the issue of replacing obsolete parts and prototyping new parts. By using Additive Manufacturing (AM), we have been able to reduce supplier costs, as our innovative technology allows us to constantly iterate and improve existing designs on specific parts.

ENHANCING PASSENGER EXPERIENCE

Our industry-defining £900 million procurement project for Greater Anglia, financing a fleet of Class 720 Bombardier Aventra EMUs, also demonstrates how we have been paving the way for the future of rail.

The new state-of-the art fleet will transform the passenger experience for thousands of commuters. With improved passenger features such as plug and USB sockets, air-conditioning, real-time information screens, improved accessibility, underfloor heating and passenger door safety features, the Class 720s will help provide a travel experience for the future.

This incredible milestone not only demonstrates our commitment to investing in sustainable rolling stock, it also shows the value we place in providing innovative fleets for modern passenger needs.

RAIL PEOPLE, REAL EXPERTISE

Trains may be our business, but it is people who are our greatest asset, and we pride ourselves on the calibre of talent within our company. With over 45 qualified engineers, making up a third of our employees, our unrivalled team of experts are on the pulse, working to deliver the best asset management programmes.

We are proud to be a leading investor in UK rail, developing the capabilities of our fleets to meet growing passenger demands for decades to come. We are planning a long-term steady flow of work and innovations that incorporate new technologies to ensure Angel Trains plays its part in the transformational change in the UK railway in the years to come. ■

Bombardier Aventras for Greater Anglia: Angel Trains is financing a £900 million fleet of Class 720s..

IN ASSOCIATION WITH

porterbrook

Innovative approach: Porterbrook's Innovation Hub (left) and HydroFLEX trains at Long Marston.

At the heart of Britain's railway for over 25 years, Porterbrook owns almost one-third of the national passenger train fleet. Its rolling stock supports around 1.5 million passenger journeys and travels over a million miles a day when the railway operates at full capacity.

Porterbrook currently has almost 4,500 vehicles on lease or on order. Since privatisation, Porterbrook has invested over £3 billion in 2,500 new passenger and freight vehicles. The company is looking to invest a further £1 billion in UK rail over coming years. Porterbrook see its role as being an innovative asset manager as well as a financier. It is a long-term player in the UK rail sector – its rolling stock assets have an expected service life of 30-35 years. Making full use of a train's asset life, supported by periodic refurbishments to the latest standards, optimises value to passengers and taxpayers whilst minimising the impact on the environment.

Innovation is at the heart of Porterbrook's whole life asset management approach. In collaboration with its customers and suppliers, Porterbrook is constantly looking ahead to anticipate future needs and help government and industry meet demanding air-quality and decarbonisation targets.

Porterbrook has a reputation for developing and delivering a range of enhancements to existing trains that address these challenges. These include battery and hybrid powered rolling stock, as well as fitment of exhaust after-treatment technology to older fleets. Porterbrook has also introduced the UK's first hydrogen-powered train, HydroFLEX, in partnership with the University of Birmingham.

Porterbrook is committed to supporting and developing the UK rail supply chain. Every week Porterbrook invests £3 million to maintain and upgrade its existing fleets, supporting circa 7,000 jobs spread across over 100 companies.

Its business is not just about managing trains, it's also about its people. Almost three-quarters of Porterbrook's workforce are specialist engineers and rolling stock managers. The company understands its assets.

In partnership with their supply chain and customers, Porterbrook's mission is to provide high-quality, digitally enabled rolling stock that helps deliver a safe, reliable and sustainable railway.

FLEX

A recent initiative from Porterbrook is the bi-mode Class 769 FLEX train. This variant of a Class 319 electric multiple-unit is designed to operate seamlessly over electrified and non-electrified routes, spreading the benefits of electrification to more rail users. Class 769 units have been delivered to Northern, Transport for Wales Rail Services and Great Western Railway during 2020, while Rail Operations Group has also ordered two of the type for its Orion High Speed Logistics services, which will be delivered in 2021.

The 'FLEX' concept is to create a bi-mode train by fitting two diesel powered alternators, one under each of the driving trailer cars. The diesel alternators provide power to the existing traction and auxiliary equipment to allow the EMU to operate without an overhead or third rail supply. The systems will provide power through the train's DC bus, avoiding any significant changes to the existing equipment. This creates a unit capable of operating from a number of different power sources whilst maintaining its full capabilities on electrified routes.

ALTERNATIVE TECHNOLOGIES

From the original electro-diesel bi-mode, Porterbrook has developed its FLEX portfolio to include a variety of innovative projects.

In September 2020 HydroFLEX became the first full size hydrogen train to operate on the UK main line network. The project has been led by Porterbrook and its partner Birmingham Centre for Railway Research and Education. The HydroFLEX train undertaking main line testing is a demonstrator unit, and the production version will be configured for operation using both overhead electric wires and hydrogen for non-electrified routes. This will make HydroFLEX particularly attractive to regions and routes where there is only partial electrification of the network.

Work on the next stage of HydroFLEX is already well advanced, with the University of Birmingham developing a hydrogen and battery power module that can be fitted underneath the production version of the train, which will create increased capacity for passengers in the train's saloon area. The HydroFLEX main line testing programme has been supported by Innovate UK, which has provided funding to two of the development workstreams.

Other projects being developed by Porterbrook include HybridFLEX, which involves fitting Rolls Royce MTU Hybrid Power Packs to a Chiltern Railways Class 168 Turbostar for conversion to hybrid-electric operation; BatteryFLEX, involving conversion of Class 350/2 EMUs currently operated by West Midlands Trains to battery/electric bi-modes; and ElectroFLEX, involving fitment of batteries to Class 377 Electrostars for operation on non-electrified routes on the southern region (which has the added benefit of removing diesel train operation from London Bridge station), without the need for expensive infrastructure upgrades.

Porterbrook has also partnered with Eminox, the exhaust manufacturer, to install ground-breaking emissions-reducing technology on a number of its units. Eminox retrofit technology helps reduce diesel particulate matter from the rail network, delivering environmental benefits to communities served by the railways. On a recent trial with South Western Railway on one of Porterbrook's Class 159 vehicles, NOx (nitrous oxide) emissions were reduced by over 80% and CO (carbon monoxide) and hydrocarbons by over 90% from current levels. This trial was supported by the Department for Transport through InnovateUK's first-of-a-kind funding (FoaK2). Plans are already in place to fit this technology to other fleets in the Porterbrook portfolio, which will offer improved air quality to passengers, rail staff and the communities the railway serves.

COMMITMENT

Porterbrook's commitment to collaboration was affirmed in early 2019 when the company secured ISO 44001 accreditation. The company's supplier conference, first held in 2018 and now an annual event, took place online in 2020 due to the restrictions of the Covid pandemic.

As part of its engagement with the supply chain, Porterbrook created the UK's first on-track Innovation Hub. An off-lease Class 319 electric multiple-unit based at Long Marston has been converted, making a successful debut in 2019 where 25 companies showcased their products. Plans to relaunch Innovation Hub for 2020 were affected by the Covid pandemic, but the company remains committed to the concept.

Porterbrook believes that as an industry we are stronger when we work together and collaborate. The company is an active Patron member of Rail Forum Midlands, partner of the Rail Freight Group and member of the Railway Industry Association.

Porterbrook employs over 140 people, three-quarters of whom are highly specialised engineers or project managers. As an established rail partner, Porterbrook is committed to an ongoing programme of investment. The company takes an industry-leading approach, driven by innovative thinking and future planning. Its extensive experience and knowledge of the rail industry gives the company a strong base to deliver value for money across the range of rolling stock products and services the company delivers.

FINANCE AND LEASING

Eversholt Rail, a member of Eversholt UK Rails Group, is owned by UK Rails S.A.R.L., a company jointly owned by CK Infrastructure Holdings Limited and CK Hutchison Holdings Limited.

Eversholt Rail owns UK passenger and freight rolling stock and has more than 25 years of experience in the rail industry. It currently leases trains to 14 train operators and three freight operators within the UK.

Since privatisation Eversholt Rail has invested more than £3 billion in new trains and continues to introduce its newest fleets on the UK network.

In March 2020, Eversholt Rail completed delivery of 12x5-car Class 397 CAF EMU trains ordered for TransPennine Express. These trains operate services from Manchester Airport and Liverpool to Glasgow and Edinburgh via Preston.

Eversholt Rail also completed delivery of its Class 331 EMU fleet to Northern Trains Ltd in 2020; these are based out of Allerton and Neville Hill depots. By autumn 2020 56 units out of 58 of the Class 195 fleet had been accepted, with the last two expected by the end of 2020. These are all based out of Newton Heath depot.

2020 continued to be a busy year for re-leasing of Eversholt's trains with lease extensions signed with Great Western Railway on the Class 802 fleet, which will see them continue until 2023; Southeastern for Class 375s, Class 376s, Class 465s and Class 395s until later in 2021; TransPennine Express for 15 Class 185s until the end of 2020; and LNER for seven IC225 trains until summer 2023. The leases on Class 321 and Class 315 fleets have also been extended.

Eversholt Rail continuously invests in maintaining the quality and reliability of its existing assets through heavy maintenance and major enhancement programmes to deliver better passenger experience and minimise through-life costs.

In partnership with ScotRail, Eversholt Rail is investing in refurbishing its Class 380 fleet. Key elements of the 'makeover' include the installation of new flooring, new seat upholstery including prominent priority seating, a paint refresh, and general repairs to tables, bins and handrails. The overhaul is taking place at ScotRail's Shields Road depot in Glasgow, with each train taking around two weeks to complete.

2020 also saw the start of the TBOX services on Eversholt Rail's fleet of 22 Class 320 units which are operated by ScotRail. The work is being carried out by Brodie Engineering. The TBOX services include safety-critical overhauls on components including brakes, doors, traction equipment, pantograph equipment and an exterior repaint. The programme is on schedule and is due to complete at the end of 2021.

Following the signature of the lease extensions, Eversholt Rail is investing in fleet enhancement packages for both its Class 375 and Class 395 fleets. For the Class 375 fleet this is to include saloon LED lighting, at-seat USB charging, energy meters, forward-facing CCTV, replacement of the on-train data recorder and a trial (on one unit only) of a bioreactor toilet. For the Class 395 fleet this similarly includes saloon LED lighting, at-seat USB charging, energy meters, but also CCTV, DCO and passenger load measurement systems and a 10-year interior refresh.

Eversholt Rail has also awarded Wabtec Faiveley UK contracts to undertake the overhaul of the LNER IC225 fleet at its Doncaster facility. The 12 Class 91 locomotives will receive a 'G' exam, comprising an overhaul of the bogies including gearboxes and wheelsets, cardan shafts, compressors and traction motors. A number of reliability improvement modifications are also planned. The seven rakes of Mk 4 coaches will receive an OH1 exam including the overhaul of bogies, couplers and doors and an interior saloon and vestibule exam. This work will be complete in January 2022.

In Scotland Eversholt Rail has awarded Alstom the contract to carry out the mileage-based overhaul of both vehicles and bogies on the Class 334 fleet – this work will be undertaken at Alstom's Polmadie, Glasgow site.

Eversholt Rail continues to invest in several innovation workstreams focused on assisting the delivery of the UK Government's decarbonisation commitments. These include adaptation of some of its electric multiple-unit fleets with on-board batteries to allow operation on unelectrified lines.

In July 2020, Eversholt Rail and Alstom announced a further £1 million investment in the Breeze hydrogen train programme. The current phase of work will ensure readiness for the first fleet order. Once converted from Class 321 EMUs, the trains will become Class 600 hydrogen multiple-units (HMUs).

The Revolution VLR (very light rail) programme is progressing well with the build of the demonstrator underway. Once complete, the vehicle will relocate to a test track for extensive performance and validation tests. The Revolution VLR vehicle is ideally matched to the need for lightweight, energy-efficient system solutions to deliver affordable service growth and extension of the UK's rail capacity. ∎

Receiving a makeover: the Eversholt Rail-owned ScotRail Class 380 EMU fleet. **COURTESY SCOTRAIL**

IN ASSOCIATION WITH

West Coast inter-city fleet: Rock Rail is the funder for Class 805 bi-mode and Class 807 electric trains for Avanti West Coast. COURTESY AVANTI WEST COAST

Rock Rail is an independent developer, investor and asset manager of rolling stock and other rail infrastructure. Established in 2014, Rock Rail has transformed the market for rolling stock funding, leading the way in partnering with major institutional investors (pension funds and insurance companies) and opening up a major new source of funding for the rail industry.

Since 2016 Rock has secured £3 billion of institutional investment in new, state-of-the-art rolling stock fleets. Accounting for around 40% of UK passenger rolling stock orders over the period, it represents over 1,500 modern, technology enabled vehicles that are already transforming passenger journeys, delivering better value for the public sector and supporting a more sustainable railway.

Working closely with its institutional investor, operator and manufacturer partners, Rock provides a complete range of specialist asset management services for its fleets across their full life cycle, managing long-term residual value and ensuring they meet passengers' and rail partners' needs over the long-term.

While Rock's initial focus has been on rolling stock, it is extending its approach to transform the design and delivery of other essential rail infrastructure, including electrification, digital signalling and depots, as well as other new technologies to bring track and train closer together.

NEW APPROACHES

Rock Rail and its investor partners take a long-term view to investment, delivering highly competitive funding over the full life of its trains and contributing to the significant reduction in rolling stock leasing costs since its entry into the market.

Rock is also working with partners across the global supply market to deliver the very best of new technologies from around the world in areas such as decarbonisation, power upgrades, European Train Control System (ETCS) and wider traffic management systems, for the benefit of UK passengers.

Safety assurance is a critical element of Rock's asset management role and it is committed to supporting the rail industry by providing industry-leading safety expertise in existing areas such as 'design for safety' and emerging ones including cyber security.

NEW FLEETS

Rock Rail's first transaction, in February 2016, was for the 25 six-carriage Class 717s built by Siemens for Govia Thameslink Railway's Great Northern route, representing an investment of over £200 million. The rollout of the EMUs was completed in September 2019, replacing mainland Britain's oldest electric trains and seeing passenger satisfaction soar by 22 percentage points.

In October of the same year, Rock Rail secured the £700 million contract for 58 new Stadler BMU and EMU trains for use on Greater Anglia's regional, inter-city and Stansted Express routes (Class 745 and 755). The first trains entered service in July 2019 with rollout continuing through 2020.

Rock Rail went on to secure its largest deal, the £1 billion financing of 90 new Bombardier trains (Class 701) for South Western Railway, in June 2017. The recently named 'Arterio' fleet will run across south west London, Surrey and Berkshire and the first units were due to enter service in late 2020.

2019 saw Rock Rail secure its latest two new rolling stock deals. The first of these in August was the £400 million, 33x5-car BMU Hitachi inter-city fleet (Class 810) for East Midlands Railway. The trains are due in service in 2023, making use of existing and future electrification on the Midland main line and replacing the existing diesel-only vehicles. The full fleet will be built in the UK, supporting hundreds of jobs at Hitachi's Newton Aycliffe factory as well as benefitting local suppliers.

Most recently, in December 2019, Rock secured the £350 million financing for the 135-vehicle Hitachi inter-city fleet for Avanti West Coast. The 10 seven-carriage electric trains (Class 807) and 13 five-carriage bi-modes (Class 805) are due to enter service on the West Coast main line in 2022, serving the West Midlands, North Wales and Liverpool and replacing the current diesel-powered fleet.

SUSTAINABILITY

Rock Rail is committed to delivering responsible investments with sustainable benefits for the environment, local communities and wider society. This strongly aligns with its institutional investor partners, who have at their core a requirement for responsible economic, social and governance-based investment.

Rock's modern fleets are already contributing to a more sustainable railway. They are set to replace many hundreds of diesel vehicles and deliver significant energy efficiencies. In its first year of operation, Rock's Great Northern fleet is estimated to have saved the equivalent of over 4,000 tonnes of CO_2 emissions through the trains' advanced regenerative braking technology.

Rock is also working in partnership with Birmingham Centre for Railway Research and Education and the Technical University of Dresden in Germany to explore opportunities for greener rail traction solutions.

EUROPE AND BEYOND

Over recent years, Rock Rail has also extended its focus to other markets, setting up operations in Germany and Australia in 2020. It is actively working with local rail partners and global manufacturers on rolling stock and rail infrastructure financing opportunities in Europe and Australia, including the purchase of greener battery and hydrogen powered trains. ∎

FINANCE AND LEASING

BRITAIN'S ROLLING STOCK
WHO OWNS IT?

Competition to the traditional ROSCOs continues

New rolling stock lessors continue to make inroads into in the UK market, challenging the three major rolling stock leasing companies (ROSCOs).

The three ROSCOs were established at railway privatisation in 1994 to take over ownership of rolling stock from the nationalised British Rail and were sold to the private sector with their initial fleet leases in place.

The aim was for each ROSCO to have a reasonably diversified portfolio, with comparable fleets allocated to each. Larger fleets of a single type were divided, but smaller fleets were allocated to a single ROSCO. This gave each a range of customers and gave most train operating companies (TOCs) a relationship with at least two ROSCOs. At privatisation approximately 38% of passenger rolling stock was allocated to Eversholt, 32% to Angel and 30% to Porterbrook.

A boom in recent orders has seen in excess of 7,000 vehicles ordered since 2014. Of the more than 4,000 vehicles ordered since 2016, 39% will be owned by Rock Rail, with the three original ROSCOs only accounting for a combined total of 38% of the remainder.

Some passenger rolling stock is owned by train operating groups: FirstGroup owns HST power cars and Mk 3s which form some of GWR's 2+4 'Castle' class HSTs, while Arriva owns Mk 3 vehicles used on Chiltern Railways' London to Birmingham service.

In an unusual move, August 2019 saw the Department for Transport take ownership of 40x4-car Class 365 EMUs from Eversholt Rail. A special purpose vehicle had been created to hold the Class 365s until 2021, which transferred to Eversholt at privatisation, but with 19 of the units in store the SPV was unable to make its lease payment, triggering guarantees in the contract and leading to the transfer of the fleet to DfT. The other 21 units remain in service with Govia Thameslink Railway. The Department set up Train Fleet Ltd, an offshoot of its Operator of Last Resort function, as the fleet's owner.

LOCAL OWNERSHIP

Most London Underground rolling stock is owned rather than leased. Crossrail's Class 345 trains were initially owned by Transport for London, before being sold in early 2019 to 345 Rail Leasing, a consortium of Equitix Investment Management Ltd, NatWest and SMBC Leasing, in a 20-year sale and leaseback deal which TfL said released £1 billion to reinvest into the capital's transport network.

The local ownership model has been followed on Merseyside, where the 52 new Stadler-built Class 777 EMUs will be owned by Merseytravel (which also led the procurement) and leased to Merseyrail.

In 2016 Kilmarnock-based firm Brodie Engineering completed repairs to a Class 156 DMU written off after a 2014 accident, and now leases it to ScotRail through a new leasing company, Brodie Leasing Ltd.

The Welsh Government initially intended to finance new trains for the Wales and Borders franchise itself, but subsequently received a cheaper offer involving private finance.

CROSS LONDON TRAINS

A new generation of train owners has steadily established itself. Prominent among them are those providing trains for the Thameslink and Intercity Express Programmes.

Cross London Trains is a consortium comprising Siemens Project Ventures GmbH, Innisfree Ltd and 3i Infrastructure plc set up (and appointed in 2011) to finance and purchase Class 700 Desiro City trains from Siemens for Thameslink services – a total of 1,140 vehicles in eight- and 12-car sets. In 2019 3i Infrastructure sold its 33.33% stake in the business to a consortium of Dalmore Capital and Equitix Investment Management.

Eversholt Rail was appointed to provide project and asset management services, including project management during the build and delivery of the rolling stock, and then long-term asset management, including both technical and commercial support.

INTERCITY EXPRESS PROGRAMME (IEP)

Agility Trains – a consortium of Hitachi and John Laing – secured the contract (confirmed in 2012) to supply Britain with the next generation of inter-city trains under the Intercity Express Programme (IEP).

Shareholders in Agility Trains West (for the Great Western route's trains) are Hitachi Rail Europe (70%), John Laing Infrastructure Fund (15%) and AXA (15%); John Laing Group sold its remaining interest in Agility Trains West in early 2018. Shareholders in Agility Trains East (for the East Coast route's trains) are Hitachi Rail Europe (70%) and AIP Management P/S (30%); John Laing Group divested its 30% share to AIP in September 2020 for a total consideration of up to £421 million, although the transaction is taking place in two stages, each comprising a 15% interest, and was not due to fully complete for up to 12 months.

Sources of IEP finance are: European Investment Bank, Japan Bank for International Co-operation, Bank of Tokyo Mitsubishi UFJ, Development Bank of Japan, HSBC, Lloyds, Mitsubishi Trust, Mizuho, Sumitomo Mitsui Banking Corporation (SMBC), Societe Generale and Credit Agricole.

BEACON RAIL

Beacon Rail Leasing Limited was established in January 2009 by BTMU Capital Corporation as its business entity for freight rolling stock leasing in the European market, including the former European portfolio of HSBC Rail (UK). In May 2014, Pamplona Capital Management announced the purchase of Beacon for a consideration of approximately $450 million. In

'803s' for East Coast Trains: Beacon Rail is the financier for this Hitachi fleet, now under construction at the manufacturer's Newton Aycliffe plant in County Durham. COURTESY HITACHI

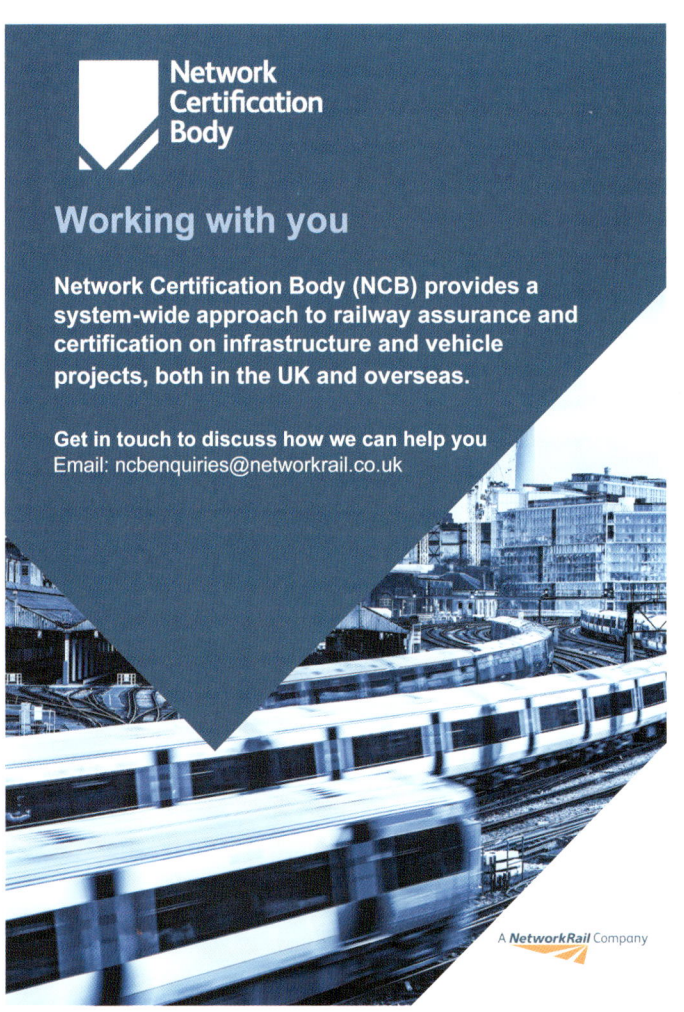

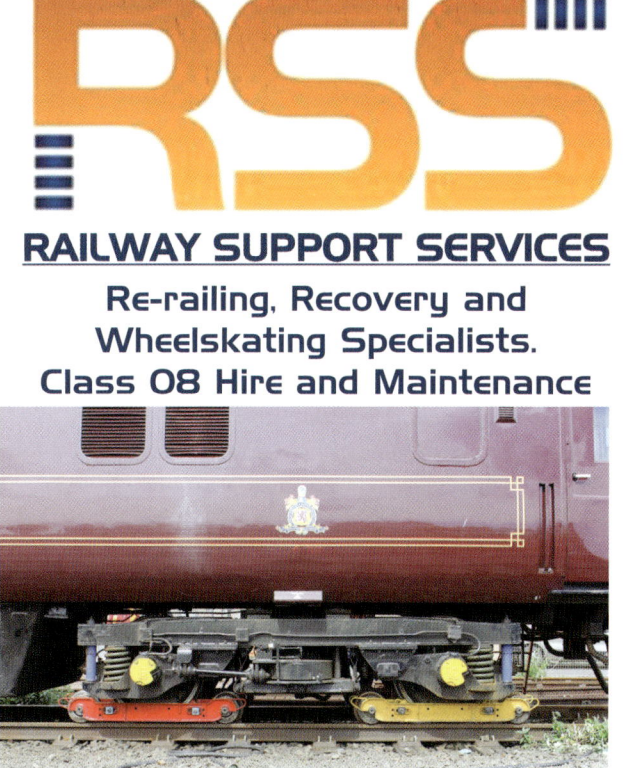

FINANCE AND LEASING

New trains for the West Midlands: Corelink Rail Infrastructure is funding two new train types for West Midlands Trains, including these Bombardier-built Class 730 EMUs. COURTESY WMT

To be assembled in Wales: bodyshell of a CAF Class 197 DMU for Transport for Wales Rail Services. New fleets for TfW are being funded by a consortium of SMBC Leasing and Equitix Ltd.

April 2017, Pamplona sold Beacon Rail to institutional investors advised by JP Morgan Asset Management in a transaction valued at around €1 billion.

Headquartered in Luxembourg with additional offices in London and Boston, Beacon Rail's portfolio includes over 200 locomotives, over 1,000 freight wagons, 55 passenger units, 67 double decker coaches and 13 sets of five-car inter-city carriages on lease in the UK, Germany, Denmark, France, Belgium, Norway, Sweden, Austria and the Netherlands.

In Britain, Beacon Rail leases eight Class 66s to Freightliner and five Class 66s to Direct Rail Services. Two Class 66s, transferred from Germany, entered service with GBRf in 2013, and a further nine GBRf Class 66s were sold to Beacon and leased back to GBRf in 2014. In 2018 GBRf agreed a sale and leaseback deal with Beacon for 10 Class 60 locomotives purchased from Colas Rail. GBRf has since introduced a further three Beacon-owned Class 66s transferred from Sweden and converted to UK specification, with five more from Germany to follow in 2021.

Beacon Rail has worked with Direct Rail Services (DRS) on the development of Vossloh Eurolight diesel locomotives, with 34 Class 68s now in the UK. These have been followed by 10 electric/diesel dual-mode Class 88 locomotives from Vossloh (now Stadler).

Beacon's first passenger trains were acquired in 2012 – 20 three-car Class 313 dual-voltage electric multiple-units, which had been retained by HSBC when it sold rolling stock company Eversholt Rail. Govia Thameslink Railway leases 19 of the Class 313s, and Network Rail leased the 20th as a test train for European Train Control System equipment.

In May 2016 Beacon agreed to purchase 66 Mk 5a carriages, manufactured by CAF, to run in 13 five-car sets for TransPennine Express (TPE). Beacon-owned Class 68 diesel locomotives haul the carriages, which entered service in August 2019 between Liverpool and Scarborough, with a pool of '68s' sub-leased from DRS to TPE.

In July 2017 Beacon purchased 78 Class 220 and 221 Voyager DEMUs from Voyager Leasing, a company established when the fleet was ordered. Of the 352 vehicles, 20 five-car Class 221s work for the West Coast franchise and the remainder of the four- and five-car units with CrossCountry.

In March 2019 Beacon was confirmed as financier for a fleet of 5x5-car Class 803 electric trains built by Hitachi for a new open access service to be operated by FirstGroup between London King's Cross and Edinburgh. The £100 million deal includes full provision of maintenance for 10 years.

In May 2020 Beacon awarded a contract to British locomotive manufacturer Clayton to build 15 Hybrid+ CBD90 shunting locomotives, along with options for a period of three years. Although the purchase is understood to be a speculative one, it is thought there will be no shortage of customers for the locos.

CALEDONIAN RAIL LEASING

Hitachi Rail Europe has built and is maintaining 46 three-car and 24 four-car Class 385 electric multiple-units for the ScotRail franchise. The contract is financed by Caledonian Rail Leasing Ltd, a Special Purpose Vehicle created by SMBC Leasing, involving KfW IPEX-Bank of Frankfurt and RBS/Lombard. The order was placed by SMBC Leasing (UK) Ltd.

CALEDONIAN SLEEPERS RAIL LEASING LTD

The fleet of 75 new Mk 5 Caledonian Sleeper coaches was manufactured by CAF. The project was funded with £60 million from Scottish Ministers, with additional financing by Caledonian Sleepers Rail Leasing Ltd, a subsidiary of Lombard North Central plc, part of RBS. The contract was valued at approximately €200 million for CAF, which supplies and manages spares, while the coaches are maintained by Alstom.

CORELINK RAIL INFRASTRUCTURE

West Midlands Trains is to introduce new fleets of CAF Civity DMUs (Class 196) and Bombardier Aventra EMUs (Class 730), totalling 413 carriages. Financing of the £680 million investment is by Corelink Rail Infrastructure Ltd, a ROSCO jointly owned by Infracapital and Deutsche Asset Management.

SMBC LEASING AND EQUITIX LTD

In 2018 SMBC Leasing (UK) Limited and Equitix Limited (SMBC-EQ) together succeeded in securing the financing of an £860 million fleet replacement programme as part of the 15-year Wales and Borders contract, awarded to KeolisAmey. The deal involved procurement of 148 units (421 vehicles) across four different fleet types from two manufacturers and due to enter service from 2021.

CAF will supply 51x2-car and 26x3-car Class 197 Civity DMUs, while Stadler will build 11x4-car Class 231 Flirt DEMUs, 36x3-car Class 398 tram-trains and 17x4-car and 7x3-car Class 756 Flirt tri-mode multiple-units. The companies say the agreements provide a whole-life asset management approach and a high level of long-term investment security beyond the current lease and usage undertaking terms.

QW RAIL LEASING

QW Rail Leasing, a joint venture between SMBC and National Australia Bank, leases Class 378 electric multiple-units to Arriva Rail London for Transport for London's London Overground concession. It also owns the 57 additional carriages used to increase all the trains to five-car length in 2015.

AKIEM GROUP

In November 2012, Macquarie Group announced that Macquarie Bank Ltd had established a new business, Macquarie European Rail, and agreed to acquire the European rolling stock leasing business of Lloyds Banking Group. In April 2020 the acquisition of Macquarie European Rail by Akiem Group was completed, comprising 137 locomotives, 30 EMUs, 16 DMUs and 110 wagons within the UK and Europe.

UK rolling stock which transferred includes 30 four-car Class 379 EMUs operated by Greater Anglia, plus a UK rail freight portfolio comprising 19 Freightliner Class 70s, 17 Freightliner Class 66s and 14 Direct Rail Services Class 66s. The acquisition gives Akiem the largest loco fleet on the continent with more than 600 locos operated by 65 customers. ■

caf.net

WHEN YOU NEED A HIGH SPEED SOLUTION…

The Oaris platform uses the latest technology to offer an inter-operable, high speed, high comfort travel for every passenger. With capacity to operate at speeds over 350 km/h - combined with the advantages of proven reliability, comfort and safety - Oaris is the Hero of High Speed.

Fast. Reliable. **Oaris**.

FINANCE AND LEASING

ROSCO FLEETS

New suburban fleet for Anglia: Angel Trains is funding a large order for Class 720 Aventra EMUs built by Bombardier for Greater Anglia. This is No 720511 on test in May 2020; the first six units were accepted by the operator in August, and entry into service was planned before the end of 2020. **COURTESY GREATER ANGLIA**

Multiple-unit vehicles, HST power cars and locomotives and their owners

345 RAIL LEASING
Class	Number of vehicles
MTR ELIZABETH LINE	
345	408

AGILITY TRAINS
Class	Number of vehicles
GWR	
800	369
LNER	
800	167
801	330

AKIEM GROUP
Class	Number of vehicles
DIRECT RAIL SERVICES	
66	14
FREIGHTLINER	
66	17
70	19
GREATER ANGLIA	
379	120

ANGEL TRAINS
Class	Number of vehicles
AVANTI WEST COAST	
390	574
C2C	
357	112
CHILTERN RAILWAYS	
165	89
172	8
CROSSCOUNTRY	
43	7

EAST MIDLANDS RAILWAY	
43	20
153	4
156	8
158	32
180	20
GRAND CENTRAL	
180	50
GREAT WESTERN RAILWAY	
43	11
150	2
165	88
166	63
GREATER ANGLIA	
317	184
360	84
720	30
HULL TRAINS	
802	25
MERSEYRAIL	
507	96
508	75
NORTHERN	
142	24
150	144
153	12
156	58
158	70
333	64
SCOTRAIL	
43	54
153	5
156	84

SOUTH WESTERN RAILWAY	
442	90
444	225
450	508
707	150
SOUTHEASTERN	
465	200
466	86
TRANSPENNINE EXPRESS	
802	95
TFW RAIL SERVICES	
142	28
153	5
158	48
175	70
WEST MIDLANDS TRAINS	
172	16
350	200

BEACON RAIL
Class	Number of vehicles
AVANTI WEST COAST	
221	100
COLAS RAIL	
56	5
66	5
67	2
70	7
CROSSCOUNTRY	
220	136
221	116

DIRECT RAIL SERVICES	
66	5
68	34
88	10
FREIGHTLINER	
66	8
GB RAILFREIGHT	
60	10
66	14
GOVIA THAMESLINK RAILWAY	
313	57
NETWORK RAIL	
313	3

BRODIE LEASING
Class	Number of vehicles
SCOTRAIL	
156	2

CALEDONIAN RAIL LEASING
Class	Number of vehicles
SCOTRAIL	
385	234

CROSS LONDON TRAINS
Class	Number of vehicles
GOVIA THAMESLINK RAILWAY	
700	1,140

EVERSHOLT RAIL
Class	Number of vehicles
CHILTERN RAILWAYS	
168	9

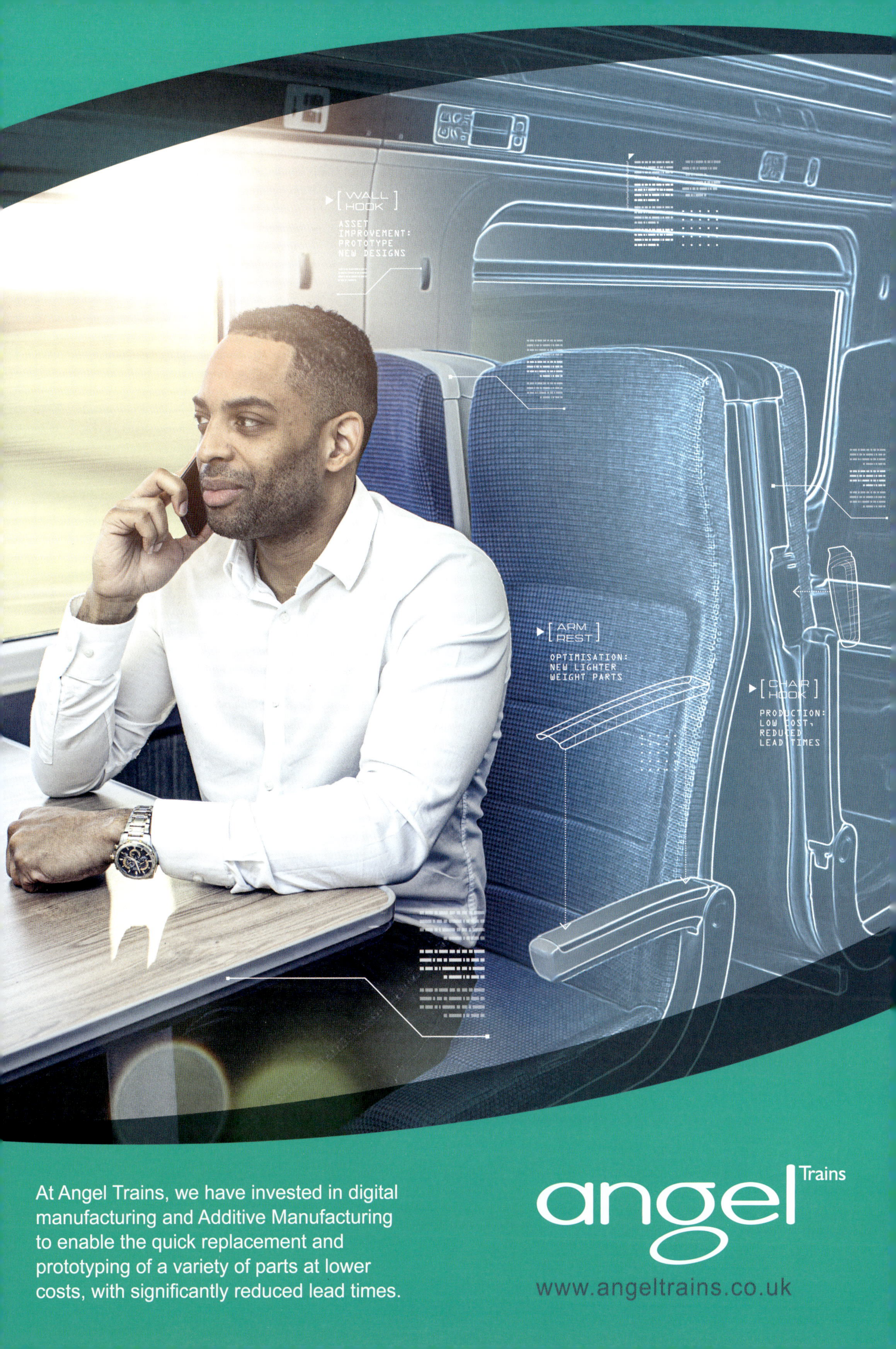

WALL HOOK
ASSET IMPROVEMENT: PROTOTYPE NEW DESIGNS
ARM REST
OPTIMISATION: NEW LIGHTER WEIGHT PARTS
CHAIR HOOK
PRODUCTION: LOW COST, REDUCED LEAD TIMES
At Angel Trains, we have invested in digital manufacturing and Additive Manufacturing to enable the quick replacement and prototyping of a variety of parts at lower costs, with significantly reduced lead times.
angel Trains
www.angeltrains.co.uk

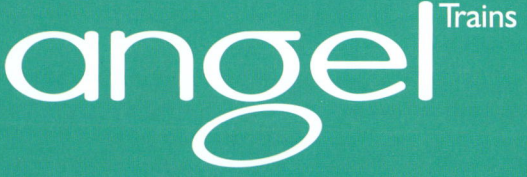

FINANCE AND LEASING

EAST MIDLANDS RAILWAY
Class	Number of vehicles
170	15
222	143

FREIGHTLINER
Class	Number of vehicles
66	56

GB RAILFREIGHT
Class	Number of vehicles
66	27

GOVIA THAMESLINK RAILWAY
Class	Number of vehicles
171	12
455	184

GREAT WESTERN RAILWAY
Class	Number of vehicles
802	236

GREATER ANGLIA
Class	Number of vehicles
321	420
322	20

LNER
Class	Number of vehicles
91	12

MTR ELIZABETH LINE
Class	Number of vehicles
315	80

NORTHERN
Class	Number of vehicles
158	20
195	149
331	141

RAIL OPERATIONS GROUP
Class	Number of vehicles
91	2

SCOTRAIL
Class	Number of vehicles
318	63
320	102
334	120
380	130

SOUTHEASTERN
Class	Number of vehicles
375	438
376	180
395	174
465	388

TRANSPENNINE EXPRESS
Class	Number of vehicles
185	153
397	60

FIRSTGROUP
Class	Number of vehicles
GREAT WESTERN RAILWAY	
43	16

LOMBARD FINANCE
Class	Number of vehicles
COLAS RAIL	
70	10

PORTERBROOK
Class	Number of vehicles
C2C	
357	184
387	24
CHILTERN RAILWAYS	
168	76
COLAS RAIL	
43	2
CROSSCOUNTRY	
43	5
170	74
DIRECT RAIL SERVICES	
57	2
EAST MIDLANDS RAILWAY	
43	8
153	7
156	40
158	20
FREIGHTLINER	
66	32
86	10
90	10
GB RAILFREIGHT	
66	9
GOVIA THAMESLINK RAILWAY	
171	44
377	894
387	224
GREAT WESTERN RAILWAY	
57	4
143	10
150	34
158	43
387	180
NETWORK RAIL	
43	3
NORTHERN	
150	22
153	8
155	14
156	36
158	24
170	48
319	44
323	51
ORION HIGH SPEED LOGISTICS	
319	4
RAIL OPERATIONS GROUP	
57	4
SCOTRAIL	
158	80
170	102
SOUTH WESTERN RAILWAY	
57	1
158	20
159	90
455	364
456	48
458	180

SOUTHEASTERN
Class	Number of vehicles
377	68

TFW RAIL SERVICES
Class	Number of vehicles
143	22
150	72
153	17
170	32

WEST MIDLANDS TRAINS
Class	Number of vehicles
139	2
153	8
170	51
172	69
319	64
323	78
350	148

QW RAIL LEASING
Class	Number of vehicles
LONDON OVERGROUND	
378	285

ROCK RAIL
Class	Number of vehicles
GOVIA THAMESLINK RAILWAY	
717	150
GREATER ANGLIA	
745	240
755	138

TRAIN FLEET (2019) LTD
Class	Number of vehicles
GOVIA THAMESLINK RAILWAY	
365	84

Note: information believed correct as at October 2020. These tables represent a snapshot of a constantly changing situation.

Electrostar upgrade: a £55 million modernisation of Porterbrook-owned Class 377 and 387 EMUs operated by Govia Thameslink Railway began in autumn 2020, covering a total of 270 trains. This is Nos 377211/208 arriving at Bletchley with the 10.10 East Croydon to Milton Keynes Central service on 27 April 2019. **PHILIP SHERRATT**

TRAIN FLEET MAINTENANCE AND MANUFACTURE

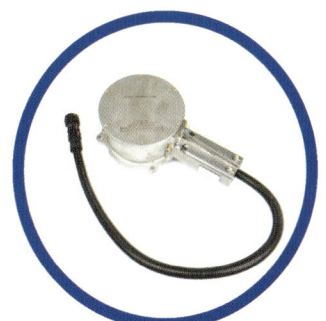
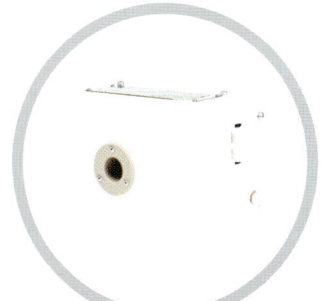

IN ASSOCIATION WITH

Rowe Hankins Ltd.

TRAIN FLEET MAINTENANCE AND MANUFACTURE

Pandemic threatens to reset rolling stock market

Modern Railways Industry and Technology Editor **ROGER FORD** assesses the prospects for rolling stock suppliers in an uncertain year

With delivery of the large orders placed following the 2013 reform of franchising starting to wind down, the ongoing Covid-19 pandemic overshadows any consideration of the new contracts needed to maintain continuity of production on assembly lines in the UK rolling stock plants. The franchise reforms added a quality factor to bid assessment, making new trains an essential feature of a winning bid, encouraging mass fleet replacement.

Now, the resulting boom in orders has come to an abrupt end. In the case of the South Eastern franchise, total fleet replacement would have required over 1,300 new electric multiple-unit (EMU) vehicles. But even before the pandemic, the potential rolling stock suppliers shortlisted by bidders had already seen the expected replacement of the fleet slip back and reduce in scale as it proved impossible to relet the franchise on acceptable terms. Similarly, the long-standing requirement to increase the capacity and upgrade the quality of the CrossCountry fleet had also stalled.

At the same time, the continuing mass fleet replacements by LNER, Northern, TransPennine Express and Greater Anglia have been flooding the market with surplus trains. Some, such as the Pacers and older EMUs, including the Class 314s in Scotland and Class 315s serving London, are life expired and are being scrapped or sent to preservation. However, there is a growing number of fleets, ranging in age from almost new, which their owners will hope to keep on lease.

PROVEN

These surplus fleets represent a threat to near-term procurement of new trains. Finding new applications for trains displaced by the 'mass extinction' fleet replacement policies of new franchisees may have been assisted by the impact of the pandemic on ridership.

With procurement of new trains on hold, surplus stock can be used to augment fleets or enhance quality by replacing an operator's oldest and least reliable trains. And in a buyer's market, they are likely to be cheap.

Newest of the fleets to be replaced are the Siemens Desiro City Class 707 EMUs procured by South West Trains and due to be replaced by the successor franchisee, South Western Railway, with a new fleet of Bombardier Aventra units. The Class 707s have already been identified for transfer to Southeastern, where they could replace ex-British Rail Class 465 first-generation AC drive trains.

Another relatively new train coming off lease is the Bombardier Electrostar Class 379 fleet, supplied for Greater Anglia's Stansted Express service in 2010. These are likely to be the last of the Greater Anglia units to be released as the replacement Class 720 Aventra fleet is delivered through 2021.

Also coming off lease are Porterbrook's Siemens Class 350/2 EMUs from West Midlands Trains. These are slightly older than the Class 379s, but a proven design with an excellent reliability record. Here Porterbrook's focus on what operators are going to need in the longer-term is reflected in discussion on conversion to battery-electric traction configuration.

FUTURE PROOFING

Retrofitting batteries to the Class 350/2 fleet is just one example of the rolling stock companies investing in upgrades aimed at meeting new demands in a changing world, at the same time as competing with more expensive new equipment. For example, while the UK Government has an aspiration to remove all diesel-powered traction by 2040, diesel multiple-units (DMUs) with the lowest emissions will be last to be withdrawn during the transition to electrification or alternative traction.

Anticipating this changing demand, Porterbrook is fitting a Chiltern Class 168 DMU with an MTU battery hybrid traction package. The aim is to cut CO_2 emissions by 24%, nitrous oxides (NOx) by 74% and, with battery power supplementing the diesel engine, reduce journey times by up to 7%.

More ambitious is Angel Trains' £4 million Hydrive project to convert a Class 165 DMU to a battery-electric hybrid. A new three-phase electric

Modern EMU going off lease: Siemens-built Class 350/2 No 350263 at Norton Bridge with the 08.56 Stafford to Crewe service on 27 May 2020. **JOHN WHITEHOUSE**

TRAIN FLEET MAINTENANCE AND MANUFACTURE

Delayed by software issues: Bombardier Aventra EMU Nos 710108/121 for London Overground approach Bethnal Green with the 13.15 Liverpool Street to Chingford service on 3 March 2020. **PHILIP SHERRATT**

Civity in service: CAF DMU No 195009 departs Sheffield with Northern's 12.09 Leeds to Nottingham service on 7 February 2020. **PHILIP SHERRATT**

traction drive will replace the existing hydro-mechanical transmission, improving performance and further reducing energy consumption through regenerative braking.

Also looking to the long-term is Hitachi, which has signed an agreement with North East-based battery specialist Hyperdrive Innovation. Under the exclusive deal, Hyperdrive will develop battery packs for rail traction and create a battery hub in the North East.

One 800 Series bi-mode owner is already discussing a trial conversion, replacing one diesel generator unit with a battery power pack. Also being considered is fitting battery packs to some of LNER's Class 801 all-electric Azuma fleet. This would allow operation to Lincoln, for example, just 17 miles beyond the wires.

HYDROGEN

While the Traction Decarbonisation Network Strategy (TDNS, p119) emphasises the niche contribution of hydrogen fuel cell traction and battery power, substantial resources are being invested in converting surplus legacy electric multiple-units to fuel cell traction. First to run on the main line was the Porterbrook HydroFlex – one in the company's series of Class 319 Conversions.

Being developed in conjunction with the University of Birmingham, the HydroFlex retains its electric traction equipment. The fuel cell traction package is seen as a 'range extender', powering the EMU beyond the electrified network. This 'bi-mode' capability has potential applications during the rolling

TABLE 1: OUTSTANDING DELIVERIES

OPERATOR	CLASS	TYPE	SETS	VEHICLES	FORMATION	ORDER PLACED	FULL FLEET IN SERVICE
Bombardier							
Greater Anglia	720	Aventra EMU	133	665	133x5-car	August 2016	Mid-2021
c2c	720/6	Aventra EMU	6	60	6x10-car	December 2017	December 2021
South Western Railway	701	Aventra EMU	90	750	30x5-car, 60x10-car	June 2017	Mid-2021
West Midlands Trains	730	Aventra EMU	81	333	36x3-car, 45x5-car	December 2017	December 2021
Total vehicles				1,808			
CAF							
West Midlands Trains	196	Civity DMU	26	80	12x2-car, 14x4-car	October 2017	May 2021
Transport for Wales	197	Civity DMU	77	180	51x2-car, 26x3-car	June 2018	Spring 2023
Transport for London	DLR		43	215	43x5-car	June 2019	February 2026
Total vehicles				475			
Hitachi							
East Coast Trains	803	AT300 EMU	5	25	5x5-car	March 2019	December 2021
Avanti West Coast	805	AT300 bi-mode	13	65	13x5-car	December 2019	December 2022
Avanti West Coast	807	AT300 EMU	10	70	10x7-car	December 2019	December 2022
East Midlands Railway	810	AT300 SXR bi-mode	33	165	33x5-car	July 2019	Summer 2023
Total vehicles				325			
Siemens							
London Underground		Inspiro tube train	94	846	94x9-car	November 2018	
Stadler							
Merseyrail	777	Metro EMU	52	208	52x4-car	February 2017	December 2021
Transport for Wales	231	Flirt DEMU	11	44	11x4-car	June 2018	September 2022
Transport for Wales	398	Citylink tram-train	36	108	36x3-car	March 2019	December 2022
Transport for Wales	756	Flirt tri-mode MU	24	89	7x3-car, 17x4-car	June 2018	
Tyne and Wear Metro (Nexus)		Metro EMU	42	210	42x5-car	February 2020	2024
Glasgow Subway		Underground train	17	68	17x4-car	March 2016	
Total vehicles				727			
Porterbrook							
Transport for Wales	769	Flex bi-mode	9	36	9x4-car	July 2017	Autumn 2021
Great Western Railway	769	Flex tri-mode	19	76	19x4-car		
Total vehicles				112			
Vivarail							
South Western Railway	484	EMU	5	10	5x2-car	September 2019	Spring 2021
Transport for Wales	230	Hybrid MU	5	15	5x3-car	October 2018	
Total vehicles				25			

Aurora: Hitachi is supplying 33x5-car Class 810 bi-modes for East Midlands Railway, which unveiled the brand name for the fleet in October 2020.

programme of electrification leading up to decarbonisation in 2050.

In contrast, the Alstom/Eversholt Breeze Class 321 fuel cell conversion is aimed at the long-term diesel replacement market for lines where electrification may not be justified. The installation draws on Alstom's proven Coradia iLint fuel cell powered multiple-unit, currently in service in Germany and with more on order.

Alstom is hoping to obtain an early order for an initial batch of Breeze conversions. The work would be carried out at its new Widnes facility. This would also see Widnes become the group's centre of excellence for hydrogen power.

Finally, Transport Scotland and Scottish Enterprise are funding a project to convert a Class 314 EMU to hydrogen power. The project is being carried out by the University of St Andrews' Hydrogen Accelerator research group. It is intended to support the Scottish Government's plans to decarbonise passenger rail transport by 2035 – five years ahead of current British Government targets.

PROSPECTS

Table 1 shows the current order books and delivery status of the manufacturers active in the UK rolling stock market. Note that of the nearly 3,000 vehicles for the national rail network, some 1,800 are represented by late-running Bombardier Aventra contracts. These are scheduled to be delivered by the end of 2021.

Bombardier enters 2021 with six production lines running at its Litchurch Lane, Derby factory. Any follow-on orders are unlikely to require this level of output. The company had formed an alliance with Hitachi to bid for the rolling stock for HS2, but the status of this venture is unclear following the acquisition of Bombardier by Alstom.

CAF's new plant in Newport, South Wales, has work for Transport for Wales; the Docklands Light Railway order will be built in Spain. The small assembly facility at Newport can survive on a low production rate, but with room to expand if required.

At its Newton Aycliffe plant Hitachi has been running a single production line with a 'beat rate' of four to five vehicles a week. While the company has won several contracts for its AT300 EMUs and bi-modes, these are for relatively small quantities. However, there should be sufficient work to take the plant through to 2022 at current capacity.

LNER is also going out to tender for 10 inter-city high-speed trains. This order is expected to be competed.

Stadler supplies the UK from its European plants and has seen its prudence in not seeking to influence

TABLE 2: NEW TRAIN RELIABILITY, 2020-21 PERIOD 6

OPERATOR	CLASS	TRACTION	MAKER	NUMBER OF UNITS/ TRAINSETS	NUMBER OF TECHNICAL INCIDENTS (TIN)	UNIT MILES	MILES PER TECHNICAL INCIDENT (MTIN)	MTIN MOVING ANNUAL AVERAGE
South Western Railway	Class 707	EMU	Siemens	30	1	208,262	208,262	81,340
ScotRail	Class 385	EMU	Hitachi	70	5	421,446	84,289	48,704
LNER	Class 801	EMU	Hitachi	42	28	597,952	21,355	19,084
Hull Trains	Class 802	bi-mode	Hitachi	5	2	26,780	13,390	18,972
Govia Thameslink Railway	Class 700	EMU	Siemens	115	63	1,220,610	19,375	17,923
LNER	Class 800	Bi-mode	Hitachi	57	56	739,666	13,208	15,238
Great Western Railway	Class 800	Bi-mode	Hitachi	23	20	293,395	14,670	12,632
Great Western Railway	Class 802	Bi-mode	Hitachi	36	42	511,058	12,168	11,986
Govia Thameslink Railway	Class 717	EMU	Siemens	25	9	156,483	17,387	11,407
TransPennine Express	Class 802	bi-mode	Hitachi	19	12	160,513	13,376	8,615
TransPennine Express	Nova 3 train set	Diesel	CAF	5	11	36,826	3,348	7,848
ScotRail	HST Set	Diesel	BREL/Wabtec	19	23	112,429	4,888	6,781
TfL Rail (Crossrail)	Class 345 RLU	EMU	Bombardier	30	24	215,980	8,999	6,301
Great Western Railway	HST set	Diesel	BREL/Wabtec	11	17	108,451	6,379	6,234
TransPennine Express	Class 397	EMU	CAF	12	15	151,859	10,124	6,010
Northern	Class 331/0	EMU	CAF	29	20	234,066	11,703	4,968
Arriva Rail London	Class 710/2	EMU	Bombardier	14	14	85,344	6,096	4,803
Greater Anglia	Class 745/0	EMU	Stadler	8	17	96,162	5,657	4,658
Northern	Class 195/0	DMU	CAF	24	29	133,068	4,589	4,370
Greater Anglia	Class 755/4	Bi-mode	Stadler	19	46	195,011	4,239	3,955
Northern	Class 195/1	DMU	CAF	30	53	235,562	4,445	3,949
Greater Anglia	Class 755/3	Bi-mode	Stadler	13	26	117,935	4,536	3,796
Greater Anglia	Class 745/1	EMU	Stadler	3	27	77,245	2,861	3,766
Northern	Class 331/1	EMU	CAF	12	12	61,089	5,091	3,192
Arriva Rail London	Class 710/1	EMU	Bombardier	24	32	123,312	3,854	2,401
West Midlands Trains	Class 230	DMU	Vivarail	3	2	4,602	2,301	1,607
TfL Rail (Crossrail)	Class 345 FLU	EMU	Bombardier	29	78	32,921	422	781

TIN=technical incident, where a train is stopped for three minutes or more due to a vehicle problem. RLU=reduced length unit, FLU=full length unit

TRAIN FLEET MAINTENANCE AND MANUFACTURE

procurement by setting up a UK assembly facility rewarded. However, it is assured of a long-term UK presence through maintenance contracts.

While not currently assembling new trains, Alstom's Widnes Transport & Technology Centre has the £127 million contract to refurbish the Avanti West Coast Class 390 Pendolino fleet. This will provide a base load of work into 2023. As reported above, the conversion of Class 321 EMUs for fuel cell traction would also be centred on Widnes.

Penalty for late delivery: Stadler has paid compensation to Greater Anglia relating to its contract for Flirt EMUs and bi-modes. No 755415 departs Hoveton & Wroxham with the 14.36 Norwich to Sheringham service on 1 January 2020. **PHILIP SHERRATT**

RELIABILITY

Highlighted in last year's traction and rolling stock overview was the unreliability of many of the new train fleets. This was compounded by late deliveries increasing the pressure on commissioning schedules and curtailing shakedown running.

During 2020 it became clear that reliability from the products of manufacturers active in the UK rolling stock market has polarised. As Table 2 shows, in part benefiting from their long-term presence in the UK, Hitachi and Siemens fill the top 10 places in the new train reliability ranking. They also have a record of continuing improvement (Figure 1).

A rule of thumb among operators is that reliability ceases to have a significant influence on service performance once a fleet reaches a failure rate around 15,000 miles per casualty. On the UK network a Technical Incident (TIN) is recorded once a train has been stopped for three minutes.

Of the top 10 fleets, just over half have passed the 15,000 MTIN moving annual average mark, and all but one are over 10,000 MTIN MAA and improving.

Contrast this with the foot of Table 1, where the bottom 12 are below 5,000 MTIN MAA. In some cases, the new trains are recording reliability figures under half those of the legacy rolling stock they are replacing.

PENALTIES

Late delivery and commissioning has also required extensions to existing short-term derogations for ex-British Rail rolling stock not compliant with the Persons with Reduced Mobility Technical Specification for Interoperability (PRM-TSI). PRM-TSI compliance became mandatory for all passenger rolling stock from 1 January 2020 and late deliveries in 2020 had already required limited exemptions.

Apart from the reputational damage, the combination of late delivery and poor performance has resulted in substantial penalties for manufacturers. Stadler, for example, has reported 'mid-to-high double-digit Swiss Francs millions' payments to Greater Anglia. This is estimated at £40-70 million.

In addition to manufacturers, the funders of the new rolling stock are also under threat from the impact of the pandemic on passenger ridership. Procurement of the 'mass extinction' fleet replacements was floated on a wave of cheap money, with pensions providers and other financial institutions seeing investment in rolling stock as generating reliable returns.

With the passenger industry now actively looking at rationalising services to bring operating costs closer to income, the prospect looms of rolling stock being taken out of service. 2021 promises to be a difficult time for the rolling stock industry. ■

FIGURE 1: HITACHI AND SIEMENS NEW TRAIN FLEET RELIABILITY IMPROVEMENT

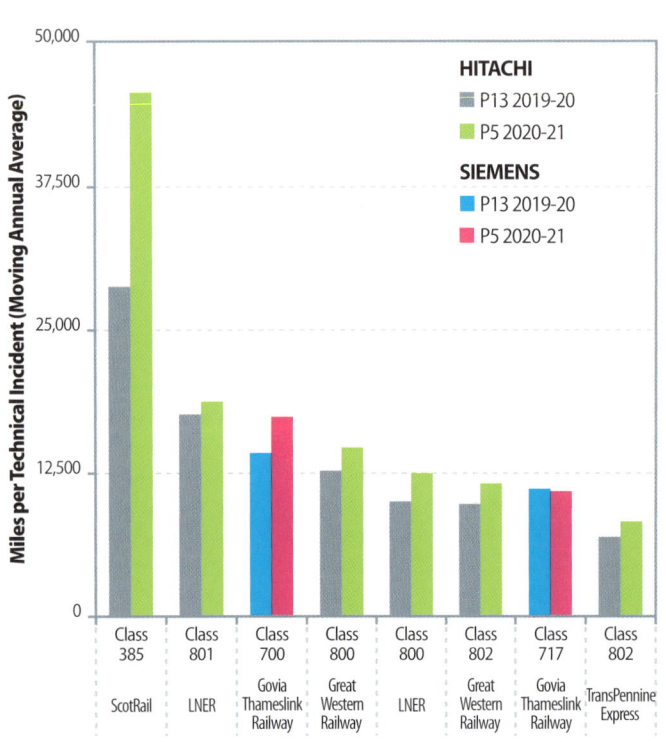

FIGURE 2: BOMBARDIER, CAF AND STADLER NEW TRAIN FLEET RELIABILITY IMPROVEMENT

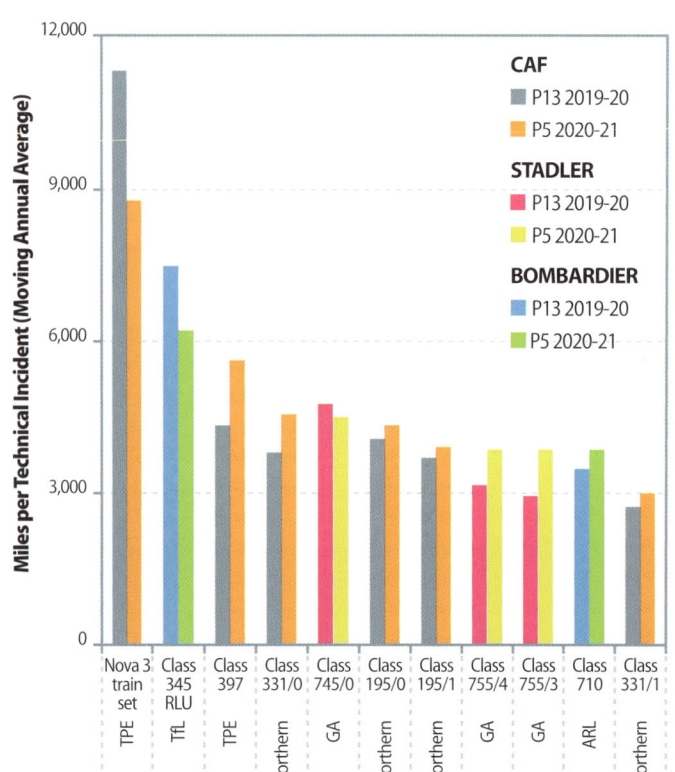

IN ASSOCIATION WITH

Precision Engineering with the iWFL and ToRFM Systems

Rowe Hankins Ltd. has supplied a UK Government-backed rail project with an award-winning intelligent modular system that enables asset managers to extend the lifecycle of wheel wear and rail infrastructure that makes passenger journeys greener and screech-free

2020 has been a year that has changed the way we all work and operate in this 'new normal'. Despite this, many advances in technologies have been made within the traction industry. Track conditions still continue to be a main offender in train and plant derailments.

However, Rowe Hankins Ltd's Intelligent Wheel Flange Lubrication (iWFL) changes that. The on-board dispensing systems improve safety and rail wear and significantly extend wheel life.

The iWFL system and the Top of Rail Friction Modifier system (ToRFM) are on-board line replacement units for all types of railway vehicles, both new build and retrofit. The systems can be used independently or controlled by the vehicles train management system, with laptop based on-site customisation and easy installation and maintenance. Using the railway vehicle (or a dedicated) antenna for GPS signals also means there is minimum disruption to the train infrastructure.

The technical team designed the iWFL system to apply predefined amounts of lubricant, creating an energy efficient use of lubricant compared to existing stick lubricants. Environmental impact was a big consideration during the planning process of the iWFL and the lubricants. As a result, the system has been developed to enhance asset life, reduce wheel and track wear and reduce the need for maintenance as often.

Engineered for national rail networks and urban tram services, by using geographical location-based dispensing of flange lubrication. The intelligent design senses the location and intensity of track curves using a combination of GPS signals, track balise beacons and speed and distance sensors.

In addition, the ToRFM system is designed to reduce curve squeal noise and short pitch corrugation. ToRFM can work independently or in conjunction with the iWFL to extend track life and reduce asset maintenance. ToRFM is a customised friction modifier system that applies a friction modifier to the top of the rail. This combination means that both the top of the rail track and the wheels flanges are sprayed with the exact amount of lubricant needed. Rowe Hankins Ltd. has also designed a biodegradable lubricant and friction modifier to work with the iWFL and ToRFM systems to ensure the maximum lifecycle of wheel wear and infrastructure.

By considering the need for both the mechanical interface solution and the environmental impact of noise, an intelligent, self-diagnostic connected solution has also been implemented; to pinpoint the precise application point, for lubrication to be dispensed. Selected wheels can have flange, back of flange and top of rail, that are pre-treated before wheel rail contact occurs. Chief Engineer Tariq Latif says: 'The use of iWFL and ToRFM work to extend service and maintenance intervals, reducing downtime and costs, whilst also using a predefined amount of lubrication to create a greener system'.

The innovative eco-friendly systems are already in use on rail networks across Europe. In the UK, Rowe Hankins Ltd. has also been approved as the preferred supplier for Crossrail's Elizabeth Line, the high frequency, high capacity railway for London and the South East.

Rowe Hankins Ltd. is committed to continual improvement, development and growth. This year has also seen a change to include a more customer focused and dynamic management team, to continue to pioneer the technologies within the traction industry. Alex Emmerson, Engineering Manager, says 'In the last year we have had a breakthrough in the development of new specialised electromagnetic components, leading the way to a vast new product range expected in 2021-22'. In addition, key progress is also underway for a new Non-intrusive Current Monitor and 4 Channel Speed Sensor, which are to be presented at InnoTrans in 2022. ∎

Rowe Hankins Ltd. is a supplier of specialised rail technologies, working with rolling stock manufacturers, train operating companies, track owners and infrastructure contractors. The company has been operating in the rail industry for over 30 years, providing innovative trainborne and wayside electromechanical equipment for safer and more efficient operations as well as having service capabilities specifying in engineering and design to overhaul and repair.

CONTACT INFORMATION
Phone: +44(0)161 765 3000
Email: sales@rowehankins.com
Website: www.rowehankins.com

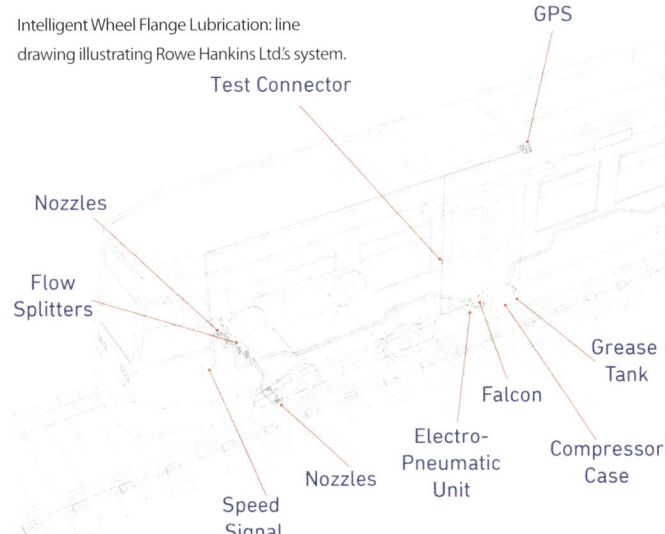

Intelligent Wheel Flange Lubrication: line drawing illustrating Rowe Hankins Ltd's system.

Labels: GPS, Test Connector, Nozzles, Flow Splitters, Grease Tank, Falcon, Electro-Pneumatic Unit, Compressor Case, Nozzles, Speed Signal

RICHARD SYKES
Managing Director

PAUL BRISCOE
Finance Director

JENNIFER TOTTEY
Compliance and Assurance Manager

ALEX EMMERSON
Engineering Manager

TARIQ LATIF
Chief Engineer

LEE WALKER
Sales Manager

Focus: Rowe Hankins Ltd. has recently made changes to its management team.

TRAIN FLEET MAINTENANCE AND MANUFACTURE

CAF builds for the future

CAF has continued to consolidate its reputation as one of the leading train manufacturers in the UK market. 2020 saw good progress with a range of contracts, from delivery of new trains to completion of key design phases. CAF also celebrated the official opening of its manufacturing facility in Newport, South Wales, which has been up and running now for over two years.

NEW TRAINS IN SERVICE

One of CAF's largest UK contracts has now been fully executed with the delivery of the last Civity trains for Northern. CAF has supplied a total of 101 trains – Class 195 DMUs and Class 331 EMUs, which are owned by Eversholt Rail and began entering service in July 2019. In addition to the Northern fleets, CAF's pivotal role in transforming rail journeys across the North of England is emphasised by its supply of new trains for TransPennine Express, in the form of Class 397 Civity EMUs and Mk 5a coaches, both also now in service.

In April 2020 CAF delivered the first of 26 Class 196 DMUs for West Midlands Trains, which has begun testing the new trains on the UK network. These units are also from CAF's Civity platform – the order comprises 12x2-car and 14x4-car units, with three-quarters of the vehicles being built at the factory at Newport.

An important milestone in CAF's contract to supply Civity DMUs for the Wales and Borders franchise was reached during 2020 with the achievement of design approval. The fleet of 51x2-car and 26x3-car units will all be built at Newport and will form the backbone of inter-urban and long-distance services within the franchise when they enter service from 2022.

CAF continues to enjoy success in the light rail market, with two UK contracts in progress. Twenty-one new trams will be supplied for the West Midlands Metro network, adding to the 21-strong CAF Urbos fleet already operating on the system. There is an option for up to 29 more trams to follow, with CAF also providing technical support services and the supply of spares.

Progress has continued with CAF's order to supply 43 new trains for the Docklands Light Railway in London. Despite the disruption caused by Covid-19, 2020 saw completion of a full-size virtual reality model of one of the new trains, a key design accomplishment.

CAF has further cemented its relationship with Northern Irish operator Translink with the extension of a maintenance contract for the Class 3000 diesel train fleet. The deal is valued at over €60 million and runs for a term of 15 years, with maintenance activities undertaken at workshops at York Road and Adelaide in Belfast City. CAF's relationship with Translink dates back to 2002, and an additional 56 intermediate carriages for the Class 4000 DMU fleet are currently under construction for delivery during 2021.

BATTERY TECHNOLOGY

CAF is a leader in battery technology and is actively looking to roll out this technology in the UK. The company has been producing catenary-free trams since 2010; these use Greentech, the on-board energy storage system product developed by CAF's Power and Automation division.

The technology is already in service on the CAF Urbos trams operating on the West Midlands Metro network, where the 21-strong fleet has been fitted with an on-

Royal opening: His Royal Highness the Prince of Wales (right) and CAF CEO Andrés Arizkorreta welcome the opening of CAF's factory at Newport on 21 February 2020.

Civity DMU for the West Midlands: CAF is supplying 26 Class 196 units for West Midlands Trains.

IN ASSOCIATION WITH

Batteries included: the fleet of CAF Urbos trams operating on West Midlands Metro has been fitted with an on-board energy storage system to support catenary-free operation. This tram is leaving the Town Hall stop on the Centenary Square extension, opened in December 2019 and entirely catenary-free. **PHILIP SHERRATT**

board energy storage system to support catenary-free operation. In December 2019 an extension of the West Midlands Metro from Grand Central to Centenary Square opened, on which the CAF trams operate entirely under battery power. This has been very successful and has proven the use of this technology within the UK. CAF also has an on-board energy storage system support contract for the West Midlands Metro fleet. As further extensions of the network are opened, the extent of catenary-free operation on the West Midlands Metro will grow further, with plans for over 25km of routes to use battery power out of a full planned network amounting to 95km in length.

Decarbonisation continues to be an important topic across the rail industry, and CAF is ready to play its part. The publication of Network Rail's Traction Decarbonisation Network Strategy sets out a path to reducing the use of diesel trains in the UK, and battery technology will have an important role to play as both an interim solution and no doubt as part of the long-term answer.

In Spain CAF has a contract for 31 metric gauge trains for Renfe, five of which will be dual-type and able to run on both electric and catenary-free lines. These will be designed so they can in future be converted to use battery or fuel cell technology, proving the development of the technology for main line applications. CAF is actively exploring potential applications for batteries within the UK, with possibilities including retro-fitment to existing fleets for operation on branch lines away from overhead wires.

HIGH-SPEED POTENTIAL

In June 2019 CAF submitted a bid to HS2 Ltd for the contract to design, build and maintain circa 54 trains for Phase One of the high-speed line. The company is proposing its Oaris platform to meet the exacting requirements of the £2.75 billion contract, combining capability of operation at over 360km/h with the advantages of proven reliability, comfort and safety. The award of the HS2 contract is due in spring 2021, and if successful it would secure the future of its Newport factory.

CAF has five high-speed train fleets in traffic around the world, including in Spain, Turkey and Norway. For the latter, Flytoget has recently taken delivery of four-car EMUs for its Airport Express, which represent the latest development of the Oaris platform.

Through a decade-long process of continuous investment by CAF, Oaris has seen the evolution of a modular platform, for which Flytoget is the latest customer. The platform is a non-articulated electric multiple-unit with distributed power designed for 220mph running, with an in-service speed of at least 200mph. The design is such that Oaris' power equipment can be adapted for any of the main overhead line electrification systems used across Europe. From a passenger perspective, Oaris is a modular design which allows customers to create different configurations depending on the requirements.

NEWPORT FACTORY OPENED

On 21 February 2020 His Royal Highness the Prince of Wales officially opened CAF's factory at the Celtic Business Park near Newport, South Wales.

The factory is the result of a £30 million investment by CAF with grant support from the Welsh Government's Inward Investment Programme. The Prince was given a tour of the factory by CAF's CEO Andrés Arizkorreta, allowing him to inspect the construction of Civity DMUs for Northern and West Midlands Trains, which has been followed at the site by the assembly of Civity DMUs for the Wales and Borders franchise.

Newport is the base for the CAF UK rolling stock division. The factory houses a staff of over 200 which is set to grow to around 300 as CAF expands, particularly towards the Wales and Borders contract. CAF has adopted a similar production process to that found at its other factories worldwide, but one difference is that Newport is a digital factory, free from paperwork.

While the current focus is on building DMUs, Newport is set up to build a range of CAF products from light rail to high-speed, including for export abroad. The factory has scope to expand, including the setup of further production lines and options for additional land within the Celtic Business Park if needed.

As important as the construction of trains is the legacy the factory creates and the economic stimulus it delivers to the South Wales area and beyond. This not only includes development of the local supply chain, but also the employment of apprentices and the development of partnerships with local education facilities, creating a skills legacy which extends beyond train building to fields such as research and development, infrastructure, testing and planning.

GLOBAL GROWTH

The growth of CAF within the UK is only part of the company's global

AWARDS SUCCESS

CAF's reputation as a leading manufacturer was confirmed with multiple award wins at the Global Light Rail Awards in 2019. CAF was named Manufacturer of the Year, a prestigious award which recognises the company's reputation as a world-leading provider of products, services and solutions for the railway sector. In addition, the company received the Project of the Year Under €50 million accolade for its contract to supply six state-of-the-art vehicles for the first catenary-free light rail system in passenger operation in Oceania. CAF was also awarded highly commended in two other categories. CAF has previously won the Manufacturer of the Year Award in 2017 and 2016.

growth story, which has seen it win new contracts worldwide. Successes since 2019 have included the award of contracts to supply CAF vehicles for systems as diverse as Naples Metro, Jerusalem Tram and EMUs for French national operator SNCF. CAF is part of the Momentum Trains consortium awarded a contract by Transport for New South Wales to supply a new fleet of 29 diesel-electric units, with the deal also including provision of two simulators and construction and fit-out of a new maintenance facility in Dubbo, north-west of Sydney.

Highlights of 2020 included contract wins to supply 37 metric gauge trains for Spanish operator RENFE, a further nine trams to Amsterdam (on top of an original order for 63 vehicles) and five M300 series metro units for Helsinki (in addition to 20 already in service).

The extent of CAF's full service offering is emphasised by the addition of maintenance contracts for light rail, metro, suburban and high-speed vehicles in a range of locations across Europe. ■

TRAIN FLEET MAINTENANCE AND MANUFACTURE

STADLER IN THE UK

Since 1942, Stadler has been making trains that are tailored to its customers' requirements and represent smart investment. Its comprehensive range of products includes both heavy rail and commuter rail and it is the world's leading manufacturer in the rack-and-pinion rail vehicle industry.

Featuring state-of-the-art technology, Stadler trains are reliable, safe, and offer maximum comfort for passengers. Every day, its 10,900 strong workforce at its production, component and service locations around the world strive to improve performance, enhance efficiency and achieve maximum precision. To date, Stadler has sold more than 8,000 units in 41 countries. To ensure a responsible use of resources, Stadler applies eco-design principles in development, production and maintenance, as well as low-emission drive technologies.

Following a strategic decision to penetrate the UK, Stadler has secured several orders over the last ten years in this market. The first saw VARIOBAHN trams enter service on the Tramlink network in Croydon in 2012. Following two subsequent orders, there are now 12 Stadler VARIOBAHNs serving this network. In 2016, Strathclyde Partnership for Transport awarded Stadler the contract to build and supply 17 METRO trains for the Glasgow Subway. A year later, Stadler delivered seven Class 399 CITYLINK vehicles for the tram network in Sheffield, the first tram-trains in this country. Also in 2017, it won the bid to deliver 52 new METRO trains for the Liverpool City Region.

Two years later, in 2019, Stadler was awarded the contract by KeolisAmey to supply 71 trains for Wales & Borders, comprising 36 CITYLINKs and 35 FLIRTs. In 2020, Nexus handed Stadler the contract to build 42 METRO trains for the Tyne and Wear Metro. This means that within a few years, there will be 166 light rail and METRO vehicles operating in the UK. Passengers on all underground trains in the UK outside London – in Liverpool, Glasgow and now Newcastle-upon-Tyne – will soon be travelling on Stadler trains.

FLIRTS FOR GREATER ANGLIA

In 2016, Stadler won the tender to build and supply 58 brand new trains for the Greater Anglia network. The contract was for 14 Class 755/3 three-car and 24 Class 755/4 four-car bi-modes, 10 12-car Class 745/0 electric and 10 12-car Class 745/1 electric trains. These new trains are replacing Greater Anglia's inter-city, rural and Stansted Express trains. They were delivered in 2019 and 2020, and by autumn 2020 almost all were in passenger service. Stadler has full service and maintenance responsibility for the new fleet.

The trains are reliable, fast, comfortable, attractive and can carry more passengers. Greener than the legacy fleet, they rely on the latest environmentally friendly technology. With 20% more seats, they feature bigger, 'picture style' windows to improve the passenger experience and create a more spacious feel. They offer vastly improved accessibility, particularly for wheelchair users and people with pushchairs, bikes or luggage. Customers can walk easily along the whole length of the train, making them feel safer. Mobile phone reception is better and plug and USB sockets are installed at every seat. Wi-Fi is free and faster than previously. All trains are fully air-conditioned, with accessible toilets and bicycle spaces.

Revolutionary and innovative, the 38 bi-modes running on rural routes in Norfolk, Suffolk, Essex and Cambridgeshire can switch seamlessly between diesel mode and electricity power. Diesel engines, fitted into the middle of the units, meet the latest higher standards for emissions and are quieter than the diesel engines that they have replaced.

METRO TRAINS FOR GLASGOW SUBWAY

In 2016, Strathclyde Partnership for Transport awarded Stadler in consortium with Ansaldo (now Hitachi) the contract to supply 17 METRO trains for the Glasgow Subway, one of the oldest and smallest underground networks in the world. With its unusually narrow track and tunnel gauges, Glasgow Subway operates solely within its original Victorian tunnels, and has a track gauge of 1.22 metres and a tunnel gauge

Bi-modes in service: a Greater Anglia Class 755 at Lowestoft in summer 2019.

The Modern Railway

of just 3.4 metres in diameter. This makes the contract highly complex.

Tailormade to suit the network, trains will have a maximum speed of 58km/h. They will be the same length and size as existing rolling stock, but made up of modern four-car sets, as opposed to the current three-car sets. They will feature open gangways to maximise space and will be equipped for fully automatic, unattended train operation. This is the first time that Stadler is manufacturing trains for a driverless system.

The project is in the test phase and there are now three new trains in Glasgow. The new wheel lathe supplied by Stadler is ready and the carriage-wash is currently being installed. Train production is set to restart in early 2021.

New Subway train: Stadler is supplying 17 four-car trains for to meet the unique requirements of the Glasgow Subway.

METRO TRAINS FOR THE LIVERPOOL CITY REGION

In 2017, Stadler signed a contract to manufacture and deliver 52 trains for the Liverpool City Region. Replacing one of the oldest fleets in the UK, the trains will run on the Merseyrail network.

They will boast the latest advances in safety and technology, such as live-streamed CCTV, Wi-Fi and air-conditioning, dramatically improving the passenger experience. Open, airy compartments will be entirely walk-through, with wider aisles and larger vestibules at the doorways.

They will provide step-free access for all passengers, making Merseyrail the most accessible traditional network in the UK and a game-changer for people in wheelchairs and with prams or luggage. The driver's cab will feature enhanced sight lines, an ergonomic desk arrangement and all of the functionality required for versatile, modern trains.

The trains will be faster, cutting journey times by 10% – up to eight minutes on some end-to-end routes. With the same number of seats, they will be able to carry 486 people, 60% more than the legacy trains.

With the fleet set to start entering passenger service from 2021, there are now eight trains in Liverpool. Testing started on the Merseyrail network earlier this year and is taking place overnight. More trains will arrive from Switzerland and Poland over the next few months.

Stadler assumed service and maintenance of the legacy fleet in 2017 and will look after the new trains, once they are in operation.

CITYLINK TRAM-TRAINS AND FLIRTS FOR WALES & BORDERS

In 2019, KeolisAmey/Transport for Wales Rail Services awarded Stadler the contract to supply 71 trains for Wales & Borders. This major contract is for 36 three-car CITYLINK tram-trains and 35 FLIRT trains.

CITYLINK three-car tram-trains will operate from Cardiff to Treherbert, Aberdare and Merthyr Tydfil. These trains will bring back on-street running to Cardiff for the first time in 70 years and will be equipped with batteries to bridge the gap resulting from intermittent electrification of the Valley Lines. They will rely on 25kV AC as well as battery power, underscoring Stadler's commitment to decarbonisation and supporting the rail industry in reducing its carbon footprint.

The remaining 35 units will be FLIRTs, 11 of which will be diesel-operated and used on South Wales Metro services to Maesteg, Ebbw Vale and Cheltenham. The other 24 units will be tri-mode, capable of running on diesel, overhead electric wires and battery power. The tri-mode fleet consists of seven three-car and 17 four-car trains.

Trains will be longer and seats will be ergonomically-designed to maximise passenger comfort. Each seat will be fitted with power sockets. Saloons will be light, bright and feature air-conditioning throughout. Wide passenger information screens will provide customers with up-to-the-minute travel information. Noise and vibrations will be kept to a minimum, with the new trains quieter than the current ones. Other benefits include space for up to six bikes on each train.

With electrical pre-assembly on the FLIRTs recently having started and work on bodyshells having just begun, final assembly of the first unit was due to kick off by the end of 2020.

METRO TRAINS FOR THE TYNE AND WEAR METRO

Stadler's latest order was secured earlier this year, when it signed the contract with public body Nexus for the delivery and maintenance of 42 METRO trains for the Tyne and Wear Metro. This is Stadler's third METRO contract in Great Britain in just shy of four years.

Entirely replacing the 40-year old legacy fleet, trains will be bright and open, with special multi-functional areas for wheelchairs, prams, luggage and bicycles. They will feel more secure, featuring video surveillance, protection systems for door operation and clear warning displays. Good thermal and acoustic insulation will regulate

Merseyrail train on test: a Class 777 EMU at Hamilton Square on an overnight test trip in May 2020.

on-board temperatures for the comfort of passengers, and newly developed air-sprung bogies will reduce noise.

The 60-metre long trains will each consist of five carriages, which can accommodate up to 600 passengers. Eight large double doors will allow passengers to get on and off quickly. Power will be supplied via an overhead line with 1,500V DC and the maximum speed is 80km/h. The lightweight vehicle, the recovery of braking energy and the use of highly efficient traction converter technology will all help reduce energy consumption. Trains will be built to accommodate an energy storage system, enabling them to operate on an extended network in future.

In October 2020, 120 staff based at Gosforth depot transferred from Nexus to Stadler. At the same time, Stadler assumed responsibility for servicing and maintaining trains for the Tyne and Wear Metro. Initially, this will be the current fleet, and within a few years, it will be the new trains, set to be introduced into passenger service from 2023. ■

TRAIN FLEET MAINTENANCE AND MANUFACTURE

Hitachi Rail looks to the future

Since opening its state-of-the-art factory in Newton Aycliffe five years ago – just a stone's throw away from the birthplace of the railway – Hitachi Rail's presence across the UK has continued to grow. With more than 250 Hitachi Rail-built trains in service across the UK, the company employs over 2,500 people across 15 locations.

And its presence is more far-reaching than just direct employment. Hitachi Rail has opened the door to the rail industry for a whole new supply chain, investing £1.8 billion with UK suppliers since 2013.

Having successfully delivered 192 new trains, the factory is now a proven manufacturer of high quality rolling stock and is capable of building the entire family of Hitachi Rail trains – from the metro-style AT100 to the very high-speed AT400. The factory will soon be working on 23 new trains for Avanti West Coast and 33 of the new AT300 SXR model for East Midlands Railway. A recent investment of £8.5 million in new painting and welding capability at the site demonstrates Hitachi Rail's ongoing commitment to the UK as well as enhancing capabilities for future export.

Covid has had a global impact on all our lives, but despite the challenges teams across the UK have adopted Covid secure working practices and continue to deliver for passengers and customers. Maintenance contracts continue for customers, with train maintenance centres servicing inter-city fleets across England, Scotland and Wales and reliability continuing to improve. Hitachi Rail is particularly proud of the performance of the Class 385 commuter train, built for Abellio ScotRail. The fleet has topped the 'New Train TIN-watch' reliability charts in *Modern Railways* for months and won the Fleet Excellence award at the National Rail Awards. The Class 395 high-speed fleet continues to be popular with passengers, added to which HS1 is set to run entirely on renewable energy, a UK first.

And as new technologies continue to emerge, Hitachi Rail is continuing to expand its signalling offering. One area where signalling and rolling stock contracts are integrated is Hitachi Rail's new driverless metros in Copenhagen.

Reliability award winner: Hitachi Rail's Class 385 EMUs for ScotRail are one of the most reliable new train fleets in the UK.

Featuring cutting edge technology, signalling and communication systems, the new trains have lower running costs, improved comfort and safety, and increased capacity and efficiency. The Communications-Based Train Control (CBTC) technology offers flexibility for the operator and passengers, giving the option to increase services during peak hours to offer more departures.

SUSTAINABILITY AND PARTNERSHIP

Hitachi Rail's vision for the future is based on sustainability and partnership.

Climate change remains a major challenge for our time and the rail industry needs to play its part. Hitachi Rail can help reduce emissions by offering new battery trains which cut carbon, improve air quality and make electrification simpler.

Hitachi Rail has been developing alternative train traction solutions for over 17 years and successfully introduced one of the world's first battery fleets into Japanese passenger service in 2016.

A new partnership with Hyperdrive Innovation has further enhanced Hitachi Rail's offer, with its market-leading battery technology creating opportunities for decarbonising trains in the UK. Meanwhile, Hitachi ABB's experience of the power sector allows battery trains to incorporate charging, storage and grid management.

Another way to reduce carbon emissions is the global drive for

Battery potential: in July 2020 Hitachi announced it has signed an exclusive agreement with Hyperdrive Innovation to develop battery packs to power zero-emission trains and create a battery hub in the North East.

modal shift to rail as an alternative to air travel or personal vehicles. Hitachi has many decades of experience making inter-city rail travel more attractive. The evolution of Japan's Shinkansen bullet trains, the world's very first high-speed train, and the Frecciarossa ETR1000 in Italy, Europe's fastest passenger train, are prime examples of pioneering international experience in high-speed rail.

Trenitalia's high-speed fleet, built through a partnership of Hitachi Rail and Bombardier, has enabled the number of passengers carried on Italian high-speed services to rise from 6.5 million in 2008 to 40 million in 2018, an increase of 517%.

As rail becomes increasingly digitised and integrated into other sectors, other key partnerships with innovative technology are key. Hitachi's agreement to acquire technology firm Perpetuum will support predictive analytics of train performance, improving reliability and availability of existing trains in service. Perpetuum's product utilises wireless condition monitoring to spot faults and fix them before they delay passenger journeys.

The rapid evolution of new technology means the engineers of the future will be working in sectors that may not have been imagined in the rail industry yet. With increased demand for AI and robotics, Hitachi is a proud co-founder of the South Durham University Technical College (UTC), which has a focus on practical engineering, advanced manufacturing and business skills.

Inspiring this next generation, with innovative and diverse ideas, into the rail industry is vital to compete with advances in other transport sectors. The future of rail is exciting, and the foundations are there for it to be at the forefront of new technology and the mode of transport of choice. ■

Keeping Rail Journeys Moving Since 1985

Rowe Hankins Ltd. specialises in innovative trainborne and wayside products for the world's railways. Working closely with rolling stock manufacturers, fleet operators, track owners and infrastructure contractors for Light and Heavy Rail Vehicle projects; as well as having service capabilities in engineering and design to overhaul and repair.

- Intelligent Wheel Flange Lubrication Systems
- Top of Rail Friction Modifier Systems
- 1, 2 and 4 Channel Speed Sensors
- Circuit Breakers
- Non-Intrusive Current Monitors
- AC/DC Earth Leakage Units
- Tachometers
- RCBO's, Residual Current Breakers with Over-Current

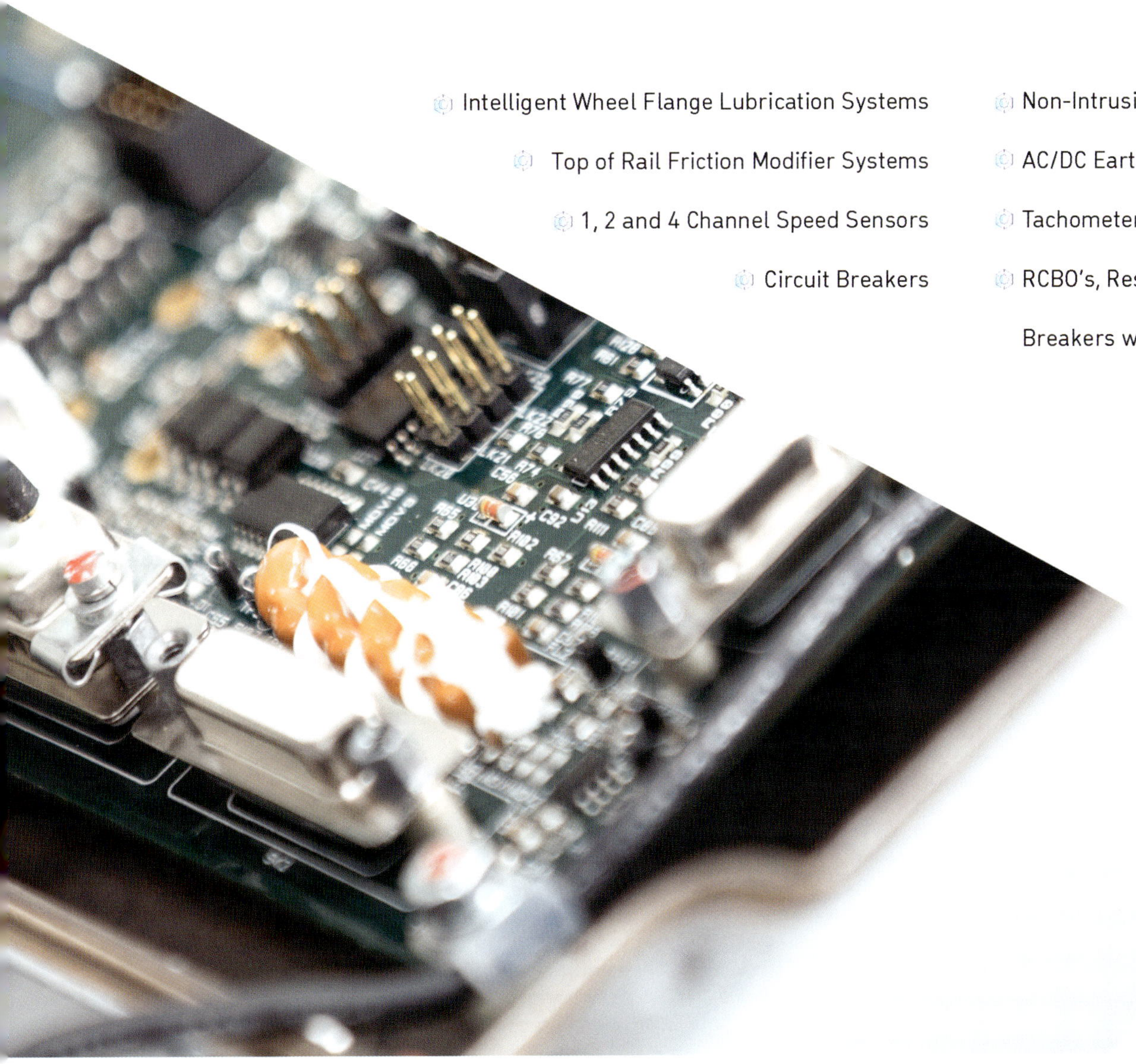

www.rowehankins.com +44(0) 161 765 3000 sales@rowehankins.com ISO 9001 & 14001 - 2015

TRAIN FLEET MAINTENANCE AND MANUFACTURE

BOMBARDIER
UK RAIL ENGINEERING AND MANUFACTURE

Bombardier is the UK's leading rail solutions company, headquartered at the iconic Litchurch Lane facility in Derby, the heart of the largest cluster of rail-connected businesses anywhere in the world. A global leader in the rail industry, the company offers a comprehensive product portfolio spanning the full spectrum of rail solutions.

In 2020 the acquisition of Bombardier's Transportation business by Alstom was confirmed, with the transaction receiving approval from the European Commission in July. The transaction is expected to close in the first half of 2021.

Bombardier is the only company in the UK able to design, develop, manufacture, test and service trains for UK and export markets. In 2019 a Bombardier-led consortium signed a major new order to build and supply the new Cairo Monorail system in Egypt. In 2021 work will start at Derby on the monorail cars, the first UK rolling stock export by any company in over a decade – since Bombardier's export order for Gautrain in South Africa.

The Aventra trains for the Elizabeth Line, London Overground, and the East Anglia, South Western, West Midlands and Essex Thameside rail franchises are designed and built in Britain. The trains Bombardier's services teams maintain from 18 sites across the country keep Britain moving on one of the busiest and most complex networks in the world.

In the UK, Bombardier employs around 4,000 people, comprising around 2,000 at Derby including over 400 specialised engineers, almost 1,000 in London, and its Rail Control Solutions engineering and manufacturing facility at Plymouth produces products for the UK and for export. Bombardier's rail control solutions business manufactures a range of railway signalling products for the UK and the global market, with a portfolio including train detection systems and associated test tools, signals, European Rail Traffic Management System (ERTMS) products and level crossings, including enhanced user worked crossings.

Bombardier has supplied just under half of the modern fleet and maintains more than 3,000 vehicles across the UK. It has submitted a joint venture bid with Hitachi to supply the next generation of high-speed trains for HS2 Phase One.

Export order beckons: Bombardier is to build monorail vehicles in Derby for export to Cairo.

Bombardier's installed product base includes:
- 2,660 Aventra Electric Multiple-Units cars built or on order for the Elizabeth Line, London Overground, and the East Anglia, South Western, West Midlands and Essex Thameside rail franchises;
- 2,805 Electrostar Electric Multiple-Units cars in operation on London Overground and on the Essex Thameside, East Anglia, Great Western, South Eastern and Thameslink, Southern & Great Northern rail franchises – as well as the Gautrain operation in South Africa;
- 456 Turbostar Diesel Multiple-Unit cars in operation on London Overground, and on the Chiltern, Cross Country, East Anglia, East Midlands, ScotRail, Thameslink, Southern & Great Northern and West Midlands rail franchises;
- 352 Voyager and Super Voyager Diesel Multiple-Unit cars in operation with the Inter-city West Coast and Cross Country rail franchises, and 143 Meridian Diesel Multiple-Unit cars in operation on the East Midlands franchise;
- 1,375 Movia 'S' stock cars in operation on the London Underground Circle, District, Hammersmith & City and Metropolitan Lines;
- 376 Movia 2009 stock cars in operation on the London Underground Victoria Line;
- 162 Flexity light rail vehicles in operation for Manchester Metrolink, Croydon Tramlink and Blackpool Transport, with a further 27 on order for Manchester Metrolink. ■

Aventra line-up: from left, EMUs of Classes 701 for South Western Railway, 720 for Greater Anglia, 710 for London Overground and 345 for Crossrail at Bombardier's Derby factory.

IN ASSOCIATION WITH

Class 600: Alstom and Eversholt Rail have continued to progress their 'Breeze' hydrogen conversion of Class 321 EMUs.

ALSTOM UK AND IRELAND

Alstom has been at the heart of the UK's rail industry for over 100 years. Today Alstom employs a workforce of 2,000 people across 20 major sites in the UK and Ireland.

Alstom provides the smartest range of solutions in the UK rail market, from innovative trains, metros and tramways to maintenance, modernisation, infrastructure and signalling solutions. Every day, up to one-third of all rail journeys in the UK are made on Alstom trains. The company keeps the West Coast main line service running for around 34 million passengers every year and services over 100 tube trains a day on London's Northern Line, carrying nearly one million passengers daily.

In Ireland, Alstom supplied the trams used by Dublin's Luas system, including the longest ever 55-metre Citadis vehicles, supported the introduction of the new Luas Cross City line, and works every day to maintain the fleet and keep it running smoothly.

Alstom has developed the world's smartest engineering and rail technology. From TrainScanner, its world-leading virtual train health checker developed in Manchester, to Appitrack, the fastest track-laying machine in the world, its engineers are helping to make Britain's railways better.

BOMBARDIER ACQUISITION

After an attempted merger of Alstom and Siemens was blocked by the European Commission in 2019, the acquisition by Alstom of Bombardier's Transportation division received approval in July 2020. Completion of the transaction is expected during the first half of 2021.

EC approval was based on a number of conditions concerning rolling stock production sites in continental Europe, access for other manufacturers to parts of Bombardier's signalling portfolio and transfer of Bombardier's design rights and contribution to the V300 Zefiro high-speed train. Production at the Bombardier Derby site is not expected to be affected by the deal, at least initially.

The original price Alstom agreed was around €6.2 billion, but this is likely to be reduced following significantly worse than expected Q2 2020 results from Bombardier. Canadian state-owned investor Caisse de dépôt et placement du Québec (CDPQ), which owned 32.5% of Bombardier Transportation, will become Alstom's biggest shareholder, with around 18% of the company. The expanded Alstom group will have an order backlog of €79 billion and combined sales of €15.5 billion, making it the second largest rolling stock manufacturer in the world after Chinese firm CRRC.

WIDNES

Alstom has opened a new Technology Centre at Widnes, in the Liverpool area. It is part of Alstom's ambition to make its operations in the UK more modern and efficient to support its growth in this market and is the UK's largest and most sophisticated modernisation facility.

The first contract for Widnes was the repainting of the Class 390 Pendolino fleet for the West Coast franchise, which concluded in December 2019. As part of the Avanti West Coast franchise Alstom has a £127 million contract to refurbish all 56 Pendolinos, reported to be the largest refurbishment programme ever undertaken in the UK. The contract will see 100 jobs created at Widnes, while Alstom also has a seven-year deal for ongoing maintenance of the fleet for Avanti.

Alstom is also carrying out a £6.7 million refurbishment of the 27 Class 175 DMUs operated by Transport for Wales at the site, including exterior rebranding and a range of interior improvements. Refresh work and repainting was carried out on Class 90/Mk 4 sets for Grand Central, which were planned to be used on London Euston to Blackpool services before GC abandoned plans for the service due to the Covid crisis.

HS2

In June 2019 Alstom submitted its bid in the competition to build the first trains for HS2. The company said its proposal is designed to meet all HS2's requirements 'for a world class, modern and flexible train which is as comfortable on the conventional network as it is on the new HS2 infrastructure'. The company cited its high-speed rail expertise supplying trains for the TGV network in France, the Avelia Liberty in the USA and AGV in Italy, combined with its UK expertise with the Pendolino fleet operating on the West Coast main line.

If successful, Alstom plans to build the fleet at its Widnes plant.

BREEZE

Alstom and Eversholt Rail have continued to develop their hydrogen conversion of Class 321 electric multiple-units.

In 2020 the companies committed a further £1 million of investment to develop the concept and confirmed converted 'Breeze' units would be Class 600s. They say the first converted trains could enter service in 2024.

The conversion will take place at Alstom's Widnes facility, which Alstom says will become its worldwide centre of excellence for hydrogen conversion when the project is in series production. Hydrogen tanks and fuel cells will be fitted to the trains, with work ongoing to develop business cases and evaluate detailed introduction plans for the units along with the associated fuelling infrastructure. Alstom's plan involves shortening the '321s' to three carriages and giving up some of the passenger space to the equipment required for hydrogen power but retaining the equivalent passenger capacity to a two-car DMU. Prospective uses include the Tees Valley, where Alstom and Eversholt Rail were working with Northern to introduce a dedicated hydrogen fleet.

The project builds on Alstom's experience of introducing the Coradia iLint train in Germany, where the hydrogen-battery hybrid has operated in passenger service since September 2018. ■

TRAIN FLEET MAINTENANCE AND MANUFACTURE

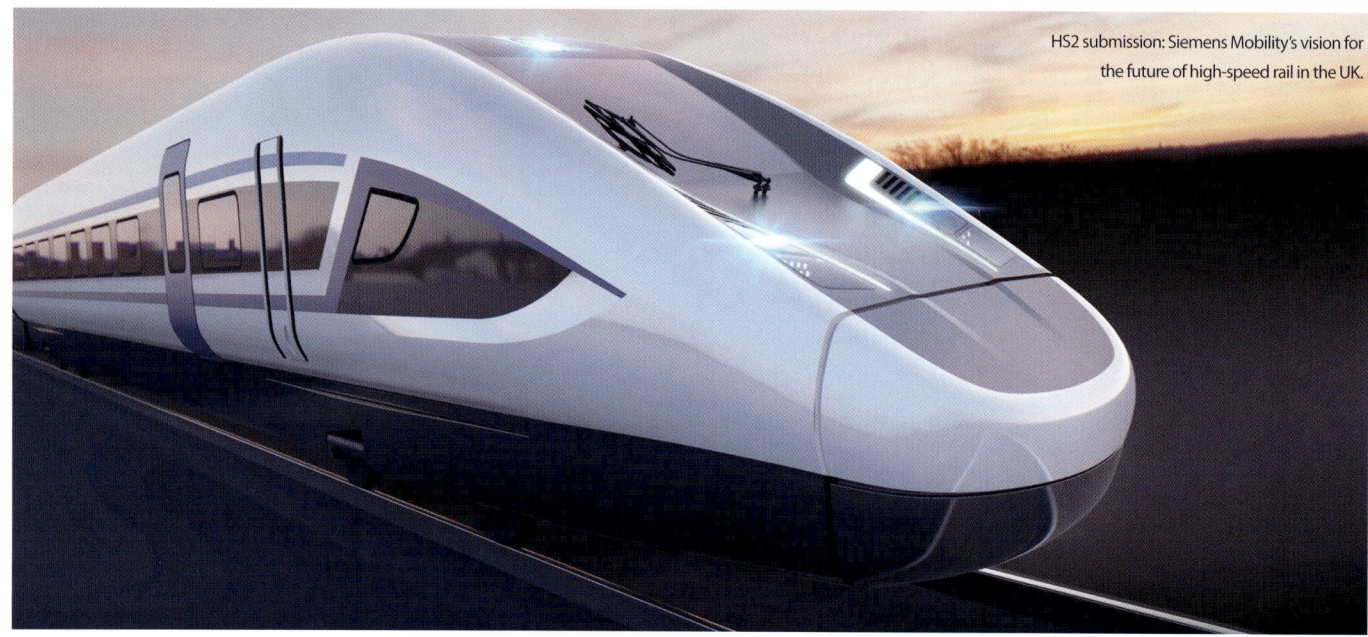

HS2 submission: Siemens Mobility's vision for the future of high-speed rail in the UK.

SIEMENS MOBILITY LIMITED

Siemens Mobility has long-standing expertise in managing the movement of people, goods and services sustainably, economically and effectively. The company is constantly developing new, intelligent mobility solutions that increase availability of infrastructure, optimise throughput and improve the passenger experience.

This enables train operators to shape today's and tomorrow's transportation needs, with Siemens Mobility offering trains, infrastructure, automation and electrification solutions, and turnkey systems as well as related services. The company has a strong focus on digitalisation, bringing together the very best innovation, data science, analytics and software development to improve quality and reduce cost for customers, solving real business problems.

In the UK, Siemens Mobility has some 4,500 employees, of which 200 are graduates and apprentices. In addition, it also supports over 22,000 jobs in the UK supply chain. The company operates from around 75 locations nationwide, including eight purpose-built rail maintenance depots and manufacturing facilities in Chippenham (for signalling, control and automation equipment) and Poole (train cab radio and communications equipment manufacture), both of which serve overseas needs as well as domestic requirements.

KEEPING THE UK RAIL INDUSTRY MOVING

Siemens Mobility continues to lead the way in developing trains for the UK, priding itself on building technologically advanced and cost-effective trains that shape the future of commuter and regional services. Decarbonisation of the industry is a key priority, with the company looking to offer low-emission alternatives and EMU fleets that can be part-powered by either batteries or hydrogen.

The company's record in train development is clear. The trailblazing Desiro family of trains frequently top industry reliability tables and are firm favourites with passengers. The Desiro City, the UK's first second generation train, now has three variants in service, increasing capacity and improving the traveller experience. The company also built the Eurostar e320 – the UK's only very high-speed train – and is committed to playing a key role in supporting the UK's high-speed ambitions. It has extensive experience in building high-speed rolling stock and infrastructure globally, including the Velaro platform of high-speed trains, which operate in countries such as Spain, China, Russia and Germany, as well as forming the base platform for the Eurostar fleet.

The company is making excellent progress on building its new rail manufacturing site in Goole, East Riding of Yorkshire, which will play a pivotal role in supply 94 new underground trains for London's Piccadilly Line. The brand new £200 million facility, which is due to open in 2023, will create up to 700 permanent, skilled jobs in engineering and manufacturing. It will also facilitate employment for a further 250 during the construction phase and generate up to 1,700 indirect jobs throughout the UK supply chain. The company also plans for space to be provided for small- and medium-sized enterprises with a view to creating a 'railway-village' with shared warehousing and logistics. When built, a £6 million building will form the headquarters of RaisE (Rail Accelerator and Innovative Solutions Hub for Enterprise) with a key focus on research and development for the UK. This will create lasting skills and a hub of railway expertise and innovation.

FOCUSED ON UK RAIL INFRASTRUCTURE

In addition to its rolling stock expertise, Siemens Mobility is a global leader in the design, supply, installation and commissioning of digital signalling, control and rail communications solutions. It is the only company in the UK to have full R&D, manufacturing, testing and delivery capabilities for signalling.

The company develops, designs and deploys a range of world-class technology to deliver safe, efficient railway operation. This includes cab radios and communication systems for trains. It also includes the technology which equips Thameslink trains with a combination of Automatic Train Operation (ATO) and European Train Control System (ETCS) to enable automatic operation through the London core, and London Underground to achieve a world-class 36 trains per hour service on the Victoria Line. Both systems deliver significant performance and capacity benefits to passengers and operators. Additionally, it is providing a signalling system for the Elizabeth Line, one of the three systems that the Crossrail trains will operate under when the full service opens.

Siemens Mobility has an unparalleled successful project delivery record. In 2020 the company was awarded framework contracts to deliver major signalling renewal programmes across two of Network Rail's five regions – Scotland and North West & Central – the maximum able to be granted to one individual supplier. In Scotland, the company is also providing a broad range of intelligent infrastructure for the Edinburgh Tram to Newhaven project contract. Building on the work it delivered for the first phase of the network, it will be extending the electrification, supervisory control and data acquisition (SCADA), telecoms and signalling systems, as well as installing new, and modifying existing, traffic and tram signals.

Opening up new routes and increasing capacity and performance requires state-of-the-art rail electrification. Siemens Mobility's products and services cover the complete spectrum of requirements for AC and DC electrified railways, including an innovative lightweight catenary system. The company is fully committed to driving the delivery of sustainable electrification solutions across the UK. ■

To find out more visit:
www.siemens.co.uk/mobility

IN ASSOCIATION WITH

NOMAD DIGITAL

Nomad Digital is the leading provider of wireless connectivity and ICT solutions to the transportation sector. Employing over 300 people at our development facilities in the UK, Germany and Portugal. Nomad boasts a rich suite of passenger and operational applications and services, which enable operators to significantly enhance the passenger experience, while delivering improved levels of reliability, safety and operational efficiencies. The business provides passenger information systems, on-board entertainment platforms and Remote Online Condition Monitoring, serving customers in more than 40 countries.

Nomad Digital technology is used on:
- more than 11,000 vehicles, representing 47% global market share for passenger Wi-Fi;
- 38,000 passenger information screens provide infotainment to 1.7 billion passengers;
- systems that carry out seven million Wi-Fi sessions each month;
- 50,000 miles of track annually;
- over 50 customers in more than 40 countries.

SOLUTIONS

We offer a broad solutions portfolio to both train operators and train builders which facilitates a significantly enhanced passenger experience. The integration of Nomad's products and services into the on-train environment improves passenger experience and delivers efficient technology, both operating on one common platform. Our offerings include but are not limited to:
- trackside networks;
- real-time reporting;
- security-as-a-service;
- Wi-Fi and internet access;
- passenger and on-board information systems;
- remote online condition monitoring;
- on-board data centre;
- CCTV;
- engage portal;
- fleet and rail connectivity.

Nomad is completely focused on a seamless, smart and enjoyable journey for everyone.

Connecting everything: Nomad's vision is extending from connecting passengers to vehicle operators, maintainers and on-board staff.

GREENER TRAVEL

The future will see greener transport becoming a main method of travel, and Nomad's products will enhance journeys and provide data and intelligence for operators. As train operators strive to provide a digitally autonomous service which does not require on-board staff, Nomad will continue to support operators by integrating industry leading digital solutions. The main advantages of Automatic Train Operation (ATO) consist of a reduction in cost and energy consumption, whilst an increase in capacity and greener mobility. Nomad envisions the digital enablement of the first and last mile and how you can use technology to provide a seamless solution.

PASSENGER EXPERIENCE

Passenger experience has always been at the forefront of what Nomad does. This focus will continue as solutions evolve to provide seamless connectivity such as trackside radio networks as well as passenger engagement through media portals.

Connecting to a wider base of stakeholders plays a valuable role in enriching the passenger experience, by responding to market needs and solving connectivity challenges. Passengers are crucial to the train operating companies – yet train guards, drivers, conductors, caterers and maintainers all serve to enhance the passenger experience too. Bringing together passenger connectivity, information and entertainment will transform a passenger's experience.

Intelligent journey: Nomad is the pioneer of an approach which provides a shared and secure network infrastructure.

COST REDUCTIONS FOR OPERATORS

Nomad will continue to support operators by providing cost reducing solutions.

Remote online condition monitoring provides in-depth and real-time information on the performance of crucial equipment and components on-board. Alongside this, it is partnered with diagnostic alerts which provide fleet operators and owners intelligence and sufficient time required to take pro-active action. Reduced costs and increased revenue are key factors for many but with such a solution implemented, it is about improving the overall reliability of fleets, which is primary. All trains share the same purpose – transportation, but it is how that raw data from a train is used to reap the benefits.

Trackside radio networks could revolutionise the rail industry by providing a flawless connection for the end consumer and providing rail providers with savings in long-term use. Helen Murray, Customer Liaison Officer admits: 'Capital cost is the initial outlay; however, potential customers can expect to save money in the long-term; in the future we could see the government provide funding'. The process involves setting up radio transmitters along the trackside, the train's antenna can then connect to the radio transmitter providing a regular strong signal. This process employs a train-to-ground trackside network solution which eradicates the transmission delay of connecting to phone masts.

FINAL THOUGHTS

Nomad's ground-breaking vision from 2007, 'connecting everything', remains relevant today. Now, the opportunity is not just to connect the passengers, but also vehicle operators, maintainers and on-board staff.

Nomad is the pioneer of the intelligent journey – a shared and secure network infrastructure to which all authorised on-board systems and passenger devices may connect. Our aim is 'To be the world leader in connected transport, renowned for continuous innovation of technology and provision of quality solutions to deliver the intelligent journey'. We strive to deliver the best possible solutions which the industry has to offer. ∎

TRAIN FLEET MAINTENANCE AND MANUFACTURE

SECTOR SPECIALISTS

TALGO

Spanish manufacturer Talgo has set up a UK division and established a head office at Barrow Hill Roundhouse in Chesterfield.

The company says the move reaffirms its commitment to the UK, 'true manufacturing' and an 'all Britain' strategy. In June 2019 it submitted a bid for the contract to build new trains for HS2, which is due to be awarded in spring 2021.

Talgo has also entered into a framework agreement with Chesterfield Borough Council, with plans to develop an Innovation Centre, co-located with Barrow Hill Roundhouse. Talgo has said it intends to introduce 'true manufacturing', sourcing from the UK supply chain rather than assembling kits from overseas. A key part of its strategy is 'knowledge transfer' – building UK domestic capacity for Research and Development. A feasibility and stage two design study has been commissioned to develop the innovation and training centre, which would deliver over 3,400 square metres of floorspace, 190 jobs and capacity for 1,800 learners over 10 years.

Also planned as part of the company's UK presence is a manufacturing facility on the former Longannet power station in Fife, for which Fife Council has granted planning consent. Talgo UK, the Scottish Enterprise and Transport Scotland have signed a jointly agreed framework to establish part of the site for manufacturing rail vehicles.

Talgo operates in more than 44 countries and has a permanent industrial presence in North America, Europe and Asia. Its bid for HS2 is based on its AVRIL platform, representing the latest evolution of very high-speed vehicles. It claims its trains feature unique technology to ensure a world-class passenger experience and comfort while maximising seating capacity and minimising carbon footprint and maintenance costs. Talgo's high-speed trains are already in operation in Spain, Saudi Arabia and Central Asia, with an order secured from Deutsche Bahn for up to 100 trains. As well as very high-speed trains, Talgo's portfolio includes regional and commuter vehicles.

Spanish vehicle in the Midlands: to mark its UK commitment, Talgo gifted a 250km/h coach to Chesterfield Borough Council; the company has set up its UK headquarters in Chesterfield. COURTESY TALGO

ELECTRO-MOTIVE DIESEL TECHNOLOGY

Progress Rail company Electro-Motive Diesel delivered a final seven new Class 66 locomotives to UK rail freight company GB Railfreight (GBRf) in 2016. Due to changes in EU emissions standards, the locos were the last Class 66s to be built.

UK subsidiary EMDL signed a 10-year contract with GBRf in 2012 to maintain its Class 66s – the company's first full maintenance contract. It provides a full range of post-delivery services for Class 66s, including full service maintenance, spare parts, modernisation and technical support, and has also converted '66s' from continental Europe for GBRf for service in the UK.

Parent company Progress Rail signed a contract with GBRf in April 2019 for the repowering of 16 Class 56 locomotives the operator purchased from UK Rail Leasing in 2018. The repowered locos will be designated as Class 69s. Work is taking place at Progress Rail's facility at Longport, Stoke-on-Trent, and will see the locos' existing Ruston-Paxman RK3 engines and control gear upgraded to EMD 12-710 Series engines, rated for EU Stage IIIA emissions certification, with updated electronic controls, based on the Class 66.

GEMINI RAIL GROUP

Gemini Rail Group comprises the former Knorr-Bremse Rail Services and Kiepe Electric UK businesses. This included the transfer of the former KB facilities at Springburn near Glasgow and Wolverton near Milton Keynes, branded as Gemini Rail Services, although the company has since closed the Springburn works. The Kiepe Electric business is now known as Gemini Rail Technology and is based in Birmingham.

The Wolverton works continues to operate, with Gemini planning a transition to a new business model. Traditional renovation contracts have included installation of new

New trains for the Isle of Wight: Class 484 EMUs under construction at Vivarail's original base at Long Marston; of the five units the last two are being assembled at its new Southam facility. PHILIP SHERRATT

RAISING STANDARDS
RAILWAY LIFTING JACKS

With 40 years' experience in heavy duty lifting solutions, TotalKare combines world class products with industry leading support to facilitate effective maintenance and repair, keeping you on track for success.

CALL 0121 585 2724
VISIT WWW.TOTALKARE.CO.UK

TOTALKARE
POWERED BY EMANUEL

TRAIN FLEET MAINTENANCE AND MANUFACTURE

traction equipment on 18 Class 442 EMUs for South Western Railway, a C6 heavy overhaul on Class 150s and refurbishment of Class 323 EMUs. Wolverton has also been used a base for commissioning of Bombardier's new Class 720 EMUs for Greater Anglia, with testing undertaken on the West Coast main line.

Gemini has also set up a new sub-brand, GemEco, which is working on developing decarbonisation projects including hybrid technology and alternative propulsion.

Property developer St Modwen, which owns Wolverton works, has obtained outline planning consent to demolish most of the buildings in favour of housing. The lifting shop is planned to be extended and another two bays added, creating a four-track modern fleet maintenance facility. This, along with the Royal Train shed, incident repair and high-voltage test bay, will be the focus of Gemini's future operations.

Knorr-Bremse has retained its UK component and aftermarket business and plans to focus on connected on-board railway subsystems and related services.

VIVARAIL

Vivarail was set up in 2015 with the aim of producing low-cost, low maintenance rolling stock. After being based for five years at the Quinton Rail Technology Centre at Long Marston, in October 2019 the company announced plans to relocate to Southam, near Leamington Spa, and it planned to end production at Long Marston by the end of 2020.

The company is producing new trains rebuilt from former London Underground 'D' stock trains. While the aluminium bodyshells and bogies of the tube trains are reused, the traction equipment is all new, while Vivarail says it can deliver an interior specified to the requirements of its customers.

In April 2019 Vivarail's first Class 230 entered passenger service as part of a contract to deliver 3x2-car diesel-electric multiple units to West Midlands Trains for the Bedford to Bletchley line. Next to be delivered are 5x3-car diesel/battery hybrid units for Transport for Wales Rail Services, which will be used on the Wrexham to Bidston line; these are planned to enter service in 2021.

Vivarail also has an ordered from South Western Railway for 5x2-car Class 484 EMUs powered by third rail for the Island line between Ryde and Shanklin on the Isle of Wight. The trains are part of a wider £26 million investment in the island's railway and will be introduced in April 2021 following a three-month closure of the line to carry out infrastructure upgrades.

Vivarail has pledged it will not incorporate diesel engines in trains it builds in future. It is advancing the use of battery power, with future plans including the testing of a 25kV AC overhead/battery hybrid unit on the main line network and the development of a battery module which could replace diesel engines on legacy DMUs. The company has created a prototyped fast charge system for battery units, based on the London Underground four-rail system.

Vivarail has opened a production facility at Seaham in County Durham, specialising in genset manufacture and overhaul.

WABTEC FAIVELEY UK

The combined resources of Wabtec and Faiveley Transport have created one of the world's largest public rail equipment companies, with a presence in all key rail freight and passenger markets worldwide.

The company's transit segment designs, manufactures, markets and services a large range of high added-value components, systems and services which the company believes help customers build and maintain trains that are safe, reliable and cost efficient throughout their life cycle. The group includes UK subsidiaries Wabtec Rail Limited, Brush Traction, LH Group, including the Hunslet Engine Company, and Brecknell Willis.

LH is a leading supplier of multiple-unit train products and services. A key activity is overhaul of rail vehicles, engines and transmission systems. The Hunslet Engine Company is a designer and manufacturer of quality industrial shunting, tunnelling and specialised locomotives.

The group undertakes the construction, refurbishment and maintenance of railway rolling stock, locomotives, passenger trains and freight wagons. Brush Traction's facilities at Loughborough provide locomotive overhaul, rebuilding and re-tractioning services and aftermarket components.

Recent major refurbishment contracts undertaken include the conversion of Class 319 EMUs to bi-mode Class 769s for Porterbrook at Brush Traction, and upgrades to HSTs for CrossCountry, Great Western Railway and ScotRail, where modifications have included provision of power doors. Both projects faced technical and resource challenges but were approaching completion by the end of 2020.

Wabtec has refocused its traditional refurbishment business in the UK following changes within the market. This included the closure of the wheelset and vehicle overhaul facility at Kilmarnock, which Wabtec acquired in 2011; the facility has since been taken over by Brodie Engineering. The company intends to consolidate its operations at its Doncaster site, although here it also plans to cut up to 450 jobs in a gradual workforce reduction concluding in the first quarter of 2021. Wabtec said it proposes to 'realign the site to focus on projects best suited for its operational strengths and better position the facility for long-term success'.

In February 2019 Wabtec completed its merger with GE Transportation, formerly a business unit of GE. The combined company has around 27,000 employees in 50 countries and is based in Wilmerding, Pennsylvania. GE had supplied 36 Class 70 UK PowerHaul Series locomotives to the UK. The original order for 19 locomotives was placed by Freightliner Group in 2007, subsequent to which Colas Rail acquired 17 more of the type.

BRODIE ENGINEERING

Brodie Engineering is a Kilmarnock-based rolling stock engineering business employing around 100 staff at its offices and workshops. The design and project office is immediately adjacent to the four-road, 14-vehicle capacity workshop.

In mid-2020 the company supplemented its existing Bonnyton Rail Depot facility by taking over the former Wabtec plant, a 100,000 square foot facility which originally opened in 1840. The company has said it is developing its plans for the site. The two facilities, separated by the railway line to Troon, are the last remaining independent overhaul facilities in Scotland.

Having traditionally focused on specialist work such as corrosion and collision damage repairs, Brodie Engineering has broadened its portfolio to include longer-term overhaul programmes and mobile engineering, dispatching teams to outside locations to support customers in delivery of current projects. A headline project is the conversion of five Class 153s for ScotRail into carriages for cycles and large sporting equipment, to be introduced in 2021 on scenic routes in Scotland. ■

'153' for scenic routes: Brodie Engineering is converting five carriages to carry cycles and large luggage for use on routes in the Scottish Highlands, the first of which was unveiled in October 2020. **COURTESY SCOTRAIL**

PASSENGER TRAIN OPERATORS

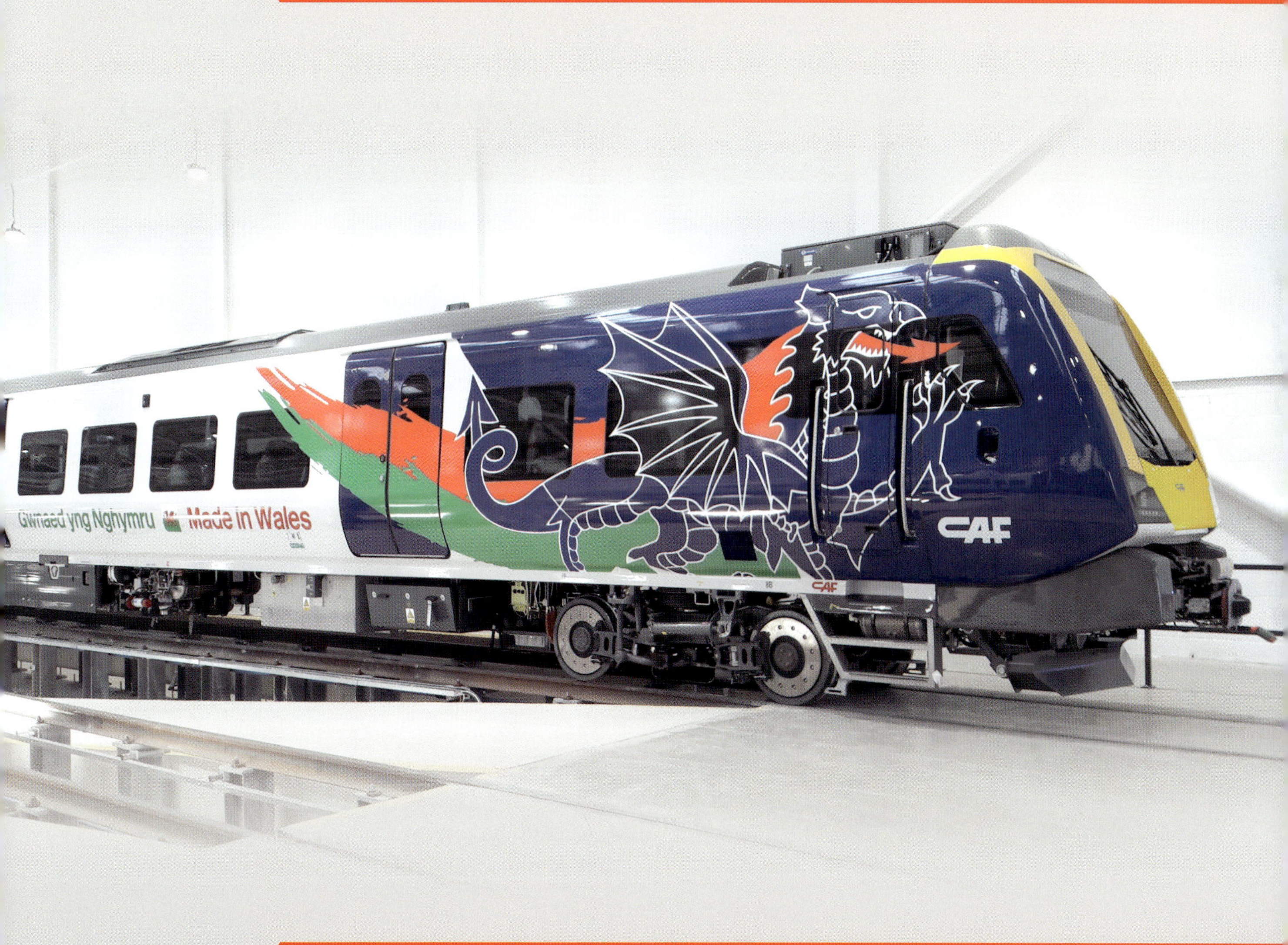

IN ASSOCIATION WITH

PASSENGER TRAIN OPERATORS

Emergency measures for franchises

Rail franchising has been turned upside-down by the coronavirus pandemic. Indeed, in September 2020 the UK Government declared traditional franchises were at an end as it planned a pathway to introduction of concessions.

Change began in March 2020 at the onset of the pandemic. Faced with rapidly falling demand, the Department for Transport introduced Emergency Measures Agreements (EMAs) for all its franchises, with DfT taking revenue and cost risk and paying a management fee of up to 2% to operators. The EMAs ran until 20 September, with the exception of CrossCountry's EMA which continued for a further four weeks to run concurrent with the end of its direct award franchise.

Exceptions to this rule within England were Transport for London's London Overground and Crossrail concessions and Merseytravel's Merseyrail concession, all of which continued under pre-existing terms.

The Scottish Government followed suit in April by introducing EMAs for the ScotRail and Caledonian Sleeper franchises. These EMAs were both extended upon expiry in September to run until January 2021.

The Welsh Government took a slightly different approach for the Wales and Borders contract, initially retaining pre-existing contract terms but providing short-term support before moving to a six-month EMA running from May to November, with total support amounting to up to £105 million. In October 2020 it confirmed a further extension of the EMA to February 2021, after which operations would become the responsibility of a publicly owned subsidiary of Transport for Wales.

With the EMAs in England coming to an end in September, the Department for Transport replaced most of them with Emergency Recovery Measures Agreements (ERMAs). These were described as 'transitional contracts' with a lower management fee of a maximum of 1.5% of the cost base of the franchise and a stronger weighting towards performance delivery.

Discussions then continued between operators and DfT over a longer-term agreement. DfT aimed to reach terms with operators by 13 December to terminate pre-existing franchise agreements, with the ERMAs then transitioning to directly awarded contracts. The termination is based on reaching agreement about how much parent company support or other payments would be required to end the franchise contracts. If a sum is agreed, it would fall due at the end of the ERMA term, at which point the franchise contract would also terminate by agreement. If a termination sum was not agreed by December, DfT could terminate the ERMA and revert to the pre-existing franchise terms from January 2021, although in some cases the financial state of franchises means it is likely the Operator of Last Resort would take over. Exceptions are GWR and Southeastern, which both have a longer EMA term and who begun new franchise contracts in April 2020, and CrossCountry, which began a new Operating Contract Franchise Agreement (OCFA) in October 2020.

The table below sets out the status of all franchises and concessions in the UK, showing both their pre-pandemic franchise status and emergency measures status at the time of going to press. ■

INDEX OF TRAIN OPERATING COMPANIES

COMPANY	OWNING GROUP	PRE-EXISTING FRANCHISE STATUS	EMERGENCY ARRANGEMENT	PAGE
Avanti West Coast	FirstGroup/Trenitalia	West Coast Partnership to March 2026, option to 2031	ERMA to March 2022	73
Great Western Railway	FirstGroup	Direct award franchise to March 2023, option to 2024	EMA to June 2021	75
South Western Railway	FirstGroup/MTR	Franchise to August 2024	ERMA to March 2021	75
TransPennine Express	FirstGroup	Franchise to April 2023	ERMA to March 2021, option to September 2021	76
Hull Trains *	FirstGroup	Open access agreement to 2029	n/a	78
c2c	Trenitalia	Franchise to November 2029	ERMA to March 2021	79
Merseyrail * (a)	Serco/Abellio	Concession to July 2028	None	80
Caledonian Sleeper * (b)	Serco	Franchise to April 2030	EMA to January 2021	80
East Midlands Railway	Abellio	Franchise to August 2027	ERMA to March 2022	82
Greater Anglia	Abellio/Mitsui	Franchise to October 2025	ERMA to September 2021	83
ScotRail * (b)	Abellio	Franchise to April 2022	EMA to January 2021	84
West Midlands Trains	Abellio/JR East/Mitsui	Franchise to March 2026	ERMA to September 2021	86
London North Eastern Railway	Operator of Last Resort	Direct award contract to June 2023, option to 2025	n/a	87
Northern		Operator of Last Resort	n/a	88
Chiltern Railways	Arriva	Franchise to December 2021	ERMA to December 2021	90
CrossCountry	Arriva	Operating Contract Franchise Agreement to October 2023		91
London Overground * (d)	Arriva	Concession to November 2024	n/a	92
Grand Central *	Arriva	Open access contract to 2026	n/a	94
Govia Thameslink Railway	Govia	Management contract to September 2021	ERMA to September 2021	96
Southeastern	Govia	Management contract to October 2021, option to March 2022	EMA to October 2021, option to March 2022	98
Transport for Wales Rail Services * (c)	KeolisAmey (e)	Operator and Development Partner contract to 2033	EMA to February 2021	99
MTR Elizabeth line (TfL Rail) * (d)	MTR	Concession to May 2023	n/a	100
Heathrow Express *	FirstGroup (GWR)	Management contract to 2028	n/a	101
Getlink (Eurotunnel) *	n/a	n/a	n/a	101
Eurostar *	n/a	n/a	n/a	102

Notes: * not franchised by Department for Transport; (a) concession agreement with Merseytravel; (b) devolved to Scottish Government; (c) devolved to Welsh Government; (d) concession agreement with Transport for London; (e) day-to-day operation to be taken over by an agency of the Welsh Government in February 2021

Finances before Covid

The pandemic interrupted a strong period of growth in passenger numbers, as **Chris Cheek** of Passenger Transport Monitor explains

Until the onset of the Covid-19 pandemic in March 2020, demand on the rail network had been continuing its now long-established period of growth. The quarter year ended 31 December 2019 showed an overall patronage increase of 6.5%, with numbers on the regional networks up by a whopping 12.6% as performance began to recover and industrial relations problems eased.

The rolling year numbers were around 3.8% ahead, and there seemed little reason to suppose this trend would not continue. The total number of journeys was a whisker below 1.8 billion, a number last seen in the aftermath of the First World War. True, there were uncertainties ahead as the economy flatlined in the final quarter of the year, and retail sales were looking a bit shaky. Nobody quite knew what life outside the EU would look like. But the market had shown itself to be virtually recession-proof last time, and employment levels were at record highs.

Twelve weeks later, and the whole scene had changed, probably for ever. Numbers for the January to March quarter were 11.4% down, thanks to a plunge in the second half of March. According to Department for Transport (DfT) estimates, demand collapsed from being at 'normal' levels on 9 March to just 5% of normal by the last day of the quarter. Six months later, it had crept back up to just below 40%. In the face of an upsurge of Covid-19 cases, nobody knew by when and by how much patronage could recover further.

For the record, the patronage in 2019-20 was 1.742 million, 0.7% down on the previous year. The sharpest fall was on the long-distance inter-city routes, down 2.6% to 142.8 million, whilst the London commuter routes saw a fall of 2.6% to 1,201 million. The regional services still saw a small 1.6% gain over the previous year, giving them a total of 398 million.

On the revenue front, the total stayed above £10 billion, but was 0.3% down on the previous year at £10,208 million. Gains on regional services of 2.3% took the total to £1,632 million, whilst London and the South East revenue was 0.2% up at £5,129 million. Long-distance revenue took a hit of 2.3%, down to £3,447 million.

PROFITS STABLE

Train operator profits were stable during the year, with margins very slightly lower at 3.1%, down from 3.2% a year earlier. According to Office of Rail and Road financial figures, the Government was a net contributor to train operators for the first time for a number of years, paying out a net total of £416 million in subsidies across the industry. This is attributed to the support required for new rolling stock and other investments around the country. This is then supplemented by another £4.1 billion in grants to Network Rail.

According to the latest analysis from passenger transport specialist Passenger Transport Intelligence Services, profits at Britain's privatised train operating companies increased in cash terms in 2018-19. Overall, the figures show operating profits were 7.3% lower during the year, though margins slipped back slightly.

The analysis covers all the TOCs lodging accounts with financial year ends between 31 December 2018 and 30 June 2019. Across the franchised train operating companies as a whole, turnover rose by 13.2% to £12,793 million, whilst operating profits totalled £393 million (last year: £366 million on £11,297 million), to give an operating margin of 3.1% (last year: 3.2%).

Operating costs reached a total of £12,400 million, 13.4% higher than the 2017-18 total of £10,931 million.

Net interest earnings for the year also fell, by 46.2%, to £3.6 million. This compares with restated earnings of £6.7 million during the previous year. Pre-tax profits were 8.3% up at £389 million (2018: £359 million). Pre-tax profit margins were 3.0% (last year: 3.2%).

Total capital expenditure by the TOCs during the year fell by 12.2%, from the previous year's £280 million to £246 million. The value of net assets employed by the operators increased by 9.6% from £171 million to £188 million.

FOUR LOSS-MAKERS

As is often the case, however, there were sharp variations between

Still the most profitable TOC: Merseyrail's Nos 508127/112 form the 13.08 New Brighton to West Kirby service at Wallasey on 19 July 2020. **JAMIE SQUIBBS**

PASSENGER TRAIN OPERATORS

Expensive new trains to pay for: GWR IET No 800307 at Bristol Parkway with the 09.45 Paddington to Swansea service on 3 July 2019. **PHILIP SHERRATT**

different rail industry sectors and between train operators. Overall, four of the 20 trading TOCs made an operating loss, unchanged from last year. c2c Rail recorded a loss of 3.6%, whilst north of the border, Caledonian Sleeper and Abellio ScotRail recorded losses of 2.2% and 0.8% respectively. TransPennine Express just failed to get it into the black but improved considerably compared with the previous year's pre-exceptional loss.

Inter-city operators saw margins improve to 4.6% (last year 4.2%). Total turnover amongst the companies rose by 9.9% to £4,500 million, whilst operating costs rose by 9.5% to £4,294 million. The resulting operating profit of £205.6 million compared with £173.4 million in 2017-18. Biggest earner in all this was the Department for Transport, which extracted a net £339 million in premium payments from the operators.

Operators in London and the South East saw margins fall as operating profits fell by 12.5%. Again, the Government was a big winner, extracting premium payments worth a net £339 million from the sector as a whole, plus a £33 million profit on the Thameslink, Southern and Great Northern operation where it is taking revenue risk. Of the commuter operators, only Southeastern and West Midlands Trains are now in receipt of subsidy from DfT, with London Overground and TfL Rail getting their concession payments from Transport for London.

Turnover at these commuter companies rose by 16.8%, taking the total to £6,079 million, whilst operating costs rose by 17.7% to £5,954 million. The resulting operating profit of £125.1 million compared with £143.1 million in the previous year, at a margin of 1.1% (last year: 2.7%). Margins remain below the peak they hit before the recession – this was the 4.8% achieved in 2006-07.

The regional franchises saw something of a recovery in profit levels as new operators and agreements settled in in Scotland, Wales and Northern England. Turnover rose by 10.8% to £2,214 million, whilst operating costs were 10.4% higher, totalling £2,152 million. Operating profits were 26.5% up at £61.9 million (last year £49.0 million), at a margin of 2.8% (2.4%). As usual, this sector consumed the bulk of the subsidy paid to train operators, soaking up a whopping £982 million worth of taxpayer funding, up from £755 million the year before.

Individually, the most profitable TOC was once again the Merseyrail Electrics operation, which returned an operating margin of 11.0%. Next came Arriva Trains Wales, which earned 8.4% during the last 10 months of its franchise. Two more earned over 7%: state-owned LNER on 7.7% and new operator, the Abellio/JR East/Mitsui joint venture West Midlands Trains, which achieved 7.4%.

In the summaries below, figures are extracted from accounts lodged at Companies House. Practice concerning the declaration and calculation of different cost and revenue items varies between train operators. This occasionally makes interpretation and reconciliation difficult: major issues are noted in the brief commentaries.

Note: Turnover per Employee figures are absolute, while all other amounts are stated in thousands.

LONG DISTANCE OPERATORS

CROSSCOUNTRY
The company continued to trade profitably during the year as income and costs moved in line, though margins slipped very slightly. Passenger revenue grew roughly in line with inflation and the company benefited from £8.5 million in support from DfT for the first time in a number of years. The cost of track access and rolling stock charges increased by almost 11%.

PERIOD TO	31/12/2018	31/12/2017
	£000	£000
Turnover	553,410	533,796
Operating Costs	524,524	505,385
Operating Profit	28,886	28,411
Operating Margin	5.2%	5.3%
Turnover per Employee	303,238	£294,752
Rail contracts	230,156	207,956
Revenue Grant	8,467	0

GREAT WESTERN RAILWAY
The company saw profits increase by a quarter during the year, as revenue and costs grew. Passenger revenue grew in line with inflation but rolling stock leasing charges trebled as new trains entered service, and track access charges rose by over one-third. These increases were funded by £193 million worth of Government support, whilst the premium payable was halved.

PERIOD TO	31/03/2019	31/03/2018
	£000	£000
Turnover	1,257,285	1,019,613
Operating Costs	1,203,364	976,574
Operating Profit	53,921	43,039
Operating Margin	4.3%	4.2%
Turnover per Employee	211,344	173,906
Track Access	143,970	104,826
Rolling stock lease	349,681	111,697
Revenue Grant	193,766	0

VIRGIN TRAINS EAST COAST
These accounts cover the last three months of operation of the Inter-city East Coast franchise by this Stagecoach subsidiary. On 24 June 2018, the franchise was taken over by London North Eastern Railway (LNER), a Government-owned company (see below). The company recorded further operating and pre-tax losses during its final period. In the previous year, there was also a £40.4 million exceptional item which was an onerous contract provision against future losses.

PERIOD TO	23/06/2019	31/03/2018
	£000	£000
Turnover	207,698	842,346
Operating Costs	210,178	822,384
Operating Profit	(2,480)	19,962
Operating Margin	-1.2%	2.4%
Turnover per Employee	275,827	260,546
Track Access	13,492	27,245
Rolling stock lease	18,590	79,651

LONDON NORTH EASTERN RAILWAY
This was a new company, established by the Department for Transport to take over the Inter-city East Coast franchise from Stagecoach on 24 June 2018. This was therefore the company's first 40-week trading period, during which it traded profitably, including making a £128 million premium payment to DfT.

PERIOD TO	31/03/2019
	£000
Turnover	680,760
Operating Costs	628,229
Operating Profit	52,531
Operating Margin	7.7%
Turnover per Employee	224,525
Franchise premium payments	128,368
Track Access	94,959
Rolling stock lease	63,495

CALEDONIAN SLEEPER
The company changed its accounting reference date to 31 March, and lodged a set of accounts for a three-month period ended 31 March 2018 followed by a set for the following 12 months.

For analysis purposes, these two sets have been summed, to provide a 65-week period. The previous accounts were for a 67-week period. The financial performance of the business has continued to disappoint, with increased operating losses recorded, even ahead of an exceptional provision for future losses of £48.9 million made in the accounts to December 2017.

PERIOD TO	31/03/2019	31/12/2017
	£000	£000
Turnover	55,586	53,244
Operating Costs	56,817	53,604
Operating Profit	(1,231)	(360)
Operating Margin	-2.2%	-0.7%
Turnover per Employee	319,460	330,708
Revenue Grant	27,570	22,797

VIRGIN TRAINS WEST COAST

This was the last full year of the company's operation of the Inter-city West Coast franchise, which finished on 7 December 2019 when the business was transferred to the new FirstGroup/Trenitalia joint venture, Avanti West Coast.

During the year in question, the company saw profits dip as increased operating costs outstripped revenue growth, despite a 7.3% rise in passenger income. Notable cost increases were in track access (28%) and power costs (32%).

PERIOD TO	31/03/2019	31/03/2018
	£000	£000
Turnover	1,317,627	1,225,207
Operating Costs	1,266,369	1,162,064
Operating Profit	51,258	63,143
Operating Margin	3.9%	5.2%
Turnover per Employee	393,321	372,517
Rolling stock lease	333,864	322,949
Track Access	214,655	166,720
Franchise premium payments	243,581	250,129

EAST MIDLANDS TRAINS

This was the company's last full year of trading before the end of the franchise. Operations were transferred to Abellio on 15 August 2019. The company traded profitably during the year, achieving improved margins. Passenger income growth was very sluggish at just 0.8%, whilst there were substantial increases in track access charges (34.8%), power costs (23.6%) and train maintenance costs (18%). These were offset by a fall in premium payments to the Government.

PERIOD TO	27/04/2019	28/04/2018
	£000	£000
Turnover	438,490	433,345
Operating Costs	416,026	413,845
Operating Profit	22,464	19,500
Operating Margin	5.1%	4.5%
Turnover per Employee	178,902	188,084
Track Access	67,008	49,705
Rolling stock lease	39,520	36,353
Franchise premium payments	22,804	65,195

LONDON AND SOUTH EAST OPERATORS

GREATER ANGLIA

The company saw profits dip slightly during the year, as operating cost increases were marginally higher than otherwise strong revenue growth. The main cost increase was a 41% rise in track access charges, whilst ORR figures show the premium payable to Government also increased to £176.9 million (last year: £134.7 million). Passenger revenue grew by 7.4%, and other income sources also showed increases.

The company restated its 2018 accounts to reflect changes in the accounting treatment of defined benefit pensions. The effect was to reduce operating costs by £7.1 million compared with the previously published result.

PERIOD TO	31/03/2019	31/03/2018
	£000	£000
Turnover	701,135	650,232
Operating Costs	694,573	643,107
Operating Profit	6,562	7,125
Operating Margin	0.9%	1.1%
Turnover per Employee	230,107	216,168
Rolling stock lease	158,412	151,803
Track Access	231,476	163,142

WEST MIDLANDS TRAINS

This was the company's first full year of trading, after taking over the operation of the West Midlands rail franchise from Govia on 10 December 2017. The company traded profitably during the period, despite major increases in rolling stock and track access charges, mainly funded by an increase in subsidy.

PERIOD TO	31/03/2019	4 MONTHS TO 31/03/2018
	£000	£000
Turnover	563,036	157,463
Operating Costs	521,220	147,097
Operating Profit	41,816	10,366
Operating Margin	7.4%	6.6%
Turnover per Employee	206,316	60,867
Track Access	85,421	19,859
Rolling stock lease	85,279	24,269
Revenue Grant	133,389	38,567

CHILTERN RAILWAYS

Strong passenger revenue growth of 6.9% was more than swallowed by increasing operating costs, including premium payable to Government, track access charges and other leasing charges. As a consequence, the company saw profits fall by more than half.

PERIOD TO	31/12/2018	31/12/2017
	£000	£000
Turnover	246,178	230,689
Operating Costs	242,725	223,472
Operating Profit	3,453	7,217
Operating Margin	1.4%	3.1%
Turnover per Employee	289,621	272,360
Rolling stock lease	27,297	27,320
Track Access	37,934	33,272
Revenue Grant	0	0

LONDON OVERGROUND

This was the second full year of Arriva's operation of the London Overground concession. It saw the company's profit levels more than double as strong revenue growth outstripped increases in operating costs. The increased profit is attributed to the margins earned on the additional costs following the delays to introduction of the Class 710 trains and on increased service levels. Improved performance regime income was also reported.

PERIOD TO	31/03/2019	31/03/2018
	£000	£000
Turnover	214,221	189,204
Operating Costs	205,112	184,789
Operating Profit	9,109	4,415
Operating Margin	4.3%	2.3%

Loss into profit: loss-making Virgin Trains East Coast was replaced in 2018 by state-owned LNER, which has turned a profit. Azuma Nos 801103/101 head through Belle Isle just after leaving King's Cross with the 14.33 to Leeds on 10 October 2019. **PHILIP SHERRATT**

PASSENGER TRAIN OPERATORS

Turnover per Employee	146,928	131,300
Rolling stock lease	18,747	14,949

SOUTH WESTERN RAILWAY

This was the company's first full year of trading, having taken over the operation of the South Western franchise in August 2017. The company continued to trade profitably, albeit at sharply reduced margins, ahead of a large exceptional provision of £145.9 million against future losses. This charge represented an onerous contract provision against future expected losses through to the end of the contract. This arose because patronage and revenue were below forecast levels, exacerbated by industrial action and delays to planned improvements.

PERIOD TO	31/03/2019	32 WEEKS TO 31/03/2018
	£000	£000
Turnover	1,108,526	650,500
Operating Costs	1,100,425	640,854
Operating Profit	8,101	9,646
Operating Margin	0.7%	1.5%
Turnover per Employee	218,472	129,170
Franchise premium payments	250,236	117,672
Rolling stock lease	191,240	110,557
Track Access	99,254	36,430

GOVIA THAMESLINK RAILWAY

The company saw no profit during the year as a result of an agreement with DfT to mitigate failures during the implementation of the May 2018 timetable changes. Turnover for this business represents the fee income received from DfT for running the Thameslink, Gatwick Express, Southern and Great Northern networks. Income goes to DfT, which takes the revenue risk. According to ORR figures, the DfT took in £33 million more in income than it paid to GTR in costs in the year to 31 March 2019.

PERIOD TO	29/06/2019	30/06/2018
	£000	£000
Turnover	1,840,880	1,427,310
Operating Costs	1,840,880	1,423,876
Operating Profit	0	3,434
Operating Margin	0.0%	0.2%
Turnover per Employee	252,487	199,987

SOUTHEASTERN

The company saw cash profits grow though margins remained unchanged as revenue and costs moved in line. In June 2019, following the cancellation of the competition for a new franchise, the previous agreement was extended, firstly to 10 November 2019 and then to 1 April 2020.

The directors report that growth in passenger income of 7% was achieved, comprising 3% passenger volumes, 2.3% from a yield increase, and a one-off settlement from Transport for London over Travelcard income during the period January 2015 to April 2019 (1.8%). Passenger demand growth was above the 10-year trend, which is attributed to the completion of the rebuilding of London Bridge station. There was also an increase in revenue grant which covered higher track access and rolling stock charges.

PERIOD TO	29/06/2019	30/06/2018
	£000	£000
Turnover	1,030,869	920,785
Operating Costs	972,439	868,189
Operating Profit	58,430	52,596
Operating Margin	5.7%	5.7%
Turnover per Employee	235,466	213,342
Track Access	355,947	319,140
Rolling stock lease	172,358	161,556
Revenue Grant	132,221	67,315

TFL RAIL

The company, which holds the concession to operate Crossrail until 2023, currently runs the TfL Rail operation comprising Great Eastern suburban routes and suburban services into Paddington, including the Heathrow Connect stopping service from the airport. The company traded profitably during the year.

PERIOD TO	31/03/2019	31/03/2018
	£000	£000
Turnover	187,575	125,663
Operating Costs	183,131	123,788
Operating Profit	4,444	1,875
Operating Margin	2.4%	1.5%
Turnover per Employee	202,128	191,268
Track Access	44,413	18,315
Rolling stock lease	12,129	15,783

ESSEX THAMESIDE (C2C RAIL)

The company saw improved results during the year as strong revenue growth outstripped the rise in operating costs. As a result, the previous year's losses were halved – though the company remained quite heavily in the red. The improvement came despite hefty increases in track access charges and premium payments to Government, offset by reduced rolling stock leasing charges.

PERIOD TO	31/12/2018	31/12/2017
	£000	£000
Turnover	186,509	179,723
Operating Costs	193,266	190,586
Operating Profit	(6,757)	(10,863)
Operating Margin	-3.6%	-6.0%
Turnover per Employee	266,441	275,227
Track Access	10,837	6,924
Rolling stock lease	20,104	31,156

REGIONAL OPERATORS

SCOTRAIL

The company changed its accounting reference date during the year, so this year's figures are for a 15-month period, making comparisons difficult. However, it is clear from the margins that losses increased during the period. On an estimated annualised basis, revenue and costs were both around 19% higher, but costs rose at a slightly faster rate, resulting in the increased operating and pre-tax losses shown.

Onerous contract provision made: SWR's Nos 444043/030 speed through Raynes Park with the 10.40 Haslemere to Waterloo service on 20 January 2020. **PHILIP SHERRATT**

IN ASSOCIATION WITH CAF

PERIOD TO	31/03/2019	31/12/2017
	£000	£000
Turnover	989,628	668,914
Operating Costs	997,479	670,422
Operating Profit	(7,851)	(1,508)
Operating Margin	-0.8%	-0.2%
Turnover per Employee	201,103	137,241
Rolling stock lease	127,788	78,860
Track Access	291,058	143,995
Revenue Grant	482,838	296,613

NORTHERN

The company saw an improvement in its trading results during the year ahead of exceptional provisions for the early termination of the franchise in March 2020, after which the business was operated by a new DfT subsidiary.

The improvement in 2018-19 performance came despite the operational problems caused by the late completion of infrastructure projects, ongoing industrial action and delayed delivery of new trains – all of which contributed to a significant fall in reliability and punctuality, especially in the wake of the new timetable introduced in May 2018.

From the profit shown must be deducted exceptional items charged, which represented an onerous contract provision against costs arising on early termination (£180 million, mainly in respect of the loans made to the company by its parent) and an impairment charge of £71.35 million following an assessment of the realisable value of fixed and intangible assets on transfer – £60.920 million against fixed assets and £9.4 million against intangible assets.

PERIOD TO	31/03/2019	31/03/2018
	£000	£000
Turnover	739,000	628,883
Operating Costs	709,501	615,575
Operating Profit	29,499	13,308
Operating Margin	4.0%	2.1%
Turnover per Employee	123,105	109,124
Track Access	67,921	44,773
Rolling stock lease	66,926	69,115
Revenue Grant	370,279	284,736

TRANSPENNINE EXPRESS

The company improved its performance during the year, as strong passenger revenue growth of 7.1% outstripped rising operating costs. The company absorbed a 55% increase in track access charges, but benefited from reduced premiums payable and sharply reduced train leasing charges, presumably in part compensation for the delays in delivery of new trains on order.

In 2017-18, the company had made an exceptional onerous contract charge of £106 million, providing for expected losses over the remaining life of the franchise.

PERIOD TO	31/03/2019	31/03/2018
	£000	£000
Turnover	268,616	258,561
Operating Costs	268,714	265,715
Operating Profit	(98)	(7,154)
Operating Margin	-0.0%	-2.8%
Turnover per Employee	231,566	234,416
Track Access	66,139	42,635
Rolling stock lease	38,170	74,556
Franchise premium payments	16,905	21,632
Revenue Grant	0	0

ARRIVA TRAINS WALES

This was the final period of the company's operation of the Wales and Borders franchise, which was transferred to a new company from 18 October 2018. The company continued to trade profitably during the 10 months, albeit at reduced margins. No figures were lodged by the new operator for the rest of the financial year.

PERIOD TO	41 WEEKS TO 31/12/2018	52 WEEKS TO 31/12/2017
	£000	£000
Turnover	251,692	290,427
Operating Costs	230,642	263,261
Operating Profit	21,050	27,166
Operating Margin	8.4%	9.4%
Turnover per Employee	139,596	134,769
Rolling stock lease	33,645	42,008
Track Access	30,211	20,142
Revenue Grant	99,732	113,913

MERSEYRAIL ELECTRICS

The company continued to trade profitably during the year, though margins slipped slightly as cost increases outstripped revenue growth. Engineering works and industrial action constrained passenger income, whilst ORR figures show subsidies increased by around £6 million.

PERIOD TO	05/01/2019	06/01/2018
	£000	£000
Turnover	161,212	151,941
Operating Costs	143,421	134,785
Operating Profit	17,791	17,156
Operating Margin	11.0%	11.3%
Turnover per Employee	139,698	122,632
Track Access	8,223	5,519
Rolling stock lease	12,580	12,562

NON-FRANCHISED OPERATIONS

GRAND CENTRAL

The company improved its profitability during the year, despite reduced income, as operating costs were reduced at a faster rate. The directors report passenger revenue increased as patronage topped 1.5 million in 2018-19 for the first time, but income from other sources fell. However, neither figure is quantified in the accounts. On the other hand, ORR figures show passenger revenue in the year to 31 March 2019 was £49.91 million, up from £43.0 million in the previous year. Other income fell from £8 million to £3.6 million.

PERIOD TO	31/12/2018	31/12/2017
	£000	£000
Turnover	51,413	53,061
Operating Costs	42,016	45,014
Operating Profit	9,397	8,047
Operating Margin	18.3%	15.2%
Turnover per Employee	317,364	353,740
Rolling stock lease	6,627	7,378

Reliability travails: poor performance of its Class 180s created a difficult year for Hull Trains; they have now been replaced by new Hitachi Class 802 bi-modes. No 180111 passes Alexandra Palace on 16 August 2019 with the 09.48 King's Cross to Hull service. PHILIP SHERRATT

HULL TRAINS

The company endured a difficult year with breakdowns, fires and weather damage to its fleet of Class 180 trains. This prompted difficulty running the timetable and resulted in additional costs of hiring rolling stock and replacement buses/coaches. Despite this, the company remained in the black, albeit with much lower profit levels on the back of reduced revenue – though passenger numbers stayed above the one million mark for the third successive year.

PERIOD TO	31/03/2019	31/03/2018
	£000	£000
Turnover	30,795	31,328
Operating Costs	29,398	27,934
Operating Profit	1,397	3,394
Operating Margin	4.5%	10.8%
Turnover per Employee	250,366	270,069
Rolling stock lease	2,035	2,035

EUROSTAR INTERNATIONAL

The company performed strongly during the year, with double-digit revenue growth outstripping increases in costs to produce an increase of almost two-thirds in operating profits. Passenger numbers increased from 10.3 million to 11.0 million, including the new Amsterdam service, launched in April 2018.

PERIOD TO	31/12/2018	31/12/2017
	£000	£000
Turnover	1,020,900	915,700
Operating Costs	924,300	857,100
Operating Profit	96,600	58,600
Operating Margin	9.5%	6.4%
Turnover per Employee	678,790	618,298

PASSENGER TRAIN OPERATORS

TRAIN OPERATOR OWNING GROUPS

ABELLIO
Abellio is a subsidiary of Dutch national passenger operator NS. It has run the ScotRail franchise since April 2015, and won a new Greater Anglia franchise from October 2016, subsequently selling a 40% share to Mitsui. The new West Midlands franchise was awarded in August 2017 to Abellio and a joint venture of East Japan Railway Company and Mitsui, while in August 2019 Abellio began operating the East Midlands franchise in its own right. It also holds a 50% share alongside Serco in the 25-year Merseyrail operating concession.
MD, Abellio UK Dominic Booth

ARRIVA
Arriva is the division of the German state rail group Deutsche Bahn (DB) responsible for regional passenger transport outside Germany. UK Trains operating profit (EBITDA adjusted) in 2019 was €220 million (2018: €112 million). DB has stated it wishes to divest its Arriva subsidiary.

Arriva operates four UK rail contracts: the Arriva Rail London concession was launched in 2016; the CrossCountry franchise was won prior to 2010; and Arriva has run Chiltern Railways since acquiring its parent Laing Rail in 2008. Open access train company Grand Central was acquired in 2011. Arriva operated the Northern franchise until March 2020, when it transferred to the Department for Transport's Operator of Last Resort. The company was a bidder for the East Midlands franchise before being disqualified in April 2019; it initially brought a legal challenge against this decision but settled out of court just before the trial began in January.

The train maintenance, overhaul and servicing company Arriva TrainCare (formerly LNWR) is based in Crewe, with other locations at Bristol, Eastleigh, Cambridge and Tyne Yard.
Acting MD, Arriva UK Trains David Brown

FIRSTGROUP
FirstGroup operates long-distance, regional, commuter and sleeper services in the UK. The group operates four UK franchises as well as open access company Hull Trains.

In August 2019 the company (in a joint venture with Trenitalia) was awarded the West Coast Partnership franchise, running from December 2019, which will also include initial operation of high-speed services when HS2 opens. The South Western Railway franchise (in a joint venture with MTR) began in September 2017. The TransPennine Express franchise launched in April 2016. The company has operated Great Western Railway under a series of direct award agreements, the latest of which was agreed in March 2020 to run until at least 2023.

An open access service between London and Edinburgh via the East Coast main line is due to launch in autumn 2021. The group also operates London Trams on behalf of Transport for London. FirstGroup's other major businesses are in the UK bus market and North America.

Revenue in FirstGroup's rail division was £3,185.9 million in 2019-20 (2018-19: £2,666.7 million), with like-for-like passenger revenue growth of 0.2%. Adjusted operating profit of £68.9 million (2018-19: £68.8 million) represents a margin of 2.2% (2018-19: 2.6%).
UK Rail Managing Director Steve Montgomery

Dutch ownership: the East Midlands franchise is the most recent addition to Abellio's UK franchise portfolio. In interim EMR livery, Meridian No 222018 passes Syston with the 14.00 Sheffield to Leicester service on 22 August 2020. **PHILIP SHERRATT**

IN ASSOCIATION WITH

GOVIA

Govia is a joint venture partnership between British company The Go-Ahead Group and Keolis. Go-Ahead, the 65% majority partner, is a major bus operator with contracts in Singapore and Ireland as well as the UK. Keolis – in which French Railways (SNCF) is a major shareholder – operates trains, buses and metros across the world.

The Govia Thameslink Railway franchise, running to 2021, is the largest in the UK. Govia also operates Southeastern, the latest direct award agreement having begun in April 2020.

Majority shareholder Go-Ahead saw profit for its rail operations decline to £8.9 million in the year to 27 June 2020 (2019: £25.4 million). Total revenue for rail was up 8% to £2,885.5 million, but passenger revenue fell by 17.3%. Go-Ahead has also begun operation of rail contracts in Germany and Norway, the former having experienced what the company described as 'significant operational challenges'.
Go-Ahead Group Chief Executive David Brown

GRAND UNION TRAINS

Grand Union is an open access operator founded by former Alliance Rail Managing Director Ian Yeowart with the aim of providing 'a new customer-focused standard of train service'. The company has applied to the Office of Rail and Road to operate new services between London and Llanelli via the Great Western main line and between Stirling and London via the West Coast main line; if approved, it hopes both could start in 2021.

JR EAST AND MITSUI

One of the seven Japan Railways group companies, JR East operates a range of passenger services in the country including all Shinkansen high-speed services north of Tokyo. Mitsui is a Japanese company which operates across a range of sectors, including machinery and infrastructure.

The two companies are part of a venture led by Abellio which won the West Midlands franchise, starting in December 2017. Abellio holds a 70.1% stake, with JR East and Mitsui sharing the remaining stake equally. A joint venture of the same three companies was in the bidding for the South Eastern franchise before this was cancelled by the Department for Transport. In addition, in March 2017 Mitsui completed the acquisition of a 40% stake in Abellio's Greater Anglia franchise.

KEOLISAMEY

Keolis, in which French Railways (SNCF) is a major shareholder, formed a joint venture with infrastructure firm Amey to successfully bid for the 15-year Operator and Development Partner (ODP) contract for the new Wales and Borders franchise, which began in October 2018. In October 2020, the Welsh Government confirmed day-to-day operations would be taken in-house from February 2021, but Keolis and Amey will continue to lead on infrastructure upgrades on the Core Valley Lines north of Cardiff. A partnership of Keolis and Amey operates the Metrolink light rail network in Manchester under a concession arrangement with Transport for Greater Manchester and the Docklands Light Railway under a Transport for London concession, while Keolis is a partner in the consortium which operates the Nottingham Express Transit light rail system.
Keolis UK Chief Executive Alistair Gordon

MTR

The MTR Corporation was established in 1975 as the Mass Transit Railway Corporation with a mission to construct and operate an urban metro system to help meet Hong Kong's public transport requirements. MTR has an average weekday patronage of about 5.6 million passengers.

In the UK, MTR's first involvement in rail operations was as a partner with Arriva subsidiary Laing in London Overground Rail Operations Ltd (LOROL), which ran the London Overground concession from 2007 until November 2016. In May 2015 the company began operating TfL Rail services as part of its concession to operate Elizabeth Line services, with the operating company now named MTR Elizabeth line.

MTR joined with FirstGroup in a successful bid for the South Western franchise, which commenced operation in August 2017, MTR holding a 30% stake in the venture. However, it was unsuccessful as lead partner in a bid for the West Coast Partnership franchise, losing out to FirstGroup and Trenitalia.
Chief Executive Officer, MTR UK Steve Murphy

OLR HOLDINGS

DfT OLR Holdings Ltd (DOHL) is the Department for Transport subsidiary which provides an operator of last resort function, maintaining continuity of passenger rail services if a passenger rail franchise terminates and is not immediately replaced, fulfilling the Secretary of State's requirements under the Railways Act.

Following the termination of the Virgin Trains East Coast franchise in June 2018, DOHL took over the East Coast franchise through wholly owned subsidiary London North Eastern Railway (LNER). A new three-year deal began in June 2020, with the option of a further two-year extension.

OLR added Northern to its portfolio in March 2020 following the early termination of the Arriva Rail North franchise due to financial difficulties.
Chair, DfT OLR Holdings Limited Richard George

SERCO

Serco is a 'business to government' company with transport as one of its five specialist sectors. Since March 2015 it has operated the Caledonian Sleeper franchise under contract to the Scottish Government, while it holds a 50% share alongside Abellio in Merseyrail, a 25-year concession running to 2028. Serco Rail Technical Services offers services including vehicle testing and condition monitoring.

STAGECOACH AND VIRGIN

Stagecoach Group operates across three main divisions – UK Bus (regional operations), UK Bus (London) and UK Rail, having sold its North American division. However, the only remaining business within the UK Rail division is now the Supertram light rail network in Sheffield, which Stagecoach operates in a concession running to 2024.

In late 2019 Stagecoach exited the UK rail franchise market with the end of the Virgin Trains franchise on the West Coast main line, which had been operated by Virgin Rail Group, a 51/49 joint venture of Virgin and Stagecoach. Earlier that year Stagecoach's last solely owned UK franchise, East Midlands Trains, had also ended. The company has said it has no intention to bid for new UK rail contracts on the current risk profile offered by the Department for Transport and has surrendered its passport to bid for franchises.

Stagecoach had challenged DfT's decision in April 2019 to disqualify it from three franchise competitions (East Midlands, South Eastern and West Coast Partnership), the latter in a joint venture with Virgin and SNCF, due to non-compliances concerning pensions; the South Eastern competition was later cancelled. However, the High Court ruled against Stagecoach's claims and said the decision to disqualify the bids was lawful.

In its preliminary results for the year ended 2 May 2020, the UK Rail division recorded revenue of £161.1 million (2019: £589.5 million), with operating profit of £4.4 million on a margin of 2.7% (2019: £26.4 million, margin 4.5%). Stagecoach's 49% share of Virgin Rail Group operating profit was £18.9 million after tax (previous year: £25.7 million).
Stagecoach Group Chief Executive Martin Griffiths

TRENITALIA

Trenitalia is the primary train operator in Italy and is owned by Ferrovie dello Stato Italiane, itself owned by the Italian Government. The company entered the UK rail market in February 2017 when it acquired the c2c franchise from National Express for a total consideration of £72.6 million. The franchise had been awarded to National Express starting from November 2014 for a 15-year term.

Trenitalia holds a 30% stake in the joint venture with FirstGroup which took over the West Coast franchise in December 2019. The companies originally formed a similar venture for the East Midlands franchise but subsequently withdrew from the competition, while Trenitalia was also shortlisted for the South Eastern franchise but again withdrew. ∎

PASSENGER TRAIN OPERATORS

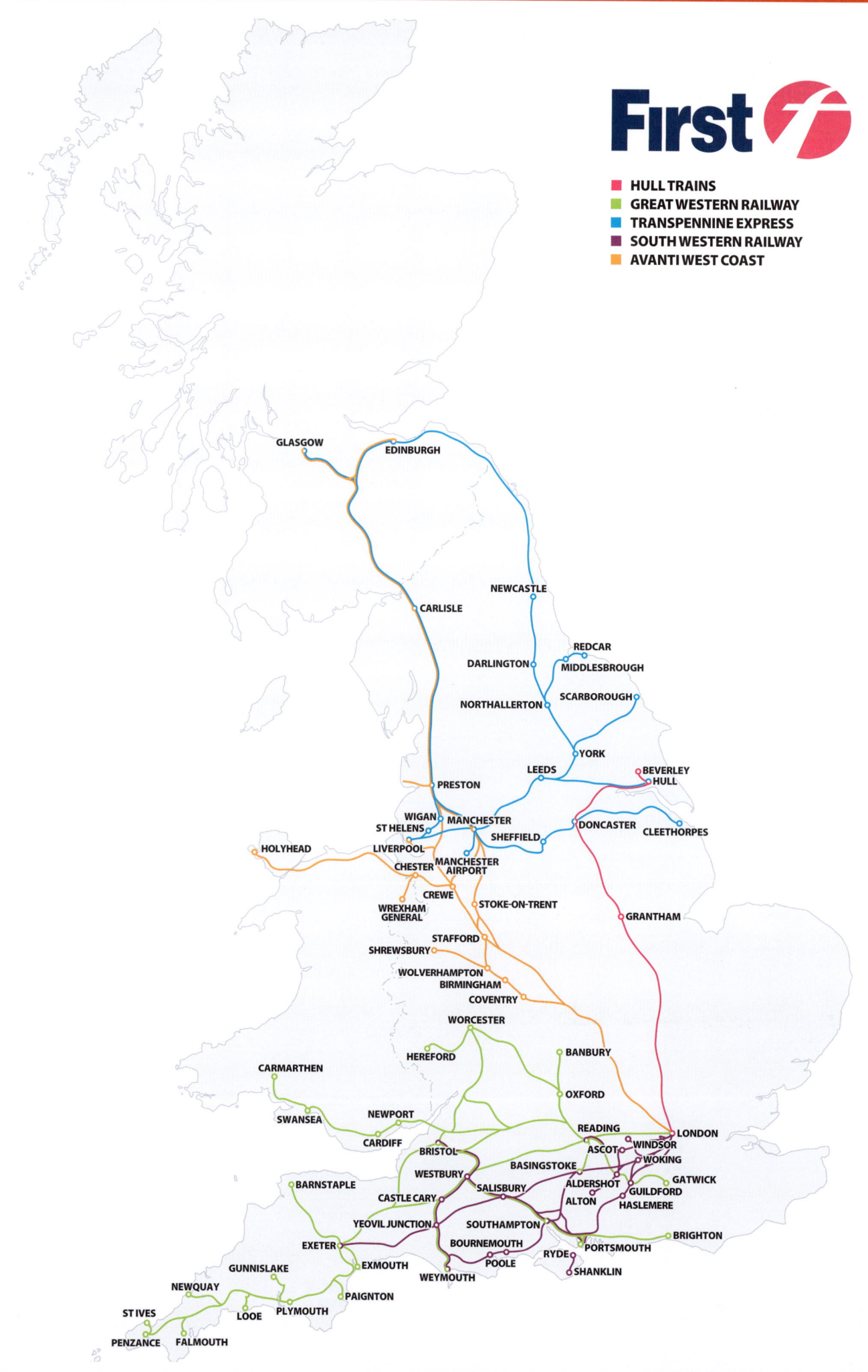

WEST COAST PARTNERSHIP FROM DECEMBER 2019

Avanti West Coast, a joint venture of FirstGroup (70% majority partner) and Trenitalia, is the operator of the West Coast Partnership franchise, having taken over from Virgin Trains on 8 December 2019. Following the impact of the coronavirus pandemic the West Coast Partnership franchise was moved onto an Emergency Recovery Measures Agreement (ERMA) contract which could last until March 2022.

The contract is in two phases, although with ongoing uncertainty over timescales for HS2 the exact date for the switch between the phases remains unclear. The initial timescale showed the joint venture operating Inter-city West Coast services until March 2026, before the second phase, running to March 2031, would see First Trenitalia operating HS2 services alongside reshaped conventional services on the West Coast main line. The Department for Transport has the option to extend the first phase, which should also see Avanti acting as shadow operator for HS2, providing a range of design, development and mobilisation services, for up to five years. The second phase has the option of an extension period of up to three years.

The West Coast Partnership represented a move away from the previous franchising system, according to DfT, with the Forecast Revenue Mechanism (FRM) helping avoid a repeat of the issues that affected the East Coast franchise, where multiple operators have failed to meet financial targets. An annual review process will ensure partnership working is 'effective, collaborative and continually improving'. During the first phase of the contract, First Trenitalia will share revenue risk with DfT through a GDP-based revenue protection mechanism and an additional Forecast Revenue Mechanism (FRM) from April 2021.

The first phase was expected to see First Trenitalia deliver £1.6 billion real Net Present Value in premium payments to the Government. The second phase of the franchise will be a management contract through which First Trenitalia will operate classic West Coast services alongside HS2 services as an integrated operation. Revenue and cost risk will pass to DfT, with First Trenitalia earning a management fee which it says will be 'equivalent to a low single digit margin per annum, with additional incentive payments for good performance'.

Initially, Avanti is operating services from London Euston to Glasgow, Liverpool, Manchester and Birmingham with the existing fleet of 35 eleven-car and 21 nine-car Class 390 Pendolino electric tilting trains and 20 five-car Class 221 diesel Super Voyager units. A £23.8 million programme to repaint the Pendolino fleet has been completed and the interiors will be extensively refurbished in a £117 million investment that will include new seats and additional luggage space. No 221101 became the first Voyager to be refurbished in an £8.3 million deal with Bombardier, entering service following work at Bombardier's Ilford facility on 10 August 2020. Work includes new standard class seats covers and carpets as well as a revamped toilet area and new LED lighting.

WEST COAST PARTNERSHIP DEVELOPMENT

First Trenitalia will be a key partner to HS2 Ltd, DfT and other stakeholders to develop world-class high-speed services and maximise the benefits of the new high-speed line.

The West Coast Partnership will be a 'shadow operator' for the design and development of the new HS2 services. Work will include advising on the design of the new trains and developing options for a new fares system for HS2 services with tickets that are integrated with the wider rail ticket system.

WCP will develop a 'passenger-focused timetable' making best use of the capacity and speed of the new infrastructure and deliver the smooth launch of the HS2 services along with the redesigned Inter-city West Coast services that will run after HS2 is launched. It will also advise on setting up the future structure for the next contract after the initial five years of HS2 operation.

KEY STATISTICS
AVANTI WEST COAST

	2018-19	2019-20
Punctuality (0-10min)	84.0%	77.7%
Passenger journeys (millions)	39.5	37.5
Passenger kilometres (millions)	7,673.2	7,388.3
Passenger train kilometres (millions)	36.0	35.3
Route kilometres operated	1,310	1,310
Number of stations managed	16	16
Number of employees	3,724	3,383

Trent Valley tilt: Pendolino No 390156, named *Pride and Prosperity* at the franchise launch event in December 2019, passes Tamworth Coton Lane with the 14.55 Manchester Piccadilly to Euston service on 29 May 2020. **JOHN WHITEHOUSE**

PASSENGER TRAIN OPERATORS

The Voyagers will be replaced in 2022 by 13 five-car bi-mode Class 805 units and 10 seven-car electric Class 807 sets which are being assembled at Hitachi's Newton Aycliffe facility in the North East. Funded by Rock Rail and ASI in a £350 million deal, the '807s' will operate between London Euston, the West Midlands and Liverpool Lime Street, while the '805s' will run from Euston to North Wales.

First Trenitalia says the first phase of its contract will include enhancements to conventional services, notably a timetable change in December 2022 which will see the introduction of over 260 extra services a week. Subject to Office of Rail and Road approval, services between Liverpool and London will be doubled from hourly to half-hourly. Other enhancements planned include new direct services from London to Llandudno and Gobowen, a new inter-city service to Walsall with an extra northbound service two years later, more trains calling at Motherwell and Rugby and introduction of hourly calls by the franchise at Liverpool South Parkway from December 2022.

Improvements at stations include more car park spaces and greater accessibility, along with new First Class lounges at Preston, Stockport and Rugby and remodelled ticket offices at Glasgow Central, Preston and Rugby. Ticketing improvements promised include flexi season ticket products, Delay Repay 15 compensation, the increased use of smart ticketing, the removal of the administration fee for changes to Advance tickets and seat reservations and making on-the-day changes possible.

Joint working with Network Rail through an alliance agreement is planned in advance of the December 2022 timetable. Plans will be developed to reduce major and minor incidents, along with installation of on-train and trackside infrastructure monitoring equipment. ■

SENIOR PERSONNEL
AVANTI WEST COAST

Managing Director Phil Whittingham (in photo)
Executive Director Finance Mark Whitehouse
Executive Director Commercial Sarah Copley
Executive Director Operations Gus Dunster
Executive Director Customer Experience Natasha Grice
Executive Director People Pauline Whitehead *
Employee Director Lizzie Power
Partnerships and Strategy Director Richard Scott *
Executive Director Projects Andy Barnes
Operations Director Nick Westcott
Safety Director Dave Whitehouse
Marketing and Brand Director Gill Corley
Revenue Director Michael Stewart

WEST COAST PARTNERSHIP DEVELOPMENT
Managing Director Caroline Donaldson
Train Services Director Russell Evans
Customer Experience Director Joost Noordewier
Finance & Contracts Director Gary Miller
PMO Director Eileen Abbess
Rolling Stock Director Adriano Scapati
Business Design & Organisation Director Sue Whaley

* shared with West Coast Partnership Development

IN ASSOCIATION WITH

DIRECT AWARD UNTIL MARCH 2023

FirstGroup runs the Greater Western franchise under a Direct Award contract with the Department for Transport, the latest of which began in April 2020. From September 2015 the business was rebranded from First Great Western to Great Western Railway (GWR).

The present contracts run to April 2023, with an option to extend this to by another year at the Department for Transport's discretion. On 30 March 2020 the company moved to a six-month Emergency Measures Agreement with the DfT due to the coronavirus pandemic, which was subsequently extended to June 2021. DfT has an option to extend this, with GWR also having the right to revert to operating with revenue risk but with protection provided though the Forecast Revenue Mechanism until at least 2023.

GWR is completing the process of introducing new or updated trains in every area of the network, with inter-city services now provided by 36 Class 800/0 five-car bi-mode Hitachi Intercity Express trains (IETs) and 21 nine-car Class 800/3 sets procured by the Department for Transport. These are supplemented by 22x5-car and 14x9-car Class 802 bi-mode sets procured by GWR.

GWR is now retaining 35 Class 43 HST power cars along with 63 modified and refurbished Mk 3 coaches to be formed into 14 2+4 Class 255 sets, branded 'Castle Class' trains. These sets will work inter-regional services in the West Country. Class 387 EMUs have taken over most local services out of Paddington, with the majority of services onto branch lines in the Thames Valley provided by diesel-powered shuttles from main line stations.

KEY STATISTICS
GREAT WESTERN RAILWAY

	2018-19	2019-20
Punctuality	84.7%	88.5%
Passenger journeys (millions)	100.1	97.0
Passenger kilometres (millions)	6,001.6	5,965.2
Passenger train kilometres (millions)	41.7	45.2
Route kilometres operated	1,997.2	1,997.2
Number of stations managed	196	197
Number of employees	6,343	6,452

In August 2020 GWR received its first Class 769 tri-mode unit. Nineteen sets are on order and will be able to work on overhead and third rail electric lines, as well as under their own diesel power. Present plans will see the trains deployed between Reading and Basingstoke; Reading, Redhill and Gatwick Airport; and on the Henley and Bourne End lines. Their introduction will enable the release of some Turbo units to add capacity in the Bristol area and support the ability to launch new routes through the city.

The new direct award contract will see Class 165 and 166 Turbo DMUs receive an interior refresh to make them better suited for longer-distance journeys, with GWR also exploring options for fitting new traction equipment. The operator is expected to bring forward proposals for the replacement for its Class 150 and 158 DMUs, and to look at options to replace the current overnight fleet of sleeping cars and locomotives. Work to refurbish London to Penzance sleeper vehicles was completed in mid-2018 with all cabins fitted with keycard door locks and offering free Wi-Fi. The sleeper trains feature a redesigned lounge bar and each service has one accessible cabin and an adjacent accessible toilet.

December 2019 saw the biggest timetable change on the Great Western Railway network since 1976, with changes to local and long-distance services. Highlights included 'super-fast' services between London and Bristol/South Wales and regular hourly services between London and the West of England, the North Cotswolds and South Cotswolds. The Castle HSTs have provided a capacity uplift between Cardiff and Taunton and on services between Exeter and Plymouth/Penzance, whilst the Exeter to Paignton service became half-hourly. Both the Looe and Barnstaple branches have seen service frequency improved to hourly.

In April 2018 GWR launched mobile ticketing across its network with customers able to travel with their ticket on their smartphone or tablet. The scheme covers all single and return tickets, standard and first class, adult and child. ∎

Masked IET: No 800321 works the 11.02 London Paddington to Bristol Temple Meads service at Swindon South Marston Junction 15 June 2020. **KEN BRUNT**

SENIOR PERSONNEL
GREAT WESTERN RAILWAY

Interim Managing Director Matthew Golton (in photo)
Interim Commercial Development Director Tom Pierpoint
Engineering Director Simon Green
Director of Sales & Marketing Phil Delaney
Customer Service & Operations Director Richard Rowland
Business Assurance Director Joe Graham
Finance Director Duncan Rimmer
Human Resources Director Ruth Busby

South Western Railway

SEVEN-YEAR FRANCHISE TO AUGUST 2024

FirstGroup plc and MTR Corporation began operating the new South Western franchise as South Western Railway (SWR) on 20 August 2017. The 70:30 joint venture is due to hold the franchise for seven years, to 18 August 2024, with an extension option of up to 11 months. Following the impact of the coronavirus pandemic the SWR franchise was moved onto an Emergency Recovery Measures Agreement (ERMA) contract which could last until March 2021.

SWR provides commuter services from London Waterloo to south west London, suburban and regional services in the counties of Surrey, Hampshire and Wiltshire as well as regional services in Devon, Somerset, Berkshire and Wiltshire.

PASSENGER TRAIN OPERATORS

Arterio EMU: No 701004 at Wimbledon depot during the event to unveil the brand name for the new suburban fleet on 24 August 2020. **PHILIP SHERRATT**

multiple-units (EMUs) (60x10-car and 30x5-car) for suburban routes was unveiled on 24 August when SWR announced Arterio as the name for the trains. The first sets from the order valued at £895 million were due to enter service on the Reading line by December 2020.

The first of 18 refurbished Class 442 trains (90 carriages) was put into service in the summer of 2019 although technical problems with these units saw them removed from service between September 2019 and January 2020 until the issues were resolved. This was followed by a decision to place the sets in store pending the end of the pandemic. The £45 million project is seeing life-expired DC traction equipment replaced with an AC package incorporating IGBT technology from Kiepe Electric Düsseldorf, with the re-tractioning work undertaken by Gemini Rail Services at Wolverton. New brake controls from Knorr-Bremse enable regenerative braking on the units. Internally the sets have been

Its subsidiary Island line operates services on the Isle of Wight.

Over the life of the franchise SWR expects to deliver investment of £1.2 billion with a key step the provision of 'longer, faster and more reliable trains with 52,000 more seats across the morning and evening peak every day at Waterloo'. In May 2019 SWR introduced more than 300 extra services per week across its network and it reports that by working closely with Network Rail its performance has begun to improve.

After arriving on the SWR network on 11 June 2020, the first of the 90-strong fleet of new Bombardier Aventra Class 701 electric

SEVEN-YEAR FRANCHISE TO APRIL 2023

Awarded to FirstGroup, the TransPennine Express (TPE) franchise runs from 1 April 2016 for seven years, with a possible two-year extension. Between 2004 and 2016 First operated the contract in a 55/45 partnership with Keolis. Delivery of the franchise is co-managed by the Department for Transport and Rail North Partnership, which brings together representatives from 29 local transport authorities. Following the impact of the coronavirus pandemic the TransPennine Express franchise was moved onto an Emergency Recovery Measures Agreement (ERMA) contract which could last until March 2021.

The new franchise sees TPE focusing on running inter-city services in the North of England and between Manchester and Scotland. Investment of more than £500 million to transform services with new and refurbished trains supports a series of timetable improvements which see a 55% increase in the number of services connecting the largest cities in the North of England and Scotland. Around 75% of the company's revenue comes from leisure passengers, with 15% derived from regular commuters and 10% from business travellers.

The May 2018 timetable change saw Manchester to Leeds local trains transferred from Northern and changes to the routeing of services from the North East to Manchester Airport via Manchester Victoria station and over the Ordsall Chord. This was a key part in delivering TPE's franchise commitments, which include a 24% increase in services on Saturdays and 52% on Sundays, and an eventual 110% increase in train miles operated by the company.

Congestion on several parts of the network saw punctuality fall significantly and from December 2019 a number of changes were made to TPE's timetables. This included the introduction of a new service between Liverpool and Glasgow via the West Coast main line, the extension of Liverpool to Newcastle services onwards to Edinburgh and the extension of Manchester Airport to Middlesbrough services to Redcar Central. Problems with crew training and availability, connected to the delayed introduction of the new train fleets, saw some of

KEY STATISTICS
TRANSPENNINE EXPRESS

	2018-19	2019-20
Punctuality (0-10min)	76.3%	76.5%
Passenger journeys (millions)	29.2	28.6
Passenger kilometres (millions)	2,081.7	2,058.5
Passenger train kilometres (millions)	20.6	21.1
Route kilometres operated	1,039.6	1,252.9
Number of stations managed	19	19
Number of employees	1,258	1,459

IN ASSOCIATION WITH

KEY STATISTICS
SOUTH WESTERN RAILWAY

	2018-19	2019-20
Punctuality (0-5min)	82.3%	80.5%
Passenger journeys (millions)	216.0	203.7
Passenger kilometres (millions)	6,039.6	5,705.8
Passenger train kilometres (millions)	39.0	38.2
Route kilometres operated	997.8	997.8
Number of stations managed	184	184
Number of employees	5,177	5,308

fitted with Wi-Fi, LED lighting and real-time passenger information systems whilst new carpets have been laid and seats reupholstered.

On 9 January 2020 SWR announced that the £70 million refurbishment programme for its 172 Class 444 and 450 Desiro trains had been completed. The refurbishment was completed by the trains' original manufacturer, Siemens, and includes improved Wi-Fi, on-board entertainment access, new inductive charging tables and power sockets, refreshed toilets and ergonomically designed seats throughout.

Orders for new and refurbished trains will see a number of EMU fleets released; 91 four-car Class 455s, 24 two-car Class 456s, and 36 five-car Class 458/5s converted from original Class 458/0 and Class 460 trains. Also to be released are 30 new Class 707 five-car Desiro City trains, ordered in 2014 in a £210 million contract with Siemens and Angel Trains, which will transfer to Southeastern.

The £26 million investment plan for the 13.7km Island line linking Ryde with Shanklin, agreed with DfT, will see an upgrade to power supplies, platform upgrades, track improvement work including a new passing loop at Brading and the replacement of the 80-year-old fleet of Class 483 EMUs with five Class 484 two-car EMUs from Vivarail which use the bodyshells and bogies from former London Underground D78 units originally constructed in 1978-81. Infrastructure work will take place during a complete closure of the line from 4 January until 31 March 2021, and after reopening with the new trains a 30-minute interval service will be introduced in May 2021, rather than the uneven 20/40-minute split currently provided.

On 1 April 2020, Romsey, Dean, and Mottisfont and Dunbridge stations transferred to SWR from GWR ownership.

On 28 August 2020 SWR ran a special 'fact-finding' train over the Fawley branch line in Hampshire, more than 50 years since regular passenger services ceased. This followed a successful submission to the DfT's 'Restoring your Railway Fund' by Hampshire County Council which will see funds provided for a feasibility study into reopening the route, which is also known as the Waterside line. ■

SENIOR PERSONNEL
SOUTH WESTERN RAILWAY

Interim Managing Director Mark Hopwood (in photo)
Chief Operating Officer Mike Houghton
Operations & Safety Director Jacqui Dey
Engineering Director Neil Drury
Customer Experience Director Alan Penlington
Finance Director Chris Cornthwaite
Commercial & Business Development Director Peter Williams
Performance & Planning Director Steve Tyler
HR Director Sharon Johnston

these timetable improvements deferred into early 2020.

Testing and introduction of the three new 'Nova' train fleets has taken considerably longer than first anticipated. Acceptance of the full 13-strong Nova 3 fleet, comprising new CAF Mk 5a coaches powered by Class 68 locomotives leased from Direct Rail Services, is not expected to be completed until 2021. On 24 August 2019 a Nova 3 train carried its first passengers, but the reduced timetable due to Covid-19 saw use of the sets accepted held at three daily diagrams.

The first passenger working of a Class 802 Hitachi bi-mode Nova 1 set was on 28 September 2019, followed by regular service introduction in October. This was also the first TPE service to operate at 125mph, achieving this southbound between Newcastle and York. The 19-strong fleet is now fully accepted and being used on TPE's Manchester Airport – Newcastle and Liverpool Lime Street – Edinburgh services.

On 30 November 2019 Nova 2 set No 397007 operated the fleet's first passenger service, running from Manchester Airport to Edinburgh.

Nova 2 in service: CAF-built EMU No 397011 at Manchester Airport as it prepares to work the 15.07 service to Glasgow Central on 2 March 2020. **PHILIP SHERRATT**

PASSENGER TRAIN OPERATORS

The 12-strong fleet of EMUs is now fully in service working all trains between Manchester/Liverpool and Glasgow/Edinburgh via the West Coast main line.

Together the three new 'Nova' fleets are providing 13 million extra seats a year, with 10,000 more morning and evening seats into key Northern cities, an 80% increase in capacity at the busiest times of the day.

All 51 Class 185 three-car DMUs were fully refurbished with the installation of Wi-Fi and TPE's on-board entertainment system, 'Exstream'. At least 36 of the 185s are due to remain with the franchise, although this number could increase in the light of increased passenger demand and possible additions to the services the company operates. Real-time passenger information screens are fitted to all trains and a new mobile app with journey planner will be introduced, with real-time seat availability information. ■

SENIOR PERSONNEL
TRANSPENNINE EXPRESS

Interim Managing Director	Liz Collins (in photo)
Finance Director	Carolann James
Commercial Director	Darren Higgins
Fleet Director	Paul Staples
Major Projects Director	Chris Nutton
Operations Director	Paul Watson
Customer Experience Director	Kathryn O'Brien
Service Planning Director	Jerry Farquharson
Strategy Director	Louise Ebbs
Head of HR	Nicola Buckley

OPEN ACCESS AGREEMENT UNTIL 2029

Currently the UK's smallest open access operator, Hull Trains launched in September 2000 when three daily return services operated between Hull and London King's Cross.

From carrying just 80,000 passengers in its first year, the 92 trains a week operated by Hull Trains were carrying over one million passengers a year when services were suspended on 30 March 2020 due to the coronavirus pandemic. Trains began running again on 21 August with a simplified timetable pending a further increase in customer numbers. Prior to the pandemic the company had extended two of its five services a day to serve Beverley, having obtained approval for a further 10-year open access agreement which runs until 2029.

Hull Trains says its customer-focused ethos has been key to its success, consistently demonstrating values which has seen it ranked highly among customers and winning awards along the way. It states: 'Our people are what set us apart and we are proud to have become one of the most innovative, enterprising and dynamic long-distance train operating companies in the UK. From our customer service advisors to our train drivers, everybody plays their part in looking after the small details and making sure every journey is a great experience.'

A £60 million investment has seen Hull Trains introduce five new Class 802 bi-mode trains built by Hitachi, replacing its four Class 180 DMUs, which suffered frequent reliability problems. Maintained by Hitachi at its Doncaster Carr depot, Hull Trains has named the new trains the 'Paragon' fleet. The first of the new trains entered service on 5 December 2019, with all services operated by the new trains by the end of February 2020. The investment has increased seating capacity and improved the operator's environmental credentials, whilst the ability to run on diesel power over non-electrified routes will also enable services to keep running if the overhead wires are damaged. ■

KEY STATISTICS
HULL TRAINS

	2018-19	2019-20
Punctuality (0-10min)	71.4%	77.8%
Passenger journeys (millions)	1.0	1.0
Passenger kilometres (millions)	244.6	245.2
Passenger train kilometres (millions)	1.4	1.6
Route kilometres operated	342.8	344.4
Number of employees	122	129

SENIOR PERSONNEL
HULL TRAINS

Managing Director	Louise Cheeseman (in photo)
Production Director	Louise Mendham
Finance Manager	Glenn McLeish-Longthorn
Head of HR & People Support	Deborah Birch

Paragon: one of Hull Trains' new bi-mode units pulls away from its stop at Grantham with the 09.48 King's Cross to Hull service on 29 January 2020. **PHILIP SHERRATT**

IN ASSOCIATION WITH

Thameside franchise: running on the edge of the estuary, No 357208 approaches Chalkwell with the 10.20 Fenchurch Street to Southend Central service on 13 November 2013. **ANTONY GUPPY**

c2c

15-YEAR FRANCHISE UNTIL NOVEMBER 2029

c2c provides commuter services from its London terminus Fenchurch Street, and on occasion from Liverpool Street, to the northern Thames Gateway area of southern Essex, with the main service groups being from Fenchurch Street to Shoeburyness via Basildon, to Southend via Ockendon/Tilbury and to Grays via Rainham.

The c2c Essex Thameside franchise was acquired by Trenitalia UK from National Express Group (NX) on 10 February 2017. NX had operated the franchise since 2000 and won a new 15-year term starting on 9 November 2014. Following the impact of the coronavirus pandemic the c2c franchise was moved onto an Emergency Recovery Measures Agreement (ERMA) contract which could initially last until March 2021. At the height of the Covid-19 pandemic c2c reduced its timetable to focus on serving key workers; however, it reinstated its standard weekday timetable from 18 May 2020.

Facing demand for more capacity, the company adapted 20% of its vehicles into a 'metro' style in 2015 with 2+2 instead of 3+2 seating. This increased the passenger capacity of these carriages by increasing the amount of available standing space. Further capacity was provided with the introduction of six four-car Bombardier Class 387 trains on a short-term lease, while a new timetable from January 2017 included faster journeys between Southend and London and longer trains for many stations.

The Class 387s will be replaced by a new £100 million fleet of 6x10-car Class 720/6 Bombardier Aventra trains, which are due to be delivered in the summer of 2021. Once they have joined the existing fleet of 74 Class 357 EMUs, the new units will provide capacity for 5,000 additional passengers, with 20% more seats.

c2c has led the way with many of its ticketing and customer-facing processes. It provides automatic compensation for registered smartcard customers for delays over two minutes and operates a Delay Repay 15 (DR15) scheme which entitles every c2c passenger to compensation if their train is delayed for as little as 15 minutes, paid automatically to holders of c2c smartcards.

The company also launched the country's first flexible season ticket in June 2016 – a digital carnet of 10 individual tickets. Each provides a typical 5% discount on the peak-time price of daily travel, with an additional 10% reward if used off-peak. Purchased online, tickets are loaded onto smartcards at the ticket gate. By late 2017, half of all annual season tickets were being sold on smartcards.

c2c's new Pico4UK ticketing system is the UK's first single ticketing solution, combining five different channels for buying tickets – ticket office machines, ticket vending machines, the website, app and new handheld devices – into a single system. Smart ticketing is available across every sales channel for the most popular c2c products. This is particularly important as c2c and other rail operators are driving customers towards digital tickets as the industry's preferred approach, as part of the strategy for recovery from the impact of coronavirus.

c2c has invested in better customer information and improved facilities at its stations whilst its work to retain its crown as the UK's most punctual train operator paid off when it won the rail industry's coveted 'Golden Whistle' award for best operational performance in London and the South East at the 2020 ceremony organised by *Modern Railways* magazine. Over the previous year, 83.5% of c2c trains arrived within one minute at each station, the best performance in the UK.

c2c has continued to adjust its timetable, with amendments in December 2018 and May 2019, using detailed information on passenger loadings and service reliability data for every train service. More train drivers have been recruited to reduce the risk of cancellations following sickness or short-term unavailability. The company is also investing over £17 million in its stations over the next three years in projects which will see improvements for passengers and staff at every station it operates, albeit with changes to the opening times of a number of ticket offices. ■

KEY STATISTICS
C2C

	2018-19	2019-20
Punctuality (0-5min)	94.6%	95.1%
Passenger journeys (millions)	49.1	47.3
Passenger kilometres (millions)	1,237.8	1,201.0
Passenger train kilometres (millions)	7.3	7.2
Route kilometres operated	125.5	125.5
Number of stations managed	25	25
Number of employees	690	643

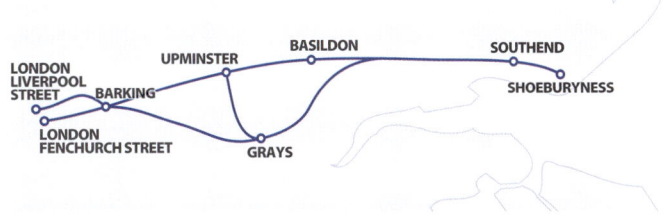

SENIOR PERSONNEL
C2C

Managing Director Ben Ackroyd (in photo)
Delivery Director Laura McEwen
Commercial Director Claire McCaffrey
Engineering Director Jeff Baker
Finance Director Rob Taylor
Head of Communications Chris Atkinson

PASSENGER TRAIN OPERATORS

New train for Liverpool: the first Class 777 to be delivered for Merseyrail, No 777003, on display in January 2020. COURTESY MERSEYTRAVEL

 Merseyrail

25-YEAR CONCESSION FROM JULY 2003

The 25-year contract to run the Merseyrail Electric network, with a total value of £3.6 billion, was awarded in 2003 to a Serco and Abellio joint venture, subject to five-yearly reviews.

The 75-mile network, which operates over 600 regular services per day, serves 68 stations and carries approximately 34 million passengers a year. Merseyrail forms the most heavily used urban railway network in the UK outside London. Services operate at 15-minute intervals, increasing to every five minutes through the city centre sections.

Merseytravel, the transport executive body of Liverpool City Region Combined Authority (CA), manages the unique operating concession for this self-contained 750V DC third rail electrified railway. The Northern line links Southport, Ormskirk and Kirkby to Hunts Cross, and the Wirral line serves West Kirby, New Brighton, Chester and Ellesmere Port. A 6.5-mile central Liverpool loop line miles runs through a tunnel, with four underground stations in Liverpool and one in Birkenhead.

A £460 million project to replace the fleet of 59 three-car Class 507 and Class 508 trains, which date back to 1978-79, was approved by the Combined Authority in December 2016. Stadler is supplying a fleet of 52 Class 777 trains which have been designed specifically for the Merseyrail network and will include pioneering sliding step technology, making Merseyrail one of the most accessible networks in the country. Merseytravel will own the trains, and lease them to the operator, with the project being financed through a reserve fund and loans, including from the Public Works Loan Board and European Investment Bank. Growth, operational efficiencies and improved reliability are expected to help recover additional costs and the order includes an option for 60 further units. Power supply, track and station upgrades are also part of the programme.

The fleet will be based at a new depot at Kirkdale as well as the refurbished Birkenhead North facility. The 65-metre long four-car EMUs will be three metres longer

15-YEAR OVERNIGHT SERVICE FRANCHISE

The 15-year franchise for overnight services between London Euston and Scotland, awarded to Serco Caledonian Sleepers Limited, began operation on 31 March 2015. At its launch Serco said the franchise was expected to deliver revenue of up to £800 million over 15 years. Trains run nightly except on Saturday nights on two routes: the Lowland Sleeper to/from Glasgow and Edinburgh, and the Highland Sleeper to/from Aberdeen, Inverness and Fort William.

A new fleet of 75 Mk 5 coaches, built by CAF, was introduced from 2019. Valued at approximately £150 million,

KEY STATISTICS
CALEDONIAN SLEEPER

	2018-19	2019-20
Punctuality (0-10min)	89.7%	81.1%
Passenger journeys (millions)	0.3	0.3
Passenger kilometres (millions)	201.0	206.0
Passenger train kilometres (millions)	1.4	1.4
Route kilometres operated	1,470.9	1,470.9
Number of employees	174	195

the new fleet was part-funded by a £60 million grant from the Scottish Government. The vehicles offer five different accommodation types including berths with an en-suite shower and WC, double, twin and single beds variants as well as reclining seats. A brasserie-style Club Car enables a hospitality service which Serco says 'offers an outstanding hospitality service that is emblematic of the best of Scotland'. The vehicles are 22.2 metres long, so a 16-vehicle train can just be accommodated at London Euston.

An updated sales and reservation system offers a broader range of fares to help growth in passenger numbers, and the ability to book 12 months ahead has proved popular. Serco says it is aiming to market the service as a high quality hotel experience with its fares reflecting the uplift in quality it is aiming to deliver.

The Covic-19 pandemic had a significant impact on services with a reduced timetable in operation through to the autumn of 2020 alongside the temporary closure of the Club Car and the seated vehicles, the latter meaning Caledonian Sleeper trains were unable to provide their usual daytime services on the Fort William line and also from Kingussie, Aviemore and Carrbridge to Inverness. The impact of the pandemic also saw the Scottish

SENIOR PERSONNEL
CALEDONIAN SLEEPER

Managing Director Kathryn Darbandi (in photo)
Operations Director Magnus Conn
Guest Experience Director Graham Kelly
Finance Director Chris Gemmell
Legal Director John Frame
Business Performance Director Anne Jack

EDs in the Highlands: rebuilt electro-diesels Nos 73967/968 work the London Euston to Inverness sleeper at Dalwhinnie on 8 August 2020. JAMIE SQUIBBS

IN ASSOCIATION WITH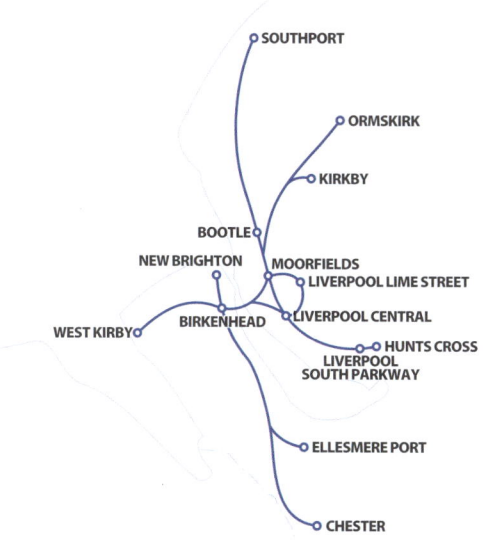

KEY STATISTICS
MERSEYRAIL

	2018-19	2019-20
Punctuality (0-5min)	95.5%	96.7%
Passenger journeys (millions)	42.1	42.6
Passenger kilometres (millions)	666.9	683.1
Passenger train kilometres (millions)	6.4	6.5
Route kilometres operated	120.7	120.7
Number of stations managed	66	66
Number of employees	1,206	1,168

than the existing trains and able to carry 60% more passengers (486 per train), while retaining the same number of seats. Wide through gangways will increase standing space. Train bodies will be tailored for Merseyrail, with lower train floors, platform and track improvements, and a sliding step from the train giving almost level access. A red and green light system around the doors will indicate when it is safe to get on and off and the doors themselves will have sensitive edges to ensure nothing is trapped as they close.

The Class 777s will be six tonnes lighter than the current 105-tonne trains, with energy consumption expected to be 20% lower; they will be able to operate on 25kV AC, beyond the Merseyrail third rail system, after a simple modification programme, and two will be fitted with batteries for energy recycling trials. The first unit, No 777003, was delivered to Kirkdale depot on 15 January 2020, with testing starting on the Kirkby branch of the Northern line on 16 March.

Average fares on Merseyrail are among the cheapest in the country and rises are capped at the Retail Price Index level. The operator has modernised significantly in recent years, launching trials for its smart ticketing scheme in 2017, working towards moving to online ticketing in the future with just a contactless bank card required.

City centre stations have undergone refurbishment over the last five years, and a new station (Maghull North) was opened on the network in June 2018, while Ainsdale station reopened in the same year following an extensive refurbishment that has seen it become Merseyrail's most eco-friendly station.

Merseyrail was recognised as the best performing regional rail operator at the 2020 Golden Whistle Awards, having recorded an annual performance of 96.36% of trains running on time. ■

SENIOR PERSONNEL
MERSEYRAIL

Managing Director Andy Heath (in photo)
Finance and Transformation Director Emma Cowan
People Director (Deputy MD) Jane English
Chief Operating Officer Zoe Hands
Commercial Director Suzanne Grant

Government move the contract onto an Emergency Measures Agreement (EMA) until 10 January 2021, with discussions taking place over the future of the contract after that date.

Rolling stock maintenance is carried out under contract by Alstom whilst traction and traincrew are provided by GB Railfreight. GBRf has a refurbished fleet of 10 Class 92 locomotives for the main legs of the journey over the West Coast main line to Glasgow/Edinburgh, with six rebuilt Class 73/9 locomotives for non-electrified sections to Fort William, Aberdeen and Inverness. On occasion Class 66 locomotives are used along with a Class 73/9 on the Inverness portion. ■

PASSENGER TRAIN OPERATORS

EMR

EIGHT-YEAR FRANCHISE TO AUGUST 2027

The East Midlands franchise is operated by Abellio under an eight-year contract which began on 18 August 2019 and runs until 21 August 2027, with an optional extension of two years at the discretion of the Secretary of State. East Midlands Railway replaced East Midlands Trains, which had been run by Stagecoach from 11 November 2007. Following the impact of the coronavirus pandemic the EMR franchise was moved onto an Emergency Recovery Measures Agreement contract which could last until March 2022.

EMR operates inter-city services from London St Pancras over the Midland main line to Leicester, Nottingham, Derby and Sheffield with limited extensions to Lincoln, Leeds and York. Local and inter-regional services include trains between Liverpool and Norwich; this service is to be split at Nottingham to improve service performance. Whilst the Department for Transport had announced another operator would take over the Nottingham to Liverpool section, in August 2020 it informed EMR this will no longer happen. Services on the line to Barton-on-Humber branch are due to transfer to EMR from Northern in May 2021.

Abellio plans to invest £600 million in the new franchise including the replacement of the entire rolling stock fleet with new or refurbished trains. EMR plans to operate longer trains and more services on many routes, providing an 80% increase in peak capacity into Nottingham, Lincoln and St Pancras.

Twenty-one four-car Class 360/1 Desiro EMUs refurbished and upgraded to 110mph operation will be introduced on services from St Pancras to Corby in May 2021, following completion of electrification north of Bedford. At this point the Midland main line timetable will be recast, providing six per trains per hour from St Pancras, with two each to Corby, Nottingham and Sheffield.

The changes in May 2021 will enable EMR to withdraw its HSTs from Midland main line services. In mid-2020 it had nine 2+8 and three 2+6 sets, which were not compliant with Persons with Reduced Mobility (PRM) regulations and operated under a dispensation. A Department for Transport initiative has seen cascaded 2+8 HSTs from LNER introduced as they have a lesser degree of PRM non-compliance, but introduction has been slower than planned. Four five-car Class 180 sets released by Hull Trains were due to be introduced by EMR in December 2020 for up to three years, enabling a reduction in HST usage and the withdrawal of the 2+6 sets.

EMR Intercity services will eventually be operated by 33 Class 810 bi-mode trains built by Hitachi at its Newton Aycliffe factory in County Durham, due to be introduced in 2023 and branded as 'Aurora'. According to Hitachi, the '810s' represent an 'evolution' of the AT300 design supplied to other UK operators, with 24-metre vehicles rather than 26-metre and a slightly modified nose profile. Each five-car set will have four underfloor diesel generator modules rather than the three used in the Class 800s and 802s. Abellio expects the units to operate 'regularly' in 10-car formations, providing increased seating capacity. The air-conditioned trains will have Wi-Fi and at-seat charging facilities, as well as enhanced passenger information displays. Introduction of the '810s' will see the transfer of part of Etches Park depot in Derby to Hitachi as the maintenance base for the new bi-mode trains.

For regional routes, incoming rolling stock comprises Class 170 DMUs released by ScotRail and West

KEY STATISTICS
EAST MIDLANDS RAILWAY

	2018-19	2019-20
Punctuality	89.5%	89.1%
Passenger journeys (millions)	26.7	25.4
Passenger kilometres (millions)	2,415.0	2,249.5
Passenger train kilometres (millions)	22.8	22.4
Route kilometres operated	1,549.8	1,549.8
Number of stations managed	90	90
Number of employees	2,460	2,440

SENIOR PERSONNEL
EAST MIDLANDS RAILWAY

Managing Director Will Rogers (in photo)
Operations Director Paul Barnfield
Fleet Director Neil Bamford
Customer Services Director Neil Grabham
Commercial Director Chris Wright
Finance Director Tim Gledhill
HR Director Kirsty Derry
Transition & Projects Director Lisa Angus

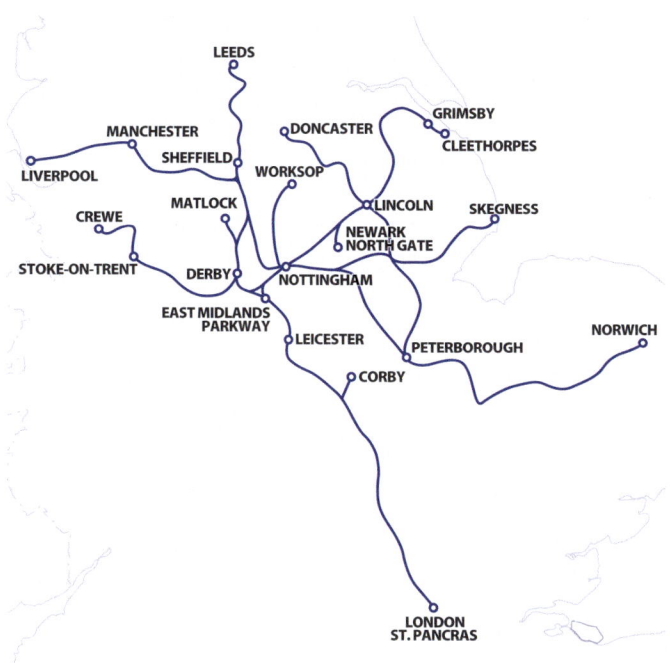

Midlands Trains and Class 171 DMUs from Govia Thameslink Railway which will be converted to Class 170 units before entering service with EMR. The first Class 170 entered service with EMR on the Robin Hood line from Nottingham to Mansfield and Worksop on 2 November 2020. The full fleet is planned to comprise 33x2-car and 11x3-car units, but now it is retaining the Nottingham to Liverpool service EMR will also have to resource additional trains for that route.

EMR will upgrade ticketing and accessibility. It has launched an improved 'Delay Repay 15' compensation scheme and has plans for smart ticketing and a new 'Flexipass' part-time season ticket.

Soldiering on: 2020 saw EMR introduce cascaded ex-LNER HSTs on the Midland main line. Power car Nos 43320/316 work the 10.45 Nottingham to St Pancras service at Attenborough nature reserve on 18 May 2020. PHILIP SHERRATT

These will be supported through a new website and mobile app.

At least £17 million will also be spent on station improvements, with larger schemes at Leicester, London St Pancras, Market Harborough and Sheffield; many stations will see upgraded waiting areas, cafes and shops and every station will have a ticket vending machine provided. ■

greateranglia
NINE-YEAR FRANCHISE TO OCTOBER 2025

Operated by Abellio, the Greater Anglia franchise runs from October 2016 to October 2025, with the option of an additional year. In March 2017 a 40% stake was sold to Mitsui. Following the impact of the coronavirus pandemic the Greater Anglia franchise was moved onto an Emergency Recovery Measures Agreement (ERMA) contract which could last until September 2021.

Greater Anglia provides the majority of commuter/regional services from London Liverpool Street to Essex, Suffolk, Norfolk and parts of Hertfordshire and Cambridgeshire, as well as regional services throughout the East of England. It also operates long-distance trains from London to Norwich via Ipswich and the Stansted Express service.

Services that used to be part of the franchise between Liverpool Street and Enfield Town, Cheshunt (via Seven Sisters) and Chingford, as well as Romford to Upminster, transferred to London Overground from 31 May 2015. Liverpool Street to Shenfield stopping services switched to TfL Rail operation by MTR Elizabeth line on the same date.

The franchise is delivering on a commitment to replace its entire train fleet in a £1.5 billion programme that will see 1,043 new carriages introduced. A total of 133 five-car Class 720 Aventra suburban electric trains are being built by Bombardier in Derby; the order originally featured 22 10-car sets but was amended in September 2020. Swiss manufacturer Stadler has delivered 378 carriages of a new Flirt UK design – 10 12-car Class 745/0 inter-city EMUs, 10 12-car Class 745/1 Stansted Express EMUs, plus 24 four-car Class 755/4 and 14 three-car Class 755/3 bi-mode regional trains. Both manufacturers will be responsible for maintenance and all trains will have air conditioning, Wi-Fi, plug points and controlled emission toilets. The accessible features on the Stadler trains, including ramps which deploy at doorways,

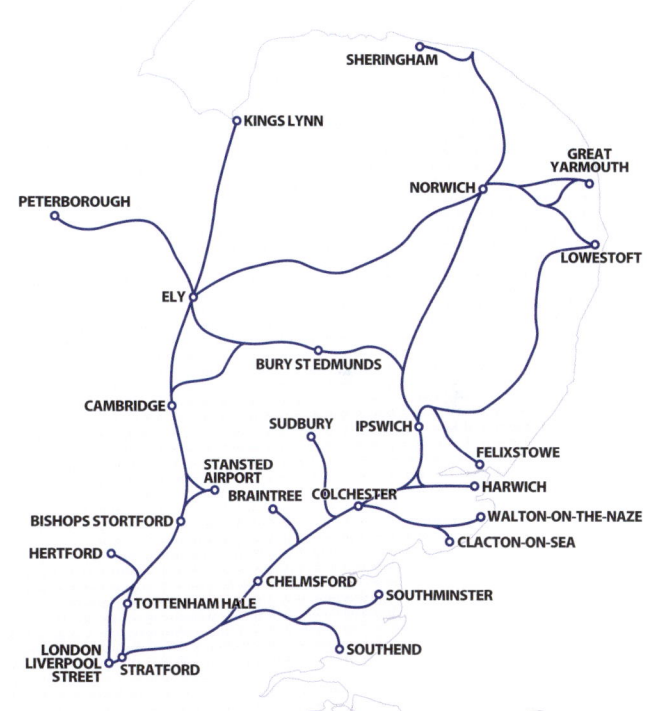

KEY STATISTICS
GREATER ANGLIA

	2018-19	2019-20
Punctuality	87.9%	89.0%
Passenger journeys (millions)	84.9	84.9
Passenger kilometres (millions)	3,925.2	3,868.4
Passenger train kilometres (millions)	28.5	29.1
Route kilometres operated	1,591.6	1,591.6
Number of stations managed	133	133
Number of employees	3,103	2,913

PASSENGER TRAIN OPERATORS

All change at Norwich: Stadler EMU No 745007 (left) waits to form the 12.30 to Liverpool Street on the day the type entered service, 8 January 2020. Next to it is No 90005 with a rake of Mk 3s on the 12.00 to Liverpool Street; all these sets were withdrawn within less than three months of this date. PHILIP SHERRATT

were developed with the support of a group of disabled passengers.

On 29 July 2019 the first of the new Stadler bi-mode sets entered service, with the full fleet in service by 1 February 2020. The first 12-car Class 745/0 EMU carried passengers between Norwich and Liverpool Street on 8 January 2020, and with a rapid rollout of the fleet the final Class 90/Mk 3 loco-hauled set, powered by pioneer locomotive No 90001, operated in service on 24 March. Class 745/1s were initially introduced to Norwich to London services before the type made its debut on the Stansted Express service on 28 July.

Testing of the first Class 720 Bombardier unit began in March 2020, with the first set running into Liverpool Street on 30 March 2020. Entry of the first sets into service was due before the end of 2020.

Greater Anglia committed to run at least two trains per weekday each way between London and Norwich in a 90-minute journey time and two between London and Ipswich in 60 minutes, with these services introduced in May 2019. A full recast of timetables on both the Great Eastern and West Anglia main lines is planned. Following a reduction in services at the start of the Covid-19 pandemic, Greater Anglia reintroduced most of its scheduled services from Monday 6 July, although the Stansted Express and Norwich to London inter-city services continued to operate at a reduced frequency pending an uplift in demand.

All stations are being refreshed or refurbished in a £60 million programme which includes new customer information screens, more ticket machines and more parking for cars and cycles. In October 2018 Greater Anglia ceased issuing paper season tickets as it moved to the use of durable plastic smartcards. ■

SENIOR PERSONNEL
GREATER ANGLIA

Managing Director Jamie Burles (in photo)
Train Service Delivery Director Jay Thompson
Business Readiness Director Andrew Goodrum
Engineering Director Martin Beable
Commercial, Customer Service and Train Presentation Director Martin Moran
Franchise and Programmes Director Ian McConnell
Asset Management Director Simone Bailey
HR and Safety Director Katy Bucknell
Finance Director Matt Dolphin

SEVEN-YEAR FRANCHISE TO MARCH 2022

Abellio was awarded the ScotRail franchise by the Scottish Government from April 2015. The seven-year contract included the option for a three-year extension contingent on performance criteria being met, but in December 2019 Scottish Transport Secretary Michael Matheson announced this option would not be taken up, the 'break clause' would be activated and the franchise will conclude in March 2022. The impact of the coronavirus pandemic saw the Scottish Government move ScotRail onto an Emergency Measures Agreement (EMA) until 10 January 2021, with discussions taking place over the contractual arrangements following this date.

Abellio established a 'deep alliance' with Network Rail, aimed at delivering improved performance and efficiencies, and the two parties are led by a single MD. ScotRail says it is working to create 'the best railway Scotland has ever had'. Over 2,300 inter-city, regional and suburban rail services a day serve more than 350 stations on a network which is vital to Scotland's communities and to the country's booming tourist industry.

The completion of a number of infrastructure projects, particularly the electrification of key routes, allowed ScotRail to replace many diesel trains with new, more reliable and environmentally friendly electric units, with the company now providing over 115,000 more seats per day than it did at the start of the franchise. The £120 million redevelopment of Glasgow Queen Street continued through 2020, although completion was hampered by the coronavirus pandemic. As well as electrification, the most significant changes at Queen Street were the extension of platforms 2 to 5 back into the station concourse towards West George Street and the construction of a completely new frontage along with improvements to the concourse area within.

New additions to the fleet during the franchise include 26 refurbished

KEY STATISTICS
SCOTRAIL

	2018-19	2019-20
Punctuality (0-5min)	87.4%	88.5%
Passenger journeys (millions)	97.8	96.4
Passenger kilometres (millions)	2,978.8	2,908.9
Passenger train kilometres (millions)	47.6	49.0
Route kilometres operated	3,120.5	3,120.5
Number of stations managed	354	354
Number of employees	5,168	5,162

IN ASSOCIATION WITH

SENIOR PERSONNEL
SCOTRAIL

Managing Director, Scotland's Railway Alex Hynes (in photo)
Chief Operating Officer Alex White
Commercial Director Lesley Kane
Operations Director David Simpson
Engineering Director Syeda Ghufran
Head of Communications David Ross
Head of Customer Operations Phil Campbell
Sustainability & Safety Assurance Director David Lister
Finance Director Paul Wright
Human Resources Director Gerry Skelton

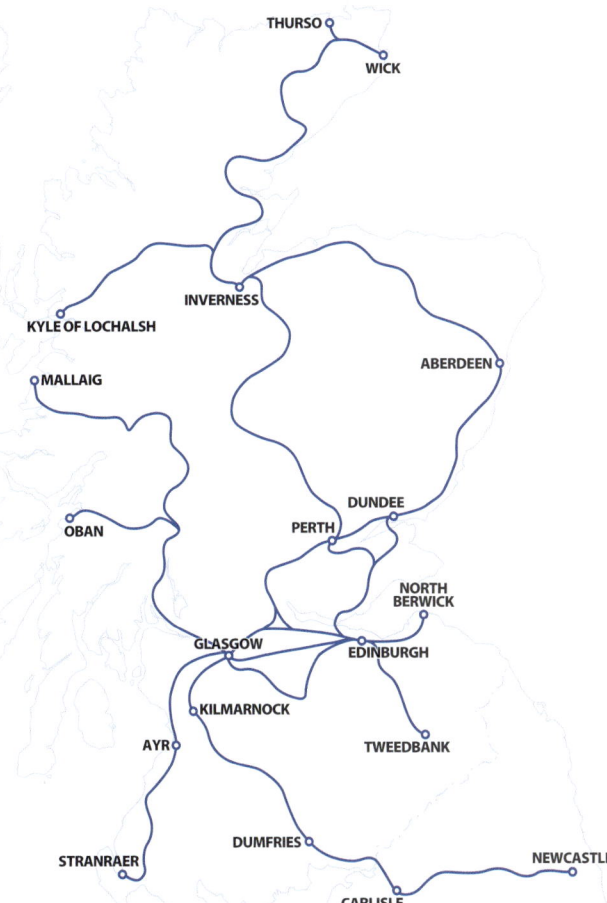

High Speed Trains, 17 2+5 and nine 2+4 sets, branded Inter7City. The first refurbished HST entered service between Aberdeen and Edinburgh on 15 October 2018, and by August 2020 ScotRail diagrammed 14 sets in daily service. Significant delays to the refurbishment programme led ScotRail to use 'classic' unrefurbished HSTs until March 2020.

The rollout of 46x3-car and 24x4-car Class 385 EMUs built by Hitachi was completed by the end of 2019, the first passenger service having been on 24 July 2018. The sets operate on a range of routes in the central belt, including the flagship Edinburgh to Glasgow via Falkirk line and newly electrified routes between Edinburgh and Glasgow via Shotts and to Stirling, Alloa and Dunblane.

In December 2019 the last Class 314 EMU was taken out of service, with the final working being a charity 'farewell tour' on 18 December which included various routes around Strathclyde. On 12 June 2020 ScotRail announced all trains on Scotland's Railway were fully accessible, following the withdrawal of its Class 68 loco-hauled services on 31 May.

Still to come is the introduction of five modified Class 153s able to carry up to 20 bikes and with space for large items of luggage, skis and snowboard equipment, working initially on the West Highland line. These will be coupled to Class 156s to support tourism on the line, and the first completed carriage was unveiled in October 2020. Additional services have also been added to the West Highland line on Sundays through the winter period between Glasgow, Fort William and Mallaig.

Work on the £14.5 million redevelopment of Motherwell station began in June 2020, with the project delivering an enhanced station forecourt and building with glazed roof and brighter, larger concourse. The £8 million redevelopment of Aberdeen station began in 2020 with the project seeing the relocation of the existing ticket office and First Class lounge, the creation of an improved station entrance and better connectivity with Union Square and the wider Aberdeen city centre. Works to enhance the listed station building will be delivered in partnership with the Railway Heritage Trust.

On 2 September 2019 ScotRail became one of the first operators in the UK to introduce WhatsApp as a customer contact channel, enabling passengers to communicate directly with the company through the most used multi-platform messaging service in the world.

The railway industry was united in sorrow on 12 August 2020 when the 06.38 Inter7City HST service from Aberdeen to Glasgow Queen Street derailed near Stonehaven after hitting a landslip. Three people lost their lives: the driver (Brett McCullough), conductor (Donald Dinnie) and a passenger (Christopher Stuchbury). It was the first accident in the United Kingdom in which a passenger lost their life on a train since 2007. ∎

Out with the old: ScotRail's oldest and newest train types side by side at Glasgow Central on 25 September 2019. At left is No 314209 in its final few months of operation prior to the class's withdrawal at the end of the year, while next to it is No 385023, one of 70 new Hitachi EMUs now in service in the central belt. PHILIP SHERRATT

PASSENGER TRAIN OPERATORS

wmtrains
FRANCHISE TO MARCH 2026

The eight years and three months contract for the West Midlands franchise to March 2026 is held by West Midlands Trains Ltd, a consortium of Abellio (70%), JR East (15%) and Mitsui (15%). WMT replaced London Midland, which had been operated by Govia, on 10 December 2017. Following the impact of the coronavirus pandemic the WMT franchise was moved onto an Emergency Recovery Measures Agreement (ERMA) contract which will could run until September 2021.

Trains are operated under two distinct brand names, each with a unique livery. London Northwestern Railway is the brand name for longer distance services on the West Coast main line including those running between London Euston and Crewe and between Birmingham New Street and Liverpool, as well as the Watford to St Albans Abbey and Bletchley to Bedford branch lines. Trains in the Birmingham and West Midlands region carry the West Midlands Railway brand and services include suburban trains centred around Birmingham, regional services from Birmingham to Shrewsbury and Hereford and local services on the Coventry to Nuneaton and Coventry to Leamington Spa lines. The Stourbridge Town branch is operated on behalf of WMT by Pre Metro Operations using the unique Parry People Mover railcars.

Services operating in the West Midlands area are jointly managed by the Department for Transport and the West Midlands Rail Executive, a partnership of 16 Metropolitan District, Shire and Unitary local transport authorities. The creation of the two separate operating units within WMT will enable the West Midlands Railway service group to be let separately in the future, with an option for this process to be managed locally rather than from London via the Department for Transport.

From May 2019 a number of timetable and service initiatives saw additional trains operating between Birmingham and Shrewsbury and the linking up of Birmingham to London Euston and Birmingham to Liverpool/Rugeley Trent Valley (Chase line) services as through trains. The aim was to reduce the number of services terminating at Birmingham New Street and to provide more journey opportunities for passengers crossing the city. The Crewe to Euston Trent Valley service now runs directly from Crewe to Stafford instead of running via Stoke-on-Trent. Many Cross City line services were extended from Longbridge to the new Bromsgrove station and the hourly shuttle between Leamington Spa and Coventry began serving the new station at Kenilworth, which opened in April 2018.

Problems with the timetable, particularly with the long-distance services passing through Birmingham onto the WCML, saw service punctuality fall significantly and WMT had already agreed to a remedial plan, splitting many of these services at Birmingham New Street once again, when Covid-19 arrived. The improvement in performance from the interim timetables led to a decision to retain many of the timetable changes in the long-term, and some reduced service frequencies will continue but with longer trains.

At its launch WMT announced orders totalling £680 million for 107 new trains which will increase the size of its fleet by 25% by the end of the franchise, financed by Corelink Rail Infrastructure, a company jointly owned by Infracapital and Deutsche Asset Management.

Bombardier is supplying 36 Class 730/0 three-car Aventra EMUs for inner suburban services on Birmingham's Cross City line and 45 Class 730/1 and 730/2 five-car trains, which will operate outer-suburban and longer-distance services on the WCML. These trains are being constructed in Derby and are planned to begin entering service in 2021. The first set arrived at the Velím test track in July 2020 ahead of an extensive test programme.

CAF is delivering 12 Class 196/0 two-car and 14 Class 196/1 four-car Civity DMUs for the Birmingham to Hereford and Birmingham to Shrewsbury lines. Testing of the first set on the Velím test track began in mid-December 2019, with No 196101 delivered to WMR's Tyseley depot in April 2020 ahead of test running which began in July; service entry is planned in 2021.

By early April 2020 WMT had received 10 Class 350/4 Desiro EMUs released by TransPennine Express. On 23 April 2019 the first Class 230 unit, converted by Vivarail from ex-London Underground D78 sets, entered service on the Marston Vale line, with three two-car units available to cover two daily diagrams. ■

New train for the Cross City line: the first Bombardier-built Class 730 EMU under construction at the Litchurch Lane factory in Derby on 6 March 2020. PHILIP SHERRATT

KEY STATISTICS
WEST MIDLANDS TRAINS

	2018-19	2019-20
Punctuality (0-5min)	86.7%	78.9%
Passenger journeys (millions)	78.7	79.5
Passenger kilometres (millions)	2,919.4	3,147.6
Passenger train kilometres (millions)	25.6	27.9
Route kilometres operated	899.6	899.6
Number of stations managed	149	149
Number of employees	2,834	2,915

SENIOR PERSONNEL
WEST MIDLANDS TRAINS

Managing Director Julian Edwards (in photo)
Customer Experience Director, LNR & Deputy MD Lawrence Bowman
Customer Experience Director, WMR Jonny Wiseman
Operations Director Darren Ward
Engineering Director Zena Dent
Transition and Projects Director Jane Fisher
Safety & Environment Director Tim Sayer
HR Director Jo MacPhail
Finance Director David Lindsay

LNER
LONDON NORTH EASTERN RAILWAY

OPERATOR OF LAST RESORT TO JUNE 2023

Run by the Government's Operator of Last Resort, LNER took over from Virgin Trains East Coast on 24 June 2018 when Stagecoach and Virgin confirmed they would be unable to meet their financial obligations to the Department for Transport. Initially it had been suggested by the Department for Transport that a new public-private partnership for the franchise would be established in 2020. In June 2020 the Department for Transport announced LNER had been given a direct award contract to continue running services for a further three years, with an optional extension period of up to 26 rail periods (equivalent to two years).

When the company was launched the Secretary of State confirmed that LNER would be the long-term identity for the Inter-city East Coast franchise as well as indicating that Great Northern services into King's Cross could be integrated into LNER when the Govia Thameslink Railway franchise expires.

LNER operates long-distance inter-city services on the East Coast main line from London King's Cross to North East England and Scotland. It manages 11 stations and its trains call at 53 stations. Principal services operate between London and Aberdeen, Edinburgh, Newcastle, Leeds and Lincoln, with less frequent trains to Inverness, Glasgow, Skipton, Bradford, Harrogate, Hull and Sunderland.

LNER is delivering two major projects – the replacement of the train fleet with new electric and bi-mode trains and the transformation of the timetable with additional services to a number of key destinations.

Delivery of 65 Hitachi 'Azuma' trains was completed in September 2020. The fleet comprises 10x5-car and 13x9-car Class 800 bi-mode multiple-units and 12x5-car and 30x9-car Class 801 electric sets. These have replaced LNER's HSTs and the majority of its Class 91/Mk 4 sets. LNER is to retain seven sets of Mk 4 coaches along with 12 Class 91 locomotives (ultimately reducing to 10) until additional new trains are procured, which is likely to be in 2024. The intention had been to retain 10 Mk 4 sets, but the number was reduced following the drop in demand caused by Covid-19. A Prior Information Notice published in October 2020 indicated LNER is seeking at least 10 new trains with self-powered capability.

The withdrawal of the HST fleet in December 2019 was marked by the repainting of a set into original British Rail InterCity 125 livery before it operated a farewell tour which ended with a final journey from Leeds to London King's Cross on Saturday 21 December. The last regular HST-worked passenger service ran on 15 December.

The Azumas began entering service on 15 May 2019 when a bi-mode set took over a diagram between Leeds and London King's Cross; the same week also saw Azumas taking over the LNER service between Hull and London. The new units started working between Edinburgh and London on 1 August 2019. Azumas took over services between London King's Cross and Glasgow Central on

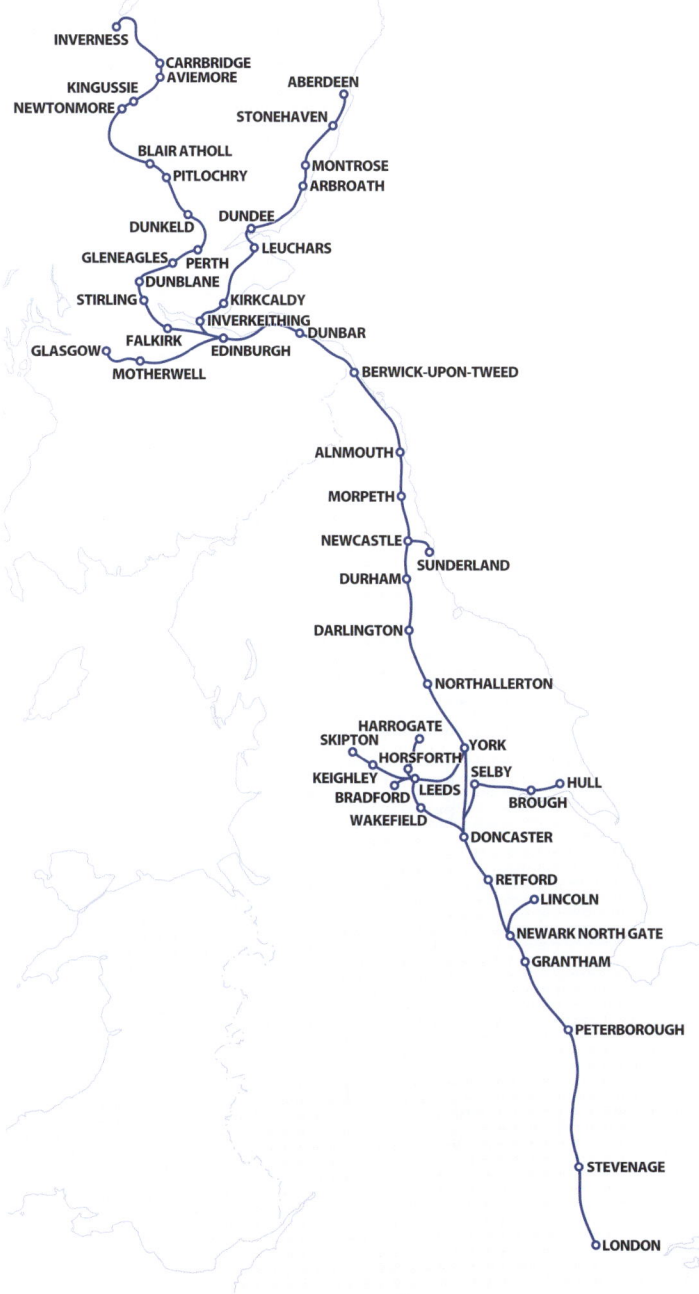

Anglo-Scottish farewell: loco No 91119 in InterCity livery heads the 08.00 King's Cross to Edinburgh service past Ulgham Lane, Morpeth on 3 September 2020. LNER ceased using its Class 91/Mk 4 sets on services north of York during September 2020. BILL WELSH

PASSENGER TRAIN OPERATORS

KEY STATISTICS
LNER

	2018-19	2019-20
Punctuality (0-10min)	74.8%	78.2%
Passenger journeys (millions)	22.3	21.2
Passenger kilometres (millions)	5,807.3	5,499.7
Passenger train kilometres (millions)	23.4	23.4
Route kilometres operated	1,480.6	1,480.6
Number of stations managed	11	11
Number of employees	3,012	3,055

SENIOR PERSONNEL
LNER

Managing Director David Horne (in photo)
Commercial Director Suzanne Donnelly
Communications Director Kate McFerran
Engineering Director John Doughty
Chief Digital & Innovation Officer Danny Gonzalez
Customer Experience Director Claire Ansley
Safety & Operations Director Warrick Dent
People Director Karen Lewis
Finance Director James Downey

23 September 2019, with Aberdeen, Harrogate and Inverness all following before the end of the year. Services between Lincoln and London King's Cross saw their first Azuma sets on 21 October 2019 alongside the introduction of additional daily direct services from Lincoln to London, with more added in December. The full 'Azuma timetable' is due to be implemented in May 2022, after completion of infrastructure works as part of the East Coast route upgrade.

In a first for the UK rail industry, LNER began trials of an 'at-seat' catering offer on-board its trains in August 2020, which enables customers to order and pay for food and drinks from their phone and was due to be rolled across the fleet later in 2020. ■

 NORTHERN

OPERATOR OF LAST RESORT SINCE MARCH 2020

Northern Trains has been operated by the Government's of Operator of Last Resort since 1 March 2020 following the termination of the Arriva Rail North franchise. Arriva took over the Northern franchise on 1 April 2016, under a nine-year contract, with an option for an additional year which is dependent on performance, but on 9 January 2020 the Secretary of State announced the Northern franchise was 'no longer financially viable' and opted to remove the franchise from Arriva and place it under the control of the Operator of Last Resort. Northern is jointly managed from Leeds by the Department for Transport and Rail North, which represents 29 local authorities across the region.

Since the transfer, OLR has begun a programme to 'restore the confidence of passengers', although many of the commitments made by Arriva are continuing. These include the delivery of a new £400 million fleet of trains, the refurbishment of all trains remaining with the franchise and the withdrawal of the Class 142 and 144 Pacer DMUs.

Arriva ordered 101 new trains from Spanish manufacturer CAF, financed by Eversholt Rail. The new 100mph trains comprise 31 three-car and 12 four-car EMUs (Class 331) and 25 two-car and 33 three-car DMUs (Class 195). This is three DMUs more than the originally announced order as additional three-car sets were added in November 2018 following a decision to deploy them on services to Windermere. Delays in manufacturing, testing and commissioning the new trains saw their entry into service significantly delayed, but the first Class 195 and 331 sets entered passenger service on 1 July 2019. By the beginning of October 2020 all the Class 331s and all bar one of the Class 195 DMUs were in service, with set No 195021 undergoing repair work after it derailed while shunting at Edge Hill depot earlier in the year.

Turbostar DMU: Arriva's franchise plan for Northern included the addition of 16 Class 170s transferred from ScotRail, which usually work on the Harrogate line and on services from Sheffield to East Yorkshire. No 170453 at York on 21 October 2019 is preparing to work the 17.11 service to Leeds via Harrogate. **PHILIP SHERRATT**

SENIOR PERSONNEL
NORTHERN

Managing Director Nick Donovan (in photo)
Chief Operating Officer Tricia Williams
Safety and Environment Director (Interim) Paul Bennett
People Director Brian Currie
Commercial and Customer Director Mark Powles
Strategic Development Director Rob Warnes
Engineering Director Jack Commandeur
Finance Director Matt Williams (from January 2021)
Programmes Director Emma Yates

KEY STATISTICS
NORTHERN

	2018-19	2019-20
Punctuality (0-5min)	80.7%	78.2%
Passenger journeys (millions)	101.3	108.0
Passenger kilometres (millions)	2,584.6	2,893.0
Passenger train kilometres (millions)	48.5	56.4
Route kilometres operated	2,800.3	3,194.0
Number of stations managed	478	477
Number of employees	6,183	6,351

The removal of Pacers began on 12 August 2019 with the withdrawal of Nos 142005/046. Completion was planned for May 2020, but the onset of coronavirus and the need to provide additional capacity for social distancing saw some Pacers reinstated for the remainder of the year. The pandemic also added further delays to the introduction of eight bi-mode Class 769 'Flex' units, which were also due to enter service in mid-2020.

Northern is retaining its 17 Class 323 EMUs and taking on 17 of the 26 sets due to be released by West Midlands Trains in preference to the Class 319 units Arriva originally planned to use. This decision meant the Northern units would need refurbishment and modification work to make them compliant with accessibility regulations; the first set completed, No 323234, returned to service in October 2019. All existing trains which will remain with the company, including those joining the Northern fleet, are being fully refurbished and fitted with free Wi-Fi, improved passenger information systems and at-seat power sockets.

Having begun to deliver on its commitment to introduce additional services, Northern found it was suffering significant performance issues due to congestion on parts of its network. It had also started to introduce the first of its 12 new longer distance 'Northern Connect' routes aimed at connecting major centres. The problems encountered with the May 2018 timetable and a recognition that capacity is not available for all the proposed services without infrastructure improvements has led to a rethink of this programme.

It is likely future timetables will see a small reduction in some service frequencies with capacity maintained through the operation of longer trains. Prior to the pandemic Northern had targeted December 2021 for a significant overhaul of schedules with a move to a performance-led timetable. ■

PASSENGER TRAIN OPERATORS

Chiltern main line: No 168001 at High Wycombe on 15 August 2018 with the 13.38 Oxford to London Marylebone service. **PHILIP SHERRATT**

Chiltern railways by arriva

20-YEAR FRANCHISE TO DECEMBER 2021

Having operated the franchise since July 1996, Chiltern Railways began operating the current franchise on 3 March 2002 with the contract, awarded by the former Strategic Rail Authority, due to run for 20 years to December 2021, conditional on various investments being made. The company is now owned by Arriva UK Trains and a five-year extension option is available to the Secretary of State. Following the impact of the coronavirus pandemic the Chiltern franchise was moved onto an Emergency Recovery Management Agreement (ERMA) contract which could run until the scheduled franchise end date in December 2021.

Chiltern Railways operates trains via the Chiltern main line between Birmingham Snow Hill and London Marylebone and the second main line route between Aylesbury and the capital, along with branch lines linking Princess Risborough and Aylesbury, Leamington Spa and Stratford-upon-Avon, and Oxford and Bicester. Some London to Birmingham services are extended to serve Kidderminster in the morning and evening peaks, including at weekends.

A new through route between Oxford and London Marylebone started in December 2016 when the £259 million Evergreen 3 project to link London Marylebone with Oxford via Bicester and Oxford Parkway was completed. The project included reinstatement of double-track over most of the line and the construction of a new 0.75-mile chord to link into the Chiltern main line at Bicester. Renamed to reflect the name of the nearby designer retail outlet, Bicester Village station has proved particularly popular, with almost 1.78 million passengers using the station in 2018-19.

The May 2019 timetable saw the number of direct trains between Stratford-upon-Avon and London Marylebone increased in both directions from three to six, with additional services also operating at weekends.

In 2019 Chiltern announced a significant spend on improving stations; Warwick Parkway and Leamington Spa stations were officially reopened on Tuesday 11 June following several months of extensive improvement work valued at over £1.3 million. The stations have new open plan ticket offices designed to help improve customer service and allow Chiltern staff to offer better information and ticket retailing to customers. Other modernised facilities at both stations include new LED lighting, part of a wider project aimed at reducing Chiltern Railways' carbon footprint.

KEY STATISTICS
CHILTERN RAILWAYS

	2018-19	2019-20
Punctuality (0-5min)	92.9%	92.6%
Passenger journeys (millions)	29.3	28.4
Passenger kilometres (millions)	1,652.4	1,579.5
Passenger train kilometres (millions)	12.2	12.0
Route kilometres operated	354.1	349.2
Number of stations managed	35	35
Number of employees	852	850

SENIOR PERSONNEL
CHILTERN RAILWAYS

Managing Director Richard Allan (in photo)
Commercial & Customer Strategy Director Eleni Jordan
Engineering and Safety Director Ian Hyde
Operations Director Mark Goodall
HR Director Maria Zywica
Finance Director Richard Johnson

IN ASSOCIATION WITH CAF

crosscountry

NEW FRANCHISE CONTRACT TO OCTOBER 2023

The CrossCountry (XC) network is the most extensive GB rail franchise. Owned by Arriva Trains UK, it operates inter-city services between the south of England and the north of England or Scotland via Birmingham, and inter-urban services between Birmingham and other cities in the Midlands, as well as some longer runs to Wales and West Anglia.

Having started on 11 November 2007, Arriva's franchise was initially due to run until 31 March 2016. In September 2016 the Department for Transport (DfT) announced a new directly awarded contract, extending the franchise to 2019, and subsequent extensions took the franchise through to October 2020.

In October 2020 a further three-year award was confirmed with an optional one-year extension. This takes the form an Operating Contract Franchise Agreement (OCFA), similar to the ERMAs introduced for other operators but with slightly different terms. DfT continues to take revenue and cost risk with the operator paid a management fee to run services.

Stretching from Scotland to Cornwall, Manchester to the south coast of England, and Wales to Stansted Airport, the CrossCountry franchise serves seven out of the 10 major cities in Great Britain but does not serve London. Its 3,860km network includes many university towns and airports with approximately 300 services each weekday, including the UK's longest daily service, the 1,162km (722-mile) 08.20 Aberdeen to Penzance, which includes 33 stops on its 13hr 15min journey.

Inter-city services are operated by four-car and five-car Voyager DEMUs and five seven-car HST sets, while inter-urban services are operated by two-car and three-car Turbostar DMUs. CrossCountry does not manage any stations,

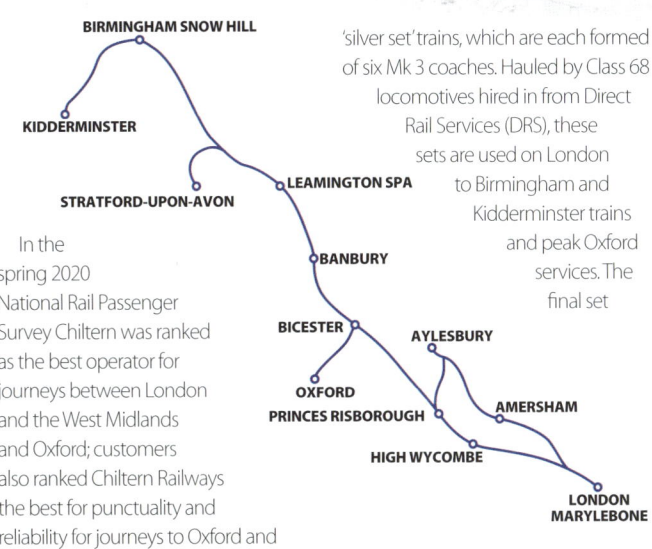

In the spring 2020 National Rail Passenger Survey Chiltern was ranked as the best operator for journeys between London and the West Midlands and Oxford; customers also ranked Chiltern Railways the best for punctuality and reliability for journeys to Oxford and the West Midlands, and overall 87% of customers were satisfied with the train company's punctuality, higher than the national average of 74%.

Chiltern's train fleet comprises 39 two- and three-car Class 165/0 DMUs, 28 two-, three- and four-car Class 168 DMUs and four two-car Class 172 Turbostar DMUs, along with a number of rakes of loco-hauled Mk 3 coaches. From late July 2019 Chiltern began a program of heavy maintenance work on the four Mainline 'silver set' trains, which are each formed of six Mk 3 coaches. Hauled by Class 68 locomotives hired in from Direct Rail Services (DRS), these sets are used on London to Birmingham and Kidderminster trains and peak Oxford services. The final set returned to service in December 2019. A loco-hauled Mk 3 set which operates a daily commuter service from/to Banbury retains slam doors; an original rake of Mk 3s was withdrawn by Chiltern at the onset of Covid in March 2020 and is being replaced by a rake of coaches released by Greater Anglia which are more compliant with accessibility regulations; these were due to enter service by the end of 2020. ■

91

PASSENGER TRAIN OPERATORS

New contract confirmed: a pair of CrossCountry Voyagers pass Clay Cross, south of Chesterfield, with the 09.41 Newcastle to Bristol Temple Meads service on 27 May 2020. PHILIP SHERRATT

KEY STATISTICS
CROSSCOUNTRY

	2018-19	2019-20
Punctuality (0-10min)	84.4%	83.1%
Passenger journeys (millions)	40.7	39.8
Passenger kilometres (millions)	3,715.8	3,638.6
Passenger train kilometres (millions)	32.7	32.8
Route kilometres operated	2,710.1	2,710.1
Number of stations managed	0	0
Number of employees	1,915	1,978

although it serves 122, and does not directly maintain any of its own trains. Government statistics indicate around 64% of CrossCountry journeys are for leisure, 13% are for business and 23% are for commuting purposes.

CrossCountry trains are serving the new Worcestershire Parkway station which opened on 23 February 2020. The two-level station is sited at the intersection of the North Cotswold line and the CrossCountry route between Birmingham and Cardiff via Cheltenham Spa and Gloucester.

Prior to the coronavirus pandemic it had been accepted by the Department for Transport that much-needed improvements in capacity through the leasing of additional rolling stock are needed. In the short-term CrossCountry has worked on some more immediate solutions to both the capacity shortfall and service performance.

Recognising the fact the size of the company's train fleet has stayed largely the same since the start of the franchise, a £2.4 million funding agreement with the DfT, announced on 24 February 2020, will see CrossCountry gain six Class 170 Turbostar centre cars and two extra HST power cars. The latter was to allow four of the five seven-car HST sets to be diagrammed to work every day from December 2020, with the fifth set on standby as a 'hot spare'. The lengthening of six two-car Class 170 Turbostars, along with the use of many of the remaining two-car sets as coupled pairs and improved availability through a changed maintenance programme, should see a significant reduction in the operation of two-car trains from May 2021. The cascade of Voyagers from Avanti West Coast or Meridians from East Midlands Railway in 2022-23 provide further options to bolster CrossCountry's fleet and increase capacity.

Following the arrival of new Managing Director Tom Joyner in June 2019 a significant reorganisation of the management team saw the creation of four Regional Director positions, which the company said would enable it to respond more effectively to local demands and concerns.

A new mobile app was introduced in May 2017 for ticket purchase and live running information whilst free Wi-Fi is now provided on all CrossCountry trains, using 4G for faster downloads. The 'Advance Purchase On the Day' (APOD) initiative enables purchase of discounted advance purchase fares (and seat reservations on many services) on the day of travel, up to 15 minutes before boarding a train. ∎

SENIOR PERSONNEL
CROSSCOUNTRY

Managing Director	Tom Joyner (in photo)
Head of Corporate Affairs	Sally Gillespie
Commercial Director	Ben Simkin
Finance Director	Gillian Ingham
Head of Transformation	Bryony Govan
Network Services Director	Lee Paxton
Head of Executive Support	Nicola Wall
HR Director	Karen Doores
Regional Director – North East & Scotland	Anna Weeks
Regional Director – West Midlands & North West	John Robson
Regional Director – East Midlands & East Anglia	Richard Morris
Regional Director – West & Wales	Sarah Kelley

OVERGROUND

EIGHT-YEAR CONCESSION TO 2024

Arriva Rail London has operated London Overground services since 14 November 2016. The eight-year concession was awarded by TfL, which sets fares, procures rolling stock and decides service levels. The operator takes only a small element of revenue risk (10%), with TfL taking 90%. In common with other TfL services, the Overground is denoted by its own colour, a vivid orange which was inherited from the former East London line prior to its transfer from Underground to Overground.

On 31 May 2015 the Liverpool Street to Enfield Town, Cheshunt (via Seven Sisters) and Chingford services, as well as trains between

Romford and Upminster, were transferred from the Greater Anglia franchise to TfL to become part of the London Overground network.

Initially services were all operated by a 57-strong fleet of Class 378 electric trains, all extended to five-car length in 2015. Twenty DC-only units operate on services over the East London line and between Euston to Watford Junction, with 37 dual-voltage AC/DC units operating on the East, North and West London lines. A refresh programme has begun, including application of a revised livery.

In July 2015 a £260 million order for 45 four-car Class 710 Bombardier Aventra EMUs was placed by TfL for use on the West Anglia routes and the Watford DC, Gospel Oak to Barking and Romford to Upminster lines. With an option for up to 24 additional sets, nine were ordered in February 2018. The complete order now comprises 30x4-car AC-only units and 18x4-car and 6x5-car dual-voltage sets.

The Gospel Oak to Barking service was worked by Class 172 DMUs from 2010; these were finally replaced by four-car Class 710/2 EMUs in 2019 following delays completing the electrification of the route and problems commissioning the new trains. In the interim some services were worked by Class 378 EMUs reduced in length to four cars. The first two Class 710s entered service on the Gospel Oak to Barking line on 23 May 2019 with the remaining six on the line all in traffic by August.

Services out of Liverpool Street were initially worked by a mix of Class 315 and 317 EMUs until the arrival of the first Class 710 units allowed the withdrawal of the older sets. The first Class 710 carried passengers on the London Euston to Watford route on 9 September 2019, before the new units entered service on the Lea Valley lines out of London Liverpool Street on 3 March 2020, with all Class 315/317 units withdrawn by mid-October 2020. A Class 710 took over the Romford to Upminster shuttle on 5 October 2020.

KEY STATISTICS
LONDON OVERGROUND

	2018-19	2019-20
Punctuality (0-5min)	93.8%	92.6%
Passenger journeys (millions)	188.1	186.0
Passenger kilometres (millions)	1,287.6	1,273.4
Passenger train kilometres (millions)	8.7	8.7
Route kilometres operated	167.4	167.4
Number of stations managed	81	81
Number of employees	1,451	1,502

From December 2017, night services were introduced on the Overground on Fridays and Saturdays, running into the early hours of Saturday and Sunday mornings. Trains operate between New Cross Gate and Highbury & Islington, enabling passengers to connect into the Victoria Line Night Tube service, although all-night services were suspended at the onset of the pandemic. Boxing Day services on

Refreshed '378': in revised livery, No 378232 crosses the river Lea approaching Hackney Wick with the 14.23 Stratford to Clapham Junction service on 18 September 2020. **ANTONY GUPPY**

PASSENGER TRAIN OPERATORS

London Overground ran for the first time in 2019, with trains running from Highbury & Islington to West Croydon and Clapham Junction to Hackney Wick. Enhancement of East London line services to 20 trains per hour is also planned, with work including signalling alterations and construction of a new station at Surrey Canal Road.

A Transport and Works Act Order for a new 1.6km branch from Network Rail's Tilbury line to a station at Barking Riverside was granted in 2017. The extension will add 4.5km to the London Overground Gospel Oak to Barking line. Due to be completed in time to enable services to begin in 2022, the £263 million project is being partially funded by Barking Riverside Limited (£172 million), with the remainder coming from TfL. The line will be constructed so that it can later be extended across the river Thames to Thamesmead and Abbey Wood, and passive provision is to be made for an intermediate station. The extension will be served by four trains per hour from Barking station along the existing Tilbury line used by c2c between Fenchurch Street and Grays. After passing under the Renwick Road bridge, the extension will then head south to a new station in the heart of the Barking Riverside development. ■

SENIOR PERSONNEL
ARRIVA RAIL LONDON/LONDON OVERGROUND

Managing Director Paul Hutchings (in photo)
Customer Experience Director Stella Rogers
Engineering Director Kate Marjoribanks
Finance Director Steve Best
HR Director Oli Gant
Performance Director Matt Pocock

OPEN-ACCESS CONTRACT TO 2026

Grand Central Rail (GC) has been operating for almost 13 years, and its extended open access contract runs until 2026. GC's first open access service, from Sunderland to London King's Cross, was launched in December 2007, and by 2012 the company was providing five return journeys. The West Riding service started in May 2010, offering three trains a day between Bradford Interchange and King's Cross. A fourth West Riding service was introduced in December 2013, and in April 2017 all West Riding trains began calling at the new Low Moor station. A series of changes in ownership culminated in GC becoming part of Arriva in November 2011.

The company operates an all Class 180 'Adelante' fleet comprising 10 sets, with sufficient sets to allow a capacity boost on the busiest trains by running 10-coach formations. GC recently completed a £9 million refresh of its trains, with revamped catering facilities and the first leather trimmed standard class seats in a UK fleet. GC has worked with Alstom, Angel Trains and Network Rail to fit the latest European Train Control System (ETCS) equipment, the first in service since the mid-Wales project in 2010. One of GC's Class 180s was to due to enter service in late 2020 with dual-fuel technology following a project led by the operator and G-volution Technology.

Grand Central continues to achieve high scores for passenger satisfaction; the spring 2020 National Rail Passenger Survey revealed 95% its passengers were satisfied or very satisfied. GC was ranked top for value for money with feedback from passengers demonstrating satisfaction with ticket prices, helpfulness and attitude of staff and the extra legroom available on its services.

Having secured access rights in 2018, GC was due to start operating a new open access service between Blackpool North and London Euston in spring 2020 using Class 90 locomotives and Mk 4 coaches. Having suspended testing and training due to the impact of Covid-19, the company announced in September 2020 it had taken the difficult decision to abandon its plans to launch the service as there was no possibility of it being viable for many years. The pandemic saw all GC trains on its pre-existing Sunderland and Bradford routes suspended from 4 April until 26 July, with a full service restored in September. ■

KEY STATISTICS
GRAND CENTRAL

	2018-19	2019-20
Punctuality (0-10min)	78.2%	78.6%
Passenger journeys (millions)	1.5	1.4
Passenger kilometres (millions)	418.4	389.0
Passenger train kilometres (millions)	2.5	2.4
Route kilometres operated	762.8	762.8
Number of employees	193	222

SENIOR PERSONNEL
GRAND CENTRAL

Managing Director Richard McClean (in photo)
Chief Operating Officer Sean English
Fleet Director Dave Hatfield
Commercial & Customer Policy Director Louise Blyth
Finance Director Carol Bainbridge
Head of HR Angela Newsome

Sunderland route: Grand Central's No 180103 at York on 21 October 2019 with the 15.30 Sunderland to King's Cross service. PHILIP SHERRATT

PASSENGER TRAIN OPERATORS

MANAGEMENT CONTRACT UNTIL 2021

Govia Thameslink Railway (GTR) is the largest rail franchise in the UK in terms of passenger numbers, trains, revenue and staff. It is operated by Govia, a joint venture between the British Go-Ahead Group (65%) and French company Keolis (35%).

The basis of the franchise, which began on 14 September 2014, is a management contract; this means Govia passes ticket revenue directly to the Government and receives a payment for the operation of services. The arrangement was chosen because of the extensive work being carried out on the Thameslink route through the centre of London, including resignalling of the central part of the route and the extensive rebuilding of London Bridge station. Following the impact of the coronavirus pandemic the franchise was moved onto an Emergency Recovery Measures Agreement (ERMA) contract, due to last until the planned franchise end date in September 2021.

Initially GTR replaced the previous Thameslink & Great Northern franchise held by First Capital Connect (FCC). From 26 July 2015, GTR incorporated Southern and Gatwick Express, which had previously been operated as a separate franchise by Govia. Separate branding is used for Thameslink, Great Northern, Southern and Gatwick Express. The impact of Covid-19 led to the suspension of all Gatwick Express services from 30 March 2020 along with reductions in other services operated by GTR, and as of autumn 2020 the airport service was still suspended.

The Thameslink and Great Northern routes connect regional centres north and south of London such as Peterborough, Cambridge, Bedford, Luton and Brighton. They provide rail links to Gatwick and Luton airports, and to Eurostar at St Pancras International. Southern services operate into London Bridge and London Victoria from south London and the south coast, and between Milton Keynes and Croydon via the West London line.

Performance regimes incentivise or penalise Govia to meet a range of service quality targets (including for punctuality, customer experience at stations and on train, and revenue protection). Bonus payments have also been made for delivery of key performance milestones in the Thameslink Programme.

In October 2019 GTR completed its five-year £2 billion fleet transformation programme as the last of its Class 313 EMUs was withdrawn from suburban services into Moorgate. The programme saw the introduction of four new fleets of trains and the acquisition of additional sets for another. The new fleets comprise 29 four-car Class 387/1 EMUs on Great Northern services, 27 four-car Class 387/2 EMUs for the Gatwick Express, 60 eight-car Class 700/0 and 55 12-car Class 700/1 EMUs for Thameslink, and 25 six-car Class 717 EMUs for Great Northern suburban services. Transferring from ScotRail were 4x3-car Class 170 DMUs, which were modified and reformed to become 2x2-car and 2x4-car Class 171 sets.

The programme included the removal of 44 Class 313s as well as fleets of Class 319s and 442s and reductions in the size of the Class 365 and 377 fleets, as well as the cascade of 880 vehicles within the GTR network as the programme progressed. The regenerative braking system on the Class 700 and 717 units means GTR's trains are now returning over 50% more energy to the network than the fleets they replaced, with the figure calculated to be 15.8 GWh every four weeks.

The 2018 reopening of Thameslink's improved London Bridge route enabled a major revamp of timetables and service patterns across the GTR network, with new cross-London Thameslink services introduced on many existing Great Northern, Southern and Southeastern routes. These included direct trains from Cambridge to Brighton and Peterborough to Horsham, both via Gatwick Airport. Timetable

IN ASSOCIATION WITH CAF

KEY STATISTICS
GOVIA THAMESLINK RAILWAY

	2018-19	2019-20
Punctuality (0-5min)	82.7%	84.9%
Passenger journeys (millions)	341.5	348.9
Passenger kilometres (millions)	9,206.8	9,342.6
Passenger train kilometres (millions)	63.3	69.1
Route kilometres operated	1,287.5	1,287.5
Number of stations managed	235	235
Number of employees	7,276	7,427

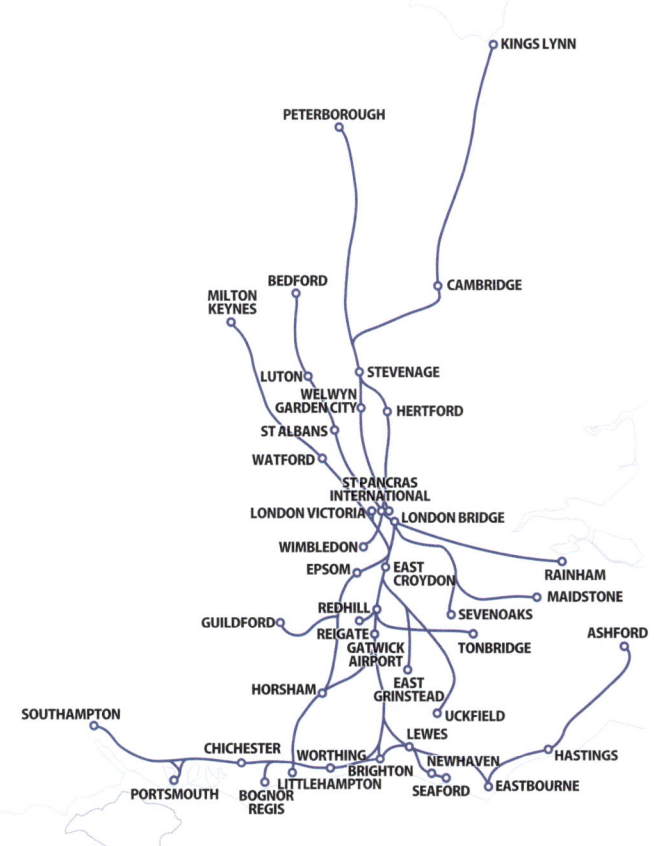

improvements in September and December 2018 took Thameslink to 19 trains per hour (tph) through the core in the peak, out of a planned 24. In May 2019 GTR doubled the frequency of the new Cambridge to Brighton cross-London service with two trains an hour running in each direction throughout the day, taking Thameslink core frequency to 20tph. Weekend Thameslink frequencies were also increased, whilst the Gatwick Express timetable changed to a half-hourly through service between Brighton, Gatwick Airport and London Victoria, alternating every 15min with services between Gatwick and Victoria only.

The opening hours of the Moorgate branch were extended on weekdays, and trains now serve it at weekends. The introduction of the new Class 717 sets has enabled an increase in peak frequencies to Moorgate and the doubling of the off-peak frequency on the Hertford loop, trains from which now run into a new bay platform at Stevenage, opened in August 2020.

A £27 million programme funded by the Department for Transport to increase capacity on the busy Fen line route between Cambridge and King's Lynn began in the summer of 2019. Improvements to the power supply plus two platform extensions at Waterbeach and one at Littleport were due to allow eight-car formations to call at intermediate stations at peak times from December 2020.

Notwithstanding the temporary timetable changes due to Covid-19, the two-year £150 million programme to rebuild Gatwick Airport station had required a reduction in services through the station from 17 May 2020. Key alterations included removal of off-peak Southern services between Brighton and Victoria and the ending of splitting and joining of trains for the West and East Coastway at Haywards Heath.

In September 2020 a new electric vehicle charging hub was opened at Hatfield station; GTR believes that with 27 charging points it is the largest EV charging hub on the UK rail network. Along with 12 new points at Haywards Heath station, it brought the total number on the GTR network to more than 150.

As part of As National Apprenticeship & Careers Week in February 2020, GTR announced that after beating its target of 140 apprentices in 2019 it would be doubling the number of apprenticeships offered in 2020 to over 300. These are being provided across 14 different roles ranging from drivers, engineers and operations to business administration and marketing. Open to people of all ages and backgrounds, including current GTR employees, the schemes reflect the true diversity of opportunities and possibilities that a career in rail can offer. GTR's 'Get into Railways' training programme, delivered with young people's charity The Prince's Trust, generated £1.6 million of social benefit over five years. 182 18-25 year olds were helped to gain skills and work experience since the start of the partnership in 2014; 164 of these young people completed the course and secured sustainable, permanent jobs within the GTR network. ■

Pandemic praise: Thameslink unit No 700111 with 'NHS We Thank You' vinyls parallels the M1 motorway at Mill Hill Broadway forming the 10.55 Brighton to Bedford service on 28 July 2020. **ANTONY GUPPY**

SENIOR PERSONNEL
GOVIA THAMESLINK RAILWAY

Chief Executive Officer Patrick Verwer (in photo)
Chief Operating Officer Steve White
Chief Financial Officer Ian McLaren
Managing Director, Great Northern & Thameslink Tom Moran
Managing Director, Southern & Gatwick Express Angie Doll

PASSENGER TRAIN OPERATORS

Masked Javelin: No 395017 working the 13.25 St Pancras International to St Pancras International rounder service arrives at Rochester on 17 September 2020. JAMIE SQUIBBS

southeastern.

DIRECT AWARD UNTIL OCTOBER 2021

Operated by Govia, a joint venture between Go-Ahead (65%) and Keolis (35%), the Southeastern franchise serves Kent, south east London and part of East Sussex and includes high-speed domestic services on High Speed 1 (HS1). Originally scheduled to end in 2014 after performance targets had been met, a direct award contract until June 2018 was agreed. In late 2016 the DfT announced a further direct award extension to December 2018, and this was subsequently extended to April 2019 and again to 10 November 2019.

In August 2019 the Department for Transport announced that the bidding process to operate the South Eastern rail franchise had been cancelled. Pending a decision over the future of the franchise, the direct award was further extended to 1 April 2020. With Covid-19 causing further difficulties it was announced on 30 March 2020 that the direct award would run to 16 October 2021, with DfT able to extend this further to 31 March 2022 at its discretion. An Emergency Measures Agreement was introduced at the same time, which may run until October 2021.

Southeastern operates on three main routes: the main line from London Cannon Street and London Charing Cross to Dover via Sevenoaks; the Chatham main line between London Victoria and Dover/Ramsgate via the Medway towns; and High Speed 1 from London St Pancras. It runs a completely electric train fleet and is committed to managing its traction energy, with over 70% of its main line and metro fleets fitted with regenerative braking.

The reopening of London Bridge station in January 2018 after the five-year £1 billion rebuilding programme paved the way for a timetable change which affected the entire Southeastern network. The Thameslink Programme also saw several of the routes formerly operated by Southeastern becoming Thameslink routes, with services to Sevenoaks and Gillingham running to/from Bedford through the Thameslink core via London Bridge. At the same time a small number of Thameslink services transferred to Southeastern.

Southeastern introduced a full timetable of domestic high-speed services over the High Speed 1 line between London St Pancras and Ashford International on 13 December 2009; branded Southeastern Highspeed, the services call at Stratford International and Ebbsfleet International. Trains from London to the Medway towns and Faversham leave the high-speed line at Ebbsfleet and continue via the North Kent line and Chatham main line. Trains for Dover Priory and Margate leave the high-speed line at Ashford International. A limited peak-hour service operates between St Pancras and Maidstone West via Ebbsfleet and Strood.

Southeastern introduced a number of timetable improvements in December 2019, including faster journey times on a number of routes. Some train lengths were also changed to alleviate overcrowding on services seeing high demand, with other trains shortened where capacity was less needed, or where the capacity being provided was only fully used for a short part of the journey.

As part of the latest direct award agreement Southeastern is to introduce 30x5-car Siemens Class 707 EMUs on its metro routes once they are released by South Western Railway. ∎

KEY STATISTICS
SOUTHEASTERN

	2018-19	2019-20
Punctuality (0-5min)	88.4%	89.4%
Passenger journeys (millions)	183.2	179.5
Passenger kilometres (millions)	4,693.1	4,629.1
Passenger train kilometres (millions)	31.9	31.6
Route kilometres operated	748.3	748.3
Number of stations managed	164	164
Number of employees	4,410	4,511

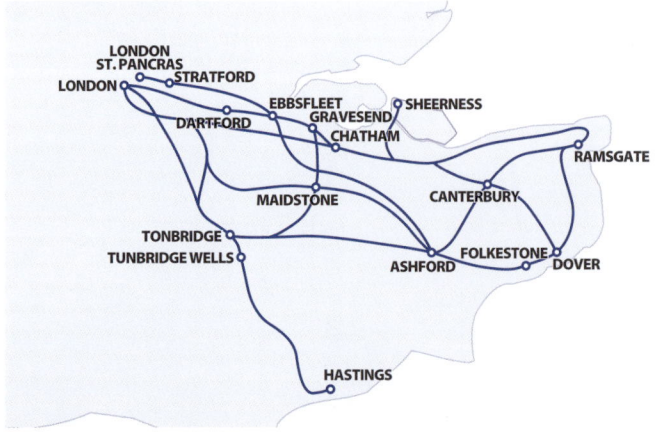

SENIOR PERSONNEL
SOUTHEASTERN

Managing Director David Statham (in photo)
Engineering Director Mark Johnson
Passenger Services Director David Wornham
Commercial Director Alicia Andrews
Train Services Director Scott Brightwell
HR Director Scott Maynard
Finance Director Felix Beeson
Head of Safety and Environment Colin Clifton
Head of Communications and Publicity Alison Nolan

**TRAFNIDIAETH CYMRU
TRANSPORT FOR WALES**
Gwasanaethau Rheilffyrdd
Rail Services

IN-HOUSE OPERATION FROM FEBRUARY 2021

Awarded by Transport for Wales on behalf of the Welsh Government, rather than by the Department for Transport, the new Wales and Borders franchise is branded as Transport for Wales Rail. Operated by KeolisAmey, it commenced on 14 October 2018 and was due to run for 15 years.

The impact of the coronavirus pandemic saw the Welsh Government move the TfW Rail contract onto an Emergency Measures Agreement (EMA). In October 2020 the Government announced day-to-day operations would transfer in-house to an agency of Transport for Wales upon expiry of an extended EMA in February 2021.

Despite this, the Government says commitments made within the original contract will continue. Highlights include an £800 million plan to replace every train operating in Wales by 2023 in a programme that will see 95% of journeys made on brand new rolling stock and the remainder on refurbished trains.

Ownership of the Core Valley Lines transferred from Network Rail to the Welsh Government on 28 March 2020, through a transfer scheme enabled by a Transport and Works Act Order. Amey Keolis Infrastructure Ltd (AKIL) is the new network licence holder for the CVL, and although no longer responsible for operations will continue to lead the infrastructure upgrades on these routes. The CVL comprise Cardiff Queen Street station and all lines north thereof, including the freight-only line from Ystrad Mynach to Cwmbargoed and the disused line from Aberdare to Hirwaun (Tower). Also included in the asset transfer were the City line from Radyr to near Ninian Park station and the spur from Queen Street to Cardiff Bay. Other lines in south Wales, such as that to Ebbw Vale, have not transferred but will be part of the wider South Wales Metro.

The asset transfer enabled the start of the £738 million upgrade of the lines, which began in August 2020. Plans include electrification of over 170km of track and station and signalling upgrades.

In terms of new trains, CAF will supply 51x2-car and 26x3-car Class 197 Civity DMUs to be used on regional and inter-urban services, which will be assembled at the manufacturer's Newport facility, which was officially opened by the Prince of Wales on 21 February 2020.

The rest of the new trains will come from Stadler. Eleven four-car Flirt bi-mode diesel and electric sets will work Maesteg to Cheltenham Spa and Cardiff Central/Newport to Ebbw Vale services from 2022. Twenty-four tri-mode variants (7x3-car and 17x4-car), which will also work on battery power, will cover services on routes linking the Vale of Glamorgan and destinations north of Cardiff. They will run on AC mode north of Cardiff and diesel to the south, providing a cross-city connection. On the Rhymney line they will switch to battery power beyond Ystrad Mynach and are expected to have a battery charge range of around 40 miles.

Finally, 36 three-car Stadler Citylink tram-trains, capable of 25kV and battery operation, will operate from Cardiff to Treherbert, Aberdare and Merthyr Tydfil once the lines are electrified. On-street running under line of sight signalling will be employed for the new section of around 300 yards to a new station opposite the Wales Millennium Centre in Cardiff Bay. By 2022 four tram-trains an hour are planned to run into Cardiff, bringing significant journey time reductions.

Other rolling stock new to the franchise includes 4x2-car and 8x3-car Class 170s cascaded from Greater Anglia, now in use in south Wales. Due to enter service by the end of 2020 on the Rhymney line, after some delay, were nine Class 769 trains. Twelve Mk 4 coaches and four driving van trailers, formed into three rakes hauled by Class 67 locomotives for Cardiff to Holyhead services, were also due in service in December 2020. Following in May 2021 will be five Class 230 three-car battery/diesel hybrid sets from Vivarail for the Borderlands line between Wrexham and Bidston. Short-term additional capacity has been delivered through the transfer of five Class 153 single-car sets released by GWR for rural routes in west Wales.

Service improvement plans include the operation of 285 additional services every weekday across Wales, with improvements on the Ebbw Vale line, North Wales Metro (Wrexham to Bidston), Cambrian and Heart of Wales lines. Most significantly there will be an additional

KEY STATISTICS
TFW RAIL SERVICES

	2018-19	2019-20
Punctuality (0-5min)	91.4%	88.1%
Passenger journeys (millions)	34.1	31.8
Passenger kilometres (millions)	1,257.3	1,170.2
Passenger train kilometres (millions)	23.8	23.8
Route kilometres operated	1,784.8	1,826.6
Number of stations managed	247	247
Number of employees	2,293	2,495

North Wales coast: No 158819 approaches Conwy with the 09.10 Birmingham International to Holyhead service on 31 August 2020. **PHILIP SHERRATT**

PASSENGER TRAIN OPERATORS

294 services across Wales on Sundays, an increase of 61%, creating a true seven-day service for the first time.

A new seven-day hourly Chester to Liverpool service over the upgraded Halton curve commenced in May 2019, with trains serving Helsby, Frodsham, Runcorn, and Liverpool South Parkway en-route to Liverpool Lime Street.

£194 million will be spent on station improvements, including the modernisation of all 247 existing stations on the network and the building of five new stations, with four of these in Cardiff. More than 170 stations in Wales have been fitted with a Welsh language information system called 'Geraint' which can provide clear Welsh language journey announcements and up to the minute changes.

Transport for Wales has launched a new WhatsApp number for customer enquiries, as a key step in its commitment to transform the customer experience for the Wales and Borders rail service. In August 2020 TfW confirmed the start of a programme to install new ticket vending machines and introduce smartcards on many of its routes; the new machines have improved Welsh language components and include raised pictograms for visually impaired customers. ■

SENIOR PERSONNEL
TFW RAIL SERVICES

Chief Executive Officer	Kevin Thomas (in photo)
Chief Operating Officer	Andy Thomas
Deputy Chief Operating Officer	Colin Lea
Chief Financial Officer	Sam Hawkins
Transformation Director	Frank Renault
Infrastructure Director	Simon Rhoden
People and Engagement Director	Marie Daly
Safety and Assurance Director	Leyton Powell

CROSSRAIL CONCESSION TO MAY 2023

Crossrail is the construction project to build the infrastructure for Elizabeth Line services. TfL Rail, the precursor to Elizabeth Line services, is operated by MTR Corporation under contract to Transport for London (TfL). The name for the route, Elizabeth Line, along with its purple logo, was announced in February 2016 at a time when the full route, which will pass through 41 stations and stretch for some 100km from Reading and Heathrow in the west through central tunnels across to Shenfield and Abbey Wood in the east, was due to open in 2018-19.

TfL Rail was introduced in May 2015 when it took control from Abellio Greater Anglia of 'metro' services on the 32.5km route between London Liverpool Street and Shenfield. In May 2018 TfL Rail also took over operation of the Heathrow Connect service over the 26.5km section between Paddington in central London and Heathrow Airport (Heathrow Terminal 4 station being the terminus) and in December 2019 it took over two trains an hour between London Paddington and Reading from GWR, complementing the existing TfL Rail branded service running between Hayes & Harlington and Paddington.

All services will be worked by a fleet of 70 nine-car Class 345 EMUs manufactured by Bombardier in Derby; initially services were introduced with seven-car units due to platform constraints at Liverpool Street. The first Class 345 EMUs took over from Class 360 sets on Heathrow Connect services in the summer of 2020, with TfL Rail taking all '360s' out of service during September. The complex software used on these trains has caused significant reliability issues, but TfL Rail was hopeful software upgrades planned for autumn 2020 would finally resolve many of the outstanding problems. Once fully in service each full-length train provides 450 seats and four wheelchair spaces, whilst offering a maximum capacity of 1,500 passengers.

A series of problems with the completion of the new Crossrail route have seen its opening delayed and the budget for the project rise. At the height of the Covid-19 pandemic Crossrail announced it would not meet its revised opening date in 2021 for the opening of the central section between Paddington and Abbey Wood, and that the temporary pause of all physical work on all sites would mean opening of this section would not be before 2022. When the central section does finally open it will link the West End, the City of London, Canary Wharf and south east London, initially with 12 trains per hour. ■

KEY STATISTICS
TFL RAIL / MTR ELIZABETH LINE

	2018-19	2019-20
Punctuality (0-5min)	93.8%	95.2%
Passenger journeys (millions)	51.3	55.5
Passenger kilometres (millions)	642.8	705.6
Passenger train kilometres (millions)	3.8	4.7
Route kilometres operated	59.5	98.8
Number of stations managed	24	24
Number of employees	1,401	1,515

SENIOR PERSONNEL
TFL RAIL / MTR ELIZABETH LINE

Managing Director	Nigel Holness (in photo)
Programme Director	Richard Schofield
Operations Director	Andy Boyle
Engineering Director	Kevin Jones
HR Director	Alison Bell
Finance Director	Andy King
Concession Director	Mark Eaton
Customer Experience Director	Paul Parsons

'345' on the Western: No 345013 in the bay at Hayes & Harlington on 21 May 2018 before working a TfL Rail service to Paddington. **PHILIP SHERRATT**

GWR MANAGEMENT CONTRACT TO 2028

Heathrow Express launched in 1998 and for some years the non-stop service has carried an average of 17,000 passengers a day. The non-franchised service is the fastest rail link from London to Heathrow. Trains usually depart every 15 minutes for most of the day with a journey time of just 15 minutes between Paddington and Terminals 2 & 3 and 21 minutes to Terminal 5. However, from the start of the coronavirus pandemic the significant reduction in air passengers saw the service frequency cut back to every 30 minutes.

Trains reach the airport on a dedicated line, tunnelling from Stockley near Hayes & Harlington on the Great Western main line, for about 3.5km to Heathrow Terminals 2 & 3. A 1.8km branch from Terminals 2 & 3 to Terminal 5 opened in 2008 and Terminal 4 (opened in 1998) is reached by a free transfer service from Terminal 2 & 3. Heathrow Express reports that approximately 55% of its customers are business passengers.

In March 2018 it was announced that operation of the service would be outsourced to the Great Western franchise, currently operated as GWR by FirstGroup, under a contract running from August 2018 until 2028. Heathrow Airport Ltd continues to own the service and is responsible for managing the stations at the airport. Heathrow Express also retains the commercial aspects including marketing, ticket pricing and revenue and it is expected the operating arrangement will transfer to any future holder of the Great Western franchise. The 14 Class 332 Heathrow Express trains have generally run in pairs, making up eight- or nine-car trains, with Siemens carrying out train maintenance at a purpose-built depot at Old Oak Common, near Paddington.

Under the new agreement with GWR, services will be worked by a fleet of 12 of GWR's Bombardier-built Class 387 Electrostar EMUs. The dedicated fleet of EMUs has been specially converted so customers will continue to enjoy a premium airport experience complete with First Class accommodation, high speed Wi-Fi, additional luggage racks and on-board entertainment. The first sets, which carry the Heathrow Express silver and purple livery, were due to enter service by the end of 2020, although this was subject to any Covid-19 related issues. This agreement means the Old Oak Common maintenance facility can be demolished to make way for the High Speed 2 project.

In 2019 Heathrow Express installed ticket barriers at Paddington, enabling customers to use pay-as-you-go Oyster and contactless ticketing. The introduction of Elizabeth Line services in future will increase rail services to Heathrow from 18 to at least 22 trains per hour, with Heathrow Express remaining the only non-stop and fastest connection between London Paddington and Terminals 2 & 3.

The Heathrow Connect service which was operated jointly by Heathrow Express and GWR transferred to TfL Rail on 20 May 2018 in advance of becoming part of the Elizabeth Line. ■

Set to replace '332s': Heathrow Express liveried No 387130 passes Caledonian Road & Barnsbury while traversing the North London line behind Rail Operations Group loco No 57310 as the 12.17 Ilford EMUD to Reading depot working on 18 September 2020. **ANTONY GUPPY**

SENIOR PERSONNEL
HEATHROW EXPRESS

Business Lead Sophie Chapman
Commercial Strategy Lead Karan Suri
Head of Customer Experience Mike Morgan-Batney

CHANNEL TUNNEL GROUP

The Channel Tunnel carries cars, coaches and lorries on shuttle trains between terminals at Folkestone and Coquelles. In November 2017 the operator of the trains and the tunnel itself, Groupe Eurotunnel, announced it had changed its name to Getlink.

The 50.45km (31.35-mile) Channel Tunnel has twin railway tunnels and a service tunnel and is operated by Getlink under a 100-year concession signed in 1986 with the French and British Governments. 2019 marked the 25th anniversary of the cross-channel fixed link.

Eurostar and freight train operators also run long-distance international trains through the tunnel; pre-Covid a total of approximately 500 trains ran through the tunnel each day.

Eurotunnel has nine passenger shuttles for cars and coaches and 18 for trucks or lorries, each powered by two locomotives; the truck shuttles carry either 31 or 32 heavy goods vehicles of 44 tonnes whilst the passenger shuttles can transport up to 120 cars and 12 coaches. During 2019 Eurotunnel shuttle services carried 1,595,241 trucks, 2,601,791 cars and 50,268 coaches. Eurostar services carried slightly more than 11 million passengers through the tunnel alongside 2,144 freight trains.

As part of its mid-term strategic thinking for Eurotunnel, the Group is working on optimising availability of the tunnel itself and believes it will be possible to increase capacity to allow more services to operate through the Channel Tunnel following a series of improvement schemes.

Revenue from Shuttle Services fell by 2% in 2019 compared to 2018 whilst revenue for the Eurotunnel segment of the overall Getlink business, which operates and directly markets the Shuttle Services and also provides access, on payment of a toll, for High-Speed Passenger Trains (Eurostar) and the Train Operators' Rail Freight Trains through its Railway Network, fell by 0.3%. In 2019 Eurotunnel's revenue amounted to €958 million, a fall of €3 million compared to 2018, whilst its operating costs rose to €406 million for the year. The Getlink Group's net result for 2019 was a profit of €159 million, an improvement of €27 million.

In its annual financial statement Getlink reported it had achieved its highest net result since 2007 on a like-for-like basis and expressed confidence in its economic model. However, it cautioned 'The economic context is however still uncertain following the United Kingdom's exit from the EU on January 2020 and the possible consequences of the Covid-19 coronavirus crisis.' ■

SENIOR PERSONNEL
GETLINK (EUROTUNNEL)

Chairman of the Board of Governors Jacques Gounon
Chief Executive Officer Yann Leriche
Deputy Chief Executive Officer François Gauthey
Chief Operating Officer, Eurotunnel Laurent Fourtune
Chief Corporate Officer Michel Boudoussier
Director of Rolling Stock Supply Chain and Energy Unit, Eurotunnel Patrick Etienne
Chief Operating Officer, Security Philippe de Lagune
Chief Executive Officer, ElecLink Steven Moore
Chief Operating Officer, Chair of Europorte Pascal Sainson

PASSENGER TRAIN OPERATORS

CHANNEL TUNNEL INTER-CITY TRAINS

Eurostar runs trains through the Channel Tunnel to link St Pancras International, Ebbsfleet International and Ashford International in the UK with Paris, Brussels, Rotterdam, Amsterdam, Lille and Calais. Less frequent services run to Disneyland Resort Paris, Bourg St Maurice, and Lyon, Avignon and Marseille. Normal timetables offer a London to Paris non-stop timing of 2hr 16min, whilst the new Netherlands services which began in 2018 offer journey times of 3hr 29min to Rotterdam and 4hr 9min to Amsterdam.

2019 marked the celebration of 25 years of Eurostar with over 190 million passengers since services began in 1994. Launched by state railway companies, the British interest was sold to London & Continental Railways (LCR) by the Government in 1996. As it prepared to sell the Channel Tunnel Rail Link (HS1), the Government took control of LCR in 2009, and in 2010 a new standalone joint venture company, Eurostar International Limited (EI), replaced the unincorporated joint venture of the three national companies.

In 2015 the UK Government sold its entire interest in EI for £757 million. A consortium comprising Caisse de dépôt et placement du Quebec (CDPQ) and Hermes Infrastructure acquired the Government's 40% stake in Eurostar for £585.1 million. Eurostar also agreed to redeem the Government's preference share, providing a further £172 million for the exchequer. SNCF (French Railways) holds 55% of EI, and SNCB (Belgian Railways) 5%. A shareholders' agreement in 2015 saw SNCF take sole managerial control of Eurostar subject to conditions set by the European Commission to avoid obstruction to future competitors.

A twice-daily service between London and The Netherlands was launched on 4 April 2018 using the new e320 trains which are compatible with the Netherlands high-speed infrastructure. Growing demand for the service saw a third daily train launched on the route in June 2019, with the company noting that a high-speed rail journey from London to Amsterdam emits 80% less carbon per passenger than the equivalent flight. Initially passengers returning from The Netherlands were required to change trains at Brussels for border and security checks to be carried out, but with work completed to resolve this the launch of a through service in both directions from Amsterdam was set for 20 April 2020 and from Rotterdam from 18 May 2020. The intervention of Covid-19 saw this pushed back to 26 October, whilst the pandemic also saw a significant reduction in services to Paris and Brussels, falling to a single daily service on each route at the height of the crisis.

The popular seasonal service between London and Marseille via Avignon did not operate in the summer of 2020 due to Covid-19 and Eurostar has confirmed it will remain suspended in 2021. In September 2020 Eurostar announced it would be reducing its timetable for 2021 and will not be reopening Ashford International or Ebbsfleet International stations before 2022. The company stated 'The environment remains very unpredictable and has been exacerbated by quarantine restrictions which are now across all of our markets. Given the uncertain outlook, it is crucial that we adapt and take action to reduce our costs so that we protect our business for the future. In 2021, therefore, we will reduce our timetable, focusing only on our core routes and destinations where we see the highest demand.' The company has created a new role of Managing Director, with the post holder working specifically on a recovery programme following the impact of the pandemic.

The first of Eurostar's 17 new Siemens Velaro-based 'e320' trains entered service in November 2015. Offering approximately 150 more seats than the original Class 373 'e300' sets, the new Class 374 units have a higher top speed of 320km/h. Ten of the original Class 373 sets have been refurbished for continued use, as their ability to operate under 1,500V DC electrification is required for services to Bourg St Maurice and Avignon. The KVB signalling system has been installed at Ashford International so the e320 trains, which are not fitted with the UK's Train Protection and Warning System (TPWS), can continue to call there.

In November 2019 Eurostar ran its first ever plastic-free train between London and Paris as a demonstration of the company's environmental ambitions for its on-board experience. The train featured new wooden cutlery, recyclable cans of water, glass wine bottles, alternative paper-based coffee cups and environmentally friendly packaging for food served to customers. From 1 January 2020, Eurostar has pledged to plant a tree for every train service it operates across its routes. Working in partnership with the Woodland Trust, ReforestAction and Trees for All, 20,000 additional trees will be planted every year in woodlands across Eurostar's markets of the UK, France, Belgium and the Netherlands.

After record performance in 2018, sales revenues in 2019 were slightly lower (£987 million, against £989 million in 2018), although year-on-year passenger numbers continued to rise with 2019 seeing 11.1 million against 11 million in 2018. Eurostar's preliminary unaudited operating profit for 2019 was £92 million. ∎

SENIOR PERSONNEL
EUROSTAR

- **Chief Executive Officer** Jacques Damas (in photo)
- **Managing Director** Olivier Fortin
- **Chairman** Dominique Reiniche
- **Chief Operating Officer** Philippe Mouly
- **Chief Customer Officer** Marc Noaro
- **Chief Information Officer** Laurent Bellan
- **Business Optimisation Director** François Le Doze
- **Customer Engagement Director** Richard Sherwood
- **Customer Experience Director** Amber Kirby
- **Strategy Director and Company Secretary** Gareth Williams
- **Director of Communications** Mary Walsh
- **Chief Financial Officer** James Cheesewright

Return from Amsterdam launched: Transport Secretary Grant Shapps (centre) joins then Eurostar CEO Mike Cooper (second left) in welcoming a media preview of the direct Eurostar from Amsterdam to St Pancras on arrival in London on 4 February 2020. The launch of commercial services was delayed due to the Covid pandemic and took place in October. **PHILIP SHERRATT**

FREIGHT AND HAULAGE

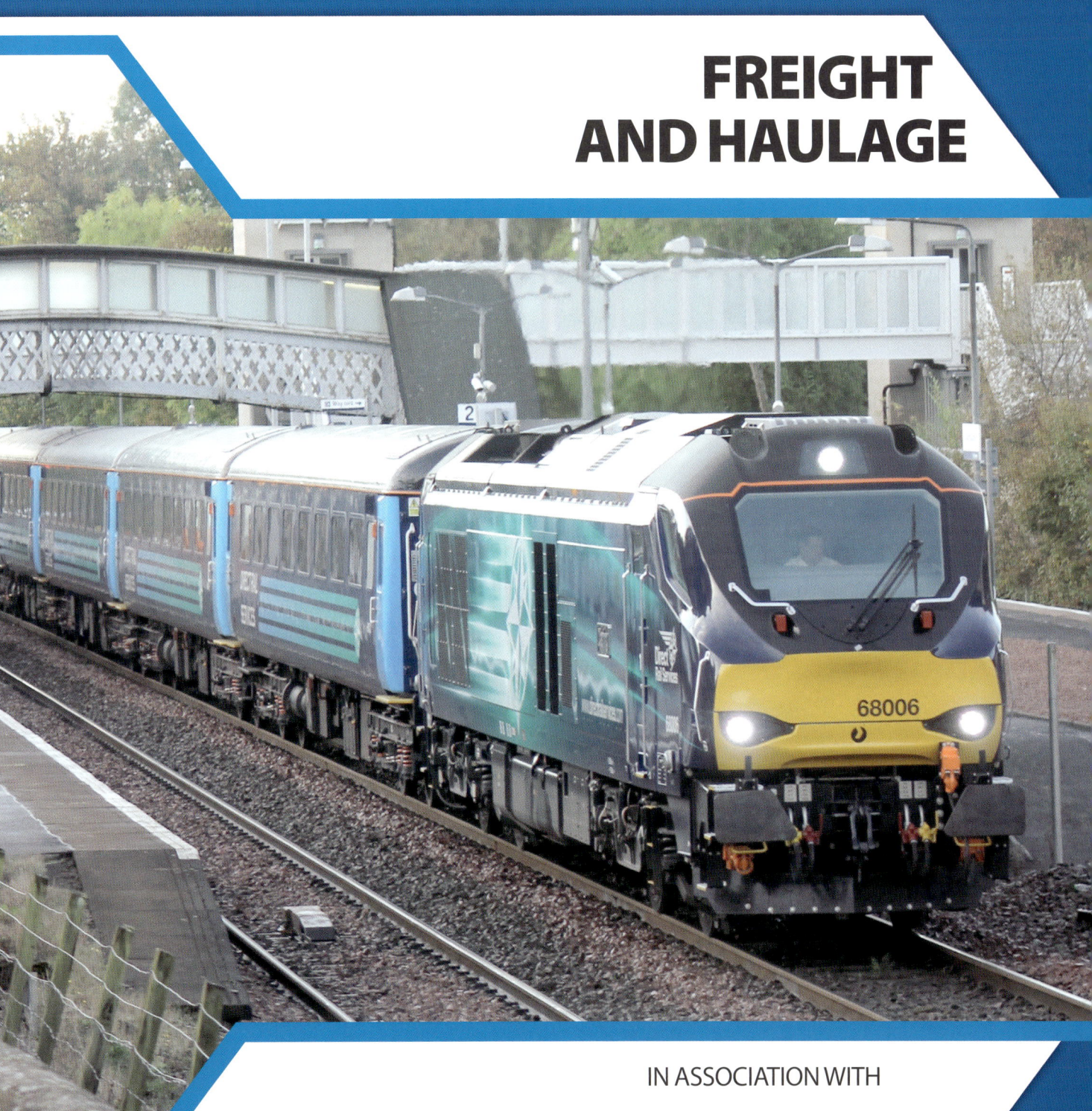

IN ASSOCIATION WITH

STADLER

FREIGHT AND HAULAGE

RAIL FREIGHT'S DECARBONISATION OPPORTUNITY

Haulage has bounced back well from Covid, but urgent action to tackle capacity constraints is needed, suggests Julian Worth

Rail freight heads into 2021 in good heart, with volumes running at over 90% of normal levels, Covid-19 notwithstanding. In total contrast to the passenger business which, before the pandemic's resurgence in autumn 2020 had only just recovered to 38% of pre-existing volume, freight never fell below 72%, even at the height of the pandemic in spring 2020.

Office of Rail and Road statistics for Q1 2020-21 record that freight was at 74% of the level recorded a year earlier and the recovery from this point was rapid, with levels rising to 85% and then to over 90% in subsequent months, albeit these numbers were subject to official confirmation. As private sector businesses receiving no Government support, this was still painful for freight operating companies (FOCs) and other companies in the freight sector, but it was nothing like the financial distress suffered elsewhere in the economy, let alone in passenger rail.

COVID IMPACT

The way in which Covid affected the various commodities within rail freight is instructive and shows how the sector reflects the performance of its customers – it is a bellwether of the British economy. The automotive sector, which was already suffering weak demand prior to Covid, was worst affected and shut all its plants almost immediately. As a result, there were no automotive trains at all in April and only a very small number in May – about 5% of normal. As car manufacturing restarted, this grew to around 50% in early summer and about 80% by late summer, led by BMW at Oxford.

Petroleum was also badly affected as the demand for fuel collapsed, with rail volumes falling by nearly 50% in April, but recovering to around 75% of normal by late summer as road traffic levels rose and more fuel was needed. In contrast, with air travel remaining severely depressed, movements of aviation spirit remained suspended, as the pipelines to Heathrow were more than able to cope with demand. Timber was also slow to recover as sources of timber close to the board mills were able to meet reduced demand and the longer hauls by rail were not needed. The flow to Kronospan at Chirk restarted at a modest level in early autumn.

At the other extreme, tonnages of biomass and domestic waste actually rose during lockdown as people were at home using more power and generating more refuse. Aided by additional capacity coming on stream at Drax, biomass was

IN ASSOCIATION WITH

37% up in April and May compared with 2019, albeit volumes tailed off as electricity demand reduced in the summer. Domestic waste was similarly 25-30% higher at the height of lockdown but eased back a little as people started to return to work.

The steel industry generally continued to produce at levels close to normal. Electric arc furnaces, producing mostly construction steel such as reinforcing bar, can be turned down – or off – when demand falls, but blast furnaces have to be kept running. Accordingly, production at Port Talbot and Scunthorpe continued largely unabated, with iron ore and coking coal running at a higher level than the previous year. Demand for steel from customers (not least in automotive) was, of course, down, so production initially filled up the domestic supply chain, with stocks increasing, and then diverted to export. Newport Docks, in particular, was handling 15,000 to 20,000 tonnes a week and further tonnages were moving through nearby Birdport and via the Channel Tunnel, with a weekly train of coil to Belgium – the first such move for several years. The fall in the value of sterling against the euro makes British steel more competitive, but export margins are rarely exciting, and it remains to be seen how sustainable this strategy is.

Other than electricity coal which – due to energy policy rather than the pandemic – has effectively ceased, the other sectors of rail freight took a knock in the spring but recovered well and in some cases very well. Just prior to lockdown, in March, construction recorded its highest ever tonnages – 13% up on the same month a year earlier. As building activity ceased in April, traffic levels predictably fell sharply and in Q1 were 37% down on 2019. From the end of May, however, the rebound was rapid with June and July volumes recovering to around 80% of 2019 levels and by August things were almost back to normal, with 90% to 95% of 2019 tonnages. As construction accounts for around 30% of all rail freight, this boosted the overall numbers significantly.

CONTAINER CONTRASTS

ORR stats combine maritime and domestic intermodal, but these two sectors experienced markedly different fortunes through 2020. The former (mostly deep sea containers) was first to see a decline, as Chinese factories closed in the face of coronavirus at the end of 2019. However, with the long sea voyage and a lot of containers in the pipeline, overall rail container volumes were only 5% to 10% down in the early months of the year, but 25% to 30% down in May as the flow from China stopped. With the Chinese factories reopening, June improved to around 85% of normal and overall volumes were almost back to normal by July, with 95% of the 2019 level recorded.

What these overall numbers mask, however, is that domestic intermodal – essentially retail goods moving between distribution centres and thence to stores – operated at high levels throughout. Consumers initially stripped supermarket shelves bare and then, through store purchases or home delivery, continued buying a lot of food and drink, substituting for eating out. Whilst only a small number of additional domestic intermodal trains operated, loadings on scheduled services were very heavy and many trains were increased in length to take more swap bodies. On the key Anglo-Scottish route from Daventry to Mossend and Coatbridge, trains were stretched to within a whisker of half-a-mile long. Interestingly, this had virtually no effect on performance, which was excellent throughout.

POSITIVE PROSPECTS

Intermodal is now the largest sector in UK rail freight, accounting for over 40% of tonne miles and along with construction making up 70% of overall volume. The fact these two businesses were running at 95% of normal levels by autumn 2020 meant rail freight overall was in a good place – but what are the prospects for 2021 and beyond?

The short answer is good, and perhaps very good. Consumer goods demand seems likely to remain buoyant as people spend money on themselves and their homes instead of entertainment and overseas holidays. Demand for cars remains low, but many buyers are waiting to see how electric and hybrid cars develop and, when this is clearer, demand should recover as deferred purchases feed through. With the Prime Minister and Chancellor declaring the strategy is to 'build, build, build' and 'build back

Electric freight: Direct Rail Services uses Class 88s on long-haul intermodal services. During mid-2020 closures of the West Coast main line caused some services to be diverted via the East Coast, marking a debut for the class on this route. This is No 88010 crossing Sopers viaduct on the Hertford loop on 17 May 2020 with a Daventry to Mossend container working. **KEN BRUNT**

FREIGHT AND HAULAGE

International freight: No 92019 powers the 6L25 Dollands Moor to Ripple Lane working at Lenham on HS1 on 15 September 2020. JAMIE SQUIBBS

better', the prospects for construction seem very bright. HS2 alone looks set to generate some 25 million tonnes of extra business over the next five years or so, in aggregates, cement and spoil from the Chiltern tunnels.

Biomass and domestic waste are likely to continue at current levels or expand gradually. The decline of coal is now largely complete and it may even grow a little if the new coking coal mine in West Cumbria receives the go-ahead – Cumbria County Council gave its approval, but the proposal was 'called in' by Westminster. Petroleum is on a trajectory of gradual decline, which will probably continue and accelerate as we move towards electric cars and vans.

The only major uncertainty is with steel – neither Port Talbot nor Scunthorpe can be regarded as wholly secure and five to 10 million tonnes per annum of rail traffic depends on their continued existence. This only amounts to around 8% of total tonne miles, but the product characteristics of steel (and its associated raw materials) mean it is very well-suited to rail and generates reasonable margins for the FOCs involved, notably DB Cargo.

CROSS-CHANNEL CHALLENGES

So much for industry-specific factors, but what of macro level changes? Setting aside Covid-related matters, the major challenges facing the UK are Brexit and decarbonisation.

In autumn 2020, the former looked set to go the wire, with the real possibility of major congestion at Dover and Cheriton as the new documentation regime delayed the throughput of HGVs. Even the prospect of delays has caused many companies to review their supply chains and conclude that the cost of driver-accompanied movement in a trailer is not justified and that unaccompanied movement, by trailer or – increasingly – swap body, meets their needs.

This has produced significant growth in short sea ferry traffic to East Coast ports on the Thames, Humber and Tees. At some of these ports, swap bodies account for 50% of unitised traffic and the proportion is growing, as swap bodies can be double stacked on ro-ro (roll on, roll off) freight ferries, doubling revenue per metre of deck space compared with trailers. Trailers are a – probably insuperable – challenge for UK railways, although the continental gauge of HS1 means piggyback is feasible as far as Barking.

The Lohr system of moving trailers on flat wagons is now established on routes from Calais, notably to Spain, and investigations are underway to extend these through the Channel Tunnel and up HS1 to Barking. This is fine for loads destined for London and the South East but less than ideal for those heading for the Midlands, the North, Wales and the South West – trailers will have to be hauled a long distance on UK roads. There may be some scope for 'cross docking' into/out of domestic rail equipment for the onward movement, which sounds counter-intuitive but already occurs with export tinplate from south Wales. Hauliers are reluctant to drive all the way down the M4, so conventional rail vans take the coils to Tilbury where they are cross docked into trailers for the journey across the Channel and on to destinations in Northern Europe.

GAUGING ISSUES

In general, though, it is far preferable from the rail perspective if goods arrive at East Coast ports in swap bodies rather than trailers. To clarify the distinction between containers and swap bodies, the former – used on all deep sea transits – are built to ISO dimensions of 20/40 feet long and eight feet wide. Swap bodies, on the other hand, can be up to 45 feet (13.6 metres) long (in UK domestic use they can be up to 50 feet/15.5 metres long) – effectively a stretched container. Crucially, swap bodies – at 2.5, 2.55 or even 2.6 metres – are also wider than ISO containers and can take two full width pallets across the unit, which is impossible with an ISO unit. Both types are commonly 9'6" high.

The greater width of swap bodies is not an issue on the continental network and many hundreds of loads per day are conveyed by rail to Zeebrugge, Amsterdam and Rotterdam to be shipped to the UK. The same applies in Scandinavia, but the UK's tighter loading gauge presents significant challenges. Only a small number of wagons (FLA and IDA) can carry 13.6 metre swap bodies within W8a gauge and then only at 2.5 metre width. If W9a gauge is available, the much larger pool of FKA/IKA megafret wagons can be used and swap bodies up to 2.6 metres wide can be conveyed. W10a allows 9'6" deep sea ISO boxes to be carried on standard height wagons, but is of no assistance with the wider short sea swap bodies – only if W12a gauge is available can these be carried on standard height wagons.

The busy F2N&M route: DB Cargo loco No 66142 *Maritime Intermodal Three* passes Elmswell with the 4L45 Wakefield Europort to Felixstowe service on 22 September 2020. **ANTONY GUPPY**

This all sounds arcane, but is crucial in determining the competitiveness of rail against road haulage, which has no such gauge constraints. Thus in late 2020 a lively debate was taking place about the trans-Pennine route, where the plan was for minimum intervention points to W8a as the preferred gauge, whereas W9a at least – and preferably W12a – is required for rail to compete with HGVs on the M62/M60, particularly on relatively short-distance routes from Immingham and Hull to the North West.

COMPETITIVE

It has already been demonstrated that – with gauge clearance – rail can compete effectively for short sea traffic. PD Ports has successfully built up a range of rail services from Teesport, with two trains a day to Scotland, one to Daventry (in conjunction with Tesco) and two to Doncaster – a haul of barely 100 miles, demonstrating that, with efficient use of rail assets, rail can compete over much shorter distances than many believed possible. PD Ports and its customers are keen to

Coal lingers on: although greatly reduced in number, some coal trains still persist. This is DB Cargo's No 66074 crossing Bebside viaduct at Bedlington on the Northumberland line en-route from Tees New Yard to North Blyth on 27 August 2020. **BILL WELSH**

FREIGHT AND HAULAGE

Biomass working: immaculate GB Railfreight loco No 600021 *Penyghent* passes Northumberland Park Metro station on North Tyneside with a loaded working from Tyne Coal terminal to Lynemouth power station on 30 June 2020. **BILL WELSH**

see a service to Manchester and, had Covid not intervened and disrupted trade patterns, a nightly train to Trafford Park would very probably have commenced in summer 2020, using low floor wagons on the W8 route over Diggle. Short sea services from Hull, this time to the Midlands and Scotland, were also rumoured to be close but were again frustrated by the advent of Covid.

In the south, daily trains operate from Tilbury to Daventry for Stobart and Forth Ports, with an extension to Grangemouth at weekends. These are in addition to the Tesco trains from Daventry to Barking and Purfleet, which connect with short sea ferry services at the latter location. Forth Ports has invested heavily in Tilbury2 – a brand new freight ro-ro terminal on the site of the former Tilbury power station. This went live in autumn 2020 and has excellent rail facilities capable of taking 775-metre trains. It also has an aggregates facility, which is planned to become operational in spring 2021, with trains of imported aggregates being forwarded to rail terminals across London and the South East. Ahead of this, new short sea intermodal services are in prospect, with the Great Western main line/M4 corridor being of particular interest.

The Thames is the main port for short sea unitised cargo from northern Europe to Wales and the West Country, with scores of HGVs a day heading down the M4 from Purfleet and Tilbury. Until autumn 2020 rail had little to offer on this route due to gauge constraints, but the clearance of Chipping Sodbury tunnel (to W12) in late summer 2020 opened up a W9 route all the way from Tilbury to Cardiff, allowing 13.6 metre x 2.55 metre wide boxes to be moved on the Great Western using megafrets. The first such service will hopefully not be too long in starting.

Worth mentioning too, in passing, that container movements from Liverpool also look set to increase, in this case deep sea ISO boxes primarily with traffic to/from the USA. Peel Ports already has a twice-weekly train to Scotland, primarily for whisky exports but, with the new Liverpool2 river-front berths being commissioned and better rail facilities following close behind, is rumoured to be looking at trains to other regions, such as the Midlands and Yorkshire. The Trans-Pennine Route Upgrade enhancements are of considerable relevance to the latter, as well as to short sea swap body moves from East Coast ports.

REACHING NET ZERO
The main drivers of modal switch to rail are the rising costs of road haulage, not least due to motorway congestion, and growing concern about climate change. This is often driven by manufacturers and retailers whose supply chains are being served – they will hardly ever pay more for a sustainable transport solution but, if the price is competitive, are more than interested in the sustainability credentials of rail. This has been given a substantial boost by the UK adopting a legal commitment to achieve net zero by 2050. Some sectors, notably agriculture and aviation, look very difficult indeed to decarbonise and it is likely that other sectors, including surface transport, will need to achieve zero carbon if the country overall is to get to net zero.

Transport is now the largest contributor (28%) to UK greenhouse gas emissions, of which road transport accounts for over 90%. Decarbonising passenger and light goods road transport looks achievable, with electric cars and vans already a reality and light trucks being trialled. Decarbonising long-distance HGVs, on the other hand, presents enormous challenges, since the energy density of diesel fuel is far superior to that offered by batteries, hydrogen or alternative fuels. Thoughts about motorway electrification and lorries fitted with pantographs are starting to emerge, but there are major technical and operational challenges to be overcome before this can be considered a remotely viable option.

It is conceivable that, as battery technology improves, medium weight battery lorries with reasonable range between charges will emerge. Local distribution of lighter products such as consumer goods over a range of 100 kilometres could be feasible and, potentially, regional distribution up to 150 kilometres. Beyond this range, however, medium weight loads look to be beyond battery propulsion and heavy loads of bulk products would probably have a working range of less than 100 kilometres.

DECARBONISATION
Rail is thus the only mode with proven zero-carbon capability in moving freight over longer distances, with renewable (or nuclear) energy being supplied to traction units via catenary or third rail. Even in advance of electrification, rail emits substantially less carbon (and other pollutants such as particulates) per tonne moved than HGVs, to the tune of about 70% less. Modal switch to rail is thus very probably the easiest way of decarbonising a supply chain available to manufacturers and retailers, both today and in the future. It is no exaggeration to say that decarbonisation offers the best opportunity rail freight has had in a century.

Network Rail published Phase One of its Traction Decarbonisation Network Strategy (TDNS) in autumn 2020, setting out the case to electrify around 85% of the network that remains unwired, with freight a major plank of the strategy. TDNS would see virtually all freight routes of any significance electrified, with the remaining 15% of lines that will remain unwired consisting of remote rural routes and branch lines that are of very limited relevance to freight.

Operation in terminals and along branch lines requires an electric loco to have a 'last-mile' capability to work off the wires. Currently, locos such as the Class 88 use a small diesel engine to achieve this but, whilst the diesel power unit can be 'clean', it is clearly not zero-carbon and the problem is exacerbated by the fact that many freight terminals are in urban areas – the very places where zero-emission operation is most important. Accordingly, power for 'last mile' operation of the next generation of electric locos, replacing Class 66 diesels, is likely to be battery.

The same power packs used by Vivarail for local passenger trains would enable a heavy freight train to be moved at low speed over reasonable distances, perhaps up to 10 miles from an electrified line. Batteries would be charged from the catenary prior to leaving the wires and could, if necessary, be charged at terminals whilst the train was discharged/loaded. Regenerative braking could also be used to charge batteries when the loco is off the main line.

But how can modal switch be achieved in practical terms? The challenge for rail freight is, of course, that many origins and destinations of freight are not connected to the rail

'70' in the North East: Freightliner's No 70001 powers the 6F23 South Bank Tees Dock to Boulby empty polyhalite fertiliser train at Hunt Cliff on 20 March 2020. **JAMIE SQUIBBS**

New terminal in the East Midlands: Freightliner loco No 66599 arrives at East Midlands Gateway with an intermodal service from Felixstowe on 21 August 2020. **PHILIP SHERRATT**

FREIGHT AND HAULAGE

network and, in many cases, never can be. Intermodal equipment – containers and swap bodies – is the obvious and well-tried solution and offers the most viable option for supply chains of the future: long-distance trunk haulage by electric train coupled with local and, for lighter loads, regional distribution by electric lorry.

TERMINALS

The higher the proportion of major origins and destinations of freight that can be directly connected to the freight network the better. Most major ports are already rail connected, along with some distribution complexes and manufacturing plants. The latter cannot generally be relocated, so rail sidings need to be provided, wherever possible, at or close to the plant. If it is not possible to directly connect the plant, there should ideally be a private haul road to the rail siding to avoid using public roads.

Warehouses, on the other hand, can be – and often are – relocated over a 20-year time horizon as supply chain requirements evolve. Over 50 million square feet of rail-connected warehousing is in the planning pipeline for the Golden Triangle of Distribution in the Midlands, where many National Distribution Centres (NDCs) are located. Many NDCs will, therefore, have rail connectivity in the future, but the Regional Distribution Centre (RDC) clusters around the UK will also need rail-connected warehousing, of which only a small amount is currently available.

Warehousing complexes, rail-connected or not, almost always attract strong local opposition. Classifying Strategic Rail Freight Interchanges (SRFIs) as Nationally Significant Infrastructure Projects (NSIPs) streamlines the planning process for major warehousing developments and a similar approach is needed for smaller scale facilities. This is particularly important in urban areas, where there is considerable pressure to build more housing. Planning policy guidelines need to ensure land alongside the main railways with good road access is preserved for logistics use, so that modal transfer can take place efficiently. Unlike NDCs and RDCs, urban modal transfer points do not require warehousing and are merely compact terminals where swap bodies can be transferred from rail to road and vice versa.

CAPACITY CONSTRAINTS

Achieving this optimum multimodal zero-carbon system will also need sufficient track capacity on key freight routes. Analysis of DfT road freight data reveals that 54% of heavy goods vehicle tonne kilometres are generated by trips of a type that rail already successfully operates – consumer goods over 120 miles and heavy bulk materials over 60 miles. It would be unrealistic to expect all such road movements to switch to rail, but it is estimated around 30% to 35% could do so.

This would roughly treble current UK rail tonnes and tonne kilometres and – due to the lighter nature of much of the new rail traffic – quadruple the number of trains. This sounds daunting, but is only double the tonnage moved by rail as recently as 2003, and such tonnages were seen in the 1960s. The difference now is that the additional trains would mostly be on main lines from the ports and between major urban areas, rather than a significant proportion being in dense industrial areas, as was the case in former times.

To put the extra demand in context, two extra freight paths in each direction per off-peak hour would be required on most main lines to accommodate this level of growth. On two routes – F2M&N from Felixstowe to the Midlands and North and the West Coast main line – the increase would be around four extra paths an hour in each direction. HS2 is thus essential to free up capacity on the WCML for freight switching modes and it is imperative that the major upgrade of F2M&N goes ahead as quickly as possible.

At present, progress on upgrading the latter route is glacial – Haughley Junction, north of Stowmarket, will hopefully be doubled in the next few years but Network Rail has embarked on a second round of public consultation about the layout and level crossings at Ely and the most urgent enhancement – doubling of the single track from Soham to Ely – is not even at first base in the industry planning process. This becomes even more important in the context of East West Rail, which will provide – for the first time – direct access from Felixstowe to the Golden Triangle, using F2N&M as far as Newmarket. This route is amongst the heaviest HGV corridors in the UK, with 1,000 containers on a typical day – equating to a maximum size container train every off-peak hour of the day.

RAIL'S OPPORTUNITY

To create extra capacity, we should always look first at good operating practice – the track and signalling must allow trains, both freight and passenger, to join and leave the main line at speed. All too often, turnouts onto freight lines, loops and platform lines have a very low maximum speed and associated restrictive approach control signalling. Increasing turnout speeds to 40mph or 60mph allows the main line to be cleared much more quickly. Similarly, if a driver can apply full power when signalled onto the main line, instead of a long train having to crawl out of a loop, precious minutes of trunk route capacity are saved.

Once these tactical measures have been banked, strategic capacity enhancement is usually best achieved by the grade separation of junctions, to eliminate conflicting moves and thereby create extra paths. European Train Control System (ETCS) can increase plain line capacity between junctions by allowing trains to run closer together but is of limited value if trains then cannot get through the next junction efficiently. Accordingly, the priority is to grade separate the junctions and derive the benefits of ETCS in due course as it becomes available.

It follows that a package of measures – electrification, additional distribution terminals and private sidings, plus capacity enhancement – can enable the railway to convey the numbers of additional freight trains required to decarbonise trunk haulage, interfacing with battery trucks for local/regional deliveries, which necessarily have to be undertaken by road.

The UK is not noted for speed (or efficiency) in delivering major infrastructure enhancements and there is lot to be done. If we start now, it's all eminently feasible by the 2040s, but now is the time for action, not further analysis and endless optioneering. A sharp focus on delivery is required if we are to achieve net zero by 2050. ■

Julian Worth has spent 41 years in the rail freight industry in a wide variety of roles, including Managing Director, Transrail Freight and Marketing Director, English Welsh & Scottish Railway. He is Chairman of the Chartered Institute of Logistics and Transport's Rail Freight Forum.

Construction by the canal: No 59005 works a train of empties from Acton to Merehead Quarry near Crofton on the Berks and Hants line on 3 March 2020. **KEN BRUNT**

RAIL FREIGHT FIGHTS BACK

While the sector is still loss-making there are signs of improvement, reports **CHRIS CHEEK**

Losses reduced: DB Cargo's No 66104 works the 12.55 Goonbarrow Junction to Fowey Dock Carne Point, arriving at Lostwithiel to run round on 14 February 2020. **KEN BRUNT**

The rail freight industry's run of losses continued into 2018-19, albeit at a much-reduced level, as the industry's enforced restructuring in the wake of the abrupt closure of coal-fired power stations continued to work through. The industry's combined losses halved during the year, according to analysis undertaken by consultant PTIS in *Rail Industry Monitor* (RIM).

Cash operating losses reduced from last year's £21.5 million to £10.8 million, with margins going from -2.5% to -1.2% – a great improvement but still clearly unsustainable and requiring ongoing support from parent companies. The good news is that four of six main players did actually turn a profit, though these were dwarfed by losses at DB Cargo and Freightliner Heavy Haul.

The combined turnover of the companies analysed was 6.1% down at £895.4 million, whilst operating costs rose by 4.7%, taking the total to £906.2 million. The companies were once again net earners of interest, though the sums involved fell to less than £200,000, down from £12.5 million. As a result, pre-tax losses amounted to £10.7 million at a margin of -1.2% (last year: £9.0 million at -1.1%).

RIM also reports on market share, as measured by turnover. DB Cargo's share fell to 36%, the lowest by some margin since privatisation. It is interesting to reflect that this figure stood at over 80% in the late 1990s. Freightliner was next with 34%. The two post-privatisation new entrants continued to build up their market shares. GB Railfreight, then owned by Swedish company Hector Rail but now by Infracapital, reached a new record high of 21.1%. Meanwhile, the Nuclear Decommissioning Authority's rail arm Direct Rail Services got to 9.3%.

Note: Turnover per Employee figures are absolute, while all other amounts are stated in thousands.

GB RAILFREIGHT

The company saw significant revenue increases of almost 30% on the back of winning several new contracts. However, costs rose by 32%, outstripping the revenue gains this year, so depressing profits by a quarter.

PERIOD TO	31/12/2018	31/12/2017
	£000	£000
Turnover	189,065	147,468
Operating Costs	182,104	137,942
Operating Profit	6,961	9,526
Operating Margin	3.7%	6.5%
Turnover per Employee	229,727	225,832
Rolling stock lease	23,654	19,988

DIRECT RAIL SERVICES

The company achieved some revenue growth during the year, which was marginally higher than the costs incurred, so improving operating profits. A small reduction in interest costs contributed to a much improved pre-tax result.

PERIOD TO	31/03/2019	31/03/2018
	£000	£000
Turnover	83,392	77,992
Operating Costs	81,557	76,334
Operating Profit	1,835	1,658
Operating Margin	2.2%	2.1%
Turnover per Employee	188,244	185,695
Rolling stock lease	19,814	17,910
Revenue Grant	140	203

DB CARGO INTERNATIONAL

The company saw profits slip during the year as increased operating costs outstripped revenue growth that was just above inflation, even though the workforce was reduced by over 30% and materials costs were also reduced substantially. No explanation is given in the accounts for the increase in other cost items.

PERIOD TO	31/12/2018	31/12/2017
	£000	£000
Turnover	21,890	21,400
Operating Costs	15,669	13,733
Operating Profit	6,221	7,667
Operating Margin	28.4%	35.8%
Turnover per Employee	280,641	189,381

DB CARGO UK

The company improved its financial performance during the year, reducing operating losses by over 40%, reaping the benefits of the previous year's restructuring and further cost reductions of almost 10% during the year. However, the rail freight market continued to be challenging, depressing income by another 4.8%. The losses shown here were reduced by exceptional items totalling £6 million (last year £24 million).

PERIOD TO	31/12/2018	31/12/2017
	£000	£000
Turnover	297,000	312,000
Operating Costs	319,000	350,000
Operating Profit	(22,000)	(38,000)
Operating Margin	-7.4%	-12.2%
Turnover per Employee	159,249	147,937

FREIGHTLINER

The company returned to the black in 2018, recording a substantial operating profit in lieu of previous losses. This followed revenue growth of 7.1%, whilst cost increases were constrained to 1% by reducing the workforce, lowering leasing costs and reducing administrative costs.

PERIOD TO	31/12/2018	31/12/2017
	£000	£000
Turnover	218,935	204,374
Operating Costs	208,006	205,489
Operating Profit	10,929	(1,115)
Operating Margin	5.0%	-0.5%
Turnover per Employee	207,521	172,613

FREIGHTLINER HEAVY HAUL

The group's trainload freight business saw results deteriorate further during the year, recording very heavy operating and pre-tax losses. Otherwise strong revenue growth of 5.6% was hit by a hefty increase in operating costs, notably wage and pension costs, leasing charges and administration costs.

PERIOD TO	31/12/2018	31/12/2017
	£000	£000
Turnover	85,118	80,614
Operating Costs	99,854	81,867
Operating Profit	(14,736)	(1,253)
Operating Margin	-17.3%	-1.6%
Turnover per Employee	149,068	145,250

FREIGHT AND HAULAGE

DB Cargo UK is part of a large international network of rail freight companies run by Deutsche Bahn. Operating in 16 different countries, DB is Europe's number one provider of rail logistics solutions.

Based in Doncaster, DB Cargo UK is the largest rail freight company operating in Great Britain. With over 2,000 highly trained and dedicated employees, the company provides freight haulage services to a variety of sectors.

The company's core markets are metals, waste, automobiles, chemicals and aggregates. DB Cargo UK is the biggest mover of metal products in the UK, providing a continuous pipeline of raw materials to local manufacturers. Specially adapted trains transport 90% of UK car manufacturers' finished vehicles, taking them fresh from the production line to UK and international markets. The company also transports fuels and chemicals from UK refineries to the frontline, as well as moving huge volumes of aggregates and building materials to support some of the UK's largest construction projects. DB Cargo's intermodal services connect ports, terminals and distribution centres, ensuring the speedy delivery of some of Britain's biggest High Street brands to Britain's consumers.

New contracts in 2020 included a five-year 'hook and haul' deal to transport biomass to Drax power station from the ports of Immingham and Hull; a three-year contract with Puma Energy for rail haulage and the supply of rail tank wagons, involving the movement of fuel from Milford Haven and Immingham to Theale and Westerleigh; and a new aggregates service for Cemex from the Peak Forest site in Derbyshire to Small Heath in Birmingham.

In addition, DB Cargo UK also provides track maintenance to Network Rail and a rail breakdown recovery service to other operators, along with charter and steam services for passengers. Among the latter, DB Cargo has the charter to operate the Royal Train for HRH The Queen and her Family.

LOGISTICS

In October 2018, UK manufacturing was given a major boost with the opening of DB Cargo UK's new steel logistics centre in the West Midlands. Construction took more than 12 months and saw the German-owned freight operator more than double the size of its existing facility in Knowles Road, Wolverhampton, which receives imported steel from as far afield as Holland and Sweden.

The £6 million project was one of the largest investments in rail freight in the past five years and seen as a major vote of confidence in the UK's continuing ability to trade and attract inward investment post-Brexit. The state-of-the-art logistics centre is now used by some of the world's biggest steel companies including ArcelorMittal, Tata Steel and SSAB, providing a major boost to local businesses that use their products in their manufacturing processes.

INTERMODAL AGREEMENT

In April 2019 DB Cargo UK announced a major new agreement with road haulier Maritime Transport Ltd, which saw two of the UK's largest freight operators combine their expertise to increase rail freight capacity and competition in the intermodal market. Under the terms of the proposed agreement, DB Cargo UK was contracted to run Maritime Intermodal's rail operations out of Felixstowe and Southampton, while Maritime Intermodal took on responsibility for DB Cargo UK's terminals in Trafford Park, Manchester and Wakefield in West Yorkshire, thus strengthening the road haulier's national network of strategic hubs. Maritime Intermodal also took responsibility for DB Cargo UK's existing intermodal customers on its Felixstowe and Southampton services. The number of intermodal services operated by Maritime Intermodal continues to grow.

TRACK INFRASTRUCTURE RENEWALS

In August 2019, DB Cargo UK started work on a multi-million programme of investment to improve track and rail infrastructure at three key sites.

The UK's largest rail freight operator is replacing more than 20km of track at its depots at Immingham in North Lincolnshire, Rotherham in South Yorkshire and Toton in Nottinghamshire. The investment will further improve the safety and reliability of services.

INNOVATION IN CUSTOMER SERVICE

In November 2018 DB Cargo UK launched an industry-leading new service that enables customers to view their rail freight deliveries in real time via an online tracking system.

The new web-based portal allows DB Cargo UK customers to see the number and type of wagons on their service, as well as exactly what progress the loco is making at any given time. Responsive to all mobile devices, the portal is easy to use and can be accessed on the go.

The system was designed by customers for customers and is the product of collaboration with some of DB Cargo UK's existing partners including Mendip Rail, British Steel, Tarmac and Puma Energy. ∎

SENIOR PERSONNEL
DB CARGO UK

Chief Executive Officer Andrea Rossi
Head of Sales Roger Neary
Chief Operating Officer Dirk Nolte
Head of Human Resources Gaynor Westwell

New service from Newhaven: DB Cargo is the operator of services from the Newhaven Marine Aggregates Terminal, on the site of the former Newhaven Marine station. Trains from the terminal carry aggregate sand and gravel for the construction industry. The first train on 18 June 2020 was hauled by No 66113, adorned with a special livery recognising the efforts of key workers during the Covid pandemic. COURTESY NETWORK RAIL

Supporting the NHS: GB Railfreight has named loco No 66731 as Captain Tom Moore, with the loco also bearing 'Thank you NHS' branding.

GB Railfreight

GB Railfreight was founded in 1999 in the post-privatisation era, unlike other freight operators which date from British Rail days. Since then its story has been one of continued growth and expansion. Since September 2019 the company has been owned by Infracapital, having been sold by EQT.

Intermodal operations are at the heart of GBRf's business. Highlights in 2020 included the launch of a fifth daily rail freight service to the iPort Rail interchange near Doncaster, operated by GBRf and running from Felixstowe.

Supporting GBRf's expansion in the intermodal sector is procurement of additional wagons. The operator had already confirmed it would take 32 Ecofret2 triple-deck wagons, each capable of accommodating either two 20ft or one 40ft container, with work to modify the wagons being undertaken by WH Davis at Shirebrook. GBRf subsequently confirmed it would order a further 52 wagons, taking the total order to 84; the wagons are leased from VTG Rail, which manages operations and maintenance.

GBRf has started operations from new intermodal sidings at Peterborough, which the company delivered in partnership with Balfour Beatty and contractor MLP Railway Maintenance Ltd. This project followed the opening of a new control room at Peterborough and an upgrade to the fuelling system, with plans to further develop the site by altering existing sidings and installing additional infrastructure to provide improved access to the East Coast main line. A new training facility has also been opened at Peterborough, including two training simulators which were unveiled in 2019. Nearby at March, a wagon maintenance and stabling depot has been created for stock used on sand trains originating at Middleton Towers, near King's Lynn.

Construction has also yielded new and renewed deals for GBRf. Among these are a new service from Dove Holes quarry to Crawley for building materials supplier Cemex, which began in April 2020. Late 2019 saw GBRf sign a seven-year continuation deal with Hanson Cement for services from Ketton cement works in Rutland and Ribblesdale cement works in Lancashire to terminals at London King's Cross, Avonmouth (Bristol) and Mossend (Glasgow). Also renewed was a contract with Etex Building Performance for transportation of gypsum to Ferrybridge, now running until July 2023.

But perhaps the headline for GBRf in the construction sector was the start of a contract to deliver material to Washwood Heath for HS2. The first train ran on 25 August 2020 for Rail Stone Solutions, HS2's preferred aggregates supplier, which selected GBRf as its rail haulage partner. In the latter part of 2020 it was expected 150 trains would bring up to 235,000 tonnes of stone to Washwood Heath from quarries in the Peak District.

Expansion at GBRf is supported by continued additions to the locomotive fleet. The company has introduced three Class 66s which previously operated in Sweden and were converted for UK operations. In October 2020 it confirmed plans to draft in a further five such locos from Germany in conjunction with Beacon Rail Leasing. The locos, which will be numbered 66973-797, will be converted at Electro-Motive Diesel's Doncaster and Longport facilities. The first two will be low-geared heavy haul 60mph locos, and the last three 75mph locomotives, with entry into service planned from April 2021.

Also in progress is the repowering of 16 Class 56 locos by Progress Rail's EMD subsidiary at Longport with updated engines and control gear. Following the work, the locomotives will be reclassified as Class 69s. The Class 56s were purchased by GBRf from UK Rail Leasing in June 2018.

GBRf has trialled the use of a Class 319 EMU for express delivery of parcels into London Euston. Following the trial in April 2020, the operator said it was discussing with Government how the service could play a role in helping with the logistical challenge of delivering supplies to hospitals during the coronavirus crisis. The trial saw parcels carried in standard roll cages, which were loaded and offloaded to and from the '319'. GBRf believes delivery into city centres could be combined with 'last mile' operations using electric vehicles. ∎

SENIOR PERSONNEL
GB RAILFREIGHT

Managing Director John Smith (in photo)
Finance Director Karl Goulding-Davis
Production Director Ian Langton
Commercial Director Liam Day
Business Development Director Tim Hartley
Asset Director David Golding
Engineering Director Bob Tiller

FREIGHT AND HAULAGE

Freightliner, a subsidiary of Genesee & Wyoming Inc. (G&W), is an established, award-winning freight transportation provider, specialising in rail, with businesses in the United Kingdom and Continental Europe. Offering customers a wide range of rail freight solutions to cater for the requirements of a diverse market sector, Freightliner provides a safe, reliable and cost-effective rail freight partnership.

As a leading provider of intermodal and bulk freight haulage, with depots and terminals spread nationwide, Freightliner operates services across the entire UK rail network as well as offering rolling stock and infrastructure maintenance solutions.

Running more than 100 services daily, the company moves more than 770,000 maritime containers per year from the deep-sea ports of Felixstowe, Southampton and London Gateway to all major conurbations in the UK, offering total coverage of the UK network.

Through deep-sea and inland terminals, third party sites and road depots, Freightliner provides customers with the choice of booking a rail only or a rail/road solution, enhancing the efficiency and effectiveness of their transport operations.

As a leading UK rail freight company with more than two decades' experience transporting bulk freight, Freightliner has set new standards of reliability, flexibility and customer service whilst continuing to invest in innovative solutions for every business need.

With 99.9% reliability on all services, Freightliner operates 200 bulk trains per week, moving 12 million tonnes of bulk freight annually, offering haulage solutions for rail infrastructure maintenance, cement, aggregates, waste, industrial minerals, rail industry services and more.

Freightliner is the largest user of electric locomotives to haul freight, having recently acquired 13 Class 90 locomotives from Porterbrook Leasing to complement its existing 10 electric locomotives, and is at the forefront of other initiatives aimed at reducing carbon, such as trialling longer trains. As the largest operator of carbon neutral traction, it is continually developing solutions to deliver decarbonisation targets, working in collaboration with customers.

Supporting this is Freightliner's in-house maintenance division, with specialist facilities located around the country offering packages for the repair and maintenance of rolling stock and track, including diesel locomotive maintenance in Leeds and electric locomotive maintenance at a purpose-built facility in Crewe, a wagon maintenance facility in Southampton and a wagon overhaul facility in Manchester.

With proven delivery levels, and the highest concentration of chartered engineers in the rail freight industry, Freightliner's team of in-house experts utilise years of knowledge and experience to diagnose, repair and maintain its traction, rolling stock and infrastructure, which means it can provide best in class services to its customers.

Freightliner is also rightly proud of its industry-leading safety performance in the UK. Safety is at the heart of everything it does, and all aims, actions and activities are focused on the goal of 'zero injuries'. Since the G&W acquisition, Freightliner's safety performance has improved dramatically from an already industry-leading position on almost every safety metric. In fact, 38 of its sites in the UK and Europe were injury free at 2019 year-end. ∎

Electric addition: the first of 13 newly-acquired Class 90 locomotives to wear Freightliner livery, No 90014, was named *Over the Rainbow* in honour of the efforts of key workers during a ceremony at Crewe on 30 July 2020. **COURTESY FREIGHTLINER**

SENIOR PERSONNEL
FREIGHTLINER GROUP

CEO – UK/Europe Gary Long (in photo)
Chief Financial Officer Patrick Taylor
HR Director Glynis Appelbe
Managing Director – Terminal Services Chris Lawrenson
General Counsel Geraint Harries
Managing Director – UK Rail Neil McNicholas
Safety Development Director Stephen Evans-Howe
European Engineering & Operations Services Director Tim Shakerley

West Coast containers: Freightliner loco Nos 86638/608 pass Searchlight Lane Junction, north of Stafford, with a Felixstowe to Garston container working on 14 May 2020. **JOHN WHITEHOUSE**

COLAS RAIL FREIGHT

Colas Rail Freight is part of the Colas Group, a subsidiary of the French-based multinational Bouygues, a prominent provider of railway infrastructure construction and maintenance services.

The company has won haulage contracts within Network Rail's Control Period 6 (CP6) portfolio, including network, bulk ballast and possession trains and rail head treatment trains (RHTTs). In December 2018 Colas won a deal from Network Rail for operation of rail grinding trains.

Freight flows include cement workings for Tarmac from Dunbar (Oxwellmains) to Aberdeen, Inverness, Viewpark (Uddingston), Seaham and West Thurrock, along with bagged cement between Aberthaw (south Wales) and Moorswater in Cornwall. Flows from Lindsey oil refinery convey bitumen to Total UK's Preston production plant, to Colnbrook in west London and Rectory Junction, Nottingham and oil tank flows to Aberthaw and West Burton. Colas also moves aviation fuel from the Ineos refinery at Grangemouth to Prestwick Airport and petroleum products from this plant to Dalston in Cumbria. Trains of timber for building materials manufacturer Kronospan are operated to Chirk from Baglan Bay in south Wales and Carlisle.

Launched in 2020 was a new trial service from Aberdeen to Spalding, conveying calcium carbonate for use in a paper plant at King's Lynn. The first service ran on 19 May and was planned to move to weekly operation; it is thought to be the first freight train to serve Spalding for over 35 years.

The Pullman Rail rolling stock overhaul and engineering facility in Cardiff is also part of the Colas Rail group. The group holds various infrastructure contracts, including track and rail systems alliance and signalling deals for CP6 from Network Rail, and Colas is part of the Midland Metro Alliance which is developing and building extensions to the light rail network in the West Midlands.

DIRECT RAIL SERVICES

A wholly-owned subsidiary of the Nuclear Decommissioning Authority, Direct Rail Services (DRS) was established to provide British Nuclear Fuels Limited with a strategic rail transport service. The company is also active in general rail freight, mainly in retail distribution. In 2020 the NDA announced plans to bring DRS together with its other subsidiary organisations International Nuclear Services (INS) and its subsidiary Pacific Nuclear Transport Ltd (PNTL) into a single division to simplify structures within the group.

Intermodal is a key market for DRS, with trains operated for Tesco in conjunction with Stobart Rail from Daventry to Mossend, Purfleet and Wentloog. In September 2018 Stobart launched a new service from the Port of Tilbury to Tesco's site in Daventry, and thence to Mossend, also operated by DRS. A new service for Forth Ports in partnership with Eddie Stobart began in June 2019 linking Tilbury and Grangemouth, while in 2020 DRS won a new contract to transport cars from the Ford factory at Dagenham to the rail terminal at Garston, near Liverpool.

Haulage contracts for Network Rail in Control Period 6 include network, bulk ballast and possession trains, rail head treatment trains and seasonal winter treatment trains.

In the passenger sector the company provides support and traction for franchised and charter passenger operators. Contracts for franchised operators have reduced, with operation of Class 37-hauled trains for both Greater Anglia and Northern ending in 2019, followed by the cessation of Class 68-hauled ScotRail trains round the Fife Circle in 2020.

Fleet modernisation has been led by Stadler (formerly Vossloh) locomotives, with 34 diesel-powered Class 68s. Some are used for passenger services, including sub-leases to Chiltern Railways and TransPennine Express. These have been supplemented by 10 bi-mode Class 88 locomotives. Rated at 5,360hp under 25kV AC supply and at 900hp in diesel mode from a Caterpillar 12-cylinder engine, they offer 'last mile' operation on non-electrified lines. In September 2017 DRS published a tender notice for supply of a further 10 mixed traffic diesel-electric locomotives, but a contract has yet to be awarded.

In January 2020 DRS won the 'Golden Whistle' award for best performing freight operator at the event organised by *Modern Railways* and the Institution of Railway Operators for the seventh consecutive year.

RAIL OPERATIONS (UK) LTD

Rail Operations Group (ROG) began operation in 2015, handling train movements relating to rolling stock delivery, testing, maintenance, modification and refurbishment programmes. Clients include rolling stock companies, passenger operators and the supply industry. Now under the Rail Operations (UK) Ltd banner, the company has expanded with subsidiaries Traxion, focusing on storage regimes for stock, and Orion, the high-speed logistics business.

ROG principally uses Class 37 and 47 locomotives leased from Europhoenix, equipped with Dellner drophead couplers and electrical translating equipment to eliminate the use of barrier/translator vehicles for electric multiple-unit haulage. The company is also diversifying into infrastructure testing, and has worked with Network Rail and Data Acquisition and Testing Services on the test programme for the new overhead wires on the Midland main line between Bedford and Corby, with a specially configured train including HST power cars, two Class 91s and a Class 90 to test the infrastructure at varying configurations and speeds.

Recent contract wins as test operator have included the new Stadler Class 745 EMUs and Class 755 BMUs for Greater Anglia, Class 710 Bombardier Aventra EMUs for London Overground, Class 769 bi-mode units for Northern and CAF-built Class 397 EMUs for TransPennine Express.

In August 2020 Orion unveiled the first Class 319 converted for its high-speed logistics operation to convey parcels and light freight. Two bi-mode Class 769s are also being converted, with the plan being to operate a '319' coupled to a '769' between the port at London Gateway and Liverpool Street, the diesel engines of the '769' providing traction on the unelectrified Gateway branch. The aim is for the service to launch in early 2021 with a single daily service; paths have been identified for a further two services in future while other routes being examined include London Gateway to Birch Coppice and Daventry to Mossend.

Parent company Rail Operations (UK) Ltd intends to order 10 or more tri-mode Class 93 locomotives from Stadler to allow further expansion in high-speed freight. The Class 93 is an adaptation of the Class 88 dual-mode design supplied to DRS, but with a bigger diesel alternator supported by lithium titanate (LTO) batteries. The

High-speed logistics launch: on 10 August 2020 Rail Operations (UK) Ltd's Orion subsidiary unveiled a converted Class 319 to carry parcels and light freight, with two Class 769 bi-mode sets to follow. A service between London Gateway and Liverpool Street is due to launch in early 2021. **KEN BRUNT**

FREIGHT AND HAULAGE

plan is for the '93s' to be capable of 110mph operation and have Dellner couplers with adjustable height.

WEST COAST RAILWAYS

With its main base at Carnforth and a subsidiary depot at Southall, west London, WCR specialises in operating charter trains both on its own account and for other tour operators, using diesel and steam traction.

In addition to an extensive programme of tours throughout the year, WCR runs two regular seasonal steam-hauled trains – the Fort William to Mallaig 'Jacobite' and the York to Scarborough 'Scarborough Spa Express'. Traction is also occasionally provided for stock and plant moves.

A highlight of 2020 was a six-week trial carrying timber freight on the Far North line in Scotland from forests in Caithness to the Norbord plant at Dalcross, near Inverness, in conjunction with Victa Railfreight, with traction provided by Class 37 locomotives (see below).

The registered diesel fleet includes Classes 33, 37, 47 and 57, not all operational. WCR also manages the operation of steam locomotives belonging to various owners. Its pool of coaching stock includes four main line registered rakes – one of Metro-Cammell 1960s-built Pullman carriages.

VICTA RAILFREIGHT

Victa Railfreight has been providing a wide range of support services to rail freight customers,

Cappagh company: DCRail's third Class 60, No 60028, was unveiled in the livery of its parent Cappagh Group in December 2019. The company said the loco was used to haul trains of construction materials to the new Cappagh rail facility under development near Wembley, London.

operators and suppliers since 1995. It operated its first trains over Network Rail infrastructure in January 2015, soon after award of its train operator licence.

A highlight of 2020 was a trial service for movement of timber on the Far North line in Scotland from forests in Caithness to the Norbord plant at Dalcross near Inverness. The six-week trial during August and September followed the award to Victa of a Freight Fund Grant worth £195,000 by Transport Scotland. Trains operated up to three times per week using wagons supplied by DB Cargo and locomotives and drivers from West Coast Railways. The main flow was from the freight terminal at Georgemas Junction to Milburn freight yard at Inverness for onward delivery by road, the timber coming from Munro Harvesting.

Other recent contracts wins have included a deal with Cemex UK which sees Victa providing shunting services at Dove Holes in the Peak District, working in conjunction with freight operators providing trunk haulage. Victa is also providing 'last mile' services within the Port of Tilbury for Direct Rail Services in connection with a new service from the Port to Daventry and Mossend, launched by Stobart Rail in September 2018.

As well as providing shunting and train preparation for freight operating companies and a number of train operating companies at locations across the country, Victa supplies operations staff on an ad-hoc basis to perform similar duties on engineering possession sites.

INTERCITY RAILFREIGHT

InterCity RailFreight provides for deliveries of goods to and from London using high-speed passenger trains. The first service launched between Nottingham and London, latterly carrying bio samples, and shellfish and other seafood have been transported from Cornwall to London. In 2020 ICRF said it had access to more than 100 125mph daily rail services across the East Midlands, Great Western and CrossCountry networks. The model is based on a door-to-door service, with local couriers using electric vehicles and cargo bikes to connect to trains.

DEVON AND CORNWALL RAILWAYS

Formerly a subsidiary of British American Railway Services Ltd and now part of the Cappagh Group of companies, Devon and Cornwall Railways Ltd (DCRail) is a freight operator based in Derby. Services provided include operation of bulk freight trains and terminals in London. The company recently introduced four Class 60 locomotives to supplement its fleet.

VARAMIS RAIL

Varamis Rail is a new freight operating company which is aiming to deliver a new concept in parcel delivery and provide huge environmental benefits to the country. Based in Doncaster, the company initially plans a concept service between London, Doncaster and Newcastle, followed by expansion to Edinburgh and Glasgow. It would use off-lease passenger EMUs retrofitted to carry parcels. ■

Timber trial: a highlight for the rail freight sector in 2020 was the return of freight to the Far North line in Scotland. Funded by a Scottish Government grant, Victa Railfreight co-ordinated the service from forests in Caithness to the Norbord plant at Dalcross, near Inverness, with trains operated by West Coast Railways. Here Nos 37516/669 head the 6Z69 Georgemas Junction to Inverness loaded timber train at Lothmore on 8 August 2020. **JAMIE SQUIBBS**

INNOVATION AND ENVIRONMENT

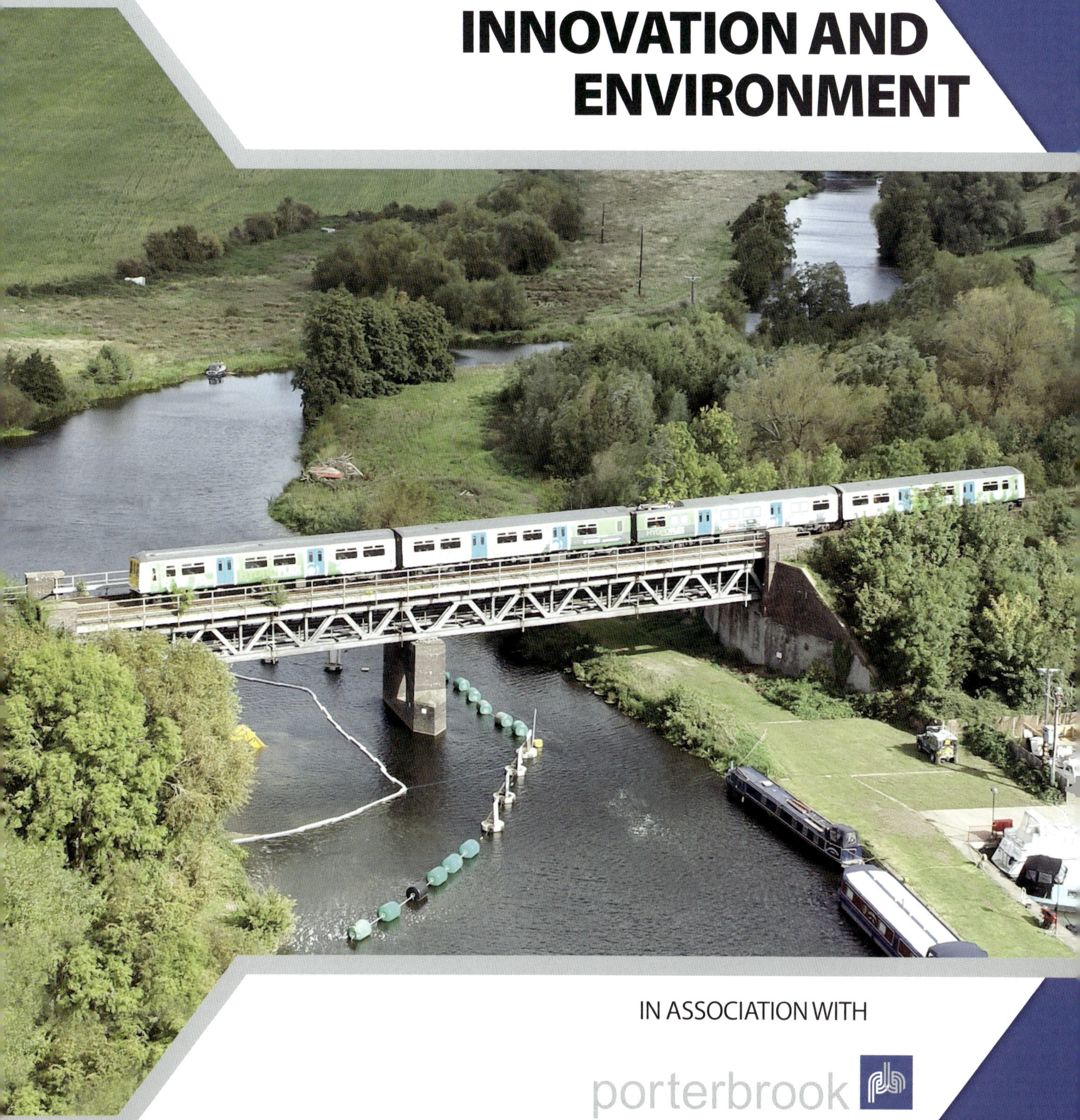

IN ASSOCIATION WITH

porterbrook

INNOVATION AND ENVIRONMENT

The future of Britain's railway depends on people and skills

Porterbrook has been at the heart of Britain's railway for over 25 years.

We own almost one-third of the national passenger train fleet. Our rolling stock supports around 1.5 million passenger journeys and travels over a million miles a day when the railway operates at full capacity.

We see our role as being innovative asset managers as well as financiers. We are long-term players in the UK rail sector – our rolling stock assets have an expected service life of 30-35 years. Making full use of a train's asset life, supported by periodic refurbishments to the latest standards, optimises value to passengers and taxpayers whilst minimising impact on the environment.

Our business is not just about managing trains, it's about our people. Almost three-quarters of our workforce are specialist engineers and rolling stock managers. In addition, over one-third of our workforce is female, including a number of our executive team, which compares favourably to the UK rail industry average of 16%.

Running a railway requires a dedicated and adaptable workforce. That's why we are committed to developing the skills and wellbeing of our people.

Porterbrook recognises the work being done by the government and the industry to ensure rail maintains and develops the number of engineers, technicians, and operational staff it needs to work successfully in the future. The industry's ambitions were set out four years ago in the Rail Sector Skills Delivery Plan.

The National Skills Academy for Rail (NSAR) has identified the industry's key skills requirements in areas such as digital, software and systems engineering as well as leadership and management. The railway also provides employment with a high socio-economic value, so we welcome NSAR's plan to target 20% of the industry's new recruits as coming from 'disadvantaged backgrounds'.

One of the rail industry's great strengths is the collaboration which takes place on skills among operators, asset managers and suppliers. In addition, rail has a relatively low staff turnover, which is beneficial in terms of the retention of institutional memory, although it can lead to a hindering of opportunities for the next generation of talent.

Skills and innovation are key to driving productivity improvements so the rail industry's focus on this is essential for the future. Improving productivity helps to reduce costs and improve output. A key emphasis is on more initial training for young people, more reskilling for people leaving other sectors, as well as a requirement for digital skills at every level. It is vital that specific training targets are established for those workplace roles currently dependent on EU labour. At the higher level, more managerial skills and more training to support the implementation of innovation must be prioritised.

The challenge grows all the more acute with the shifting demography of an ageing workforce, which means there is an urgent need for rail to recruit more widely, particularly in roles ranging from project management to customer service, as well as system specialists and in engineering disciplines. It is critical that rail attracts the right talent at the outset and provides strong support for career development.

There is still much more to be done to attract a broader range of people into the sector at various levels. Recent research for NSAR showed just three in 10 young people are interested in a career in rail, and despite doubling the proportion of women in the industry over the last five years, rail is still perceived as a largely male environment. Furthermore, the industry will need much more focus on technical skills at level 4 and 5. The new management of the National College for Advanced Transportation and Infrastructure (NCATI) can deliver the core skills priorities in rail in the short-term, as well as address wider transport skills in the longer-term.

The industry is working hard to bring about change through outreach work, internships and apprenticeships to build the pipeline of talent. All of us within rail have a responsibility to promote rail and highlight the many benefits that a career on the railway can bring. ∎

Developing skills for the future: Porterbrook CEO Mary Grant (right) and Nottingham South MP and former Transport Committee Chair Lilian Greenwood (left) congratulate the team from Aston University Engineering Academy who won the Porterbrook-sponsored 2018 iRail Grand Skills Challenge.

Workforce development: Porterbrook is committed to advancing the skills and wellbeing of its workforce.

Decarbonisation strategy published

Electrification programme recommended to remove diesel trains

Plans to decarbonise Britain's rail network have advanced, despite the onset of Covid. In September Network Rail published its initial Traction Decarbonisation Network Strategy (TDNS), setting out how to remove diesel trains. This followed the publication in July of the Scottish Government's 'Rail services decarbonisation action plan', explaining ambitions for electrification and alternative traction north of the border (see overleaf).

The roots of the TDNS can be traced back to Rail Minister Jo Johnson's challenge in February 2018 that there should be no diesel-only trains operating on the British network by 2040. This led to the formation of the Rail Industry Decarbonisation Task Force, which produced interim and final reports outlining the feasibility of achieving this ambition. Network Rail then took up the mantle within its System Operator team, systematically examining what the optimum traction solution would be for each line and setting out an end state ambition in the TDNS.

Since 2016, transport has been the largest emitter of greenhouse gases in the UK. While the bulk of that is accounted for by private cars, there is a recognition that rail will need to make its contribution to driving down emissions. RSSB research demonstrates that 85% of energy use in rail is attributable to traction, so while work is underway on decarbonising infrastructure and property it is clear where the priority must lie.

RSSB's research was a key input to the Decarbonisation Task Force. For alternatives to diesel traction, it identified the only technologies likely to be suitable are battery and hydrogen power or electrification. Electrification is the optimal solution for most routes, with the role of battery and hydrogen power likely to emerge as these technologies develop, although as an extensive electrification programme will be take a long time to deliver, batteries and hydrogen will have a role during the transition period, including in bi-mode trains.

Electrification: the Traction Decarbonisation Network Strategy calls for a major programme of wiring. These structures were erected on the Midland main line as part of the Bedford to Corby scheme. **COURTESY NETWORK RAIL**

TDNS OUTPUT

The TDNS suggests that of the 15,400 single track kilometres (stk) of unelectrified rail network in Great Britain today, at least 11,700stk should be electrified.

Of the remainder, the TDNS suggests battery operation for over 400stk and hydrogen for over 900stk. This leaves 2,300stk with no clear technical choice where 'multiple options' could be delivered, and the TDNS identifies an additional 1,340stk of electrification, 400stk of battery operation and 400stk of hydrogen operation for these routes, leaving only 260stk with no clear decision yet.

In the latter scenario, 96% of passenger unit kilometres would be operated using electric traction and the remaining 4% by hydrogen and battery units, while for freight around 90% of train kilometres could be operated electrically, with the remainder requiring diesel or alternative traction. Modelling suggests the residual emissions in this scenario would be around 50 million kg CO_2e per year, equivalent to just 3% of today's total traction emissions.

TDNS estimates delivering on these recommendations is likely to cost between £18 and £26 billion at 2020 prices, most of which comes from the cost of electrification. This is 1.7 to 2.4 times the total Control Period 6 (2019-24) enhancements budget and would be spread over at least five Control Periods. Capital costs for battery charging points and hydrogen refuelling locations were also estimated based on an RSSB study.

PATHWAYS

Five pathways to deliver are identified based on differing rates of delivering electrification (Table 1). Pathways 3, 4 and 5 see all passenger emissions removed, with some residual emissions from freight operation. Removing these freight emissions as well would require an additional 2,100stk of electrification at a capital cost increase of £3 to £4 billion. The TDNS estimates associated rolling stock costs as £15 to £17 billion for passenger trains (3,600 to 3,800 electric and 150 to 200 battery and hydrogen trains) and £3 to £4 billion for freight locomotives, leading to a combined capital cost of £36 to £47 billion. However, the need for interim solutions will likely increase the number of battery and hydrogen trains needed in the short-term.

Of the five pathways, pathway 4, with the highest rate of electrification needed, is not considered feasible unless there is 'an unprecedented change in delivery capability'. The target rate of electrification is around 450stk per year, which is at the upper end of recent periods of significant electrification delivery as highlighted in the Railway Industry Association's Electrification Cost Challenge. The TDNS cautions that while it appears in principle to be feasible to deliver the volumes of electrification needed to achieve zero emissions by 2050, consideration needs to be given 'around the efficiency of delivery and the disruption impact on the rail network'. It also highlights the challenge of rebuilding the capability to efficiently deliver electrification, with RIA analysis suggesting this requires a gradual build-up over several years and a commitment to 'a stable and efficient programme of work'. It is recommended specialist delivery teams are employed who consistently move from project to project, each delivering 75 to 100 stk per year.

Capital costs for the programme were estimated by dividing the unelectrified network into 151 segments and estimating based on a cost of between £1 million and £2.5 million per stk, dependent on complexity. The highest Net Present Values (NPV) are for pathways 2, 3 and 5, which are also found to be the most cost-efficient.

DON'T BUY DMUs

Among further recommendations made in the TDNS is that diesel-only trains should not be bought unless there are 'clear strategic and economic reasons for doing so', and if this is the case diesel engines should be replaceable with a zero-carbon solution in future. It is also recommended any new railways should consider the need to operate using zero-carbon rolling stock. The TDNS urges that battery and hydrogen train operations should start 'wherever this is possible to ensure standards are developed, whole-system operational experience is gained, and lessons are learned'. Projects and programmes should be continued to support modal shift to rail, drawing on the strategic and economic benefits of decarbonisation and modal shift in their business case, particularly for freight projects because of the significant modal shift they deliver. ■

TABLE 1: PATHWAYS TO DECARBONISATION – ELECTRIFICATION REQUIREMENT

TRACTION DECARBONISATION PATHWAY	AVERAGE ANNUAL STK OF ELECTRIFICATION	MAXIMUM STK OF ELECTRIFICATION IN ANY ONE YEAR
Pathway 1 (-80%)	259	377
Pathway 2 (-95%)	303	447
Pathway 3 (net-zero by 2050)	355	691
Pathway 4 (net-zero by 2040)	658	922
Pathway 5 (net-zero by 2061)	303	447

Source: TDNS; stk = single track kilometres

INNOVATION AND ENVIRONMENT

Alternative traction locations set out

CrossCountry and freight drive TDNS recommendations

An overriding theme of the Traction Decarbonisation Network Strategy is the way freight and CrossCountry drive its recommendation for an extensive electrification programme.

The TDNS sets out proposals for which technology (electrification, battery or hydrogen) should be applied on which routes, with a more detailed prioritisation to follow in a Programme Business Case, which was due for completion in October 2020.

Proposals within the TDNS for Scotland were aligned with those in the Scottish Government's own decarbonisation plan (see opposite).

EASTERN

Eastern Region requires the most significant volumes of electrification. A starting point is existing projects on the Midland main line and trans-Pennine routes. Freight is also a key determinant of requirements, with major routes from Teesport, Felixstowe, London Gateway, Doncaster and Immingham all requiring electrification, as do routes serving aggregates flows in Yorkshire and the Midlands. Other key passenger considerations are major CrossCountry flows, while the Leeds suburban network is proposed to be fully electrified. Alternative traction is proposed for areas around the North East and coastal areas of East Anglia.

SOUTHERN

Within Southern region most of the network is currently electrified at 750V DC third rail, so introducing 25kV overhead electrification would require new skills and experience in delivery and maintenance, and the study says further work on this is needed. A key consideration is the Southampton to Basingstoke corridor, currently electrified at third rail but also used by CrossCountry and freight services, with options including residual diesel emissions through to conversion to 25kV overhead line.

The TDNS says providing a 25kV overhead system on infill sections between third rail in Sussex and Kent 'does not make operational sense'. Work is underway between NR, RSSB and the Office of Rail and Road to establish the feasibility of providing a modern-day conductor rail system for these areas, which is due to report in late 2021. The role of third rail in supporting freight services is also suggested as a topic for further investigation. Once TDNS projects are completed, the possibility of converting third rail routes to overhead electrification is mooted, but this is highly unlikely until 2050-2060 at the earliest.

WALES AND WESTERN

Requirements within the Wales and Western Region are determined by complex freight movements from quarries, wharfs and ports. Extension of Great Western electrification beyond Cardiff and Bristol is required, as is coverage of the CrossCountry network. Diversionary routes are also a key consideration, while deployment of alternative traction is focused on Devon and Cornwall branch lines and regional routes in central Wales, with battery and hydrogen both required.

NORTH WEST AND CENTRAL

Freight routes are also critical within the North West and Central region, with the West Coast main line being one of the busiest freight corridors in the UK, while the CrossCountry network is again a key consideration. Electrification of the Chiltern main line from London to Birmingham is suggested to be followed by routes to Aylesbury, Stratford-upon-Avon and north of Birmingham Snow Hill, while existing WCML services into Shrewsbury and North Wales would also convert to electric operation. Further north, routes into Manchester via the Castlefield corridor are highlighted for electrification, with existing North West and trans-Pennine projects providing an opportunity to retain skills and experience. Although not currently committed, it is assumed East West Rail will be electrified 'to some extent', meaning wider electrification would be needed beyond the EWR core. Most routes not provided with electrification are likely to utilise battery operation. ■

AREAS FOR ALTERNATIVE TRACTION – SINGLE OPTION SOLUTIONS

BATTERY
- Bishop Auckland to Darlington and Whitby
- Ulceby to Barton-on-Humber
- Sheffield to Huddersfield via Penistone
- Derby to Matlock
- Thames Valley branches (Marlow, Henley and Windsor)
- Cornish branches (Gunnislake, Looe, Falmouth and St Ives)
- Bidston to Wrexham

HYDROGEN
- Norwich to Great Yarmouth/Lowestoft
- Norwich to Sheringham

AREAS FOR ALTERNATIVE TRACTION – MULTIPLE OPTION SOLUTIONS

These areas have no clear technological choice for decarbonisation technology development, although in some cases the TDNS suggests an optimal solution.

ELECTRIFICATION OPTIMAL
- Deepcar freight branch
- Derby to Stoke-on-Trent
- Norwich to Ely
- Fawley branch
- Par to Newquay
- Droitwich Spa to Birmingham Snow Hill
- Stratford-upon-Avon to Chiltern main line
- Marylebone to Aylesbury via Amersham
- Mid-Cheshire line (east of West Coast main line)

BATTERY OPTIMAL
- Dorchester to Castle Cary
- Llandudno to Blaenau Ffestiniog
- Ebbw Vale branch

HYDROGEN OPTIMAL
- Shrewsbury to Aberystwyth/Pwllheli
- Central Wales line (Craven Arms to Llanelli)

ELECTRIFICATION OR BATTERY
- Scarborough to York
- Leeds to York via Harrogate (electrification to Harrogate)
- Newmarket to Cambridge
- Mark's Tey to Sudbury
- Severn Beach branch
- Windermere to Oxenholme
- Morecambe/Heysham branch (electrification to Morecambe)
- Colne to Blackburn
- Blackpool South branch
- Southport to Wigan
- Mid-Cheshire line (west of West Coast main line)

ELECTRIFICATION OR HYDROGEN
- Saltburn to Middlesbrough
- Skegness to Grantham
- Barnstaple to Exmouth

ELECTRIFICATION AND BATTERY OR HYDROGEN
- Hull to Scarborough (electrification to Beverley)

THIRD RAIL ELECTRIFICATION OR BATTERY
- Isle of Grain branch
- Aldershot to Wokingham
- Redhill to Guildford
- Uckfield branch
- Ashford to Hastings

IN ASSOCIATION WITH porterbrook

SCOTLAND'S PLAN TO MEET 2035 DECARBONISATION TARGET

All inter-city routes to be electrified north of the border

Scotland's plan to decarbonise its rail network is more ambitious than that of the UK Government. Set out in the 'Rail services decarbonisation action plan' published in July 2020, the aim is that by 2045 the only non-electrified routes in Scotland would be the Far North line north of Tain, the Kyle of Lochalsh line, the West Highland line and the stretch from Girvan to Stranraer. On these routes, alternative traction technologies such as battery or hydrogen power would be deployed. Achieving this end state would require 130 single track kilometres of electrification per year.

As of early 2020 just over 40% of Scotland's track was electrified, although 76% of passenger journeys were made using electric traction and around 45% of Scottish rail freight journeys were electrically hauled from origin to destination. The Scottish Government has invested extensively in electrification in recent years, and the action plan states that in the last two years the number of ScotRail passengers carried on electrified services has increased by around 23%. Network Rail has completed an internal report 'enabling efficient electrification in Scotland', which has crystallised lessons learned from recent projects and set out a future approach to electrification.

In addition to electrification, Scotland intends to adopt alternative traction technologies, including electric/battery bi-modes, which could unlock the benefits of using electric traction earlier in the rollout, as well as non-diesel traction types such as battery or hydrogen power. A project to develop a hydrogen prototype through conversion of a redundant Class 314 EMU is underway.

Given the scale of ambition, the electrification programme is not expected to be completed by 2035, the Scottish Government's deadline for a decarbonised rail network. Instead, alternative traction, potentially bi-modes, will be used as a transition solution on parts of the network, including the central section of the Aberdeen to Inverness line, the Far North line between Inverness and Tain and Ayr to Girvan in south west Scotland. These routes would all be electrified by 2045, leaving only a few routes using either hydrogen or battery power.

Early candidates for electrification are the routes from Glasgow to East Kilbride and Barrhead, where planning has already commenced, and onward to Kilmarnock, as well as Glasgow to Anniesland via Maryhill, the Borders line from Edinburgh to Tweedbank, the Levenmouth branch (proposed for reopening) and discrete sections in Fife as a precursor to a fully electrified route. Design and development work was also being progressed during 2020 for the route from Dunblane to Perth.

The aim by 2035 is to have fully electrified routes from the central belt to both Aberdeen and Inverness. The route between Glasgow and Carlisle via Gretna is also slated for full electrification, providing strategic capacity for rail freight and a diversionary route when the West Coast main line is closed. The action plan highlights that electrification is the only viable option for rail freight to decarbonise.

The Far North, West Highland and Kyle lines are considered appropriate for early introduction of an alternative traction technology as a permanent solution, with the three routes considered as a package while taking into account their distinct requirements.

Network Rail's Traction Decarbonisation Network Strategy mirrors the conclusions of the Scottish Government's action plan in its recommendations for Scotland.

ROLLING PROGRAMME

Detailed cost analysis by route has not yet been undertaken, but the Scottish Government says it will maintain its previous level of commitment to rail investment. The plan will be updated and refined as schemes progress, with a further review planned in spring 2023 to cover Control Periods 7 and 8 (2024-34).

While it is accepted that the proposed rate of electrification is challenging, the action plan highlights recent delivery of a number of electrification projects in the central belt. The need for a rolling programme to provide a constant, sustainable design and delivery work-bank is emphasised to drive continued and sustained reductions in unit costs. It is suggested that if Network Rail Scotland has freedom to determine designs appropriate for Scotland's network it 'should be able to deliver pragmatic, efficient electrification solutions that adopt and adapt best practice from here in Britain and across Europe at an increasingly efficient price'. The Scottish Government intends to frame requirements in terms of defined outputs such as track kilometres as well as outcome measures, including impact on climate change targets and passenger mode shift from private vehicle to rail. ■

Early electrification candidate: the line from Glasgow to Kilmarnock. This is ScotRail's No 156511 at Kilmarnock on 25 September 2019 with the 14.13 Glasgow Central to Stranraer service. **PHILIP SHERRATT**

INNOVATION AND ENVIRONMENT

Top innovations celebrated

Network Rail leads the field at the Railway Industry Innovation Awards

The 23rd annual Railway Industry Innovation Awards was unique. After successive ceremonies held in London as part of *Modern Railways* Fourth Friday Club meetings, the Covid pandemic meant the awards moved online for the first time. After being postponed from the summer, the celebration of the top innovations in the rail industry was held on 23 October.

Following a keynote speech from Helen Waters, Associate Director at Steer Group, prizes were presented in eight categories. In addition to the usual seven awards, the judges created an eighth category recognising innovations responding to the Covid crisis.

It was an excellent year for Network Rail at the awards, amid a strong field of entries. Recognising the breadth of innovation going on within the company, the award for a Large Project was presented to Network Rail's R&D portfolio. The company also picked up two other trophies – its work to monitor tree health through hyperspectral remote sensing earned it the Environment award, while the rapid production of 40,000 protective visors picked up the prize in the special Covid response category.

There was a varied mix of winners in the other five categories. Resonate's Luminate Traffic Management System, in use on Network Rail's Western Route, picked up the Operations and Performance award, while LNER's 'Let's Eat – At Your Seat' took the Passenger Experience prize. ActiWheel GS, a novel technical solution to reducing wheel wear, saw Stored Energy Technology Ltd pick up the Engineering and Safety award, while Porterbrook's Innovation Hub was recognised for the collaboration it fostered and took the Cross-Industry Partnership prize. Lastly, One Big Circle's Automated Intelligent Video Review platform, described as a Google Earth for rail, won the prize for a Small Scale project.

GOLDEN SPANNERS HIGHLIGHT RISING RELIABILITY

Awarded each year at a ceremony in November, the *Modern Railways* Golden Spanner awards celebrate the achievements of rolling stock depots in increasing the reliability of their fleets. Awards are made in categories based on the type and age of train concerned, with awards for the most reliable and most improved fleets plus the fleet generating the fewest delay minutes per incident. The 2020 awards were held online on 27 November.

The National Task Force (NTF) is the pan-industry body responsible for improving reliability of the railway. Within NTF, 'ReFocus' covers traction and rolling stock and publishes a monthly report for each fleet, which is the basis for the Golden Spanners. A casualty is reported if a train is stopped by a technical issue for more than three minutes, when a Technical Incident Notice (TIN) is recorded.

GOLDEN WHISTLES FOR BEST PERFORMERS

Skilful operators can make the trains run safely and on time – and the best operators deserve recognition.

For this reason, the Institution of Railway Operators and *Modern Railways* magazine joined forces to launch the Golden Whistle Awards. These awards acknowledge best practice and congratulate railway operators and infrastructure managers (including passenger and freight operators, Network Rail, London Underground and Irish Rail) that have done a good job by rewarding them with that ultimate symbol of smart operating – a whistle.

Based on objective data, awards are presented for best and most improved performance in categories including on time performance and minimising delays. Awards for outstanding operator are also given out, based on nominations judged by a panel of senior figures from the IRO.

The 2020 awards, held on 24 January, once again adopted the industry's new 'On Time' figures which measure performance at every recorded station stop.

THE FOURTH FRIDAY CLUB

The *Modern Railways* Fourth Friday Club provides a unique networking forum for executives from all sectors in the railway industry. As well as the three awards events, three regional conferences focus on developments in the Midlands, the North of England, and Wales and the West. Since the first meeting in 2003, the growing reputation of the club for attracting senior policy makers and top railway managers as guest speakers has seen membership expand rapidly. For more information visit www.keymodernrailways.com/fourth-friday-club. ∎

RVE SUCCUMBS TO COVID

The Covid pandemic forced the cancellation of Modern Railways RVE 2020, the original dedicated show for the rolling stock sector. Due to take place on 5 November, the show will instead return bigger and better on 4 November 2021.

Although the exhibition could not take place, the industry leading RVE Meet The Buyer event was held in an online format. RVE Meet The Buyer is co-ordinated by Rail Forum Midlands and gives companies from the supply chain the opportunity to pitch their products and services to buyers from leading organisations in the rolling stock sector. Eighteen companies participated as buyers in the 2020 event, continuing the success of this major attraction within Modern Railways RVE.

Fourth Friday Club: due to the Covid pandemic, the only in-person event held during 2020 was the Golden Whistle awards on 24 January. The keynote speaker was Alex Hynes, MD of Scotland's Railway, while a morning conference featured a presentation from Network Rail Chief Executive Andrew Haines. **TONY MILES**

NEW WEBSITE LAUNCH

YOUR ONLINE HOME FOR MODERN railways

Key Modern Railways is the **NEW** online home of rail industry content, brought to you by Key Publishing, publishers of *Modern Railways* magazine.

You'll find all the latest industry news, written with authority, on Key Modern Railways - plus detailed analysis, in-depth features and website exclusives.

UNLIMITED access to this exciting online content from our dedicated team starts from just £41.99/year for UK customers. And registering couldn't be simpler. For instant access to the latest *Modern Railways* magazine features and industry-leading content, visit:

www.keymodernrailways.com

Philip Sherratt
Editor - *Modern Railways* Magazine
& Key Modern Railways

FREE ACCESS FOR ALL **modern railways** SUBSCRIBERS*

Visit: www.keymodernrailways.com/subscribe

Free access available for a limited time only – sign up today!

We value your feedback! Let us know your thoughts on *Key Modern Railways* – drop us a line at subs@keypublishing.com today

INNOVATION AND ENVIRONMENT

BACK TO BASICS?

Community Rail Partnership Chairman **Alan Williams** warns that, with a rail funding crisis looming, we need to remind ourselves why community rail first came into being and what it has shown it can do

From six Partnerships tasked 15 years ago with promoting services on branch lines perceived as threatened with closure, what is now the Community Rail Network supports over 70 Community Rail Partnerships and over 1,000 station adoption groups, all expanding the role and influence of the railway across the country by engaging in and supporting social, environmental and economic initiatives. There are now thousands of people actively supporting these groups – collectively more than any single Train Operating Company (TOC) – providing their time and considerable expertise for free in a way most industries can only dream of. But it all came shuddering almost to a halt in March when the Prime Minister announced the lockdown.

Timetables were slashed, promotional events were summarily cancelled, station adopters were banned from platforms – even those who lived in the adjacent station houses – and the remainder of the active volunteer workforce ordered to stay at home, many being, by virtue of their age, required to self-isolate.

But, undeterred by fewer trains and even fewer passengers, within days those that could concentrated on helping others in their communities who couldn't. Some prepared and delivered meals to those who were housebound by the pandemic, others made and sold masks to raise funds, while yet others maintained contact with their communities online, for example organising online conversations for the lonely. Nor were local businesses ignored. Groups posted details of which local shops and other essential services remained available. Thus many more people were introduced to community rail activity for the first time.

Nevertheless, Partnerships which had spent years actively encouraging and promoting rail travel now found themselves required to support the various TOC versions of the Government's 'Don't travel unless it is really necessary' messages, the exact opposite of what they were set up to do. Instead of promoting services, Groups concentrated on advising those 'essential workers' of the seemingly almost weekly changes to timetables as first lockdown reduced numbers to near-zero, and then later, as restrictions were eased, trains were added back in.

On my rural line services went from six trains a day, including a new early morning train that had only been introduced weeks earlier, first to three and then to just one each way. On some lines, services were withdrawn altogether, with either a bus replacement or, if you were really unlucky, nothing at all. These draconian reductions were driven not only by shortage of crews but exacerbated by the apparent insistence of the Department for Transport that available rolling stock be used to strengthen remaining

services on lines into city centres to allow social distancing to continue.

That decision seemed unfair to many. It was certainly roundly condemned in rural areas where, unlike in urban environments, no alternative public transport was available. In the event, despite the continued demand from Government that people should still not travel by rail, even though other restrictions were relaxed, the sheer number of people furloughed or otherwise not at work, coupled with ongoing uncertainty about overseas travel, meant leisure travel by rail, particularly to coastal resorts, recovered more quickly than commuter traffic. Community Rail Partnerships reported leisure travel outside the peak was becoming greater than commuter travel, with the result that while almost empty 12-coach trains served largely deserted city centre termini in London and elsewhere, trains on lines to the coast, including mine, had to be doubled in length to maintain social distancing.

All this means the almost total shutdown of some lines has not only left Community Rail Partnerships needing to re-establish their activities in a post-Covid environment, but also going back to basics in rebuilding ridership almost from scratch. The exceptional temporary peak summer levels of leisure ridership have faded away and CRPs are now faced with the long-term task of attracting customers anew back to rail. Months of being told not to go near a railway station, coupled with a dramatic fall in road fuel prices and a hike in rail ticket prices threatened for the turn of the year, has made this a big ask. People have been persuaded that they are safer in their cars when, as Jools Townsend, Chief Executive of Community Rail Network points out, in reality you are many, many more times safer on a train compared to on the road, whether in a car, walking or cycling.

After a further series of timetable changes as services were restored, my own line is now back to where it was in March 2020. But not yet in ridership. It is clear it is going to take time to get back to anything like the previous normal level. Some predictions are that it might be several years. Government has made it clear that in the longer-term

Supporting the Shakespeare line: the Shakespeare Line Promotion Group is the CRP for the lines to Stratford-upon-Avoun. Launching a new poster advertising the group's work are Ian Taylor, Station Manager for Dorridge & Stratford lines at West Midlands Railway (left) and Fraser Pithie, Secretary of the Shakespeare Line Promotion Group. **COURTESY SLPG**

Serving the Portsmouth Direct line: the Surrey Hills to South Downs CRP gained accreditation in 2020 for its work covering the Haslemere to Farnscombe area, having been formed 12 months earlier. **COURTESY SWR**

Hope Valley: the Manchester to Sheffield line is served by the High Peak and Hope Valley Community Rail Partnership, which also covers routes to Buxton and Glossop. Northern's Nos 150113/222 pass Edale with a Sheffield to Manchester Piccadilly service on 24 June 2020. **PHILIP SHERRATT**

the country cannot go on subsidising rail at anything like the level seen in the first few months of the pandemic. There is a fear that if further surges in the virus require the imposition of more restrictions, services may again be reduced or even withdrawn altogether, not necessarily directly because of the pandemic but in the face of financial crisis, and that despite the damage to local communities that would result, CRP lines may again be in the frontline for cuts.

TRY THE TRAIN!

Promoting more rail travel in all its forms – commuting, business, and particularly leisure – is therefore once more the primary objective of the movement. In this it needs the wholehearted support of Government. However you see it, at present the railway has only two sources of financial support – passengers through the farebox and taxpayers through the Treasury. Worryingly, the Train Operating Companies have not so far seemed to be as swift in actively promoting rail travel again, with for example special offers and fares, as they were to encourage people not to travel when the lockdown descended.

Early indications are that the reduction in peak time commuting and the greater demand for rural services that we saw when lockdown was lifted is continuing. This implies city centres will become more leisure orientated and less business focused, with remote, home-based working meaning commuting may never return to pre-March 2020 levels. In contrast, estate agents are already reporting a definite and so far undiminished surge in demand for rural properties, suggesting the beginning of a permanent population drift away from traditional suburban commuting, in turn implying a growing demand for rural transport services in the future.

One result of the pandemic that is already clear is the huge increase in the number of people walking and cycling for leisure. On my line, a large part of which is in a National Park, support has been secured from

INNOVATION AND ENVIRONMENT

the National Lottery funded 'Land of Iron' project to provide permanent displays on each station, including maps detailing walks to the various local industrial heritage sites. Catering for the growing band of cyclists wishing to travel with their machines is however more of a problem in that the current generation of trains provide scant accommodation for bikes. For several years CRPs, including mine, have been pushing for the conversion of redundant rolling stock into 'bike carriers' which can be coupled to existing services on those lines where the demand is greatest. The idea has been taken up in Scotland for services in the Highlands, but not yet south of the border.

Community rail leaders at both local and government level will need to emphasise these unprecedented and quite possibly permanent changes in demand to planners and ensure they react appropriately. One issue already becoming apparent is that, if commuter services fail to recover to pre-Covid levels, the present glut of not yet life expired electrically powered rolling stock will be compounded, whereas the ongoing shortage of almost entirely diesel-powered trains that are currently required for most secondary and rural lines, let alone any additional resources that may be needed, will inevitably be worsened. With still no Government commitment to major new rail electrification, the race is on to develop battery or hydrogen sources of power for electric trains.

Experience has shown that direct exhortations to 'support our line' or 'use it or lose it' garner less ongoing media interest and therefore less public support than the organisation of social events that bring people back onto the railway – even some for the first time. These may take the form of music and ale trains, special trains with entertainment for children or, as on my line, for those in society who do not or are not normally able to travel by train, such as people with learning difficulties or living with dementia, so community rail people will be anxious to resume such activities as soon as practicable.

Environmental concerns, too, are increasingly coming to the fore. The renewed rise in private car use as a result of the pandemic and the associated increase in pollution levels back to or even above the pre-March 2020 level is pushing government decarbonisation targets firmly in the wrong direction. However, the near collapse of the aviation industry and the associated demise of many domestic flights and those to destinations on the near continent present a new opportunity for long-distance rail travel, particularly if it can capitalise on the huge environmental advantages in the reduction of CO_2 that rail travel offers over air. But the last few miles are just as important. The old adage, ignored for so long in the Beeching era and for several decades after, that success requires 'both robust routes and healthy branches' remains as true as ever.

YOUR RAILWAY NEEDS YOU!

Surviving the effects of the pandemic and building anew are not the only challenges facing community rail. Another is the decline in volunteers, becoming evident even before Covid-19 forced many into self-isolation. The gradual increase in the age at which people now retire plus the ever expanding number of organisations looking for volunteer assistance, particularly those in the health and rescue sectors, means there are simply fewer and fewer people with time available.

Another concern among many in the community rail movement is the apparent decline in interest at the Department for Transport and the implications, given that Government is now funding the network. Look at the DfT's own chart of its top 200 people – who it modestly describes as 'brilliant' – and you will find those in charge of such nationally important issues as the Government Car Service. But not a mention anywhere of community rail. Such concerns are now increasingly left to the Train Operating Companies, which display varying degrees of interest and support, both physical and financial, for community rail. And with all the TOCs financially distressed as a result of Covid-19 and beholden to Government for support, there are important questions about continued levels of funding for community rail in the future.

Those concerns are linked to the question of visibility of community rail within the rail industry, and specifically within individual TOCs. I know from my own experience that the awareness of what community rail does, what it can offer and how it can help those in the industry tackle their jobs more effectively still varies enormously – some are very helpful and supportive but others far less so, giving the impression they would rather you went away. Since community rail sits alongside but is not part of the Train Operating Companies it works with, and therefore has no specific authority beyond its accreditation and thus relies essentially on goodwill to proceed and progress, that can sometimes prove to be difficult.

Community rail undoubtedly has an important role to play in the recovery of both the rail network and the communities it serves. But for best effect, it requires the fulsome support of both Government and rail industry, please. ■

Alan Williams is Chairman of the Esk Valley Rail Development Company, established in 2003 and the Community Rail Partnership for the Middlesbrough to Whitby line.

Tyne Valley line: No 158817 works Northern's 10.23 Carlisle to Newcastle service at Riding Mill on 14 September 2020. BILL WELSH

MAJOR PROJECTS

IN ASSOCIATION WITH

TOTALKARE
POWERED BY EMANUEL

MAJOR PROJECTS

HS2 gets building

High-speed line gets the go-ahead

2020 was certainly a landmark year for HS2. After starting the year with its future hanging in the balance, the project to construct a new high-speed line received Government backing and then got the green light to begin main construction works on the Phase One route from London to the West Midlands.

The Government had commissioned the Oakervee review to examine the project in detail. While the review suggested further work is needed on some elements of the specification, it was clear the project should not be cancelled. Prime Minister Boris Johnson confirmed the Government was giving HS2 the 'green signal' in February, although his statement was laced with criticism for some of HS2 Ltd's actions, particularly its engagement with lineside neighbours.

The Oakervee review suggested the full HS2 network is needed to realise the scheme's benefits, with Phase One alone making 'little sense'. Design optimisation is suggested for Phase 2b to reduce costs and negative impacts, for example by redesigning alignments. The review also ruled out making Old Oak Common the permanent southern terminus for HS2 but suggested the design for the central London terminus at Euston should be reviewed and therefore Old Oak Common would be used as a temporary terminus initially.

Following the approval from Government, 'Notice to Proceed' was issued in April, meaning HS2 could fully mobilise its main works civils contracts and get construction underway on Phase One, announced as formally starting in September. Phase 2a, from the West Midlands to Crewe, needs to complete its legislative journey before receiving approval, and is planned to be completed concurrent with Phase One. Phase 2b, covering Crewe to Manchester and the West Midlands to Leeds, is the subject of further review.

COST AND SCHEDULE

With publication of the business case for Phase One of HS2, Government has confirmed the cost and schedule for opening of the high-speed line.

Phase One is expected to cost between £35 and £45 billion, while Phase 2a, planned to open at the same time, has a central cost estimate of £4.4 billion. A phased opening will start with passenger services between Old Oak Common in west London and Birmingham Curzon Street between 2029 and 2033. This initial service is planned to comprise six trains per hour (tph), with 3tph from London to Birmingham and 1tph each to Liverpool, Manchester and Glasgow.

The stretch from Old Oak Common into the central London terminus is planned to open between 2031 and 2036. Once the line to Euston is complete, HS2 services would increase to 10tph from London, with 3tph to each of Manchester and Birmingham, 1tph to Liverpool, 1tph to Glasgow, 1tph to Macclesfield via Stafford and Stoke-on-Trent and 1tph splitting at Crewe with portions for Liverpool and Lancaster. The Macclesfield service would use the Handsacre connection from HS2 onto the West Coast main line in Staffordshire; this was recommended for removal in the Oakervee review, although Government has chosen not to accept this recommendation. Most high-speed services would continue via Phase 2a to join the West Coast main line further north.

PHASE 2B UNDER REVIEW

The business case stated Phase 2b has a central cost estimate of £28.7 billion, but its future is uncertain and Phase 2b is set to be broken down into a series of smaller hybrid bills to speed up the legislative process.

A clear indication that the Crewe to Manchester link would be prioritised came in October 2020 when HS2 Ltd began consultation on changes to this section. These included changes to station designs at Manchester Airport and Manchester Piccadilly, aimed to align HS2 with emerging Northern Powerhouse Rail proposals and provide better interchange with the Metrolink light rail network. Also added was a Crewe Northern Connection, supporting plans for a Crewe Hub station, and a train stabling facility at Annandale in Dumfries and Galloway.

This consultation raised fears the eastern leg of HS2 from the West Midlands to Leeds via the East Midlands and South Yorkshire may be removed from the scope altogether, although this has been consistently denied by ministers. An Integrated Rail Plan setting out the best phasing for HS2 with Northern Powerhouse Rail, Midlands Engine Rail and other enhancements was due to be published by the end of 2020.

Another suggestion in the Oakervee review was to cut the planned frequency when HS2 is complete to 14tph, but HS2 Minister Andrew Stephenson confirmed the Government does not favour this option, suggesting it would save only a 'very small amount of cost'. The Oakervee review proposed a 14tph service with the potential to move to 16tph later.

HS2's business case suggests a 17tph service from London when the full network opens with an 18th path for redundancy.

MAIN WORKS MOBILISED

The issuing of Notice to Proceed in April 2020 granted formal approval for the main design and construction phases of HS2 to get underway. HS2 Ltd awarded four main works civils contracts to joint venture organisations in July 2017 covering the route from London to the West Midlands, and having initially focused on scheme design and site preparation these have transitioned to full detailed design and construction.

The four contracts are together valued at £12 billion. Beginning at the south end of the route, SCS Railways (Skanska, Costain and Strabag) has the contracts covering Euston Tunnels and Approaches and Northolt Tunnels, valued together at £3.298 billion.

The contract for the Chiltern Tunnels and Colne Valley viaduct (package C1) is held by the Align JV comprising Bouygues Travaux Publics, Sir Robert McAlpine and VolkerFitzpatrick, valued at £1.6 billion. This section starts around 20km west of central London and features 21.6km of high-speed line, including the 3.37km viaduct across the Colne Valley and a 16.04km twin-bored tunnel with five ventilation shafts.

EKBF JV, comprising Eiffage, Kier, Bam Nuttall and Ferrovial Agroman, is the contractor for lots C2 and C3, covering the North Portal Chiltern Tunnels to Brackley and Brackley to South Portal of Long Itchington Wood Green Tunnel sections, totalling 80km in length. The section includes 15 viaducts, 5km of green tunnels, 22km of road diversions, 67 overbridges and 30 million cubic metres of excavation, with a total contract value of £2.269 billion.

The fourth contractor, and most significant by value, is the BBV JV of Balfour Beatty and Vinci. Valued at £4.8 billion, it holds the contracts covering Long Itchington Wood

Chiltern tunnel TBMs: Herrenknect in Germany is supplied two tunnel boring machines for the twin Chiltern tunnels, named *Florence* (foreground) and *Cecilia*.

Preparing for tunnelling: work in progress on the south portal site for the long tunnel through the Chilterns.

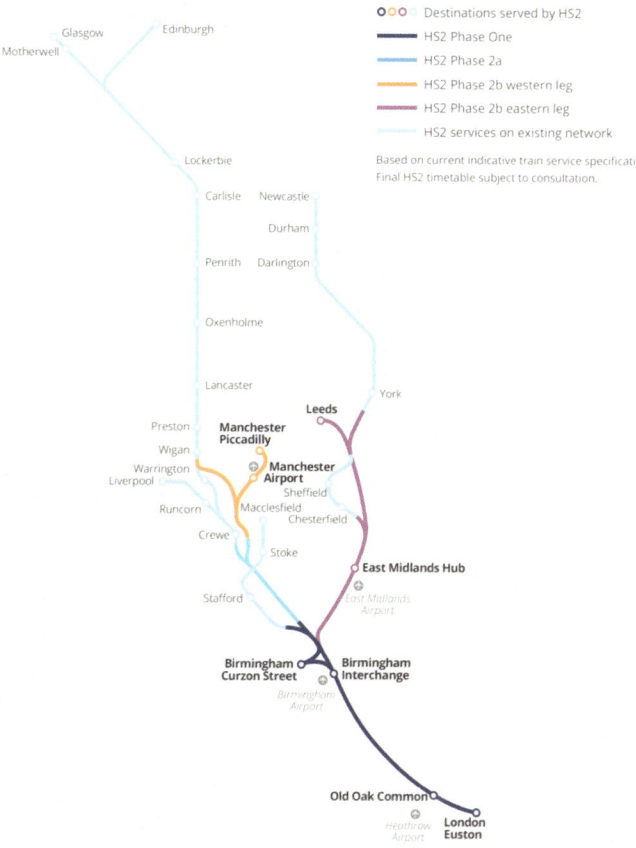

Route map: plan of HS2 routes; note how Phase 2b has been divided into distinct sections, reflecting the prioritisation of the Crewe to Manchester stretch.

MAJOR PROJECTS

First freight delivery: the maiden rail freight delivery of aggregate arrived at HS2's Washwood Heath site in Birmingham on 25 August 2020. Rail Stone Solutions and haulage partner GB Railfreight are delivering stone from quarries in the Peak District to the site. HS2 Ltd says over the next decade up to 15,000 freight trains will haul 10 million tonnes of aggregate to HS2 construction sites.

Green Tunnel to Delta Junction and Birmingham Spur and the Delta Junction to West Coast main line tie-in (Handsacre Junction), totalling 90 route kilometres.

TUNNELS

A major milestone for HS2 will be the start of tunnelling on the 16km Chiltern tunnels, the longest on HS2, scheduled for April 2021. Herrenknecht in Germany is supplying two tunnel boring machines (TBMs), which will be named *Florence* and *Cecilia*. The Align JV's work during summer 2020 concentrated on preparing the South Chalfont portal for the launch.

The Align JV will also build the longest of more than 50 viaducts on the Phase One route – the 3.4km structure crossing the Colne Valley.

Construction work on Phase One will require 10 TBMs in total, six of them to work in the London area. In October the SCS JV awarded the first contracts for TBMs for the London area, with two machines to be delivered by Herrenknecht by the end of 2021. These two TBMs will be launched from West Ruislip and will travel east for five miles to Greenford, creating the west section of the Northolt Tunnel, with tunnelling running from mid-2022 to the start of 2024. A further two TBMs will build the eastern section of Northolt Tunnel while two more will excavate the tunnels between Old Oak Common and Euston.

August 2020 saw the installation of HS2's first permanent structure – a bridge over the M42 near Solihull in the West Midlands. This is part of work on the delta junction towards the northern end of Phase One where the line into central Birmingham will diverge from that continuing northwards towards Crewe and to Handsacre, where trains can join the West Coast main line. The delta junction will be 9.5km long and consists of seven bridges and viaducts spanning three rail lines, eight roads, five rivers and canals and the M6 motorway. A second structure, a bridge over the A446, was driven into place in late October.

STATIONS

Work is also progressing on the four stations on Phase One.

At Euston, the joint venture of Mace and Dragados appointed by HS2 as construction partner in March 2019 moved onto the site to begin work in July 2020. Early works include piling for the basement wall of the station in advance of large-scale excavations and sub-structure works in 2021.

The Old Oak Common site in west London was handed over to station construction partner BBVS (a joint venture of Balfour Beatty, Vinci and Systra) in July 2020, following enabling works by a joint venture of Costain and Skanska. The station will have a total of 14 platforms serving the high-speed line and the Great Western main line and is expected to be used by 250,000 passengers per day. Planning approval for the high-speed station was received in May 2020 from the Old Oak and Park Royal Development Corporation (OPDC).

For Curzon Street station in Birmingham, a shortlist of three bidders was announced in June 2020 to tender for a two-stage design and build contract valued at £570 million, which is due to be awarded in 2021. In April 2020 the station received planning approval from Birmingham City Council based on designs developed by Grimshaw Architects and WSP.

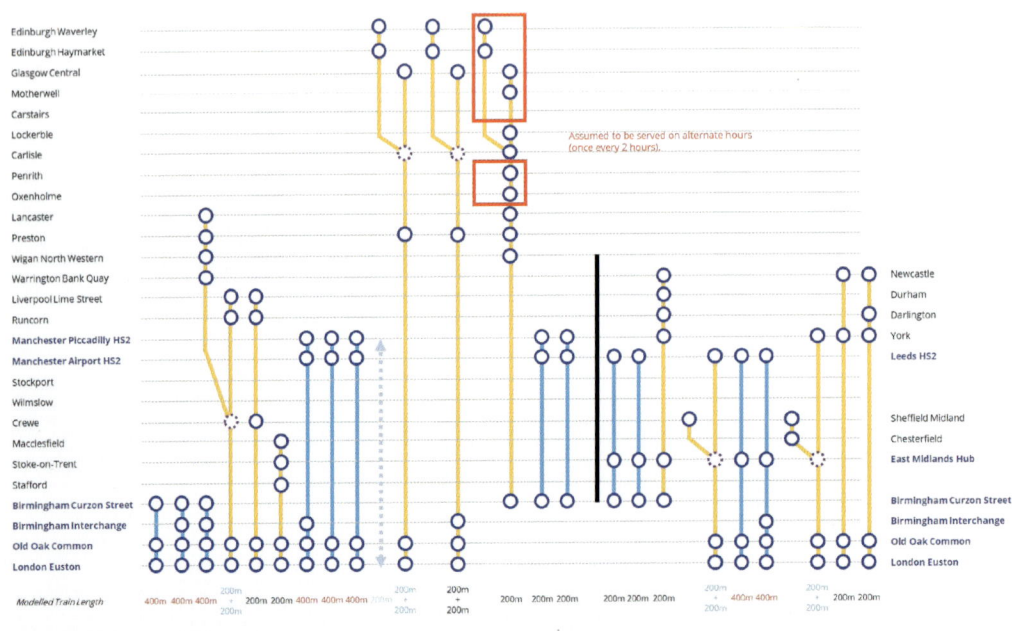

Planned service pattern: the 17 trains per hour service currently planned for HS2 when the full network is open, as set out in the Phase One business case published in April 2020.

IN ASSOCIATION WITH

Interchange station in Solihull followed Curzon Street in receiving planning approval from Solihull Metropolitan Borough Council in August 2020. The application covered the station, surrounding landscape and public realm and an automated people mover linking it to the NEC, Birmingham International station and Birmingham Airport along a 2.3km route. Design work on the station was led by Arup, with a construction partner contract planned to be awarded in 2022 ahead of the start of construction in 2024.

CONTRACT OPPORTUNITIES

The issuing of Notice to Proceed prompted a raft of contract opportunities for Phases One and 2a.

First to be announced in April was a contract to design, deliver and maintain 168 lifts and 128 escalators at HS2's four stations. Valued at up to £465 million, the contract is divided into separate packages for lifts and escalators, with the winners to be appointed to frameworks. Contract awarded is expected in 2021.

The first of two contracts launched in May was the competition to deliver around 280km of slab track. Four track packages will be awarded, covering urban sections in London and Birmingham, two sections of open route (central and north) and the Phase 2a route from the West Midlands to Crewe, with a combined value of nearly £2 billion. A shortlist was expected in late 2020, with contract award planned for 2022.

On the theme of track, in October 2020 HS2 awarded a contract to PORR UK Ltd and Aggregate Industries UK to design and manufacture the modular track system for Phases One and 2a. Valued at £260 million, the companies will use a system known as Slab Track Austria, with track manufactured at a new purpose-built factory at Shepton Mallet in Somerset and then transported to site. There will also be separate contracts covering rail and switches and crossings.

Also launched in May was a contract for signalling and control systems across Phases One and 2a. With a combined value of £540 million, the contract covers European Train Control System (ETCS) signalling and Traffic Management (TM) technology, with the potential for the extension of TM to cover Phase 2b as well. A shortlist is expected in 2021 with contract award in 2022.

Valued at £300 million, a tender was launched in June for delivery of 230km of telecommunications systems across the Phase One and Phase 2a routes. The scope of the work includes 2,760km of fibre optic cabling, 140 trackside cabinets, dozens of equipment cabins and radio coverage across the route. The winning bidder will also deliver a separate contract for the provision of technical support services. Separate contract opportunities to be launched in 2021 will cover third party communications, including mobile phone coverage for passengers on trains and in stations, Wi-Fi and an emergency services network.

In July HS2 Ltd launched the search for a contractor to deliver the overhead catenary system for the high-speed line. The deal covers 589 single track kilometres of route from London to Crewe and is valued at £300 million. HS2 will use the V360 design range under licence from SNCF Reseau, the first system in Europe to be certified for speeds of up to 360km/h. A shortlist was expected to be announced in late 2020, with contract award planned for 2022.

August saw the start of a search for a contractor to deliver the high voltage power supply systems for HS2, in a deal valued at £523 million. The winner of the contract will be responsible for the design as well as manufacture, supply, installation, testing, commissioning and maintenance of the HV power supply systems, with around 50 traction substations to be built along the Phase One and Phase 2a routes. A shortlist is expected to be announced in 2021 with contract award in 2022.

Still ongoing is the competition to supply the first trains for HS2. Five bidders submitted tenders for this contract in June 2019: Alstom; CAF; a joint venture of Bombardier and Hitachi; Siemens; and Talgo. The contract covers the construction and maintenance of at least 54 200-metre-long conventional-compatible trains, capable of operating at up to 360km/h and able to run on both the high-speed line and the classic network. Announcement of a preferred bidder was delayed until spring 2021, which HS2 Ltd said matched the general shift to the right of timescales on the project. A separate competition will be launched for a contractor to build the depot and control centre at Washwood Heath, Birmingham.

JOBS BOOST

Announcing the start of formal construction on Phase One, HS2 Ltd pledged a 22,000 jobs boost arising from the project. The BBJV contractor responsible for the north end of the route expects to create around 7,000 jobs, while the EKFB JV building the central section expects to recruit over 4,000 roles in the next two years. Contractors at the southern end of the route – the Align JV building the Chiltern tunnels and Colne Valley viaduct together with SCS Railways which is building the southern stretch into Euston and the two London station contractors – collectively plan to recruit over 10,000 new jobs. HS2 Ltd is directly recruiting for 500 new roles over the next three years, mostly based in Birmingham, and the company expects to create at least 2,000 apprenticeships on Phase One. ■

HS2 PHASE ONE CONTRACTORS

STATIONS	
Euston	
Master Development Partner	Lendlease
Design	Ove Arup and Partners/Grimshaw
Construction	Mace/Dragados
Old Oak Common	
Design	WSP/Wilkinson Eyre
Construction	Balfour Beatty/Vinci/Systra
Interchange	
Design	Ove Arup and Partners/Arup/Wilkinson Eyre
Birmingham Curzon Street	
Design	WSP/Grimshaw
Construction (shortlist)	Bam Nuttall/Ferrovial; Laing O'Rourke; Mace/Dragados
CIVILS WORKS	
Area South (Euston Tunnels and Approaches and Northolt Tunnels)	SCS Railways (Skanska/Costain/Strabag)
Area Central (Chiltern Tunnels and Colne Valley Viaduct)	Align JV (Bouygues Travaux Publics/VolkerFitzpatrick/Sir Robert McAlpine)
Area Central (North Portal Chiltern Tunnels to Brackley and Brackley to South Portal of Long Itchington Wood Green Tunnel)	EKFB JV (Eiffage/Kier/Bam Nuttall/Ferrovial Agroman)
Area North (Long Itchington Wood Green Tunnel to Delta Junction and Birmingham Spur and Delta Junction to West Coast main line tie-in)	BBV JV (Balfour Beatty/Vinci)

First HS2 structure: this precast bridge over the M42 was installed in August 2020.

MAJOR PROJECTS

Crossrail opening slips to 2022

Two further delays to Elizabeth Line opening

The route to platform level: the escalator barrel at Whitechapel station linking to the Elizabeth Line platforms, as seen on 25 February 2020. PHILIP SHERRATT

Since the publication of our last yearbook, there have been two further slippages in Crossrail's opening plan.

Towards the end of 2019, Crossrail Ltd confirmed it had abandoned any hope of opening the central section of the Elizabeth Line between Paddington and Abbey Wood in 2020. It also confirmed the funding package agreed between parent company Transport for London and Government in December 2018 would be insufficient, with at least an additional £400 million required to complete the line, taking the project's total cost to over £18 billion.

At the time, Crossrail Ltd promised the line would open 'as soon as practically possible in 2021'. An update in early 2020 confirmed a planned 'summer 2021' opening, with trial running due to start in autumn 2020.

Then Covid came along. The pandemic forced Crossrail to bring all its worksites to a safe stop on 24 March 2020. The company began remobilising in May, bringing staff back to sites in reduced numbers to comply with social distancing and resuming dynamic testing, but the stoppage clearly had an impact on the schedule to get the line open.

By the July meeting of Crossrail's board, the inevitable was confirmed – the summer 2021 opening date announced only six months earlier was no longer achievable. Crossrail Ltd said the pandemic had made the existing pressures on an already challenging programme more acute.

Another month later, and the schedule impact became clear, with the promise now being for a Paddington to Abbey Wood opening in the first half of 2022, at least three years later than the originally planned December 2018 opening. Crossrail Ltd suggested there may be an opportunity to review and bring forward the opening, 'subject to progress during the intensive operational testing phase'. Trial running would begin 'at the earliest opportunity in 2021'.

With more time comes more money, and on top of its previous November 2019 estimate Crossrail suggested it would need another £450 million to complete the project, taking the total cost increase to £3.25 billion compared with the original budget aligned to the December 2018 opening.

Opening of the central section is a key milestone as it introduces trains through the new tunnels under London. It will be followed, as per Crossrail's phased opening plan, by the extension of services from the central section over the Great Western main line to Reading and Heathrow airport and on the Great Eastern main line to Shenfield, with these introductions to be aligned with National Rail timetable changes in either May or December.

To help recover lost time, Crossrail paused dynamic testing for six weeks in summer 2020 to focus on completing remaining construction works in the central section. With this complete, testing of signalling software resumed, with the aim of reaching a stable state before trial running can begin. A key cause of the delay has also been the decision to phase the handover of the 10 central section stations to Transport for London, due to the magnitude of this task. While there have been further delays, Crossrail Ltd has made progress in handing over shafts and portals to TfL, and during 2020 the track was also handed over to TfL as infrastructure owner.

A concern for the project during October 2020 was the lack of funding certainty. Mirroring TfL's own financial problems, Crossrail Ltd was running out of committed funding through which it would be able to continue construction, with a worst-case scenario that this could grind to a halt.

INTEGRATED INTO TFL

A notable landmark came on 1 October 2020, when Crossrail Ltd was integrated into Transport for London. Previously a subsidiary organisation, the change means TfL will manage directly the remaining phases of the project, with Crossrail CEO Mark Wild reporting directly to TfL Commissioner Andy Byford.

The change meant the abolition of Crossrail Ltd's board, under the chairmanship of Tony Meggs, which met for the last time in September 2020. Instead, a TfL Elizabeth Line Delivery Group chaired by Mr Byford will oversee progress, along with higher level and more public scrutiny form a special purpose committee of the TfL board, known as the Elizabeth Line Committee.

'345s' REACH HEATHROW

The delays to opening mean Crossrail's neatly devised operating sequence has fallen somewhat out of sync.

Crossrail concessionaire MTR Elizabeth line has taken over operation of suburban services west of the capital from Paddington to Heathrow Airport and Reading. However, issues with European Train Control System meant the '345s' were initially unable to reach the airport, with the legacy Class 360s retained.

Nine-car '345s', with a more advanced software interface compared to the seven-car reduced length sets, were introduced from Paddington in July 2019. Office of Rail and Road approval for their use under ETCS was achieved in May 2020, only for the type to be withdrawn en masse in June due to a software issue, with seven-car sets substituting. With this resolved, nine-car '345s' finally worked to the airport in passenger service for the first time on 30 July, with the '345s' taking over all stopping services to the airport from the '360s' during September. With '345s' now in place on airport services, the half-hourly Paddington to Hayes & Harlington stopping services were due to be extended to the airport.

Seven-car sets were originally created to operate east of the capital between Shenfield and Liverpool Street, whose terminal platforms cannot yet accommodate nine-car sets. Replacement of seven-car units with nine-car variants in the west enabled more '345s' to transfer to the eastern side, displacing legacy Class 315 EMUs. Work to extend platforms 16 and 17 at Liverpool Street was due to begin during Christmas 2020, allowing nine-car '345s' to operate on the east side of the capital as well from mid-2021. ■

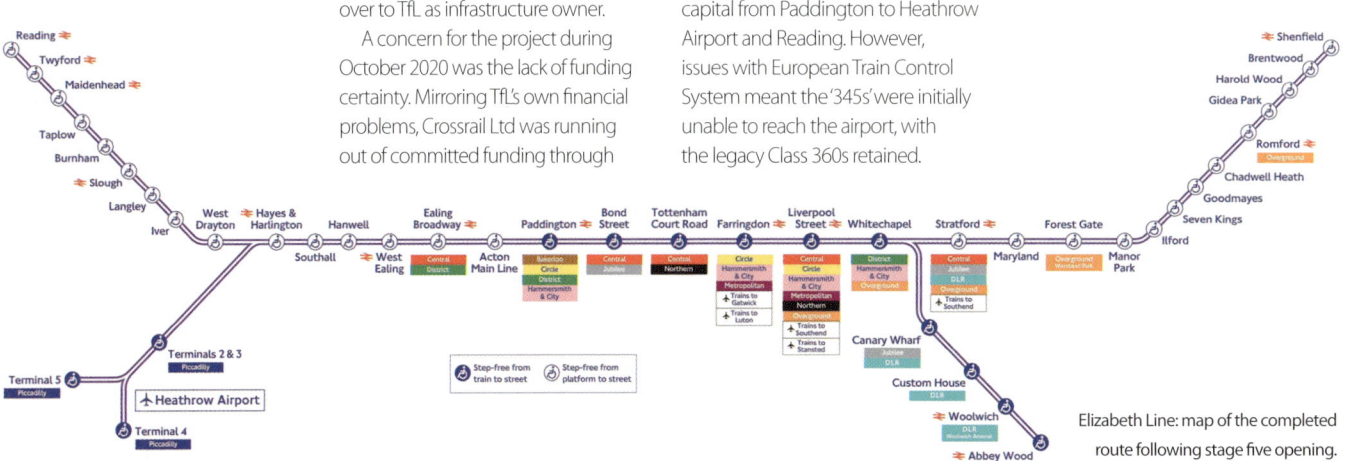

Elizabeth Line: map of the completed route following stage five opening.

IN ASSOCIATION WITH

EAST WEST RAIL
CONSTRUCTION UNDERWAY

The project to connect Oxford and Cambridge by a direct rail link is gathering momentum at last. East West Rail (EWR) received planning permission to complete the route from Bicester to Bedford in early 2020, while route selection for the new-build Bedford to Cambridge section continues to progress.

EWR aims to restore train services over new, improved and reopened sections of railway between Oxford, Bletchley and Cambridge. The East West Rail Company was launched in 2017 as a special purpose vehicle to secure private sector involvement to design, build and operate the route as an integrated organisation. The company was chaired on an interim basis by Network Rail Non-Executive Director and former Chiltern Railways Managing Director Rob Brighouse, with a permanent chair due to be appointed by early 2021. The National Infrastructure Commission (NIC) had previously given strong support to the project as part of its work on the Oxford to Cambridge corridor.

WESTERN SECTION

The EWR route is divided into three sections. The western section runs from Oxford to Milton Keynes and Bedford. The western extremity of the route between Oxford and Bicester has already been upgraded as part of work to enable Chiltern Railways' services from Oxford to London Marylebone. The remainder of the western section comprises upgrades to freight-only routes and reinstatement of mothballed lines, along with some upgrades between Bletchley and Bedford.

The East West Rail Alliance, comprising Atkins, Laing O'Rourke, VolkerRail and Network Rail, is responsible for delivery of the western section, while the EWR Company has taken over the client role for the project from the Department for Transport. In July 2018 the alliance applied to the Secretary of State for a Transport and Works Act Order for the section east of Bicester, with approval received in January 2020. Pre-Covid, the aim

Bletchley flyover: work to remove redundant spans from the 1960s structure was a main focus of East West Rail during 2020. **COURTESY NETWORK RAIL**

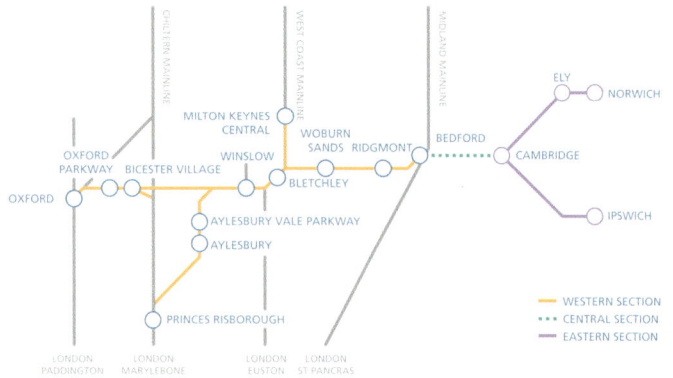

Built in three phases: map of East West Rail; the Aylesbury section is rumoured to have been removed from the project's scope.

was to start passenger services by 2024, proposed to be half-hourly services between Oxford and Milton Keynes and hourly services from Oxford to Bedford and from Aylesbury to Milton Keynes.

The scheme involves upgrading and reinstating 78km of existing and mothballed lines, along with a new station at Winslow, new platforms at Bletchley and Aylesbury Vale Parkway and platform extensions at Woburn Sands and Ridgmont. Electrification of the line has been removed from the project scope, but passive provision will be made for wires to be installed at a later date.

The estimated cost of the scheme as of July 2018 was £1.084 billion, following a cost challenge exercise that saw changes to the scope and a reduction in cost. However, reports in 2020 suggested further scope reductions would see the Aylesbury section removed from the project, leaving only services to and from Oxford.

A key focus of early works has been at Bletchley, where the EWR Alliance is rebuilding parts of the flyover which will carry EWR tracks over the West Coast main line. Fifteen of the 37 spans are being rebuilt to rectify construction defects, with lifting out of old spans taking place progressively across the summer of 2020; the other 22 spans are reported to be in a serviceable condition, with their main structural elements to be retained but the parapets renewed.

CENTRAL SECTION

EWR's central section links Bedford to Cambridge and will comprise a new railway, with the alignment of the former Varsity line no longer in place.

After a period of consultation, in early 2020 EWR confirmed its preferred route out of five options. This would use the existing Bletchley to Bedford Marston Vale line into the current Bedford Midland station, providing interchange with Thameslink and Midland main line services. It would then leave Bedford to the north, with a new interchange station on the East Coast main line between Sandy and St Neots before continuing east through a further station at Cambourne and joining the West Anglia main line to enter Cambridge from the south. The estimated capital cost of this option is £3.7 billion, with a suggested journey time of 33 minutes from Bedford to Cambridge and 1hr 28min from Oxford to Cambridge. A more detailed preferred route alignment will be identified ahead of submission of a development consent order application, with the aim of securing consent in 2024 and starting construction of the central section in 2025. EWR aims to begin running direct trains between Oxford and Cambridge by the end of the decade.

The eastern section of EWR beyond Cambridge is expected to comprise upgrades to existing routes towards Ipswich and Norwich.

SELF-POWERED TRAINS

With electrification removed from the project's scope, EWR will initially be served by self-powered trains. 2020 saw the launch of an Invitation to Tender for a fleet of 12 or 14 three-car self-powered units with modifications including European Train Control System (ETCS) Level 2 and Driver Controlled Operation capability, supported by a full maintenance package (under a wet lease). The lease duration is four years, with an option to extend for two years. These trains would provide an interim solution, allowing time to explore green energy technologies to power trains and for a smoother transition to electrification across the line, should this be chosen as a longer-term solution. EWR is aiming to be a net zero carbon railway by the time passenger services run along the full length of the route between Oxford and Cambridge. ■

MAJOR PROJECTS

Cross-Pennine connectivity in focus

Go-ahead for Trans-Pennine upgrade as Northern Powerhouse Rail development continues

The Manchester to Leeds/York route upgrade is underway, after Government released £589 million of funding for the Trans-Pennine route upgrade in July 2020.

The full project is valued at £2.9 billion, with the aim of increasing capacity between Manchester and Leeds from six to eight trains per hour and cutting six minutes from Leeds to Manchester schedules and seven or eight minutes from York to Manchester journeys.

Full electrification of the route is not presently confirmed but remains an ambition. It is expected the stretches from Manchester to Stalybridge and Huddersfield to Leeds will be electrified, while Network Rail is already progressing plans to install overhead wires between Church Fenton and the intersection with the East Coast main line at Colton Junction, with this five-mile stretch due to be upgraded by October 2022.

Detailed plans have been set out for the stretch between Huddersfield and Dewsbury, for which Network Rail intends to submit a Transport and Works Act Order application. A second round of consultation was launched in autumn 2020 on these plans, which include electrification and quadruple tracking. Some remodelling will be required at Huddersfield station, there will be new platforms at Deighton, Mirfield station will be rebuilt and Ravensthorpe station relocated 300 metres to the west so it can be served by trains to and from Wakefield as well as those from Leeds. Thornhill Junction, where these routes diverge, will be grade separated, and a new viaduct will be built over the Calder & Hebble Navigation, Spen Valley Greenway and river Calder to allow a faster linespeed. Other structures will be four-tracked, electrified and strengthened.

A significantly longer list of upgrade options is being developed beyond the confirmed programme which will be brought back for further investment decisions in 2021. These include investigation of the feasibility of full electrification and cutting a further couple of minutes off the journey time. Also within the potential additional scope is digital signalling and further sections of three- or four-tracking.

Huddersfield: the station layout will be remodelled as part of the Trans-Pennine Route Upgrade. Loco No 68026 leads a TransPennine Express Nova 3 set into the station with the 10.41 Scarborough to Liverpool Lime Street service on 30 August 2019. **PHILIP SHERRATT**

Where a chosen solution is confirmed, work is underway on the next phase of design ahead of the start of early construction works, with the aim of delivering the first benefits of the scheme in 2024. Those elements of scope still under discussion would follow later in the 2020s.

NORTHERN POWERHOUSE RAIL

Transport for the North's flagship Northern Powerhouse Rail scheme is aimed at transforming the region's railways through a mix of new and upgraded lines.

The project will build on the Trans-Pennine Route Upgrade and then the arrival of HS2, with which it is closely linked, and the phasing of HS2 Phase 2b and NPR is being examined as part of the Government's Integrated Rail Plan, which was due to be published by the end of 2020.

TfN's ambition is to operate six trains an hour in each direction between Liverpool, Manchester and Leeds, with a new NPR line planned from Liverpool to Manchester Airport before trains join HS2's tracks into Manchester Piccadilly. A new line will run across the Pennines via Bradford to Leeds, with major upgrades east of Leeds to connect to Hull, York and Newcastle. To the south of the Pennines, an upgraded Hope Valley line is planned to help reduce journey times between Manchester and Sheffield. NPR is planned to be a fully electrified railway with 200-metre-long trains operating at speeds of up to 125mph. Under NPR it is planned to cut the Manchester to Leeds journey time by 21 minutes while providing an additional two fast trains each hour between the cities.

The target is for TfN's board to approve the Strategic Outline Business Case for NPR in March 2021, the board having selected its preferred option from four phasing scenarios identified for delivery. While work on new sections of railway is unlikely to start until at least 2030 due to the need to achieve planning consents, work to upgrade existing lines could begin in the mid-2020s under permitted development rights.

QUICK WIN PROJECTS

More widely TfN has called for Government commitment to 'quick win' projects on the existing network in addition to NPR. Part of its submission to the National Infrastructure Commission's call for evidence ahead of the formulation of the Integrated Rail Plan, TfN suggests reliability and resilience are key to restoring the confidence of the travelling public and helping build new markets for rail.

TfN's Strategic Transport Plan calls for up to £70 billion of investment in the region's transport network by 2050, including road as well as rail. It sets desirable minimum standards for rail services in the region, along with a target for improvement in the average speed of freight services and gauge clearance enhancements. An integrated and smart travel plan also features, beginning with the introduction of smartcards on rail and concluding with a move to account-based travel. ■

INFRASTRUCTURE ENHANCEMENT & RENEWAL

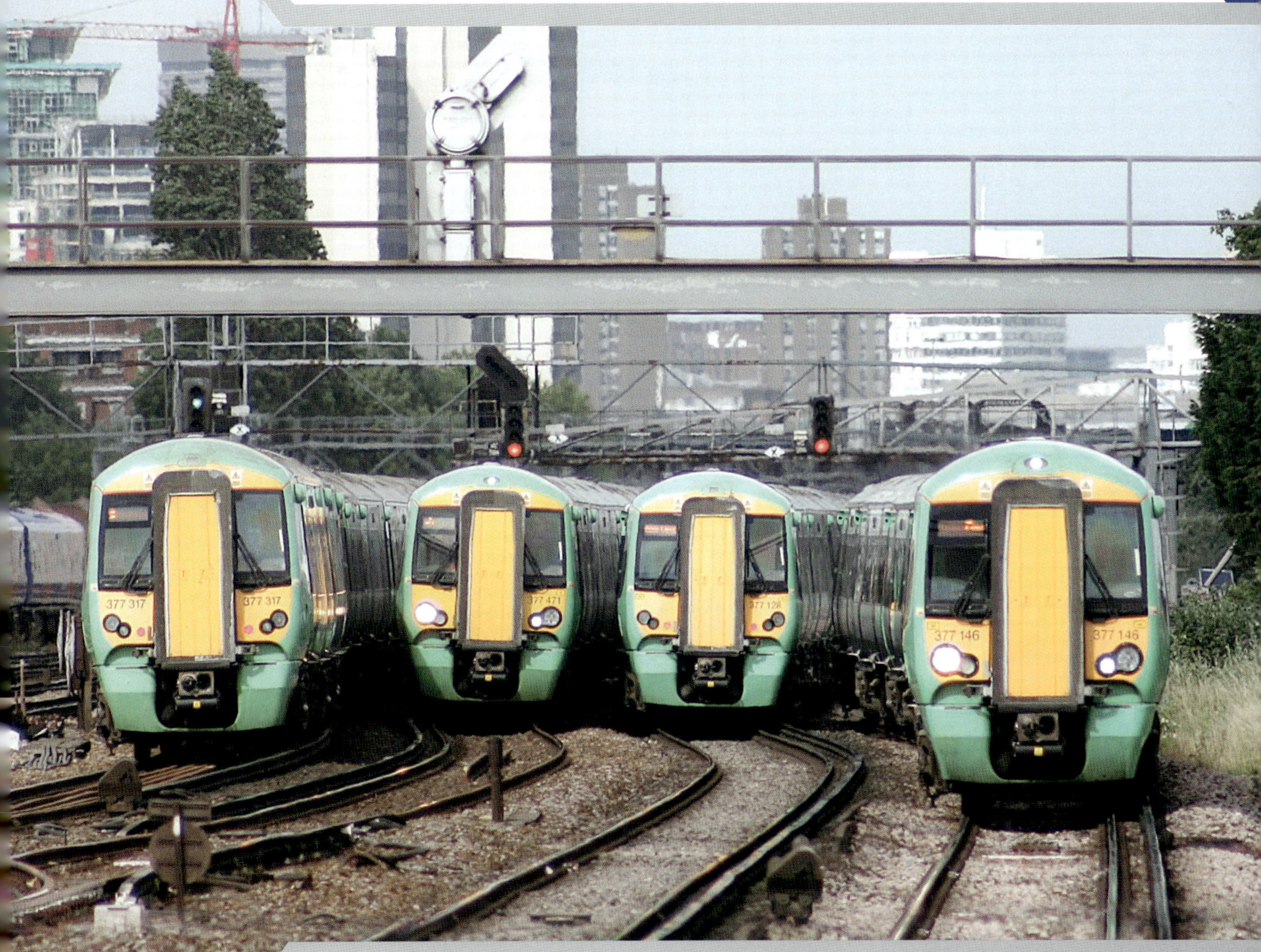

IN ASSOCIATION WITH

INFRASTRUCTURE ENHANCEMENT & RENEWAL

RESILIENCE
COPING WITH A CHANGING WORLD

Modern Railways Industry and Technology Editor **ROGER FORD** reports on how the railway is responding to change

Railway infrastructure's vulnerability to extremes of weather first came to public attention with the celebration of the orange army's 'herculean' efforts to reopen the line at Dawlish in 2014, just eight weeks after the sea front trackbed was washed away in a storm. Having the West Country cut off from the national rail network for this time also highlighted the importance of rail connections. One study estimated the cost to the economy of Devon and Cornwall at several hundred million pounds.

Having restored the rail link, Network Rail began a programme of work to maintain the long-term operation of this section of main line under worsening climatic conditions. The focus changed from maintenance to resilience. Already the first sections of a new sea wall along the front at Dawlish are in place.

Plans are also advanced for a programme of work at a nearby location where the line is bordered by steep cliffs on one side and the sea on the other. This adds the risk from cliff falls and landslips to damage caused by rough seas. Realigning the railway will provide space for corrective measures to stabilise the cliffs and provide better protection from storms.

Resilience is not just about future-proofing the existing railway. Parallel studies are investigating the restoration of an inland route between Exeter and Plymouth on existing alignments. A shorter, entirely new inland route has also been mooted.

Railway lines in coastal areas, such as Dawlish and North Wales, are easily identified as requiring investment in resilience. However, inland, the vulnerability of cuttings and embankments to heavy rainfall represents a much greater threat. This has been reflected in rising expenditure since the turn of the century (Figure 1).

CARMONT

In August 2020 the torrential rainfall at Carmont on the Dundee to Aberdeen main line resulted in large volumes of water pouring down an embankment towards the railway. The flood overwhelmed a drainage ditch, washing gravel and stones, derailing an inter-city train with the loss of three lives. This was despite £1.8 million having been spent on improving drainage at the cutting and reinforcing and protecting.

On Network Rail's earthworks hazard matrix, the Carmont embankment was rated B/C. As Table 1 shows, this rating band covers over 80,000 individual assets.

Following the accident Network Rail investigated 584 sites with similar characteristics to Carmont. None of these investigations identified any significant issues requiring emergency intervention. At around 1% of the sites deterioration was noted, requiring remedial action sooner than originally planned.

EVALUATION

Most cuttings and embankments date from the Victorian railway age and were built by navvies with pick and shovel. Embankments used whatever material was available, tipped from the top as the embankment advanced. Cuttings were excavated with steep sides to minimise the volume of material excavated. In

Earthworks challenge: aerial view of the Carmont site where a ScotRail HST derailed on 12 August 2020. **COURTESY NETWORK RAIL**

some cases, landslips were happening before the new line opened.

For today's civil engineers, the key task is to determine the condition of what was laid down up to 150 years ago. Network Rail has developed its Global Stability and Resilience Appraisal (GSRA) tool, which brings together in one set of data the many factors that determine the stability of an embankment or cutting and enables the risks to be compared with the modern equivalent.

In effect, GSRA is allowing Network Rail to quantify the vulnerability of its legacy earthwork assets and plan remedial action. This work can draw upon a range of techniques for strengthening earthworks and rock faces.

MONITORING

But, as Carmont showed, today's extreme weather can overwhelm even a location where £1.8 million had been spent on preventative measures 10 years ago. Extremes of weather and dry, hot summers exacerbate the stresses on earthworks, making monitoring of at-risk sites increasingly important. Here technology is on the railway's side in the form of a growing armoury of monitoring equipment.

Network Rail categorises earthwork failure under three headings:

Cliff stability concern: GWR's No 158952 approaches Parsons Tunnel, between Teignmouth and Dawlish, on 25 June 2019 with the 12.53 Paignton to Cardiff Central service. Network Rail has consulted on a scheme to move the railway out to sea and away from the cliffs, but in October 2020 put on hold plans to submit a Transport and Works Act Order application in the face of local opposition. **PHILIP SHERRATT**

slow; rapid; and instantaneous. 'Slow' is over a time period of, typically, days to years; 'rapid' covers minutes to hours; 'instantaneous' failures happen in seconds.

Each type of failure has its own range of monitoring tools. One of the current developments is the deployment of GPS devices on embankments and cuttings which are capable of measuring movement down to millimetres. These can be set to issue an alert if movement is detected.

However, as numerous landslips in recent years have demonstrated, the key challenge remains the immediate detection of instantaneous failures and the provision of a warning to the signaller controlling the location.

PEOPLE

Working through the pandemic has highlighted another aspect of resilience. Consolidation of signalling and control at a small number of Rail Operating Centres (ROCs) has long been seen as the ideal. Such concentration should lead to improving efficiency and reduced costs.

This philosophy is now under review following experience during the pandemic. One major ROC, in an area with a high level of Covid-19 infections, is reported to have had over 30 signallers off-duty on one day – either infected, self-isolating or shielding.

With modern software-configured workstations, it is theoretically possible to control a route from any location with compatible equipment. Provision of such a back-up facility has been considered previously, but as a response to a major signalling centre being closed down, for example by a terrorist attack. Long-term shortage of staff could be a more mundane event encouraging such provision.

Similarly with other activities involving key workers. Driver training has been halted during the pandemic due to the close proximity of driver and instructor in the cab during train handling and route learning sessions. Add this to the age profile of drivers, where age requires shielding, and some operators have been struggling to cover all services.

Great advances have been made in the use of driving simulators. However, driving experience on the track remains an essential part of training.

Also affected by social distancing and related protocols are rolling stock maintenance depots. While the Government had been pressing passenger train operators to run as close to a full service as possible, constraints on drivers and rolling stock availability have frustrated this aspiration.

As with other transport services, the railway has kept running during the pandemic. But its resilience has been challenged on all fronts. ■

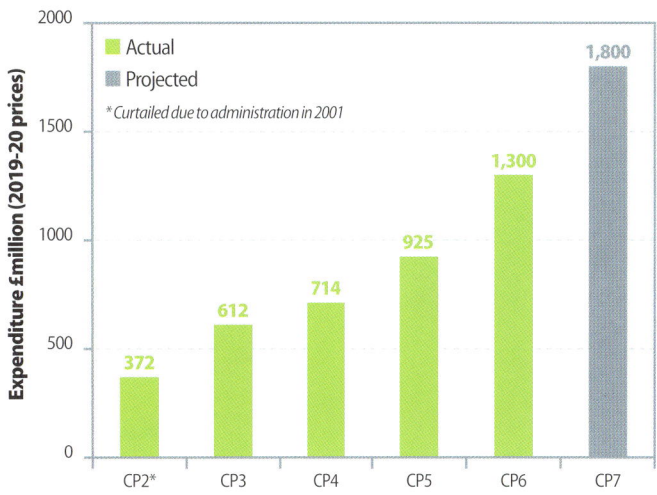

FIGURE 1: NETWORK RAIL'S EARTHWORKS AND DRAINAGE EXPENDITURE

*Curtailed due to administration in 2001

CP2*: 372
CP3: 612
CP4: 714
CP5: 925
CP6: 1,300
CP7: 1,800 (Projected)

TABLE 1: EARTHWORKS BY HAZARD RATING

RATING	QUANTITY
A	98,000
B	46,000
C	38,000
D	8,000
E	1,000
Total	**191,000**

PUTTING PASSENGERS FIRST

Network Rail completes devolution journey

Network Rail's reorganisation to a new devolved structure was due to be fully complete by the end of 2020.

Initiated by Chief Executive Andrew Haines, the plans were announced in February 2019. Under the moniker 'Putting passengers first,' Mr Haines aimed to create the opportunity for devolved decision-making, with accountability and authority for decisions at route level.

This involves shrinking the central functions of the company and aligning its operations more closely with those of train operators. The restructuring has included the abolition of NR's Infrastructure Projects division, whose responsibilities are shared between the routes. Elements of the System Operator, Safety, Technical & Engineering and Group Digital Railway functions are also devolved on a phased basis. The Route Services directorate has been retained for services that benefit from economies of scale and those best managed at a national level. It is supplemented by a new Network Services directorate, incorporating the 'virtual' route for freight and national passenger operators as well as elements of Group Digital Railway and other national services.

Routes, each led by a route director, are responsible for day-to-day delivery of train performance and the relationship with operators. Regions, each led by a managing director, support the routes and absorb the devolved functions, with responsibility for relationships with stakeholders and funders.

Phase One of the reorganisation was completed in September 2019, comprising the set up of the 14 routes and five regions and the establishment of Network Services. Phase Two in November 2019 saw more teams transfer to the regions, Network Services, Route Services and the Chief Financial Officer directorate. A third phase of nationally co-ordinated changes in June 2020 left only changes at regional level to be completed, some of which were put back slightly due to Covid but were due to follow in the latter part of the year. ■

Managing directors – Network Rail regions

Eastern
Rob McIntosh

North West & Central
Tim Shoveller

Scotland's Railway
Alex Hynes

Southern
John Halsall

Wales & Western
Mark Langman
(due to retire December 2020)

Route directors

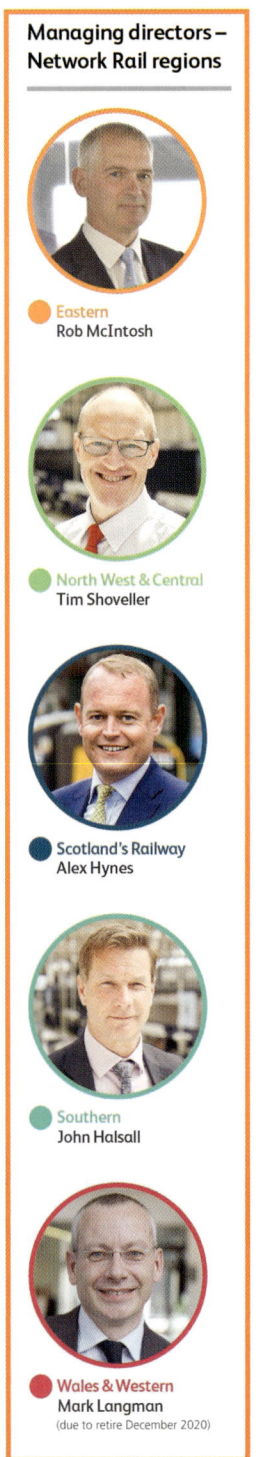

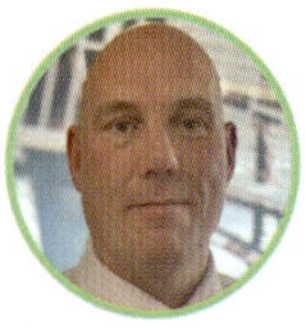

5 North West
Phil James

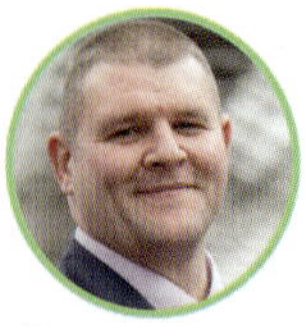

6 Central
Dave Penney

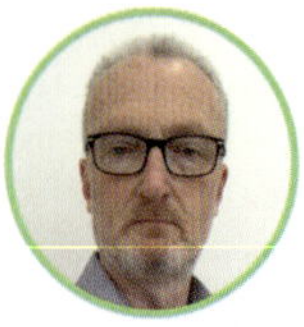

7 West Coast Mainline South
James Dean

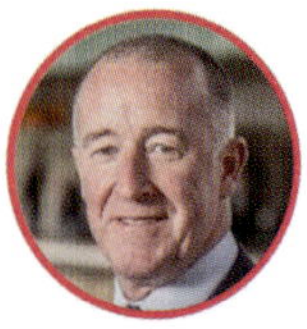

13 Wales & Borders
Bill Kelly

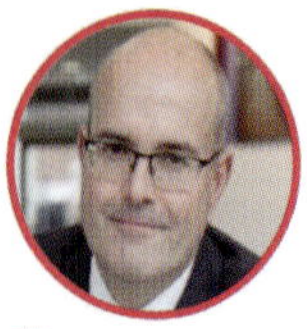

14 Western
Mike Gallop

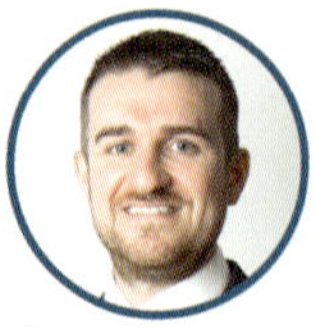

8 Scotland
Liam Sumpter

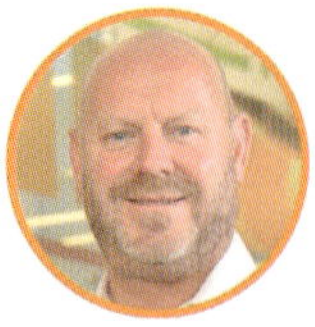

1 East Coast
Paul Rutter

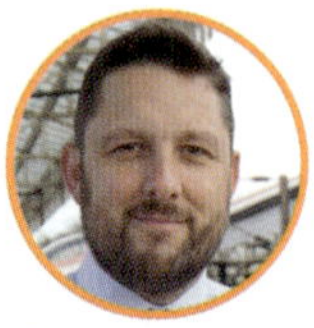

2 North & East
Matthew Rice

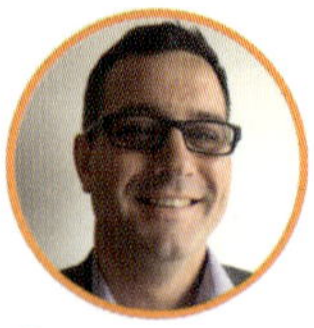

3 East Midlands
Gary Walsh

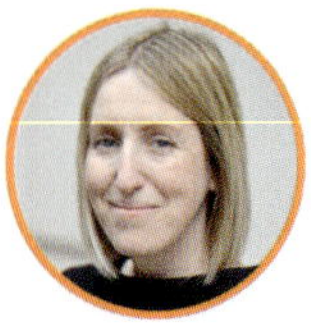

4 Anglia
Ellie Burrows

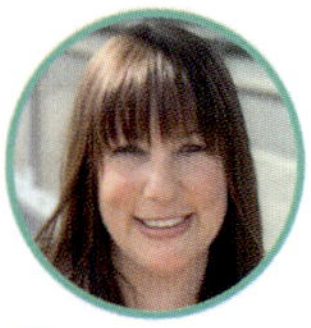

10 Network Rail High Speed
Katie Frost

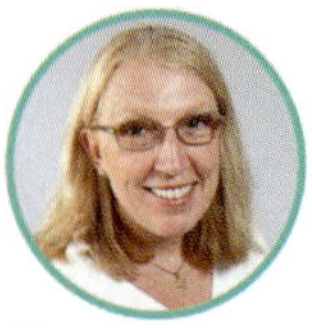

9 Kent
Fiona Taylor

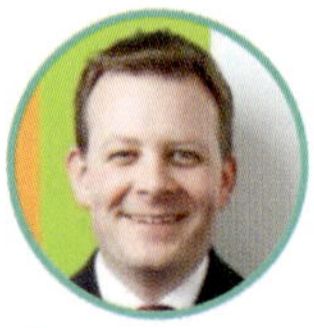

12 Wessex
Mark Killick

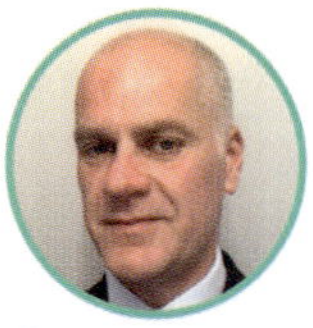

11 Sussex
Shaun King

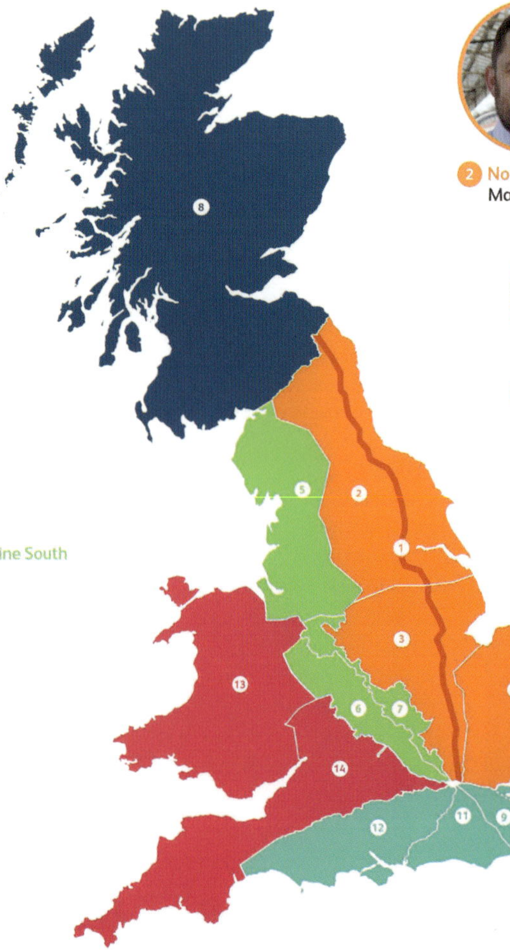

IN ASSOCIATION WITH porterbrook

Midland main line wires live: EMR Meridian No 222018 leads the 12.49 Sheffield to St Pancras service at Sharnbrook on 18 October 2020. **KEN BRUNT**

PROJECTS BEAT THE PANDEMIC

Delivery and development of infrastructure schemes has continued through 2020

Despite the challenges of Covid, the railway pressed on with delivering infrastructure projects during 2020. Overhead wires were switched on, new stations opened and work on a number of long-term schemes continued. Clearly the viability of some projects may be reconsidered in the light of reduced passenger demand, but the response of the industry in pressing ahead augurs well for the future.

During Control Period 6 (2019-24) Network Rail's central focus is on operations, maintenance and renewals, with an allocation of £42 million. The sad events of the derailment of a ScotRail HST at Stonehaven will likely create a sharper focus on how railway infrastructure is maintained, and in particular resilience to the effects of climate change.

While enhancement projects include some schemes initiated in Control Period 5, the development of future schemes is determined by progress through the Department for Transport's Rail Network Enhancements Pipeline, with its five stages of determine, develop, design, deliver and deploy. Progress and visibility of schemes through this pipeline has been patchy; in autumn 2019 DfT published a list of schemes in the pipeline, but a year later no further update had been forthcoming, a matter highlighted by the Railway Industry Association, which is anxious to ensure the pipeline is visible.

PROJECT SPEED

A strong emphasis in the Covid crisis has been to 'build back better', with a focus on the way infrastructure schemes are delivered.

The rail industry's response to this has included the development by Network Rail of a 'Project Speed' initiative to halve the time and slash the cost of delivering projects. Although there had not been a formal announcement during the autumn, it is understood Network Rail identified an initial six programmes to which it is applying the Project Speed ethos:
■ Croydon Area Remodelling (CARS);
■ Trans-Pennine Route Upgrade;
■ Manchester reliability improvements;
■ Northumberland line reopening;
■ Oxford Connect; and
■ Midland main line electrification to Sheffield.

The aim of Project Speed is to articulate and demonstrate how enhancements can be delivered more quickly and effectively using real-time live projects at varying states of the early delivery cycle, and to change the culture, processes and risk appetite in delivering projects.

Work on the initial set of six projects was under development during summer 2020, and by the autumn a second subset of projects had been identified as Project Speed candidates. Again, although a list had not been formally confirmed, it is thought these included electrification of the Uckfield line and restoration of regular passenger services between Exeter and Okehampton.

In parallel with this, Transport Secretary Grant Shapps launched a new Acceleration Unit to speed up delivery of transport projects. Led by Darren Shirley, formerly Chief Executive of the Campaign for Better Transport, the unit will engage experts with 'significant experience in delivery of infrastructure projects'. Its creation follows the establishment of a Northern Transport Acceleration Council targeted at levelling up infrastructure across the north's towns and cities.

MIDLAND MAIN LINE WIRES GO LIVE

Perhaps a highlight for enhancement projects in 2020 was the switching on of overhead wires on the Midland main line over the weekend of 22-23 August.

Electrification from Bedford to Corby is a headline element of the

INFRASTRUCTURE ENHANCEMENT & RENEWAL

Werrington dive under: work in progress on the north ramp, east of the East Coast main line, on 12 March 2020. **PHILIP SHERRATT**

Midland main line upgrade, which has also featured reinstatement of a fourth track between Sharnbrook and Kettering (now complete), station upgrades, including platform extensions and construction of a fourth platform at Wellingborough, provision of new substations and construction of an electric stabling facility at Kettering. Switching on the overhead wires has enabled a programme of testing and assurance to begin, with a specially formed test train used for this purpose.

The upgrade will allow East Midlands Railway to launch a new half-hourly electric service between Corby and London St Pancras in May 2021, delayed from December 2020 due to the impact of the pandemic. This means EMR will operate six rather than five trains per hour out of St Pancras.

Ground investigation works are taking place ahead of a planned extension of electrification from Kettering to Market Harborough. This is being progressed to provide a connection to the power supply feed at Braybrooke, south of Market Harborough, the site of which was chosen before electrification north of Kettering was cancelled in 2017. Completion of this element is planned for 2023, with further electrification north of Market Harborough the subject of a Project Speed initiative.

EAST COAST UPGRADE

Work also continues on the £1.2 billion East Coast Upgrade, a programme targeted at increasing capacity on the East Coast main line. A new timetable is planned to feature eight long-distance paths per hour out of King's Cross instead of the current six, although implementation has been deferred from December 2021 to May 2022.

In September 2020 Network Rail confirmed key closure dates in 2021 for the two most significant individual projects – remodelling the station throat at King's Cross and building a new dive-under at Werrington. The original plan was to carry out the majority of work at King's Cross in the early part of 2021, but this will now take place between March and early June. The work to remodel the station throat will increase capacity, bringing back into use the third bore of Gasworks Tunnel.

The project at Werrington is creating a grade-separated junction, removing the conflict posed by trains crossing the flat junction from the Stamford lines on the west side to access the so-called 'Joint' line to Spalding, a manoeuvre chiefly undertaken by long freight trains. A nine-day closure of the East Coast main line from 16 to 24 January 2021 will be used to install an 11,000-tonne curved concrete box for the dive-under, with a further three-day closure to complete the project in mid-2021. Morgan Sindall is the principal contractor for the Werrington project.

The most tangible achievement within the East Coast upgrade during 2020 was the opening of platform 5 at Stevenage on 2 August. The 130-metre-long platform serves terminating services from the Hertford loop, which are segregated from main line services.

The last element of the upgrade is power supply works. A £216.2 million contract has been awarded to the Rail Electrification Alliance, comprising VolkerRail, J Murphy & Sons, Jacobs, Systra, Siemens Mobility and Network Rail, for power supply enhancements between Doncaster and Edinburgh, following on from works already completed south of Doncaster.

A new platform 0 at Leeds station was due to be brought into service by the end of 2020, helping increase capacity for local and long-distance services. Network Rail has also completed improvements to the station façade.

At the southern end of the ECML, a six-month programme to clean tunnels, renew track and refresh stations on the Northern City line between Finsbury Park and Moorgate was completed during 2020. Network Rail and Govia Thameslink Railway carried out the work, which included cleaning almost 17km of tunnels, renewing over 3.4km of track and replacing more than 1km of ballast.

In the north east, meanwhile, changes are planned at Middlesbrough station to accommodate direct LNER services from London. Tees Valley Mayor Ben Houchen has announced a £35 million project, the first phase of which will see platform 2 extended to accommodate LNER's Azumas.

Next phase of the coastal resilience programme: visual of the work planned between Coastguards and Colonnade breakwaters at Dawlish. **COURTESY NETWORK RAIL**

GREAT WESTERN WIRES COMPLETED

2020 saw the culmination of the long-running and challenging Great Western Electrification Programme. Great Western Railway has increased the proportion of electric running, including the first main line electric services into Wales.

A blockade through Cardiff and Newport over the Christmas 2019 period enabled the operation of electric services into south Wales to begin in the New Year, with the electrification work delivered by Balfour Beatty. The previous western limit of electric operation had been Bristol Parkway, since January 2019.

Pan up in Wales: a GWR Intercity Express Train crosses the river Usk into Newport with the 13.18 Paddington to Cardiff Central service on 23 January 2020. **PHILIP SHERRATT**

However, this excluded the Severn Tunnel as further testing continued of electrification equipment here, with GWR's bi-mode Intercity Express Trains switching to diesel power. Full electric operation through the tunnel began in June, completing the electrified route between the English and Welsh capitals. The tunnel proved a challenging environment to electrify, and corrosion between the aluminium overhead conductor bar supplied by Furrer+Frey and the copper contact wire led to NR replacing the latter with an aluminium contact wire, a first for the UK.

One project on the western now mired in uncertainty is the Western Rail Link to Heathrow (WRLtH). Network Rail has delayed submission of a development consent order application for the 6.5km link from the Great Western main line near Langley to the airport, which would allow direct trains to Heathrow from Slough and Reading. Uncertainty caused by the impact of Covid on the aviation industry has been cited as the reason for the delay, meaning a DCO submission will not now be made until winter 2021-22.

METROWEST TRAVAILS

Ambitions to improve local rail services in the Bristol area continue to progress, albeit slowly. The major achievement for the MetroWest scheme, promoted by the West of England Combined Authority, is the closure of a funding gap.

First up will be a frequency increase on routes to Severn Beach and Westbury. Reopening of the Portishead line is expected to follow, involving upgrades to the Portbury Dock freight line and revival of 5km of disused track. Cost challenges have led to

New frontage at Glasgow Queen Street: work in progress on the improved concourse in summer 2020. **COURTESY NETWORK RAIL**

descoping of the scheme, meaning an hourly service will be provided instead of half-hourly. In November 2019 a Development Consent Order application was submitted, although progress has been slowed by the pandemic. The current plan sees the line reopening in March 2024.

A second phase of MetroWest covers reopening of the Henbury line with new stations at North Filton and Henbury and an improved frequency from Bristol to Yate and Gloucester, along with an additional station on the Filton bank at Ashley Down. Four-tracking of the Filton bank was recently completed by Network Rail as part of the wider Great Western programme.

Intertwined with MetroWest is remodelling of Bristol East Junction, where the line east towards Bath divides from the Filton bank route in the station throat north-east of Bristol Temple Meads station. The main works are planned for an eight-week period in summer 2021, with the closure to also be used to advance work on a new eastern entrance at Temple Meads, although completion of this is not scheduled until autumn 2023. A refurbishment of the station roof at Temple Meads is being carried out by Taziker on behalf of Network Rail, again with completion in 2023.

CORE VALLEY LINES MODERNISATION

Infrastructure works to modernise the Core Valley Lines in south Wales are now underway. The process to transfer the infrastructure from Network Rail to the Welsh Government concluded on 28 March 2020. Although day-to-day operation of the Wales and Borders franchise is to be taken in-house by the Welsh Government in February 2021, Keolis and Amey will continue to deliver the modernisation of the CVL, and Amey Keolis Infrastructure Ltd (AKIL) is the new network licence holder for the CVL.

Modernisation works on the CVL began in August 2020. The aim of the £738 million programme is to provide four trains per hour from each heads of the Valleys terminus, operated by new tram-trains and tri-mode units, with no use of diesel power over CVL infrastructure. Overhead electrification

INFRASTRUCTURE ENHANCEMENT & RENEWAL

At the heart of the Core Valley Lines upgrade: visual of the new tram-train depot and control centre at Taff's Well. COURTESY TFW

will be provided, but there will be stretches where the tram-trains and tri-mode units will switch to battery operation, particularly where rebuilding of structures would be costly. The scheme is also to see tram-trains operating on street to a new terminus at Cardiff Bay.

The routes concerned are the lines north from Cardiff Queen Street, including freight lines, the City line from Radyr to near Ninian Park station and the spur from Queen Street to Cardiff Bay. Construction works are principally taking place overnight on Sundays to Thursdays, supplemented by weekend closures and longer blockades.

A particular challenge is that elements of the CVL upgrade are reliant on European Union funding, which is time-limited. A later than planned asset transfer was exacerbated in 2020 by the impact of Covid.

An infrastructure hub at Treforest opened in January 2020, and a tram-train depot and CVL control centre is being built at Taff's Well, with Siemens Mobility awarded a contract for renewal of CVL signalling and creation of the control centre. An early milestone will be commissioning of a section of track in the Taff's Well area on which tram-trains can be tested.

The Ebbw Vale line is not part of the scope of CVL, but in autumn 2020 Network Rail commenced rebuilding of the river bridge at Crumlin to enable the second track over it to be reinstated. Plans to increase frequency on the line have faltered in recent years; the Welsh Government's stated ambition is for a frequency enhancement in 2021.

Elsewhere in Wales, Network Rail has begun a major programme of work to upgrade Barmouth bridge on the Cambrian Coast line. The £25 million programme will include replacement of many of the timber and metal elements of the viaduct as well as replacement of track along the length of the structure. A closure of 2½ weeks in autumn 2020 will be followed by longer closures over consecutive autumns in 2021 and 2022, with timbers renewed in the first two blockades and steel spans in the third.

DEVON COAST RESILIENCE

Another landmark of 2020 was the completion of the first phase of coastal resilience work on the railway between Exeter and Newton Abbot.

An event on 25 September marked the completion of construction of a new sea wall between Dawlish station and Kennaway Tunnel alongside Marine Parade. Network Rail and contractor Bam Nuttall have raised the height of the sea wall and installed a new recurve in the face of the wall with the aim of reducing wave overtopping onto the railway.

Attention is now turning to the second phase, covering the 415-metre stretch between Coastguards and Colonnade breakwaters. As well as the higher sea wall here, upgrades at Dawlish station will include construction of a new seaward platform and a new Access for All footbridge.

Development work continues on further elements of the scheme, covering sections between Dawlish and Teignmouth and focusing chiefly on cliff stability. Most significant are plans to move the railway out to sea and away from the cliffs on the Parsons Tunnel to Teignmouth (PT2T) stretch. After analysing the outcome of a consultation held in early 2020, Network Rail has paused plans to submit a Transport and Works Act Order application

Ely enhancement planned: consultation has begun on a major capacity improvement scheme. CrossCountry's No 170110 arrives on 1 January 2020 with the 07.22 Birmingham New Street to Stansted Airport service. PHILIP SHERRATT

IN ASSOCIATION WITH porterbrook

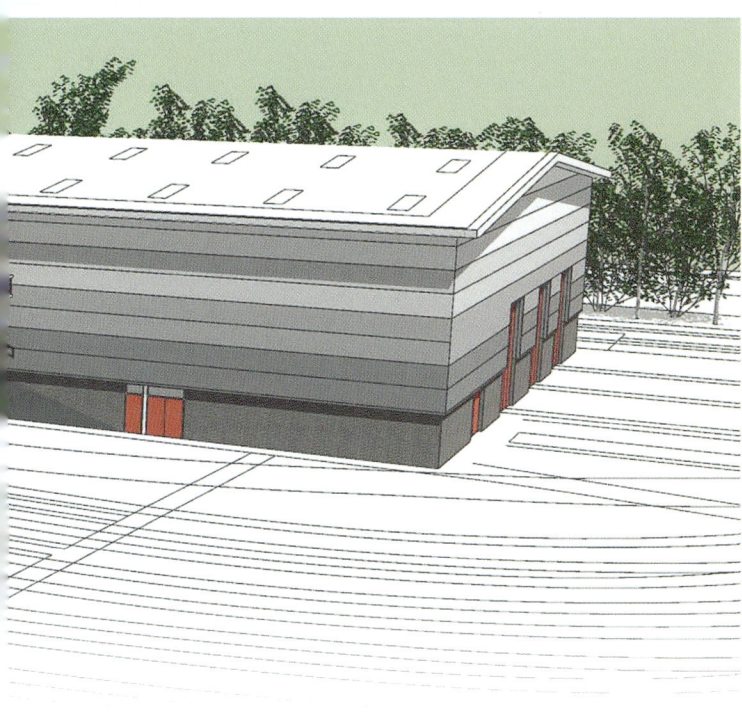

for the PT2T works as it considers feedback on these proposals.

ISLAND LINE UPGRADE

2021 will herald some of the most significant infrastructure changes in the history of the Island line, the Isle of Wight's railway linking Ryde and Shanklin.

The work is part of an overall £26 million upgrade which also sees South Western Railway introduce replacement Class 484 trains built by Vivarail. SWR is largely responsible for the infrastructure on the island and is leading on the project to upgrade the railway.

A closure of the line from 4 January to 31 March 2021 will be used to carry out a range of upgrades in preparation for the introduction of the Class 484s. The headline project is the reinstatement of a passing loop at Brading, enabling SWR to provide an even interval half-hourly service rather than the previous uneven alternating 20/40-minute intervals. Platform and track heights will be adjusted to suit the Class 484s, with level access at most stations. Replacement signalling will be provided between Smallbrook Junction and Shanklin, with axle counters and colour light signals introduced along with Train Protection and Warning System (TPWS), replacing the tripcocks previously used. A significant amount of track will also be renewed.

Work carried out in parallel by Network Rail will include bridge refurbishment work and a power supply upgrade. NR is also undertaking a £30 million programme of strengthening works to the pier at Ryde.

SCOTTISH PROJECTS MOVE FORWARD

The positive approach to railway enhancements in Scotland continued to manifest itself during 2020. Pre-existing projects continued, with some perturbation caused by Covid, while electrification and expansion of the network is in development.

A particular highlight is the rebuilt Glasgow Queen Street station, whose completion marks the formal end of the Edinburgh Glasgow Improvement Programme (EGIP), which saw electrification of the line via Falkirk and introduction of new Hitachi Class 385 EMUs. While the operational elements in terms of lengthening platforms to accommodate eight-car '385s' had already been tackled, work to complete the new station concourse was affected by Covid but was drawing to a close in the latter part of 2020.

Design work is underway on enhancements at Edinburgh Waverley, with a masterplan under development which envisages a new mezzanine concourse across the whole station and extensions to seven platforms.

East of Edinburgh, a second platform at Dunbar station was opened in December 2019. Network Rail and contractor AMCO built a 271-metre-long platform, which avoids the need for northbound stopping services to cross the southbound line to call at the station.

A project targeted at clear operational benefits was a £5 million programme to extend platforms at Milngavie station. The work, which began in summer 2020, was prompted by the Donovan review into ScotRail's performance and acts on one of its recommendations. Extending the platforms will enable a longer layover of terminating trains, improving reliability of services across the central belt. The benefits were due to be reaped with a timetable recast in December 2020.

Two significant reopening schemes are being investigated north of the border. One is the 5.5-mile Levenmouth branch in Fife, leaving the existing network at Thornton with stations at Cameron Bridge and Leven. Meanwhile, the West of Fife enhancement project could see the return of passenger trains east of Alloa to Longannet. The target is an eastward extension from the current terminus at Alloa with new stations at Clackmannan, Kincardine and Longannet. This plan is contingent upon Talgo delivering its proposal to build a new rail-connected manufacturing facility at Longannet, which the reopening would support.

The Scottish Government has also published its rail decarbonisation action plan (p121), and among the commitments is enhancement and electrification of the lines to East

Serving the Commonwealth Games: visual of the new transport interchange at Perry Barr, due to open in 2022. **COURTESY WMCA**

Repairing storm damage: work in progress at Polmont on the Edinburgh to Glasgow line, which was shut for six weeks during August and September 2020. **COURTESY NETWORK RAIL**

INFRASTRUCTURE ENHANCEMENT & RENEWAL

Kilbride and Barrhead in the Glasgow conurbation. As well as electrification, this is to include partial or full double-tracking between East Kilbride and Busby, a new station building at East Kilbride, relocation of Hairmyres station 600 metres to the west and platform extensions to accommodate longer trains. The ultimate ambition is for a four trains per hour eight-car zero emissions service at peak periods.

WEST MIDLANDS SCHEMES PRESS ON

The most visible example of positive progress in the West Midlands conurbation was the opening of the first phase of the new station building at Wolverhampton in May 2020. The contractor for the work is Galliford Try, which is due to complete the second phase by early 2021. The £150 million interchange is designed to improve connections between train, tram and bus services; an extension of the West Midlands Metro tram network will be completed once the station redevelopment is finished.

Authorities in the West Midlands are developing plans for major upgrade projects at two stations and reopening of others. The upgrades are at Perry Barr and University, both with an eye on the forthcoming 2022 Commonwealth Games. Perry Barr will serve the Alexander Stadium, and plans for the new transport interchange were submitted to Birmingham City Council in October 2020. For University, the full business case for a £56 million redevelopment has been approved by the West Midlands Combined Authority with VolkerFitzpatrick appointed as contractor.

The new stations are on the Camp Hill and Walsall to Wolverhampton lines. On the former, the aim is to reintroduce local services calling at Moseley, Kings Heath and Hazelwell stations, all of which closed in 1941 but have now received planning permission for reinstatement. On the Walsall to Wolverhampton line, the intention is to introduce a two trains per hour service calling at new stations at Darlaston and Willenhall; again both have planning permission, with opening targeted for 2023.

BRIGHTON MAIN LINE ENHANCEMENTS

In May 2020 Network Rail began the major element of the £150 million station enhancement project at Gatwick Airport. Costain is delivering the project, which will create a new station concourse so arriving and departing passengers can be segregated. A phased approach is taking platforms out of use in stages until May 2022, with the fully upgraded station due to open in 2023.

Next up is a plan to build a new third platform at Reigate for terminating services, potentially paving the way for direct Thameslink services from London. The current short platforms at the station limit train lengths to four carriages, something the proposed works would address, and a consultation showed broad support for the scheme. A power supply upgrade would also feature.

Both these schemes pale into insignificance compared with the Croydon Area Remodelling Scheme (CARS). The basis of the plan is grade separation of flat junctions at Windmill Bridge, north of East Croydon station, which place a major constraint on capacity. Refined proposals were presented by Network Rail in 2020, which include moving East Croydon station slightly northwards and providing grade separation for down East Grinstead trains, which was previously absent from the plans. The scheme would also involve significant alterations at Norwood Junction. It is the subject of a Project Speed initiative, potentially aiding acceleration of its delivery.

ELY AND WISBECH

There has been progress in advancing plans for tackling one of the railway's most notorious bottlenecks, with a consultation launched about the Ely area capacity enhancement (EACE) scheme.

EACE offers a much wider scope than a previous plan to remodel Ely North Junction. The aim is to increase capacity through Ely from 8.5 trains per hour (tph) to 10tph, with a suite of interventions including removal of speed restrictions across bridges, remodelling of the track layout, modifications to platforms at Ely, remodelling of Ely North Junction, signalling upgrades and upgrades to or closures of level crossings. The aim is to complete an outline business case by the end of 2021, with a current delivery date for the programme of 2031, although Network Rail is hoping this can be accelerated.

Bound up with the Ely scheme is a plan to restore passenger services between March and Wisbech.

Kintore revival: the first train calls at the reopened station on 15 October 2020, marking the return of rail services to the Aberdeenshire town after almost 60 years. **COURTESY NETWORK RAIL**

Support regeneration: a new station is being built on the Midland main line at Brent Cross West, with opening scheduled for 2022.

Proposals are being developed by the Cambridgeshire and Peterborough Combined Authority, which after examining options concluded heavy rail would be preferable to a tram-train scheme. The preference would be to provide direct services from Wisbech to Cambridge, but this will be constrained until improvements are made at Ely and a shuttle to March may be the interim solution.

Enhancements on the Fen line between Cambridge and King's Lynn were completed in 2020, enabling longer eight-car trains to run from December. The £29 million project included provision of a new siding outside King's Lynn and lengthened platforms at Littleport and Waterbeach and was delivered by Network Rail and contractor VolkerFitzpatrick.

STORMS BATTER THE RAILWAY

The effects of extreme weather on the railway were thrown into sharp focus in 2020. As well as the derailment of a ScotRail HST at Stonehaven on 12 August in which three people lost their lives, there were a number of lengthy closures due to flooding and landslips, notably in the early part of the year. In the case of the Conwy Valley line in north Wales an extended seven-month closure allowed more extensive repairs on a line frequently affected by severe weather, the line eventually reopening on 28 September.

In addition to the derailment at Stonehaven, severe weather in Scotland on the night of 11 August caused major damage to the main Edinburgh to Glasgow route in the Polmont area, with water cascading onto the railway following a breach of the Union Canal. The major repairs took just over six weeks, with the line reopening on 21 September.

The response to the Stonehaven derailment was more extensive. An interim report from Network Rail Chief Executive Andrew Haines to Transport Secretary Grant Shapps outlined actions including immediate inspection of sites at risk, changes to operating procedures and emergency instructions to signallers and controllers. Two task forces were also established: a weather action task force led by Dame Julia Slingo, and an earthworks management task force headed by Lord Robert Mair.

WORKING THROUGH COVID

Covid has posed significant challenges for infrastructure projects due to social distancing requirements. However, Network Rail and its contractors have adapted to the changed way of working and projects have continued, even if some tasks take longer than they otherwise would.

One advantage of the severe reduction in passenger numbers during the spring was the opportunity to close the railway and bring forward works. The best example of this was at Kilsby tunnel, five miles south east of Rugby on the West Coast main line, where Network Rail worked with operators to carry out work addressing longstanding drainage issues, allowing the linespeed to be raised from 90mph to 110mph. The work was organised over a two-week period, with services diverted over the slower Northampton route.

Another project taking advantage of Covid was a nine-day closure on the West of England line between Yeovil Junction and Gillingham in June 2020 to secure an embankment at Templecombe following a landslip in December 2019, allowing removal of two speed restrictions. The work was planned at short notice by Network Rail in conjunction with South Western Railway.

BEECHING REVERSAL FUND

In January 2020 the Government launched the £500 million 'Restoring your Railway' fund, which it says aims to kickstart reversal of the Beeching cuts. The headline element is an 'Ideas' fund, providing support to consultancy studies into reopening and enhancement projects; submissions must be backed by an MP.

Sixty proposals were submitted for the first round. The 10 successful schemes announced on 23 May included a range of stations reopening schemes, reinstatement of passenger services on freight-only or mothballed lines and enhancements to existing routes. In connection with one of the successful submissions, South Western Railway organised a fact-finder trip on the Fawley branch line in Hampshire on 28 July 2020. The branch last saw regular passenger services in 1966, with freight services ceasing in 2016.

Two further rounds of the Restoring your Railway scheme were promised, while a fresh round of the New Stations Fund has been announced with £20 million allocated.

One reopening scheme which is further advanced is the restoration of passenger services from Newcastle to Blyth and Ashington on the freight-only Northumberland line.

Fact-finder trip: South Western Railway arranged a special working on the Fawley branch on 28 July 2020 to promote the campaign to reopen the line for passenger services. From left, SWR MD Mark Hopwood, Network Rail Chair Sir Peter Hendy and Rail Minister Chris Heaton-Harris pose for a photo prior to departure from Southampton Central. **COURTESY SWR**

INFRASTRUCTURE ENHANCEMENT & RENEWAL

New station in the north east: Horden station on the Durham Coast line opened to passengers on 29 June 2020. **COURTESY NETWORK RAIL**

This scheme, awarded Government funding early in 2020, is now the subject of a Project Speed initiative.

NEW STATIONS

A number of new stations have opened in the last 12 months.

December 2019 saw two stations added to the network – Warrington West and Robroyston. The £19 million Warrington West station in Chapelford is served by Northern, with the station delivered in partnership with Warrington Borough Council, Network Rail and Balfour Beatty. Robroyston station in Glasgow cost £14 million and is on the Glasgow to Cumbernauld route. The main contractor was AMCO, working with ScotRail, Network Rail, Transport Scotland, Strathclyde Partnership for Transport and Glasgow City Council.

After a series of delays, Worcestershire Parkway station opened on 23 February 2020. The station is located at the intersection of the Cotswold line and the Cross Country line linking Birmingham with Cheltenham, with platforms on both routes. Worcestershire County Council led the project to deliver the station, with Buckingham Group the lead contractor.

On 29 June 2020 Horden station on the Durham Coast line was opened. The £10.55 million station was a joint project between Network Rail, operator Northern and Story Contracting, with funding from Durham County Council, the Department for Transport's New Stations Fund and a grant from the North East Local Enterprise Partnership.

The most recent addition to the network came on 15 October 2020 with the opening of Kintore station at the eastern end of the Aberdeen to Inverness line. The £15 million station was built by Network Rail and main contractor Bam Nuttall with funding from Transport Scotland, Aberdeenshire Council and Nestrans. A second new station towards the western end of the line at Dalcross, near Inverness airport, is in development.

MORE IN THE PIPELINE

Numerous new station schemes are in development, at varying stages.

Construction is underway on a new station at Reading Green Park, on the Reading to Basingstoke line. Balfour Beatty is the contractor, and after a delay due to Covid it is hoped the station will open in 2021.

Work continues on a new £40 million station at Brent Cross West on the Midland main line. Preparatory works including the realignment of the existing railway and alterations to sidings at Cricklewood, with piling beginning in October 2020. Barnet Council is leading this project and has appointed VolkerFitzpatrick as the construction contractor for the five-platform station; opening is scheduled for 2022.

Network Rail has appointed J Murphy and Sons to build a new station at Soham, east of Ely. Funding for the £18.6 million project is led by the Cambridgeshire and Peterborough Combined Authority, with a target opening date of December 2021.

Kent County Council has granted planning permission for a new Thanet Parkway station on the Ashford to Ramsgate line, planned to open in 2023, with main works planned to start in March 2021. The council's rail strategy also features ambitions to restore passenger services to the Isle of Grain.

Work continues to develop a new station at Cambridge South, serving the adjacent biomedical campus. The aim is to submit a Transport and Works Act Order application in 2021, and subject to further consultation and achievement of consents construction work could begin in 2023 with the station opening in 2025.

On the Great Eastern main line, a new station is in prospect at Beaulieu Park, north of Chelmsford. Housing Infrastructure Fund support was awarded to Essex County Council in 2019, supporting a new development of up to 14,000 homes. The station is planned to include loops where fast trains can overtake slower services.

In east London, a new station at Beam Park is planned on c2c's Tilbury branch between Dagenham Dock and Rainham, serving a major new housing development. Opening is due in 2022.

Devon County Council has ambitions to open further new stations around Exeter, notably Marsh Barton, west of Exeter St Thomas. In May 2020 Restoring your Railway funding was awarded for studies into reopening Cullompton and Wellington stations, the former in Devon and the latter in Somerset.

Transport for Wales is building a park and ride station at Bow Street, near Aberystwyth, which was due to open in 2020 but appears to have been delayed by the pandemic. Other new stations in prospect in Wales include Deeside Parkway on the Wrexham to Bidston line and several in south Wales as part of the Core Valley Lines modernisation.

North of the border, a planning application for a new station on the East Coast main line at Reston was submitted by Network Rail to Scottish Borders Council in September 2020. East Lothian and Scottish Borders Councils aim to open new stations at Reston and East Linton, to be served by a local service between Edinburgh and Berwick-upon-Tweed. It is hoped Reston station could open in late 2021, although a planning application for East Linton was yet to be submitted as of autumn 2020.

Authorities in West Yorkshire have secured Transforming Cities funding for a new White Rose station, between Leeds and Dewsbury on the trans-Pennine route. Pre-Covid, the aim was to begin construction in early 2021 and complete the station in mid-2022. White Rose would be located 750 metres from the current Cottingley station, which may close. ∎

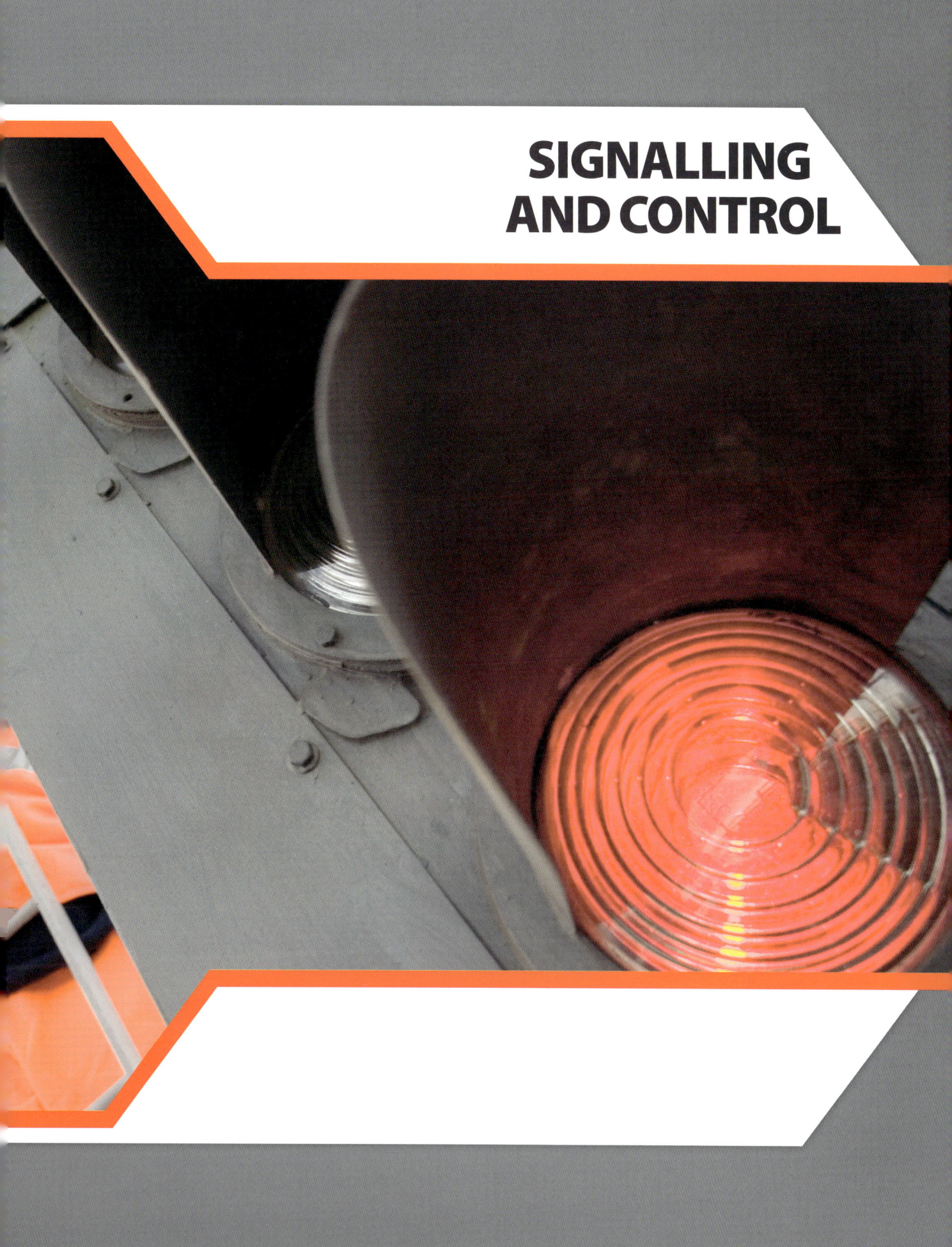

SIGNALLING AND CONTROL

MAIL ORDER

Key Books

366/20

LOCO-HAULED PASSENGER TRAINS

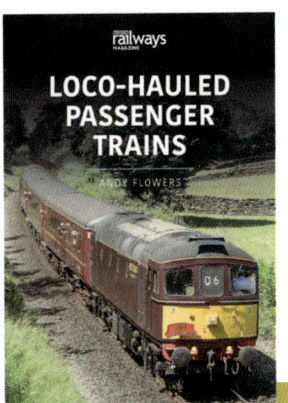

British Railways Series, Volume 1
A richly illustrated portrait of locomotive-hauled trains over four decades, from the 1980s to the present day. Softback, 96 pages.

Subscribers call for your £2 discount

ONLY £14.99 Code: B689

INTERNATIONAL PASSENGER LOCOMOTIVES

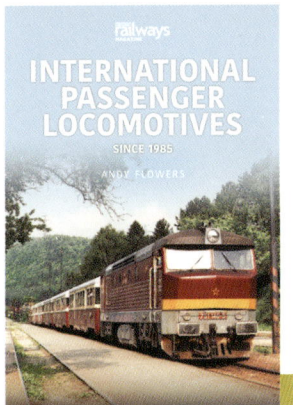

The World's Railway Series: Volume 1
This book summarises some of the more popular destinations and locomotives that enthusiasts travel abroad for. Softback, 96 pages

Subscribers call for your £2 discount

ONLY £14.99 Code: B697

RAIL FREIGHT NORTH WEST ENGLAND

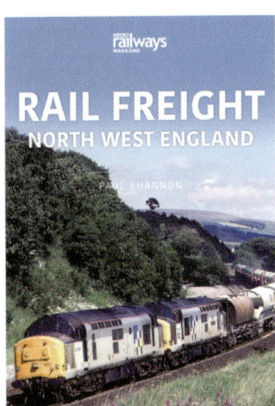

The Railways and Industry Series, Volume 3
A highly illustrated portrait of rail freight in a major industrial region over the last 40 years. Softback, 96 pages.

Subscribers call for your £2 discount

ONLY £14.99 Code: B690

CLASS 47S IN THE 1980S

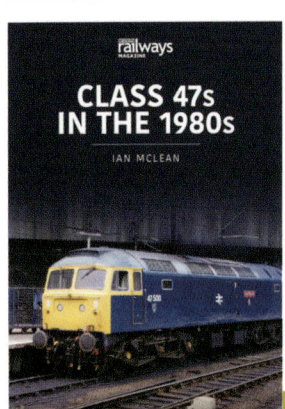

Britain's Railways Series: Volume 5
The Class 47 diesel locomotives were a mainstay of British Rail with 512 built in the 1960s. Softback, 96 pages

Subscribers call for your £2 discount

ONLY £14.99 Code: B701

RAILWAYS OF CENTRAL SCOTLAND

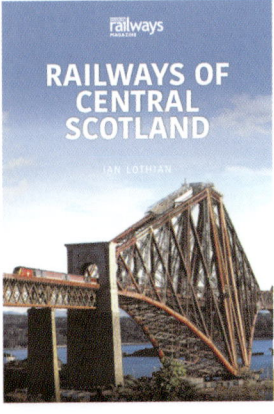

Britain's Railways Series, Volume 2
A unique portrait of the main lines of Central Scotland. Softback, 96 pages.

Subscribers call for your £2 discount

ONLY £14.99 Code: B692

BR: FROM GREEN TO BLUE

Britain's Railways Series: Volume 4
The many varied livery styles worn by British Rail's locomotives, units and coaching stock during from mid 1960s-1980s. Softback, 96 pages

Subscribers call for your £2 discount

ONLY £14.99 Code: B700

TO VIEW OUR FULL RANGE OF BOOKS, VISIT OUR SHOP

shop.keypublishing.com/books

Or call UK: 01780 480404 - overseas: +44 1780 480404

Monday to Friday 9am-5:30pm GMT. Free 2nd class P&P on all UK & BFPO orders. Overseas charges apply.
All publication dates subject to change

Signalling schemes press on

Highlights of 2020 included the culmination of the Wherry lines and Hither Green schemes

As with all infrastructure schemes, the Covid pandemic created challenges for delivering signalling projects during 2020.

Perhaps the best example is the resignalling in the Hither Green area, planned to be completed during the Easter bank holiday weekend but deferred to a week-long intervention in the summer.

Hither Green was a significant project as it marked the closure of the London Bridge Area Signalling Centre (ASC) with a recontrol to Three Bridges Rail Operating Centre (ROC). The signal box was built in 1974 and began controlling trains the following year. It once employed as many as 60 people, but the Thameslink programme was the catalyst for the transfer of signalling panels away from London Bridge, starting at Christmas 2014. After the Angerstein recontrol, only Panel 7 covering the Hither Green area was left at the ASC, covering the Southeastern main line as far as Chislehurst, the Dartford line as far as Mottingham and the Bromley North branch.

The commissioning was the culmination of a longer project lasting two years and featuring 21 stages. Siemens Mobility was the main contractor with Balfour Beatty engaged for the civils side. The project introduced 190 new signalling equivalent units (SEUs), 58 new signals, 20 ground position lights, 26 point conversions, five relocatable equipment buildings (REBs) and 20 location cabinets, 26 new signal posts and nine refurbished signal structures. The method of train detection was changed from track circuits to axle counters, and power supply improvements were made.

At the same time, the opportunity was taken to introduce flexibility in the signalling system to provide turnback opportunities for use at times of perturbation or during engineering works, with two at Hither Green, two at Grove Park and one at Lee. Moving the signal on platform 3 at Grove Park has enabled a 12-car train to be accommodated, rather than the previous 10-car maximum.

The original plan was for a 103-hour possession for the final commissioning over Easter weekend, but Network Rail concluded the amount of work required could not be completed while complying with social distancing requirements. Instead, commissioning was moved to a nine-day closure from 25 July to 2 August.

WHERRY LINES

Renewing life-expired equipment was the driver for the Wherry lines project, which was completed in February 2020. This scheme had suffered some delays, the original intention having been for completion in March 2019. Atkins was awarded a £29 million contract for the work, covering 42km of route between Norwich and Great Yarmouth/Lowestoft. Prior to that the line had been slated for a 'proof of concept' for digital railway technology, before those plans were reassessed.

The conclusion of the resignalling brought to an end over 130 years of operation using semaphore signals. A blockade during February marked the culmination of the project, with Alstom's ElectroLogIXS interlocking technology introduced and control transferred to Colchester signalling centre. The blockade began on 1 February, with the Norwich to Yarmouth line and the north end of the East Suffolk line from Beccles to Lowestoft reopening on 17 February, followed a week later by the Norwich to Lowestoft line and the branch from Reedham to Great Yarmouth via Berney Arms. The latter, a single line route, had been scheduled to close from October 2018 to March 2019 to allow works at Reedham Junction to take place, but in the event was shut for some 16 months.

Mechanical signal boxes at Brundall, Acle, Great Yarmouth, Cantley, Reedham, Oulton Broad North and Lowestoft all closed, with all the new hardware remote-monitored and controlled from Colchester. The system uses Frauscher axle counters for train detection while the GSM-R (railway mobile telecommunications) on the route is solar-powered, with diesel generator back-up.

While Atkins was lead contractor on the signal and telecommunications work, the opportunity was taken during the blockades to relay some track and renew points, with the Southern Rail Systems Alliance (Colas) undertaking this work. Track renewal and modifications were made at Lowestoft station and additional track renewal work completed at Hassingham, Acle and Oulton Broad North. Plans to renew a road bridge at Postwick were postponed due to poor weather during the blockade.

Level crossing upgrades were a key feature of the Wherry project. Control of six road level crossings (Lingwood Station Road and Chapel Road; Cantley; Brundall; Strumpsall; Oulton Broad North) transferred from local boxes to Colchester. In addition, 11 user worked crossings (UWCs) were upgraded.

NEW STREET ON THE HORIZON

Far more modern than the legacy Wherry lines technology but equally

On borrowed time: panel 7 at London Bridge ASC on 5 March 2020. This was the last remaining panel at the ASC, which ceased controlling trains with the Hither Green commissioning during the summer. **PHILIP SHERRATT**

SIGNALLING AND CONTROL

Historic scene: the date may only be 2 August 2019, but both the train and semaphore signals at Lowestoft have now been modernised. No 153322 arrives with the 10.17 from Ipswich. PHILIP SHERRATT

Control moving to Saltley: the final operational panel at Birmingham New Street power signal box, covering the station area, on 20 December 2019. TONY MILES

in need of replacement is signalling in the Birmingham New Street area. The scheme to resignal one of the busiest rail hubs in the country will be a landmark in Control Period 6.

It will lead to the closure of the Grade II listed New Street power signal box at the western end of the station, which was built in 1964 and opened two years later. The box is the last in the country to be relying on the Westpac Mk 1 signalling system, with its obsolete mechanical relays and associated equipment.

New Street marks the culmination of a series of resignalling projects across the West Midlands since 2007, with control transferring to the West Midlands Signalling Centre at Saltley. New Street is the final control area to transfer and the seventh phase of the programme.

After assessing options ranging from life extension of the existing equipment at New Street to creating an island of European Rail Traffic Management System, Network Rail opted to retain the existing layout with targeted enhancements and provision for future growth. Siemens is the framework contractor for the installation of its Westlock system, track circuits will be replaced by Thales axle counters and additional train despatch points through the station will improve the despatch process. Many mid-platform signals will be relocated to better suit modern operations. Once the work is complete, it is hoped to raise exit speeds in the station from the current 10mph to 15mph, potentially reducing platform reoccupation times by around 30 seconds.

Commissioning is planned for Christmas 2022. A series of Christmas blockades in consecutive years will be supplemented by a 'platform out of use' programme to enable to work to progress across the station.

METRO TRAVAILS
Schemes to introduce new signalling equipment on the London Underground and Glasgow Subway have both faced challenges, exacerbated by the Covid pandemic.

On LU, the Four Lines Modernisation programme is equipping the Circle, District, Hammersmith & City and Metropolitan Lines with new Communications Based Train Control (CBTC) equipment supplied by Thales. Introduction is progressive across a series of Signalling Migration Areas (SMAs), but despite initial sections going live in 2019, progress in 2020 was slow.

First to see automatic control was the western end of the Hammersmith branch as far as Latimer Road on 17 March 2019. Then at the beginning of September 2019 the new signalling reached the central area of the Circle Line for the first time, extending the boundary as far east as Euston Square and also bringing in the Metropolitan Line northwards to Finchley Road. Next up is a continuation eastward from Euston Square to Stepney Green and round the Circle Line to Monument (SMA 3), a large area including major junctions around Aldgate and six new signalling equipment rooms. However, technical challenges have delayed implementation and now the Covid pandemic has caused difficulties for the programme to train District Line train operators, as this section introduces the CBTC system to part of the main District Line trunk for the first time.

Nonetheless, LU has pressed on with installation of CBTC equipment where possible. The approach of the programme has been to concentrate on the sections in central London first, before moving out to areas where the lines interoperate with other services. Unconfirmed reports during 2020 suggested some of the latter elements of 4LM had been descoped, potentially alleviating some of these complications.

Also required is fitment of the CBTC equipment to trains, including the 192 Bombardier-built 'S' stock trains used on the four lines and LU's engineering trains. A series of timetable uplifts is planned once sufficient migration has been completed, with the final uplift scheduled for May 2023. The end state is a 32 trains per hour (tph) service over key sections of the four lines, up from a maximum 28tph today.

There have been challenges too with plans to introduce a new CBTC system on the Glasgow Subway. Strathclyde Partnership for Transport contracted a joint venture of Ansaldo (now Hitachi) and Stadler to provide new signalling and trains respectively. The original plan was that the new trains would run under the new signalling system from the outset, but this has now been revised and a software modification will allow them to operate under the legacy signalling until the new system is ready to go live. The current signalling on the Subway already uses automatic control but with a fixed block system.

The eventual plan on the Subway is for unattended train operation to be introduced. The new Stadler trains will initially have a temporary driver's cab at the end of the vehicle, but this can be removed later once the new signalling system is live and ready for a shift to unattended operation.

SIGNALLING FRAMEWORKS AWARDED
In early 2020 Network Rail awarded five framework contracts for signalling during Control Period 6 (2019-24). Worth an estimated £2.4 billion, the deals include an option to extend to 2026, potentially increasing contract value to £3.6 billion.

The frameworks went live on 31 January 2020 and are split into five geographical lots. Alstom has the contract for the Southern and Eastern Regions, Siemens Mobility for Scotland and North West & Central, and a joint venture of Hitachi Rail and Linbrooke Services for the Wales & Western Region.

The major signalling frameworks are the final awards in a three-tier approach to signalling delivery for CP6, following contracts in 2019 for minor signalling and refurbishments and for signalling and telecoms. NR says the frameworks are part of a wider new approach to commerciality with a focus on securing better deals with the supply chain, saving £3.5 billion over CP6. ■

DIGITAL RAILWAY
COST REDUCTION PLAN

Network Rail is aiming to drive down the cost of renewals

Plans to introduce digital signalling in the UK continue to gather pace. Network Rail is advancing its flagship East Coast digital programme, including implementation of European Train Control System (ETCS) and Traffic Management (TM), with contracts awarded in early 2020. In the longer-term, the aim is to reduce the cost of digital signalling to address the bow-wave of renewals due in Control Period 7 (2024-29) and beyond, for which NR believes implementation of conventional renewals would be impractical.

EAST COAST DIGITAL GO-AHEAD

2020 was a busy year for the East Coast digital programme (ECDP) as Network Rail awarded three contracts. Siemens Mobility was named as Train Control Partner (TCP), with the contract taking the form a framework agreement under which contracts will be called off for specific schemes replacing existing signalling with ETCS. The first such contract will cover the outline design for installation of ETCS Level 2 between London King's Cross and Peterborough North, plus a design, build and maintain contract for the Northern City line branch from Finsbury Park to Moorgate. Two lots are covered by the TCP framework, the East Coast main line resignalling and the Trans-Pennine Route Upgrade (TRU), and Siemens was awarded both lots.

Siemens Mobility has also been announced as the winner of the Traffic Management Partner framework which has been procured as part of the ECDP. Procurement has been managed on behalf of the Routes and is based on the requirements of the York and Manchester Rail Operating Centres (ROC).

Completing the ECDP is a third framework contract for a Railway Systems Integration Partner (RSIP), whose role will be to help co-ordinate the industry change in delivering the programme. The RSIP framework has been awarded to a consortium of consultants Atkins, Ramboll and PwC.

SIGNALS AWAY

In the summer the Government backed the ECDP with £350 million of funding, including for train fitment. Delivery of the programme will be in a series of tranches, starting with the Northern City line branch. Tranche 2 includes all the work required to fit trains with ETCS equipment and achieve operational readiness and will be complete by December 2024 ahead of the first 'signals away' deployment.

Current plans envisage Welwyn Garden City to Biggleswade being used as an overlay section, with ETCS installed but colour light signals retained, for the purposes of driver training and vehicle/infrastructure integration testing. The first area with no lineside signals is proposed to be Biggleswade to Holme, which would be part of the Tranche 4 'progressive rollout and transition to ETCS'. Tranche 3 involves the implementation of a Traffic Management System based at the York Rail Operating Centre (ROC). Tranche 5, 'optimisation and planning of operations', sees the full benefits of digital signalling realised by all users of the route.

The aim is to remove all lineside signals southward from Fletton Junction, just south of Peterborough, meaning only trains equipped with ETCS could operate here. From Fletton Junction through Peterborough station and to Stoke Tunnel, south of Grantham, the plan is to implement ETCS Level 2 but retain lineside signals, so trains not fitted with ETCS can run conventionally. This installation will include a recontrol of Peterborough Power Signal Box to York ROC. The ambition is to complete the transition to ETCS Level 2 between King's Cross and Stoke Tunnel by the end of 2029.

Partners in the ECDP have been keen to emphasise the practical benefits of the programme. LNER, the main inter-city operator on the ECML, has undertaken extensive driver scenario modelling work which suggests ETCS could save 44,000 minutes of unattributed delay over a typical four-week period.

TARGET 190 PLUS

The ECDP is the flagship digital railway project, taking advantage of the synergy of most trains on the route being ETCS-ready and renewals of signalling coming due, providing the opportunity to gain maximum benefit from thw switch to digital signalling.

Digital signalling coming: contracts have been awarded and funding confirmed for the East Coast digital programme. LNER Azuma No 800102 heads through Alexandra Palace with the 10.06 King's Cross to Newark Northgate service on 16 August 2019. **PHILIP SHERRATT**

SIGNALLING AND CONTROL

But there is also concern around the impending level of signalling renewals in CP7, and this is the basis behind Network Rail's Long Term Deployment Plan (LTDP) for digital signalling. Conventional signalling renewals require extensive access to the railway, whereas with a digital alternative much of the work can be carried out offline, reducing requirements for access and disruption to services.

Under the LTDP, the aim is to ramp up digital signalling renewals to a rate of 3,000 signalling equivalent units (SEUs) per year by Control Period 8 (2029-34). The Department for Transport has responded positively to the LTDP, and NR has identified two tranches of initial schemes as part of this programme.

Nine schemes have been identified in the LTDP where action is required in CP6 (2019-24) for delivery in CP7. These are:
- Midland main line – starting with the Bedford area;
- Extensions to the East Coast digital programme – Peterborough to Ely and King's Lynn;
- West Coast main line north – starting with the Warrington and Wigan area.

A further 22 schemes have been identified for which work should start in CP7 for delivery either in that funding period or into CP8 (2029-34).

While with conventional renewals the challenge is workload, in the LTDP the challenge shifts to cost. Network Rail has identified £190,000 per SEU as the target rate for the renewals it is planning. To drive towards this figure, it has initiated 'Target 190 plus', which is looking at how different delivery methods and reduced access can help drive out cost. This ambition sits alongside the Rail Sector Deal, driving further efficiencies and feeding back into the LTDP.

TRAIN FITMENT

Central to the success of the digital railway programme is fitment of the required technology to trains. Some trains are delivered with ETCS fitted, while others require retro-fitment – the East Coast programme includes examples of both. One example of a confirmed change during 2020 was the decision that East Midlands Railway's new Class 810 bi-modes built by Hitachi should be fitted with ETCS from the outset, rather than with passive provision as originally intended. This is because a section of the Midland main line is planned

Operating under ETCS: Class 345s have taken over from Class 360s on stopping services between Paddington and Heathrow Airport. COURTESY TFL

for ETCS fitment in CP7 as part of the LTDP, as explained above.

Perhaps the biggest challenge is fitting ETCS to freight locomotives. Siemens Mobility has a contract from Network Rail to fit the national freight locomotive fleet, totalling 745 locomotives. This covers 20 classes of locomotive along with further sub-classes, each requiring a bespoke design. Siemens has been carrying out design work for first in class installations for each type, and by mid-2020 design work was substantially complete for Class 66 and 67 locos. The next stage was for laboratory testing and then on-track testing at Network Rail's Rail Innovation and Development Centre. The programme aims to fit the complete national freight fleet by 2029.

THAMESLINK AND HEATHROW PROGRESS

Existing ETCS programmes have made progress over the past year.

Deployment of digital technology through the Thameslink core between Blackfriars and St Pancras represents a world-first in the use of Automatic Train Operation with ETCS. Siemens was the contractor for this programme, and also built the Class 700 trains used on Thameslink services.

Govia Thameslink Railway first used the ATO/ETCS technology in passenger service in March 2018, but deployment in day-to-day service was not a regular feature until December 2019, when ATO was switched on for final testing and validation. The use of ATO/ETCS is a requirement when service frequencies rise above 20 trains per hour (tph), although the timing of such a change is uncertain and likely to be even more so following the Covid pandemic. By mid-2020 GTR reported around 1,000 trips through the Thameslink core in passenger service had been made under ETCS and ATO, with the pause on driver training due to social distancing requirements a limiting factor in growing this number.

West of the capital, work has continued to introduce trains running under ETCS on the branch from the Great Western main line to Heathrow Airport. TfL Rail Class 345s began operating to Heathrow under ETCS from 30 July 2020, with the Bombardier-built trains taking over fully from the legacy Class 360s used on stopping service to the airport in September. Introduction of the '345s' on the airport branch has taken longer than planned due to compatibility issues with the trains.

Extensive testing has also been underway with Class 387 EMUs which were due to be introduced on Heathrow Express services by the end of 2020, replacing Class 332s. A sub-fleet of 12 '387s' has been retrofitted with ETCS and refurbished by Bombardier for use on the airport service, and as with the '345s' ETCS operation is needed on the airport branch. Operation of the Heathrow Express is now sub-contracted to Great Western Railway, which has worked with Porterbrook, Bombardier and other testing partners on the project. The first in class fitment to the '387s' could allow ETCS to be rolled out to other Bombardier Electrostar fleets.

In the longer term there are ambitions to convert the section of the Great Western main line into Paddington to ETCS as well.

CAMBRIAN ERTMS UPGRADE

The first in-service deployment of digital railway technology is getting an upgrade: Network Rail has received £3 million from the Department for Transport to assess the feasibility of updating the trackside software on the Cambrian lines.

The UK's pilot European Rail Traffic Management System (ERTMS) deployment was fully introduced on the lines in 2011. The driver for the work is the introduction by Transport for Wales Rail Services of new CAF-built Class 197 DMUs, which are not compatible with the current ERTMS software; a sub-fleet of Class 158s was retro-fitted to work Cambrian line services. Network Rail aims to complete the software change by December 2022, although it will be backwards compatible with the '158s', meaning the legacy fleet can continue in service until the new trains are introduced.

The £3 million fund received is to support software design and a series of laboratory tests required to validate the software compatibility between trackside and on-board ERTMS systems.

ETCS TO FENCHURCH STREET?

Could ETCS be coming to the Essex Thameside route? c2c's owner Trenitalia has developed a business case for introducing ETCS Level 2 between Upminster and Fenchurch Street, which could allow a frequency increase from 20 trains per hour to 24tph at peak times by May 2025, with the capability to support a 28tph service if needed. While Network Rail's Long Term Deployment Plan suggests ETCS would not be introduced on the route for around 20 years (when the current signalling becomes due for renewal), earlier introduction of digital signalling could provide a crucial capacity boost. This option found favour in Network Rail's Essex Thameside study, published in 2020, although what impact the pandemic may have on these plans to increase capacity is not yet clear.

LUMINATE DEAL

Following its successful deployment on Network Rail's Western Route, Resonate is to introduce its Luminate Integrated Traffic Management at the Liverpool Street signalling control centre. Following a one-year trial on the Western, the use of Luminate will become permanent, with NR licensing the Luminate software and Resonate providing maintenance and support. At Liverpool Street the rollout will build on the provision of Resonate's IECC Scalable platform, with Luminate covering all routes managed from the control centre, extending to Marks Tey, Stansted/Elsenham and Shenfield.

Under a separate contract, Resonate is to upgrade the Upminster IECC to Scalable. Thales' ARAMIS TM system at Romford Rail Operating Centre is providing an isolated TM facility at Upminster. ∎

LIGHT RAIL AND METRO

IN ASSOCIATION WITH

STADLER

LIGHT RAIL AND METRO

TRANSPORT for LONDON

Transport for London (TfL) is a statutory body created under the Greater London Authority Act 1999. This Act gives the Mayor a general duty to develop policies for safe, integrated and efficient transport in London.

TfL's role is to deliver the Mayor's strategy and to manage the services concerned. Currently there are around 8.9 million people living in Greater London, a figure which is expected to rise by around 12% to 10 million by the 2030s.

TFL COMPANIES

London Underground Ltd is the principal TfL rail operator and is a wholly owned subsidiary; it serves 270 stations. It became part of TfL on 15 July 2003. In the 2019-20 year, the Underground carried 1,337 million people, representing a continuing drop from the record carryings of 2017-18.

TfL is thus responsible for running the trains, stations and control centres, maintaining and renewing the infrastructure (except that of Network Rail), making sure the Underground is safe and secure, and collecting and protecting fares revenue.

Other TfL companies include Docklands Light Railway Ltd, which owns the land on which the DLR is built and is responsible for the operation of the railway, Rail for London Ltd (London Rail), Crossrail Ltd and London Transport Museum.

Transport Trading Ltd is the holding company for all TfL's operating transport companies. It receives and allocates revenues from the sale and use of Oystercards, contactless payments, Travelcards and similar.

The traditional home of London Transport and its successors, at 55 Broadway, is no longer part of TfL.

Large scale passenger growth over time has resulted in the system becoming ever more crowded; very exceptionally the Underground has carried over five million passengers a day. It has been said that the regular carriage of four million a day in future is a possibility.

The key requirement is to deliver a safe and reliable service day-in, day-out, irrespective of the performance of the ageing and often obsolete assets. The investment programme thus needs to make good the deficiencies in asset quality, and to build in sufficient new capacity to meet future demand. There also needs to be an ability to recover from the delays that do occur and customers need to be broadly satisfied with the overall results.

COVID-19

Covid-19 has had a similar effect on London Underground in terms of passenger loss as with national rail. Volumes fell precipitately from an early stage to around 5% of normal carryings, with recovery slightly quicker.

This has resulted in serious financial problems, and a Government rescue package on 14 May was contingent upon fares rising by RPI+1% in 2021 (as opposed to no change for the previous four years of the Mayor's office), restrictions on free travel for the under-18s and over-60s, and an increase in the road congestion charge.

The value of this package was up to £1.9 billion, covering the period from 1 April until 17 October. A review of TfL's future financial position and structure was commissioned by Government, but as of the autumn it had yet to be published or any outcomes confirmed.

With carryings and therefore revenues still significantly reduced, negotiations took place regarding a further Government support deal. As an interim measure, the package agreed in May was extended for a further two weeks until 31 October.

On 1 November Government and TfL confirmed a further support package. The funding is for a core amount of £1 billion for the period to 31 March 2021, with provision for this to rise to up to £1.8 billion dependent on ridership and therefore revenue. As part of the funding package, TfL committed to

LONDON UNDERGROUND
KEY STATISTICS

	2018-19	2019-20
Passenger journeys (millions)	1,384	1,337
Passenger kilometres (millions)	12,127	11,754
Passenger revenue (£ million, 2019-20 prices)	2,823	2,732

Wear a face covering: poster at Waterloo Underground station. COURTESY TFL

contribute approximately £160 million of the forecast funding shortfall, either through additional income or savings. Temporary changes to the congestion charge were maintained, as was the removal of free morning peak travel for 60+/older persons freedom pass holders.

BUSY STATIONS

The busiest Underground stations are, in descending order of passenger volumes, King's Cross St Pancras, Waterloo, Oxford Circus, Victoria, and London Bridge, with Liverpool Street close behind. All see between 70 million and 100 million entries and exits in a normal year.

King's Cross St Pancras is served by six Underground lines, feeding into (and fed by) the services of eight operators at the two main line stations above. Of the busiest stations, only Oxford Circus is not directly connected to a main line station. This indicates the very real pressures that interchanging passengers to and from National Rail put on the Underground in its role as urban distributor of commuters and others.

When services are operational on the Elizabeth Line (Crossrail) as well as Thameslink, there is likely to be further growth in Underground traffic. From where these lines intersect, at Farringdon, there will be direct services to the airports at Heathrow, Gatwick and Luton, and with a single change of train at Liverpool Street, Stansted and Southend. Reaching London City Airport takes a little more effort.

SOCIAL DISTANCING

TfL's advice in light of Covid indicated: 'Our network is at its busiest between the hours of 05.45-09.15 and 16.00-17.30'. There followed a list of stations which were said to be amongst the busiest at these times. The listing was separate for entry and for interchange. Interestingly, the hotspots mentioned above were omitted.

The restricted entry list showed Barking, East Ham, Lewisham DLR, Leyton, Liverpool Street LU, London Bridge LU, West Croydon, Wood Green and Woolwich Arsenal. That for interchange featured Canada Water, Clapham Junction, North Acton, Walthamstow Central and West Ham.

The others – Brixton, Canning Town, East Croydon, Seven Sisters and Stratford – were included in both categories.

Passengers were warned they might be asked to queue for entry, and to try and avoid interchanging at the stations so marked.

Bank upgrade: in October 2020 TfL confirmed tunnelling had been completed for the station capacity improvement project, due for completion in 2022. COURTESY TFL

TRAINS IN SERVICE

Off-peak travel, though less than that at the Monday to Friday peak, is now a very considerable part of the total. That includes the situation on Saturdays and Sundays. Table 1 shows that the maximum peak requirement for 542 trains remains at above 80% of that level during the day and for the maximum requirement at weekends. Fewer trains are needed at the ends of the day, particularly in the evenings.

The number of trains in use is not directly related to the numbers of passengers carried. Overall, though, the peak/off-peak service variations, in central and inner London anyway, are of little consequence. In terms of lateral thinking, it also suggests pricing of fares to encourage off-peak rather than peak travel has its limitations. It is no longer as effective as once it was.

As always, such figures conceal large variations. The Northern Line requires a maximum of 96 trains, followed by the Piccadilly at 78 and the Central at 77. The essentially urban Circle/Hammersmith & City Lines' train requirement varies only between 33 and 31 at the different time periods, while the Metropolitan with its large suburban/outer-suburban catchment drops sharply from 48 trains to 36.

Unsurprisingly, the Waterloo & City remained the odd one out by not running at all on Sundays, though it had an all-day service during the week; it was suspended in spring 2020 due to the pandemic, and remained so as of the autumn.

The problem has thus become the total volume of passengers, irrespective of when they choose to travel.

NIGHT TUBE

All night services at around six per hour have been run on the main sections of the Central, Jubilee, Northern, Piccadilly and Victoria Lines, on Friday and Saturday nights only and requiring a total of 76 trains in service. Both the Night Tube and Night Overground services were suspended during the coronavirus pandemic, a situation which is expected to continue until at least March 2021.

PICCADILLY NEW TRAINS

Siemens Mobility has been awarded the contract to design and build 94 new generation Inspiro trains for the Piccadilly Line, replacing the increasingly unreliable 1973 stock. The new trains will be walk through and air-cooled and complemented by investment in supporting infrastructure. This includes the modernisation and extension of depot facilities at Cockfosters and Northfields, as well as power upgrades. Intermediate driving cabs are no longer required, as all trains on all lines now run at full length. Capital costs are thus saved, with the space being made available for passenger use. Train frequencies are expected to increase to 27 trains per hour once the fleet is in service.

TfL would like to introduce new signalling on the Piccadilly Line to capitalise on the investment in new trains, potentially allowing frequencies of up to 36tph. A tender for new signalling was cancelled due to lack of funding certainty, for which TfL continues to lobby. Any such proposal would also require a significant upgrade to increase capacity at Holborn station.

OTHER TUBE LINES

Further train builds to a uniform if not identical design to that for the Piccadilly were anticipated for the Bakerloo, Central and Waterloo & City Lines, but these have all been 'paused' as a result of Covid-19. Uniform fleets allow trains to be transferred between lines should requirements change over time, though differing platform lengths between lines are just one of the many items that would have to be considered.

A more recent TfL proposal is to build 73 new trains for the Jubilee Line. Some of the current Jubilee Line trains could then be transferred to the Northern Line, whose services would be split into two separate lines based on the two routes through central London. This would require an upgrade of Camden Town station.

NORTHERN TO BATTERSEA

The twin tunnels of the 3.2km Northern Line extension run from step plate junctions on the terminal loop of the Charing Cross branch of the Northern

TABLE 1: TRAINS REQUIRED FOR SERVICE, LONDON UNDERGROUND, SEPTEMBER 2020

	NUMBER	AS INDEX
Mondays to Fridays at 09.00	542	100
Mondays to Fridays at 12.00	452	83
Saturdays, maximum	473	87
Sundays, maximum	449	83

Source: LU Working Timetables

LIGHT RAIL AND METRO

To be replaced by new trains for Siemens: a 1973 stock train on the Piccadilly Line arrives at Covent Garden on 29 July 2019. **PHILIP SHERRATT**

Line at Kennington to new stations at Nine Elms and Battersea Power Station.

Opening towards the end of 2021 is anticipated. The two new stations will not have platform doors, as in any event there is insufficient space to install them at other Northern Line stations. Some reconstruction of the junction station at Kennington has been completed.

Trains will be run as an extension of the Charing Cross services; it will not be possible to run between the new branch and the line via Bank. It is not intended, at present anyway, to extend the new spur west of Battersea.

BANK/MONUMENT

Bank/Monument might be termed a combined station. The 10 platforms there are served, at various levels, by the Central, Circle, District, Northern and Waterloo & City Lines, plus the Docklands Light Railway.

The station complex (337,000 passengers a day) is being extensively reconstructed. The southbound Northern Line tunnel is being diverted to a new tunnel, with the space vacated used by a new long concourse. Travelators will speed passengers from one end of the station (District/Circle Lines) to the other (Central Line). Bringing all this into operation will cause a prolonged closure of the Northern Line City branch. There are also new street level station entrances.

Completion is expected during 2022.

FOUR LINES MODERNISATION

The Circle, Hammersmith & City, District and Metropolitan Lines are now operated exclusively by Bombardier 'S' stock. The 192 air-conditioned trains consist of eight-car sets for the Metropolitan (S8) and seven-cars for the remainder (S7).

On the sub-surface railway, which constitutes nearly 40% of the total, all signalling equipment is being replaced. Thales is installing the digital signalling and train control systems.

Line capacities will be increased by around one-third. An example target is 32 trains per hour on both sides of the traditional Circle Line. The new Service Control Centre for all four lines is at Hammersmith and controlled from seven desks.

Trains will be driven automatically. The train operator in the cab will open and close the doors and will be responsible for managing customer information and safety. Completion in 2023 is expected.

The introduction of regenerative braking has allowed a reduction in the overall power consumption on the District. Other work has included strengthening power supplies generally, lengthening platforms, laying new track and rebuilding the rolling stock depots.

ESCALATORS

Otis holds a contract for the procurement and maintenance of new escalators throughout their 30-year life. At least 50 heavy duty metro-type will be installed on LU over the next 10 years, excluding those for Crossrail. A major aim is to improve reliability, given that most operate for 20 hours a day and each runs for an average of 46 days between failures. The whole life cost of a single escalator is around £2.5 million.

FARES AND TICKETING

Payments for all TfL services are dominated by Oystercard, although contactless payments are rising fast. Oystercard acts as a prepaid credit card, topped up by the user as necessary. The Oystercard is now 17 years old.

Underground ticket offices are now all but extinct. Cash fares are available from ticket machines, but these are priced to discourage usage. Typically, the charge is about twice Oyster levels.

BAKERLOO EXTENSION

The proposed Phase One extension of the Bakerloo Line is to take it south from Elephant & Castle in tunnel via the Old Kent Road (two stations) to New Cross Gate (reconstruction) and Lewisham (new integrated station). A Transport and Works Act application has yet to be made and the work is presently unfunded. This scheme is presently paused.

LONDON RAIL

Transport for London's London Rail deals with the National Rail network in London. Tasks include overseeing major new rail projects related to London Overground, managing the Overground concession and also the operation of the Docklands Light Railway and London Tramlink. It supports and develops Crossrail and Thameslink and supports Network Rail's contribution to the public transport system.

It also works with the DfT and the rail industry to improve national rail services in London and liaises with the rail freight industry. The Mayor's Transport Strategy seeks the devolution of a number of passenger services on National Rail to TfL control.

The Mayor also seeks to develop a series of mini-radial hubs on the National Rail network with strategic interchanges at Willesden Junction/ Old Oak, Stratford, Lewisham and Clapham Junction, together with improved orbital rail links.

These include a new West London Orbital rail route over existing and upgraded Network Rail infrastructure as part of London Overground. This might run from Cricklewood and Hendon via Dudding Hill to Old Oak Common, Acton Wells Junction, South Acton and Hounslow. This scheme is presently paused.

The Mayor would also wish to see the Elizabeth Line extended from Abbey Wood towards Ebbsfleet. Construction of the 4.5km Barking Riverside branch as an extension of Tottenham & Hampstead line Overground services is already underway.

CROSSRAIL 2

The Crossrail 2 proposal envisages a route in new tunnelling between Wimbledon and Tottenham Hale, with a branch to New Southgate. Elements of the route remain undetermined, but in general it would serve Clapham Junction, King's Road Chelsea, Victoria, Tottenham Court Road, a combined station with exits to both Euston and St Pancras main line stations, Angel and Dalston.

At the outer ends, it would extend over Network Rail lines to Epsom, Chessington South, Hampton Court and Shepperton, and in the north over a newly four-tracked Lea Valley line to Broxbourne.

This approach, with the use of full-sized rolling stock, is similar to that of both Crossrail and Thameslink. Euston would be important, to cater for the additional traffic of HS2 passengers.

Various cost saving measures have been suggested, such as dispensing with the New Southgate branch. A less ambitious but wholly urban version of Crossrail 2, which did not extend onto Network Rail tracks at either Tottenham or Wimbledon, might also be possible.

The National Infrastructure Commission has endorsed the project, but both construction powers and funding are lacking. In October 2020 it was confirmed work on the scheme was formally paused.

LONDON TRAVELWATCH

London Travelwatch is the statutory organisation representing transport users in and around the capital. It is sponsored and funded by the London Assembly. It promotes integrated transport policies and presses for higher standards of quality, performance and accessibility. It also deals with user complaints.
Director Emma Gibson

IN ASSOCIATION WITH **STADLER**

Edinburgh Trams: a service for York Place approaches Haymarket on 30 July 2019. **PHILIP SHERRATT**

Light rail developments

The light rail sector was hit as hard as national rail by the Covid-19 outbreak, with passenger numbers falling and service cutbacks the order of the day from March 2020. Table 1 summarises the overall situation to the end of the years 2015-16, 2018-19 and 2019-20. These figures are derived from national statistics issued by the Department for Transport. They cover the 10 major systems operating in Britain as set out in this chapter and exclude London Underground. All except Edinburgh Trams and Glasgow Subway are in England.

The severity of the decline in 2019-20 will be noted, given Covid-19 only affected the last part of the year ended 31 March 2020. Provisional results for operations until July suggest both patronage and revenues declined to a mere 5% of their pre-Covid values – this seems to have been general throughout the sector.

The results for the rest of 2020 were showing signs of a slow recovery. Government support for operators was forthcoming for the initial period. It may be noted that total route kilometres open have changed little over the whole of this period.

The interworking of light and heavy rail looks likely to be extended on Tyne and Wear on the South Shields branch, this time with freight operations. Transport for Greater Manchester has shown an interest in tram-train operation on some of its suburban railways and trials of the concept may be conducted. Technical advances include battery operation over a short section of the West Midlands tram system, with more likely to follow. Many tram systems have now been in operation for several years; amongst these has been Nottingham Express Transit, where extensive infrastructure renewal has been necessary.

What scope might there be for innovations such as Very Light Rail (VLR) and is there a market? The rough and tumble encountered with operational systems always needs to be remembered, and experimentation with VLR will be watched with interest.

More efficient operation is always a goal, and the Glasgow Subway seems to be well on the way to having unstaffed trains. Elsewhere, the duties of on-train staff may be confined to commercial roles. With unsegregated systems, which includes most tramways, the post of at least the driver would seem to be secure. Who or what else is needed?

LIGHT RAIL AND METRO NETWORKS

KEY STATISTICS	2018-19	2019-20
Passenger journeys (millions)	5.2	4.8
Passenger kilometres (millions)	22.7	21.0
Passenger revenue (£ million, 2019-20 prices)	7.2	6.7

Blackpool trams alone survive from the first generation tramways, but only one of the original routes remains, the 18km from Starr Gate, Blackpool to the Ferry Terminus, Fleetwood. This is a 600V DC overhead system. Operation is by the municipally owned Blackpool Transport Services Ltd under contract to Blackpool Borough Council.

The 18 Bombardier 'Flexity 2' trams are housed at Starr Gate depot. Each has five articulated sections. These 32.2-metre long vehicles have 74 seats plus a standing capacity of 148. They are fully accessible, with level access at the 37 stops. End-to-end journey times are about 58 minutes and all trams carry conductors.

There are also some vintage double-deckers and a heritage fleet.

Passenger journeys seemed to be stabilising at around the levels reached in the early 1990s. However, stormy weather in summer 2019 resulted in heavy reductions in both services and patronage. On Sunday 29 March 2020, Covid-19 resulted in the complete closure of the tramway. Services did not resume until Sunday 19 July, 17 weeks later.

The £22 million extension of the tramway system from North Pier to a new terminus at Blackpool North station has been funded by the Local Enterprise Partnership and Blackpool Council. This sum includes the cost of two additional 'Flexity 2' trams. Work started in 2017 and completion is not now expected until 2022.

KEY STATISTICS	2018-19	2019-20
Passenger journeys (millions)	121.4	116.8
Passenger kilometres (millions)	656.6	620.7
Passenger revenue (£ million, 2019-20 prices)	174.9	168.8

The Docklands Light Railway dates from 1982 when the London Docklands Development

TABLE 1: LIGHT RAIL IN BRITAIN, ALL SYSTEMS

	2015-16	2018-19	2019-20
Passenger journeys (millions)	263.7	295.4	283.3
Passenger kilometres (millions)	1,760.0	1,933.0	1,853.2
Passenger revenue (£ million, 2019-20 prices)	390.9	423.6	413.3
Route kilometres open	364	372	378

LIGHT RAIL AND METRO

Metrolink extension opens: on the first day of operation for the Trafford Park line, 22 March 2020, tram No 3092 heads away from the Trafford Centre towards Pomona after calling at the first stop at Barton Dock Road. **TONY MILES**

New fleet for the Metro: visual of the trains Stadler will build for the Tyne and Wear Metro.

Corporation was formed to co-ordinate the redevelopment of the extensive and very rundown area. The docks themselves had all moved downstream.

The 12km first stage of the Docklands Light Railway opened in 1987 with two routes, from both Tower Gateway and Stratford to Island Gardens. There were 15 stations and a fleet of 11 two-section articulated cars. Extensions have since taken the system to its present length of 38km with 45 stations and three-car length trains. Trains are driven automatically, but the Passenger Service Agent is responsible for closing the doors.

The third rail 750V DC electrification uses underside contact. There are many grade-separated junctions, keeping operational conflicts to the minimum. Alcatel Seltrac moving block signalling is used.

The system is operated by Keolis Amey Docklands, the extended contract now continuing until April 2025. The company is paid a fixed fee for operating the railway to agreed levels and standards of service, with adjustments for performance. The Lewisham extension remains in the hands of City Greenwich Lewisham Railway until that contract expires during 2021.

An order for 43 new 87-metre long trains has been placed with CAF of Spain, for delivery from 2023. Of these, 33 will replace the B90/B92 fleets, with the other 10 catering for traffic growth. As a consequence, Beckton depot is being enlarged.

The newer B07 vehicles will remain in service; these have been converted to all-longitudinal seating. This is to increase unit capacity, as seen in the builds of more recent Underground trains.

To serve the Royal Docks development, infrastructure and service enhancements are planned. Under consideration is a new cross-river branch of the DLR to serve Thamesmead.

The Network Rail Essex Thameside study of July 2020 suggested passenger growth at Fenchurch Street makes a six (instead of four) platform station highly desirable. This might be achieved by moving the station site 350 metres further east, which would result in the forced closure of the DLR's Tower Gateway terminus.

KEY STATISTICS	2018-19	2019-20
Passenger journeys (millions)	7.5	7.1
Passenger kilometres (millions)	1.4	1.4
Passenger revenue (£ million, 2019-20 prices)	16.0	15.9

Edinburgh Trams is the operator and infrastructure manager of the city's tramway. Transport for Edinburgh is the holding company for the local authority owned operator.

Services commenced on the 14km line from the Airport to York Place on 31 May 2014. End-to-end journey time is about 35 minutes for the 15 stops. The 27 seven-section 42.8-metre trams built by CAF are based at Gogar depot and are the longest in use in Britain. Ticketing Services Assistants on trams check, but do not issue, tickets. Penalty fares are in operation. In normal times, there is a core service frequency of every 7½ minutes, enhanced at peak periods.

The project had a difficult construction period involving cost over-runs, construction delays and delivery of a lesser system than was planned. A public inquiry was established in June 2014 to ascertain why matters went so badly wrong, but six years later its report was still awaited when this book went to press.

Work has now commenced on the original proposal for Line 1a, a 5km extension from York Place to Leith and Newhaven, with eight additional stops. The cost is £207 million and opening in 2023 is expected.

KEY STATISTICS	2018-19	2019-20
Passenger journeys (millions)	13.1	12.7
Passenger kilometres (millions)	41.9	40.7
Passenger revenue (£ million, 2019-20 prices)	18.9	20.2

The circular 10.6km route of the Glasgow Subway has 15 stations and is wholly underground. Broomloan depot alone is on the surface, reached by ramps between Ibrox and Govan stations. The busiest stations are Buchanan Street and St Enoch with 5.2 million and 3.8 million passenger entries and exits respectively in 2018, followed by Hillhead at 3.7 million and Kelvinbridge with 2.0 million.

Presently, a round trip will take 24 minutes, with a train every four minutes in each direction at peak. Two separate running tunnels (inner circle and outer circle) are built to the restrictive diameter of 3.35 metres, and track gauge is a unique 1,220mm (4ft). The present three-car trains are a mere 38.3 metres long.

This 600V DC third rail system is owned and operated by Strathclyde Passenger Transport (SPT). It opened with cable traction in 1896, was electrified in 1935 and refurbished in 1980.

Transport Scotland and SPT have made grants for system modernisation. The 17 new trains from Stadler are in course of delivery, with three pre-series trains undergoing testing on a track behind Broomloan depot. Each is of four cars, formed of two articulated pairs, with wide inter-car gangways available for passenger use. All seating is longitudinal.

This £288 million contract includes the associated signalling, communication and control systems in a consortium with Ansaldo (now Hitachi). Tunnel linings and water ingress problems have also been addressed, while a station modernisation package is now complete. Platforms will eventually have 1.7-metre-high screen doors.

Trains in operation will be increased from 12 to 16. Later, temporary drivers' cabs will be removed and Unattended Train Operation (UTO) will be introduced.

KEY STATISTICS	2018-19	2019-20
Passenger journeys (millions)	28.7	27.2
Passenger kilometres (millions)	149.2	141.3
Passenger revenue (£ million, 2019-20 prices)	23.9	22.7

London Trams links Croydon to Wimbledon, Beckenham Junction and Elmers End with three branches; formerly these were for the most part heavy rail on a reserved formation. A further line serves New Addington. The core is a one-way street level loop around central Croydon.

The system is 28km long and became fully operational in May 2000. There are 39 stops. Electrification is at 750V DC. The original 24 three-section trams were built by Bombardier, later supplemented by 10 Variobahn trams from Stadler. Selective double tracking has been undertaken, with the aim of offering a more reliable and resilient tram network. Higher frequencies are in prospect generally, with more trams, for which a second depot will be needed.

Operation is by FirstGroup subsidiary Tram Operations Ltd; tram maintenance is in house at Therapia Lane depot. The assets are owned by Transport for London.

Extensive changes have been made to both systems and operations since the Sandilands derailment in 2016, but traffic volumes have yet to recover.

The preferred route for system extension is an on-road route from Colliers Wood to Sutton, crossing the existing Tramlink branch from Wimbledon at Belgrave Walk. This is as yet unfunded and has been paused.

KEY STATISTICS	2018-19	2019-20
Passenger journeys (millions)	43.7	44.3
Passenger kilometres (millions)	457.3	463.0
Passenger revenue (£ million, 2019-20 prices)	83.7	82.6

Manchester's Metrolink began operations in 1992 using the rail infrastructure on the radial Bury and Altrincham lines and combining them using street running through the city centre. This is a 750V DC high-floor system.

Extensions have taken Metrolink to five groups of routes. The Second City Crossing was opened in 2015, enhancing capacity, but also giving some operating flexibility and benefits to reliability. More recently, the 5.4km branch from Pomona to Trafford Park was opened on 22 March 2020. There are six new stops, and the line is mostly segregated. Larger infrastructure works include the Pomona viaduct and the Bridgewater Canal crossing. The expanding network has resulted in substantial growth in passenger usage.

A fleet of 120 Bombardier M5000 'Flexity Swift' trams provides all services. A further tranche of 27 vehicles is to be delivered to support future passenger growth. These are 28.4-metre six-axle vehicles in two sections, with a capacity of 206 passengers in total. Depots are at Queen's Road and Trafford Bar.

Metrolink is owned by Transport for Greater Manchester and the system is operated and maintained by KeolisAmey.

A zonal fares system features four concentric zones, based around Manchester city centre. Metrolink now has 99 stops, more than any other British light rail network.

Future opportunities include an extension to Manchester Airport Terminal 2 and beyond, while it is intended to evaluate tram-train opportunities through 'pathfinder' trials on up to three selected routes. In the much longer-term, a city centre Metrolink tunnel is a possibility.

Manchester Metrolink was the only light rail system to show a modest increase of 1.4% in passenger journeys from 2018-19 to 2019-20.

KEY STATISTICS	2018-19	2019-20
Passenger journeys (millions)	18.8	18.7
Passenger kilometres (millions)	123.9	123.3
Passenger revenue (£ million, 2019-20 prices)	21.0	21.3

The 32km Nottingham Express Transit (NET) system has 51 stops. It consists of three lines and all trams serving the city centre call at Nottingham station. Line 1 to Hucknall and Phoenix Park opened in 2004, and Line 2 to Clifton South and Line 3 to Toton Lane in 2015.

The original fleet consisted of 15 articulated five-section 33.0-metre Bombardier vehicles, later supplemented by a further 22 five-section Alstom Citadis 302 trams. Each pair of cars has around 56 seats. The depot is at Wilkinson Street. Electrification is at 750V DC.

NET serves a number of park and ride sites, together accommodating around 5,400 parking spaces.

The Tramlink Nottingham consortium holds a Private Finance Initiative concession to finance, build, operate and maintain NET Lines 2 and 3, as well as the operation and maintenance of Line 1 until the end of 2033. Track wear in the central area after 16 years of use saw extensive closures to enable replacement during 2020.

In the future, Line 3 could be extended by around 2km to the site of the planned HS2 station at Toton, subject to the future of that part of the high-speed scheme.

Stagecoach SUPERTRAM

KEY STATISTICS	2018-19	2019-20
Passenger journeys (millions)	11.9	10.5
Passenger kilometres (millions)	77.4	68.2
Passenger revenue (£ million, 2019-20 prices)	14.3	13.8

The 750V DC Supertram network was opened in 1994-95. About half the 29 route kilometres of the original system are fully segregated, with on-street running for the rest. Curvature is tight, with maximum gradients of 10%.

Services are operated by Stagecoach from the city centre to Middlewood, Meadowhall Interchange, Halfway and Herdings Park. Passenger journeys reached 15 million in 2010-11 but have since declined very substantially. The present operating contract with Stagecoach continues until 2024.

Operation is by 25 three-section Siemens/Duewag cars, each of 34.8 metres in length and based at Nunnery Square. These 80-seat vehicles can accommodate around 200 standing passengers.

The Citylink tram-train project is testing the operation of specialist tramway-type vehicles on both a conventional tram network and the national rail system. Inaugurated on 25 October 2018, tram-trains run at three services per hour from Sheffield Cathedral over the existing tram line to Meadowhall South, thence by the Tinsley chord to the freight-only railway to Rotherham Central and a terminus beyond at Parkgate Retail Centre. The throughout journey takes about 27 minutes.

Operation is by seven Class 399 three-section 37.2-metre Citylink tram-train vehicles, built by Vossloh (now Stadler) in 2015-16. They have 25kV AC as well as 750V DC capability, but the present application uses DC only.

The difficulties of uniting heavy and light rail were considerable. They included the wheel/rail profiles of each, technical standards variations such as crashworthiness, vehicle detection for signalling purposes, use of sanders for adhesion and the use of magnetic track brakes. Platform heights can differ, too, with light rail systems using low level stops (as in Sheffield) or high level (as in Manchester).

This Government-funded project has been developed by a partnership led by South Yorkshire Passenger Transport Executive. The PTE manages the legal framework, maintains the tram line part of the tram-train route, owns the vehicles and looks after the operating contract. Network Rail maintains the heavy rail part. Stagecoach runs the services, employs the staff and maintains the vehicles.

The pilot project was for two years, but in October 2020 it was confirmed the service would continue. Transport Focus has recorded 100% passenger satisfaction with the tram-train service.

KEY STATISTICS	2018-19	2019-20
Passenger journeys (millions)	36.4	33.1
Passenger kilometres (millions)	318.6	289.1
Passenger revenue (£ million, 2019-20 prices)	52.9	49.1

The Tyne and Wear Metro reinvigorated previously electrified suburban lines operated by British Rail. These were linked by underground construction in Newcastle city centre and a new bridge over the river Tyne. The first services started in 1980 and successive enhancements have taken the system to its present length of 78km. There are 60 stations and electrification is at 1,500V DC overhead.

Substantial early patronage with a high of 59.1 million in 1985-86 dwindled, with a low of 32.5 million passengers in 2000-01. Usage subsequently recovered to around 40 million, but this has not been sustained.

The Green line runs from Airport to South Hylton, the Yellow line from St James to South Shields via Whitley Bay. They overlap in the central area. The section from Pelaw towards Sunderland and South Hylton is on Network Rail infrastructure, which is in part shared with National Rail trains.

Nexus is the public body delivering local transport services for Tyne and Wear on behalf of the North East Joint Transport Committee. Metro is an in-house operation. Nexus has always owned the Metro, set fares and determined services. Metro's 'All Change' package 2010-21 was funded by Government, providing an operating subsidy and extensive modernisation and renewals.

The original fleet is to be replaced by new trains from Stadler, for delivery from 2022 and with full operation from

LIGHT RAIL AND METRO

Catenary-free operation: a West Midlands Metro tram calls at the Town Hall stop on the Centenary Square extension on 31 December 2019. The short extension from the previous Grand Central terminus sees trams operate under battery power. PHILIP SHERRATT

Midland Metro's 20.4km Line 1 between Birmingham Snow Hill and Wolverhampton opened in 1999, mostly over the reserved formation of the Great Western Railway.

Line 1 has been diverted at the Birmingham end via Bull Street to Grand Central (for New Street station) and thence to Centenary Square. The latter part uses battery operation and opened in December 2019. It will be further extended to Edgbaston Village by the end of 2021.

At Wolverhampton, the St Georges terminus will continue to be served, but an extension from The Royal is following a new 700-metre route to the bus and railway stations. Completion is linked to the latter's redevelopment.

An eastside extension is from a new Bull Street junction to New Canal Street (for HS2) and High Street Deritend, for which a Transport and Works Act Order was issued in January 2020. The Secretary of State is satisfied that funds should be available. Eventually, it is intended this line should reach Birmingham International (rail and airport), the NEC and Birmingham Interchange (again for HS2).

The enabling Transport and Works Act Order for the 11km extension from Wednesbury to Dudley and Brierley Hill over the former heavy rail route was received in July 2020 and operations are expected to commence in 2023.

The Midland Metro Alliance is planning, designing and delivering all four extensions for the West Midlands Combined Authority.

Services are provided by a fleet of 21 CAF Urbos 3 trams, capable of operation under battery and overhead electric power. These are 33 metres long and can carry a total of around 200 passengers. An additional 21 trams have been ordered from CAF to support future extensions, with an option for a further 29 on top of that.

Services are operated by West Midlands Metro Ltd, a company wholly owned by the West Midlands Combined Authority. A 10 trams per hour service during the day reduces to four per hour early, late and on Sundays. Electrification is at 750V DC overhead and the operations centre and depot are at Wednesbury.

2024. This 42-strong fleet will have all longitudinal seating, air-conditioning and battery power capability. The five-section trains will be 60 metres long and the contract covers both their supply and maintenance for 35 years. In October 2020 Stadler took over maintenance of the legacy fleet ahead of delivery of the new trains.

In March 2020, Metro Flow was announced. The whole of the branch from Pelaw to South Shields will be converted to double track, electrified, and shared with freight services on a similar basis to the present operation from Pelaw to Sunderland. Four additional trains are planned to be ordered to support the service enhancement this will permit.

Stadler is leading the rebuilding of the South Gosforth depot, a five-year project. A new satellite depot has been built at Howden in North Tyneside to assist with maintenance during the rebuilding. A skills centre is being constructed at South Shields.

KEY STATISTICS	2018-19	2019-20
Passenger journeys (millions)	8.3	8.0
Passenger kilometres (millions)	86.9	84.3
Passenger revenue (£ million, 2019-20 prices)	10.9	11.3

STOURBRIDGE SHUTTLE
Pre-Metro Operations Ltd (PMOL) runs the 1.2km self-contained single-track Network Rail branch between Stourbridge Junction and Stourbridge Town. This is the shortest branch line in Britain, run by the smallest train operating company. The only pointwork on the branch is that connecting it to the main line, which is not in regular use.

A four-wheeled Class 139 Parry People Mover is used, with a second as a spare. These hybrids have a small Ford engine powered by LPG and flywheel stored energy. The vehicles are 8.7 metres long and weigh 12.5 tonnes, with a maximum speed of 45mph. There are 21 seats and a total carrying capacity of around 50. During the 2020 lockdown, passenger numbers were limited to eight per journey and services reduced from six to four an hour, with breaks for vehicle cleaning. Running time is three minutes and service reliability better than 99%.

PMOL operates on behalf of West Midlands Railway, employs the operating staff and maintains the vehicles.

In 2018-19, 592,000 passenger entries and exits were recorded at Stourbridge Town. The vast majority interchanged with other rail services at Stourbridge Junction National Rail station.

UK TRAM
UK Tram is a not for profit trade body for all light rail and other guided transport systems in the British Isles. Its purpose is to provide a single industry voice in dealing with Government and statutory bodies.

The objectives are to address underperformance or cost escalation of some tram and light rail schemes and to help develop a co-ordinated and structured approach to regulation, procurement and standardisation. At the same time best practice is to be shared, while enhancing the industry's reputation.

Investigations include those which could speed up and reduce the cost of network construction, or result in lower energy and operating costs.

There are advisory groups on safety, operations, engineering, heritage systems and the promotion of light rail.
Managing Director James Hammett

LIGHT RAIL SAFETY & STANDARDS BOARD (LRSSB)
A subsidiary of UK Tram, the LRSSB's purposes are to enable UK-wide co-operation on safety matters, to develop tram standards and good practice, and to provide authoritative and impartial advice. LRSSB was established following the Rail Accident Investigation Branch report on the 2016 accident at Sandilands, Croydon.
Chief Executive Carl Williams

VERY LIGHT RAIL
Light rail is costly in terms of both vehicles and infrastructure. Could cheaper forms be developed? A Very Light Rail research and development programme aims to deliver the benefits of trams, but at a fraction of the cost. Funding of £14.7 million from the West Midlands Combined Authority and the Coventry and Warwickshire Local Enterprise Partnership has been secured.

A key feature will be low cost track, quickly installed and designed to minimise the need to relocate utilities. A lightweight battery powered rail guided demonstrator vehicle with a capacity for 56 passengers is under construction, with driverless operation the ultimate aim. It is to be tested at the National Innovation Centre in Dudley in 2021.

A permanent 7km tracked route is planned for Coventry, from the station via the city centre to the University Hospital, using a fleet of production vehicles. Around 80% of the route would operate in mixed traffic.

Such schemes are also known as Ultra Light Rail.

A separate initiative is aimed at developing a lightweight diesel railcar for heavy rail application. ■

INTO EUROPE

For sale: Bombardier will be acquired by Alstom in early 2021. The Talent 3 EMU platform and part of the Hennigsdorf site near Berlin are for sale; this is Talent 3 EMU No 4758 002 for ÖBB in Austria and Bombardier Traxx3 multi-system four-voltage prototype loco No 188 002 at Hennigsdorf in September 2018. **KEITH FENDER**

began moving containerised fruit from Spain to London in 2020 on behalf of UK supermarkets.

Freight operators across Europe continued to invest in new locomotive fleets in 2020, despite in some cases massive losses due to traffic decline, with Siemens Vectron/Smartron and Bombardier Traxx designs dominating deliveries. New bi-mode locos entered service (Stadler Eurodual in Germany) and were ordered (100 Vectron dual-mode for DB Cargo in Germany). Financial support from government for freight operators was announced in several countries although, whilst both France and Austria did, many chose to not waive track access charges for freight operators.

LIGHT RAIL AND METRO INVESTMENT

In Germany, central Government decisions taken pre-pandemic to increase public transport funding as a means of combatting climate change will result in substantial new investment funds being available for rail reopening and light rail construction in the next decade. By contrast, the loss of farebox revenue due to the pandemic may severely impact expansion and fleet renewal plans in many other countries.

A wide variety of existing projects will see new vehicles or infrastructure delivered across Europe in 2021.

In Milan the first section of the new metro line M4 will open in early 2021, and Hitachi is supplying 47 four-car automatic EMUs for the new line, which serves Linate airport. In Naples the majority of 19 six-car metro EMUs being supplied by CAF will enter service on line 1, replacing older trains during 2021.

Delivery and commissioning of new Flexity light rail vehicles for the Swiss city of Zürich was delayed by the pandemic; all 27 trams should be introduced by the end of 2021. In Luxembourg the tram system has continued to expand, serving Luxembourg main station since December 2020. In Ireland planning for the extension of the Dublin Luas system to Finglas and the construction of a new cross-city Luas line in the southern city of Cork will be completed in 2021.

In Poland, multiple cities are due to receive new tram vehicles during 2021. The first of 123 vehicles being built by Hyundai Rotem in South Korea will be delivered to Warsaw, and Krakow will receive more Stadler Tango Kraków Lajkonik II trams – 50 are due for delivery in 2020/21 to enable replacement of older vehicles, with another 60 to follow in 2023.

In Portugal, the first Chinese-built light rail vehicles in Europe will enter service when Metro do Porto introduces the 18 vehicles being built by CRRC Tangshan; deliveries are due from June 2021 onwards. In Spain tram-train operation is due to begin in Cadiz using the 1,668mm gauge main line network for the first time.

Many German cities are receiving new trams; in Bremen the first of 77 Siemens-built Avenio trams are due to enter service during 2021, replacing older vehicles, whilst Mannheim/Heidelberg operator RNV will take delivery of the first of 80 'ForCity Smart' vehicles built in Finland by Škoda Transtech. In Berlin the two biggest changes to the city's rail transport network for 15 years were finally opened in late 2020; the new railways serving the new Berlin Brandenburg Airport opened in late October, whilst the extension of metro line U5 under the historic city centre opened in December. In Wuppertal the unique 'Schwebebahn' suspension railway should reopen for daily traffic in August following warranty repairs on the new train fleet delivered by Stadler and Kiepe in 2016 plus extensive infrastructure repairs.

In Paris, the extension of automatic metro line 14 from St Lazare to Mairie de Saint-Ouen was due to open in late 2020. The first of the fleet of new MP14 EMUs supplied by Alstom entered service in late 2020, with another 19 scheduled to enter service during 2021. The extension of line 14 has been incorporated in the 'Grand Paris' programme, now being built, to add four brand new orbital metro lines; line 14 will be extended south to Orly airport and north from its new terminus to the new transport interchange with future lines 15 and 16 at Saint Denis Pleyel in time for the 2024 Olympics, which will be largely held in the Saint Denis area.

In Bulgaria, Siemens will complete delivery of all 30 Inspiro EMUs for the Sofia Metro system, which was expanded in 2020 when the 7.8km central section of new line M3 opened with eight stations; extensions are planned at both ends. In Athens the first of 25 five-section Citadis X05 trams supplied by Alstom will enter service in February 2021; all 25 vehicles should be delivered by May 2021.

The southern Swedish city of Lund gained a 5.5km tramway from December 2020, operated using a fleet of seven five-section Urbos trams built by CAF. In Gothenburg the fleet of 40 new Type M33 Flexity trams built by Bombardier will enter service in 2021, replacing older vehicles. In neighbouring Finland, the city of Tampere will see its first trams when the first section of the new light rail system opens; Škoda Transtech is supplying 19 three-section Arctic X34 vehicles. ■

change in risk appetite from bidders and levels of uncertainty generally may negatively impact tendering in countries where this is a new development, for example in France, where three regional governments have announced tendering plans, often based on sub-regional networks. A range of potential new French operators have established bidding teams, including a new joint venture between Channel Tunnel operator Getlink and Paris metro operator RATP.

In some countries the pandemic led to major service reductions, in some cases not reversed after the initial lockdown; in Hungary multiple rural branch and secondary lines lost all services, with only 10 regaining skeleton services in August 2020. More positively, active plans to reopen potentially large numbers of closed secondary lines are being developed in Poland and Germany, with governments there prioritising funding for this. In France, less well-used regional lines are being transferred to the management of the regional governments and in some cases reopening lines is being considered.

More Avenios in 2021 for Munich and Bremen: Munich operator MVG already has a fleet ranging from two- to four-section vehicles; this is two-car Avenio No 2707 on 13 August 2020. KEITH FENDER

NEW TRAIN FLEETS ENTERING SERVICE

In Germany the last of the Pesa Link DMUs ordered by DB Regio were due to enter service in Bavaria from December 2020. The original 2012 contract had options for up to 470 trains, but after delivery and approval delays only 72 of the Class 632/633 DMUs were ordered by DB. Multiple new train fleets are due to enter service in Germany in 2021; DB will replace the last Class 143 electric locos used for Nuremberg S-Bahn services with new Alstom Coradia Continental EMUs, while Go-Ahead will start its first contract in Bavaria in late 2021 with a fleet of 22 four-car Flirt3 EMUs operating services from Munich to Lindau. DB Regio may finally introduce its fleet of Škoda-built 189km/h double deck push-pull trains operating fast regional services between Munich and Nuremberg; originally due in service in 2016, these have faced extensive approval delays.

In France, Bombardier-built Regio2N/Omneo part double deck EMUs will replace electric locos and Corail coaches operating most Paris – Orleans – Tours services; the first of 48 on order for TER Center-Loire Valley services entered service in 2020. The inter-city version of the Omneo EMU entered service between Paris and Normandy in 2020 in limited numbers; they are expected to replace the majority of the remaining loco-hauled services on the route during 2021.

Dutch operator NS plans to start introduction of its new Alstom-built 'ICNG' (Intercity Nieuwe Generatie, or Inter-city New Generation) EMUs. In neighbouring Belgium, the new Bombardier/Alstom-built type M7 double deck trainsets should enter regular service after the pandemic delayed introduction in 2020; 90 sets comprising 445 vehicles are on order.

In Slovenia the first of 42 Stadler Flirt and 10 Kiss double deck EMUs will enter service in October 2021, replacing older EMUs and some older locos. In Hungary more Stadler Kiss double deck EMUs will enter service, displacing older loco-hauled push-pull trains operating regional services from Budapest. In southern Hungary the first of eight Stadler 'Citylink' bi-mode (600V DC (city tramway) and diesel) tram-trains will enter service on the new Szeged – Hódmezővásárhely tram-train system in autumn 2021; the initial order was increased by four vehicles in 2020, and these will be delivered in 2022.

SUPPLY INDUSTRY CONSOLIDATION

The acquisition of Bombardier by Alstom, likely to be complete by mid-2021, will leave Alstom as the biggest single rolling stock and signalling supplier in Europe. The conditions imposed by the EU Commission when approving the Alstom purchase have also strengthened Hitachi, as it has obtained the design and other rights to the Italian ETR1000 high-speed trains (which it already built in partnership with Bombardier). The Bombardier Talent 3 and Alstom Coradia Polyvalent EMU designs plus the former Bombardier and Alstom sites in Reichshoffen (France) and part of the Hennigsdorf site near Berlin are for sale, with Škoda, CAF, Talgo and Transmashholding (based in Russia but 20% owned by Alstom) reportedly interested in acquiring one or both sites.

Chinese rail equipment conglomerate CRRC took over the Vossloh Locomotives business in Kiel, northern Germany during 2020 and delivered a further battery/diesel hybrid loco from China for use by German national infrastructure manager DB Netze during the year. CRRC's plans for manufacturing in Europe are not clear, with the Kiel factory currently only producing locomotives, most of which were ordered prior to the CRRC acquisition. CRRC won an order to build eight five-car metro EMUs for the Ukrainian city of Kharkiv during 2020; these trains will be built in China and delivered by the end of 2021.

FREIGHT FALTERS

Whilst European rail freight volumes fell in mid-2020 in reaction to the Covid disruption to manufacturing industry, 'New Silk Road' container traffic between China and Europe rebounded during 2020 after coronavirus lockdowns in China in January and February led to major disruption. The Chinese Government is reducing subsidies available to fund the trains, with only certain routes now eligible, but the Russian Government, keen to create transit traffic, has begun offering subsidies for traffic via the Russian Railways network.

Regular direct trains from China to the UK have not been established despite previous test operations, however containers are transported weekly by rail from China to North Sea ports in Germany or the Netherlands, where they are then moved by sea to UK ports. 2021 may herald more rail freight opportunities, importing food and other consumer goods to the UK via the Channel Tunnel if rail can offer time and cost advantages compared to road transport once the new Brexit frontier and customs regime applies; DB-owned Transfesa

INTO EUROPE

new sub-contractors replacing its previous partners, having suspended services during the 'lockdown' period.

Italian-based open access operator Thello, owned by Italian national operator Trenitalia, announced it was ceasing its daytime Milan – Nice/Marseille service from early 2021; its Paris – Venice overnight service has been suspended due to the pandemic since March. Trenitalia has other open access expansion plans, however, and in 2020 ordered 23 ETR1000 trains from Hitachi/Bombardier for new open access 'ILSA' high-speed services in Spain (from 2022). Future use of the ETR1000 for services from Italian cities to Paris also is likely, with 14 more due for delivery from 2021 for use in/from Italy. Testing of the ETR1000 design in France continued in 2020.

Open access high-speed competition will arrive in Spain in March 2021 when French Railways (SNCF) subsidiary Ouigo España starts services, branded as 'Falbalá', between Madrid and Barcelona. Modified TGV Euroduplex trains will be used. Spanish national operator RENFE plans to respond to the new competition with both a low cost operation branded 'Avlo', the 2020 launch of which was shelved due to the pandemic, and by introducing new Talgo-built Class S106 high capacity 'Avril' 330km/h trains featuring 3+2 seating.

New trains and locomotives are due to enter service with Czech open access operators Regiojet (15 Traxx3 Class 388 locomotives) whilst Leo Express plans to introduce its three Chinese-built 'Sirius' EMUs. Chinese manufacturer CRRC has completed the first of these trains, but the pandemic and associated travel restrictions severely delayed approval testing. Leo Express may also find new investors during 2021 as talks with the Czech Government in 2020 about national operator ČD taking over the company fell through and the economic reality hasn't improved since.

HIGH-SPEED DEVELOPMENTS

German operator DB will introduce the seven-car Class 412.2 version of its ICE4 train in 2021. The trains will replace older ICE2 trains operating in pairs between Berlin and the Ruhr. Later in 2021 DB intends to introduce the 13-coach version of the ICE4. DB placed an order with Siemens for 30 new Velaro high-speed EMUs in July 2020 as part of plans to expand its fleet for the future 'Deutschland Takt' regular interval timetable. As a first step towards this, more frequent services were to be introduced between Berlin and Hamburg from December 2020, offering a half-hourly frequency for much of the day.

The first of French operator SNCF's 100 new Alstom Avelia Horizon high-speed trains, which will be called TGV M, should be completed during 2021; introduction is planned from 2023. In Denmark national operator DSB will introduce its new Class EB Siemens Vectron electric locos, replacing the few remaining Class EA electric locos and eventually all remaining Class ME diesel locos, whilst in Bulgaria national operator BDZ will start using 10 Siemens 'Smartron' locos. In Greece national operator Trainose, which is owned by Trenitalia, will introduce second-hand 'Pendolino' EMUs no longer required by its owner in Italy.

INFRASTRUCTURE DEVELOPMENTS

Construction work continues on multiple major projects across Europe, including the Semmering and Koralm base tunnels in Austria, Brenner base tunnel (Austria/Italy), Fehmarn link (Germany/Denmark), and new high-speed lines in Italy (Naples – Bari plus Brescia – Verona), but all these remain several years from completion.

In Spain the 25km-long new base tunnel and high-speed line under the Pajares Pass on the line between Madrid and Gijon should open in 2021, with the two tunnels each equipped with different gauge track; one standard, the other 1,668mm gauge.

Substantial planning work is underway in several countries to expand or create high-speed networks, notably in Germany, where several new lines are planned as part of plans to introduce the Deutschland Takt regular interval timetable. In both the Czech Republic and Poland planning for multiple sections of new high-speed line is now well advanced.

REGIONAL MARKETS DEVELOP

Whilst 2021 marks the start of deregulation for regional rail services EU-wide, the economics of operating such services have been challenged like never before by the pandemic. In countries with established concession systems, transport authorities have had to find substantial sums to offset lost passenger revenue, although short-term revenue losses for train operators have in some cases been small as they have operated the contracted service, albeit with far fewer passengers. In Germany some operators, notably Abellio, faced multiple problems due to staff shortages, higher than expected costs and late delivery of new train fleets.

In late 2020 even small concession contracts with revenue risk for the train operator were resulting in no bids being offered; revenue risk is unlikely to be a feature of new contracts awarded in 2021. The

An increasingly common sight in Germany and Bulgaria: Siemens Smartron locos are all delivered in overall blue livery. No 192 010, leased to TX Logistik by North Rail, passes Munich Ost on 13 August 2020 with an eastbound intermodal service. **KEITH FENDER**

have seen passenger numbers fall by 80% or more and service levels reduced to a handful of trains daily. In the UK Eurostar has reduced staff numbers and has no plans to serve Ashford or Ebbsfleet during 2021.

The pandemic has caused a major but probably temporary fall in rail usage, especially for passenger services, although freight serving manufacturing industry was also badly hit in mid-2020. The policy and economic trends pre-pandemic have not changed; the European Union and individual countries have committed to ambitious climate protection goals which cannot be achieved without increasing public transport's share of overall mobility – with electric powered railways and light rail fundamental in most countries to achieving the decarbonisation targets. Rail usage in most European countries had returned to 50% to 70% of pre-pandemic levels prior to the 'second wave' series of lockdowns seen in October/November; in multiple cases operators or government bodies were imposing 50% maximum social distancing capacity on services, such was the demand for travel.

In October 2020 the European Parliament designated 2021 as European Year of Rail, recognising

Regional reopening Polish style: Koleje Dolnośląskie DMU No SA132 002 at Bielawa Zachodnia on 25 February 2020, weeks after the reinstated branch line was reopened, with a service to Wrocław. **KEITH FENDER**

Brand new: seven-car ICE4 set No 9210 at Berlin Hbf on 16 September 2020; from December these were due to operate in pairs working services from Berlin to Cologne. **KEITH FENDER**

the rail industry's contribution to the 'European Green Deal' decarbonisation strategy. This calls for 90% of all transport-related greenhouse emissions to be removed by 2050; transport (all modes) represents 25% of all EU emissions. The European Green Deal calls for 75% of current road freight to be shifted to either rail or inland waterways by 2050. Rail currently represents no more than 17% of domestic freight measured EU-wide, and less in some major countries such as France. 2021 is also the first full year for full implementation of the 'Fourth Railway Package', mandating passenger rail deregulation in all EU member states.

BRIGHTER FUTURE FOR INTERNATIONAL SERVICES?

In September 2020 the German Government, holding the rotating EU Presidency, proposed a new 'Trans Europe Express' (TEE) network, dubbed 'TEE2.0' after the original TEE system created in the late 1950s. A network of long-distance high-speed routes spanning the continent (eg Warsaw to Paris or Rome to Amsterdam) is proposed, to be operated by a new jointly-owned company using existing trains and crew from participating national operators.

Existing planned major infrastructure improvements such as the new Brenner Base Tunnel (Austria to Italy) and the Fehmarnbelt Link (Denmark to Germany) would make some of the routes possible or faster. Possibly more significantly, a new overnight network that would offer high quality sleeper/couchette trains on multiple lengthy routes is also proposed. The motivation behind both the day and night TEE2.0 networks is to reduce dependency on short haul flights – in part motivated by the Swedish Flygskam (flight shaming) movement, which has gained popularity in northern Europe in particular, plus the actual reduction in short haul flights in 2020 due to the pandemic.

In 2021 new international overnight services are expected to begin operating (some from the December 2020 timetable change), with the ÖBB Nightjet network expanded to include daily trains to Amsterdam, in part funded by the Dutch Government. Swedish open access operator Snälltåget, owned by Transdev, plans to offer commercial Stockholm to Berlin services. German open access operator RDC Deutschland, owned by Railroad Development Corporation in the USA, plans to expand the overnight service it launched in summer 2020 between Germany and Austria, whilst in the Czech Republic open access company Regiojet plans several new overnight routes linking Prague with Polish and Slovak cities using a fleet of former DB overnight coaches. Regiojet, acting quickly, introduced an overnight service from Prague to Rijeka in Croatia in mid-2020 as Czech holidaymakers sought summer holidays despite the pandemic; the service was so successful it will operate again in 2021.

From December 2020 services between Munich and Zurich were to switch from conventional loco-hauled Eurocity trains to SBB-operated Class 503 'Pendolino' EMUs following completion of electrification between Munich and Lindau in Germany. Removal of loco changes plus use of tilting trains will reduce journey times by an hour to 3hr 30min by December 2021, when a new through station opens in Lindau. Six train pairs daily will operate, compared to three previously.

OPEN ACCESS STRUGGLES

Whilst EU Governments have provided privately owned airlines, operating commercial networks, with multi-million pandemic funding (sometimes attaching the condition that some short haul flights cease where rail connections are available), no government has offered funding to private rail operators with commercial open access services.

Reduction or removal of track access fees for commercial passenger and freight operations has been permitted EU-wide since October 2020 following initial plans for this announced in Austria and France; whilst helpful, this move is optional and has not been adopted in every country. It does not overcome the fundamental problem of running socially distanced open access trains (as mandated for example in Italy for all operators), namely passenger loads at 50% or less. In most countries open access operators have had to reduce services to a bare minimum, laying off staff in the process. One exception was FlixTrain's restarted German operation which, using compulsory reservations, operated some services at full capacity. FlixTrain restarted its services in mid-2020, with

INTO EUROPE

Europe looks to post-pandemic world

Despite the challenges of Covid, projects in continental Europe have progressed, as *Modern Railways* Europe Editor **KEITH FENDER** explains

The global Covid pandemic has changed many things in Europe. But equally, many anticipated developments in the rail industry have gone ahead and the industry continues to plan for a more prosperous, stable future post-pandemic as decarbonisation takes centre stage as a policy objective.

Infrastructure enhancements in Switzerland to create a transit corridor suitable for four-metre high containers continued as planned, with the Ceneri Base Tunnel officially opened on 4 September 2020; this plus the shorter Eppenburg Tunnel west of Zürich are now in use. Not obvious a year ago, but not entirely surprising either, was the announcement from Alstom in February that it was acquiring Bombardier; the final purchase price was marked down by €300 million to around €5.5 billion in the deal signed in September. The full acquisition will be completed early in 2021.

SPUR FOR NEW GROWTH?

The coronavirus pandemic hit rail operators Europe wide. Individual countries adopted differing approaches ranging from near total lockdowns in Spain and Italy through to a much more permissive approach in Sweden, with most countries falling somewhere between the two extremes. Passenger operators Europe wide had to deal with plummeting passenger numbers, the need for additional cleaning and longer trains for social distancing, with government mandated occupancy levels in some but not all countries. In most cases 'national' (ie state-owned) railway companies received sometimes substantial additional funding to cover all or some of the revenue lost and costs incurred, although this was not uniform across the EU.

In most cases, private open access commercial operators received no financial assistance, with the notable exception of Austria, where private company Westbahn and national operator ÖBB shared an emergency public service obligation (PSO) contract on the Vienna – Salzburg route, which is the only major route operated by ÖBB on a commercial basis; existing subsidy covered operation elsewhere.

In countries such as the Netherlands and Germany, where many regional passenger services are operated under concession contracts, operators were frequently paid to operate very empty trains and thus lost less revenue than the transport authorities paying them, which ordinarily retain the (suddenly depleted) ticket revenue. Long-distance revenues plummeted across Europe and international services largely ceased operation between March and June. Even when borders reopened, travel patterns did not return to previous levels and specialist international high-speed operators such as Thalys and Eurostar

INTO EUROPE

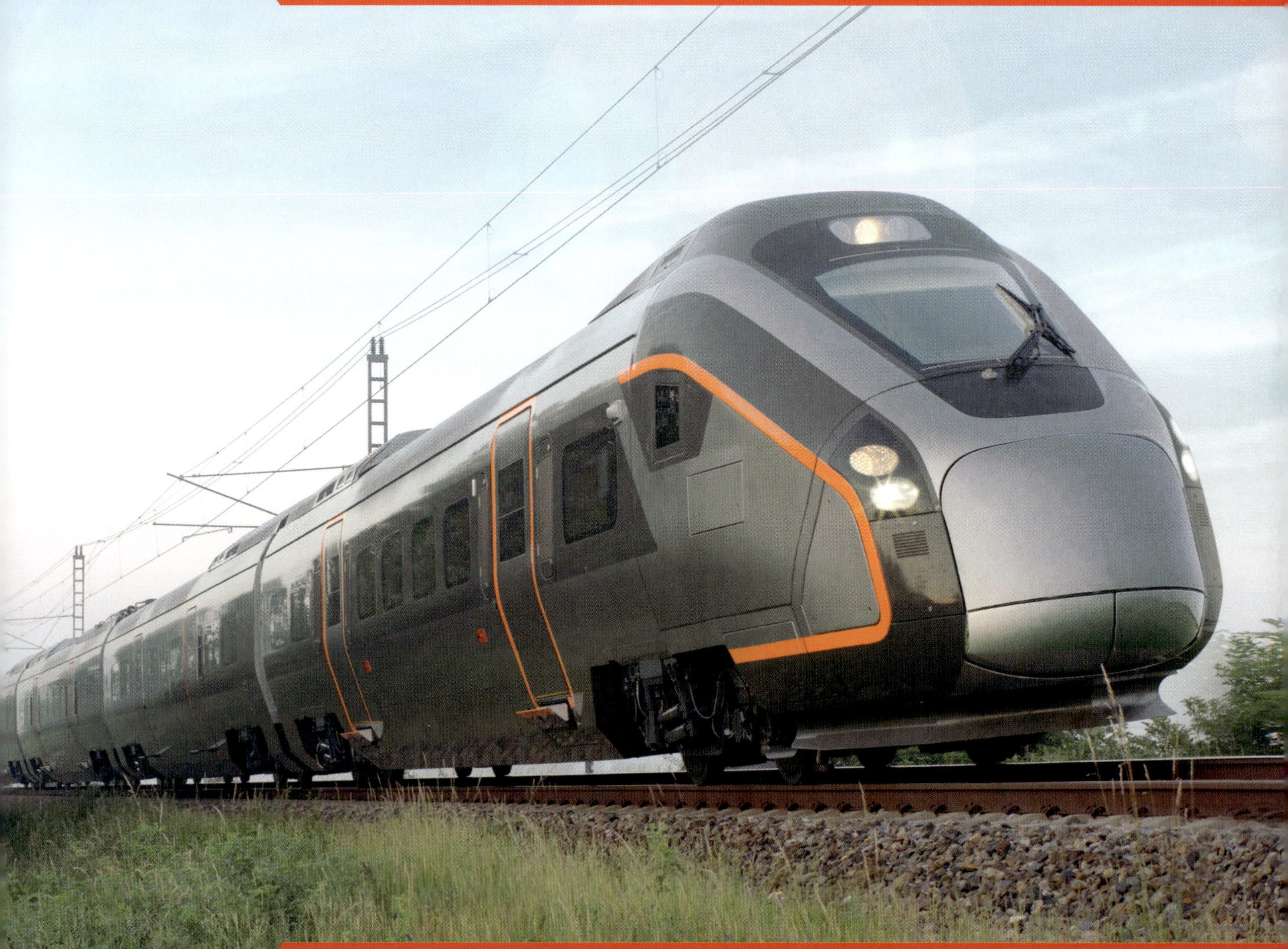

IN ASSOCIATION WITH

DIRECTORY
THE UK RAIL INDUSTRY IN YOUR HANDS

IN ASSOCIATION WITH

Nomad Digital

1Spatial Group
Tennyson House, Cambridge Business Park, Cambridge, CB4 0WZ
T: 01223 420414
W: https://1spatial.com/

1st Solutions
1st Solutions House, Cwm Cynon Business Park, Mountain Ash, CF45 4ER
T: 0844 561 7419
F: 0844 561 0933
E: daniel.munn@shortermgroup.com
W: www.1sr.co.uk/

1stinrail
1D North Crescent, Cody Road, London, E16 4TG
T: 0845 527 8440
F: 0845 527 8441
W: www.1stinrail.co.uk/

21st Century Technology plc
12 Charter Point Way, Ashby-de-la-Zouch, Leicestershire, LE65 1NF
T: 0844 871 7990
E: info@21stplc.com
W: www.21stplc.com

345 Rail Leasing
10-11 Charterhouse Square, London, EC1M 6EH

360 Vision Technology Ltd
Unit 7, Seymour Court, Manor Park, Runcorn, Cheshire, WA7 1SY
T: 0870 903 3601
F: 0870 903 3602
E: info@ipx360solutions.com
W: www.360visiontechnology.com

3D Laser Mapping
1a Church St, Bingham, Nottingham, NG13 8AL
T: 0870 442 9400
F: 0870 121 4605
E: info@3dlasermapping.com
W: www.3dlasermapping.com

3DVSL (3D Visual Simulations Ltd)
Suite 5.9 Techcube, 1 Summerhall, Edinburgh, EH9 1PL
M: 07730 417111
E: hello@3dvsl.com
W: www.3dvsl.com

3M CPPD
Standard Way, Northallerton, N.Yorks, DL6 2XA
T: 01609 780170
F: 01609 780438
W: www.copon.co.uk

3M United Kingdom PLC
3M Centre, Cain Rd, Bracknell, Berks, RG12 8HT
T: 01344 858704
E: railsolutions@mmm.com
W: www.3m.co.uk/railsolutions

3Squared
Fountain Precinct, Balm Green, Sheffield, S1 2JA
T: 0333 121 3333
E: info@3squared.com
W: www.3squared.com

42 Technology
Meadow Lane, St Ives, Cambridgeshire, PE27 4LG
T: 01480 302700
F: 01480 302701
E: answers@42technology.com
W: www.42technology.com/

4Silence
Vliegveldstraat 100-C38, 7524 PK Enschede, Netherlands
T: +31 53 303 4888
E: info@4silence.com
W: www.4silence.com

50026 Indomitable

A & J Fabtech Limited
700 Bretton Way, Bretton Park Industrial Estate, Dewsbury, West Yorkshire, WF12 9BS
T: 01924439614
E: info@ajfabtech.com
W: www.ajfabtech.com

A&J Electrical Services
3 Greenshields Industrial Estate, Bradfield Road, London, E16 2AU
T: 020 7366 6519
F: 020 7476 3638
W: www.ajeltd.com/

Aalco Metals Ltd
25 High Street, Cobham, KT11 3DH
T: 01932 576820
E: info@aalco.co.uk
W: www.aalco.co.uk

Aardvark Site Investigations Ltd
See Screwfast Foundations Ltd

Aaron Rail
Pepper House, Pepper Road, Hazel Grove, Stockport, SK7 5DP
T: 0161 638 3283
E: enquiries@aaronrail.co.uk
W: www.aaronrail.co.uk

AATI Rail Ltd
11 Swinborne Drive, Springwood Ind. Est, Braintree, Essex, CM7 2YP
T: 01376 346278
F: 01376 348480
E: info@aati.co.uk
W: www.aati.co.uk

AB Connectors Ltd
Abercynon, Mountain Ash, Rhondda Cynon Taff, CF45 4SF
T: 01443 743403
F: 01443 741676
E: sales@ttabconnectors.com
W: www.ttabconnectors.com

AB Hoses & Fittings Ltd
Units 6-7, Warwick St Ind Est., Chesterfield, Derbyshire, S40 2TT
T: 01246 208831
F: 01246 209302
E: info@abhoses.com
W: www.abhoses.com

ABA Surveying
Lansbury Est., Lower Guildford St, Knaphill, Woking, Surrey, GU21 2EP
T: 01483 797111
F: 01483 797211
E: info@abasurveying.co.uk
W: www.abasurveying.co.uk

Abacus Lighting Ltd
Oddicroft Lane, Sutton-in-Ashfield, Notts, NG17 5FT
T: 01623 511111
F: 01623 552133
E: sales@abacuslighting.com
W: www.abacuslighting.com

ABB Ltd
Tower Court, Foleshill Enterprise Park, Courtaulds Way, Coventry, CV6 5NX
T: 02476 368500
E: lv.enquiries@gb.abb.com
W: www.abb.com/railway

Abbey Pynford Foundation Systems Ltd
IMEX, First Floor, West Wing, 575-599 Maxted Road, Hemel Hempstead, Herts, HP2 7DX
T: 0870 085 8400
F: 0870 085 8401
E: info@abbeypynford.co.uk
W: www.abbeypynford.co.uk

Abbeydale Training Ltd
26 Stonewood Grove, Sheffield, S10 5SS
T: 0114 230 4400
E: abbeydale.training@btconnect.com
W: www.abbeydaletraining.co.uk

Abbi Access Services Ltd
Clwyd Close, Hawarden Industrial Estate, Manor Lane, Hawarden, CH5 3PZ
T: 01244 629919
F: 01244 676557
M: 07733 216036
E: admin@abbiaccess.com
W: www.abbiaccess.com

Abbott Risk Consulting Ltd
Audley House, 13 Palace Street, London, SW1E 5HX
M: 07789 176401
E: rail@consultarc.com
W: www.consultarc.com

ABC Electrification
Myson House, Rugby, Warks, CV21 3HT
T: 01788 545654
E: jo.evans@chq.alstom.com
W: abcel.co.uk/

Abellio
5th Floor, The Culzean Building, 36 Renfield Street, Glasgow, G2 1LU
T: 020 7430 8270
F: 020 7430 2239
E: info@abellio.com
W: www.abellio.com

Abellio ScotRail
Atrium Court, 50 Waterloo St, Glasgow, G2 6HQ
T: 0344 811 0141
E: customer.relations@scotrail.co.uk
W: www.scotrail.co.uk/

ABET Ltd
70 Roding Rd, London Ind. Park, London, E6 4LS
T: 020 7473 6910
F: 020 7476 6935
E: sales@abet.ltd.uk
W: www.abetuk.com

Abloy UK
Portobello Works, School St, Willenhall, West Midlands, WV13 3PW
T: 01902 364500
F: 01902 364501
E: sales@abloy.co.uk
W: www.abloy.co.uk

ABM Precast Solutions Ltd
Ollerton Rd, Tuxford, Newark, Notts, NG22 0PQ
T: 01777 872233
E: precast@abmeurope.com
W: www.abmprecast.co.uk

Abracs Ltd
Abracs House, Unit 3, George Cayley Drive, Clifton Moor, York, YO30 4XE
T: 01904 789997
F: 01904 789996
E: abracs@abracs.com
W: www.abracs.com

ABS Consulting
EQE House, The Beacons, Warrington Rd, Birchwood, Warrington, WA3 6WJ
T: 01925 287300
F: 01925 287301
E: enquiriesuk@absconsulting.com
W: www.eqe.co.uk

Abtus Ltd
Falconer Rd, Haverhill, Suffolk, CB9 7XU
T: 01440 702938
F: 01440 702961
E: chris.welsh@abtus.com
W: www.abtus.com

Acal BFI UK Limited
3 The Business Centre, Molly Millars Lane, Wokingham, RG41 2EY
T: 01189788878
E: sales-uk@acalbfi.co.uk
W: www.acalbfi.co.uk

Access Design & Engineering Ltd
Marsh Road, Middlesbrough, TS1 5JS
T: 01642 245151
E: sales@access-design.co.uk
W: www.access-design.co.uk

Access IS
18 Suttons Business Park, Reading, Berks, RG6 1AZ
T: 0118 966 3333
F: 0118 926 7281
E: carol.harraway@access-is.com
W: www.access-is.com

Acciona Infrastructure
Avda. Europa 18, Parque Empresarial La Moraleja, 28108 Alcobendas (Madrid), Spain
T: +34 91 663 28 50
F: +34 91 663 30 99
E: webmail-infraestructuras@acciona.es
W: www.acciona-infrastructure.com/

Acetech Personnel Ltd
Pembroke House, Pegasus Bus. Park, Castle Donnington, Derby, DE74 2TZ
T: 01509 676962
F: 01509 676867
E: rail@acetech.co.uk
W: www.acetech.co.uk

Achilles Information Ltd (Link-Up)
30 Park Gate, Milton Park, Abingdon, Oxon, OX14 4SH
T: 01235 820813
F: 01235 838156
E: link-up@achilles.com
W: www.achilles.com

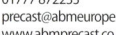

ACIC International Ltd
14 Blacknest Business Park, Blacknest, Nr Alton, Hants, GU34 4PX
T: 01420 23930
F: 01420 23921
E: sales@acic.co.uk
W: www.acic.co.uk

ACM Bearings Ltd
Derwent Way, Wath West Ind Est, Rotherham, S Yorks, S63 6EX
T: 01709 874951
F: 01709 878818
E: sales@acmbearings.co.uk
W: www.acmbearings.co.uk

ACO Technologies Plc
ACO Business Park, Hitchin Rd, Shefford, Beds, SG17 5TE
T: 01462 816666
F: 01462 815895
E: technologies@aco.co.uk
W: www.aco.co.uk

ACOREL S.A.S
Technopar Pole 2000, 3 Rue Paul Langevin, 07130 St Peray, France
T: 0033 475 405979
F: 0033 475 405771
E: info@acorel.com
W: www.acorel.com

Acorn People
7 York Rd, Woking, Surrey, GU22 7XH
T: 01483 654463
F: 01483 723080
E: sarah.griffiths@acornpeople.com
W: www.acornpeople.com

ACT Informatics Ltd
One St Peters Rd, Maidenhead, Berks, SL6 1QU
T: 0870 114 9800
F: 0870 114 9801
E: admin@act-consultancy.com

Acumen Design Associates Ltd
1 Sekforde St, Clerkenwell, London, EC1R 0BE
T: 020 7107 2900
F: 020 7107 2901
E: info@acumen-da.com
W: www.acumen-da.com

AD Engineering
Unit 1, Saxon Shore Business Park, Castle Road, Eurolink Industrial Estate, Sittingbourne, Kent, ME10 3EU
T: 01795 435900
F: 01795 435940
W: www.adengineering.co.uk

Adamson Associates
6th Floor, One Canada Square, Canary Wharf, London, E14 5AB
T: 020 7418 2068
F: 020 7418 2517
E: mroyston@adamson-associates.com
W: www.adamson-associates.com/

Adaptaflex
Station Rd, Coleshill, Birmingham, B46 1HT
T: 01675 468222
F: 01675 464276
E: sales@adaptaflex.com
W: www.adaptaflex.com

ADAS UK Ltd
Woodthorn, Wergs Rd, Wolverhampton, WV6 8TQ
T: 01902 754190
E: sam.lowe@adas.co.uk
W: www.adas.co.uk

THE 2021 MODERN RAILWAY DIRECTORY - THE MOST COMPREHENSIVE DIRECTORY OF BUSINESSES INVOLVED IN THE OPERATION OF THE UK RAIL INDUSTRY

KEY TO SYMBOLS

TRAIN OPERATORS
Passenger and Freight Train Operators, TOC Owning Groups, Light Railway, Metro and Tramway Operators, Rail Tour Operators, Passenger Transport Authorities/ Executives, Freight Forwarders/Brokers.

ROLLING STOCK MANUFACTURE, SUPPLY AND DELIVERY
Locomotive, Light Rail, Metro, Carriage and Wagon Manufacture, Locomotive, Wagon and Coaching Stock Hire, Chartering, Rolling Stock Leasing Companies, Rolling Stock Delivery.

INFRASTRUCTURE
Infrastructure Maintenance and Renewal, Lineside Equipment, Construction Projects, Electrification, Electrical Components Misc.,Trackwork, Ground Protection and Safety, Workshop Equipment, Fencing & Security, Lighting (except rolling stock), Platforms, Access Systems, Walkways & Gantries, Cable Management, Power Supply, Carriage Washing, Freight Terminals, Level Crossings and Associated Components, Passenger Information Displays, Signs and Notifications, Car Parking, Cleaning, Weighing & Lifting, Grafitti Removal, Pest Control, Ticketing, CCTV, Public Address, Test Facilities, Fares and Collection. Customer Accessibility, Route Management and Ownership, Noise and Vibration Control.

INFRASTRUCTURE MATERIAL SUPPLIES
Buildings & Building Refurbishment, Plant, Tools, Welding, Paints & Coatings, Clothing & Boots, Chemicals and Lubricants, Scaffolding and Safety Netting, Temporary Bridges, Roads, Buildings and Containers, Flooring, Weighing & Lifting.

ON TRACK PLANT & MISCELLANEOUS
On Track Plant Manufacturers, Misc.

ROLLING STOCK MAINTENANCE/PARTS
Locomotive, Carriage and Wagon Maintenance, Component supply, Lighting and Cabling, Decals and Transfers, De-Icing, Sanding, Upholstery, Disposal, Textiles, Fuel Technology, In Train Entertainment, Train Monitoring Systems, Train Branding ,Vinyls and Wraps, Depot Equipment, Carpeting & Insulation.

HUMAN RESOURCES INCLUDING CATERING, TRAINING & HEALTH
Recruitment and Training Companies/ Consultancies, Personnel Supply, Retirement and Convalescence, Catering.

SIGNAL & TELECOMMUNICATION
S&T Installation and Equipment, Wireless Technology and Datacoms, Training Simulators.

PROFESSIONAL ADVICE, CONSULTANCY AND SERVICES
Consultants, Legal Services, Economists, Industry Reporting, Insurance, Accreditation & Compliance, Verification & Validation, Assessment, Test & Development, Systems & Software, IT Services, Architects and Design Agencies, Surveying, Data Management, Financial Services, Property, Solutions and Turnkey Providers, Mapping, Vehicle Acceptance, Video & Film Production, Photography, Journey Planning, Conferences & Exhibitions, Specialist Media, Project Management, Marketing, PR & Branding, Weather Forcasting, Simulation, Drugs and Alcohol Testing, Research Organisations.

INDUSTRY AND REGULATORY BODIES
Trade Associations, Alliances and Authorities, Advisory Boards, Government Departments, Customer Organisations, Accident Investigators, Campaigning Organisations, Passenger Watchdogs, Trade Unions, Port Authorities and Development Agencies.

ROAD TRANSPORT SERVICES
Fleet Management, Heavy Haulage, Replacement Buses and Vehicle Hire

IN ASSOCIATION WITH Nomad Digital

Addleshaw Goddard
Milton Gate, 60 Chiswell Street, London, EC1Y 4AG
T: 020 7606 8855
F: 020 7606 4390
W: www.addleshawgoddard.com/

Adeo Construction Consultants
Unit 16, Oakhurst Business Park, Wilberforce Way, Southwater, Horsham, RH13 9RT
T: 01403 821770
F: 01403 733405
E: enquiries@adeo.uk.com
W: www.adeo.uk.com

Adey Steel Group
Falcon Industrial Park, Meadow Lane, Loughborough, Leicestershire, LE11 1HL
T: 01509 556677
F: 01509 828622
E: mail@adeysteel.co.uk
W: www.adeysteelgroup.co.uk/

Adien Ltd
Delta Court, Sky Business Park, Robin Hood Airport, Doncaster, DN9 3GB
T: 01302 802200
F: 01302 802201
E: jane.glastonbury@adien-utility-detection.com
W: www.adien-utility-detection.com/

ADT Fire & Security
Security House, The Summit, Hanworth Rd, Sunbury on Thames, TW16 5DB
T: 01932 743229
F: 01932 743047
W: www.adt.co.uk/

Advance Consultancy Ltd
St Mary's House, Church St, Uttoxeter, ST14 8AG
T: 01889 561510
F: 01889 561591
E: enquiry@advance-consultancy.com
W: www.advance-consulting.com

Advance Training & Recruitment Services
2nd Floor, Stamford House, 91 Woodbridge Rd, Guildford, GU1 4QD
T: 01483 361061
F: 01483 431958
E: info@advance-trs.com
W: www.advance-trs.com

Advanced Handling Ltd
Northfields Ind. Est, Market Deeping, Peterborough, PE6 8LD
T: 01778 345365
F: 01778 341654
E: sales@advancedhandling.co.uk
W: www.advancedhandling.co.uk

Advanced Micro Peripherals
1 Harrier House, Sedgeway Business Park, Witchford, Cambridge, CB6 2HY
T: 01353 659500
F: 01353 659600
E: sales@ampltd.com
W: www.ampltd.com

Advanced Selection Ltd
Cooper House, The Horsefair, Romsey, Hants, SO31 8JZ
T: 02380 744455
F: 01794 518549
E: sam@advancedselect.co.uk
W: www.advancedselect.co.uk

Advantage Technical Consulting
See Atkins

Advante Strategic Site Services
4th Floor, Phoenix House, Christopher Martin Rd, Basildon, SS14 3HG
T: 01268 280500
F: 01268 293454
E: sales@advante.co.uk
W: www.advante.co.uk

Advantech
Unit 3 Gunnery Terrace, Duke of Wellington Avenue, Royal Arsenal, Woolwich, London, SE18 6SW
T: 02083197683
F: 02088369732
E: brian.lin@advantech.com
W: www.advantech.eu

Adventis Consulting
3 Chiswick Park, 566 Chiswick High Rd, Chiswick, London, W4 5YA
T: 020 8878 3454
W: adventis.co.uk

AE Petsche
Unit 8, Suttons Business Park, Sutton Park Avenue, Earley, Reading, Berkshire, RG6 1AZ
T: 0118 969 3230
E: contactaep@aepetsche.com
W: www.aepetsche.com/

AECOM
AECOM House, 63-77 Victoria St, St Albans, Herts, AL1 3ER
T: 0141 3545722
E: ian.hay@aecom.com
W: www.aecom.com

Aedas Group Ltd
5-8 Hardwick St, London, EC1R 4RG
T: 020 7837 9789
F: 020 7837 9678
E: london@aedas.com
W: www.aedas.com

AEG Power Solutions Ltd
Suite 16, Wenta Business Centre, 1 Electric Avenue, Enfield, Middx, EN3 7XU
T: 01992 719200
F: 01992 702151
E: kevin.pateman@aegps.com
W: www.aegps.com

Aegis Certification Services Ltd
29 Brunel Parkway, Pride Park, Derby, DE24 8HR
T: 01332 384302
E: info@aegis-cert.co.uk
W: www.aegis-cert.co.uk

Aegis Engineering Systems Ltd
29 Brunel Parkway, Pride Park, Derby, DE24 8HR
T: 01332 384302
E: info@aegisengineering.co.uk
W: www.aegisengineering.co.uk

AEI Cables Ltd
Durham Rd, Birtley, Chester-le-Street, Co. Durham, DH3 2RA
T: 0191 410 3111
F: 0191 410 8312
E: info@aeicables.co.uk
W: www.aeicables.co.uk

Aerco Ltd
16-17 Lawson Hunt Ind. Park, Broadbridge Heath, Horsham, West Sussex, RH12 3JR
T: 01403 260206
F: 01403 259760
M: 07767 002298
E: chenderson@aerco.co.uk
W: www.aerco.co.uk

Aerial Facilities Ltd
Aerial House, Asheridge Rd, Chesham, Bucks, HP5 2QD
T: 01494 777000
F: 01494 777002
E: sales@aerial.co.uk
W: www.aerialfacilities.com

Aerosystems International
See BAE Systems

AES
The Old Warehouse, Park St, Worcester, WR5 1AA
T: 01905 363520
E: contact@aesco.co.uk
W: www.aesco.co.uk

Agant Ltd
T: 020 8123 9401
E: contactus@agant.com
W: www.agant.com

AGC AeroComposites Derby
Unit 10a, Sills Rd, Willow Farm Business Park, Castle Donington, DE74 2US
T: 01332 818000
F: 01332 818089
E: sales@paulfabs.co.uk
W: www.agcaerocomposites.com

AGD Equipment Ltd
Avonbrook House, 198 Masons Rd, Stratford Enterprise Park, Stratford upon Avon, Warks, CV37 9LQ
T: 01789 292227
F: 01789 268350
E: info@agd-equipment.co.uk
W: www.agd-equipment.co.uk

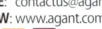

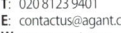

Aggregate Industries UK Ltd
Bardon Hill, Bardon Hill Quarry, Coalville, Leics, LE67 1TL
T: 01530 510066
F: 01530 510123
E: corporate.communications@aggregate.com
W: www.aggregate-uk.com

Aggreko UK Ltd
2 Voyager Drive, Cannock, Staffs, WS11 8XP
T: 08458 247365
F: 01543 437772
E: enquiries@aggreko.co.uk
W: www.aggreko.co.uk

AGH Engineering Ltd
Mill House, North Street, York, North Yorkshire, YO1 6JQ
T: 01904 545040
E: info@aghengineering.co.uk
W: www.aghengineering.co.uk/

Agilia
71 Central Street, Clerkenwell, London, EC1V 3AR
T: 020 7971 1014
E: info@agilia.co.uk
W: www.agilia.co.uk

Agility Trains
7th Floor, 40 Holborn Viaduct, London, EC1N 2PB
T: 020 7970 2700
E: enquiries@agilitytrains.com
W: www.agilitytrains.co.uk

Aikona Management Ltd
Windsor House, Lodge Place, Sutton, SM1 4AU
T: 020 8770 9393
F: 020 8770 9555
E: training@aikona.com
W: www.aikonatraining.com

Ainscough
Bradley Hall, Bradley Lane, Standish, Lancs, WN6 0XQ
T: 0800 272 637
F: 01257 473286
E: heavy.cranes@ainscough.co.uk
W: www.ainscough.co.uk

Airedale International Air Conditioning Ltd
Leeds Road, Rawdon, Leeds, LS19 6JY
T: 0113 239 1000
F: 0113 250 7219
E: connect@airedale.com
W: https://airedale.com/

Airex Composite Structures. Airex AG
Park Altenrhein, Altenrhein, 9423, Switzerland
T: 0071 858 4848
F: 0071858 4858
E: acs.info@airexcompositestructures.com
W: www.airexcompositestructures.com

Airquick (Newark) Ltd
Brunel Business Park, Jessop Close, Newark, Notts, NG24 2AG
T: 01636 640480
F: 01636 701216
E: info@airquick.co.uk
W: www.airquick.co.uk

Airtec International Ltd
40 Couper St, Glasgow, G4 0DL
T: 0141 552 5591
F: 0141 552 5064
E: akilpatrick@airtecintl.co.uk
W: www.airtecinternational.com

AJT Engineering
Craigshaw Crescent, West Tullos, Aberdeen, AB12 3TB
T: 01224 871791
F: 01224 890251
E: info@ajt-engineering.co.uk
W: www.ajt-engineering.co.uk/

Akiem Group
W: www.akiem.com/

AKS Training
Goodwill Solutions Buildings, Deer Park Road, Moulton Park Ind Est, Northampton, Northamptonshire, NN3 6RX
T: 01604 247800
E: info@akstraining.com
W: https://akstraining.com/

AKT II
100 St John Street, London, EC1M 4EH
T: 020 7250 7777
F: 020 7250 5555
W: www.akt-uk.com/

Alan Baxter
75 Cowcross Street, London, EC1M 6EL
T: 020 7250 1555
E: aba@alanbaxter.co.uk
W: alanbaxter.co.uk

Alan Dick Communications Ltd
Unit 11, Billet Lane, Normanby Enterprise Park, Scunthorpe, DN15 9YH
T: 01724 292200
F: 01724 292556
E: robert.illsley@alandickcomms.com
W: www.alandick.com

Alan Murray Architects
9 Harrison Gardens, Edinburgh, EH11 1SJ
T: 0131 313 1999
E: ama@ama-ltd.co.uk
W: www.ama-ltd.co.uk

Alandale Group
9 Selsdon Way, City Harbour, London, E14 9GL
T: 020 7005 0050
F: 020 7005 0051
W: www.alandaleuk.com

Albatros UK
Unit 9, Garamonde Drive, Clarendon Ind Park, Wymbush, Milton Keynes, MK8 8DF
T: 01908 305740
F: 01908 577899
E: sales@raildoorsolutions.co.uk
W: www.albatros-uk.co.uk

Albion Economics
Sandpiper, Kingston Road, Lewes, East Sussex, BN7 3ND

Alcad
1st Floor, Unit 5, Astra Centre, Edinburgh Way, Harlow, Essex, CM20 2BN
T: 01279 772555
E: carter.sarah@alcad.com
W: www.alcad.com

Alcatel-Lucent
Voyager Place, Shoppenhangers Rd, Maidenhead, SL5 2PJ
T: 01628 428221
F: 01628 428785
E: phil.cottom@alcatel-lucent.com
W: www.alcatel-lucent.com/railways

Alcoa Fastening Systems (Huck)
Unit 7, Stafford Park 7, Telford, TF3 3BQ
T: 01952 204603
E: matthew.dowd@alcoa.com
W: www.afsglobal.net

Alcontrol
Units 7&8, Hawarden Business Park, Manor Rd, Hawarden, Deeside, Flintshire, CH5 3US
T: 01244 528700
F: 01244 528701
W: www.alcontrol.com

Alere Healthcare Connections
Nashleigh Court, 188 Severalls Avenue, Chesham, Bucks, HP5 3EN
T: 01235 861483
W: www.alerehealthcareconnections.com/

The Alexander Partnership
Suite 47, 34 Buckingham Palace Road, Belgravia, London, SW1W 0RH
T: 0845 643 0824
E: info@thealexanderpartnership.com
W: www.thealexanderpartnership.com

Alfatronix Ltd
29-30 Newtown Business Park, Dorset, Poole, BH12 3LL
T: 01202 715517
F: 01202 715122
E: sales@alfatronix.com
W: www.alfatronix.com

Alfred Bagnall & Sons (North)
6, Manor Lane, Shipley, West Yorks, BD18 3RD
T: 01274 714800
F: 01274 530171
E: info@bagnalls.co.uk
W: www.bagnalls.co.uk

Alfred McAlpine Plc
See Carillion Rail

All Clothing & Protection Ltd
Units 6&7, Manor Park Ind Est, Station Rd South, Totton, Hants, SO40 9HP
T: 02380 428003
F: 02380 869333
E: sales@allclothing.co.uk
W: www.allclothing.co.uk

Allan Webb Limited
Bonds Mill, Stonehouse, GL10 3RF
T: 01453824581
E: info@smartditch.co.uk
W: www.allanwebb.co.uk

Allbatteries UK Ltd
Unit 20, Monkspath Business Park, Highlands Road, Solihull, West Midlands, B90 4NZ
T: 0121 506 8619
E: customerservice@allbatteries.co.uk
W: www.allbatteries.co.uk/

Allelys Heavy Haulage
The Slough, Studley, Warks, B80 7EN
T: 01527 857621
F: 01527 857623
E: robert@allelys.co.uk
W: www.allelys.co.uk

Allen & Douglas Corporate Clothing
See Sartoria Corporatewear

Allerton Steel
Thurston Road, Northallerton, North Yorkshire, DL6 2NA
T: 01609 774471
F: 01609 780364
E: contactus@allertonsteel.co.uk
W: https://www.allertonsteel.co.uk/

Allford Hall Monaghan Morris (AHMM)
Morelands, 5-23 Old Street, London, EC1V 9HL
T: 020 7251 5261
F: 020 7251 5123
W: www.ahmm.co.uk/

DIRECTORY

Alliance Rail Holdings
See Grand Central Railway Co. Ltd.

Allies & Morrison
85 Southwark St, London, SE1 0HX
T: 020 7921 0100
F: 020 7921 0101
E: newprojects@alliesandmorrison.com
W: www.alliesandmorrison.com

Allstar Business Solutions
PO Box 1463, Windmill Hill, Swindon, Wiltshire, SN5 6PS
T: 0870 182 8489
W: www.allstarcard.co.uk

Alltask Ltd
Alltask House, Commissioners Rd, Rochester, Kent, ME2 4EJ
T: 01634 298000
E: nick.covell@alltask.co.uk
W: www.alltask.co.uk

Alltype Fencing Specialists Ltd
Ye Wentes Wayes, High Rd, Langdon Hills, Essex, SS16 6HY
T: 01268 545192
F: 01268 545260
E: sales@alltypefencing.com
W: www.alltypefencing.com

Alonyx Ltd
The Mills, Canal St, Derby, DE1 2RJ
E: alexbrain@alonyx.com
W: www.alonyx.com

Alphatek Hyperformance Coatings Ltd
Head Office & Works, Unit A5, Cuba Ind. Est, Bolton Rd North, Ramsbottom, Lancs, BL0 0NE
T: 01706 821021
F: 01706 821023
E: railcoatings@alphatek.co.uk
W: www.alphatek.co.uk

Alstom Transport
The Place, 175 High Holborn, London, WC1V 7AA
T: 020 7438 9230
M: 07739 009 575
E: will.roberts@alstom.com
W: www.alstom.com

ALTE Technology
Pol. Industrial El Pla, C/ Camí de Can Gurri, 1, 08185 Lliçà de Vall, Barcelona, Spain
T: +34 938 407 012
F: +34 938 618 561
E: info@alte-technologies.com
W: www.alte-technologies.com

Altius
Wyvern Court, Stanier Way, Wyvern Business Park, Derby, DE21 6BF
T: 01332 960320
E: enquiries@altiusva.com
W: www.altiusva.com

Altran UK Ltd
2nd Floor Offices, 22 St Lawrence St, Southgate, Bath, BA1 1AN
T: 01225 466991
F: 01225 496006
E: info-uk@altran.com
W: www.altran.co.uk

Altro Ltd
Works Road, Letchworth Garden City, Hertfordshire, SG6 1NW
T: 01462 480480
F: 01462 480010
E: enquiries@altro.com
W: www.altro.com

Alucast Ltd
Western Way, Wednesbury, W. Midlands, WS10 7BW
T: 0121 556 6111
F: 0121 505 1302
E: aes@alucast.co.uk
W: www.alucast.co.uk

Aluminium Lighting Company (ALC)
Croeserw Industrial Estate, Eastern Avenue, Crymmer, Port Talbot, SA13 3PB
T: 01639852502
E: sales@alulight.com
W: www.aluminium-lighting.com

Aluminium Special Projects Ltd (ASP Group)
Unit 39, Second Ave, The Pensnett Estate, Kingswinford, W.Midlands, DY6 7UW
T: 01384 291900
F: 01384 400344
E: david@aspgroup.co.uk
W: www.aspgroup.co.uk

Aluminium Structures
Unit 5a, Aviation Park, Flint Rd, Saltney Ferry, Chester, CH4 0GZ
T: 01244 531889
F: 01244 539412
E: info@allystructures.co.uk
W: www.allystructures.co.uk

Alun Griffiths Ltd
Waterways House, Merthyr Road, Llanfoist, Abergavenny, NP7 9PE
T: 01873 857211
F: 01873 857679
E: enquiries@alungriffiths.co.uk
W: www.alungriffiths.co.uk

Alvey & Towers
Bythorn House, 8 Nether St, Harby, Leics, LE14 4BW
T: 01949 861894
E: office@alveyandtowers.com
W: www.alveyandtowers.com

AM1 Projects Ltd
8 Second Avenue, Chatham, Kent, ME4 5AU
T: 01634 400033
E: info@am1projects.co.uk
W: www.am1projects.co.uk

Amalgamated Construction Ltd (AMCO)
Whaley Rd, Barugh, Barnsley, S.Yorks, S75 1HT
T: 01226 243413
F: 01226 320202
E: info@amco.co.uk
W: www.amco-construction.co.uk

Amaro Group Ltd
Corsair Building, Marconi Way, Rochester, Kent, ME1 2XX
T: 0845 207 1190
E: wendy.meakins@amarogroup.co.uk
W: www.amarogroup.co.uk/

Amtrain Midlands Ltd
A38 Southbound, Fradley, Lichfield, Staffs, WS13 8RD
T: 01283 792633
F: 01283 792622
E: info@amtrain.co.uk
W: www.amtrain.co.uk

Ambersil (CRC UK)
Ambersil House, Wylds Road, Bridgewater, TA6 4DD
T: 01278727272
E: marketing.uk@ambersil.com
W: www.ambersil.com

Ambirad Ltd
Fens Pool Avenue, Brierley Hill, West Midlands, DY5 1QA
T: 01384 489700
F: 01384 489707
E: ambiradsales@nordyne.com
W: www.ambirad.co.uk

AMCL Systems Engineering Ltd
221 St John St, Clerkenwell, London, EC1V 4LY
T: 020 7688 2828
F: 020 7688 2829
E: enquiries@amcl.com
W: www.amcl.com

AMEC Environment & Infrastructure UK
Atlantic House, Imperial Way, Reading, RG2 0TP
T: 0800 371733
E: info.ukenvironment@amec.com
W: www.amec-ukenvironment.com/

Ameron UK Ltd
Bankside, Hull, HU5 1SQ
T: 01482 341441
F: 01482 348350
E: sales.uk@ameron-bv.com
W: www.ameron-bv.com

Amery Construction Ltd
Amery House, Third Way, Wembley, Middx, HA9 0RZ
T: 020 8903 1020
F: 020 8903 1560
E: reception@ameryrail.com
W: www.ameryrail.co.uk

Ametek Airtechnology Group Ltd
111 Windmill Road, Sunbury-on-Thames, Middlesex, TW16 7EF
T: 01932 765822
E: paul.hammond@ametek.co.uk
W: www.airscrew.co.uk/

Amey
The Sherard Building, Edmund Halley Rd, Oxford, OX4 4DQ
T: 01865 713100
F: 01865 713357
E: ais@amey.co.uk
W: www.amey.co.uk

Amicus
See Unite - The Union

AMOT
Western Way, Bury St Edmunds, Suffolk, IP33 3SZ
T: 01284 762222
F: 01284 760256
E: info@amot.com
W: www.amot.com

Amphenol Ltd
Thanet Way, Whitstable, Kent, CT5 3JF
T: 01227 773200
F: 01227 276571
E: info@amphenol.co.uk
W: www.industrial-amphenol.com

AMPL Ltd
See Carillion Rail

Amplicon Liveline Ltd
Centenary Industrial Estate, Hollingdean Rd, Brighton, BN2 4AW
T: 01273 570220
F: 01273 570215
E: sales@amplicon.com
W: www.amplicon.com

AMT Sybex Ltd
The Spirella Building, Bridge Rd, Letchworth Garden City, Herts, SG6 4ET
T: 01462 476400
F: 01462 476401
E: info@amt-sybex.com
W: www.amt-sybex.com

Anchor Systems (Europe) Ltd
Unit 45, Rowfant Business Centre, Wallage Lane, Rowfant, West Sussex, RH10 4NQ
T: 01342 719362
F: 01342 719436
E: sales@anchorsystems.co.uk
W: www.anchorsystems.co.uk

AndersElite Ltd
Dashwood House, 69, Old Broad St, London, EC2M 1NQ
T: 020 7256 5555
F: 020 7256 9898
E: rail@anderselite.com
W: www.anderselite.com

Anderton Concrete Products Ltd
Units 1 & 2, Cosgrove Business Park, Soot Hill, Anderton, Northwich, Cheshire, CW9 6AA
T: 01606 79436
F: 01606 871590
E: sales@andertonconcrete.co.uk
W: www.andertonconcrete.co.uk

Andrew Muirhead & Son Ltd
273-289 Dunn St, Glasgow, G40 3EA
T: 0141 554 3724
F: 0141 554 3724
E: sales@muirhead.co.uk
W: www.muirhead.co.uk

Andrews Signs and Engravers
Units 5 & 6, Rawcliffe Industrial Estate, Manor Lane, York, YO30 5XY
T: 01904 658322
E: sales@andrewssigns.co.uk
W: www.railsigns.com

Andromeda Engineering Ltd
14 Hurricane Court, Estuary Boulevard, Liverpool, L24 8RL
T: 0151 427 3802
E: info@andromedauk.com
W: www.andromedauk.com

Andy Waters Rail Safety
Cwm Elan, Cherry Tree Lane, Botesdale, Diss, Norfolk, IP22 1DL
T: 01379 898918
M: 07713656355
E: andy@watersrailsafety.co.uk
W: www.watersrailsafety.co.uk/

Angel Trains Limited
123 Victoria St, London, SW1E 6DE
T: 020 7592 0500
F: 020 7592 0520
E: communications@angeltrains.co.uk
W: www.angeltrains.co.uk

Anixter
3 Edmund St, Sheffield, S2 4EB
T: 0114 275 5884
F: 0114 275 7169
E: enquiries@anixteradhesives.com
W: www.infast.com

Anixter (UK) Ltd
Unit A, The Beacons, Birchwood Park, Birchwood, Warrington, Cheshire, WA3 6GP
T: 0870 242 2822
F: 01925 850292
E: railsales@anixter.com
W: www.anixter.com

Ansaldo STS
2.04 The Euston Office, One Euston Square, 40 Melton Street, London, NW1 2FD
T: 020 3574 4980
E: info@ansaldo-sts.com
W: www.ansaldo-sts.com/

Anstee & Ware Ltd - Midlands
Unit 15, Willow Rd, Trent Lane Industrial Est, Castle Donington, Derbys, DE74 2NP
T: 01332 850346
M: 01332 850686
E: john.alden@ansteeware.co.uk
W: www.ansteeware.co.uk

A-Plant Rail
102 Dalton Avenue, Birchwood Park, Warrington, WA3 6YE
T: 01925 281000
E: enquiries@aplant.com
W: www.aplant.com

Antagrade Electrical Ltd
6 Verity Court, Middlewich, Cheshire, CW10 0GW
T: 01606 833299
F: 01606 836959
E: enquiries@antagrade.co.uk
W: www.antagrade.co.uk

Antal International Network
170 Lanark Rd West, Currie, Edinburgh, EH14 5NY
T: 0870 428 1745
F: 0870 428 1745
E: edinburgh@antal.com
W: www.antal.com

Antislip Antiwear Treads Int.
See AATI Rail Ltd

AP Diesels Ltd
25a Victoria Street, Englefield Green, Egham, Surrey, TW20 0QY
T: 01784437228
E: office@apdiesels.com
W: www.apdiesels.com

AP Webb Plant Hire Ltd
Common Rd, Stafford, ST16 3DQ
T: 01785 241335
F: 01785 255178
E: mail@apwebbplanthire.co.uk
W: www.apwebbplanthire.co.uk

APB Group Ltd
Ryandra House, Ryandra Business Park, Brookhouse Way, Cheadle, Stoke-on-Trent, Staffordshire, ST10 1SR
T: 01538 755377
F: 01538 755010
E: apbgroup@aol.com
W: www.apbgroup.co.uk

APCOA
Wellington House, 4-10 Cowley Road, Uxbridge, Middlesex, UB8 2XW
T: 01895 272500
W: www.apcoa.co.uk/

APD Communications Ltd
Newlands Centre, Inglemire Lane, Hull, HU6 7TQ
T: 01482 808300
F: 01482 803901
E: info@apdcomms.com
W: www.apdcomms.com

Aperio Ltd
See Fugro GeoServices

Apex Cables Ltd
St Johns Rd, Meadowfield Ind Est, Durham, DH7 8RJ
T: 0191 378 7908
F: 0191 378 7809
E: apex@apexcables.co.uk
W: www.apexcables.co.uk

API Capacitors Ltd
Leyden Works, Station Road, Great Yarmouth, NR31 0HB
T: 01493 652752
F: 01493 655433
E: info@api-capacitors.com
W: www.api-capacitors.com

Application Solutions (Safety & Security) Ltd
Unit 17, Cliffe Ind. Est, Lewes, E Sussex, BN8 6JL
T: 01273 405411
F: 01273 405415
E: contactus@asl-control.co.uk
W: www.asl-control.co.uk

Applied Card Technologies Ltd
Langley Gate, Kington Langley, Chippenham, Wilts, SN15 5SE
T: 01249 751200
F: 01249 751201
E: info@weareact.com
W: www.weareact.com

Applied Inspection Ltd
Mosley Business Park, Mosley Street, Burton upon Trent, DE14 1DW
T: 01283 515163
F: 01283 539729
E: mark@appliedinspection.co.uk
W: www.appliedinspection.co.uk

APT Skidata Ltd
The Power House, Chantry Place, Headstone Lane, Harrow, Middlesex, HA3 6NY
T: 020 8421 2211
F: 020 8421 3951
E: d.murphy@aptskidata.co.uk
W: www.aptcontrols-group.co.uk

Aqua Fabrications Ltd
Belmont House, Garnett Place, Skelmersdale, Lancs, WN8 9UB
T: 01695 51933
F: 01695 51891
E: sales@aquafab.co.uk
W: www.aquafab.co.uk

Aquaforce Jetting Ltd
Innovation House, Euston Way, Telford, TF3 4LT
T: 01952 201790
W: www.aquaforcejetting.co.uk/

ANGEL Trains Limited
123 Victoria Street
London SW1E 6DE
T: 0207 592 0500
E: communications@angeltrains.co.uk

www.angeltrains.co.uk

Aquarius Railroad Technologies Ltd
Old Slenningford Farm, Mickley, Ripon, N Yorks, HG4 3JB
T: 01765 635021
F: 01765 635022
E: enquiries@railrover.com
W: www.railrover.com

Arbil Lifting Gear
Providence St, Lye, Stourbridge, West Midlands, DY9 8HS
T: 01384 424006
F: 01384 898814
E: info@arbil.co.uk
W: www.arbil.co.uk

Arcadia Alive Ltd
8 The Quadrant, 99 Parkway Avenue, Sheffield, S9 4WG
T: 0845 260 0126
E: talk@arcadiaalive.com
W: www.arcadiaalive.com

Arcadis LLP
Arcadis House, 34 York Way, London, N1 9AB
T: 020 7812 2000
E: kimberley.richardson@echarris.com
W: www.arcadis.com

Archer Safety Signs
Unit 6 Daniels Way, Hucknall, Nottingham, NG15 7LL
T: 0115 968 1152
F: 0115 976 1110
E: sales@archersigns.co.uk
W: www.archersafetysigns.co.uk

Archerdale Ltd
Hirstwood Works, Hirstwood Road, Shipley, West Yorkshire, BD18 4BU
T: 01274595783
E: sales@archerdale.com
W: www.archerdale.com

Arco Ltd
Head Office, PO Box 21, Waverley St, Hull, HU1 2SJ
T: 01482 222522
F: 01482 218536
E: sales@arco.co.uk
W: www.arco.co.uk

Arcola Energy
24 Ashwin Street, Dalston, London, E8 3DL
T: 020 7503 1386
E: sales@arcolaenergy.com
W: www.arcolaenergy.com

Arentis Limited
2 Wortley Road, Deepcar, Sheffield, S36 2UZ
T: 0114 218 0470
E: sales@arentis.co.uk
W: www.arentis.co.uk

Areva Risk Management Consulting Ltd
Suite 7, Hitching Court, Abingdon Business Park, Abingdon, Oxon, OX14 1RA
T: 01235 555755
F: 01235 525143
E: abingdon@arevamc.com
W: www.arevamc.com

170

Ark Signalling Consultancy
Lower Granary, Cornwells Farm, Marden, Kent, TN12 9NS
T: 01622 902880
M: 07917 697185
E: enquiries@arksignalling.co.uk
W: www.arksignalling.co.uk

Arlington Fleet Services Ltd
Railway Works, Campbell Rd, Eastleigh, Hants, SO50 5AD
T: 02380 696789
F: 02380 629118
E: info@arlington-fleet.co.uk
W: www.arlington-fleet.co.uk

ARM Engineering
Langstone Technology Park, Langstone Rd, Havant, Hants, PO9 1SA
T: 02392 228283
F: 02036 978 434
E: ibe@arm.co.uk
W: www.arm.co.uk

Arm4 Rail
Unit 7 Prescot Business Park, Sinclair Way, Prescot, Merseyside, L34 1QL
T: 0151 431 1369
F: 0151 430 7541
E: enquiries@arm4.co.uk
W: arm4.co.uk/

Arriva CrossCountry
See CrossCountry

Arriva plc
1 Admiral Way, Doxford International Business Park, Sunderland, SR3 3XP
T: 0191 520 4000
F: 0191 520 4001
E: enquiries@arriva.co.uk
W: www.arriva.co.uk

Arriva Rail London (London Overground)
Customer Services Centre, Overground House, 125 Finchley Rd, London, NW3 6HY
T: 0203 031 9315
E: overgroundinfo@tfl.gov.uk
W: www.arrivaraillondon.co.uk/

Arriva TrainCare
Crewe Carriage Shed, Off Weston Road, Crewe, Cheshire, CW1 6NE
T: 01270 508000
E: info@arrivatc.com
W: www.arrivatc.com

Arrow Cleaning & Hygeine Solutions
Rawdon Rd, Moira, Swadlincote, Derbys, DE12 6DA
T: 01283 221044
F: 01283 225731
E: sales@arrowchem.com
W: www.arrowchem.com

Arrowvale Electronics
Arrow Business Park, Shawbank Rd, Lakeside, Redditch, Worcs, B98 8YN
T: 01527 514151
F: 01527 514321
E: sales@arrowvale.co.uk
W: www.arrowvale.co.uk

Artel Rubber Company
Unit 11, Waterloo Park, Wellington Rd, Bidford on Avon, Warks, B50 4JH
T: 01789 774099
F: 01789 774599
W: www.artelrubber.com

Artelia International
26-28 Hammersmith Grove, Hammersmith, London, W6 7HA
T: +44 20 8237 1800
F: +44 20 8237 1810
W: www.uk.arteliagroup.com

Artemis Intelligent Power
Unit 3, Edgefield Industrial Estate, Loanhead, Midlothian, EH20 9TB
T: 0131 440 6260
E: enquiries@artemisip.com

Arthur D Little Ltd
Unit 18, Science Park, Milton Rd, Cambridge, CB4 0FH
T: 01223 427100
F: 01223 427101
E: info.adl@adlittle.com
W: www.adl.com

Arthur Flury (UK) Ltd
Unit 218, Milton Keynes Business Centre, Foxhunter Drive, Linford Wood, Milton Keynes, MK14 6GD, Switzerland
T: 01908 686766
E: info@aflury.co.uk
W: www.aflury.co.uk

Arthur J Gallagher
International Division, The Walbrook Building, 25 Walbrook, London, EC4N 8AW
T: +44 (0)20 7204 6000
E: ukenquiries@ajg.com
W: www.ajginternational.com

Arup
The Arup Campus, Blythe Gate, Blythe Valley Park, Solihull, West Midlands, B90 8AE
T: 0121 213 3412
F: 0121 213 3001
E: rail@arup.com
W: www.arup.com/rail

ASCO Numatics
Pit Hey Place, West Pimbo, Skelmersdale, Lancs, WN8 9PG
T: 01695 713600
F: 01695 713633
E: enquiries.asconumatics.uk@emerson.com
W: www.asconumatics.eu

Ashley Group
8 Kimpton Link, 40 Kimpton Road, Sutton, Surrey, SM3 9QP
T: 020 8644 4416
F: 020 8644 4417
E: info@ashleygroup.co.uk
W: www.ashleygroup.co.uk

Ashtead Plant Hire Co Ltd (APlant)
102 Dalton Ave, Birchwood Park, Birchwood, Warrington, WA3 6YE
T: 01925 281000
F: 01925 281001
E: enquiries@aplant.com
W: www.aplant.com

Ashurst
Broadwalk House, 5 Appold St, London, EC2A 2HA
T: 020 7859 1897
F: 020 7638 1112
E: email@ashurst.com
W: www.ashurst.com

ASL Contracts
See Pitchmastic PmB Ltd

ASL Control
Unit 17, Cliffe Industrial Estate, Lewes, East Sussex, BN8 6JL
T: 01273 405411
F: 01273 405415
E: sales@asl-control.co.uk
W: www.asl-control.co.uk/

ASLEF
75-77 St Johns St, Clerkenwell, London, EC1M 4NN
T: 020 7324 2400
F: 020 7490 8697
E: info@aslef.org.uk
W: www.aslef.org.uk

Aspin Foundations Ltd
Nexus House, Boundary Way, Hemel Hempstead, Hertfordshire, HP2 7SJ
T: 01442 236507
F: 01442 239096
E: info@aspingroup.com
W: www.aspingroup.com

Aspire Rail Consultants
See Keltbray Aspire Rail Ltd

Assertis
150 Minories, London, EC3N 1LS
T: 0207 347 5280
E: info@assertis.co.uk
W: www.assertis.co.uk

Asset International Structured Solutions
Suite 5, Brecon House, William Brown Close, Llantarnam Ind Park, Llantarnam, Cwmbran, Torfaen, NP44 3AB
T: 01633 499830
E: david.mason@assetint.co.uk
W: www.assetint.co.uk

Asset VRS
Springvale Business & Ind. Park, Bilston, Wolverhampton, West Midlands, WV14 0QL
T: 01902 499400
F: 01902 402104
E: assetvrs@hill-smith.co.uk
W: www.asset-vrs.co.uk/

Asset-Pro Ltd
Concorde House, 24 Cecil Pashley Way, Shoreham Airport, W.Sussex, BN43 5FF
T: 0845 120 2046
F: 01444 448071
E: info@asset-pro.com
W: www.asset-pro.com

Associated British Ports
Aldwych House, 71-91 Aldwych, London, WC2B 4HN
T: 020 7406 7853
F: 020 7430 1384
E: pr@abports.co.uk
W: www.abports.co.uk

Associated Rewinds (Ireland) Ltd
Tallaght Business Park, Whitestown, Dublin 24, Republic of Ireland
T: 00353 1 452 0033
F: 00353 1 452 0476
E: sales@associatedrewinds.com
W: www.associatedrewinds.com

Associated Train Crew Union
DBH Serviced Business Centres Ltd, Longfields Court, Middlewoods Way, Carlton, Barnsley, S71 3GN
T: 01226 630166
E: headoffice@atcu.org.uk
W: www.atcu.org.uk

Associated Utility Supplies Ltd
1 Dearne Park Ind Est, Park Mill Way, Clayton West, Huddersfield, HD8 9XJ
T: 01484 860575
F: 01484 860576
E: sales@aus.co.uk
W: www.aus.co.uk

Association for Project Management
150 West Wycombe Rd, High Wycombe, Bucks, HP12 3AE
T: 01494 460246
F: 01494 528937
E: info@apm.org.uk
W: www.apm.org.uk

Association of Railway Training Providers (ARTP)
Kelvin House, RTC Business Park, London Rd, Derby, DE24 8UP
T: 01332 360033
F: 01332 366367
E: info@artp.co.uk
W: www.artp.co.uk

Association of Train Operating Companies (ATOC)
See Rail Delivery Group

AST Language Services Ltd
Unit 8, Ayr st, Nottingham, NG7 4FX
T: 0115 970 5633
F: 0845 051 8780
E: office@astls.co.uk
W: www.astlanguage.com

AST Recruitment Ltd
First Floor, Chase House, Park Plaza, Heath Hayes, Cannock, Staffs, WS12 2DD
T: 01543 331331
E: iperry@ast-recruit.com
W: www.astrecruitment.co.uk

Ast Signs
The Box, Eden Business Park, Penrith, Cumbria, CA11 9FB
T: 01768 892292
M: 07725 888029
E: gareth.livingstone@astsigns.com
W: https://www.astsigns.com

Astrac Safety Training Solutions Ltd
Unit 2, Victoria Rd, Stoke on Trent, ST4 2HS
F: 01782 411490
E: train@astractraining.co.uk
W: www.astractraining.com/

At Source QX Ltd
18 Eve St, Louth, Lincs, LN11 0JJ
T: 01507 604322
F: 01507 608513
E: mick@sourceqx.com
W: www.protecthear.co.uk

ATA Rail
See TQ Technical and Vocational

ATEIS UK Ltd
10 Hacche Lane Business Park, Pathfields, South Molton, Devon, EX36 3LH
T: 0845 652 1511
F: 0845 652 2527
E: neil.voce@ateis.co.uk
W: www.ateis.co.uk

Athena Project Services
Mill Lane, Barrow on Humber, North Lincs, DN17 7BD
T: 01469 533333
F: 01469 532233
E: david.tyerman@athenaprojectservices.com
W: www.athenaprojectservices.com

Atkins
Euston Tower, 286 Euston Road, London, NW1 3AT
T: 020 7121 2000
F: 020 7121 2111
E: rail@atkinsglobal.com
W: www.atkinsglobal.com

ATL Transformers Ltd
Hanson Close, Middleton, Manchester, M24 2HD
T: 0161 653 0902
F: 0161 653 4744
E: sales@atltransformers.co.uk
W: www.atltransformers.co.uk

Atlantic Design Projects Limited
Branch Hill Mews, Branch Hill, London, NW3 7LT
T: 020 7435 1777
E: cg@atlanticdesign.uk.com
W: www.atlanticdesign.uk.com

Atlantis International Ltd
See Karcher Vehicle Wash

Atlas Copco Compressors Ltd
Swallowdale Lane, Hemel Hempstead, Herts, HP2 7HA
T: 01442 261201
F: 01442 234791
E: general.enquiries@uk.atlascopco.com
W: www.atlascopco.co.uk

Atlas Rail Components Ltd
See Associated Utility Supplies Ltd

ATOS Origin
4 Triton Square, Regents Place, London, NW1 3HG
T: 020 7830 4447
E: ukwebenquiries@atos.net
W: www.atos.net/transport

Auctus Management Group
Tech Block, Gee Business Park, Holborn Hill, Aston, Birmingham, B7 5JR
T: 0121 366 8800
E: info@auctusmg.co.uk
W: www.auctusmg.co.uk/

Aura Brand Solutions
Freemantle Road, Lowestoft, Suffolk, NR33 0EA
T: 0845 052 5241
E: info@aurabrands.com
W: www.aurabrands.com

Austin Reynolds Signs
Augustine House, Gogmore Lane, Chertsey, Surrey, KT16 9AP
T: 01932 568888
F: 01932 566600
M: 07831 465491
E: austin.reynolds@austinreynolds.co.uk
W: www.austinreynolds.com

Autobuild Ltd
See Pelma Services and Autobuild Ltd

Autoclenz Holdings Plc
See REACT Beyond Cleaning

Autodrain
Wakefield Rd, Rothwell Haigh, Leeds, LS26 0SB
T: 0113 205 9332
F: 0113 288 0999
E: mark@autodrain.net
W: www.autodrain.net

Autoglass
1 Priory Business Park, Cardington, Bedford, MK44 3US
T: 01234 273636
E: debbie.barnes@autoglass.co.uk
W: www.autoglass.co.uk

Autoglym PSV
Works Road, Letchworth Garden City, Herts, SG6 1LU
T: 01462 677766
F: 01462 686565
E: npro@autoglym.com
W: www.autoglymprofessional.com/psv/trains.asp

Autolift GmbH
Mayrwiesstasse 16, 5300 Hallwang, Salzburg, Austria
T: 0043 662 450588 11
F: 0043 662 450588 18
E: a.foelsce@autolift.info
W: www.autolift.info

Automotive Trim Developments (ATD)
Priory Mill, Charter Avenue, Coventry, West Midlands, CV4 8AF
T: 02476 695150
F: 02476 695156
E: info@autotrimdev.com
W: www.autotrimdev.com/

AV Dawson
Riverside Park Road, Middlesbrough, TS2 1UT
T: 01642 219271
F: 01642 222636
W: www.av-dawson.com

Avanti West Coast
North Wing Offices. Euston Station, London, NW1 2HS
T: 03331 031 031
W: https://www.avantiwestcoast.co.uk/

Avery Weigh-Tronix
Foundry Lane, Smethwick, West Midlands, B66 2LP
T: 0845 3070314
F: 0870 9050085
E: info@awtxglobal.com
W: www.awtxglobal.com

Avondale Environmental Services Ltd
Fort Horsted, Primrose Close, Chatham, Kent, ME4 6HZ
T: 01634 823200
F: 01634 844485
E: info@avondaleuk.com
W: www.avondaleuk.com

AWW Architects
Rivergate House, 70 Redcliff Street, Bristol, BS1 6LS
T: 0117 923 2535
E: info@aww-uk.com
W: aww-uk.com/

Axiom Rail
Whieldon Road, Stoke on Trent, ST4 4HP
T: 07801 905 799
E: sales@axiomrail.com
W: www.axiomrail.com

Axion Technologies
Lokesvej 7-9, 3400 Hillerød, Denmark
T: 0045 721 93500
F: 0045 721 93501
E: info@axiontech.dk
W: www.axiontech.dk

Axis Communications (UK) Ltd
Ground Floor, Gleneagles, Belfry Business Park, Colonial Way, Watford, WD24 4WH
T: 01923 211417
F: 01923 205589
E: pressoffice@axis.com
W: www.axis.com/trains

Axminster Carpets Ltd
Woodmead Rd, Axminster, Devon, EX13 5PQ
T: 01297 630686
F: 01297 35241
E: sales@axminster-carpets.co.uk
W: www.axminster-carpets.co.uk

Axon Bywater
See Bywater Training Ltd

Azea Ltd
6 Dilton Terrace, Amble, Morpeth, Northumberland, NE65 0DT
T: 01665 714000
E: info@azea.co.uk
W: www.azea.co.uk

AZPML
55 Curtain Road, London, EC2A 3PT
T: 020 7033 6480
F: 020 7033 6481
E: lon@azpml.com
W: www.azpml.com

Aztec Chemicals
Gateway, Crewe, CW1 6YY
T: 01270 655500
F: 01270 655501
E: info@aztecchemicals.com
W: www.aztecchemicals.com

BA Events
156 Great Charles Street, Queensway, Birmingham, B3 3HN
T: 0121 728 2193
E: info@baevents.co.uk
W: www.baevents.co.uk/

Babcock Rail
Kintail House, 3 Lister Way, Hamilton International Park, Blantyre, G72 0FT
T: 01698 203005
F: 01698 203006
E: shona.jamieson@babcock.co.uk
W: www.babcock.co.uk/rail

DIRECTORY

Bache Pallets Ltd
Bromley St, Lye, Stourbridge, West Midlands, DY9 8HU
T: 01384 897799
F: 01384 891351
E: mike@bache-palletsltd.co.uk
W: www.bache-pallets.co.uk

BAE Systems
Marconi Way, Rochester, Kent, ME1 2XX
T: 01634 844400
F: 01634 205100
E: john.hawkins@baesystems.com
W: www.baesystems.com/hybridrive

Baker Bellfield Ltd
Display House, Hortonwood 7, Telford, Shropshire, TF1 7GP
T: 01952 677411
F: 01952 670188
E: sales@bakerbellfield.co.uk
W: www.bakerbellfield.co.uk

Bakerail Services
4 Green Lane, Hail Weston, St Neots, Cambs, PE19 5JZ
T: 01480 471349
F: 01480 218044
E: info@bakerailservices.co.uk
W: www.bakerailservices.co.uk

BakerHicks
20 Timothy's Bridge Road, Stratford-upon-Avon, Warks, CV37 9NJ
T: 01789 204288
E: contact@baker-hicks.com
W: baker-hicks.com/

Baldwin & Francis Ltd
President Park, President Way, Sheffield, S4 7UR
T: 0114 286 6000
F: 0114 286 6059
E: sales@baldwinandfrancis.com
W: www.baldwinandfrancis.com

Balfour Beatty Ground Engineering
Pavilion B, Ashwood Park, Ashwood Way, Basingstoke, Hants, RG23 8BG
T: 01256 400400
F: 01256 400401
M: 07753 833200
E: neil.beresford@bbge.com
W: www.bbge.com

Balfour Beatty Rail
Kingsgate, 62 High Street, Redhill, Surrey, RH1 1SH
T: 01737 854400
E: info@bbrail.com
W: balfourbeatty.com

Balfour Kilpatrick Ltd
Lumina Building, 40 Aislie Rd, Hillington Park, Glasgow, G52 4RU
T: 0141 880 2001
F: 0141 880 2201
E: enquiry@balfourkilpatrick.com
W: www.balfourkilpatrick.com

Ballard Power
Majsmarken 1, DK-9500 Hobro, Denmark
E: marketing@ballard.com
W: www.ballard.com

Ballast Tools (UK) Ltd
7 Pure Offices, Kembrey Park, Swindon, SN2 8BW
T: 01793 697800
M: 07703 608551
E: sales@btukltd.com
W: www.btukltd.com

Ballyclare Ltd
The Forum, Hercules Business Park, Bird Hall Lane, Cheadle Heath, Stockport, Cheshire, SK3 0UX
T: 0844 493 2808
F: 0844 493 2801
E: info@ballyclarelimited.com
W: www.ballyclarelimited.com

BAM Nuttall Ltd
St James House, Knoll Rd, Camberley, Surrey, GU15 3XW
T: 01276 63484
F: 01276 66060
E: headoffice@bamnuttall.co.uk
W: www.bamnuttall.co.uk

Bam Ritchies
Glasgow Rd, Kilsyth, Glasgow, G65 9BL
T: 01236 467000
F: 01236 467030
E: ritchies@bamritchies.co.uk
W: www.bamritchies.co.uk

R Bance & Co
Cockrow Hill House, St Mary's Rd, Surbiton, Surrey, KT6 5HE
T: 020 8398 7141
F: 020 8398 4765
E: admin@bance.com
W: www.bance.com

Bank of Scotland Corporate
155 Bishopsgate, London, EC2M 3YB
T: 020 7012 8001
F: 020 7012 9455
W: www.bankofscotland.co.uk/corporate

Baqus Group Plc
2/3 North Mews, London, WC1N 2JP
T: 020 7831 1283
F: 020 7242 9512
E: enquiries@baqus.co.uk
W: www.baqus.co.uk

Barcodes For Business Ltd
Buckland House, 56 Packhorse Rd, Gerrards Cross, SL9 8EF
T: 01753 888833
F: 01753 888834
E: info@barcodesforbusiness.co.uk
W: www.barcodesforbusiness.co.uk

Bardon Aggregates
See Aggregate Industries UK Ltd

Barhale Construction Plc
Unit 3, The Orient Centre, Greycaine Rd, Watford, Herts, WD24 7GP
T: 01923 474500
F: 01923 474501
E: samantha.davis@barhale.co.uk
W: www.barhale.co.uk

Barker Ross Recruitment
24 De Montford St, Leicester, LE1 7GB
T: 0800 0288 693
F: 0116 2550 811
E: people@barkerross.co.uk
W: www.barkerross.co.uk

Barnbrook Systems Ltd
25 Fareham Park Rd, Fareham, Hants, PO15 6LD
T: 01329 847722
F: 01329 844132
E: sales@barnbrook.co.uk
W: www.barnbrook.co.uk

Barnshaw Section Bending Ltd
Tipton Rd, Tividale, Oldbury, West Midlands, B69 3HY
T: 0121 557 8261
F: 0121 557 5323
E: tony.farrington@barnshaws.com
W: www.barnshaws.com

Barrier Electrical Engineering
Pearl Buildings, Stephenson Street, Willington Quay, Wallsend, Tyne and Wear, NE28 6UE
T: 0191 262 0510
E: recruitment@barrierltd.co.uk
W: www.barriergroup.com/

Basic Solutions Ltd
See LNT Solutions Ltd

H S Bassett
Coronet Way, Enterprise Park, Morriston, Swansea, SA6 8RH
T: 01792 790022
F: 01792 790033
E: info@hsbassett.co.uk
W: www.hsbassett.co.uk

BATT Cables
The Belfry, Fraser Rd, Erith, Kent, DA8 1QH
T: 01322 441165
F: 01322 443681
E: battindustrial.sales@batt.co.uk
W: www.batt.co.uk

Bauer Consumer Media
Media House, Peterborough Business Park, Lynch Wood, Peterborough, PE2 6EA
T: 01733 468000
E: rail@bauermedia.co.uk
W: www.bauermedia.co.uk

BaxterStorey
9th Floor, 140 London Wall, London, EC2Y 5DN
T: 020 7600 3838
F: 020 7600 3121
W: www.baxterstorey.co.uk/

Bayer Environmental Science
W: www.environmentalscience.bayer.co.uk/

BCM Construction
6 Blenheim Centre, Locks Lane, Mitcham, Surrey, CR4 2JX
T: 020 8640 7887
F: 020 8640 3437
W: www.bcmconstruction.co.uk/

BCM Glass Reinforced Concrete
Unit 22, Civic Industrial Unit, Whitchurch, Shropshire, SY13 1TT
T: 01948 665321
F: 01948 666381
E: info@bcmgrc.com
W: www.bcmgrc.com/railhome

BDP (Building Design Partnership)
16 Brewhouse Yard, Clerkenwell, London, EC1V 4LJ
T: 020 7812 8000
F: 020 7812 8399
E: london@bdp.com
W: www.bdp.com/en/

Beacon Rail Leasing Ltd
111 Buckingham Palace Road, Victoria, London, SW1W 0SR
T: 0207 340 8500
E: rail@beaconrail.com
W: www.beaconrail.com

Beakbane Bellows Ltd
Stourport Rd, Kidderminster, Worcs, DY11 7QT
T: 01562 820561
F: 01562 820560
E: info@beakbane.co.uk
W: www.beakbane.co.uk

Bearward Engineering Ltd
Main Road, Far Cotton, Northampton, Northamptonshire
T: 01604 762851
F: 01604 766168
E: sales@bearward.com
W: www.bearward.com

Beaver Sports (Yorkshire) Ltd
Flint Street, Fartown, Huddersfield, HD1 6LG
T: 01484 512354
E: sales@beaversports.co.uk
W: www.royalscotsgrey.com

Bechtel Ltd
11 Pilgrim Street, London, EC4V 6RN
T: 020 7651 7777
F: 020 7651 7972
E: jgreen2@bechtel.com
W: www.bechtel.com

Beck & Pollitzer
Burnham Rd, Dartford, Kent, DA1 5BD
T: 01322 223494
F: 01322 291859
E: info@beck-pollitzer.com
W: www.beck-pollitzer.com

Becorit GmbH
PO Box 189, Congleton, Cheshire, CW4 7FB
F: 01270 269000
E: becorit@btinternet.com
W: www.becorit.de

Beejay Rail Ltd
79 Charles St, Springburn, Glasgow, G21 2PS
T: 0141 553 1133
F: 0141 552 5333
E: info@beejayrewinds.com
W: www.beejayrewinds.com

Beeswift
Delta House, Delta Point, Greets Green Road, West Bromwich, West Midlands, B70 9PL
T: 0121 524 2323
F: 0121 524 2325
E: marketing@beeswift.com
W: www.beeswift.com

Belden Solutions
Suite 13, Styal Rd, Manchester, M22 5WB
T: 0161 498 3724
F: 0161 498 3762
E: info@belden.com
W: www.belden.com

Bell & Pottinger
E: info@bell-pottinger.com

Bell & Webster Concrete Ltd
Alma Park Rd, Grantham, Lincs, NG31 9SE
T: 01476 562277
F: 01476 562944
E: bellandwebster@eleco.com
W: www.bellandwebster.co.uk/

Bellvedi
Suite 2, Berkhamsted House, 121 High St, Berkhamsted, Hertfordshire, HP4 2DJ
T: 01442 861041
E: info@bellvedi.com
W: bellvedi.com/

Belmond Luxury Trains
Shackleton House, 4 Battle Bridge Lane, London, SE1 2HP
T: 020 3117 1300
F: 020 7921 4708
E: help@belmond.com
W: www.belmond.com/luxury-trains

Belvoir Engineering Services
Unit 11, High Hazles Road, Manvers Business Park, Cotgrave, Nottingham, NG12 3GZ
T: 0115 989 2760
W: www.belvoires.com

Bemrose Booth Paragon
Stockholm Rd, Hull, HU7 0XY
T: 01482 826343
E: rfarmer@bemrosebooth.com
W: www.bemrosebooth.com/

Bender UK Ltd
Low Mill Business Park, Ulverston, Cumbria, LA12 9EE
T: 01229 480123
F: 01229 480345
E: info@bender-uk.com
W: www.bender-uk.com

Bentley Systems International Limited
2 Park Place, Upper Hatch Street, Dublin 2, Republic of Ireland
T: (+353) 1 436 4600
W: www.bentley.com

Bentley Systems UK Ltd
North Heath Lane, Horsham, W Sussex, RH12 5QE
T: 01403 259511
W: www.bentley.com

Bernstein Ltd
Unit One, Tintagel Way, Westgate, Aldridge, West Midlands, WS9 8ER
T: 01922 744999
F: 01922 457555
E: sales@bernstein-ltd.co.uk
W: www.bernstein-ltd.co.uk

Berry Systems
Springvale Business & Industrial Park, Bilston, Wolverhampton, WV14 0QL
T: 01902 491100
F: 01902 494080
E: sales@berrysystems.co.uk
W: www.berrysystems.co.uk

Best Impressions
15 Starfield Rd, London, W12 9SN
T: 020 8740 6443
F: 020 8740 9134
E: talk2us@best-impressions.co.uk
W: www.best-impressions.co.uk

Bestchart Ltd
6A Mays Yard, Down Rd, Horndean, Waterlooville, Hants, PO8 0YP
T: 023 9259 7707
F: 023 9259 1700
E: info@bestchart.co.uk
W: www.bestchart.co.uk

Beta Technology
Barclay Court, Heavens Walk, Doncaster Carr, Doncaster, South Yorkshire, DN4 5HZ
T: 01302 322633
E: info@betatechnology.co.uk
W: www.betatechnology.co.uk

BHSF Occupational Health Ltd
Banham Court, Hanbury Rd, Stoke Prior, Bromsgrove, Worcs, B60 4JZ
T: 01527 577242
F: 01527 832618
E: admin@bhsfoh.co.uk
W: www.bhsf.co.uk

Bierrum International Ltd
Bierrum House, High St, Houghton Regis, Bedfordshire, LU5 5BJ
T: 01582 845745
F: 01582 845746
E: solutions@bierrum.co.uk
W: www.bierrum.co.uk

Bijur Delimon International
Wenta Business Centre, 1 Electric Ave, Innova Science Park, Enfield, EN3 7XU
T: 01432 262107
F: 01432 365001
E: chris.riley@bijurdelimon.co.uk
W: www.bijurdelimon.co.uk

Bilfinger
Carl-Reiß-Platz 1-5, 68165 Mannheim, Germany
T: +49 621 459-0
F: +49 621 459-2366
W: www.bilfinger.com/en/

Bingham Rail
Barrow Rd, Wincobank, Sheffield, S9 1JZ
T: 0870 774 2341
F: 0870 774 5423
E: info@binghamrail.com
W: www.trainwash.co.uk

Bircham Dyson Bell LLP
50 Broadway, London, SW1H 0BL
T: 020 7227 7000
F: 020 7222 3480
E: enquirieslondon@bdb-law.co.uk
W: www.bdb-law.co.uk

Birchwood Price Tools
Birch Park, Park Lodge Rd, Giltbrook, Nottingham, NG16 2AR
T: 0115 938 9000
F: 0115 938 9010
W: www.birdwoodpricetools.com

Birley Manufacturing Ltd
Birley Vale Ave, Sheffield, S12 2AX
T: 0114 280 3200
F: 0114 280 3201
E: info@birleyml.com
W: www.birleyml.com

Birmingham Centre for Railway Research and Education (BCRRE)
University of Birmingham, Gisbert Kapp Building, Edgbaston, Birmingham, B15 2TT
F: 0121 414 4291
E: j.grey@bham.ac.uk
W: www.birmingham.ac.uk/research/activity/railway/index.aspx

Birse Rail Ltd
See Balfour Beatty Rail

Blackpool Transport Services
Rigby Rd, Blackpool, Lancs, FY1 5DD
T: 01253 473001
F: 01253 473101
E: enquiries@blackpooltransport.com
W: www.blackpooltransport.com

Blom Aerofilms Ltd
The Astrolabe, Cheddar Business Park, Cheddar, Somerset, BS27 3EB
T: 01934 745820
F: 01934 745825
E: uk.info@blomasa.com
W: www.blomasa.com

Blue I UK Ltd
See Peli Products (UK) Ltd

BMAC Ltd
Units 13-14, Shepley Ind. Est. South, Shepley Road, Audenshaw, Manchester, M34 5DW
T: 0161 304 5644
F: 0161 336 5691
E: enquiries@bmac.ltd.uk
W: www.bmac.ltd.uk

BMT Group
Goodrich House, 1 Waldegrave Road, Teddington, Middlesex, TW11 8LZ
T: 020 8943 5544
F: 020 8943 5347
E: enquiries@bmtmail.com
W: www.bmt.org/

BNP Paribas Real Estate
One Redcliff St, Bristol, BS1 6NP
T: 0117 984 8480
F: 0117 984 8401
E: realestate.press@bnpparibas.com
W: www.realestate.bnpparibas.co.uk

BOC
Customer Service Centre, Priestley Rd, Worsley, Manchester, M28 2UT
T: 0800 111 333
F: 0800 111 555
E: custserv@boc.com
W: www.bocindustrial.co.uk

Boddingtons Electrical
Prospect House, Queenborough Lane, Great Notley, Essex, CM77 7AG
T: 01376 567490
F: 01376 567495
E: info@boddingtons-electrical.com
W: www.boddingtons-electrical.com/

Boden Rail Engineering
16 Taplin Close, Holmcroft, Stafford, ST16 1NW

Bodycote Materials Testing
See Exova (UK) Ltd

Bodyguard Workwear Ltd
Adams St, Birmingham, B7 4LS
T: 0121 380 1308
E: sales@bodyguardworkwear.co.uk
W: www.bodyguardworkwear.co.uk / www.railclothing.co.uk

Bombardier Transportation UK Ltd
Litchurch Lane, Derby, DE24 8AD
T: 01332 344666
F: 01332 289271
W: www.bombardier.com

Bonar Floors Ltd
See Forbo Flooring Ltd

Bonatrans AS
Revoluční 1234, 735 81 Bohumín, Czech Republic
T: +420 597 083 112
W: www.bonatrans.cz/

Bond Dickinson LLP
4 More London Riverside, London, SE1 2AU
T: 0345 415 0000
F: 0345 415 6200
W: www.bonddickinson.com/

Bond Insurance Services
Salisbury House, 81 High St, Potters Bar, Herts, EN6 5AS
T: 01707 291200
F: 01707 291202
E: enquiries@bond-insurance.co.uk
W: www.bond-insurance.co.uk

C F Booth Ltd
Clarence Metal Works, Armer St, Rotherham, S. Yorks, S60 1AF
T: 01709 559198
F: 01709 561859
E: info@cfbooth.com
W: www.cfbooth.com

Borders Railway Project
Transport Scotland, 7th Floor, Buchanan House, 58 Port Dundas Rd, Glasgow, G4 0HS
T: 0141 272 7100
E: bordersrailway@transportscotland.gsi.gov.uk
W: www.bordersrailway.com

Bosch Rexroth Ltd
15 Cromwell Rd, St Neots, Cambs, PE19 2ES
T: 01480 223253
E: info@boschrexroth.co.uk
W: www.boschrexroth.co.uk

Bosch Security Systems
PO Box 750, Uxbridge, Middx, UB9 5ZJ
T: 01895 878094
F: 01895 878098
E: uk.securitysystems@bosch.com
W: www.boschsecurity.co.uk

Boss Cabins Limited
BCS House, Pinfold Road, Bourne, Lincolnshire, PE10 9HT
T: 0845 1801616
F: 01778 395265
M: 07854008955
E: rburchell@bosscabins.co.uk
W: www.bosscabins.co.uk

Boston Marks Insurance Brokers (London) Limited
New Loom House, 101 Back Church Lane, London, E1 1LU
T: 020 7337 4078
F: 020 7337 4061
E: aorpwood@normanbutcherjonesltd.co.uk
W: www.normanbutcherjonesltd.co.uk

Botany Weaving Mill Ltd
Vauxhall Avenue, Cork Street, Dublin 8, Republic of Ireland
T: +353 1 453 2278
E: jonathan@botanyweaving.com
W: www.botanyweaving.com

Bott Ltd
Bude-Stratton Business Park, Bude, Cornwall, EX23 8LY
T: 01288 357788
F: 01288 352692
E: i-sales@bottltd.co.uk
W: www.bott-group.com

Bowden Bros Ltd
Brickworks House, Spook Hill, North Holmwood, Dorking, Surrey, RH5 4HR
T: 01306 743355
F: 01306 876768
E: ian.bowden@bowden-bros.com
W: www.bowden-bros.com

Bowen Projects Ltd
1 Portway Close, Off Torrington Avenue, Coventry, CV4 9UY
T: 02476 695550
F: 02476 695040
E: s.bowen@bowenprojects.co.uk
W: www.bowenprojects.co.uk

Bowmer & Kirkland Ltd
High Edge Court, Heage, Belper, Derbys, DE56 2BW
T: 01773 853131
F: 01773 856710
E: general@bandk.co.uk
W: www.bandk.co.uk/

Boxwood Ltd
15 Old Bailey, London, EC4M 7EF
T: 020 3170 7240
F: 020 3170 7241
E: info@boxwood.com
W: www.boxwood.com

Bradgate Containers
Leicester Rd, Shepshed, Leics, LE12 9EG
T: 01509 508678
F: 01509 504350
E: sales@bradgate.co.uk
W: www.bradgate.co.uk

The Bradley Group
Junction 21 Business Park, Gorse Street, Chadderton, Oldham, Greater Manchester, OL9 9QH
T: 01706 621421
F: 01706 366154
E: pce@johnbradleygroup.co.uk
W: www.johnbradleygroup.co.uk

Brady UK
Wildmere Industrial Estate, Banbury, Oxon, OX16 3JU
T: 01295 228288
E: csuk@bradycorp.com
W: www.bradyeurope.com

Branch Line Society
10 Sandringham Rd, Stoke Gifford, South Gloucestershire, BS34 8NP
E: general.secretary@branchline.uk
W: www.branchline.uk

Brand-Rex Ltd
Speciality Cabling Solutions, West Bridgewater St, Leigh, Lancs, WN7 4HB
T: 01942 265500
F: 01942 265576
E: speciality@brand-rex.com
W: www.brand-rex.com

Bratts Ladders
Abbeyfield Rd, Lenton Industrial Estate, Nottingham, NG7 2SZ
T: 0115 986 6851
F: 0115 986 1991
E: stephen@brattsladders.com
W: www.brattsladders.com

Braybrook Ltd
Foremost House, Radford Way, Billericay, Essex, CM12 0BT
T: 01277 815151
E: admin@braybrookltd.co.uk
W: braybrookltd.co.uk/

Brecknell, Willis & Co Ltd
PO Box 10, Chard, Somerset, TA20 2DE
T: 01460 260700
F: 01460 66122
E: sales@brecknellwillis.com
W: www.brecknellwillis.com

Brentto Industry
See Onyxrail Ltd

Briben Products
Unit 29, Braintree Business Park, Blackwell Drive, Springwood Industrial Estate, Braintree, Essex, CM7 2PU
T: 01376 335119
E: sales@briben.com
W: https://www.briben.com

Bridgeway Consulting Ltd
Bridgeway House, 2 Riverside Way, Nottingham, NG2 1DP
T: 0115 919 1111
F: 0115 919 1112
E: enquiries@bridgeway-consulting.co.uk
W: www.bridgeway-consulting.co.uk

Briggs Equipment
Orbital Way, Cannock, Staffordshire, WS11 8XW
T: 0330 123 9814
W: www.briggsequipment.co.uk/

BriggsAmasco
Amasco House, 101 Powke Lane, Cradley Heath, B64 5PX
T: 0121 502 9600
F: 0121 502 9601
W: www.briggsamasco.co.uk/

Bright Bond (BAC Group)
Stafford Park 11, Telford, Shropshire, TF3 3AY
T: 01952 290321
F: 01952 290325
E: sales@bacgroup.com
W: www.bacgroup.com

Britannia Washing Systems
See Smith Bros & Webb Ltd

Britax PSV Wypers Ltd
Navigation Rd, Worcester, WR5 3DE
T: 01905 350500
F: 01905 763928
E: enquiries@psv-wypers.com
W: www.psv-wypers.com

British American Railway Services (BARS)
Stanhope Station, Stanhope, Bishop Auckland, Co Durham, DL13 2YS
T: 01388 526203
E: mfairburn@britamrail.com
W: www.rmslocotec.com

British Geological Survey
Kingsley Dunham Centre, Keyworth, Nottingham, NG12 5GG
T: 0115 936 3100
F: 0115 936 3200
E: enquiries@bgs.ac.uk
W: www.bgs.ac.uk

British Springs
See GME Springs

British Steel
Rail Service Centre, PO Box 1, Brigg Road, Scunthorpe, North Lincolnshire, DN16 1BP
T: 01724 404040
E: rail@britishsteel.co.uk
W: britishsteel.co.uk/rail

British Transport Police (BTP)
25 Camden Rd, London, NW1 9LN
T: 020 7830 8800
F: 020 7023 6952
E: first_contact@btp.pnn.police.uk
W: www.btp.police.uk

Briton Fabricators Ltd
Fulwood Rd South, Huthwaite, Sutton-in-Ashfield, Notts, NG17 2JW
T: 0115 963 2901
F: 0115 968 0335
E: sales@britonsltd.co.uk
W: www.britonsltd.co.uk

Brixworth Engineering Co Ltd
Creaton Rd, Brixworth, Northampton, NN6 9BW
T: 01604 880338
F: 01604 880252
E: sales@benco.co.uk
W: www.benco.co.uk

Broadland Rail
7 York Rd, Woking, Surrey, GU22 7XH
T: 01483 725999
W: www.broadlandrail.com

Broadway Malyan
Holmes House, 4 Pear Place, London, SE1 8BT
T: 020 7261 4200
W: https://www.broadwaymalyan.com/

Brockhouse Forgings Ltd
Howard St, West Bromwich, West Midlands, B70 0SN
T: 0121 556 1241
F: 0121 502 3076
W: www.brockhouse.co.uk

Brodie Engineering Ltd
Bonnyton Rail Depot, Bonnyton Industrial Estate, Munro Place, Kilmarnock, Ayrshire, KA1 2NP
T: 01563 546280
F: 01563 546281
E: sales@brodie-engineering.co.uk
W: www.brodie-engineering.co.uk/

Brodie Leasing Ltd
C/O Mr Gerry Hilferty, Montgreenan House Offices, Montgreenan, Kilwinning, Ayrshire, KA13 7QZ

Brown & Mason Ltd
Anson House, Schooner Court, Crossways Business Park, Dartford, DA2 6QQ
T: 01322 277731
F: 01322 284152
E: b&m@brownandmason.ltd.uk
W: www.brownandmason.com

Browse Bion Architectural Signs
Unit 19/20, Lakeside Park, Medway City Est, Rochester, Kent, ME2 4LT
T: 01634 710063
F: 01634 290112
E: sales@browsebion.com
W: www.browsebion.com

BRP Ltd
See Keltbray

Brush Barclay
Caledonia Works, West Langlands St, Kilmarnock, KA1 2QD
T: 01563 523573
F: 01563 541076
E: sales@brushtraction.com
W: www.brushtraction.com

Brush Traction
PO Box 17, Falcon Works, Meadow Lane, Loughborough, Leics, LE11 1HS
T: 01302 340700
F: 01302 790058
E: sales@brushtraction.com
W: www.brushtraction.com

Brush Transformers Ltd
Falcon Works, Loughborough, LE11 1EX
T: 01509 611511
E: salesuk@brush.eu
W: www.brush.eu/en/38/home/products/transformers

Bruton Knowles
Greybrook House, 28 Brook St, London, W1K 5DH
T: 0845 200 6489
F: 020 7499 8435
E: patrick.downes@brutonknowles.co.uk
W: www.brutonknowles.co.uk

Bryn Thomas Cranes Ltd
421 Chester Rd, Flint, CH6 5SE
T: 01352 733984
F: 01352 733990
E: dylan.thomas@brynthomascranes.com
W: www.brynthomascranes.com

BSP Consulting
12 Oxford St, Nottingham, NG1 5BG
T: 0115 840 2227
F: 0115 840 2228
E: info@bsp-consulting.co.uk
W: www.bsp-consulting.co.uk

BT Fleet
Parkside Business Park, Mile Lane, Coventry, CV1 2TR
T: 0800 032 0012
W: www.btfleet.com/

BTMU Capital Corporation
See Beacon Rail Leasing Ltd

BTRoS Interiors & Cabling
Litchurch Lane, Derby, Derbyshire, DE24 8AD
T: 01332 257 500
E: jshelton@btros.co.uk
W: www.btros.co.uk

C Buchanan
See SKM Colin Buchanan

Buck and Hickman
Siskin Parkway East, Middlemarch Business Park, Coventry, CV3 4FJ
T: 02476 306444
F: 02476 514214
E: enquiries@buckandhickman.com
W: www.buckandhickman.com

Buckingham Group Contracting Ltd
Silverstone Rd, Stowe, Bucks, MK18 5LJ
T: 01280 823355
F: 01280 812830
E: mail@buckinghamgroup.co.uk
W: www.buckinghamgroup.co.uk

Buildbase
Gemini One, 5520 Oxford Business Park, Cowley, Oxford, OX4 2LL
F: 01865 871700
E: tony.newcombe@buildbase.co.uk

Building Business Bridges UK Ltd
B4 Ashville Centre, Hampton Park, Melksham, Wilts, SN12 6ZE
T: 01225 707021
F: 01225 709361
E: hello@bbbuk.co.uk
W: www.bbbuk.co.uk

Bupa – Health Care Service Delivery
Battle Bridge House, 300 Grays Inn Rd, London, WC1X 8DU
T: 020 7800 6459/ 0845 600 3476
F: 0207 800 6461
E: lampkine@bupa.com
W: www.bupa.co.uk/

Bureau Veritas Weeks
Tower Bridge Court, 224-226 Tower Bridge Rd, London, SE1 2TX
T: 020 7550 8900
F: 020 7403 1590
E: transport.logistics@bureauveritas.com
W: www.bureauveritas.com

Burges Salmon LLP
Narrow Quay House, Narrow Quay, Bristol, BS1 4AH
T: 0117 939 2000
F: 0117 902 4400
E: email@burges-salmon.com
W: www.burges-salmon.com

Burgess Rail Solutions Ltd
M: 07798 858494
E: robbie@burgessrailsolutions.co.uk
W: www.burgessrailsolutions.co.uk

Burns + Nice
70 Cowcross Street, London, EC1M 6EJ
T: 020 7253 0808
F: 020 7253 0909
E: info@burnsnice.com
W: www.burnsnice.com/

Burns Carlton Plc
Simpson House, Windsor Court, Clarence Drive, Harrogate, HG1 2PE
T: 01423 792000
F: 01423 792001
E: contactus@burnscarlton.com
W: www.burnscarlton.com

Business Moves Group
4 Acre Road, Reading, Berkshire, RG2 0SX
T: 0118 933 6600
F: 0118 975 1358
W: www.businessmoves.com/

Butler & Young (BYL) Ltd
Unit 3-4 Jansel House, Hitchin Road, Luton, LU2 7XH
T: 01582 404113
F: 01582 483420
E: debbie.clark@byl.co.uk
W: www.byl.co.uk

M Buttkereit Ltd
Unit 2, Britannia Rd Ind. Estate, Sale, Cheshire, M33 2AA
T: 0161 969 5418
F: 0161 969 5419
E: sales@buttkereit.co.uk
W: www.buttkereit.co.uk

BWB Consulting
5th Floor, Waterfront House, Station Street, Nottingham, NG2 3DQ
T: 0115 924 1100
E: nottingham@bwbconsulting.com
W: www.bwbconsulting.com/

BWCS
6 Worcester Road, Ledbury, Herefordshire, HR8 1PL
T: 01531 634326
F: 01531 631443
E: ross.parsons@bwcs.com
W: www.bwcs.com/

Bywater Training Ltd
3 Furtho Manor, Northampton Rd, Old Stratford, MK19 6NR
T: 01908 543900
F: 01908 543999
E: sales@bywatertraining.co.uk
W: www.bywatertraining.co.uk

C & S Equipment Ltd
15 Wingbury Courtyard, Leighton Rd, Wingrave, Bucks, HP22 4LW
T: 0843 504 4011
F: 0843 504 4012
E: info@candsequipment.co.uk
W: www.candsequipment.co.uk

C A P Productions Ltd
The Crescent, Hockley, Birmingham, B18 5NL
T: 0121 554 9811
F: 0121 554 3791
E: sales@capproductions.co.uk
W: www.capproductions.co.uk

C P Plus Ltd
10 Flask Walk, Camden, London, NW3 1HE
T: 020 7431 4001
F: 020 7435 3280
E: info@cp-plus.co.uk
W: www.cp-plus.co.uk

C2C Rail Ltd
2nd Floor, Cutlers Court, 115 Houndsditch, London, EC3A 7BR
T: 020 7444 1800
F: 020 7444 1803
E: c2c.customerrelations@nationalexpress.com
W: www.c2c-online.co.uk

C2e Consulting
Ludlow House, The Avenue, Stratford upon Avon, Warks, CV37 0RH
E: ed.sharman@c2econsulting.co.uk
W: www.c2econsulting.co.uk

C3S Projects
Canal Mills, Elland Bridge, Elland, Halifax, HX5 0SQ
T: 01422 313800
M: 01422 313801
E: info@c3s.com
W: www.c3s.com

Cable & Wireless UK
Lakeside House, Cain Rd, Bracknell, Berks, RG12 1XL
T: 01908 845000
F: 01344 713961
E: companysecretary@cwc.com
W: www.cwc.com

Cable Detection Ltd
Unit 1, Blythe Park, Sandon Rd, Cresswell, Stoke on Trent, ST11 9RD
T: 01782 384630
F: 01782 388048
W: www.cabledetection.co.uk

Cable Dynamics Ltd
Unit 15, Binghams Park Business Centre, Potten End Hill, Water End, Hemel Hempstead, Hertfordshire, HP1 3BN
T: 01442 234808
W: www.cabledynamics.co.uk/

Cable Management Products Ltd - Thomas & Betts Ltd
CMG House, Station Rd, Coleshill, Birmingham, B46 1HT
T: 01675 468 200
F: 01675 464930
E: info@cm-products.com
W: www.cm-products.com

Cablecraft Ltd
Cablecraft House, Unit 3, Circle Business Centre, Blackburn Rd, Houghton Regis, Beds, LU5 5DD
T: 01582 606033
F: 01582 606063
E: claire@cablecraft.co.uk
W: www.cablecraft-rail.co.uk

Cabletec ICS Ltd
Sunnyside Rd, Weston Super Mare, BS23 3PZ
T: 01934 424900
F: 01934 636632
E: sales@cabletec.com
W: www.cabletec.com

Cadenza Transport Consulting Ltd
8-10 South Street, Epsom, KT18 7PF
T: 020 3793 6188
M: 07786 430420
E: info@cadenza.co.uk
W: www.cadenza.co.uk

CADFEM
Suite 173-177, Airport House Business Centre, Purley Way, Croydon, Surrey, CR0 0XZ
T: 0844 212 5900
F: 0844 212 5910
E: info@cadfemuk.com
W: cadfemukandireland.com/

Cairn Cross Civil Engineering
1 Cadman Court, Morley, Leeds, LS27 0RX
T: 0113 284 2415
E: info@cairncross.uk.com
W: www.cairncross.uk.com

Calco Services Ltd
Melrose House, 42 Dingwall Rd, Croydon, CR0 2NE
T: 020 8655 1600
F: 020 8655 1588
E: careers@calco.co.uk
W: www.calco.co.uk

Caledonian Rail Leasing
99 Queen Victoria Street, London, EC4V 4EH

Caledonian Sleepers Rail Leasing Ltd

Calmet Laboratory Services
Hampton House, 1 Vicarage Rd, Hampton Wick, Kingston upon Thames, KT1 4EB
T: 0845 658 0770
F: 020 8614 8048
E: sales@lazgill.co.uk
W: www.calmet.co.uk

Camira Fabrics Ltd
The Watermill, Wheatley Park, Mirfield, West Yorks, WF14 8HE
T: 01924 490591
F: 01924 495605
E: info@camirafabrics.com
W: www.camirafabrics.com/transport

Camlin Rail
31 Ferguson Drive, Knockmore Hill Ind. Park, Lisburn, County Antrim, BT28 2EX, Northern Ireland
T: 028 9262 6982
E: mail@camlinrail.com
W: www.camlingroup.com

Campaign for Better Transport
70 Cowcross Street, London, EC1M 6EJ
E: philippa.edmunds@bettertransport.org.uk
W: www.bettertransport.org.uk

CAN Geotechnical
Smeckley Wood Close, Chesterfield Trading Est., Chesterfield, S40 3JW
T: 01246 261111
F: 01246 261626
E: info@can.ltd.uk
W: www.can.ltd.uk

Cannon Technologies Ltd
Head Office, Queensway, Stem Lane, New Milton, Hants, BH25 5NU
T: 01425 638148
F: 01425 619276
E: sales@cannontech.co.uk
W: www.cannontech.co.uk

Capgemini UK
Forge End, Woking, Surrey, GU21 6DB
T: 01483 764764
F: 01483 786161
W: www.uk.capgemini.com

Capita Property and Infrastructure Ltd
Capita House, Wood St, East Grinstead, W. Sussex, RH19 1UU
T: 01342 327161
F: 01342 315927
E: john.mayne@capita.co.uk
W: www.capitasymonds.co.uk

Capita Architecture
90-98 Goswell Rd, London, EC1V 7DF
T: 020 7251 6004
F: 020 7253 3568
E: mervyn.franklin@capita.co.uk
W: www.capitaarchitecture.co.uk

Capital & Counties Properties plc (Capco)
15 Grosvenor Street, London, W1K 4QZ
T: 020 3214 9150
F: 020 3214 9151
E: feedback@capitalandcounties.com
W: www.capitalandcounties.com/

Capital Project Consultancy Ltd (CPC)
See CPC Project Services LLP

Capital Safety Group
Unit 7, Christleton Court, Manor Park, Runcorn, Cheshire, WA7 1ST
T: 01928 571324
F: 01928 571325
E: csgne@csgne.co.uk
W: www.uclsafetysystems.com

Capitol Industrial Batteries
22 Napier Court, Wardpark North Industrial Estate, Cumbernauld, Glasgow, G62 6HU
T: 01236 731982
W: www.capitolbatteries.co.uk/

Captec Ltd
11 Brunel Way, Segensworth, Fareham, Hants, PO15 5TX
T: 01489 866066
F: 01489 866088
E: sales@captec.co.uk
W: www.captec.co.uk

Cardev International
See Environmental Technologies Ltd.

Carlbro Group
See Grontmij

Carlisle Support Services
800 The Boulevard, Capability Green, Luton, Beds, LU1 3BA
T: 01582 692692
E: info@carlislesupportservices.com
W: www.carlislesupportservices.com

Carlow Precast Tanks UK Ltd
Gunnery House, The Royal Arsenal, Woolwich, London, SE18 6SW
T: 01538 753333
F: 0870 493 1409
E: sales@carlowprecasttanks.com
W: www.carlowprecasttanks.com

Carlton Technologies Ltd
Unit 4, Church View Business Park, Coney Green Rd, Clay Cross, Chesterfield, Derbys, S45 9HA
T: 01246 861330
F: 01246 251466
E: sales@carltontech.co.uk
W: www.carltontech.co.uk

Carter Jonas
One Chapel Place, London, W1G 0BG
T: 020 7518 3200
F: 020 7408 9238
E: chapelplace@carterjonas.co.uk
W: www.carterjonas.co.uk/

Carver Engineering Services Ltd
11 Brunel Close, Brunel Ind. Est, Blyth Rd, Harworth, Doncaster, DN11 8QA
T: 01302 751900
F: 01302 757026
E: sales@carverengineering.com
W: www.carverengineering.com

Cass Hayward LLP
York House, Welsh St, Chepstow, Monmouthshire, NP16 5UW
T: 01291 626994
F: 01291 626306
E: office@casshayward.com
W: www.casshayward.com

Catalis
See TQ Technical and Vocational

Cats Solutions Ltd
Two Rushy Platt, Caen View, Swindon, Wilts, SN5 8WQ
T: 01793 432913
F: 01793 490270
E: sales@cats-solutions.co.uk
W: www.cats-solutions.com

CB Frost & Co Ltd
Green St, Digbeth, Birmingham, B12 0NE
T: 0121 773 8494
F: 0121 772 3584
E: info@cbfrost-rubber.com
W: www.cbfrost-rubber.com

CCD Design and Ergonomics
Northdown House, 11-21 Northdown St, London, N1 9BN
T: 0207 593 2900
E: info@ccd.org.uk
W: www.ccd.org.uk

CCL Rail Training
Scope House, Weston Rd, Crewe, CW1 6DD
T: 01270 252400
E: info@ccltraining.com
W: www.ccltraining.com

CCP Composites
16/32 Rue Henri Regnault, La Defense 6, 92062 Paris La Defense cedex, France
T: 00331 4796 9850
F: 00331 4796 9986
E: kevin.louis@ccpcomposites.com
W: www.ccpcomposites.com

CDC Draincare Ltd
Unit 1, Chatsworth Ind. Est, Percy St, Leeds, LS12 1EL
T: 0845 644 6130
E: enquiries@cdc-draincare.co.uk
W: www.cdc-draincare.co.uk

CDL (Collinson Dutton Ltd)
See GHD Ltd (Gutteridge, Haskins & Davey Ltd)

CDM-UK
PO Box 7035, Melton Mowbray, Leics, LE13 1WG
T: 01664 482486
F: 01664 482487
E: info@cdm-uk.co.uk
W: www.cdm-uk.co.uk

CDS Rail Ltd
Unit 1, Fulcrum 4, Solent Way, Whiteley, Hants, PO15 7FT
T: 01489 571771
F: 01489 571985
E: sales@cdsrail.com
W: www.cdsrail.com

Cecence
Unit 6, Bunas Business Park, Hollom Down Road, Lopcombe Corner, Hampshire, SP5 1BP
T: 01264 781115
E: info@cecence.com
W: www.cecence.com

Cembre Ltd
Dunton Park, Kingsbury Rd, Curdworth, Sutton Coldfield, B76 9EB
T: 01675 470440
F: 01675 470220
E: sales@cembre.co.uk
W: www.cembre.co.uk

Cemex Rail Products
Aston Church Rd, Washwood Heath, Saltley, Birmingham, B8 1QF
T: 0121 327 0844
F: 0121 327 7545
W: www.cemex.co.uk

Censol Ltd
Forbes Close, Long Eaton, Nottingham, NG10 1PX
T: 0115 972 7070
F: 0115 973 6722
E: info@censol.co.uk

Centinal Group
The Brook Works, 174 Bromyard Rd, St Johns, Worcester, WR2 5EE
T: 01905 748569
F: 01905 420700
E: les@mfhhydraulics.co.uk
W: www.centinalgroup.co.uk/

Central Engineering & Hydraulic Services Ltd
See Centinal Group

Centre for Economics and Business Research (CEBR)
Unit 1, 4 Bath Street, London, EC1V 9DX
T: 020 7324 2850
E: enquiries@cebr.com
W: cebr.com

Centregreat Rail Ltd
Ynys Bridge, Heol yr Ynys, Tongwynlais, Cardiff, CF15 7NT
T: 02920 815662
F: 02920 813598
E: rail@centregreat.net
W: www.centregreatrail.co.uk

Centrus MDT
10 Queen Street Place, London, EC4R 1BE
T: 020 3846 5670
E: jacqui.nelson@centrusadvisors.com
W: www.centrusadvisors.com

CGI IT UK Ltd
Kings Place, 90 York Way, 7th Floor, London, N1 9AG
T: 0845 070 7765
W: www.cgi-group.co.uk/

CH2M
2nd Floor, Quarnmill House, Stores Rd, Derby, DE21 4XF
T: 01332 222620
F: 01332 222621
E: robert.kaul@ch2m.com
W: www.ch2m.com

Chapman Taylor
10 Eastbourne Terrace, London, W2 6LG
T: 020 7371 3000
E: london@chapmantaylor.com
W: www.chapmantaylor.com

Charcon
See Aggregate Industries UK Ltd

Charcroft Electronics Ltd
Dol-y-Coed, Llanwrtyd Wells, Powys, LD5 4TH
T: 01591 610408
F: 01591 562013
E: chris.leek@charcroft.com
W: www.charcroft.com

Charles Endirect Ltd
Wessex Way, Wincanton Business Park, Wincanton, Somerset, BA9 9RR
T: 01963 828400
F: 01963 828401
E: info@charlesendirect.com
W: www.charlesendirect.com

Charles Rayner Ltd
12 Drakes Mews, Crownhill, Milton Keynes, Buckinghamshire, MK8 0ER
T: 01908 565904
E: info@charlesraynerltd.co.uk
W: www.charlesraynerltd.co.uk

Charter Security Plc
Suite 6, Ensign House, Admirals Way, London, E14 9XQ
T: 020 7515 0771
E: info@charter-security.co.uk
W: www.charter-security.co.uk

Chartered Institute of Logistics and Transport (UK) (CILT)
Logistics and Transport Centre, Earlstrees Court, Earlstrees Rd, Corby, NN17 4AX
T: 01536 740100
F: 01536 740101
E: enquiry@ciltuk.org.uk
W: www.ciltuk.org.uk

CHB & W Buildings & Railway Contractors
Unit 9, Skein Enterprises, Hodsall St, Sevenoaks, Kent, TN15 7LB
T: 01732 824687
F: 01732 823285
E: admin@chbw.co.uk
W: www.chbw.co.uk

Chela Ltd
68 Bilton Way, Enfield, Middx, EN3 7NH
T: 020 8805 2150
F: 020 8443 1868
E: tony.philippou@chela.co.uk
W: www.chela.co.uk

Chester le Track Ltd
See Trainline

CHG Electrical
2 Wortley Road, Deepcar, Sheffield, S36 2UZ
T: 0114 218 0470
F: 0114 283 1874
E: info@chgelectrical.co.uk
W: www.chgelectrical.co.uk/

Chieftain Trailers Ltd
207 Coalisland Rd, Dungannon, Co Tyrone, BT71 4DP
T: 028 8774 7531
F: 028 8774 7530
E: sales@chieftaintrailers.com
W: www.chieftaintrailers.com

Chiltern Railways
2nd Floor, Western House, Rickfords Hill, Aylesbury, Bucks
T: 03456 005165
F: 01296 332126
E: marketing@chilternrailways.co.uk
W: www.chilternrailways.co.uk

Chloride Power Protection
See Emerson Network Power

Chrysalis Rail
Electra House, Electra Way, Crewe, Cheshire, CW1 6GL
T: 01270 534683
E: info@chrysalisrail.com
W: chrysalisrail.com

Chubb Systems Ltd
Shadsworth Rd, Blackburn, BB1 2PR
T: 0844 561 1316
F: 01254 667663
E: systems-sales@chubb.co.uk
W: www.chubbsystems.co.uk

MJ Church Plant Ltd
Star Farm, Marshfield, Nr Chippenham, Wiltshire, SN14 8LH
T: 01225 891591
F: 01225 891173
E: info@mjchurch.com
W: mjchurch.com/

Cintec International Ltd
Cintec House, 11 Gold Tops, Newport, S.Wales, NP20 4PH
T: 01633 246614
F: 01633 246110
E: johnbrooks@cintec.co.uk
W: www.cintec.co.uk

CIRAS
4th Floor, The Helicon, One South Place, London, EC2M 2RB
T: 0203 142 5367
E: info@ciras.org.uk
W: www.ciras.org.uk

CITI
Lovat Bank, Silver St, Newport Pagnell, Bucks, MK16 0EJ
T: 01908 283600
F: 01908 283601
E: bdu@citi.co.uk
W: www.citi.co.uk

CJ Architecture
Earl Business Centre, Office 20, E3, Dowry St, Oldham, OL8 2PF
T: 0161 620 8834
E: enquiries@cjarchitecture.co.uk
W: www.cjarchitecture.co.uk

CJ Associates Ltd
26 Upper Brook St, London, W1K 7QE
T: 020 7529 4900
F: 020 7529 4929
E: info@cjassociates.co.uk
W: www.cjassociates.co.uk

Clancy Docwra
Clare House, Coppermill Lane, Harefield, Middx, UB9 6HZ
T: 01895 823711
F: 01895 825263
E: enquiries@theclancygroup.co.uk
W: www.theclancygroup.co.uk

Clarabridge
EMEA - London, 6th Floor, 95 Aldwych, London, WC2B 4JF
T: 020 3142 8615
W: www.clarabridge.com/

Clarke Chapman Group
PO Box 9, Saltmeadows Road, Gateshead, Tyne & Wear, NE8 1SW
T: 0191 477 2271
F: 0191 478 3951
E: info@clarkechapman.co.uk
W: www.clarkechapman.co.uk/

Clarks Vehicle Conversions
Unit 16A, Carcroft Enterprise Park, Station Road, Carcroft, Doncaster, DN6 8DD
T: 01302 784490
E: sales@cvcltd.co.uk
W: www.van-conversion.co.uk/

Class 40 Preservation Society (CFPS)
The East Lancashire Railway, Bolton St, Bury, Lancs, BL9 0EY
T: 07500 040145
M: 07818 040135
E: chairman@cfps.co.uk
W: www.cfps.co.uk

Class 50 Alliance Limited
Severn Valley Railway, Number One, Comberton Place, Kidderminster, DY10 1QR
T: 01562 757900
W: www.class50alliance.co.uk

Clayton Equipment
Second Avenue, Centrum 100 Business Park, Burton Upon Trent, Staffordshire, DE14 2WF
T: 01283 524470
M: 07403 425955
E: contact@claytonequipment.co.uk
W: claytonequipment.co.uk/

CLD Fencing Systems
Unit 11, Springvale Business Centre, Millbuck Way, Sandbach, Cheshire, CW11 3HY
T: 01270 764751
F: 01270 757503
E: sales@cld-fencing.com
W: www.cld-fencing.com

CLD Services
170 Brooker Rd, Waltham Abbey, Essex, EN9 1JH
T: 01992 702300
F: 01992 702301
E: contact@cld-services.co.uk
W: www.cld-services.co.uk

Cleartrack
Salcey-EVL Ltd, The Old Woodyard, Forest Rd, Hanslope, Milton Keynes, MK19 7DE
T: 01908 516250
E: info@cleartrack.co.uk
W: www.cleartrack.co.uk

Clements Technical Recruitment Ltd t/a Clemtech
7 Falcon Court, Parklands Business Park, Denmead, Waterlooville, Hants, PO7 6BZ
T: 023 9224 2690
F: 023 9224 2692
E: rail@clemtech.co.uk
W: www.clemtech.co.uk

Clemtech
See Clements Technical Recruitment Ltd t/a Clemtech

Cleshar Contract Services Ltd
Heather Park House, North Circular Rd, Stonebridge, London, NW10 7NN
T: 020 8733 8888
F: 020 8733 8899
E: info@cleshar.co.uk
W: www.cleshar.co.uk

Cleveland Bridge Uk
PO Box 27, Yarm Rd, Darlington, DL1 4DE
T: 01325 381188
F: 01325 382320
E: info@clevelandbridge.com
W: www.clevelandbridge.com

Cleveland Cable Company
Riverside Park Road, Middlesbrough, Cleveland, TS2 1QW
T: 01642 241133
F: 01642 226171
E: sales@clevelandcable.com
W: www.clevelandcable.com/

Clifford Marker Associates
9 Warners Close, Woodford Green, Essex, IG8 0TF
T: 020 8504 2570
W: www.cliffordmarkerassociates.com

Clifton Rubber Company Ltd
Edison Road, Industrial Estate, St Ives, Cambs, PE27 3FF
T: 01480 496161
E: sales@cliftonrubber.co.uk
W: www.cliftonrubber.co.uk/

Clyde & Co LLP
St Botolph Building, 138 Houndsditch, London, EC3A 7AR
T: 020 7876 5000
E: robert.meakin@clydeco.com
W: www.clydeco.com

CML
See Construction Marine Ltd

CMS Cameron McKenna
Cannon Place, 78 Cannon Street, London, EC4N 6AF
T: 020 7367 2113
F: 020 7367 2000
E: jonathan.beckitt@cms-cmck.com
W: www.cmslegal.com

Co Channel Electronics
Victoria Rd, Avonmouth, Bristol, BS11 9DB
T: 0117 982 0578
F: 0117 982 6166
E: sales@co-channel.co.uk
W: www.co-channel.co.uk

Cobham Technical Services (ERA Technology Ltd)
Cleeve Rd, Leatherhead, Surrey, KT22 7SA
T: 01372 367030
F: 01372 367102
E: era.rail@cobham.com
W: www.cobham.com/technicalservices

Coffey Geotechnics
Atlantic House, Atls Business Park, Simonsway, Manchester, M22 5PR
T: 0161 499 6800
F: 0161 499 6802
E: andrew_smith@coffey.com
W: www.coffey.com

Cogitamus
11 Woodfield Road, Peterborough, PE3 6HD
T: 01733 767244
F: 01733 313492
E: info@cogitamus.co.uk
W: https://cogitamus.co.uk/

COLAS Rail
Dacre House, 19 Dacre Street, London, SW1H 0DH
T: 020 7593 5353
F: 020 7593 5343
E: enquiries@colasrail.co.uk
W: www.colasrail.co.uk

Coleman and Company
The Coleman Group, Shady Lane, Great Barr, Birmingham, B44 9ER
T: 0121 325 2424
F: 0121 325 2425
E: contracts@coleman-co.com
W: www.coleman-co.com/

Colin Buchanan
See SKM Colin Buchanan

Collaborative Project Management Services (CPMS)
Office 113B, New Broad Street House, 35 New Broad Street, London, EC2M 1NH
T: 0203 009 3119
E: info@cpmsrail.co.uk
W: www.cpmsrail.co.uk

Collis Engineering Civils Division
Salcombe Rd, Meadow Lane Ind. Est, Alfreton, Derbys, DE55 7RG
T: 01773 833255
F: 01773 836525
E: sales@collis.co.uk
W: www.signalhousegroup.co.uk

Collis Engineering Ltd
Salcombe Rd, Meadow Lane Ind. Est, Alfreton, Derbys, DE55 7RG
T: 01773 833255
F: 01773 520693
E: sales@collis.co.uk
W: www.collis.co.uk

Colman Rail Services
8 Fort House Business Centre, Primrose Close, Chatham, Kent, ME4 6HZ
T: 01634 888620
M: 07804 735935
E: clive@colmanrailservices.co.uk
W: www.colmanrail.co.uk

Colour-Rail
558 Birmingham Road, Bromsgrove, Worcs, B61 0HT
E: colourrail@aol.com
W: www.colourrail.com/

Colt Industrial
Colt Business Park, Witty Street, Hull, HU3 4TT
T: 01482 214244
F: 01482 215037
W: www.colt-industrial.co.uk/

Coltraco Ultrasonics
46 Mount Street, Mayfair, London, W1K 2SA
T: 020 7629 8475
F: 020 7629 8477
E: info@coltraco.co.uk
W: www.coltraco.com/

Comech Metrology Ltd
Castings Rd, Derby, DE23 8YL
T: 01332 867700
F: 01332 867707
E: sales@comech.co.uk
W: www.comech.co.uk

Commend UK Ltd
Commend House, Unit 20, M11 Business Link, Parsonage Lane, Stansted, Essex, CM24 8GF
T: 01279 872020
F: 01279 814735
E: sales@commend.co.uk
W: www.commend.co.uk

CommonTime Ltd
15 St Christophers Way, Pride Park, Derby, DE24 8JY
T: 01332 542074
E: mike.roberts@commontime.com
W: www.commontime.com

Comms Design Ltd
40 Freemans Way, Harrogate Business Park, Wetherby Road, Harrogate, North Yorkshire, HG3 1DH
T: 01423 895071
E: sales@commsdesign.net
W: commsdesign.ltd.uk/

Community Rail Network
The Old Water Tower, St George's Square, Huddersfield, HD1 1JF
T: 01484 548926
E: info@communityrail.org.uk
W: communityrail.org.uk

Compass Tours
46 Hallville Rd, Liverpool, L18 0HR
T: 0151 722 1147
F: 0151 722 0297
E: info@compasstoursbyrail.co.uk
W: www.compasstoursbyrail.co.uk

Competence Assurance Solutions Ltd
221 St John St, Clerkenwell, London, EC1V 4LY
T: 020 7688 2840
F: 020 7688 2829
E: info@casolutions.co.uk
W: www.casolutions.co.uk

Compin-Fainsa
Horta, 08107 Martorelles, Spain
T: (34) 93 5796970
E: fainsa@fainsa.com
W: www.compin.com/?lang=en

Complete Drain Clearance
49 Weeping Cross, Stafford, ST17 0DG
T: 01785 665909
F: 01785 664944
E: completedrainclearance@yahoo.co.uk
W: www.completedrainclearance.co.uk

Complus Teltronic
See Commend UK Ltd

Comply Serve Ltd
Number 1, The Courtyard, 707 Warwick Rd, Solihull, B91 3DA
T: 0121 711 2185
E: sales@complyserve.com
W: www.complyserve.com

Composites UK
Innovation House, 39 Mark Road, Hemel Hempstead, Herts, HP2 7DN
T: 01442275365
E: info@compositesuk.co.uk
W: www.composites.co.uk

CompoTech
Nová 1316, Sušice 34201, Czech Republic
T: +420 376 526 839
F: +420 376 522 350
E: enquire@compotech.com
W: www.compotech.com/

Comtest Wireless
Badgemore House, Gravel Hill, Henley on Thames, Oxfordshire, RG9 4NR
T: 01491 579512
F: 01491 576377
E: contact@comtestwireless.eu
W: www.comtestwireless.eu/

Comtrol
Unit 6/7 Bignell Park Barns, Chesterton, Bicester, Oxon, OX26 1TD
T: 01869 352740
F: 01869 351848
E: sales@comtrol.co.uk
W: www.comtrol.co.uk

Concrete Canvas Ltd
Unit 3, Block A22, Pontypridd, CF37 5SP
T: 0845 680 1908
E: info@concretecanvas.com
W: www.concretecanvas.com

Conductix-Wampfler Ltd (Insul 8)
1 Michigan Ave, Salford, M50 2GY
T: 0161 848 0161
F: 0161 873 7017
E: info.uk@conductix.co.uk
W: www.conductix.co.uk

Confederation of Passenger Transport UK
Drury House, 34-43 Russell St, London, WC2B 5HA
T: 020 7240 3131
F: 020 7240 6565
E: admin@cpt-uk.org
W: www.cpt-uk.org

Consillia Ltd
See Donfabs and Consillia Ltd

Construcciones y Auxiliar de Ferrocarriles SA (CAF)
The TechnoCentre, Puma Way, Coventry, CV1 2TT
T: 02476 158195
F: 0034 914 366008
E: caf@caf.net
W: www.caf.net

Construction Marine Ltd
The Coach House, Mansion Gate Drive, Chapel Allerton, Leeds, LS7 4SY
T: 0113 262 4444
F: 0113 262 4400
E: info@cml.uk.com
W: www.cml-civil-engineering.co.uk

Containerlift
PO Box 582, Great Dunmow, Essex, CM6 3QX
T: 0800 174 546
F: 0800 174 547
E: joostbaker@containerlift.co.uk
W: www.containerlift.com

Continental Contitech
Chestnut Field House, Chestnut Field, Rugby, Warks, CV21 2PA
T: 01788 571482
F: 01788 542245
W: www.contitech.co.uk

Cook Rail
See William Cook Rail

Cooper and Turner Ltd
Templeborough Works, Sheffield Rd, Sheffield, S9 1RS
T: 0114 256 0057
F: 0114 244 5529
E: sales@cooperandturner.co.uk
W: www.cooperandturner.com

Cooper B-Line
Walrow Ind. Est, Highbridge, Somerset, TA9 4AQ
T: 01278 783371
F: 01278 789037
E: sales@cooperbline.co.uk
W: www.cooperbline.co.uk

Cooper Bussmann (UK) Ltd
Melton Road, Burton-on-the-Wolds, Leics, LE12 5TH
T: 01509 882737
F: 01509 882786
E: bule.sales@cooperindustries.com
W: www.cooperbussmann.com

Cooper Handling
Holly Farm Business Park, Honiley, Kenilworth, Warwickshire, CV8 1NP
T: 01926 658900
F: 01926 484310
E: info@cooperhandling.com
W: www.cooperhandling.com/

Copon E Wood Ltd
See 3M CPPD

Corbett Keeling
8 Angel Court, London, EC2R 7HP
T: 020 7626 6266
F: 020 7626 7005
E: info@corbettkeeling.com
W: www.corbettkeeling.com/

Cordek Ltd
Spring Copse Business Park, Slinfold, West Sussex, RH13 0SZ
T: 01403 799600
F: 01403 791718
E: sales@cordek.com
W: www.cordek.com

Corehard Ltd
Viewpoint, Babbage Rd, Stevenage, Herts, SG1 2EQ
T: 01438 225102
F: 01438 213721
E: info@corehard.com
W: www.corehard.com

Corelink Rail Infrastructure
Suite 1, 3rd Floor, 11-12 St James's Square, London, SW1Y 4LB

Coriel Ltd
Nottingham Geospatial Building, Triumph Rd, Nottingham, NG7 2TU
T: 0115 748 4486
E: contact@coriel.co.uk
W: www.coriel.co.uk

Coronet Rail Ltd
See Portec Rail Group

Corporate College
Derby College, Prince Charles Ave, Derby, DE22 4LR
T: 01332 520145
E: enquiries@derby-college.ac.uk
W: www.corporatecollege.co.uk

Correl Rail Ltd
See SGS Correl Rail Ltd

Corus Cogifer
See Vossloh Cogifer UK Ltd

Corus Rail Infrastructure Services
See Tata Steel Projects

Corys
44 Rue des Berges, 38024 Grenoble, France
T: 0033 476 288200
F: 0033 476 288211
E: coryscom@corys.fr
W: www.corys.com

Cosalt Ltd
See Ballyclare Ltd

Costain Ltd - Rail Sector
Costain House, Vanwall Business Park, Maidenhead, Berks, SL6 4UB
T: 01628 842310
E: gren.edwards@costain.com
W: www.costain.com

Covanburn Contracts Ltd
91 Bothwell Road, Hamilton, Lanarkshire, ML3 0DW
T: 01698 200057
E: enquiries@covanburncontracts.co.uk
W: www.covanburn.com/

Covtec Ltd
Allens West, Eaglescliffe Logistics Centre, Durham Rd, Eaglescliffe, Stockton on Tees, TS16 0RW
E: info@covtec.co.uk
W: www.covtec.co.uk

Cowans Sheldon
The Clarke Chapman Group Ltd, PO Box 9, Saltmeadows Rd, Gateshead, NE8 1SW
T: 0191 477 2271
F: 0191 478 3951
E: martin.howell@clarkechapman.co.uk
W: www.cowanssheldon.co.uk

COWI
Eastfield, Church Street, Uttoxeter, Staffordshire, ST14 8AA
T: 01889 563680
E: info_uk@cowi.com
W: https://www.cowi.com/

Coyle Personnel Plc
Hygeia, 66-68 College Rd, Harrow, Middx, HA1 1BE
T: 020 8901 6619
F: 020 8901 6706
E: roger@coyles.co.uk
W: www.coylerail.co.uk

CP Films Solutia (UK) Ltd
13 Acorn Business Centre, Northarbour Rd, Cosham, PO6 3TH
T: 02392 219112
F: 02392 219102
W: www.llumar.eu.com

CPC Project Services LLP
7th Floor, 100 Wood Street, London, EC2V 7AN
T: 020 7539 4750
M: 07734 052747
E: andy.norris@cpcprojectservices.com
W: www.cpcprojectservices.com

CPR
Millburn Roads Depot, Main Street, Renton, West Dunbartonshire, G82 4PZ
T: 01389 751797
W: www.cpr-resurfacing.co.uk/

Craig & Derricott Ltd
Hall Lane, Walsall Wood, Walsall, WS9 9DP
T: 01543 375541
F: 01543 361619
E: sales@craiganderricott.com
W: www.craiganderricott.com

Cranfield University
College Rd, Cranfield, Beds, MK43 0AL
T: 01234 750111
E: info@cranfield.ac.uk
W: www.cranfield.ac.uk/soe/rail-investgation

Creactive Design (Transport)
Unit 2 Trojan Business Centre, Tachbrook Park Drive, Warwick, CV34 6RS
T: 01926 499124
E: info@creactive-design.co.uk
W: www.creactive-design.co.uk

Creative Rail Dining
PO Box 10375, Little Waltham, Chelmsford, Essex, CM1 9JW
T: 01245 364051
E: enquiries@crdltd.co.uk
W: www.crdltd.co.uk

DIRECTORY

Crécy Publishing Ltd
1a Ringway Trading Estate, Shadowmoss Road, Manchester, M22 5LH
T: 0161 499 0024
F: 0161 499 0298
E: enquiries@crecy.co.uk
W: www.crecy.co.uk/

Credit360 Ltd
Compass House, Vision Park, Cambridge, CB24 9BZ
T: 01223 237 200
W: https://cr360.com/en-gb/

Critical Power Supplies Ltd
Unit F, Howlands Business Park, Thame, Oxon, OX9 3GQ
T: 01844 340122
E: sales@critical.co.uk
W: www.criticalpowersupplies.co.uk

Critical Project Resourcing Ltd
116a, High St, Sevenoaks, Kent, TN13 1UZ
T: 01732 455300
F: 01732 458447
E: rail@cpresourcing.co.uk
W: www.cpresourcing.co.uk

Cross London Trains
210 Pentonville Road, London, N1 9JY

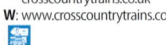

Cross Services Group
Cross House, Portland Centre, Sutton Rd, St Helens, WA9 3DR
T: 01744 458000
F: 01744 458099
E: martinclementson@crossgroup.co.uk
W: www.crossgroup.co.uk

CrossCountry
5th Floor, Cannon House, 18 Priory Queensway, Birmingham, B4 6BS
T: 0344 736 9123
F: 0121 200 6001
E: customer.relations@crosscountrytrains.co.uk
W: www.crosscountrytrains.co.uk

Crossrail 2
E: crossrail2@tfl.gov.uk
W: crossrail2.co.uk/

Crossrail Ltd
25 Canada Square, Canary Wharf, London, E14 5LQ
T: 0845 602 3813
E: helpdesk@crossrail.co.uk
W: www.crossrail.co.uk

Crouch Waterfall & Partners Ltd
The Dairy, Greenways Studios, Lower Eashing, Godalming, Surrey, GU7 2QF
T: 01483 425314
F: 01483 425814
E: office@cwp.co.uk
W: www.cwp.co.uk

Crowd Dynamics
21 Station Rd West, Oxted, Surrey, RH8 9EE
T: 01883 718690
F: 08700 516196
E: enquiries@crowddynamics.com
W: www.crowddynamics.com

Crowle Wharf Engineers Ltd (CWE)
Unit 1 & 2, Woodland Court, Coach Road, Shireoaks Triangle, Worksop, S81 8AD
T: 01909 498641
E: info@cwelimited.com
W: cwelimited.com/

Crown International
Old Mill Road, Portishead, Bristol, BS20 7BX
T: 01275 818008
F: 01275 818288
W: www.crown-international.co.uk/

Croylek Ltd
23 Ullswater Cres, Coulsdon, Surrey, CR5 2UY
T: 020 8668 1481
F: 020 8660 0750
E: sales@croylek.co.uk
W: www.croylek.co.uk

CRRC Corporation Ltd
No.16 West 4th Ring Mid Road, Haidian District, Beijing, 100036, China
T: 01522 502757
F: +86-10-63984785
M: 07836 500382
E: paul.taylor@dynexsemi.com
W: www.crrcgc.cc/en

CSC
Royal Pavilion, Wellesley Rd, Aldershot, GU11 1PZ
T: 01252 534000
F: 01252 534100
E: uk-consumer@csc.com
W: www.csc.com

Ctrack
Park House, Headingley Office Park, 8 Victoria Road, Leeds, LS6 1PF
T: 0345 055 8555
F: 0113 203 6771
E: info@ctrack.co.uk
W: www.ctrack.co.uk/

Cubic Transportation Systems
AFC House, Honeycrock Lane, Salfords, Redhill, Surrey, RH1 5LA
T: 01737 782362
F: 01737 789759
E: jennifer.newell@cubic.com
W: www.cubic.com/cts

Cubis Industries
Lurgan, Co Armagh, BT66 6LN
T: 0151 548 7900
F: 0151 548 7184
E: info@cubisindustries.com
W: www.cubisindustries.com

Cubris
Cubris ApS, Ebertsgade 2, 2, DK-2300, Copenhagen S, Denmark
T: 0330 2230 460
E: info@cubris.dk
W: www.cubris.dk/

Cudis Ltd
Power House, Parker St, Bury, BL9 0RJ
T: 0161 765 3000
F: 0161 705 2900
E: sales@cudis.co.uk
W: www.cudis.co.uk

Cummins
Yarm Rd, Darlington, DL1 4PW
T: 01327 886464
F: 0870 241 3180
E: cabo.customerassistance@cummins.com
W: www.everytime.cummins.com

Cundall
One Carter Lane, London, EC4V 5ER
T: 020 7438 1600
W: www.cundall.com

D&D Rail Ltd
Time House, Time Square, Basildon, Essex, SS14 1DJ
T: 01268 520000
F: 01268 520011
E: info@ddrail.com
W: www.ddrail.com

D2 Rail and Civils
1st Floor, Langton House, Bird St, Lichfield, WS13 6PY
T: 0161 817 5022
F: 0161 817 8006
E: info@d2rc.co.uk
W: www.d2railandcivils.co.uk

DAC Ltd
Union Mill, Watt Street, Sabden, Lancashire, BB7 9ED
T: 01282 447000
F: 0845 280 1915
E: sales@daclimited.co.uk
W: www.daclimited.co.uk

Dailys UK Ltd
See Novah Ltd

Dallmeier Electronic UK Ltd
Dallmeier House, 3 Beaufort Trade Park, Pucklechurch, Bristol, BS16 9QH
T: 0117 303 9303
F: 0117 303 9302
E: dallmeieruk@dallmeier-electronic.com
W: www.dallmeier-electronic.com

Danburykline
1A, The Old Fire Station, 150 Waterloo Road, London, SE1 8SB
M: 07747 180180
W: www.danburykline.co.uk

Danny Sullivan Group
22 Barretts Green Rd, Park Royal, London, NW10 7AE
T: 020 8961 1900
F: 020 8961 1965
E: enquiries@dannysullivan.co.uk
W: www.dannysullivan.co.uk

Darran Jacobs Limited
PO Box 7254, Wednesbury, WS10 1DU
M: 07903 999901
E: djhodgetts@darranjacobs.co.uk

Dartford Composites Ltd
Unit 1, Ness Rd, Erith, Kent, DA8 2LD
T: 01322 350097
F: 01322 359438
E: sales@dartfordcomposites.co.uk
W: www.dartfordcomposites.co.uk

Data Acquisition & Testing Services Ltd
Unit 4, Gainsborough Close, Gainsborough Business Park, Long Eaton, Nottingham, NG10 1PX
T: 01332 875450
F: 05603 137103
E: enquiries@datsltd.com
W: www.datsltd.com

Data Display UK Ltd
3 The Meadows, Waterberry Drive, Waterlooville, Hants, PO7 7XX
T: 023 9224 7500
F: 023 9224 7519
E: sales@datadisplayuk.com
W: www.datadisplayuk.com

Data Systems & Solutions
See Optimized Systems & Solutions Ltd

Datasys Ltd
See Tracsis Plc

Datum - Composite Products
22 Longbridge Lane, Derby, DE24 8UJ
T: 01332 751503
F: 01332 385487
E: composites@datum-patterns.co.uk
W: www.datum-patterns.co.uk

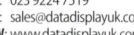

David Brice Consultancy
11 Sebastian Ave, Shenfield, Brentwood, Essex, CM15 8PN
T: 01277 221422
M: 07721 657521
E: davidpbrice@aol.com
W: www.bricerail.co.uk

David Brown Gear Systems Ltd
Park Gear Works, Lockwood, Huddersfield, HD4 5DD
T: 01484 465634
F: 01484 465587
E: steve.oldroyd@dbsantasalo.com
W: www.dbsantasalo.com

David Keay Railway & Tramway Engineering
16 Willoughby Close, Penkridge, Staffs, ST19 5QT
M: 07904 011079
E: david.keay@outlook.com

David Lane Publishing
62 North Street, Bourne, Lincolnshire, PE10 9NB
T: 01778 420888
F: 01778 421550
M: 07795 031051
E: dave@davidlanepublishing.co.uk

David Simmonds Consultancy
Suite 4, Bishop Bateman Court, New Park Street, Cambridge, CB5 8AT
T: 01223 316098
E: dsc@davidsimmonds.com
W: www.davidsimmonds.com

David Simmonds Consultancy
112 George Street, Edinburgh, EH2 4LH
T: 01223 316098
E: admin@davidsimmonds.com
W: www.davidsimmonds.com

DB Cargo (UK)
Lakeside Business Park, Carolina Way, Doncaster, DN4 5PN
T: 01302 575000
E: uk.dbcargo@deutschebahn.com
W: uk.dbcargo.com

DB ESG
Derwent House, RTC Business Park, London Rd, Derby, DE24 8UP
T: 01332 483800
E: enquiries@dbesg.com
W: www.deutschebahn.com/dbesg

DB Symmetry
Grange Park Court, Roman Way, Northampton, NN4 5EA
T: 01604 330630
W: www.dbsymmetry.com/

DB Systemtechnik
Weserglacis 2, 32423 Minden, Germany
T: +49 571 3935500
W: www.deutschebahn.com/en/business/engineering_services

dBD Communications
4 Furlongs, Basildon, Essex, SS16 4BW
T: 01268 449871
F: 01268 442390
E: npurcell@dbdcom.co.uk
W: www.dbdcom.co.uk

DBK Technitherm Ltd
Unit 11, Llantrisant Business Park, Llantrisant, CF72 8LF
T: 01443 237927
F: 01443 237867
E: info-uk@dbk-group.com
W: www.dbktechnitherm.ltd.uk

DC Airco
Opaalstraat 18, 1812 RH Alkmaar, Netherlands
T: 0031 72533 6540
E: info@dcairco.com
W: www.dcairco.com

DCA Design International
19 Church St, Warwick, CV34 4AB
T: 01926 499461
E: transport@dca-design.com
W: www.dca-design.com/

DCRail
Offices 9 & 10, Days Space Business Centre, Litchurch Lane, Derby, DE24 8AA
T: 01332 977008
E: ahickling@dcrail.com
W: www.dcrail.com

Dedicated Micros
1200 Unit, Daresbury Park, Daresbury, Warrington, WA4 4HS
T: 0845 600 9500
F: 0845 600 9504
E: customerservices@dmicros.com
W: www.dedicatedmicros.com/uk

DEG Signal Ltd
Aspect House, Crusader Park, Warminster, Wilts, BA12 8BT
T: 01985 212020
F: 01985 212053
E: info@degsignal.co.uk
W: www.degsignal.co.uk

Delay Attribution Board
1 Eversholt St, 8th Floor, London, NW1 2DN
E: admin@delayattributionboard.co.uk
W: www.delayattributionboard.co.uk

Delimon Denco Lubrication
See Bijur Delimon International

Delkor Rail
74 Harley Cres, Condell Park, NSW, Australia
T: 61 2 9709 2918
F: 61 2 9709 5934
E: george@delkorrail.com
W: www.delkorrail.com

Dellner Couplers UK Ltd
Hearthcote Rd, Swadlincote, Derbys, DE11 9DX
T: 01283 221122
E: ukinfo@dellner.com
W: www.dellner.com

Delmatic
The Power House, 6 Power Rd, Chiswick, London, W4 5PY
T: 020 8987 5900
F: 020 8987 5957
E: sales@delmatic.com
W: www.delmatic.com

Deloitte LLP
2 New Street Square, London, EC4A 3BZ
T: 020 7936 3000
F: 020 7583 1198
W: www2.deloitte.com/uk/en/

Deltic Preservation Society ltd
Barrow Hill Roundhouse, Railway Centre Campbell Drive, Barrow Hill, Chesterfield, Derbyshire, S43 2PR
E: secretary@thedps.co.uk
W: www.http://thedps.co.uk

Deltix Transport Consulting
4 Church Hill Drive, Edinburgh, EH10 4BT
T: 0131 447 7764
M: 07917 877399
E: david@deltix.co.uk
W: www.deltix.co.uk

Deltone Training Consultants
Ground Floor, 42-48 High Rd, South Woodford, London, E18 2QL
T: 020 8532 2208
F: 020 8532 2206
E: sales@deltonetraining.com
W: www.deltonetraining.com

Demco
Heyford Close, Aldermans Green Ind. Est., Coventry, CV2 2QB
T: 02476 602323
F: 02476 602116
E: info@mgs.co.uk
W: www.demco.co.uk

Denchi Power Ltd
Denchi House, Thurso, Caithness, KW14 7XW
T: 01847 808000
W: www.denchipower.com

Dentons UKMEA LLP
One Fleet Place, London, EC4M 7WS
T: 020 7242 1212
F: 020 7246 7777
W: www.dentons.com/en/

Department for Transport
Great Minster House, 33 Horseferry Road, London, SW1P 4DR
T: 020 7944 5409
F: 020 7944 2158
E: fax9643@dft.gsi.gov.uk
W: www.dft.gov.uk

Deploy UK Rail
The Podium, 1 Eversholt St, London, NW1 2DN
T: 020 7434 0300
E: info@deployuk.com
W: www.deployuk.com

Depot Rail Ltd
Mercury House, Willoughton Drive, Foxby Lane Business Park, Gainsborough, Lincs, DN21 1DY
T: 01427 619512
F: 01427 619501
E: sales@drail.co.uk
W: www.depotrail.co.uk

Derby Engineering Unit Ltd
Unit 22, Riverside Park, East Service Rd, Raynesway, Derby, DE21 7RW
T: 01332 660364
F: 01332 675191
E: enquiries@derbyengineeringunit.co.uk
W: www.derbyengineeringunit.co.uk

The Deritend Group Ltd
Cyprus St, Off Upper Villiers St, Wolverhampton, WV2 4PB
T: 01902 426354
F: 01902 711926
E: sales@deritend.co.uk
W: www.deritend.co.uk

Design & Projects Int. Ltd
2 Manor Farm, Flexford Rd, North Baddesley, Hants, SO52 9FD
T: 02380 277910
F: 02380 277920
E: colin.brooks@designandprojects.com
W: www.railwaymaintenance.com

Design and Analysis Ltd
Unit 1 H2O, Lake View Drive, Sherwood Business Park, Nottingham, NG15 0HT
T: 0115 888 2666
E: info@design-and-analysis.co.uk
W: www.designandanalysis.co.uk/

Design Triangle Ltd
The Maltings, Burwell, Cambridge, CB25 0HB
T: 01638 743070
F: 01638 743493
E: mail@designtriangle.co.uk
W: www.designtriangle.com

Designplan Lighting
16 Kimpton Park Way, Sutton, Surrey, SM3 9QS
T: 020 8254 2000
F: 020 8644 4253
E: sales@designplan.co.uk
W: www.designplan.co.uk

Det Norske Veritas
See DNV (Det Norske Veritas)

Deutsche Bahn UK
DB Vertrieb GmbH, Suite 6/7, The Sanctuary, 23 Oakhill Grove, Surbiton, Surrey, KT6 6DU
W: www.bahn.co.uk

Deuta-Werke GmbH
Paffrather Str. 140, D-51465 Bergisch Gladbach, Germany
T: 0049 2202 958 100
F: 0049 2202 958 145
E: support@deuta.de
W: www.deuta.de

DEUTZ AG - UK & Ireland
Unit 3, Willow Park, Burdock Close, Cannock, Staffs, WS11 7FQ
T: 01543 438901
F: 01543 438931
E: brocklebank.s@deutz.com
W: www.deutz.de/

Devol Engineering Ltd
Unit 2, Faulds Park Industrial Estate, Faulds Park Road, Gourock, PA19 1FB
T: 01475 657360
F: 01475 787873
E: sales.devol.uk@jameswalker.biz
W: www.devol.com

Devon & Cornwall Rail Partnership
School of Geography Earth & Environmental Science, University of Plymouth, Plymouth, PL4 8AA
T: 01752 584777
E: railpart@plymouth.ac.uk
W: www.greatscenicrailways.com

Dewalt
210 Bath Rd, Slough, SL1 3YD
T: 01753 567055
F: 01753 521312
E: reply@dewalt.com
W: www.dewalt.co.uk

DEWESoft
Meadow Brook, Summerside Road, Buckland, Faringdon, Oxfordshire, SN7 8QY
T: 01367 871000
F: 01367 871001
E: sales.uk@dewesoft.com
W: www.dewesoft.com

Dewhurst Plc
Unit 9, Hampton Business Park, Hampton Road West, Feltham, Middx, TW13 6DB
T: 020 8744 8200
F: 020 8744 8299
E: info@dewhurst.co.uk
W: www.dewhurst.co.uk

Dexeco Ltd
Brickfields Business Park, Gillingham, Dorset, SP8 4PX
T: 01747 858100
F: 01747 858153
E: sales@dexeco.co.uk
W: www.dexeco.co.uk/

DfT OLR Holdings Ltd
Albany House, 94-98, Petty France, London, SW1H 9AE
E: enquiries@olrholdings.co.uk
W: www.olrholdings.co.uk/

DG Design
Friar Gate Studios, Ford Street, Derby, DE1 1EE
T: 01332 258360
E: design@davidgordonltd.co.uk
W: www.davidgordonltd.co.uk/

DG8 Design and Engineering Ltd
Room 7, The College Business Centre, Uttoxeter New Rd, Derby, DE22 3WZ
T: 01332 869351
F: 01332 869350
E: tony.devitt@dg8design.com
W: www.dg8design.com

DGauge Ltd
Unit 5, 11 Brunel Parkway, Pride Park, Derby, DE24 8HR
T: 01332 546905
E: colin.johnson@dgauge.co.uk
W: www.dgauge.co.uk

Dhesi Group
Station House, Station Road, Southfleet, Kent, DA13 9PA
T: 01474 833388
F: 01474 831349
E: enquiries@dhesiplc.com
W: www.dhesiplc.com/

dhp11 Ltd
The Barn, Overlees, Barlow, Dronfield, Derbyshire, S18 7SN
T: 0114 289 9393
F: 0114 289 9400
E: info@dhp11.com
W: www.dhp11.com/

Diamond Point
Suite 13, Ashford House, Beaufort Court, Sir Thomas Longley Rd, Rochester, ME2 4FA
T: 01634 300900
F: 01634 722398
E: john.vaines@dpie.com
W: www.dpie.com

Diamond Seating Ltd
Unit 3, Butterthwaite Lane, Ecclesfield, Sheffield, S35 9WA
T: 0114 257 0909
F: 0114 245 7950
E: info@diamondseating.co.uk

DIEM Ltd
11 Jubilee Rd, Formby, Merseyside, L37 2HN
T: 01704 870461
M: 07737 194686
E: davidinman@diemltd.co.uk
W: www.diemltd.co.uk

Diesel Traction Group
E: info@westernchampion.co.uk
W: westernchampion.co.uk

Difuria Ltd
West Stockwith Business Park, Stockwith Road, Misterton, Doncaster, DN10 4ES
T: 01427 848712
F: 01427 848056
E: sales@difuria.co.uk
W: www.difuria.co.uk

Digitals Barriers
Enterprise House, 1-2 Hatfields, London, SE1 9PG
T: 020 7940 4740
F: 020 7940 4746
E: info@digitalbarriers.com
W: www.digitalbarriers.com/

Digital Technology International (DTI)
31 Affleck Rd, Perth Airport WA 6105, Western Australia, Australia
T: 01913 854803
F: +61 8 9479 1190
E: dti@dti.com.au
W: www.dti.com.au/

Dilax Systems UK Ltd
Unit 1, Knowlhill Business Park, Roebuck Way, Milton Keynes, MK5 8HL
T: 01908 607340
F: 020 7223 2011
E: sales.uk@dilax.com
W: www.dilax.co.uk

Dimension Data
Dimension Data House, Building 2, Waterfront Business Park, Fleet Road, Fleet, Hampshire, GU51 3QT
T: 01252 779000
W: www2.dimensiondata.com/en-uk

The Direct Group
Unit 2, Churnet Court, Churnetside Business Park, Harrison Way, Cheddleton, Staffs, ST13 7EF
T: 01538 360555
F: 01538 369100
E: dpl@direct-group.co.uk
W: www.direct-group.co.uk

Direct Link North
56 Beverley Gardens, Wembley, Middx, HA9 9QZ
T: 020 8908 0638
E: keith.gerry@directlinknorth.com
W: www.directlinknorth.com/

Direct Rail Services (DRS)
Regents Court, Baron Way, Carlisle, CA6 4SJ
T: 01228 406600
E: salesenquiries@drsl.co.uk
W: www.directrailservices.com

Direct Track Solutions Ltd
Unit C Midland Place, Midland Way, Barlborough Links, Barlborough, Chesterfield, S43 4FR
T: 01246 810198
F: 01246 570926
E: info@directtracksolutions.co.uk
W: www.directtracksolutions.co.uk

Directly Operated Railways
4th Floor, Chancery Lane, London, EC4A 1BL
T: 020 7904 5043
E: enquiries@directlyoperatedrailways.co.uk
W: www.directlyoperatedrailways.co.uk

Direx Solutions
1 Fulwith Close, Harrogate, North Yorkshire, HG2 8HP

Discover LEDs
PO Box 222, Evesham, Worcs, WR11 4WT
T: 0844 578 1000
F: 0844 578 1111
E: sales@mobilecentre.co.uk
W: www.mobilecentre.co.uk

Discovery Drilling Ltd
32 West Station Yard, Maldon, Essex, CM9 6TS
T: 01621 851300
F: 01621 851305
E: enquiries@discoverydrilling.co.uk
W: www.discoverydrilling.co.uk

DK Rewinds
Cranford Street, Smethwick, West Midlands, B66 2RT
T: 0121 555 5532
F: 0121 558 6251
E: balvinder@dkrewinds.co.uk
W: www.dkrewinds.co.uk/

DLA Piper UK LLP
Princes Exchange, Princes Square, Leeds, LS1 4BY
T: 0113 369 2468
F: 0113 369 2999
E: julie.lang@dlapiper.com
W: www.dlapiper.com

DMC Group
Unit 17, The Capstan Centre, Thurrock Park Way, Tilbury, Essex, RM18 7HH
T: 01375 845070
F: 01375 841333
E: office@dmccontracts.co.uk
W: www.dmccontracts.co.uk

DML Group
See Babcock Rail

DMS Technologies
Belbin's Business Park, Cupernham Lane, Romsey, Hants, SO51 7JF
T: 01794 525463
F: 01794 525450
E: info@dmstech.co.uk
W: www.dmstech.co.uk

DNH WW Ltd
31 Clarke Rd, Mount Farm, Bletchley, Milton Keynes, MK1 1LG
T: 01908 275000
F: 01908 275100
E: dnh@dnh.co.uk
W: www.dnh.co.uk

DNV (Det Norske Veritas)
Palace House, 3 Cathedral St, London, SE1 9DE
T: 020 7716 6593
F: 020 7716 6738
E: david.salmon@dnv.com
W: www.dnv.com

Docklands Light Railway
Castor Lane, Poplar, London, E14 0DX
T: 020 7363 9898
F: 020 7363 9708
E: enquire@tfl.gov.uk
W: www.dlr.co.uk

Docmate Services Ltd
18 Alder Tree Rd, Banchory, Aberdeenshire, AB31 4FW
T: 01330 822620
F: 01330 822620
E: info@docmates.co.uk
W: www.docmates.co.uk

Dold Industries Ltd
11 Hamberts Rd, Blackall Ind Est, South Woodham Ferrers, Essex, CM3 5UW
T: 01245 324432
F: 01245 325570
E: admin@dold.co.uk
W: www.dold.co.uk

Domnick Hunter Industrial Operations
Dukesway, Team Valley Trading Est., Gateshead, Tyne & Wear, NE11 0PZ
T: 0191 402 9000
F: 0191 482 6296
E: dhindsales@parker.com
W: www.domnickhunter.com

Donaldson Associates
Eastfield, Church St, Uttoxeter, Staffs, ST14 8AA
T: 01889 563680
F: 01889 562586
E: tunnels@donaldsonassociates.com
W: www.donaldsonassociates.com

Donfabs and Consillia Ltd
The Old Iron Warehouse, The Wharf, Shardlow, Derby, DE72 2GH
T: 01332 792483
F: 01332 799209
E: ian.moss@consillia.com
W: www.donfabsandconsillia.com

Donyal Engineering Ltd
Unit 7, Hobson Ind Est, Burnopfield, Newcastle upon Tyne, NE16 6EA
T: 01207 270909
F: 01207 270333
E: mike@donyal.co.uk
W: www.donyal.co.uk

Dorma+Kaba
Lower Moor Way, Tiverton, Devon, EX16 6SS
T: 0870 000 5625
F: 0870 000 5397
E: info.uk@kaba.com
W: www.dormakaba.co.uk

Dorset Woolliscroft
Falcon Road, Sowton Industrial Estate, Exeter, Devon, EX2 7LB
T: 01392 473037
F: 01392 473003
E: info@dorsetwoolliscroft.com
W: www.dorsetwoolliscroft.com

Dow Hyperlast
Station Rd, Birch Vale, High Peak, Derbyshire, SK22 1BR
T: 01663 746518
F: 01663 746605
E: help@dowhyperlast.com
W: www.dowhyperlast.com

Downer Group
Triniti Business Campus, 39 Delhi Road, North Ryde NSW 2113, Sydney, Australia
T: +61 2 9468 9700
F: +61 2 9813 8915
W: www.downergroup.com/

DP Consulting
Unit 4, Tygan House, The Broadway, Cheam, Surrey
T: 0845 094 2380
F: 0700 341 8557
E: info@dpconsulting.org.uk
W: www.dpconsulting.org.uk

DPSS Cabling Services Ltd
Unit 16, Chiltern Business Village, Arundel Rd, Uxbridge, UB8 2SN
T: 01895 251010
F: 01895 813133
E: airon.duke@dpsscabling.co.uk
W: www.dpsscabling.co.uk

Dragados S.A.
Regina House, 2nd Floor, 1-5 Queen St, London, EC4N 1SW
T: 020 7651 0900
F: 020 7248 9044
E: jcruzd@dragados.com
W: www.grupoacs.com

DRail
See Depot Rail Ltd

Drum Cussac
8 Hill St, St Helier, Jersey, JE4 9XB
T: 0870 429 6944
E: risk@drum-cussac.com
W: www.drum-cussac.com

DSM Demolition Group
Arden House, Arden Road, Heartlands, Birmingham, B8 1DE
T: 0121 322 2225
F: 0121 322 2227
E: info@dsmgroup.info
W: www.dsmdemolitiongroup.co.uk/

Dual Inventive Ltd
Drake House, Decoy Bank North, Doncaster, DN4 5JR
T: 01724 608020
M: 07957 880220
E: info@dualinventive.com
W: www.dualinventive.com

DuPont (UK) Ltd
Wedgwood Way, Stevenage, Herts, SG1 4QN
T: 01438 734061
F: 01438 734836
W: www.rail.dupont.com

Dura Composites
Dura House, Telford Rd, Clacton-on-Sea, Essex, CO15 4LP
T: 01255 423601
F: 01255 435426
E: info@duracomposites.com
W: www.duracomposites.com

Durapipe
Walsall Rd, Norton Canes, Cannock, Staffs, WS11 9NS
T: 01543 279909
E: enquiries@durapipe.co.uk
W: www.durapipe.co.uk

DW Windsor UK
Pindar Rd, Hoddesden, Herts, EN11 0DX
T: 01992 474600
F: 01992 474600
E: light@dwwindsor.co.uk
W: www.dwwindsor.co.uk

DWG Timber Components Ltd
2 Burrough Court, Burrough-on-the-Hill, Melton Mowbray, Leicestershire, LE14 2QS
T: 0115 939 5992
E: info@dwguk.com
W: www.dwguk.com

Dyer & Butler Ltd
Mead House, Station Rd, Nursling, Southampton, SO16 0AH
T: 02380 742222
F: 02380 742200
E: enquiries@dyerandbutler.co.uk
W: www.dyerandbutler.co.uk

Dyer Engineering Ltd
Solution House, Unit 3, Morrison & Busty North Ind Est, Annfield Plain, Stanley, Co Durham, DH9 7RU
T: 01207 234315
F: 01207 282834
E: paul.dyer@dyer.co.uk
W: www.dyer.co.uk

Dynex Semiconductor Ltd
Doddington Rd, Lincoln, LN6 3LF
T: 01522 500500
F: 01522 500020
E: power_solutions@dynexsemi.com
W: www.dynexsemi.com

Dywidag-Systems International Ltd
Northfield Rd, Southam, Warks, CV47 0FG
T: 01926 813980
F: 01926 813817
E: sales@dywidag.co.uk
W: www.dywidag-systems.co.uk

E A Technology
Capenhurst Technology Park, Capenhurst, Chester, CH1 6ES
T: 0151 339 4181
F: 0151 347 2404
E: john.hartford@eatechnology.com
W: www.eatechnology.com

E C Harris
ECHQ, 34 York Way, London, N1 9AB
T: 020 7812 2000
F: 020 7812 2001
W: www.echarris.com

EAL
Unit 2, The Orient Centre, Greycaine Rd, Watford, WD24 7GP
T: 01923 652400
F: 01923 652401
E: customercare@eal.org.uk
W: www.eal.org.uk

EAO Ltd
Highland House, Albert Drive, Burgess Hill, West Sussex, RH15 9TN
T: 01444 236000
F: 01444 236641
E: sales.euk@eao.com
W: www.eao.com

East Anglian Sealing Co Ltd
Units 3-6, Goldingham Hall, Bulmer, Sudbury, Suffolk, CO10 7ER
T: 01787 880433
F: 01787 880442
E: sales@easeals.co.uk
W: easeals.co.uk/

East Coast Trains
4th Floor, Capital House, 25 Chapel Street, London, NW1 5DH

East Lancashire Railway
Bolton St Station, Bury, Lancs, BL9 0EY
T: 0161 764 7790
E: admin@eastlancsrailway.co.uk
W: www.eastlancsrailway.org.uk

East Midlands Railway
1 Prospect Place, Millenium Way, Pride Park, Derby, DE24 8HG
T: 03457 125678
F: 01738 643648
W: https://www.eastmidlandsrailway.co.uk/

East West Rail (EWR)

East West Rail Consortium
E: info@eastwestrail.org.uk
W: www.eastwestrail.org.uk/

Eaton Electrical Ltd
270 Bath Road, Slough, Berkshire, SL1 4DX
T: 08700 545 333
E: chrisswales@eaton.com
W: https://uk.eaton.com/

EB Elektro UK Ltd
Unit 2, Shireoaks Triangle, Coach Crescent, Worksop, Notts, S81 8AD
T: 01909 483658
E: william@eb-elektro.co.uk
W: www.eb-elektro.co.uk

Ebeni Ltd
Hartham Park, Corsham, Wilts, SN13 0RP
T: 01249 700505
F: 01249 700001
M: 07776 532131
E: matthew.pearson@ebeni.com
W: www.ebeni.com

EcarbonUK
See Electrical Carbon UK Ltd

ECR Retail Systems
Church House, Church Lane, Kings Langley, WD4 8JP
T: 020 8205 7766
E: sales@ecr.co.uk
W: www.ecr.co.uk

ECT Group
See British American Railway Services (BARS)

Ecus Environmental Consultants
Brook Holt, 3 Blackburn Road, Sheffield, S61 2DW
T: 0114 2669292
E: contactus@ecusltd.co.uk
W: www.ecusltd.co.uk/

Ede and Wilkinson
Intel House, 85 London Road, Marks Tey, Colchester, Essex, C06 1EB
T: 01206 213279
F: 01206 213055
E: enquiries@ewgltd.com
W: www.edewilkinson.co.uk/

Eden Brown
222 Bishopsgate, London, EC2M 4QD
T: 020 7422 7300
F: 0845 434 9573
E: london@edenbrown.com
W: www.edenbrown.com

Eden Lea Rail
Meteor House, First Avenue, RHADS Business Park, Finningley, Doncaster, DN9 3GA
T: 01302 791750
E: info@edenlearail.co.uk
W: www.edenlearail.co.uk

Edenred
50 Vauxhall Bridge Road, London, SW1V 2RS
T: 0843 453 0206
W: www.edenred.co.uk/

EDF Energy
See UK Power Networks Services

Edgar Allen
See Balfour Beatty Rail

Edilon Sedra
See Tiflex Ltd

Edinburgh Trams Limited
55 Annandale Street, Edinburgh, EH7 4AZ
T: 0131 475 0177
W: www.http://edinburghtrams.com

Edmund Nuttall Ltd
See BAM Nuttall Ltd

Edward Barber & Jay Osgerby
37-42 Charlotte Road, London, EC2A 3PG
T: 020 7033 3884
E: info@barberosgerby.com
W: www.barberosgerby.com/

Edward Symmons
2 Southwark St, London, SE1 1TQ
T: 020 7955 8454
F: 020 7407 6423
E: info@edwardsymmons.com
W: www.es-group.com

EFD Corporate
41 Caxton Court, Garamonde Drive, Wymbush, Milton Keynes, MK8 8DD
T: 0845 1285172 / 01908 560669
F: 01908 565672
M: 07827 817205
E: enquiries@efd-corporate.com
W: www.efd-corporate.com

DIRECTORY

Efficio
22 Long Acre, London, WC2E 9LY
T: 020 7550 5677
F: 020 7550 5679
E: info@efficioconsulting.com
W: www.efficioconsulting.com/

EFI Heavy Vehicle Brakes
6/7 Bonville Rd, Brislington, Bristol, BS4 5NZ
T: 0117 977 7859
F: 0117 971 0573
E: tonyp@efiltd.co.uk
W: www.efiltd.co.uk

Egis Rail
15 avenue du Centre, CS 20538 Guyancourt, 78286 Saint-Quentin-en-Yvelines CEDEX, France
T: +33 (0)1 39 41 40 00
W: www.egis-group.com/

Eglin Concourse International
Globe Works, Victoria Rd, Sowerby Bridge, West Yorks, HX6 3AE
T: 01422 317601
F: 01422 833857
E: sales@eglinconcourse.com
W: www.eglinconcourse.com

Eiffage
163 Quai du Docteur-Dervaux, 92601 Asnières-sur-Seine, Paris, France
T: 0001 4132 8000
F: 0001 4132 8113
W: www.eiffage.com/en/

EKE Electronics
Piispanportti 7, 02240 Espoo, Finland
T: +358 9 6130 30
F: +358 9 6130 3300
E: sales@eke.com
W: https://www.eke-electronics.com/

Eland Cables
120 Highgate Studios, 53-79 Highgate Rd, London, NW5 1TL
T: 020 7241 8787
F: 020 7241 8700
E: sales@eland.co.uk
W: www.eland.co.uk

Elastacloud
138-142 Holborn, London, EC1N 2SW
M: 07918 638492
E: info@elastacloud.com

Elcot Environmental
The Nursery, Kingsdown Lane, Blunsdon, Swindon, Wilts, SN25 5DL
T: 01793 700100
F: 01793 722221
E: peterw@elcotenviro.com
W: www.elcotenviro.com

Eldapoint Ltd
Charleywood Rd, Knowsley Ind. Prk North, Knowsley, Merseyside, L33 7SG
T: 0151 548 9838
F: 0151 546 4120
E: paul.wyatt@eldapoint.co.uk
W: www.eldapoint.co.uk

E-Leather
Kingsbridge Centre, Sturrock Way, Peterborough, PE3 8TZ
T: 01733 843939
F: 01733 843940
M: 07500 609351
E: carl.watkins@eleathergroup.com
W: www.eleathergroup.com

E-Leather Ltd
Kingsbridge Centre, Sturrock Way, Peterborough, PE3 8TZ
T: 01733 843939
F: 01733 843940
M: 07500 609351
E: carl.watkins@eleathergroup.com
W: www.eleathergroup.com

Electren UK
2nd Floor, Regina House, 1-5 Queen Street, London, EC4N 1SW
T: 020 3542 8281
E: electrenuk@electren.co.uk
W: www.electren.co.uk

Electric Railway Improvement Company (ERICO)
See Pentair

Electrification Solutions Ltd
Floor 5, Building 4, Exchange Quay, Manchester, M5 3EE
T: 0161 875 1341
E: info@electrificationsolutions.co.uk
W: www.electrificationsolutions.co.uk

Electro Motive
See Progress Rail Services

Electromagnetic Testing Services Ltd (ETS)
Pratts Fields, Lubberhedges Lane, Stebbing, Dunmow, Essex, CM6 3BT
T: 01371 856061
F: 01371 856144
E: info@etsemc.co.uk
W: www.etsemc.co.uk

ELG Carbon Fibre
Cannon Business Park, Darkhouse Lane, Coseley, West Midlands, WV14 8XQ
T: 01902 406010
E: contactus@elgcf.com
W: www.elgcf.com/

Elite KL Ltd
19A Sandy Way, Amington Industrial Estate, Tamworth, Staffordshire, B77 4DS
T: 01827 300100
F: 01827 300111
E: sales@elitekl.co.uk
W: www.elitekl.co.uk/

Elite Precast Concrete
Halesfield 9, Telford, Shropshire, TF9 4QW
T: 01952 588885
F: 01952 582011
E: sales@eliteprecast.co.uk
W: www.eliteprecast.co.uk

Elliott Thomas Ltd
The Watermill, Spring Lane, Oxted, Surrey, RH8 9PB
T: 01883 732200
F: 01883 733196
E: info@elliott-thomas.co.uk
W: www.elliott-thomas.co.uk/

Ellis Patents Ltd
High Street, Rillington, Malton, North Yorkshire, YO17 8LA
T: 01944 758395
F: 01944 758808
E: sales@ellispatents.co.uk
W: www.ellispatents.co.uk/

Elmatic
Wentloog Road, Rumney, Cardiff, CF3 1XH
T: 029 2077 8727
F: 029 2079 2297
E: petercrisp@elmatic.co.uk
W: www.elmatic.co.uk

Eltek Valere UK Ltd
Cleveland Road, Hemel Hempstead, Herts, HP2 7EY
T: 01442 219355
F: 01442 245894
E: sales.gb@eltek.com
W: www.eltek.com/

Eltherm UK Ltd
Liberta House, Scotland Hill, Sandhurst, Berks, GU47 8JR
T: 01252 749910
E: sales@eltherm.uk.com
W: www.eltherm.uk.com

Embed Ltd
Viscount Centre Two, University of Warwick Science Park, Millburn Hill Road, Coventry, Warks, CV4 7HS
T: 02476 323251
E: webenquiries@embeduk.com
W: www.embeduk.com

Embedded Rail Technology Ltd
Rosehill House, Derby, DE23 8GG
M: 07967 667020
E: cp@charlespenny.com

EMEG Electrical Ltd
Unit 3, Dunston Place, Dunston Road, Whittington Moor, Chesterfield, Derbys, S41 8NL
T: 01246 268678
F: 01246 268679
E: enq@emeg.co.uk
W: www.emeg.co.uk

Emergency Power Systems
See Emerson Network Power

Emergi-Lite - Thomas & Betts Ltd
Bruntcliffe Lane, Morley, Leeds, LS27 9LL
T: 0113 281 0600
F: 0113 281 0601
E: emergi-lite.sales@tnb.com
W: www.emergi-lite.co.uk

Emerson Crane Hire
Emerson House, Freshwater Road, Dagenham, Essex, RM8 1RX
T: 020 8548 3900
F: 020 8548 3999
E: liam@emersoncranes.com
W: www.emersoncranes.com

Emerson Network Power
Ebury Gate, 23 Lower Belgrave Street, London, SW1W 0NR
T: 020 7881 1440
F: 020 7730 5085
E: uk.rail@emerson.com
W: www.emersonnetworkpower.com

Emerson Network Power Chloride Products & Services
See Emerson Network Power

Emico Ltd
Innovation House, 39 Mark Rd, Hemel Hempstead, Herts, HP2 7DN
T: 01442 213111
F: 01442 236945
E: contact@emico.co
W: www.emico.co

Eminox
Miller Road, Corringham Road Industrial Estate, Gainsborough, Lincolnshire, DN21 1QB
T: 01427 810088
E: enquiries@eminox.com
W: www.eminox.com/

Emission Solutions Ltd (EMSOL)
Sustainable Workspaces, 25 Lavington Street, London, SE1 0NZ
T: 020 3982 9440
E: info@emsol.io
W: www.emsol.io

EMKA
Patricia House, Bodmin Road, Coventry, CV2 5DG
T: 02476 616505
F: 02476 612837
E: enquiries@emka.co.uk
W: www.emka.com/uk_en/

Enable Access
Marshmoor Works, Great North Road, North Mymms, Hatfield, AL9 5SD
T: 0208 2750375
F: 02084490326
E: technical@enable-access.com
W: www.enable-access.com

Enable ID
10-12 The Courtyard, Timothys Bridge Road, Stratford-upon-Avon, CV37 9NP
T: 020 8102 9541
E: hello@enableid.com
W: enableid.com/

Encocam Ltd
5 Stukeley Business Centre, Blackstone Road, Huntingdon, Cambridgeshire, PE29 6EF
T: 01480 435302
W: www.encocam.com/industries/rail

Enerpac
Bentley Rd South, Darlaston, West Midlands, WS10 8LQ
T: 0121 505 0787
F: 0121 505 0799
E: info@enerpac.com
W: www.enerpac.com

EnerSys
Power/Full Solutions
Every train operator needs the peace of mind that all the on-vehicle battery technology contributes to a safe and reliable trip. EnerSys is proficient in the design of complex engineered systems comprising many individual components, ensuring that we supply rail power solutions to the highest standards of safety and reliability.
• Rolling Stock Maintenance/Parts
Oak Court, Clifton Business Park, Wynne Avenue, Swinton, Manchester, M27 8FF
T: 0161 794 4611
F: 0161 727 3809
E: enersys.rail@uk.enersys.com
W: www.enersys-emea-rail.com

EnerSys Ltd
Oak Court, Clifton Business Park, Wynne Ave, Swinton, Manchester, M27 8FF
T: 0161 794 4611
F: 0161 727 3809
E: enersys.rail@uk.enersys.com
W: www.enersys.com

Engineered Composites Ltd
Unit 4, Borders 2 Industrial Park, River Lane, Saltney, Chester, CH4 8RJ
T: 01244 676000
E: info@engineered-composites.co.uk
W: www.engineered-composites.co.uk

Engineering Support Group
See DB ESG

England's Economic Heartland (EEH)
c/o Buckinghamshire County Council, Walton Street, Aylesbury, HP20 1UA
T: 01296 382703
E: englandseconomicheartland@buckscc.gov.uk
W: www.englandseconomicheartland.com/

Ennstone Johnston
See FP McCann Ltd

ENOTRAC UK Ltd
Chancery House, St Nicholas Way, Sutton, Surrey, SM1 4AF
T: 020 8770 3501
F: 020 8770 3502
E: sebastien.lechelle@enotrac.com
W: www.enotrac.com

Entech Technical Solutions Ltd
56 Broadwick St, London, W1F 7AL
T: 0207 434 7370
E: saul@entechts.co.uk
W: www.entechts.co.uk

Entech Technical Solutions Ltd
1st Floor, Hamilton House, 111 Marlowes, Hemel Hempstead, Herts, HP1 1BB
T: 01442 898900
F: 01442 898990
E: info@entechts.com
W: www.entechts.co.uk

Enterprise
See Amey

Enterprise Managed Services Ltd
See Amey

Environmental Management Solutions Group Holdings Ltd (EMS)
Sigeric Business Park, Holme Lacey Road, Rotherwas, Hereford, HR2 6BQ
T: 01432 263333
F: 01432 263355
W: www.ems-asbestos.co.uk/

Environmental Resources Management (ERM) Ltd
2nd Floor, Exchequer Court, 33 St Mary Axe, London, EC3A 8AA
T: 020 3206 5200
F: 020 3206 5440
W: www.erm.com/en/

Environmental Scientifics Group Ltd (ESG)
ESG House, Bretby Business Park, Ashby Rd, Burton upon Trent, DE15 0YZ
T: 01283 554400
F: 01283 554423
E: sales@esg.co.uk
W: www.esg.co.uk

Environmental Technologies Ltd.
Grimbald Crag Road, Environmental Technologies Ltd. Grimbald Crag Road Knaresborough, HG5 8PY
T: 01423 817200
F: 01423 817400
E: admin@ecolube.co.uk
W: www.env-t.com

Envirotech
See LH Group Services

EPC Global
See Talascend Ltd

EQE International
See ABS Consulting

Equib Ltd
Fold House, The Green, Finningley, Doncaster, DN9 3BP
T: 01200 449709
E: bob.hide@equib.co.uk
W: www.equib.co.uk/

ERG Transit Systems (UK) Ltd
See Vix Technology

Ergonomics & Safety Research Institute (ESRI)
Holywell Building, Holywell Way, Loughborough, Leics, LE11 3UZ
T: 01509 226900
F: 01509 226960
E: dsoffice@lboro.ac.uk
W: www.lboro.ac.uk

Eric Wright Group
Sceptre House, Sceptre Way, Bamber Bridge, Preston, PR5 6AW
T: 01772 698822
F: 01772 628811
E: info@ericwright.co.uk
W: www.ericwright.co.uk

Erlau AG
John Wilson Business Park, Units 10-14, Thanet Way, Whitstable, Kent, CT5 3QT
T: 01227 276611
W: www.erlauuk.co.uk/

ERM Ltd
2nd Floor, Exchequer Court, 33 St Mary Axe, London, EC3 8LL
T: 020 3206 5401
F: 020 7465 7272
W: www.erm.com

Ernst & Young LLP
1 More London Place, London, SE1 2AF
T: 020 7951 1113
F: 020 7951 3167
E: gfavaloro@uk.ey.com
W: www.ey.com/uk

ESAB (UK) Ltd
Hanover House, Queensgate, Britannia Rd, Waltham Cross, EN8 7TF
T: 01992 768515
F: 01992 788053
E: info@esab.co.uk
W: www.esab.co.uk

ESP Systex Ltd
68-74 Holderness Rd, Hull, HU9 1ED
T: 01482 384500
F: 01482 384555
E: info@espsystex.co.uk
W: www.http://the-espgroup.com

ESR Technology Ltd
202 Cavendish Place, Birchwood Park, Warrington, Cheshire, WA3 6WU
T: 01925 843400
F: 01925 843500
E: info@esrtechnology.com
W: www.esrtechnology.com

ESS Rail
3rd Floor, Regal House, 70 London Rd, Twickenham, TW1 3QS
T: 0845 245 3000
F: 0845 245 3061
E: john.lynch@essengineering.com
W: www.essengineering.com

Essempy
1 Phoebe Lane, Church End, Wavendon, Bucks, MK17 8LR
T: 01908 582491
M: 07967 398431
E: norman.price@essempy.co.uk
W: www.essempy.co.uk

Essex Medical Testing
104 Haltwhistle Rd, South Woodham Ferrers, Essex
T: 01245 426042
F: 01245 425617
E: info@essexmt.co.uk
W: www.essexmedicaltesting.co.uk

E-T-A Engineering Technology
Telford Close, Aylesbury, Buckinghamshire, HP19 8DG
T: 01296 420336
F: 01296 488497
E: info@e-t-a.co.uk
W: www.e-t-a.co.uk

ETS Cable Components
Units 4-6, Red Lion Business Park, Red Lion Rd, Tolworth, Surrey, KT6 7QD
T: 020 8405 6789
F: 020 8405 6790
E: sales@etscc.co.uk
W: www.etscc.co.uk

Eurailscout GB Ltd
Unit 2, Kimberley Court, Kimberley Rd, Queens Park, London, NW6 7SL
T: 020 7372 2973
F: 020 7372 5444
E: info@eurailscout.com
W: www.eurailscout.com

Euro Cargo Rail SAS
Immeuble la Palacio, 25-29 Place de la Madelaine, 75008 Paris, France
T: 0033 977 400 000
F: 0033 977 400 200
E: info@eurocargorail.com
W: www.eurocargorail.com

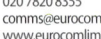

Eurochemi
Kingsbury Park, Midland Rd, Swadlincote, Derbys, DE11 0AN
T: 01283 222111
F: 01283 550177
E: info@hkw.co.uk
W: www.eurochemi.co.uk

Eurocom Ltd
W013 to W015, Westminster Business Square, Durham Street, Vauxhall, London, SE11 5JH
T: 020 7820 8344
F: 020 7820 8355
E: comms@eurocomltd.co.uk
W: www.eurocomlimited.com/

Eurofins York
Market Square, University of York, Heslington, York, YO10 5DD
T: 01904 324440
F: 01904 324434
E: enquiry@yorkemc.co.uk
W: www.yorkemc.co.uk

Eurolog Ltd
Orlando House, 3 High St, Teddington, TW11 8NP
T: 020 8977 4407
F: 020 8977 3714
E: info@eurolog.co.uk
W: www.eurolog.co.uk

Europe Rail Consultancy Ltd
North Court, Hassocks, West Sussex, BN6 8JS
T: 01273 845583
E: chris.dugdale@europerailconsultancy.com
W: www.europerailconsultancy.com

European Association of Railway Personnel
32 Greet Road, Lancing, Sussex, BN15 9NS
T: 01903 521850
E: fam.andrews@yahoo.com

European Investment Bank (EIB)
1 Royal Exchange Buildings, London, EC3V 3LF
T: 020 7375 9660
F: 020 7375 9699
W: www.eib.org

European Union

Europhoenix
Registered Address, 58a High Street, Stony Stratford, Milton Keynes, Buckinghamshire, MK11 1AQ
W: www.europhoenix.eu

Eurostar International Ltd
Times House, Bravingtons Walk, Regent Quarter, London, N1 9AW
E: press.office@eurostar.co.uk
W: www.eurostar.com

Eurotech Ltd
3 Clifton Court, Cambridge, CB1 7BN
T: 01223 403410
F: 01223 410457
E: sales.uk@eurotech.com
W: www.eurotech.com/en/

Eurox
Aqua House, Buttress Way, Smethwick, B66 3DL
T: 0121 555 7167
F: 0121 555 7168
E: sales.orders@eurox.co.uk
W: www.eurox.co.uk

Eve Trakway Ltd
Bramley Vale, Chesterfield, Derbys, S44 5GA
T: 08700 767676
F: 08700 737373
E: mail@evetrakway.co.uk
W: www.evetrakway.co.uk

Evergrip Ltd
Unit 4, Flaxley Rd, Selby, YO8 4BG
T: 01757 212744
F: 01757 212749
E: sales@evergrip.com
W: www.evergrip.com

Eversheds
1 Royal Standard Place, Nottingham, NG1 6FZ
T: 0845 497 9797
F: 0845 497 4919
W: www.eversheds.co.uk

Eversholt Rail (UK) Ltd
First Floor, 210 Pentonville Rd, London, N1 9JY
T: 020 7380 5057
E: enquiries@eversholtrail.co.uk
W: www.eversholtrail.co.uk

Evolvi Rail Systems Ltd
3rd Floor, 1 New Century Place, East St, Reading, RG1 4ET
T: 01732 598510
E: accountmanagement@evolvi.co.uk
W: www.evolvi.co.uk

EWS
See DB Cargo (UK)

Excalibur Screwbolts Ltd
Gate 3, Newhall Nursery, Lower Rd, Hockley, Essex, SS5 5JU
T: 01702 206962/207909
F: 01702 207918
E: charles.bickford@screwbolt.com
W: www.excaliburscrewbolts.com

Exide Technologies
See GNB Industrial Power (UK) Ltd

Exled ITD
Phoenix Mill, London Rd, Stroud, Glos, GL5 2BU
T: 01453 456361
F: 01453 756505
E: sales@exled.co.uk
W: www.exled.co.uk

Exova (UK) Ltd
6 Coronet Way, Centenary Park, Salford, M50 1RE
T: 0161 787 3291
F: 0161 787 3251
E: steve.hughes@exova.com
W: www.exova.com

Expamet Security Products
PO Box 14, Longhill Ind. Est. (North), Hartlepool, TS25 1PR
T: 01429 867366
F: 01429 867355
E: sales@exmesh.co.uk
W: www.expandedmetalfencing.com

Expedition Engineering
The Clove Building, 4 Maguire Street, London, SE1 2NQ
T: 020 7307 1000
F: 020 7307 1001
E: info@expedition.uk.com
W: expedition.uk.com/

Express Electrical
37 Cable Depot Rd, Riverside Ind Est, Clydebank, G81 1UY
T: 0141 941 3689
F: 0141 952 8155
E: sales@expresselectrical.co.uk
W: www.expresselectrical.co.uk

Express Medicals Ltd
8 City Business Centre, Lower Rd, London, SE16 2XB
T: 020 7500 6900
F: 020 7500 6910
E: workhealth@expressmedicals.co.uk
W: www.expressmedicals.co.uk

External Solutions Ltd
Unit 2, 5 Elwes St, Brigg, North Lincs, DN20 8LB
T: 01652 655933
F: 01652 655966
E: dawn@external-solutions.co.uk
W: www.external-solutions.co.uk

Fabric Architecture Ltd
Unit B4 Nexus, Gloucester Business Park, Brockworth, GL3 4AG
T: 01452 612800
E: info@fabricarchitecture.com
W: fabricarchitecture.com/

Factair Ltd
49 Boss Hall Rd, Ipswich, Suffolk, IP1 5BN
T: 01473 746400
F: 01473 747123
E: enquiries@factair.co.uk
W: www.factair.co.uk

Faithful & Gould
Euston Tower, 286, Euston Rd, London, NW1 3AT
T: 020 7121 2121
F: 020 7121 2020
E: info@fgould.com
W: www.fgould.com

Faiveley Transport Ltd
Morpeth Wharf, Twelve Quays, Birkenhead, Wirral, CH41 1LF
T: 0151 649 5000
F: 0151 649 5001
E: nigel.lavers@faiveleytransport.com
W: www.faiveleytransport.com

Falcon Electrical Engineering Ltd
Falcon House, Main St, Fallin, Stirlingshire, FK7 7HT
T: 01786 819920
F: 01786 814381
E: sales@falconelectrical.com
W: www.falconelectrical.com

Farrans
99 Kingsway, Dunmurry, Belfast, Co Antrim, BT17 9NU
T: 02890 551300
W: https://www.farrans.com/

Fastrack (Expamet Security Products)
PO Box 14, Longhill Ind. Est.(North), Hartlepool, TS25 1PR
T: 01429 867366
F: 01429 867355
E: sales@exmesh.co.uk
W: www.expandedmetalcompany.co.uk

FCC Construcción
Federico Salmón, 13. 28016, Madrid, Spain
T: 34 913 595 400
F: 34 913 594 923
W: www.fcc.es/

Federal Mogul Friction Products (Ferodo)
Hayfield Road, Chapel-en-le-Frith, Derbys, SK23 0JP
T: 01298 811689
F: 01298 811580
W: www.federalmogul.com

Feilden Fowles
8 Royal Street, London, SE1 7LL
T: 020 7033 4594
E: info@feildenfowles.co.uk
W: www.feildenfowles.co.uk

Fenbrook Consulting Ltd
22 Fenbrook Close, Hambrook, Bristol, BS16 1QJ
T: 0117 970 1773
E: trevor@fenbrook.com
W: www.fenbrook.com

Fencing & Lighting Contractors Ltd
Unit 21, Amber Drive, Bailey Brook Ind Est, Langley Mill, Derbys, NG16 4BE
T: 01773 531383
F: 01773 531921
E: info@fencingandlighting.co.uk
W: www.fencingandlighting.co.uk/

Fenix Signalling
18 Shottery Brook Office Park, Timothys Bridge Road, Stratford upon Avon, CV37 9NR
T: 3300 580180
E: enquiries@fenixsignalling.com
W: www.fenixsignalling.com/

The Fenning Lovatt Partnership Ltd
69-71 Newington Causeway, London, SE1 6BD
T: 020 7378 4812
F: 020 7407 4612
E: mail@fenninglovatt.com
W: www.fenninglovatt.com

Feonic Technology
3e Newlands Science Park, Inglemire Lane, Hull, HU6 7TQ
T: 01482 806688
F: 01482 806654
E: info@feonic.com
W: www.feonic.com

Fereday Pollard
30 Kings Bench Street, London, SE1 0QX
T: 020 7253 0303
E: admin@fereday-pollard.co.uk
W: https://www.fereday-pollard.co.uk/

Ferrabyrne Ltd
Fort Rd Ind. Est, Littlehampton, West Sussex, BN17 7QU
T: 01903 721317
F: 01903 730452
E: sales@ferrabyrne.co.uk
W: www.ferrabyrne.co.uk

Ferrograph Ltd
Unit 1, New York Way, New York Ind Park, Newcastle Upon Tyne, NE27 0QF
T: 0191 280 8800
F: 0191 280 8810
E: info@ferrograph.com
W: www.ferrograph.com

Ferrovial Agroman
10th Floor, BSI Building 389, Chiswick High Road, London, W4 4AL
E: pressheadoffice@ferrovial.com
W: www.faukie.com/

FGD Ltd
Smestow Bridge, Bridgnorth Road, Wombourne, Wolverhampton, Staffordshire, WV5 8AY
T: 01902 893226
F: 01902 895283
E: info@fgdltd.co.uk
W: www.fgdltd.co.uk

Fibergrate Composite Structures
5151 Beltline Rd, Ste 1212, Dallas, TX 75254, United States
T: 00 800 527 4043
F: 00 972 250 1530
E: info@fibergrate.com
W: www.fibergrate.com

Fibrelite Composites Ltd
Snaygill Ind. Est, Keighley Rd, Skipton, N Yorks, BD23 2QR
T: 01756 799773
F: 01756 799539
E: covers@fibrelite.com
W: www.fibrelite.com

Fieldfisher LLP
Riverbank House, 2 Swan Lane, London, EC4R 3TT
T: 020 7861 4000
F: 020 7488 0084
M: 07795 267789
E: nicholas.thompsell@fieldfisher.com
W: www.fieldfisher.com

Fifth Dimension Associates Ltd (FDAL)
Suite 18411, 20-22 Wenlock Road, London, N1 7GU
T: 020 7060 2332
F: 020 7060 3325
E: london@fdal.co.uk
W: www.fdal.co.uk

Findlay Irvine Ltd
Bog Rd, Penicuik, Midlothian, EH26 9BU
T: 01968 671200
F: 01968 671237
E: sales@findlayirvine.com
W: www.findlayirvine.com

Finning (UK) Ltd
Unit 3, Triangle Business Park, Oakwell Way, Birstall, Batley, West Yorks, WF17 9LU
T: 0113 201 2065
E: oillab@finning.co.uk
W: www.fluid-analysis.com

Fircroft
Trinity House, 114 Northenden Rd, Sale, Cheshire, M33 3FZ
T: 0161 905 2020
F: 0161 969 1743
E: hq@fircroft.co.uk
W: www.fircroft.co.uk

The Fire Service College
Moreton-in-Marsh, Glos, GL56 0RH
T: 01608 812130
F: 01608 651790
E: dluff@fireservicecollege.ac.uk
W: www.fireservicecollege.ac.uk

Fireclad Ltd
5th Floor, 120 Old Broad Street, London, EC2N 1AR
T: 020 7628 6500
W: www.fireclad.com/

First Call Building Services Ltd
Euston Station Office, PO Box 45544, London, N1 2WB
T: 020 7383 2002
E: sales@firstcalleuston.co.uk
W: www.firstcalleuston.com/

First Choice Protection
See Portwest Clothing Ltd

First Components Ltd
Wallows Ind Est, Wallows Rd, Brierley Hill, DY5 1QA
T: 01384 262068
F: 01384 482383
E: info@firstcomponents.co.uk
W: www.firstcomponents.co.uk

First Engineering Ltd
See Babcock Rail

First Procurement Associates
See FPA Consulting Ltd

First Rail Support Ltd
Unit 20, Time Technology Park, Blackburn Rd, Simonstone, Lancs, BB12 7TG
T: 01282 688110
F: 01282 688141
E: rail.support@firstgroup.com
W: www.firstgroup.com/firstrailsupport

Firstco Ltd
4 Celbridge Mews, Royal Oak, London, W2 6EU
T: 020 7034 0833
F: 020 7229 8002
E: info@firstco.uk.com
W: www.firstco.uk.com

FirstGroup Plc
395 King St, Aberdeen, AB24 5RP
T: 01224 650100
E: corporate.comms@firstgroup.com
W: www.firstgroupplc.com

FISA (Fabbrica Italiana Sedili Autoferroviari Srl)
Via Giovanni De Simon, 6, 33010 Rivoli di Osoppo (UD), Italy
T: +39 0432 986 071
F: +39 0432 986 086
W: www.fisaitaly.com/

Fishbone Solutions Ltd
7 Pride Point Drive, Pride Park, Derby, DE24 8BX
T: 01332 899190
F: 01332 898560
E: go-fish@fishbonesolutions.co.uk
W: www.fishbonesolutions.co.uk

Fitzpatrick Contractors Ltd
See VolkerFitzpatrick Ltd

FKI Switchgear
See Hawker Siddeley Switchgear ltd

Flash Forward Consulting
M: 07771 828 644
E: enquiries@flashforwardconsulting.co.uk
W: www.flashforwardconsulting.co.uk/

FleetwoodMay
Bramble Dene, 35 Cavendish Road, Woking, Surrey, GU22 0EP
M: 07836 720537
E: martin@fleetwoodmay.co.uk
W: www.fleetwoodmay.co.uk

Flexible & Specialist (FS) Cables
Alban Point, Alban Park, Hatfield Rd, St Albans, AL4 0JX
T: 01727 840841
F: 01727 840842
E: sales@fscables.com
W: www.fscables.com

Flexicon Ltd
Roman Way, Coleshill, Birmingham, B46 1HG
T: 01675 466900
F: 01675 466901
E: rail@flexicon.uk.com
W: www.flexicon.uk.com

FLI Structures
Francis & Lewis International, Waterwells Drive, Waterwells Business Park, Gloucester, GL2 2AA
T: 01452 722200
F: 01452 722244
E: m.jones@fli.co.uk
W: www.fliscrewpiles.co.uk

Flint Bishop Solicitors
St Michaels Court, St Michaels Lane, Derby, DE1 3HQ
T: 01332 340211
E: info@flintbishop.co.uk
W: www.flintbishop.co.uk

Flir Systems Ltd (UK)
2 Kings Hill Ave, West Malling, Kent, ME19 4AQ
T: 01732 220011
F: 01732 843707
E: flir@flir.com
W: www.flir.com

Flotec Rail Division
Unit 8, Pavilion Way, Loughborough, Leicestershire, LE11 5GW
T: 01509 230100
E: rail@floteconline.com
W: www.flotecindustrial.com

Flowcrete UK Ltd
The Flooring Technology Centre, Booth Lane, Sandbach, Cheshire, CW11 3QF
T: 01270 753000
F: 01270 753333
E: uk@flowcrete.com
W: www.flowcrete.com

Fluke UK Ltd (Tracklink)
52 Hurricane Way, Norwich, NR6 6JB
T: 020 7942 0700
F: 020 7942 0701
E: industrial@uk.fluke.nl
W: www.fluke.co.uk

Fluor Ltd
Fluor Centre, 140 Pinehurst Road, Farnborough, Hants, GU14 7BF
T: 01252 291000
F: 01252 292222
W: www.fluor.com

Focus 2000 Infrared Ltd
5a Lodge Hill Business Park, Westbury-sub-Mendip, Somerset, BA5 1EY
T: 01749 870620
F: 01749 870622
E: sales@focus2k.co.uk
W: www.focus2k.co.uk

DIRECTORY

Fone Alarm Installations Ltd
59 Albert Rd North, Reigate, RH2 9EL
T: 01737 223673
F: 01737 224349
E: enquiries@fonealarm.co.uk
W: www.fonealarm.co.uk

Forbo Flooring Ltd
High Holborn Rd, Ripley, Derbys, DE5 3NT
T: 01773 744121
F: 01773 744142
E: bob.summers@forbo.com
W: www.forbo-flooring.co.uk

Ford & Stanley Ltd
44 Royal Scot Rd, Pride Park, Derby, DE24 8AJ
T: 01332 344443
M: 07720 678521
E: rail@fordandstanley.com
W: www.fordandstanley.com

Ford Components Manufacturing Ltd
Unit 2, Monkton Business Park North, Mill Lane, Hebburn, Tyne & Wear, NE31 2JZ
T: 0191 428 6600
F: 0191 428 6620
E: shaun.gribben@ford-components.com
W: www.ford-components.com

ForgeTrack Ltd
Thistle House, St Andrew St, Hertford, SG14 1JA
T: 01992 500900
F: 01992 589495
E: sales@forgetrack.co.uk
W: www.forgetrack.co.uk

ForPeople
1 Pickle Mews, London, SW9 0FJ
T: 020 7820 6070
E: hello@forpeople.com
W: https://forpeople.com/

Forwardis UK Ltd
2nd Floor, Unit 17, 83 Crampton Street, London, SE17 3BQ
T: 020 7939 1900
E: salesuk@forwardis.com
W: www.forwardis.com

Fosroc Ltd
Drayton Manor Business Park, Coleshill Rd, Tamworth, Staffs, B78 3XN
T: 01827 262222
F: 01827 262444
E: enquiryuk@fosroc.com
W: www.fosroc.com

Fourth Friday Club
Key Publishing, PO Box 100, Stamford, Lincolnshire PE9 1XQ
T: 01780 755131
W: www.keymodernrailways.com/fourth-friday-club

Fourway Communication Ltd
Delamere Rd, Cheshunt, Herts, EN8 9SH
T: 01992 629182
F: 01992 639227
E: enquiries@fourway.co.uk
W: www.fourway.co.uk

FP McCann Ltd
Cadeby Depot, Brascote Lane, Cadeby, Nuneaton, Warks, CV13 0BE
T: 01455 290780
F: 01455 292189
E: scarson@fpmccann.co.uk
W: www.fpmccann.co.uk

FPA Consulting Ltd
1 St Andrew's House, Vernon Gate, Derby, DE1 1UJ
T: 01332 604321
F: 01332 604322
E: johnb@fpaconsulting.co.uk
W: www.fpaconsulting.co.uk

Frankham Consultancy Group Ltd
Irene House, 7b Five Arches Business Estate, Maidstone Rd, Sidcup, Kent, DA14 5AE
T: 020 8309 7777
F: 020 8306 7890
E: enquire@frankham.com
W: www.frankham.com

Franklin + Andrews
Sea Containers House, 20 Upper Ground, London, SE1 9LZ
T: 020 7633 9966
F: 020 7928 2471
E: enquiries@franklinandrews.com
W: www.franklinandrews.com

Frauscher Selectrail (UK) Ltd
Unit 58, Basepoint Business Centre, Isidore Rd, Bromsgrove, B60 3ET
T: 01527 834670
F: 01527 834671
E: info@frauscher-selectrail.com
W: www.frauscher-selectrail.com

Frauscher UK
Abbey House, 282 Farnborough Road, Farnborough, Hampshire, GU14 7NA
T: 01276 534700
E: richard.colman@uk.frauscher.com
W: www.frauscher.com

Frazer-Nash Consultancy Ltd
Stonebridge House, Dorking Business Park, Station Rd, Dorking, Surrey, RH4 1HJ
T: 01306 885050
F: 01306 886464
E: t.myall@fnc.co.uk
W: www.fnc.co.uk

Freeman Williams Language Solutions Ltd
College Business Centre, Uttoxeter New Rd, Derby, DE22 3WZ
T: 01332 869342
F: 01332 869344
E: abi@freemanwilliams.co.uk
W: www.freemanwillams.co.uk

Freeths LLP
Cardinal Square, 2nd Floor, West Point, 10 Nottingham Rd, Derby, DE1 3QT
T: 0845 634 9791
F: 0845 634 9804
E: mike.copestake@freeths.co.uk
W: www.freeths.co.uk

Freight Europe (UK) Ltd
See Forwardis UK Ltd

Freight On Rail
4 Beresford Avenue, East Twickenham, Middlesex, TW1 2PY
T: 020 8241 9982
E: philippa@freightonrail.org.uk
W: www.freightonrail.org.uk

Freight Systems Express Wales (FSEW)
South Wales International FL Terminal, Newlands Road, Wentloog, Cardiff, CF3 2EU
T: 02920 020900
E: info@fsew.com
W: www.fsew.com

Freight Transport Association (FTA)
Hermes House, St John's Road, Tunbridge Wells, Kent, TN4 9UZ
T: 03717 112 222
F: 01892 552360
E: enquiry@fta.co.uk
W: https://fta.co.uk

FreightArranger Ltd
West View, Brownshill, Stroud, Glos, GL6 8AQ
T: 01453 367150
W: www.freightarranger.co.uk

Freightliner Group Ltd
3rd Floor, 90 Whitfield Street, Fitzrovia, London, W1T 4EZ
T: 03330 169545
F: 020 7200 3975
E: info@gwrr.co.uk
W: www.freightliner.co.uk

Frequentis UK Ltd
Regal House, 70 London Road, Twickenham, TW1 3QS
T: 020 8891 1518
E: marketing@frequentis.com
W: www.frequentis.com

Freshfields Bruckhaus Deringer LLP
65 Fleet St, London, EC4Y 1HT
T: 0207 936 4000
F: 0207 832 7001
E: digitalcommunications@freshfields.com
W: www.freshfields.com

Freshwater
Raglan House, Cardiff Gate Business Park, Cardiff, CF23 8BA
T: 02920 304050
E: hello@freshwater-uk.com
W: www.freshwater-uk.com/

Freyssinet Ltd
Innovation House, Euston Way, Town Centre, Telford, Shropshire, TF3 4LT
T: 01952 201901
F: 01952 201753
E: mailto:john.kennis@freyssinet.co.uk
W: www.freyssinet.co.uk

Frontier Economics
71 High Holborn, London, WC1V 6DA
T: 0207 031 7000
E: transport@frontier-economics.com
W: www.frontier-economics.com/

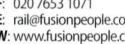

FS Cables
See Flexible & Specialist (FS) Cables

Fuchs Lubricants (UK) Plc
New Century St, Hanley, Stoke on Trent, ST1 5HU
T: 08701 203700
F: 01782 202072
E: contact-uk@fuchs-oil.com
W: www.fuchslubricants.com

Fuelcare Ltd
Suite 1, The Hayloft, Blakenhall Park, Barton under Needwood, Staffs, DE13 8AJ
T: 01283 712263
F: 01283 262263
E: sales@fuelcare.com
W: www.fuelcare.com

Fugro GeoServices
Focal Point, Newmarket Rd, Bottisham, Cambridge, CB25 9BD
T: 0870 600 8050
F: 0870 800 8040
E: info@fugro-aperio.com
W: www.fugro-aperio.com

Fujikura Europe Ltd
C51 Barwell Business Park, Leatherhead Rd, Chessington, Surrey, KT9 2NY
T: 020 8240 2000
F: 020 8240 2010
E: sales@fujikura.co.uk
W: www.fujikura.co.uk

Fujitsu
22 Baker Street, London, W1U 3BW
T: 0843 354 7998
E: askfujitsu@uk.fujitsu.com
W: www.fujitsu.com/uk/industries/rail

Fullmen
Fullmen Industrial Park, Kings Road, Canvey Island, Essex, SS8 0SF
T: 01268 683530
W: www.fullmen.co.uk/

Funkwerk Information Technologies York Ltd
See Trapeze Group Rail Ltd

Furneaux Riddall & Co Ltd
Alchorne Place, Portsmouth, Hants, PO3 5PA
T: 02392 668624
F: 02392 668625
E: info@furneauxriddall.com
W: www.furneauxriddall.com

Furrer + Frey
1st Floor, Winchester House, 19 Bedford Row, London, WC1R 4EB
T: 020 3740 5455
M: 07825 258397
E: ndolphin@furrerfrey.ch
W: www.furrerfrey.ch

Furse - Thomas & Betts Ltd
Wilford Rd, Nottingham, NG2 1EB
T: 0115 964 3700
F: 0115 986 0538
E: enquiry@furse.com
W: www.furse.com

Furtex
See Camira Fabrics Ltd

Fuse Rail
Unit D, Concept Court, Shearway Business Park, Folkestone, Kent, CT19 4RG
T: 01233 877780
E: info@fuserail.com
W: fuserail.com

Fusion People Ltd
2nd/3rd Floor, Aldermary House, 10-15 Queen St, London, EC4N 1TX
T: 020 7653 1070
F: 020 7653 1071
E: rail@fusionpeople.com
W: www.fusionpeople.com

Future Rail (formerly Future Welding)
The Rowe, Stableford, Staffs, ST5 4EN
T: 01782 411800
E: futureraildesign@gmail.com
W: www.futurerail.co.uk

Gabriel & Co Ltd
1 Cromwell Rd, Smethwick, West Midlands, B66 2JT
T: 0121 555 7615
F: 0121 555 1922
E: john.gabriel@gabrielco.com
W: www.gabrielco.com

GAI-Tronics (Hubbell Ltd)
Brunel Dr., Stretton Business Park, Burton upon Trent, DE13 0BZ
T: 01283 500500
F: 01283 500400
E: sales@gai-tronics.co.uk
W: www.gai-tronics.co.uk

Galldris
Galldris House, Pavilion Business Centre, Kinetic Crescent, Innova Science Park, Enfield, EN3 7FJ
T: 01992 763000
E: info@galldris.co.uk
W: https://galldris.co.uk/

Galliford Try Rail
Crab Lane, Fearnhead, Warrington, WA2 0XR
T: 01925 822821
F: 01925 812323
E: ron.stevenson@gallifordtry.co.uk
W: www.gallifordtry.co.uk

Gamble Rail
See Keltbray

Ganymede Solutions Ltd
26 Hershel St, Slough, SL1 1PA
T: 01753 820810
F: 0870 890 1894
E: gary.hewett@ganymedesolutions.co.uk
W: www.ganymedesolutions.co.uk

Gardiner & Theobald
10 South Crescent, London, WC1E 7BD
T: 020 7209 3000
F: 020 7209 1840
E: p.armstrong@gardiner.com
W: www.gardiner.com

Gardner Denver Ltd
Claybrook Drive, Washford Ind. Est, Redditch, Worcs, B98 0DS
T: 01527 838200
F: 01527 521140
E: hydrovane-info.uk@gardnerdenver.com
W: www.gardnerdenver.com/

Garic Ltd
Kingfisher Park, Aviation Rd, Pilsworth, Bury, BL9 8GD
T: 0844 417 9780
F: 0161 766 8809
E: sales@garic.co.uk
W: www.garic.co.uk

Garrandale Ltd
Dartmouth House, Bawtry Road, Wickersley, Rotherham, S66 2BL
T: 0800 949 9575
E: sales@gbr-rail.com
W: www.gbr-rail.com

GarrettCom Europe Ltd
See Belden Solutions

Gatecare
Unit N, Tyson Courtyard, Weldon South Industrial Est, Corby, Northamptonshire, NN18 8AZ
T: 01536 266211
F: 01536 261491
E: sales@gatecare.co.uk
W: www.gatecare.co.uk/

Gates Power Transmission
Tinwald Downs Rd, Heath Hall, Dumfries, DG1 1TS
T: 01387 242000
F: 01387 242010
E: mediaeurope@gates.com
W: www.gates.com

Gatwick Express
See Govia Thameslink Railway

Gauge Communication
Suite S1, Unit 1, Verulam industrial Estate, 224 London Road, St Albans, Herts, AL1 1JB
T: 01727 853952
E: info@gauge-communication.com
W: www.gauge-communication.com/

GAV Access Covers
PO Box 2282, Nuneaton, Warks, CV11 9ZT
T: 02476 381090
F: 02476 373577
E: gavmet@aol.com
W: www.gav-solutions.com

GB Electronics
Ascot House, Mulberry Close, Woods Way, Goring-by-Sea, West Sussex, BN12 4QY
T: 01903 244500
F: 01903 700715
E: matt.s@gbelectronics.com
W: www.gbelectronics.uk

GB Railfreight
3rd Floor, 55 Old Broad Street, London, EC2M 1RX
T: 020 7904 3393
F: 020 7983 5113
E: gbrfinfo@gbrailfreight.com
W: www.gbrailfreight.com

GDS Technology Ltd
Unit 6, Cobham Centre, Westmead Industrial Est, Westlea, Swindon, SN5 7UJ
T: 01793 498020
E: sales.gdstechnology@gds.com
W: www.gdstechnology.co.uk

GE Transportation Systems
Inspira House, Martinfield, Welwyn Garden City, Herts, AL7 1GW
T: 01707 383700
F: 01707 383701
E: getransportationinquiries@ge.com
W: www.getransportation.com

Geatech S.p.A
Via Del Palazzino 6/B, 40051 Altedo (BO), Italy
T: 0039 051 6601514
F: 0039 051 6601309
E: info@geatech.it
W: www.geatech.it

Geismar UK Ltd
Salthouse Rd, Brackmills Ind. Est., Northampton, NN4 7EX
T: 01604 769191
F: 01604 763154
E: sales-uk@geismar.com
W: www.geismar.com

Geldards LLP
Number One, Pride Place, Pride Park, Derby, DE24 8QR
T: 01332 331631
F: 01332 294295
E: michelle.craven-faulkner@geldards.com
W: www.geldards.co.uk

Gemini Rail Services Ltd
Wolverton Works, Stratford Road, Wolverton, Milton Keynes, MK12 5NT
T: 01908 574400
E: info@geminirg.co.uk
W: www.geminirailgroup.co.uk

Gemini Rail Technology Ltd
2 Priestley Wharf, Holt Street, Birmingham, B7 4BN
T: 0121 359 7777
E: info@geminirg.co.uk
W: www.geminirailgroup.co.uk

Gemma Lighting
Unit 3, Marshlands Spur, Farlington, Portsmouth, Hampshire, PO6 1RX
T: 0844 856 5201
F: 0844 856 5209
E: marketing@gemmalighting.com
W: www.gemmalighting.com

GenQuip Plc
Aberafan Rd, Baglan Ind. Park, Port Talbot, SA12 7DJ
T: 01639 823484
F: 01639 822533
E: sales@genquip.co.uk
W: www.genquip.co.uk

Gensler
Aldgate House, 33 Aldgate High Street, London, EC3N 1AH
T: 020 7073 9600
F: 020 7539 1917
W: www.gensler.com/

Genwork Ltd
See Bache Pallets Ltd

Geodesign Barriers Ltd
2 Montgomery Ave, Pinehurst, Swindon, SN2 1LE
T: 01793 538565
E: britt.warg@palletbarrier.com
W: www.geodesignbarriers.com

Geoff Brown Signalling Ltd
The Cottage, Old Lodge, Minchinhampton, Stroud, GL6 9AQ
M: 07977 265721
E: geoffbrownsignalling@btinternet.com

GeoRope
Arumindarrich, West Laroch, Ballachulish, Argyll, PH49 4JG
T: 01855 811224
E: kam@geo-rope.com
W: www.geo-rope.com

Geosynthetics Ltd
Fleming Rd, Harrowbrook Ind.Est., Hinckley, Leics, LE10 3DU
T: 01455 617139
F: 01455 617140
E: sales@geosyn.co.uk
W: www.geosyn.co.uk

Geotechnical Engineering Ltd
Centurion House, Olympus Park, Quedgeley, Glos, GL2 4NF
T: 01452 527743
F: 01452 729314
E: geotech@geoeng.co.uk
W: www.geoeng.co.uk

Geotechnics Ltd
The Geotechnical Centre, 203 Torrington Ave, Tile Hill, Coventry, CV4 9UT
T: 02476 694664
F: 02476 694642
E: mail@geotechnics.co.uk
W: www.geotechnics.co.uk

Getlink
The Channel Tunnel Group Ltd, UK Terminal, Ashford Rd, Folkestone, Kent, CT18 8XX
T: 08443 353535
F: 01303 288784
E: communication.internet@eurotunnel.com
W: www.eurotunnel.com

Getzner Werkstoffe GmbH
Herrenaus, A-6706 Burs, Austria
T: 0043 5552 2010
F: 0043 5552 201899
E: sylomer@getzner.at
W: www.getzner.at

GEW 2 Ltd
Unit 4, Office Village, Keypoint, Keys Road, Alfreton, Derbyshire, DE55 7FQ
T: 0345 508 2057
E: commercialteam@gew2ltd.co.uk
W: www.gew2.co.uk/

Gewiss UK Ltd
2020 Building, Cambourne Business Park, Cambourne, Cambridge, CB23 6DW
T: 01954 712757
F: 01954 712753
E: marketing@gewiss.co.uk
W: www.gewiss.co.uk

GGB UK
Wellington House, Starley Way, Birmingham Int. Park, Birmingham, B37 7HB
T: 0121 767 9100
F: 0121 781 7313
E: greatbritain@ggbearings.com
W: www.ggbearings.com/en

GGR Group Ltd
Broadway Business Park, Broadgate, Chadderton, Oldham, OL9 0JA
T: 0161 683 2580
F: 0161 683 4444
E: info@ggrrail.com
W: www.ggrrail.com

GGS Engineering (Derby) Ltd
Atlas Works, Litchurch Lane, Derby, DE24 8AQ
T: 01332 299345
F: 01332 299678
E: sales@ggseng.com
W: www.ggseng.com

GHD Ltd (Gutteridge, Haskins & Davey Ltd)
6th Floor, 10 Fetter Lane, London, EC4A 1BR
T: 020 3077 7900
E: sue.jackson@ghd.com
W: www.ghd.com

Giffen Group
Lyon Way, St Albans, Herts, AL4 0LQ
T: 01727 869126
F: 01727 855744
E: hazel.stubbs@giffengroup.co.uk
W: www.giffengroup.co.uk/

Gifford
See Ramboll UK Ltd

Giken Europe BV
15 Manchester Mews, London, W1U 2DX
T: 0845 260 8001
F: 0845 260 8002
E: info@giken.co.uk
W: www.giken.com

GARRANDALE RAIL
Garrandale Rail supplies Specialist Rail Depot Equipment for the servicing of trains and revolutionary products such as Cleartrak, a train toilet waste processing system.
Garrandale Rail, Dartmouth House, Bawtry Road, Wickersley, Rotherham, S66 2BL, UK
T: +44 (0) 800 949 9575
E: sales@gbr-rail.com
www.gbr-rail.com

Gilbarco Veeder-Root
Crompton Close, Basildon, Essex, SS14 3BA
T: 01268 533090
F: 01268 524214
E: uksales@gilbarco.com
W: www.gilbarco.com

Gillespies
1 St John's Square, London, EC1M 4DH
T: 020 7253 2929
W: www.gillespies.co.uk/

Gioconda Limited
Unit 10, Woodfalls, Gravelly Ways, Laddingford, Maidstone, Kent, ME18 6DA
T: 01622 872512
E: mail@gioconda.co.uk
W: www.gioconda.co.uk

GKD Technik Ltd
17 Cobham Rd, Ferndown Industrial Estate, Wimborne, Dorset, BH21 7PE
T: 01202 861961
F: 01202 861361
E: nick@gkdtechnik.com
W: www.gkdtechnik.com

GKN Hybrid Power
Po Box 55, Ipsley House, Ipsley Church Lane, Redditch, Worcs, B98 0TL
T: 01527 517715
W: www.gkn.com/landsystems/brands/hybrid-power/pages/default.aspx

Glasdon UK Ltd
Preston New Rd, Blackpool, Lancs, FY4 4UL
T: 01253 600410
F: 01253 792558
E: sales@glasdon-uk.co.uk
W: www.glasdon.com

Glazzard Ltd
Washington Centre, Halesowen Rd, Dudley, West Midlands, DY2 9RE
T: 01384 233151
F: 01384 250224
E: info@glazzard.co.uk
W: www.glazzard.co.uk/

Gleeds
95 New Cavendish St, London, W1W 6XF
T: 020 7631 7000
F: 020 7631 7001
E: london@gleeds.co.uk
W: www.gleeds.com

Glenair UK Ltd
40 Lower Oakham Way, Oakham Business Park, Mansfield, Notts, NG18 5BY
T: 01623 638100
F: 01623 638111
E: cbaker@glenair.co.uk
W: www.glenair.com

Glendale
The Coach House, Duxbury Hall Road, Duxbury Park, Chorley, Lancs, PR7 4AT
T: 01257 460461
F: 01257 460421
E: info@glendale-services.co.uk
W: www.glendale-services.co.uk/

Glenn Howells Architects
321 Bradford Street, Birmingham, B5 6ET
T: 0121 666 7640
E: mail@glennhowells.co.uk
W: glennhowells.co.uk

Glentworth Rail Ltd
Long Lane, Hawthorn Hill, Maidenhead, Berks, SL6 3TA
T: 01628 639823
F: 01628 639823
E: rgraham@william-cook.co.uk
W: glentworthrail.co.uk/

Glide (UK) Ltd
32 Clay Hill, Enfield, EN2 9AA
T: 020 8367 7350
E: info@pigeonglide.com
W: www.pigeonglide.com

Global Crossing (UK) Telecommunications Ltd
See Level 3 Communications

Global House Training Services Ltd
1 Cotswold Close, Bexleyheath, Kent, DA7 6ST
T: 01322 331617
F: 01322 341817
E: contact@globalhouse.co.uk
W: www.globalhouse.co.uk

Global Rail Construction Ltd
Unit 20, The IO Centre, Hatfield Business Park, Hearle Way, Hatfield, Hertfordshire, AL10 9EW
T: 0870 990 4074
E: enquiries@grcl.co.uk
W: www.grcl.co.uk/

Global Rail Support
8 Curzon Lane, Alvaston, Derby, DE24 8QS
T: 01332 601596
F: 01332 727494
E: ask@globalrailsupport.com
W: www.globalrailsupport.com

Global Transport Forum
3rd Floor, Petersham House, 57A Hatton Garden, London, EC1N 8JG
T: 020 7045 0900
E: marketing@globaltransportforum.com

Globalforce Group
Custom House, 1-3 Harolds Road, Harlow, Essex, CM19 5BJ
T: 01279 427898
E: enquiries@globalforcegroup.co.uk
W: www.globalforcegroup.co.uk

GlobalReach Technology
110 Cannon Street, London, EC4N 6EU
T: 020 7831 5630
E: sales@globalreachtech.com
W: globalreachtech.com/

GLS Coatings
Units 1-2 Broncoed Court, Broncoed Business Park, Mold, Flintshire, CH7 1HP
T: 0800 231 5260
E: info@glscoatings.co.uk
W: glscoatings.co.uk/

GM Rail Services Ltd
65 Somers Rd, Rugby, Warks, CV22 7DG
T: 01788 573777
F: 01788 551138
E: dwhitley@gmrail.co.uk
W: www.gmrail.co.uk

GME Springs
Unit C, GME Industrial Estate, Coventry, CV6 5NN
T: 02476 664911
F: 02476 663020
E: sales@gmesprings.co.uk
W: www.gmesprings.co.uk

GMT Manufacturing Ltd
Old Gorsey Lane, Wallasey, Merseyside, CH44 4AH
T: 0151 630 1545
F: 0151 639 0510
E: info@gmt.co.uk
W: www.gmt.co.uk

GMT Rubber-Metal-Technic Ltd
The Sidings, Station Rd, Guiseley, Leeds, LS20 8BX
T: 01943 870670
F: 01943 870631
E: sales@gmt.gb.com
W: www.gmt-rubber.com

GNB Industrial Power (UK) Ltd
Mansell House, Aspinall Close, Middlebrook, Horwich, Bolton, BL6 6QQ
T: 0845 606 4111
F: 0845 606 4112
E: sales-uk@eu.exide.com
W: www.gnb.com

GNER
See Grand Central Railway Co. Ltd.

GNWR
See Grand Central Railway Co. Ltd.

Go-Ahead Group plc
Head Office, 4 Matthew Parker St, Westminster, London, SW1H 9NP
T: 020 7799 8999
F: 020 7799 8998
E: enquiries@go-ahead.com
W: www.go-ahead.com

GOBOTiX Ltd
140B Longden Coleham, Shrewsbury, SY3 7DN
T: 01743 387030
E: sales@gobotix.co.uk
W: www.gobotix.co.uk/

Golder Associates (UK) Ltd
1 Alie Street, London, E1 8DE
T: (0)20 7423 0940
F: (0)20 7423 0941
W: www.golder.co.uk

Goldwing Cable Ltd
Unit 8A, Ellough Ind Est, Beccles, Suffolk, NR34 7TD
T: 01502 713161
F: 01502 717773
E: jon@goldwingcable.com
W: www.goldwingcable.com

GoMedia
Evergreen House North, Grafton Place, London, NW1 2DX
T: 020 3691 1873
E: enquiries@gomedia.io
W: www.gomedia.io/

GO-OP Co-operative Ltd
10 East Reach, Taunton, TA1 3EW
E: info@go-op.coop
W: www.go-op.coop

Gordon Services Ltd
Unit 8, Dawes Farm, Ivy Barn Lane, Ingatestone, Essex, CM4 0PX
T: 01277 352895
F: 01277 356115
E: enquiries@gordonservicesltd.co.uk
W: www.gordonservicesltd.co.uk

GOS Tool & Engineering Services Ltd
Heritage Court Rd, Gilchrist Thomas ind. Est, Blaenavon, NP4 9RL
T: 01495 790230
F: 01495 792757
E: enquiries@gosengineering.co.uk
W: www.gosengineering.co.uk

Goskills
See People 1st

Go-Tel Communications Ltd
See Samsung Electronics Hainan Fibreoptics

Govia
Go-ahead Group Rail, Go-ahead House, 26-28 Addiscombe Rd, Croydon, Surrey, CR9 5GA
E: contact@go-ahead-rail.com
W: www.govia.info

Govia Thameslink Railway (GTR)
1st and 2nd Floor, Monument Place, 24 Monument Street, London, EC3R 8AJ
T: 0345 026 4700
W: www.gtrailway.com/

Gradus Ltd
Park Green, Macclesfield, Cheshire, SK11 7LZ
T: 01625 428922
F: 01625 433949
E: imail@gradusworld.com
W: www.gradusworld.com

GRAHAM
1 Seaward Place, Centurion Business Park, Glasgow, G41 1HH
T: 0141 418 5550
E: glasgow@graham.co.uk
W: www.graham.co.uk

Gramm Barrier Systems Ltd
18 Clinton Place, Seaford, East Sussex, BN25 1NP
T: 01323 872243
F: 01323 872244
E: info@grammbarriers.com
W: www.grammbarriers.com

Gramm Interlink
17-19 High St, Ditchling, East Sussex, BN6 8SY
T: 01275 846397
M: 07827 947086
W: www.gramminerlinkrail.co.uk

Grammer Seating Systems Ltd
Willenhall Lane Ind. Est., Bloxwich, Walsall, WS3 2XN
T: 01922 407035
F: 01922 710552
E: david.bignell@grammer.com
W: www.grammer.com

Gramos Applied Ltd
Orapi Applied Ltd, Spring Rd, Smethwick, West Midlands, B66 1PT
T: 0121 525 4000
F: 0121 525 4950
E: info@gramos-applied.com
W: www.gramos-applied.com

Grand Central Railway Co. Ltd.
Third Floor, Northern House, Rougier Street, York, YO1 6HZ
T: 0345 603 4852
F: 01904 466066
E: customer.services@grandcentralrail.com
W: www.grandcentralrail.co.uk

Grand Union Trains
Fulford Lodge, 1 Heslington Lane, Fulford, York, YO10 4HW

Grant Rail Group
See VolkerRail

Grant Thornton UK LLP
Melton St, Euston Square, London, NW1 2EP
T: 0141 223 0731
E: taylor.ferguson@uk.gt.com
W: www.grant-thornton.co.uk

Grants of Shoreditch
Grant House, Prospect Way, Hutton, Brentwood, Essex, CM13 1XD
T: 01277 236190
F: 01277 212849
E: office@grantsint.com
W: www.grantsint.com/

Grass Concrete Ltd
Duncan House, 142 Thornes Lane, Thornes, Wakefield, WF2 7RE
T: 01924 379443
F: 01924 290289
E: info@grasscrete.com
W: www.grasscrete.com

GrayBar Ltd
10 Fleming Close, Park Farm Ind. Est, Wellingborough, Northants, NN8 6UF
T: 01933 676700
F: 01933 676800
E: sales@graybar.co.uk
W: www.graybar.co.uk

Great Western Railway
Milford House, 1 Milford St, Swindon, SN1 1HL
T: 0345 7000 125
E: fgwfeedback@firstgroup.com
W: www.gwr.com/

Greater Anglia
11th Floor, One Stratford Place, Montfitchet Rd, London, E20 1EJ
T: 020 7904 4031
F: 020 7549 5999
E: contactcentre@greateranglia.co.uk
W: https://www.greateranglia.co.uk/

Green Leader Ltd
21 Foxmoor Close, Oakley, Basingstoke, Hants, RG23 7BQ
T: 01256 781739
E: nmoore@greenleader.co.uk
W: www.greenleader.co.uk

Green Light Signalling
1 Bedford Court, Bawtry, Doncaster, South Yorkshire, DN10 6RU

Greenbrier Europe/Wagony Swidnica SA
Ul Strzelinska 35, 58-100 Swidnica, Poland
T: 0048 74 856 2000
F: 0048 74 856 2035
E: europeansales@gbrx.com
W: www.gbrx.com

Greengauge 21
28 Lower Teddington Road, Kingston-upon-Thames, Surrey, KT1 4HJ
E: co-ordinator@greengauge21.net
W: www.greengauge21.net

GreenMech Ltd
The Mill Ind. Park, Kings Coughton, Alcester, Warks, B49 5QG
T: 01789 400044
F: 01789 400167
E: sales@greenmech.co.uk
W: www.greenmech.co.uk

Grimshaw Architects
57 Clerkenwell Rd, London, EC1M 5NG
T: 0207 291 4141
E: info@grimshaw-architects.com
W: www.grimshaw-architects.com

Grinsty Rail
Arrow Business Park, Shawbank Road, Lakeside, Redditch, Worcestershire, B98 8YN
T: 01527 514151
E: sales@grinstyrail.co.uk
W: www.grinstyrail.co.uk

GripDeck UK
Unit 1, Chancers Farm, Fossett Lane, Colchester, Essex, CO6 3NY
T: 01206 242494
F: 01206 242496
E: mail@gripdeck.co.uk
W: www.gripdeck.co.uk

Groeneveld Uk Ltd
The Greentec Centre, Gelders Hall Rd, Gelders hall Ind. Est, Shepshed, Leics, LE12 9NH
T: 01509 600033
F: 01509 602000
E: info-uk@groeneveld-group.com
W: www.groeneveld-group.com

Grontmij
Grove House, Mansion Gate Drive, Leeds, LS7 4DN
T: 0113 262 0000
F: 0113 262 0737
E: enquiries@grontmij.co.uk
W: www.grontmij.co.uk

Ground Control Ltd
1st Floor, Kingfisher House, Radford Way, Billericay, Essex, CM12 0EQ
T: 01277 650697
F: 01277 630746
E: info@ground-control.co.uk
W: www.ground-control.co.uk/

Groundwise Searches Ltd
Suite 8, Chichester House, 45 Chichester Rd, Southend on Sea, SS1 2JU
T: 01702 615566
F: 01702 460239
E: mail@groundwise.com
W: www.groundwise.com

GroupCytek
The Oast House, 5 Maed Lane, Farnham, Surrey, GU9 7DY
T: 01252 715171
F: 01252 713271
E: projects@groupcytek.com
W: www.groupcytek.com

GT Engineering (Markyate) Ltd
Unit 4, Pulloxhill Business Park, Greenfield Rd, Pulloxhill, MK45 5EU
T: 01525 718585
E: sales@gtengineering.co.uk
W: www.gtengineering.co.uk

Gummiwerk
See STRAIL (UK) Ltd

Gunnebo UK Ltd
PO Box 61, Woden Rd, Wolverhampton, WV10 0BY
T: 01902 455111
F: 01902 351961
E: marketing@gunnebo.com
W: www.gunnebo.com

Gutteridge, Haskins & Davey Ltd
See GHD Ltd (Gutteridge, Haskins & Davey Ltd)

G-volution
Trym Lodge, 1 Henbury Road, Bristol, BS9 3HQ
T: 0117 959 6470
F: 0845 052 9345
E: sales@g-volution.com
W: www.g-volution.co.uk

H&M Security Services
476-478 Larkshall Road, London, E4 9HH
T: 020 8523 2227
F: 020 8523 5595
E: info@hmsecurityservices.co.uk
W: www.hmsecurityservices.co.uk/

H.A. Marks Construction Ltd
T: 020 8659 6918
E: info@hamarks.com
W: www.hamarks.co.uk

h2gogo Ltd
The Heights, 59-65 Lowlands Rd, Harrow, Middx, HA1 3AW
T: 01494 817174
E: info@h2gogo.com
W: www.h2gogo.com

HackTrain powered by Hack Partners
Hack Partners, WeWork Old St, 41 Corsham Street, London, N1 6DR
E: hello@hackpartners.com
W: hacktrain.com/

HaCon (UK)
Luminous House, 300 South Row, Milton Keynes, MK9 2FR
T: 0845 835 8688
F: 0049 511 33699-99
E: info@hacon.de
W: www.hacon.de

Hadleigh Castings Ltd
Pond Hall Rd, Hadleigh, Ipswich, Suffolk, IP7 5PW
T: 01473 827281
F: 01473 827879
E: data@hadleighcastings.com
W: www.hadleighcastings.com

Hafren Security Fasteners
Unit 23, Mochdre Industrial Park, Newtown, Powys, SY16 4LE
T: 01686 621300
F: 01686 621800
E: security@hafrenfasteners.com
W: www.hafrenfasteners.com

Haigh Rail Ltd
Unit 35, Roundhouse Court, Barnes Wallis Way, Buckshaw Village, Chorley, Lancs, PR7 7JN
T: 01772 458000
E: chris@haighrail.com
W: www.haighrail.com

A W Hainsworth & Sons Ltd
See Replin Fabrics

Haki Ltd
Magnus, Tame Valley Ind. Est, Tamworth, Staffs, B77 5BY
T: 01827 282525
F: 01827 250329
E: info@haki.co.uk
W: www.haki.co.uk

Hako Machines Ltd
Eldon Close, Crick, Northants, NN6 7UD
T: 01788 825600
F: 01788 823969
E: sales@hako.co.uk
W: www.hako.co.uk

Halfen Ltd
A1/A2 Portland Close, Houghton Regis, Dunstable, Beds, LU5 5AW
T: 01582 470300
F: 01582 470304
E: info@halfen.co.uk
W: www.halfen.co.uk

HallRail
See Trackwork Ltd

Halo Rail
See Stewart Signs Rail

Hammond (ECS) Ltd
Canal Road, Cwmbach, Aberdare, CF44 0AG
T: 01685 884813
F: 01685 888187

Hanson Springs
Hanson Place, Gorrells Way, Rochdale, Lancs, OL11 2PX
T: 01706 510600
M: 07780 496290
E: sales@hanson-springs.co.uk
W: www.hanson-springs.co.uk/

Hardstaff Barriers
Hillside, Gotham Road, Kingston on Soar, Nottingham, NG11 0DF
T: 0115 983 2304
E: enquiries@hardstaffbarriers.com
W: www.hardstaffbarriers.com/

Harmill Systems Ltd
Unit P, Cherrycourt Way, Leighton Buzzard, Beds, LU7 4UH
T: 01525 851133
F: 01525 850661
E: david.flint@harmill.co.uk
W: www.harmill.co.uk

Harmonic Ltd
The Hatchery, Eaglewood Park, Ilminster, TA19 9DQ
T: 01460 256500
F: 01460 200037
W: www.harmonicltd.co.uk

Harp Visual Communications Solutions
Unit C4, Segensworth Business Centre, Segensworth Road, Fareham, Hants, PO15 5RQ
T: 01329 844005
E: sales@harpvisual.co.uk
W: www.passengerinformation.com

Harrington Generators International (HGI)
Ravenstor Rd, Wirksworth, Derbys, DE4 4FY
T: 01629 824284
F: 01629 824613
E: sales@hgigenerators.com
W: www.hgigenerators.com

Harry Fairclough Construction
Howley Lane, Howley, Warrington, Cheshire, WA1 2DN
T: 01925 628300
F: 01925 628325
E: post@harryfairclough.co.uk
W: www.harryfairclough.co.uk

Harry Needle Railroad Company
Barrow Hill Depot, Campbell Drive, Barrow Hill, Chesterfield, S43 2PR
T: 01246 477001
F: 01246 477208
E: info@hnrail.co.uk
W: www.hnrail.co.uk/

Harsco Rail Ltd
Unit 1, Chewton St, Eastwood, Notts, NG16 3HB
T: 01773 539480
F: 01773 539481
E: uksales@harsco.com
W: www.harscorail.com/

Harting Limited
Caswell Rd, Brackmills Ind. Est, Northampton, NN4 7PW
T: 01604 827500
F: 01604 706777
E: gb@harting.com
W: www.harting.co.uk

Harvard Engineering plc
Tyler Close, Normanton, Wakefield, West Yorks, WF6 1RL
T: 0113 383 1000
F: 0113 383 1010
E: johncharles@harvardeng.com
W: www.harvardeng.com

Haskoll
39 Harrington Gardens, London, SW7 4JU
T: 020 7835 1188
F: 020 7373 7230
W: www.haskoll.co.uk/

HaslerRail AG
Unit 6, Brookside Business Park, Chadderton, Manchester, M24 1GS
M: 07575 308330
E: michael.healy@haslerrail.com
W: www.haslerrail.com

Hawker Siddeley Switchgear ltd
Unit 3, Blackwood Ind. Estate, Newport Rd, Blackwood, S.Wales, NP12 2XH
T: 01495 223001
F: 01495 225674
E: nigel.jones@hss-ltd.com
W: www.hss-ltd.com

Hawkgrove Ltd
The Rural Enterprise Centre, The Showground, Shepton Mallet, Somerset, BA4 6QN
T: 01373 710777
E: mike.duberry@hawkgrove.co.uk
W: www.hawkgrove.co.uk

Hawkins\Brown
159 St John Street, London, EC1V 4QJ
T: 020 7336 8030
F: 020 7336 8851
E: mail@hawkinsbrown.com
W: www.hawkinsbrown.com/

Hawsons
Pegasus House, 463a Glossop Road, Sheffield, S10 2QD
T: 0114 266 7141
E: email@hawsons.co.uk
W: www.hawsons.co.uk/

Hayley Rail
48-50 Westbrook Rd, Trafford Park, Manchester, M17 1AY
T: 0161 872 7466
F: 0161 877 3005
E: phil.mccabe@hayley-group.co.uk
W: www.hayley-group.co.uk

Haywood and Jackson Fabrication
Denton Drive, Northwich, Cheshire, CW9 7LU
T: 01606 47777
F: 01606 41234
E: info@haywoodandjackson.co.uk
W: www.haywoodandjackson.co.uk/

HBM Test & Measurement
1 Churchill Court, 58 Station Rd, North Harrow, Middx, HA2 7SA
T: 020 8515 6000
F: 020 8515 6002
E: info@uk.hbm.com
W: www.hbm.com

Health, Safety & Engineering Consultants Ltd (HSEC)
70 Tamworth Rd, Ashby de la Zouch, Leics, LE65 2PR
T: 01530 412777
F: 01530 415592
E: hsec@hsec.co.uk
W: www.hsec.co.uk

Healthcare Connections Ltd
Nashleigh Court, 188 Severalls Ave, Chesham, Bucks, HP5 3EN
T: 08456 773002
F: 08456 773004
E: sales@healthcare-connections.com
W: www.healthcare-connections.com

Heat Trace Ltd
Mere's Edge, Chester Rd, Helsby, Frodsham, Cheshire, WA6 0DJ
T: 01928 726451
F: 01928 727846
E: neil.malone@heat-trace.com
W: www.heat-trace.com

Heathrow Connect
See Heathrow Express

Heathrow Express
The Compass Centre, Nelson Road, Hounslow, Middlesex, TW6 2GW
T: 0345 600 1515
W: www.heathrowexpress.com

Heathrow Hub Ltd
60-62, Old London Road, Kingston on Thames, KT2 6QZ
T: (0) 207 379 5151
E: heathrowhub@maitland.co.uk
W: www.heathrowhub.com

Heathrow Southern Railway
Connect House, 133-137 Alexandra Road, London, SW19 7JY
T: 01733 767244
W: heathrowrail.com/

Heavy Haul Power International GmbH
Steigerstrasse 9, 99096 Erfurt, Germany
T: 0049 361 43046714
F: 0049 361 2629971
E: richard.painter@hhpi.eu
W: www.hhpi.eu

Hedra
See Mouchel

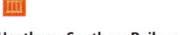

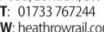

Hegenscheidt MFD GmbH & CO KG
Hegenscheidt Platz, D-41812 Erkelenz, Germany
T: 0049 2431 86279
F: 0049 2431 86480
E: info@niles-simmons.de
W: www.hegenscheidt-mfd.de

Heimda UK Ltdll
BCS House, Pinfold Road, Bourne, Lincolnshire, PE10 9HT
T: 0845 1801616
F: 01778 395265
M: 07854008955
E: rburchell@heimdalluk.co.il
W: www.heimdalluk.co.uk

Hellermann Tyton
Sharston Green Business Park, 1 Robeson Way, Altrincham Rd, Wythenshawe, Manchester, M22 4TY
T: 0161 947 2200
F: 0161 947 2220
E: sales@hellermanntyton.co.uk
W: www.hellermanntyton.co.uk

Henkel Loctite
Technologies House, Wood Lane End, Hemel Hempstead, Herts, HP2 4RQ
T: 01442 278100
F: 01442 278293
W: www.loctite.com

Henry Williams Ltd
Dodsworth St, Darlington, Co. Durham, DL1 2NJ
T: 01325 462722
F: 01325 245220
E: info@hwilliams.co.uk
W: www.hwilliams.co.uk

Hepworth Rail International
4 Merse Rd, North Moons Moat, Redditch, Worcs, B98 9HL
T: 01527 61243
F: 01527 66836
E: markjones@b-hepworth.com
W: www.b-hepworth.com

Hering UK LLP
Wessex House, Oxford Rd, Newbury, Berks, RG14 1PA
T: 01635 814490
F: 01635 814491
W: www.heringinternational.com

Herrenknecht AG
Schlehenweg 2, 77963 Schwanau, Germany
T: 0049 7824 3020
F: 0049 7824 3403
E: info@herrenknecht.com
W: www.herrenknecht.com

Hertford Controls Ltd
14 Ermine Point, Gentlemens Field, Westmill Rd, Ware, Herts, SG12 0EF
T: 01920 467578
F: 01920 487037
E: info@hertfordcontrols.co.uk
W: www.hertfordcontrols.co.uk

Hevertech
Unit 2, Treefield Industrial Estate, Gildersome, Leeds, LS27 7JU
T: 0113 238 3355
F: 0113 253 5443
E: enquiries@hevertech.co.uk
W: www.hevertech.co.uk/

Hexagon Metrology Ltd
Halesfield 13, Telford, Shropshire, TF7 4PL
T: 0870 446 2667
F: 0870 446 2668
E: enquiry.uk@hexagonmetrology.com
W: www.hexagonmetrology.com/uk

HFZ Consulting Ltd
8 Westbury Close, Bury, Lancs, BL8 2LW
E: aj@hfzconsulting.co.uk
W: www.hfzconsulting.co.uk

Hid Global

Hiflex Fluidpower
Howley Park Rd, Morley, Leeds, LS27 0BN
T: 0113 281 0031
F: 0113 307 5918
E: sales@hiflex-europe.com
W: www.dunlophiflex.com

High Speed 1 Ltd
See HS1 Ltd

High Speed 2 Ltd
See HS2 Ltd

High Voltage Maintenance Services Ltd
Unit A, Faraday Court, Faraday Rd, Crawley, West Sussex, RH10 9PU
T: 0845 604 0336
F: 01293 537739
E: enquiries@hvms.co.uk
W: www.hvms.co.uk

Highlands and Islands Transport Partnership (HITRANS)
2nd Floor, Rear, 7 Ardross Terrace, Inverness, IV3 5NQ
T: 01463 719002
E: info@hitrans.org.uk
W: https://www.hitrans.org.uk/

Hill Cannon (UK) LLP
Business Centre, Hartwith Way, Harrogate, HG3 2XA
T: 01423 813522
F: 01423 530018
E: harrogate@hillcannon.com
W: www.hillcannon.com

Hill McGlynn
See Ranstad CPE

Hilti (GB) Ltd
1 Trafford Wharf Rd, Trafford Park, Manchester, M17 1BY
T: 0800 886 100
F: 0800 886 200
E: gbsales@hilti.com
W: www.hilti.co.uk

HIMA
Albert-Bassermann-Str. 28, 68782 Bruehl, Germany
T: +49 06202 709-405
E: d.plaga@hima.com
W: www.hima.de

Hird Rail Services Ltd
Head Office & Factory, Barton Lane, Armthorpe, Doncaster, DN3 3AB
T: 01302 831339
F: 01302 300031
E: info@hirds.co.uk
W: www.hirdrail.com/

Hire Station
Fields Farm Road, Long Eaton, Nottingham, NG10 3FZ
T: 0845 604 5337
F: 0845 668 8999
W: www.hirestation.co.uk/

Hiremasters
See Quickbuild (UK) Ltd

Hitachi ABB Power Grids
Wells House, 65 Boundary Road, Woking, Surrey, GU21 5BS
T: 01483 722777
E: power-grids@hitachi-powergrids.com
W: https://www.hitachiabb-powergrids.com/

Hitachi Capital Vehicle Solutions Ltd
Kiln House, Kiln Rd, Newbury, Berks, RG14 2NU
T: 01635 574640
W: www.hitachicapitalvehiclesolutions.co.uk

Hitachi Information Control Systems Europe
Manvers House, Kingston Rd, Bradford-on-Avon, Wilts, BA15 1AB
T: 01225 860140
F: 01225 867698
E: contact_us@hitachi-infocon.com
W: www.hitachi-infocon.com/

Hitachi Rail Ltd
7th Floor, 1 New Ludgate, 60 Ludgate Hill, London, EC4M 7AW
T: 020 3904 4000
F: 020 7970 2799
E: rail.enquiries@hitachirail-eu.com
W: www.hitachirail-eu.com

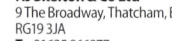

HJ Skelton & Co Ltd
9 The Broadway, Thatcham, Berks, RG19 3JA
T: 01635 866877
E: email@hjskelton.com
W: www.hjskelton.co.uk

HOCHTIEF (UK) Construction Ltd
Epsilon, Windmill Hill Business Park, Whitehill Way, Swindon, Wilts, SN5 6NX
T: 01793 755555
F: 01793 755556
E: enquiries@hochtief.co.uk
W: www.hochtief-construction.co.uk/

Hodge Clemco Ltd
36 Orgreave Drive, Handsworth, Sheffield, South Yorks, S13 9NR
T: 0114 254 8811
F: 0114 254 0250
E: sales@hodgeclemco.co.uk
W: www.hodgeclemco.co.uk

Hodgson & Hodgson Group Ltd
Crown Business Park, Old Dalby, Melton Mowbray, Leics, LE14 3NQ
T: 01664 821810
F: 01664 821820
E: info@hodgsongroup.co.uk
W: www.acoustic.co.uk/h&h/rail.htm

Hogia Transport Systems Ltd
St James House, 13 Kensington Square, London, W8 5HD
T: 020 7795 8156
E: gary.umpleby@hogia.com
W: www.hogia.com/transport

HOK International Ltd
Qube, 90 Whitfield St, London, W1T 4EZ
T: 020 7636 2006
F: 020 7636 1987
E: robyn.gilmour@hok.com
W: www.hok.com

Holdfast Level Crossings Ltd
Brockenhurst, Cheap St, Chegworth, Cheltenham, Glos, GL54 4AA
T: 01242 578801
F: 01285 720748
E: request@railcrossings.co.uk
W: www.railcrossings.co.uk

Holdtrade UK
No. 1, The Rubicon, 51 Norman Road, Greenwich, London, SE10 9QB
T: 020 8293 5999
F: 020 8293 7123
E: holdtrade@holdtrade.co.uk
W: www.holdtrade.co.uk/

Holland Company
1000 Holland Drive, Crete, Illinois, 60417 USA, United States
T: 001 708 672 2300
F: 001 708 672 0119
E: sales@hollandco.com
W: www.hollandco.com

Holmar Rail Services
Kendal House, The Street, Shadoxhurst, Ashford, Kent, TN26 1LU
T: 01233 731007
F: 01233 733221
W: www.holmar.co.uk

Holmatro Group
Lissenveld 30, P.O. Box 66, 4940 AB, Raamsdonksveer, Netherlands
T: +31 (0) 162 751 480
E: info@holmatro.com
W: www.holmatro.com/

Holophane Rail Solutions
Bond Avenue, Bletchley, Milton Keynes, Bucks, MK1 1JG
T: 01908 649292
F: 01908 367618
E: info@holophane.co.uk
W: www.holophane.co.uk

Homegrown Timber (Rail) Ltd
Courtlands, Antlands Lane, Shipley Br, Surrey, RH6 9TE
T: 01293 821321
F: 01293 772319
E: rail@homegrowntimber.com
W: www.homegrowntimber.com

Hook-up Solutions Ltd (Hooka)
Unit 1, Royston Road, Baldock, Herts, SG7 6PA
T: 01462 499642
M: 07788 594796
E: charles.sterling@hookup-solutions.com
W: www.thehooka.co.uk

Hoppecke Industrial Batteries Ltd
Unit 2, Centre 500, Lowfield Drive, Wolstanton, Newcastle-under-Lyme, Staffs, ST5 0UU
T: 01782 667306
F: 01782 667314
E: sales@hoppecke.co.uk
W: www.hoppecke.co.uk

Horizon Utility Supplies Ltd
Unit 1, Windmill Business Park, Windmill Road, Clevedon, North Somerset, BS21 6SR
T: 01275 342700
E: enquiries@hor-i-zon.com
W: www.horizonutilitysupplies.com

Hosiden Besson Ltd
11 St Josephs Close, Hove, East Sussex, BN3 7EZ
T: 01273 861166
F: 01273 777501
E: info@hbl.co.uk
W: www.hbl.co.uk

Houghton International
Ronnie Mitten Works, Shields Road, Newcastle upon Tyne, NE6 2YL
T: 0191 234 3000
E: info@houghton-international.com
W: www.houghton-international.com

House of Commons Transport Commitee
7th Floor, 14 Tothill Street, House of Commons, London, SW1H 9NB
T: 020 7219 3266
E: transcom@parliament.uk
W: www.parliament.uk/business/committees/committees-a-z/commons-select/transport-committee

Howarth & Co Consultancy Ltd
39 Ordnance Hill, St John's Wood, London, NW8 6PS
T: 020 7586 5770
F: 020 7586 6556
W: www.howarthandco.com

Howells Railway Products Ltd
Longley Lane, Sharston Ind. Est., Wythenshawe, Manchester, M22 4SS
T: 0161 945 5567
F: 0161 945 5597
E: info@howells-railway.co.uk
W: www.howells-railway.co.uk

HP Information Security
3200 Daresbury Park, Daresbury, Warrington, WA4 4BU
T: 01925 665500
F: 01925 667200
E: salessupport.infosec@hp.com
W: www.hp.com

HPR Consult
See Rendel Limited

HR Kilns Ltd
Unit 5 & 7, Gorsey Place, Gillibrands, Skelmersdale, Lancs, WN8 9UP
T: 01695 557711
E: sales@hrkilns.com
W: www.hrfibreglass.co.uk/

HRD Rail Fabrications
3 Acorn Business Centre, Northarbour Road, Portsmouth, PO6 3TH

HS Carlsteel Engineering Ltd
Crabtree Manorway South, Belvedere, Kent, DA17 6BH
T: 020 8312 1879
F: 020 8320 9480
E: sales@hscarlsteel.co.uk
W: www.hscarlsteel.co.uk

HS1 Ltd
5th Floor, Kings Place, 90 York Way, London, N1 9AG
T: 020 7014 2700
E: wendy.spinks@highspeed1.co.uk
W: https://highspeed1.co.uk/

HS2 Ltd
One Canada Square, London, E14 5AB
T: 020 7944 4908
E: hs2enquiries@hs2.org.uk
W: www.hs2.org.uk

HSBC Rail (UK)
See Eversholt Rail (UK) Ltd

HSS Training Ltd
Circle House, Lostock Rd, Davyhulme, Manchester, M41 0HS
T: 0845 766 7799
F: 0161 877 9074
E: training@hss.com
W: www.hsstraining.com

Huber + Suhner (UK) Ltd
Telford Rd, Bicester, Oxon, OX26 4LA
T: 01869 364100
F: 01869 249046
E: info.uk@hubersuhner.com
W: www.hubersuhner.co.uk

Hull Trains
Europa House, 184 Ferensway, Hull, HU1 3UT
T: 03456 769 905
E: customer.services@hulltrains.co.uk
W: www.hulltrains.co.uk

Human Reliability
1 School House, Higher Lane, Dalton, Lancs, WN8 7RP
T: 01257 463121
F: 01257 463810
E: dembrey@humanreliabilty.com
W: www.humanreliability.com

Hunslet Barclay
See Brush Barclay

Hunslet Engine Co
See LH Group Services

John F Hunt
London Road, Grays, Essex, RM20 4DB
T: 01375 366700
W: www.johnfhunt.co.uk

HurleyPalmerFlatt
NWS House, 1e High Street, Purley, Surrey, CR8 2AF
T: 020 8763 5900
W: www.hurleypalmerflatt.com/

Husqvarna Construction Products
Unit 4, Pearce Way, Bristol Rd, Gloucester, GL2 5YD
T: 0844 844 4570
E: husqvarna.construction@husqvarna.co.uk
W: www.husqvarna.co.uk

Hutchinson Team Telecom Ltd
See Indigo Telecom Group

HV Wooding Ltd
Range Rd Industrial Estate, Hythe, Kent, CT21 6HG
T: 01303 264471
F: 01303 262408
E: sales@hvwooding.co.uk
W: www.hvwooding.co.uk

HW Martin (Fencing Contractors) Ltd
Fordbridge Lane, Blackwell, Alfreton, Derbys, DE55 5JY
T: 01773 813214
F: 01773 813339
E: fencing@hwmartin.com
W: www.hwmartin.com

Hyder Consulting (UK) Ltd
Manning House, 22 Carlisle Place, London, SW1P 1JA
T: 020 3014 9000
F: 020 7828 8428
E: mahmoud.alghita@hyderconsulting.com
W: www.hyderconsulting.com

HydraPower Dynamics Ltd
St Marks Street, Birmingham, B1 2UN
T: 0121 4565 656
F: 0121 4565 668
E: info@hdl.uk.net
W: www.hydrapower-dynamics.com

Hydraulic Pumps (UK) Ltd
Summit 2, Mangham Rd, Barbot Hill Ind. Est, Rotherham, S61 4RJ
T: 01709 360370
F: 01709 372913
E: sales@hydraulicpumps.co.uk
W: www.hydraulicpumps.co.uk

Hydrex Equipment UK Ltd
See TXM Plant Ltd

Hydrotech Europe Ltd
Beaufort Court, 11 Roebuck Way, Knowlhill, Milton Keynes, MK5 8HL
T: 01908 675244
F: 01908 397513
E: enquiries@hydro-usl.com
W: www.hydro-usl.com

Hydrotechnik UK Ltd
1 Central Park, Lenton Lane, Nottingham, NG7 2NR
T: 01159 003550
F: 01159 868875
E: sales@hydrotechnik.co.uk
W: www.hydrotechnik.co.uk

Hyperdrive Innovation
Future Technology Centre, Barmston Court, Nissan Way, Sunderland, Tyne and Wear, SR5 3NY
T: 0191 640 4586
E: info@hyperdriveinnovation.com
W: https://hyperdriveinnovation.com

Hypertac UK
36-38 Waterloo Rd, London, NW2 7UH
T: 020 8450 8033
F: 020 8208 4114
E: info@hypertac.co.uk
W: www.hypertac.com

I C Consultants Ltd
58 Prince's Gate, Exhibition Rd, London, SW7 2QA
T: 020 7594 6565
F: 020 7594 6570
E: consultants@imperial.ac.uk
W: www.imperial-consultants.co.uk

IAD Rail Systems
See Network Rail Infrastructure Ltd

Ian Catling Consultancy
Ash Meadow, Bridge Way, Chipstead, CR5 3PX
T: 01737 552225
F: 01737 556669
E: ic@catling.com
W: www.catling.com

Ian Riley
See Riley & Son (E) Ltd

IBI Group (UK) Ltd
One Didsbury Point, 2 The Avenue, Didsbury, Manchester, M20 2EY
T: 0161 696 4980
F: 0844 7440 5012
E: ukandirelandcontactus@ibigroup.com
W: www.ibigroup.com

ICEE
20 Arnside Rd, Waterlooville, Hants, PO7 7UP
T: 02392 230604
F: 02392 230605
E: sales@icee.co.uk
W: www.icee.co.uk

Icomera UK
2nd Floor, Victory House, Quayside, Chatham Maritime, Chatham, Kent, ME4 4QU
T: 0870 446 0461
E: sales@icomera.com
W: www.icomera.com

Icon Silentbloc UK Ltd
Wellington Rd, Burton upon Trent, Staffs, DE14 2AP
T: 01283 741741
F: 01283 741742
E: silentblocinfo@iconpolymer.com
W: www.iconpolymer.com

ID Computing Ltd
Marble Hall, 80 Nightingale Road, Derby, DE24 8BF
M: 07734 602800
E: info@idcomputing.co.uk
W: www.idcomputing.co.uk

Ideagen
Ergo House, Mere Way, Ruddington Fields Business Park, Nottinghamshire, NG11 6JS
T: 01629 699100
W: www.ideagen.com/

Ideas Limited (Integration Design Ergonomics Applications Solutions)
PO Box 193, Thame, Oxon, OX9 0BR
T: 01844 216896
F: 0970 460 6190
E: info@ideas.ltd.uk
W: www.ideas.ltd.uk

IET
See Institution of Engineering & Technology

IETG Ltd
Cross Green Way, Cross Green Ind. Est., Leeds, LS9 0SE
T: 0113 201 9700
F: 0113 201 9701
E: ietg.info@idexcorp.com
W: www.ietg.co.uk

IFE (Innovation for Entrance Systems)
See Knorr-Bremse Rail UK

IFPL
Elm Lane, Calbourne, Newport, Isle of Wight, PO30 4JY
T: 01983 555990
F: 01983 531608
E: enquiries@ifpl.com
W: www.ifpl.com/

igus UK
Caswell Road, Northampton, NN4 7PW
T: 01604 677240
F: 01604 677242
E: sales@igus.co.uk
W: www.igus.co.uk/

iGuzzini Illuminazione UK Ltd
Astolat Business Park, Astolat Way, off Old Portsmouth Rd, Guildford, GU3 1NE
T: 01483 468000
F: 01483 468001
E: info@iguzzini.co.uk
W: www.iguzzini.co.uk

Ilecsys
Unit 4B, Tring Ind. Est, Upper Icknield Way, Tring, Herts, HP23 4JX
T: 01442 828387
F: 01442 828399
E: sales@ilecsysrail.co.uk
W: www.ilecsysrail.co.uk

iLine Technologies Ltd/ Channeline International
KG House, Kingsfield Way, Northampton, NN5 7QS
T: 01443 743402
E: hello@i-group.uk.com
W: www.iline.uk.com/

ILME UK Ltd
50 Evans Rd, Venture Point, Speke, Merseyside, L24 9PB
T: 0151 336 9321
F: 0151 336 9326
E: sales@ilmeuk.co.uk
W: www.ilmeuk.co.uk

IM Kelly Rail
Home Farm Business Park, Church Way, Whittlebury, Northants, NN12 8XS
T: 01327 855678
F: 01327 855510
E: keithgriffiths@imkellyrail.co.uk
W: www.imkelly.co.uk/

Imagerail
Reservoir House, Wetheral Pasture, Carlisle, CA4 8HR
T: 01768 800208
E: andrew@imagerail.com
W: www.imagerail.com

Imetrum Ltd
Unit 4, Farleigh Court, Old Weston Road, Flax Bourton, Bristol, BS48 1UR
T: 01275 464443
E: sales@imetrum.com
W: www.imetrum.com/

IMI Precision Engineering
Blenheim Way, Fradley Park, Lichfield, Staffordshire, WS13 8SY
T: 01543 265000
E: advantage@imi-precision.com
W: www.imi-precision.com/

Impact Reporting
2nd Floor, 24-26 Lever St, Manchester, M1 1DW
T: 0161 660 7949
W: impactreporting.co.uk/

Impreglon UK Limited
Kingsbury Link, Trinity Road, Piccadilly, Tamworth, West Midlands, B78 2EX
T: 01827 871400
F: 01827 871401
E: info@impreglon.co.uk
W: https://www.impreglon.co.uk/

Imtech Traffic & Infra UK Ltd
Hazlewood House, Limetree Way, Chineham Business Park, Basingstoke, RG24 8WZ
T: 01256 891800
F: 01256 891870
E: info@imtech.uk.com
W: www.imtech.uk.com

In2rail Ltd
Hobbs Hill, Rothwell, Northants, NN14 6YG
F: 01536 711804
E: pm@in2rail.co.uk
W: www.in2rail.co.uk

Inabensa
1 Lyric Square, London, W6 0NB
T: 0203 5427832
W: www.inabensa.com/web/en/

Inbis Ltd
Club St, Bamber Bridge, Preston, Lancs, PR5 6FN
T: 01772 645000
F: 01772 645001
W: www.inbis.com

Inchmere Design
Swan Close Studios, Swan Close Way, Banbury, Oxon, OX16 5TE
T: 01295 661000
F: 01295 277939
E: mark@inchmere.co.uk
W: www.inchmere.co.uk

Incorporatewear
Edison Rd, Hams Hall National Distribution Park, Coleshill, B46 1DA
T: 0844 257 0530
F: 0844 257 0591
E: info@incorporatewear.co.uk
W: www.incorporatewear.co.uk

Incremental Solutions
York Science Park, Innovation Centre, Innovation Way, York, YO10 5DG
T: 01904 435100
E: contact@incrementalsolutions.co.uk
W: www.incrementalsolutions.co.uk/

Independent Glass Co Ltd
540-550 Lawmoor St, Dixons Blazes Ind. Est, Glasgow, G5 0UA
T: 0141 429 8700
F: 0141 429 8524
E: toughened@ig-glass.co.uk
W: www.independentglass.co.uk

Independent Rail Consultancy Group (IRCG)
E: info@ircg.co.uk
W: www.ircg.co.uk

Independent Transport Commission (ITC)
70 Cowcross Street, London, EC1M 6EJ
T: 0207 253 5510
E: independenttransportcommission@gmail.com
W: www.theitc.org.uk/

Indigo
Oak House, Reeds Cres, Watford, Herts, WD24 4QP
T: 01908 223500
F: 01923 231914
E: info@vincipark.co.uk
W: www.vincipark.co.uk

Indigo Telecom Group
Field House, Uttoxeter Old Rd, Derby, DE1 1NH
T: 01332 375570
F: 01332 375673
E: sales@indigotelecomgroup.com
W: www.indigotelecomgroup.com

Industrial Communication Products
The Angel Business Centre, 1 Luton Road, Toddington, Bedfordshire, LU5 6DE
T: 020 3086 9569
F: 020 3002 5648
E: sales@industrialcomms.com
W: www.industrialcomms.co.uk/

Industrial Door Services Ltd
Adelaide St, Crindau Park, Newport, Gwent, NP20 5NF
T: 01633 853335
F: 01633 851989
E: enquiries@indoorserv.co.uk
W: www.indoorserv.co.uk

Industrial Flow Control Ltd
3 Ryder Way, Basildon, Essex, RM17 5XR
T: 01268 596900
F: 01268 728435
E: sales@inflow.co.uk
W: www.inflow.co.uk

Ineco
Southern Cross, Bramble Bill, Balcombe, Haywards Heath, RH17 6HR
T: 01444 811090
E: sergio.navarro@ineco.com
W: www.ineco.com/webineco/en

Inflow
See Industrial Flow Control Ltd

Infodev EDI Inc.
1995 Rue Frank-Carrel, Suite 202, Quebec G1N 4H9, Canada
T: 001 418 681 3539
F: 001 418 681 1209
E: info@infodev.ca
W: www.infodev.ca

Infor
1 Lakeside Rd, Farnborough, Hants, GU14 6XP
T: 0800 376 9633
F: 0121 615 8255
E: ukmarketing@infor.com
W: www.infor.co.uk

informatica Software Ltd
6 Waltham Park, Waltham Rd, White Waltham, Maidenhead, Berks, SL6 3JN
T: 01628 511311
F: 01628 511411
E: ukinfo@informatica.com
W: www.informatica.com

Informatiq
Gresham House, 53 Clarendon Rd, Watford, WD17 1LA
T: 01923 224481
F: 01923 224493
E: permanent@informatiq.co.uk
W: www.informatiq.co.uk

DIRECTORY

Infotec Ltd
The Maltings, Tamworth Rd, Ashby De La Zouch, Leics, LE65 2PS
T: 01530 560600
F: 01530 560111
E: sales@infotec.co.uk
W: www.infotec.co.uk

Infra Safety Services
See ISS Labour

Infrastructure Measurement Solutions Ltd
22 Mallard Way, Pride Park, Derby, DE24 8GX
E: info@bumpbox.eu
W: www.bumpbox.eu/

Infrata
One Fetter Lane, London, EC4A 1BR
T: 020 3440 5920
E: info@infrata.com
W: www.infrata.com/

Ingersoll Engineers
1 Northumberland Avenue, Trafalgar Square, London, WC2N 5BW
T: 020 7872 5666
E: info@ingersollengineersuk.com
W: www.ingersollengineersuk.com/

INIT Innovations in Transportation Ltd
49 Stoney St, The Lace Market, Nottingham, NG1 1LX
T: 0870 890 4648
F: 0115 989 5461
W: www.init.co.uk

Initiate Consulting Ltd
Edinburgh House, 40 Great Portland Street, London, W1W 7LZ
T: 020 7357 9600
F: 020 7357 9604
E: info@initiate.uk.com
W: www.initiate.uk.com

Inline Track Welding Ltd
Ashmill Business Park, Ashford Rd, Lenham, Maidstone, ME17 2GQ
T: 01622 854730
F: 01622 854731
E: david.thomson@fsmail.net

InnoTrans
Messe Berlin GmbH, Messedamm 22, D-14055 Berlin, Germany
T: 0049 303038 0
F: 0049 303038 2325
E: innotrans@messe-berlin.de
W: www.innotrans.com

Innovative Railway Safety Ltd
Ty Penmynydd, Llangennith, Swansea, SA3 1DT
M: 07974 065798
E: paul@inrailsafe.co.uk
W: www.inrailsafe.co.uk

Innovative Support Systems Ltd (ISS)
15 Fountain Parade, Mapplewell, Barnsley, S Yorks, S75 6FW
T: 01226 381155
F: 01226 381177
E: enquiries@iss-eng.com
W: www.iss-eng.com

The Input Group
Input House, 101 Ashbourne Road, Derby, DE22 3FW
T: 01332 348830
F: 01332 296342
E: info@inputgroup.co.uk
W: www.inputgroup.co.uk

Inside Out Group (Europe) Limited
190 North Gate, Nottingham, NG7 7FT
T: 0115 979 1719
E: info@insideoutgroup.co.uk
W: www.insideoutgroup.co.uk/

Insight Security
Units 1 & 2, Cliffe Ind. Est, South Street, Lewes, E Sussex, BN8 6JL
T: 01273 475500
F: 01273 478800
E: info@insight-security.com
W: www.insight-security.com

Insituform Technologies Ltd
4-8 Brunel Close, Park Farm Industrial Estate, Wellingborough, Northants, NN8 6QX
T: 01933 670500
F: 01933 689249
E: jwatson@insituform.com
W: www.insituform.co.uk

Inspectahire Instrument Co. Ltd
Unit 11, Whitemyres Business Centre, Whitemyres Ave, Aberdeen, AB16 6HQ
T: 01224 789692
F: 01224 789462
E: enquiries@inspectahire.com
W: www.inspectahire.com

Install CCTV Ltd
10 Rochester Court, Anthonys Way, Rochester, Kent, ME2 4NW
T: 01634 717784
F: 01634 718085
W: www.installcctv.co.uk

Installation Project Services Ltd
53 Ullswater Crescent, Coulsdon, Surrey, CR5 2HR
T: 020 8655 6060
F: 020 8655 6070
E: sales@ips-ltd.co.uk
W: www.ips-ltd.co.uk

Institute of Rail Welding
Granta Park, Great Abington, Cambridge, CB21 6AL
T: 01223 899000
E: iorw@twi.co.uk
W: www.iorw.org

Institute of Railway Research
University of Huddersfield, Queensgate, Huddersfield, HD1 3DH
T: 01484 472030
E: irr.info@hud.ac.uk
W: www.hud.ac.uk/irr

Institute Of Transport Studies, University Of Leeds
34-40 University Road, University of Leeds, Leeds, LS2 9JT
T: 0113 343 5325
F: 0113 343 5334
W: www.its.leeds.ac.uk

Institution of Civil Engineers (ICE)
One Great George St, Westminster, London, SW1P 3AA
T: 020 7222 7722
E: communications@ice.org.uk
W: www.ice.org.uk

Institution of Engineering & Technology
Michael Faraday House, Six Hills Way, Stevenage, Herts, SG1 2AY
T: 01438 313111
F: 01438 765526
E: postmaster@theiet.org
W: www.theiet.org

Institution of Mechanical Engineers (IMechE)
1 Birdcage Walk, Westminster, London, SW1H 9JJ
T: 020 7222 7899
F: 020 7222 4557
E: railway@imeche.org.uk
W: www.imeche.org/

Institution of Railway Operators (IRO)
The Moat House, 133 Newport Rd, Stafford, ST16 2EZ
T: 03333 440523
E: info@railwayoperators.co.uk
W: www.railwayoperators.co.uk

Institution of Railway Signal Engineers (IRSE)
4th Floor, 1 Birdcage Walk, Westminster, London, SW1H 9JJ
T: 020 7808 1180
F: 020 7808 1196
E: hq@irse.org
W: www.irse.org

Instrumentel Ltd
Leeds Innovation Centre, 103 Clarendon Road, Leeds, LS2 9DF
T: 0113 346 6223
E: enquiries@instrumentel.com
W: www.instrumentel.com/

Intamech Ltd
See Arbil Lifting Gear

Intec (UK) Ltd
York House, 76-78 Lancaster Rd, Morecambe, Lancs, LA4 5QN
T: 01524 426777
F: 01524 426888
E: intec@inteconline.co.uk
W: www.inteconline.co.uk

Integrated Transport Planning Ltd
50 North Thirtieth St, Milton Keynes, MK9 3PP
T: 01908 259718
F: 01908 605747
E: wheway@itpworld.net
W: www.itpworld.net

Integrated Utility Services
Unit 8, Brindley Way, 41 Industrial Estate,
Wakefield, West Yorks, WF2 0XQ
T: 0800 0737373
E: enquiries@ius.co.uk
W: www.ius.co.uk

Integrated Water Services Ltd
Green Lane, Walsall, WS2 7PD
T: 01543 445700
F: 01543 445717
E: contact@integrated-water.co.uk
W: www.integrated-water.co.uk

Intelligent Data Collection Ltd
4 Pocketts Yard, Cookham, Berks, SL6 9SL
T: 0845 003 8747
E: info@intelligent-data-collection.com
W: www.intelligent-data-collection.com

Intelligent Glass Protection (IGP)
16 Hillbottom Rd, High Wycombe, Bucks, HP12 4HJ
T: 0800 448 8855
F: 01494 462675
E: sales@igpsolutions.com
W: www.igpsolutions.com

Intelligent Locking Systems
Bordesley Hall, Alvechurch, Birmingham, B48 7QA
T: 01527 68885
F: 01527 66681
E: info@ilslocks.co.uk
W: www.ilslocks.co.uk

InterCity RailFreight
T: 0845 125 9659
E: info@intercityrailfreight.com
W: intercityrailfreight.com/

Interface Fabrics Ltd
See Camira Fabrics Ltd

Interfaces
2 Valley Close, Hertford, SG13 8BD
T: 01992 422042
E: reg.harman@ntlworld.com

Intermodal Logistics
Cedar House, Glade Rd, Marlow, Bucks, SL7 1DQ
T: 01234 822821
F: 01628 486800
E: derekbliss@intermodallogistics.co.uk
W: www.intermodallogistics.co.uk

Intermodality Ltd
Owlsbrook House, New Pond Lane, Heathfield, East Sussex, TN21 0NA
T: 0845 130 4388
F: 01435 867637
E: info@intermodality.com
W: www.intermodality.com

International Engineering
314 W. Pitkin Ave, Pueblo, Colorado 81004, United States
E: info@i-engr.com
W: www.i-engr.com/

International Institute of Obsolescence Management (IIOM)
Unit 3,, Curo Park, Frogmore, St Albans, Herts, AL2 2DD
T: 01727 876029
E: admin@theiiom.org
W: www.theiiom.org

International Rail
PO Box 153, Alresford, Hants, SO24 4AQ
T: 0871 231 0790
F: 0871 231 0791
E: sales@internationalrail.com
W: www.internationalrail.com

International Transport Intermediaries Club Ltd
See ITIC

Interserve plc
Interserve House, Ruscombe Park, Twyford, Berks, RG10 9JU
T: 0118 932 0123
F: 0118 932 0206
E: info@interserve.com
W: www.interserve.com

Intertek NDT
Unit 10A, Victory Park, Victory Road, Derby, DE24 8ZF
T: 01332 275700
F: 01332 275729
E: sales@ndtservices.co.uk
W: www.ndtservices.co.uk/

Intertrain (UK) Ltd
Intertrain House, Union St, Doncaster, DN1 3AE
T: 01302 815530
F: 01302 815531
E: intertraininfo@intertrain.biz
W: www.intertrain.biz

Intuitive Interim & Executive Search
22 Top o'th Lane, Brindle, Chorley, Lancashire, PR6 8PA
M: 07801 995094
E: nina.lockwood@intuitiverecruitment.com
W: www.intuitiverecruitment.com

Invensys Rail Ltd
See Siemens Rail Automation

Invertec Interiors Ltd
Trimdon Grange Industrial Estate, Trimdon Grange, County Durham, TS29 6PE
T: 01429 882210
E: sales@invertec.co.uk
W: www.invertec.co.uk

Instrumentel is a world leading manufacturer of electronics systems for Condition Based Maintenance and precision measurement in extreme environments.

Technology & Products Solutions

instrumentel
MEASURING SUCCESS

Ionbond Ltd
Unit 36, Number One Ind Est, Medomsley Rd, Consett, Co Durham, DH8 6TS
T: 01207 500823
F: 01207 590254
E: maria.beadle@ionbond.com
W: www.ionbond.com

Iosis Associates
15 Good Shepherd Close, Bishop Rd, Bristol, BS7 8NF
T: 0117 370 6313
M: 07910 519247
E: pwt@iosis.org.uk
W: www.iosis.org.uk

Ipex Consulting Ltd
1 Lower John Street, Soho, London, W1F 9DT
T: 01954 230854
E: info@ipexconsulting.com
W: www.ipexconsulting.com

IPPR
4th Floor, 14 Buckingham Street, London, WC2N 6DF
T: 020 7470 6100
F: 020 7470 6111
W: www.ippr.org/

IQM Software
Unit 2, Hove Technology Centre, St Josephs Close, Hove, East Sussex, BN3 7ES
T: 01293 226136
M: 07841 902760
E: martyn.mccormack@iqmsoftware.co.uk
W: www.iqmsoftware.co.uk

IQPC
129 Wilton Road, London, SW1V 1JZ
T: 020 7368 9300
F: 020 7368 9301
E: enquire@iqpc.co.uk
W: www.iqpc.co.uk

Iridium Onboard
Clue House, Petherton Rd, Hengrove, Bristol, BS14 9BZ
T: 01275 890140
W: www.iridiumonboard.com

iris-GMBH
Ostendstraße 1-14, Berlin, 12459, Germany
E: mail@irisgmbh.de
W: www.irisgmbh.de

Irish Traction Group
31 Hayfield Rd, Bredbury, Stockport, SK6 1DE
E: info@irishtractiongroup.com
W: www.irishtractiongroup.com

IRL Group Ltd
Unit C1, Swingbridge Rd, Loughborough, Leics, LE11 5JD
T: 01509 217101
F: 01509 611004
E: info@irlgroup.com
W: www.irlgroup.com

Ironside Farrar
111
McDonald Rd, Edinburgh, EH7 4NW
T: 0131 550 6500
E: mail@ironsidefarrar.com
W: www.ironsidefarrar.com

Irvine-Whitlock
Brickstone House, Priory Business Park, Bedford, MK44 3JW
T: 01234 832300
F: 01234 832400
W: www.irvine-whitlock.co.uk/en

ISC
Best Practice Consultancy Ltd
Lower Market Hall Offices, Market St, Okehampton, Devon, EX20 1HN
T: 01837 54555
E: isc@ischq.com
W: www.isc-bestpractice consultancy.co.uk

Ischebeck Titan
John Dean House, Wellington Rd, Burton upon Trent, Staffordshire, DE14 2TG
T: 01283 515677
F: 01283 516126
E: sales@ischebeck-titan.co.uk
W: www.ischebeck-titan.co.uk

ISEEU Global Limited
Kingsbury Square, Melksham, Wiltshire, SN12 6HL
T: 07003941006
E: mike.roberts@iseeuglobal.com
W: www.iseeurail.com

IS-Rayfast Ltd
2 Lydiard Fields, Great Western Way, Swindon, Wilts, SN5 8UB
T: 01793 616700
F: 01793 644304
E: sales@israyfast.com
W: www.israyfast.com

ISS Labour
Unit 5, Sidney Robinson Business Park, Ascot Drive, Derby, DE24 8EH
T: 01332 37082
E: info@isslabour.co.uk
W: www.isslabour.co.uk

ITAL Group Ltd
Unit 2-3, Ridgeway Office Park, Bedford Road, Petersfield, Hampshire, GU32 3QF
T: 0844 544 7449
E: info@ital-uk.com
W: www.ital-uk.com/

ITIC
90 Fenchurch St, London, EC3M 4ST
T: 020 7338 0150
F: 020 7338 0151
E: itic@thomasmiller.com
W: www.itic-insure.com

itmsoil Group Ltd
Bell Lane, Uckfield, E Sussex, TN22 1QL
T: 01825 765044
F: 01825 744398
E: sales@itmsoil.com
W: www.itmsoil.com

ITS United Kingdom
Suite 312, Tower Bridge Business Centre, 46-48 East Smithfield, London, E1W 1AW
T: 020 7709 3003
F: 020 7709 3007
E: mailbox@its-uk.org.uk
W: www.its-uk.org.uk

ITSO Ltd
Aurora House, Deltic Ave, Milton Keynes, MK13 8LW
T: 01908 255455
F: 01908 255450
E: info@itso.org.uk
W: www.itso.org.uk

ITT Water & Wastewater UK Ltd
Colwick, Nottingham, NG4 2AN
T: 0115 940 0111
F: 0115 940 0444
W: www.itwww.co.uk

IXC UK Ltd
Innovation Birmingham Campus, Faraday Wharf, Holt St, Birmimgham, B7 4BB
T: 0121 250 5717
E: connect@ixc-uk.com
W: www.ixc-uk.com

Ixthus Instrumentation Limited
The Stables, Williams Barns, Tiffield Road, Towcester, Northants, NN12 6JR
T: 01327 353437
F: 01327 353564
E: info@ixthus.co.uk
W: www.ixthus.co.uk

J.Boyle Associates Ltd
Bunch Meadows, Woodway, Princes Risborough, Bucks, HP27 0NW
F: 0870 460244
E: info@jba.uk.net
W: www.jba.uk.net

Jabero Consulting Ltd
22 Church Rd, Tunbridge Wells, TN1 1JP
T: 01892 535730
W: www.jaberoconsulting.com

Jacobs Consultancy UK Ltd
See LeighFisher

Jacobs UK Ltd
1180 Eskdale Rd, Winnersh, Wokingham, RG41 5TU
T: 0118 946 7000
F: 0118 946 7001
W: www.jacobs.com

Jactron
Northdown Business Park, Ashford Road, Lenham, Maidstone, Kent, ME17 2DL
T: 01622 852848
W: www.jactron.co.uk/

Jafco Tools Ltd
Access House, Great Western St, Wednesbury, West Midlands, WS10 7LE
T: 0121 556 7700
F: 0121 556 7788
E: info@jafcotools.com
W: www.jafcotools.com

James Fisher and Sons plc
Fisher House, PO Box 4, Michaelson Road, Barrow-in-Furness, Cumbria, LA14 1HR
T: 01229 615400
F: 01229 836761
W: www.james-fisher.com

JB Corrie & Co Ltd
Frenchmans Rd, Petersfield, Hants, GU32 3AP
T: 01730 237129
F: 01730 264915
E: mhickman@jbcorrie.co.uk
W: www.jbcorrie.co.uk

JBA Management Consultants
See J.Boyle Associates Ltd

JC Decaux UK
991 Great West Road, Brentford, Middlesex, TW8 9DN
T: 020 8326 7777
W: www.jcdecaux.co.uk

JCB
World Headquarters, Rocester, Staffs, ST14 5JP
T: 01889 590312
F: 01889 593455
W: www.jcb.co.uk

JCPii Ltd
69 Chadwick Way, Hamble, Hampshire, SO31 4FD
T: 02380 197116
E: office@jcpii.co.uk
W: www.jcpii.co.uk/

Jeanette Bowden, Network PR
PO Box 173, Harrogate, North Yorkshire, HG2 8YX
T: 01423 538699
E: jeanette@networkpr.co.uk
W: www.networkpr.co.uk

Jefferson Sheard Architects
Fulcrum, 2 Sidney St, Sheffield, S1 4RH
T: 0114 276 1651
F: 0114 279 9191
E: contactus@jeffersonsheard.com
W: www.jeffersonsheard.com

Jelf Insurance Brokers Ltd
Hillside Court, Bowling Hill, Chipping Sodbury, BS37 6JX
T: 01423 700758
M: 07827 158870
E: matthew.whitehurst@jelf.com
W: www.jelf.com

Jestico + Whiles
1 Cobourg St, London, NW1 2HP
T: 020 7380 0382
E: jw@jesticowhiles.com
W: www.jesticowhiles.com/

Jewers Doors Ltd
Normandy Lane, Stratton Business Park, Biggleswade, Beds, SG18 8QB
T: 01767 317090
F: 01767 312305
E: mjewers@jewersdoors.co.uk
W: www.jewersdoors.co.uk

Jigsaw M2M Ltd
Pemberton Business Centre, Richmond Hill, Pemberton, Wigan, Lancashire, WN5 8AA
T: 01942 621786
E: sales@jigsawm2m.com
W: www.jigsawm2m.com

JLL
30 Warwick Street, London, W1B 5NH
T: 020 7493 4933
W: www.jll.co.uk/

JMJ Laboratories
See Synergy Health Plc

JMP Consultants Ltd
See Systra UK

Jnction
Unit 1, 33 Waterson Street, London, E2 8HT
T: 020 3011 1008
E: hello@jnction.uk
W: https://jnction.uk/

Jobson James - Specialist Rail Supply Chain Insurance
148 Leadenhall Street, London, EC3V 4QT
T: 020 7983 9039
E: rail@jobson-james.co.uk
W: www.jobson-james-rail.co.uk

John Headon Ltd
Hivernia, Jackson's Hill, St Mary's, Isles of Scilly
T: 01720 423540
E: john@johnheadonltd.co.uk

John McAslan + Partners
7-9 William Road, London, NW1 3ER
T: 020 7313 6000
F: 020 7313 6001
E: marketing@mcaslan.co.uk
W: www.mcaslan.co.uk/

John Prodger Recruitment
The Courtyard, Alban Park, Hatfield Rd, St Albans, Herts, AL4 0LA
T: 01727 841101
F: 01727 838272
E: jobs@jprecruit.com
W: www.jprecruit.com

Johnson Rail
Orchard Ind Est, Toddington, Glos, GL54 5EB
T: 01242 621362
F: 01242 621554
E: stephen.phillips@johnson-security.co.uk
W: www.4dji.com/products-services/security/

Jonathan Lee Recruitment
3 Sylvan Court, Southfield Business Park, Basildon, Essex, SS15 6TU
T: 01268 455520
F: 01268 455521
E: southfields@jonlee.co.uk
W: www.jonlee.co.uk

Jonathan Roberts Consulting (JRC)
Bridge House, Wanstrow, Somerset, BA4 4TE
M: 07545 641204
E: jrc@jrc.org.uk
W: www.jrc.org.uk

Jones Garrard Move Ltd
7 Beaker Close, Smeeton Westerby, Leics, LE8 0RT
E: michael-rodber@jonesgarrardmove.com
W: www.jonesgarrardmove.com

Jotun Paints (Europe) Ltd
Stather Rd, Flixborough, Scunthorpe, N. Lincs, DN15 8RR
T: 01724 400000
F: 01724 400100
E: decpaints@jotun.co.uk
W: www.jotun.com

Journey4
Blake House, 18 Blake Street, York, YO1 8QG
T: 01823 451199
W: www.journey4.co.uk/

Journeycall Ltd
3 James Chalmers Road, Arbroath Enterprise Park, Kirkton Industrial Estate, Arbroath, DD11 3RQ
T: 01241 730300
E: journeycall@the-espgroup.com
W: www.journeycall.com

JourneyPlan c/o Logan Interactive Ltd
2 Frances Street, Langholm, DG13 0BQ
T: 01387 381046
F: 01387 381046
E: iain@logan.co.uk
W: www.journeyplan.co.uk

JR East (East Japan Railway Company)
1st Floor, Boston House, 63-64 New Broad Street, London, EC2M 1JJ
T: 020 7786 9900
W: www.jreast.co.jp/e/

JSD Research & Development Ltd
14-15 Globe Park, Moss Bridge Road, Rochdale, OL16 5EB
T: 01706 646959
F: 01904 352412
E: info@jsdrail.com
W: www.jsdrail.com

J-Trec (Japan Transport Engineering Company)
3-1 Okawa, Kanazawa-ku, Yokohama 236-0043, Japan
W: https://www.j-trec.co.jp/eng/

Judge 3d
Bellingham House, 2 Huntingdon Street, St Neots, Cambs, PE19 1BG
T: 01480 211080
F: 05601 152019
E: mary.morahan@judge3d.com
W: judge3d.com/

JUMO Instrument Co Ltd
Temple Bank, Riverway, Harlow, Essex, CM20 2DY
T: 01279 635533
F: 01279 625029
E: info.uk@jumo.net
W: www.jumo.co.uk/

Junction 9 Network Ltd
Parkgate House, Ickleton Road, Elmdon, Saffron Walden, Essex, CB11 4LT
T: 01763 838288
M: 07971 498113
E: jhall@j9imaging.co.uk
W: www.j9network.co.uk/

Jura Consultants
7 Straiton View, Straiton Business Park, Loanhead, EH20 9QZ
T: 0131 440 6750
E: admin@jura-consultants.co.uk
W: www.jura-consultants.co.uk

Kaba (UK) Ltd
Lower Moor Way, Tiverton, Devon, EX16 6SS
T: 01884 256464
F: 01884 234415
E: info@kaba.co.uk
W: www.kaba.co.uk

Kapsch Group
Unit 2 espace, 26 St Thomas Place, Ely, Cambs, CB7 4EX
T: 01353 644010
F: 01353 611001
E: ktc.uk.info@kapsch.net
W: www.kapsch.net/uk

Karcher Vehicle Wash
Karcher UK Ltd, Karcher House, Beaumont Rd, Banbury, Oxon, OX16 1TB
T: 01295 752172
F: 01295 752040
E: enquiries@karcher.co.uk
W: www.karchervehiclewash.co.uk

Kavia Moulded Products Ltd
Rochdale Rd, Walsden, Todmorden, West Yorks, OL14 6UD
T: 01706 816696
F: 01706 813822
E: enquiries@kavia.info
W: www.kavia.info

KILBORN CONSULTING

We are an independent railway engineering consultancy and design business. We specialise in the design of railway signalling and telecommunication systems for the UK and Ireland railway infrastructure.

Our core services cover technical advice, consultancy, concept, outline and detailed design of both signalling and telecommunication systems. We can provide all Signal Sighting activities and signalling risk assessments, including SORA and Suitable and Sufficient Risk Assessments for Level Crossings. We also provide EMC and E&B studies to complement our core services.

KILBORN CONSULTING LIMITED, 6th Floor, South Suite, 12 Sheep St, Wellingborough, Northamptonshire NN8 1BL
T: 01933 279909 E: pmcsharry@kilbornconsulting.co.uk

www.kilbornconsulting.co.uk

Kaymac Marine & Civil Engineering Ltd
Osprey Business Park, Byng St, Landore, Swansea, SA1 2NX
T: 01792 301818
F: 01792 645698
E: claire.williamson@kaymacltd.co.uk
W: www.kaymacmarine.co.uk

Kee Systems
Thornsett Works, Thornsett Rd, Wandsworth, London, SW18 4EW
T: 0208 874 6566
F: 0208 874 5726
E: sales@keesystems.com
W: www.keesystems.com

Kelly Integrated Transport Services Ltd
Unit 21, Kynock Rd, Eley Ind. Est, Edmonton, London, N18 3BD
T: 020 8884 6605
F: 020 8884 6633
E: kitsenquiries@kelly.co.uk
W: www.kelly.co.uk

Keltbray
St Andrews House, Portsmouth Rd, Esher, Surrey, KT10 9TA
T: 020 7643 1000
F: 020 7643 1001
E: enquiries@keltbray.com
W: www.keltbray.com

Keltbray Aspire Rail Ltd
Unit 4a/5b, Crewe Hall Enterprise Park, Weston Lane, Crewe, CW1 6UA
T: 01270 254176
F: 01270 253267
W: www.keltbray.com

Kelvatek Ltd
Bermuda Innovation Centre, St David's Way, Bermuda Park, Nuneaton, Warks, CV10 7SD
T: 02476 320100
F: 02476 641172
E: mail@kelvatek.com
W: www.kelvatek.com/

Kendall Poole Consulting
Pinewood Business Park – TS2, Coleshill Rd, Marston Green, Solihull, B37 7HG
T: 0121 779 0934
E: scm@kendallpoole.com
W: www.kendallpoole.com

Kennedy Solutions
1 Bromley Lane, Chislehurst, Kent, BR7 6LH
T: 020 8468 1016
F: 01689 855261
E: martin@kennedy-solutions.com
W: www.kennedy-solutions.com

Kent Modular Electronics Ltd (KME)
621 Maidstone Rd, Rochester, Kent, ME1 3QJ
T: 01634 830123
F: 01634 830619
E: sales@kme.co.uk
W: www.kme.co.uk

Kent PHK Ltd
Kent House, Lower Oakham Way, Mansfield, Notts, NG18 5BY
T: 01623 421202
F: 01623 421302
E: enquiries@kentphk.co.uk
W: www.kentphk.com/

Kent Stainless (Wexford) Ltd
Ardcavan, Wexford, Republic of Ireland
T: 0800 376 8377
F: 00353 53914 1802
E: info@kentstainless.com
W: www.kentstainless.com

Keolis (UK) Ltd
Evergreen Building North, 160 Euston Rd, London, NW1 2DX
T: 020 3691 1715
E: comms@keolis.com
W: www.keolis.co.uk

KeTech Ltd
Glaisdale Drive East, Bilborough, Nottingham, NG8 4GU
T: 0115 900 5600
F: 0115 900 5601
E: info@ketech.com
W: www.ketech.com

Key Fasteners
Cavalry Hill Industrial Estate, Weedon Bec, Northants, NN7 4PP
T: 01332 207342
E: enquiries@keyfasteners.co.uk
W: www.keyfasteners.co.uk/

Key Publishing
Units 1-4, Gwash Way Industrial Estate, Ryhall Road, Stamford, Lincolnshire, PE9 1XP
T: 01780 755131
F: 01780 757261
W: www.keypublishing.com/

Keyline Builders Merchants
Grove Road, Northfleet, Kent, DA11 9AX
T: 020 7473 5288
F: 020 7473 5171
E: rail@keyline.co.uk
W: www.keyline.co.uk

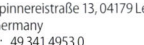

Keysight Technologies
610 Wharfedale Rd, IQ Winnersh, Wokingham, Berks, RG41 5TP
T: 0800 0260637
F: 01189 276855
E: contactcentre_uk@keysight.com
W: www.keysight.com

Kiel Seating UK Ltd
Regents Pavilion, 4 Summerhouse Road, Moulton Park, Northampton, NN3 6BJ
T: 01604 641148
F: 01604 641149
E: p.scott@kiel-seating.co.uk
W: www.kiel-sitze.de

Kiepe Electric Ltd
Kiepe-Platz 1, 40599 Düsseldorf, Germany
T: +49 (0) 211 74 97-0
F: +49 (0) 211 74 97-300
E: info.kiepe@knorr-bremse.com
W: www.kiepe.knorr-bremse.com

Kier Rail
Tempsford Hall, Station Road, Tempsford, Sandy, Beds, SG19 2BD
T: 01767 355000
F: 01767 355633
E: contact.us@kier.co.uk
W: www.kier.co.uk

Kilborn Consulting Ltd
6th Floor, South Suite, 12 Sheep Street, Wellingborough, Northants, NN8 1BL
T: 01933 279909
F: 01933 276629
E: pmcsharry@kilbornconsulting.co.uk
W: www.kilbornconsulting.co.uk

Kilbride Rail
Bury House, 1-3 Bury Street, Guildford, Surrey, GU2 4AW
T: 01483 569263
F: 01483 577379
E: info@kilbridegroup.com
W: kilbridegroup.com/

Kilfrost Ltd
Albion Works, Haltwhistle, Northumberland, NE49 0HJ
T: 01434 320332
F: 0191 230 0426
E: alex.stephens@kilfrost.com
W: www.kilfrost.com

Kilnbridge Construction Services Ltd
McDermott House, Cody Rd. Business Park, South Crescent, London, E16 4TL
T: 020 7511 1888
F: 020 7511 1114
E: sales@kilnbridge.com
W: www.kilnbridge.com

Kimberley-Clark Professional
1 Tower View, Kings Hill, West Malling, Kent, ME19 4HA
T: 01732 594000
F: 01732 594060
E: marta.longhurst@kcc.com
W: www.kcprofessional.com/uk

King Rail
King Trailers Ltd, Riverside, Market Harborough, Leics, LE16 7PX
T: 01858 467361
F: 01858 467161
E: info@kingtrailers.co.uk
W: www.kingtrailers.co.uk

Kingfisher Productions
Losinga, PO Box 110, Cullompton, Devon, EX15 9AZ
T: 0333 121 0707
E: roger@kingfisher-prods.demon.co.uk
W: www.railwayvideo.com

Kingfisher Resources Management Ltd
First Floor, Azrec Centre, Aztec West, Almondsbury, Bristol, BS32 4TD
T: 01454 612799
E: mike@kingfisherlimited.com
W: www.kingfisherlimited.com

Kingston Engineering Co (Hull) Ltd
Pennington St, Hull, HU8 7LD
T: 01438 325676
F: 01438 216438
E: sales@kingston-engineering.co.uk
W: www.kingston-engineering.co.uk

Kirow
Spinnereistraße 13, 04179 Leipzig, Germany
T: 49 341 4953 0
F: 49 341 477 3274
W: www.kranunion.de/nc/en/

KIT Design
International House, Nunnery Drive, Sheffield, S2 1TA
T: 0114 279 8136
E: sales@kitdesignworks.co.uk
W: kitdesignworks.co.uk

KJ Hall Chartered Land & Engineering Surveyors
22 Bower Hinton, Martock, Somerset, TA12 6JY
T: 01935 823423
E: admin@kjhsurvey.co.uk
W: www.kjhsurvey.co.uk

DIRECTORY

Klauke UK Ltd
Hillside Road East, Bungay, Suffolk, NR35 1JX
T: 01986 891519
E: sales@klauke.textron.com
W: www.klauke.com

Klaxon Signals Ltd
Bradwood Court, St Crispin Way, Haslingden, Lancs, BB4 4PW
T: 01706 234800
E: sales@klaxonsignals.com
W: www.klaxonsignals.com

Kluber Lubrication GB Ltd
Longbow Close, Pennine Business Park, Bradley, Huddersfield, HD2 1GQ
T: 01422 205115
F: 01422 206073
E: sales@uk.klueber.com
W: www.klueber.com

KLW - Wheelco SA
Via San Salvatore 13, PO Box 745, CH-6902 Paradiso-Lugan, Switzerland
T: 0041 91261 3910
F: 0041 91261 3919
E: info@klw-wheelco.ch
W: www.klw.biz

KM&T Ltd
The Techno Centre, Coventry University Technology Park, Puma Way, Coventry, CV1 2TT
T: 02476 236275
E: info@kmandt.com
W: www.kmandt.com

KMC International
7 Old Park Lane, London, W1K 1QR
T: 020 7317 4600
F: 020 7317 4620
E: info@kmcinternational.com
W: www.kmcinternational.com

KME
See Kent Modular Electronics Ltd (KME)

KN Network Services
4 Chancerygate Business Centre, South Ruislip, Middlesex, HA4 0JA
T: 020 8845 9292
F: 020 8845 9287
E: info@kn-group.co.uk
W: knetworkservices.com/

Knight Architects
Thame House, 9 Castle Street, High Wycombe, Buckinghamshire, HP13 6RZ
T: 01494 525 500
E: info@knightarchitects.co.uk
W: knightarchitects.co.uk

Knorr-Bremse Rail UK
Westinghouse Way, Hampton Park East, Melksham, Wilts, SN12 6TL
T: 01225 898700
F: 01225 898705
E: ukrarailenquiries@knorr-bremse.com
W: www.knorr-bremse.co.uk

Komplete Group Ltd
Suite 2, Floor 3, Southpoint, Cardinal Square, 10 Nottingham Road, Derby, DE1 3QT
T: 01332 349255
F: 01332 294688
E: enquiries@komplete-group.com
W: www.komplete-group.com

Kone UK
Global House, Station Place, Fox Lane North, Chertsey, Surrey, KT16 9HW
T: 0870 770 1122
F: 0870 770 1144
E: sales.marketinguk@kone.com
W: www.kone.com

Konecranes UK Ltd
Unit 1B, Sills Road, Willow Farm Business Park, Castle Donington, Leics, DE74 2US
T: 0844 3246 599
F: 01332 697755
E: sales.uk@konecranes.com
W: www.konecranes.co.uk/

Kontron AG
Units 5&7, Sussex Business Village, Lake Lane, Barnham, West Sussex, PO22 0AL
T: 01243 533900
E: uksales@kontron.com
W: www.kontron.com

Korec Group
Blundellsands House, 34-44 Mersey View, Brighton-le-Sands, Liverpool, L22 6QB
T: 0845 603 1214
F: 0151 931 5559
E: info@korecgroup.com
W: www.korecgroup.com

KPMG
15 Canada Square, Canary Wharf, London, E14 5GL
T: 020 7311 1000
F: 020 7311 3311
W: https://home.kpmg.com/uk/en/home.html

Kroy (Europe) Ltd
Unit 2, 14 Commercial Rd, Reading, Berks, RG2 0QJ
T: 0118 986 5200
F: 0118 986 5205
E: sales@kroyeurope.com
W: www.kroyeurope.com

KS Terminals Inc
21F-2, No 6, Lane 256, Sec 2, Xitun Road, Xitun District, 407 Taichung City, Taiwan
T: 886 2706 6260
M: 886 4758 2786
E: exp@ksterminals.com.tw
W: www.ksterminals.com.tw

KV Mobile Systems Division
See Parker KV Division

Kwik-Step Ltd
Unit 5, Albion Dockside, Hanover Place, Bristol, BS1 6UT
T: 0117 929 1400
F: 0117 929 1404
E: info@kwik-step.com
W: www.kwik-step.com

L&S Waste Management
Pegham Industrial Park, Laveys Lane, Fareham, Hampshire, PO15 6SD
T: 01329 840000
F: 01329 840001
E: info@lswaste.co.uk
W: www.lswaste.co.uk/

L.C. Switchgear Ltd
Unit 16, St Josephs Business Park, St Josephs Close, Hove, East Sussex, BN3 7ES
T: 01273 770540
E: sales@lcswitchgear.com
W: www.lcswitchgear.com/

L.E.K Consulting
40 Grosvener Place, London, SW1X 7JL
T: 020 7389 7200
F: 020 7389 7440
E: surfacetransport@lek.com
W: www.lek.com

Laboursite Group Ltd (Rail)
See Wyse Rail Ltd

Lafarge Aggregates (UK) Ltd
Portland House, Bickenhill Lane, Solihull, West Midlands, B37 7BQ
T: 0800 1 218 218
F: 0870 336 8602
E: enquiries@lafargetarmac.com
W: www.lafarge.co.uk

Lafarge Tarmac
Portland House, Bickenhill Lane, Solihull, West Midlands, B37 7BQ
T: 0845 812 6400
F: 0845 812 6200
E: customerhelpline@tarmac.com
W: www.tarmac.com/

Lagan Construction Group
Rosemount House, 21 – 23 Sydenham Road, Belfast, BT3 9HA, Northern Ireland
T: 028 9045 5531
F: 028 9045 8940
W: www.laganconstructiongroup.com/

Laing O'Rourke Infrastructure
Bridge Place, Anchor Blvd., Admirals Park, Crossways, Dartford, Kent, DA2 6SN
T: 01322 296200
F: 01322 296262
E: info@laingorourke.com
W: www.laingorourke.com

Laing Rail
Western House, 14 Rickfords Hill, Aylesbury, Bucks, HP20 2RX
T: 01296 332108
F: 01296 332126
E: enquiries@laing.com
W: www.laing.com/

Lakesmere Ltd
The Ring Tower Centre, Moorside Rd, Winnall, Winchester, Hants, SO23 7RZ
T: 01962 826500
E: enquiries@lakesmere.com
W: www.lakesmere.com

Lambert Smith Hampton
UK House, 180 Oxford Street, London, W1D 1NN
T: 020 7198 2000
F: 020 7198 2001
W: www.lsh.co.uk/

Lamifil
Frederic Sheidlaan, B-2620 Hemiksem, Belgium
T: 32 (0)3 8700 611
F: 32 (0)3 8878 059
W: lamifil.be/

Land Sheriffs
Bencroft, Dassels, Braughing, Ware, Hertfordshire, SG11 2RW
T: 0845 257 4567
E: info@landsheriffs.co.uk
W: www.landsheriffs.co.uk/

Landolt + Brown
Unit 13.2.2 The Leathermarket, 11-13 Weston Street, London, SE1 3ER
T: 020 7357 9547
W: https://landoltbrownportfolio.wordpress.com/

Lanes Group Plc - Lanes For Drains
17 Parkside Lane, Parkside Ind. Est, Leeds, LS11 5TD
T: 0800 526488
F: 0161 788 2206
E: sales@lanesfordrains.co.uk
W: www.lanesfordrains.co.uk

Lankelma Limited
Cold Harbour Barn, Cold Harbour Lane, Iden, East Sussex, TN31 7UT
T: 01797 280050
F: 01797 280195
E: info@lankelma.co.uk
W: www.lankelma.com

Lantern Engineering Ltd
Unit 4, Globe Court, Coalpit Road, Denaby Main, Doncaster, DN12 4LH
T: 01709 861008
F: 01709 863623
E: info@lantern.co.uk
W: www.lantern.co.uk

Largam
Unit 9, Oak Industrial Park, Great Dunmow, Essex, CM6 1XN
T: 01371 876121
E: plant@largam.co.uk
W: www.largam.co.uk

Laser Rail
See Balfour Beatty Rail

LB Foster Europe
Stamford St, Sheffield, S9 2TX
T: 0114 256 2225
E: sales@lbfoster.com
W: www.lbfoster.eu

Leadec Limited
2 Academy Drive, Warwick, CV34 6QZ
T: 01926 623550
F: 01926 623551
E: info-uk@leadec-services.com
W: www.leadec-services.com/uk

Leda Recruitment
See McGinley Support Services

Leewood Projects
38 Deacon Rd, Kingston upon Thames, Surrey, KT2 6LU
T: 020 8541 0715
F: 020 8546 4260
E: david.cockle@leewoodprojects.co.uk
W: www.leewoodprojects.co.uk

Legioblock (A Jansen B.V.)
Kanaaldojk Zuid 24, 5691 NL SON, Netherlands
T: 0845 689 0036
F: 0845 689 0035
E: sales@legioblock.com
W: www.legioblock.com

Legion Limited
Hamilton House, Mabledon Place, London, WC1H 9BB
T: 020 7793 0200
E: info@legion.com
W: www.legion.com

Legrand Electric Ltd
Great King St. North, Birmingham, B19 2LF
T: 0121 515 0522
E: legrand.sales@legrand.co.uk
W: www.legrand.co.uk

Leica Geosystems Ltd
Hexagon House, Michigan Drive, Tongwell, Milton Keynes, MK15 8HT
T: 01908 513400
F: 01908 513401
E: uk.sales@leica-geosystems.com
W: www.leica-geosystems.co.uk

Leidos
Skypark 1, 8 Elliot Place, Glasgow, G3 8EP
E: info@leidos.com
W: www.leidos.com

LeighFisher
New City Court, 20 St Thomas street, London, SE1 9RS
T: 0118 946 8152
E: david.bradshaw@leighfisher.com
W: www.leighfisher.com

LEK Consulting
40 Grosvenor Place, London, SW1X 7JL
T: 020 7389 7200
F: 020 7389 7440
W: www.lek.com/

LEM UK Ltd
West Lancs Investment Centre, Suite 10, Maple View, White Moss Business Park, Skelmersdale, Lancs, WN8 9TG
T: 01942 388440
F: 01942 388441
E: luk@lem.com
W: www.lem.com

Lemon Consulting
See AMCL Systems Engineering Ltd

Lendlease Consulting
20 Triton St, Regents Place, London, NW1 3BF
T: 020 3430 9000
F: 020 3430 9001
E: peter.foy@lendlease.com
W: www.lendlease.com

Lesmac (Fasteners) Ltd
73 Dykehead St, Queenslie Ind. Est, Queenslie, Glasgow, G33 4AQ
T: 0141 774 0004
F: 0141 774 2229
E: sales@lesmac.co.uk
W: www.lesmac.co.uk

Level 3 Communications
7th Floor, 10 Fleet Place, London, EC4M 7RB
T: 0845 000 1000
F: 202 7954 2385
E: europe@level3.com
W: www.level3.com

Level Crossing Installations Ltd
Suite 9, Canterbury Business Centre, 18 Ashchurch Rd, Tewkesbury, Glos, GL20 8BT
T: 01684 278022
W: www.levelcrossinginstallations.co.uk

Lexicraft Ltd
2 Bromborough Pool Business Park, Price's Way, Bromborough, Wirral, CH62 4LP
T: 0151 647 9281
F: 0151 666 1079
E: rfewtrell@lexicraft.co.uk
W: www.lexicraft.co.uk

Ley Hill Solutions
Beech House, 9 Cheyne Walk, Chesham, Bucks, HP5 1AY
T: 01494 772327
F: 0870 169 5984
E: graham.hull@leyhill.com
W: www.leyhill.com

LGM (UK) Ltd
Unit 18, Apex Court, Woodlands, Bradley Stoke, Bristol, BS32 4JT
T: 0117 321 0827
M: 07547 912197

LH Group Services
Graycar Business Park, Barton-under-Needwood, Burton upon Trent, Staffs, DE13 8EN
T: 01283 722600
F: 01283 722622
E: lh@lh-group.co.uk
W: www.lh-group.co.uk

LH Safety Footwear
Greenbridge, Rawtenstall, Rossendale, Lancs, BB4 7NX
T: 01706 235100
F: 01706 235150
E: enquiries@lhsafety.co.uk
W: www.lhsafety.co.uk

Liebherr Transportation Systems UK
Liebherr Sunderland Works Ltd, Ayres Quay, Deptford Terrace, Sunderland, SR4 6DD
T: 0191 515 4930
F: 0191 515 4936
E: alan.lepatourel@liebherr.com
W: www.liebherr.com

Life Environmental Services
4 Ducketts Wharf, South Street, Bishop's Stortford, Hertfordshire, CM23 3AR
T: 01279 503117
F: 01279 503162
W: www.lifeenvironmental.co.uk/

Light Rail Transit Association (LRTA)
138 Radnor Ave, Welling, Kent, DA16 2BY
T: 01179 517785
E: office@lrta.org
W: www.lrta.org

Linbrooke Services Ltd
Sheffield Business Park, Churchill Way, Chapeltown, Sheffield, S35 2PY
T: 0114 232 8290
F: 0844 800 0984
E: info@linbrooke.co.uk
W: www.linbrooke.co.uk

Lindapter International
Lindsay House, Brackenbeck Rd, Bradford, BD7 2NF
T: 01274 521444
F: 01274 521130
E: enquiries@lindapter.com
W: www.lindapter.com

Line Worx Ltd
2nd Floor, Afon Building, Worthing Road, Horsham, West Sussex, RH12 1TL
T: 0333 9000 939
W: www.lineworx.co.uk

Lineside Structure Maintenance
Works Depot, Lilac Grove, Beeston, Nottingham, NG9 1PF
T: 0115 922 5218
F: 0115 967 7516
E: info@lineside.co.uk
W: www.lineside.co.uk/

Liniar Retaining Systems
Flamstead House, Denby Hall Business Park, Denby, Derbyshire, DE5 8JX
T: 01332 883900
E: info@liniar.co.uk
W: www.liniar.co.uk

Link2 Ltd
2 Wortley Road, Deepcar, Sheffield, S36 2UZ
T: 0114 2180475
E: marketing@link-2.biz
W: www.link-2.biz

Linklite Systems Ltd
29 Waterloo Road, Wolverhampton, WV1 4DJ
T: 0345 862 0236
E: sales@linklite.co.uk
W: www.linklite.co.uk

Link-up
See Achilles Information Ltd (Link-Up)

LINSINGER Maschinenbau GmbH
Dr-Linsinger-Strasse 24, A-466 Steyrermühl, Austria
T: 0043 7613 8840 140
F: 0043 7613/8840-951
E: maschinenbau@linsinger.com
W: www.linsinger.com

Lionverge Civils Ltd
Unit 33, Cornwell Business Park, Salthouse Road, Brackmills Industrial Estate, Northampton, NN4 7EX
T: 01604 677227
F: 01604 677218
E: enquiries@lionverge.co.uk
W: www.lionverge.co.uk

Liquid Management Solutions Ltd
Creative Industries Centre, Wolverhampton Science Park, Glashier Drive, Wolverhampton, WV10 9TG
T: 0845 450 7373
E: client.services@liquidms.co.uk
W: www.liquidms.co.uk

Lista (UK) Ltd
14 Warren Yard, Wolverton Mill, Milton Keynes, MK12 5NW
T: 01908 222333
E: info.uk@list.com
W: www.lista.co.uk

Llumar Anti-Grafitti Coating
See CP Films Solutia (UK) Ltd

LML Products Ltd
13 Portemarsh Rd, Calne, Wilts, SN11 9BN
T: 01249 814271
F: 01249 812182
E: sales@lmlproducts.co.uk
W: www.lmlproducts.co.uk

LNT Solutions Ltd
Helios 47, Leeds, LS25 2DY
T: 0113 385 4187
F: 0113 385 3854
E: info@lntsolutions.com
W: www.lntsolutions.com

LoatesHR
32 Friar Gate, Derby, DE1 1BX
T: 01332 890345
E: hello@loates.net
W: https://loateshr.net/

Lobo Systems Ltd
Centurion Way Business park, Alfreton Rd, Derby, DE21 4AY
T: 01332 365666
F: 01332 365661
E: sales@lobosystems.com
W: www.lobosystems.com

Locomotive Services Ltd
Railway Yard, Collett Way, Great Western Industrial Park, Southall, Middlesex, UB2 4SE
W: www.locomotiveservices.co.uk/

Logic Engagements Ltd
45-47 High St, Cobham, Surrey, KT11 3DP
T: 01932 869869
F: 01932 864455
E: info@logicrec.com
W: www.logicrec.com

LogiKal Ltd
27-29, Cursitor St, London, EC4A 1LT
T: 020 7404 4826
E: admin@logikal.co.uk
W: www.logikalprojects.co.uk

Lombard Finance
PO Box 520, Rotherham, South Yorkshire, S63 3BR
T: 0345 877 8888
W: https://www.lombard.co.uk/

London & Continental Railways (LCR)
4th Floor, One Kemble Street, London, WC2B 4AN
T: 020 7391 4300
F: 020 7391 4401
E: rwillis@lcrhq.co.uk
W: www.lcrhq.co.uk/

London North Eastern Railway (LNER)
East Coast House, 25 Skeldergate, York, YO1 6DH
T: 03457 225 333
W: https://www.lner.co.uk/

London Overground
See Arriva Rail London (London Overground)

London Rail
See Transport for London

London TravelWatch
169 Union Street, London, SE1 0LL
T: 020 3176 2999
E: enquiries@londontravelwatch.org.uk
W: www.londontravelwatch.org.uk

London Underground Limited
See Transport for London

Look CCTV
Fleetwood Road North, Blackpool, Lancs, FY5 4QD
T: 01253 490399
E: enquiries@lookcctv.co.uk
W: www.look-cctv.co.uk/

Loram
3900 Arrowhead Dr., P.O. Box 188, Hamel, MN 55340, United States
T: 1-800-328-1466
W: www.loram.com/

Loram UK
RTC Business Park, London Rd, Derby, DE24 8UP
T: 01332 293035
F: 01332 331210
E: enquiries@loram.co.uk
W: https://www.loram.co.uk/

Lordgate Engineering
1 Stonehill, Stukeley Meadows Ind Est, Huntingdon, Cambs, PE29 6ED
T: 01480 455600
F: 01480 454972
E: sales@lordgate.com
W: www.lordgate.com

Lorne Stewart Plc
Stewart House, Orford Park, Greenfold Way, Leigh, Lancs, WN7 3XJ
T: 01942 683333
E: andy.vickers@lornestewart.co.uk
W: www.lornestewart.co.uk

Lowery Ltd
Ashley Place, Hanworth Lane, Chertsey, Surrey, KT16 9JX
T: 01932 564248
E: info@lowery.co.uk
W: www.lowery.co.uk/

LPA Group
Light & Power House, Shire Hill, Saffron Walden, Essex, CB11 3AQ
T: 01799 512800
F: 01799 512826
E: enquiries@lpa-group.com
W: www.lpa-group.com

LPDN - Luhn & Pulvermacher, Dittmann & Neuhaus
Voerder Strasse 38, D-58135 Hagen, Germany
T: 0039 0365 526213
E: giovannico.dore@sogefigroup.com
W: www.sogefigroup.com

LSC Group
Lincoln House, Wellington Crescent, Fradley Park, Lichfield, Staffordshire, WS13 8RZ
T: 01543 446800
F: 01543 446900
E: marketing@lsc.co.uk
W: www.lsc.co.uk/

Lucy Zodion Ltd
Chestnut Lodge, 3 Meeres Lane, Kirton, Lincs, PE20 1PS
T: 01422 317337
E: pwpsales@lucyzodion.com
W: www.lucyzodion.com

Lundy Projects Ltd
195 Chestergate, Stockport, Cheshire, SK3 0BQ
T: 0161 476 2996
F: 0161 476 3760
E: mail@lundy-projects.co.uk
W: www.lundy-projects.co.uk

LUR - Lucchini Unipart Rail Ltd
Ashburton Road West, Trafford Park, Manchester, M17 1GU
T: 0161 872 0492
F: 0161 872 2895
E: salesuk@lucchinirs.co.uk
W: www.lucchinirs.co.uk

LORAM®
UK LIMITED

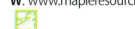

LORAM UK: Providing OTM operations & maintenance, T&RS maintenance and bespoke projects at the heart of the railway industry.

Supplying OTM operations & maintenance, rolling stock maintenance, overhauls and modifications, re-engineering, hook and haul services and seasonal treatment.

LORAM UK LTD
RTC Business Park, London Road, Derby, DE24 8UP
Phone: 01332 293035 Fax: 01332 331210
enquiries@loram.co.uk
www.loram.co.uk

Luxfer Gas Cylinders
Colwick Industrial Estate, Nottingham, NG4 2BH
T: 0115 980 3800
F: 0115 980 3899
W: www.luxfercylinders.com

Luxury Train Club
See Train Chartering (Luxury Train Club)

Lynch Plant Hire
Lynch House, Parr Rd, Stanmore, London, HA7 1LE
T: 0845 400 0000
F: 020 8733 2020
E: brucel@l-lynch.com
W: www.l-lynch.com

Lynch Plant Hire
Lynch House, Parr Rd, Stanmore, Middx, HA7 1LE
T: 020 8900 0000
F: 020 8733 2020
E: brucel@l-lynch.com
W: www.l-lynch.com

Lyndon Scaffolding
Valepits Road, Garretts Green, Birmingham, B33 0TD
T: 0121 789 7979
F: 0121 789 7034
E: enquiries@lyndonscaffolding.co.uk
W: www.lyndonscaffolding.co.uk/

M H Southern & Co Ltd
Church Bank Sawmills, Jarrow, Tyne & Wear, NE32 3EB
T: 0191 489 8231
F: 0191 428 0146
E: timber@mhsouthern.co.uk
W: www.mhsouthern.co.uk

M.A.C. Solutions (UK) Ltd
Unit 6-7, Kingfisher Business Park, Arthur St, Lakeside, Redditch, Worcs, B98 8LG
T: 01527 529774
F: 01527 838131
E: sales@mac-solutions.co.uk
W: www.mac-solutions.net

Maber Architects
85 Tottenham Court Rd, London, W1T 4TQ
T: 020 3402 2065
F: 020 7268 3100
E: info@maber.co.uk
W: www.maber.co.uk

Mabey Hire Ltd
Scout Hill, Ravensthorpe, Dewsbury, West Yorkshire, WF13 3EJ
T: 01942 460601
E: marketing@mabeyhire.co.uk
W: www.mabeyhire.co.uk

Mac Roberts LLP
Capella, 60 York St, Glasgow, G2 8JX
T: 0141 303 1100
F: 0141 332 8886
E: carly.mason@macroberts.com
W: www.macroberts.com

Mace Group
155 Moorgate, London, EC2M 6XB
T: 020 3522 3000
E: info@macegroup.com
W: www.macegroup.com

Macemain + Amstad Ltd
Boyle Rd, Willowbrook Ind. Est., Corby, Northants, NN17 5XU
T: 01536 401331
F: 01536 401298
E: sales@macemainamstad.com
W: www.macemainamstad.com

Machines with Vision
CodeBASE, 3 Lady Lawson Street, Edinburgh, EH3 9DR
M: 07481 245147
E: jan.wessnitzer@machineswithvision.com
W: www.machineswithvision.com

Mack Brooks Exhibitions Ltd
Romeland House, Romeland Hill, St Albans, Herts, AL3 4ET
T: 01727 814400
F: 01727 814401
E: railtex@mackbrooks.co.uk
W: www.railtex.co.uk/

Maclay Murray & Spens LLP
One London Wall, London, EC2Y 5AB
T: 0330 222 0050
F: 0330 222 0054
W: www.mms.co.uk/

MacRail Systems Ltd
Units One & Two, Morston Court, Aisecome Way, Weston Super Mare, BS22 8NG
T: 01934 319810
F: 01934 424139
E: info@macrail.co.uk
W: www.macrail.co.uk

Macrete Precast Concrete Engineers
50 Creagh Rd, Toomebridge, Co. Antrim, BT41 3SE
T: 02879 650471
F: 02879 650084
E: info@macrete.com
W: www.macrete.com

Maddox Consulting Ltd
34 South Molton Street, London, W1K 5RG
M: 0788 7575 254
E: info@maddoxconsulting.com
W: www.maddoxconsulting.com

MagDrill
Unit 11, Unthank Road, Bellshill, North Lanarkshire, ML4 1DD
T: 01698 333200
F: 01698 749294
E: sales@magdrill.com
W: www.magdrill.com/

Mainframe Communications Ltd
Network House, Journeymans Way, Temple Farm Ind Est, Southend on Sea, Essex, SS2 5TF
T: 01702 443800
F: 01702 443801
E: info@mainframecomms.co.uk
W: www.mainframecomms.co.uk

Mainline Resourcing Ltd
Suite 214, Business Design Centre, 52 Upper St, London, N1 0QH
T: 0845 083 0245
F: 020 7288 6685
E: info@mainlineresourcing.com
W: www.mainlineresourcing.com

Majorfax Ltd
Charles Street, Walsall, West Midlands, WS2 9LZ
T: 01922 645815
E: castings@majorfax.co.uk
W: www.majorfax.co.uk/

Majorlift
Arnolds Field Estate, Wickwar, Wotton-Under-Edge, Gloucestershire, GL12 8JD
T: 01454 299299
F: 01454 294003
E: info@majorlift.com
W: www.majorlift.co.uk/

Malcolm Rail
Fouldubs, Laurieston Rd, Grangemouth, Falkirk, FK3 8XT
T: 01324 668329
F: 01324 668312
E: turnerd@whm.co.uk
W: www.malcolmgroup.co.uk

Mammoet (UK) Ltd
The Grange Business Centre, Belasis Ave, Billingham, Cleveland, TS23 1LG
T: 0800 111 4449
E: saleseurope@mammoet.com
W: www.mammoet.com

MAN Energy Solutions UK Ltd
Hythe Hill, Colchester, Essex, CO1 2HW
T: 01206 875536
F: 01206 794325
E: phil.hoskins@man-es.com
W: uk.man-es.com / vp185enquiries@man-es.com

Manbat Ltd
Lancaster House, Lancaster Road, Shrewsbury, SY1 3NJ
T: 01743 218500
F: 01743 218511
E: sales@manbat.co.uk
W: www.manbat.co.uk

Mane Rail
UCB House, 3 St George St, Watford, WD18 0UH
T: 01923 470720
E: rail@mane.co.uk
W: www.mane.co.uk

Mansell Recruitment Group
Mansell House, Priestley Way, Crawley, West Sussex, RH10 9RU
T: 01293 404050
F: 01293 404122
E: neil@mansell.co.uk
W: www.mansell.co.uk

Maple Resourcing
Black Sea House, 72 Wilson Street, London, EC2A 2DH
T: 020 7048 0775
F: 0845 052 9357
E: info@mapleresourcing.com
W: www.mapleresourcing.com

Marcroft Engineering Services
See Axiom Rail

Maritime and Rail
E-Business Centre, Consett Business Park, Villa Real, Consett, DH8 6BP
T: 01207 693616
F: 01207 693917
W: www.maritimeandrail.com

Maritime Transport
Clickett Hill Road, Felixstowe, Suffolk, IP11 4AX
T: 01394 617300
F: 01394 617299
E: enquiries@maritimetransport.com
W: www.maritimetransport.com/

Marl International Ltd
Marl Business Park, Marcambe Road, Ulverston, Cumbria, LA12 9BN
T: 01229 582430
F: 01229 585155
E: sales@marl.co.uk
W: www.leds.co.uk

Marsh Bellofram Europe Ltd
9 Castle Park, Queens Drive, Nottingham, NG2 1AH
T: 0115 993 3300
F: 0115 993 3301
E: bellofram@aol.com
W: www.marshbellofram.eu

Marshalls plc
Landscape House, Premier Way, Lowfields Business Park, Elland, West Yorkshire, HX5 9HT
T: 01422 312000
E: info@marshalls.co.uk
W: www.marshalls.co.uk/commercial

Martek Power Ltd
Glebe Farm Technical Campus, Knapwell, Cambridge, CB23 4GG
T: 01954 267726
F: 01954 267626
E: pippa.keane@martekpower.co.uk
W: www.martekpower.com

Martifer
26 - 28 Hammersmith Grove, London, W6 7BA
T: 020 8834 1348
E: info@martifer.com
W: www.martifer.com/en/

Martin Higginson Transport Research & Consultancy
5 The Avenue, Clifton, York, YO30 6AS
T: 01904 636704
M: 07980 874126
E: mhrcgm@gmail.com
W: www.martinhigginson.co.uk

Martineau
See SGH Martineau LLP

Marubeni-Komatsu
Padgets Lane, Redditch, Worcestershire, B98 0RT
T: 01527 512512
E: customerfeedback@mkl.co.uk
W: www.marubeni-komatsu.co.uk/

Masabi
56 Ayres St, London, SE1 1EU
T: 020 7089 8860
E: kevin@masabi.com
W: www.masabi.com

Matchtech Group
1450 Park Way, Solent Business Park, Whiteley, Fareham, Hants, PO15 7AF
T: 01489 898989
F: 01489 898290
E: info@matchtech.com
W: www.matchtech.com

Matisa (UK) Ltd
PO Box 202, Dawes Lane, Scunthorpe, North Lincolnshire, DN15 6XR
T: 01724 786165
F: 01724 786159
E: melissa.carne@matisa.co.uk
W: www.matisa.ch

Mattei Compressors Ltd
Admington Lane, Admington, Shipston-on-Stour, Warwickshire, CV36 4JJ
T: 01789 450577
F: 01789 450698
E: info@mattei.co.uk
W: https://www.mattei.co.uk/

Maxim Power Tools (Scotland) Ltd
40 Couper St, Glasgow, G4 0DL
T: 0141 552 5591
F: 0141 552 5064
E: akilpatrick@maximpower.co.uk
W: www.maximpower.co.uk

May & Scofield
Stroudley Road, Basingstoke, Hants, RG24 8UG
T: 01256 306800
F: 01256 306810
E: philj@may-scofield.co.uk
W: www.may-scofield.co.uk

May Gurney Rail Services
See Kier Rail

Mayflower Engineering Ltd
Coleridge Road, Sheffield, South Yorkshire, S9 5DA
T: 0114 244 1353
F: 0114 2445977
E: info@mayflower-engineering.co.uk
W: www.mayflower-engineering.co.uk/

Maynard Design Consultancy
5 Baldwin Terrace, London, N1 7RU
T: 020 7724 9500
E: info@maynard-design.com
W: https://www.maynard-design.com/

M-Brain Ltd
County House, 3rd Floor, Friar St, Reading, RG1 1DB
T: 0118 956 5836
F: 0118 956 5850
E: response@esmerk.com
W: www.m-brain.com

MC Electronics
61 Grimsdyke Rd, Hatch End, Pinner, Middlesex, HA5 4PP
T: 020 8428 2027
F: 020 8428 2027
E: info@mcelectronics.co.uk
W: www.mcelectronics.co.uk

Sir Robert McAlpine Ltd
Eaton Court, Maylands Avenue, Hemel Hempstead, Herts, HP2 7TR
T: 01442 233444
F: 01442 230024
E: information@srm.com
W: www.srm.com

DIRECTORY

McAuley Engineering
21 Ballymena Rd, Ballymoney, County Antrim, Northern Ireland
T: 02827 666646
F: 02827 665150
M: 07730 136660
E: wesley@mcauleyengineering.co.uk
W: mcauleyengineering.co.uk

McCulloch Rail
Craigiemains, Main St, Ballantrae, Girvan, Ayrshire, KA26 0NB
T: 01465 831350
F: 01465 831350
E: enquiries@mccullochrail.com
W: www.mccullochrail.com

McGee Group Ltd
340-342 Athlon Rd, Wembley, Middx, HA0 1BX
T: 020 8998 1001
F: 020 8997 7689
E: mail@mcgee.co.uk
W: www.mcgee.co.uk

McGeoch LED Technology
86 Lower Tower Street, Birmingham, B19 3PA
T: 01229 580180
F: 0121 333 3089
E: debbie.albion@mcgeoch.co.uk
W: www.mcgeoch.co.uk

McGinley Support Services
Ground Floor, Edward Hyde Building, 38 Clarendon Rd, Watford, Herts, WD17 1JW
T: 0845 543 5953
F: 0845 543 5956
E: info@mcginley.co.uk
W: www.mcginley.co.uk

B&M McHugh Ltd
429a Footscray Rd, New Eltham, London, SE9 3UL
T: 020 8859 7706
F: 020 8859 9999
E: msg@mchughltd.co.uk
W: www.mchughltd.co.uk

McKenzie Martin Partnership Ltd
Beat House, Workhouse Lane, East Meon, Petersfield, Hampshire, GU32 1PD
T: 02380 216940
E: info@mmpartnership.co.uk
W: www.mmpartnership.co.uk

MCL (Martin Childs Ltd)
1 Green Way, Swaffham, Norfolk, PE37 7FD
T: 01760 722275
E: enquiries@martinchilds.com
W: www.martinchilds.com

McLaughlin & Harvey
15 Trench Road, Mallusk, Newtownabbey, BT36 4TY
T: +44 28 9034 2777
E: mclh@mclh.co.uk
W: www.mclh.co.uk/

McLellan & Partners
Sheer House, West Byfleet, Surrey, KT14 6NL
T: 01932 343271
F: 01932 348037
E: hq@mclellan.co.uk
W: www.mclellan.co.uk

McNealy Brown Limited - Steelwork
Prentis Quay, Mill Way, Sittingbourne, Kent, ME10 2QD
T: 01795 470592
F: 01795 471238
E: info@mcnealybrown.co.uk
W: www.mcnealybrown.co.uk

McNicholas Rail
Lismirrane Industrial Park, Elstree Road, Elstree, Herts, WD6 3EA
T: 020 8953 4144
F: 01302 380591
E: infrastructure@mcnicholas.co.uk
W: www.mcnicholas.co.uk

MCT Brattberg Ltd
Commerce St, Carrs Ind. Est, Haslingden, Lancs, BB4 5JT
T: 01706 244890
F: 01706 244891
E: info@mctbrattberg.co.uk
W: www.mctbrattberg.co.uk

MDA Rail Ltd
Millbank House, Northway, Runcorn, Cheshire, WA7 2SX
T: 01928 751000
F: 01928 751555
E: railresource@mdarail.com
W: www.mdarail.com

MDL Laser Measurement Systems
Acer House, Hackness Rd, Northminster Business Park, York, YO26 6QR
T: 01904 791139
F: 01904 791532
E: privers@mdl.co.uk
W: www.laserace.com

MDS Transmodal Ltd
5-6 Hunters Walk, Canal St, Chester, CH1 4EB
T: 01244 348301
F: 01244 348471
W: www.mdst.co.uk

Mechan Ltd
Sir John Brown Building, Davy Industrial Park, Prince of Wales Road, Sheffield, S9 4EX
T: 0114 257 0563
F: 0114 245 1124
E: info@mechan.co.uk
W: www.mechan.co.uk

Mechan Technology Ltd
See Zonegreen

MEDC Ltd
Unit B, Sutton Parkway, Oddicroft Lane, Sutton in Ashfield, Notts, NG17 5FB
T: 01623 444400
F: 01623 444531
E: medcadmin@eaton.com
W: www.medc.com

MegaTech Projects
20 Forrestfield Gardens, Newton Mearns, Glasgow, G77 6DZ
T: 0141 778 5165
E: info@megatechprojects.co.uk
W: www.megatechprojects.co.uk/

Melford Electronics Ltd
Unit 14, Blenheim Rd, Cressex Business Park, High Wycombe, HP12 3RS
T: 01494 638069
F: 01494 463358
E: info@melford-elec.co.uk
W: www.melford-elec.co.uk

Mendip Rail Ltd
Merehead, East Cranmore, Shepton Mallet, Somerset, BA4 4RA
T: 01749 881202
F: 01749 880141
E: karen.taylor@mendip-rail.co.uk
W: www.aggregate.com/

Mennekes Electric Ltd
Unit 4, Crayfields Ind. Park, Main Rd, St Pauls Cray, Orpington, Kent, BR5 3HP
T: 01689 833522
F: 01689 833378
E: sales@mennekes.co.uk
W: www.mennekes.co.uk

The Mental Wealth Company Limited
40 Hazelwood Road, Duffield, Belper, Derbyshire, DE56 4AA
M: 07305 843993
E: wendy@thementalwealthcompany.co.uk
W: www.thementalwealthcompany.co.uk

Meon LLP
Railside, Northarbour Spur, Portsmouth, PO6 3TU
T: 02392 200606
F: 02392 200707
E: mail@meonuk.com
W: www.meonuk.com

Merak
Parque Empresarial La Carpetania, C/ Miguel Faraday, 1, 28906 GETAFE - Madrid, Spain
T: +34 911 459 400
F: +34 911 459 444
W: www.merak-hvac.com/en/

Merc Engineering UK Ltd
Lower Clough Hill, Pendle St, Barrowford, Lancs, BB9 8PH
T: 01282 694290
F: 01282 613390
E: sales@merceng.co.uk
W: www.merceng.co.uk

Mercia Charters
PO Box 1926, Coventry, CV3 6ZL
T: 07535 759344
E: team@merciacharters.co.uk
W: www.merciacharters.co.uk

Merebrook Consulting Ltd
Suite 2B, Bridgefoot, Belper, Derbys, DE56 2UA
T: 01773 829988
F: 01773 829393
E: consulting@merebrook.co.uk
W: www.merebrook.co.uk

Meridian Generic Rail
8 Westerdale Road, Greenwich, London, SE10 0LW
M: 07971 486638
E: info@meridian-generic-rail.co.uk
W: www.meridian-generic-rail.co.uk/

Mermec
Via Oberdan 70, I-70043 Monopoli (Bari), Italy
T: 0039 080 9171
F: 0039 080 9171 112
E: mermec@mermecgroup.com
W: www.mermecgroup.com

Merseyrail
Rail House, Lord Nelson St, Liverpool, L1 1JF
T: 0151 702 2534
F: 0151 702 3074
E: comment@merseyrail.org
W: www.merseyrail.org

Merseytravel
PO Box 1976, Liverpool, L69 3HN
T: 0151 227 5181
E: comments@merseytravel.gov.uk
W: www.merseytravel.gov.uk

Merson Signs
2 Young Place, Kelvin Ind. Est., East Kilbride, Glasgow, G75 0TD
T: 01355 243021
E: web@merson-signs.com
W: www.railsignage.com

Met Systems Ltd
Cottis House, Locks Hill, Rochford, Essex, SS4 1BB
T: 020 3246 1000
F: 020 7712 2146
E: info@metsystems.co.uk
W: www.metsystems.co.uk

Metalweb
Unit 1, Stargate Business Park, Cuckoo Road, Nechells, Birmingham, B7 5SE
T: 0121 326 2900
F: 0121 328 3421
E: info@metalweb.co.uk
W: www.metalweb.co.uk

MeteoGroup UK Ltd
292 Vauxhall Bridge Rd, London, SW1V 1AE
T: 020 7963 7575
F: 020 7963 7599
E: uk@meteogroup.com
W: www.meteogroup.com

Meteor Power Limited
Unit 2245, Silverstone Technology Park, Towcester, Northamptonshire, NN12 8GX
E: mike.edwards@meteorpower.com
W: www.meteorpower.com/

Metham Aviation Design ltd (MADCCTV Ltd)
Unit 5, Station Approach, Four Marks, Alton, Hants, GU34 5HN
T: 01420 565618
F: 01420 565628
E: stuart@madcctv.com
W: www.madcctv.com

Metrail Construction Ltd
Unit 1, 70 Bell Lane, Bellbrook Ind. Est., Uckfield, TN22 1QL
T: 01825 761360
E: nadia@metrail.co.uk
W: www.metrail.co.uk

Metroline
ComfortDelGro House, 3rd Floor, 329 Edgware Road, Cricklewood, London, NW2 6JP
T: 020 8218 8888
F: 020 8218 8899
W: https://www.metroline.co.uk/

Metrolink (Manchester)
Metrolink House, Queens Road, Manchester, M8 0RY
T: 0161 205 8665
E: customerservices@metrolink.co.uk
W: www.metrolink.co.uk

Mettex Electronic Co Ltd
Beaumont Close, Beaumont Road Ind Est, Banbury, Oxon, OX16 1TG
T: 01295 250826
F: 01295 268643
E: sales@mettex.com
W: www.mettex.com

MF Hydraulics
See Centinal Group

MGB Electrical Ltd
See Ilecsys

MGB Engineering Ltd
MGB House, Unit D, Eagle Rd, Langage Business Park, Plympton, Plymouth, PL7 5JY
T: 0845 070 2490
F: 0845 070 2495
E: enquiries@mgbl.co.uk
W: www.mgbl.co.uk

MGF Trench Construction Ltd
Foundation House, Wallwork Road, Astley, Manchester, M29 7JT
T: 01942 402700
E: enquiries@mgf.ltd.uk
W: www.mgf.ltd.uk

Michael Evans & Associates Ltd
34 Station Rd, Draycott, Derbys, DE72 3QB
T: 01332 871840
F: 01332 871841
E: mike@mevans.co.uk
W: www.mevans.co.uk

Mick George Ltd
6 Lancaster Way, Ermine Business Park, Huntingdon, Cambridgeshire, PE29 6XU
T: 01480 498099
F: 01480 498077
E: sales@mickgeorge.co.uk
W: www.mickgeorge.co.uk/rail

Micro-Epsilon UK Ltd
Dorset House, West Derby Rd, Liverpool, L6 4BR
T: 0151 260 9800
F: 0151 261 2480
E: info@micro-epsilon.co.uk
W: www.micro-epsilon.co.uk

Micro-Mesh Engineering Ltd
Innovation House, Dabell Ave, Blenheim Industrial Estate, Nottingham, NG6 8WA
T: 01159 752929
F: 01159 751175
E: enquiries@micro-mesh.co.uk
W: www.micro-mesh.co.uk

Micromotive (A1 Results Ltd)
38 Coney Green Business Centre, Wingfield View, Clay Cross, Derbys, S45 9JW
T: 01246 252360
F: 01246 252361
E: a1micromotive@btopenworld.com
W: www.a1micromotive.co.uk

Middle Peak Railways Ltd
PO Box 71, High Peak, Derbys, SK23 7WL
T: 0870 881 6743
F: 0870 991 7350
E: info@middlepeak.co.uk
W: www.middlepeak.co.uk

Midland Metro Alliance
W: www.metroalliance.co.uk/

Midland Quarry Products
Leicester Road, Whitwick, Leicestershire, LE67 5GR
T: 01530 831000
F: 01530 832299
E: enquiries@mqp.co.uk
W: www.mqp.co.uk/

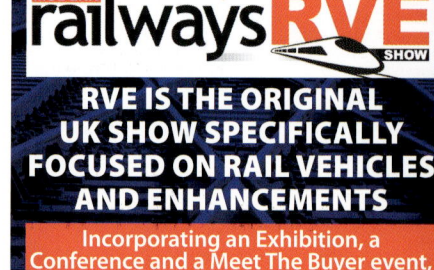

Midlands Connect
16 Summer Lane, Birmingham, B19 3SD
W: https://www.midlandsconnect.uk

Mid-West Services
44 Broadway, Stratford, London, E15 1XH
T: 020 3130 0466
F: 020 3070 0065
E: info@midwestservices.co.uk
W: www.midwestservices.co.uk

Mike Worby Survey Consultancy Ltd
37 Ramblers Way, Welwyn Garden City, Herts, AL7 2JU
T: 01707 333677
F: 01707 333677
M: 07767 456196
E: survey@mw-sc.co.uk
W: www.mw-sc.co.uk

Millar Bryce Ltd
5 Logie Mill, Beaverbank Office Park, Logie Green Rd, Edinburgh, EH7 4HH
T: 0131 556 1313
F: 0131 557 5960
E: marketing@millar-bryce.com
W: www.millar-bryce.com

Millcroft Services Plc
Salutation House, 1 Salutation Rd, Greenwich, London, SE10 0AT
T: 020 8305 1988
F: 020 8305 1986
E: sales@millcroft.co.uk
W: www.millcroft.co.uk

Millenium Site Services Ltd
Haydock Park Road, Derby, DE24 8HT
T: 01332 820003
E: lee.birkett@milleniumsiteservices.co.uk
W: www.milleniumsiteservices.co.uk

Miller Construction
Miller House, 2 Lochside View, Edinburgh, EH12 9DH
T: 0870 336 5000
E: mc.edinburgh@miller.co.uk
W: www.miller.co.uk

Mills Ltd
13 Fairway Drive, Fairway Industrial Estate, Greenford, Middlesex, UB6 8PW
T: 020 8833 2626
F: 020 8833 2600
E: sales@millsltd.com
W: www.millsltd.com

Minimise Energy
6 Stirling Park, Laker Road, Rochester Airport Estate, Rochester, Kent, ME1 3QR
T: 0330 313 3220
E: info@minimisegroup.com
W: www.minimisegroup.com/

Minova
Unit 19, Redbrook Business Park, Wilthorpe Road, Barnsley, S75 1JN
T: 01226 280567
F: 01226 731563
E: robert.fisher@minovaglobal.com
W: www.minovaglobal.com

Mirror Technology Ltd
Redwood House, Orchard Ind Est, Toddington, Glos, GL54 5EB
T: 01242 621534
F: 01242 621529
E: malcolm@mirrortechnology.co.uk
W: www.mirrortechnology.co.uk

Mission Room Ltd
Kings Meadow Campus, Lenton Lane, Nottingham, NG7 2NR
T: 0115 951 6800
F: 0115 954 1002
E: info@missionroom.com
W: www.missionroom.com

Mita (UK) Ltd
See Schneider Electric Ltd

Mitchell Bridges Ltd
London Rd, Kingsworthy, Winchester, Hants, SO23 7QN
T: 01962 885040
F: 01962 885040
E: chris@mitchellbridges.com
W: www.temporarybridges.com

MITIE
1 Harlequin Office Park, Fieldfare, Emersons Green, Bristol, BS16 7FN
T: 0117 970 8800
E: info@mitie.com
W: www.mitie.com/

Mitsubishi Electric (Melco)
Travellers Lane, Hatfield, Herts, AL10 8XB
T: 01707 276100
F: 01707 278693
W: www.mitsubishielectric.co.uk/

Mitsui & Co Europe plc
8th and 9th Floors, 1 St. Martin's Le Grand, London, EC1A 4AS
T: 020 7822 0321
W: www.mitsui.com/eu/

MLM Consulting Engineers Ltd
North Kiln, Felaw Maltings, 46 Felaw Street, Ipswich, Suffolk, IP2 8PN
T: 01473 231100
E: lee.bowker@mlmgroup.com
W: www.mlmgroup.com/

MLP Railway Maintenance Ltd
60 Brookhill Road, Pinxton, Notts, NG16 6NS
T: 01773 811977
W: https://www.mlprail.co.uk/

MMRA
10 Fleet Place, London, EC4M 7RB
T: 020 7651 0590
E: paul.bardsley@mottmac.com
W: www.mmra-cert.com

The Mobile Catering Group
The Monkey House, Kersoe, Pershore, Worcs, WR10 3JD
T: 01386 710123
F: 01386 710123
M: 07850 915959
E: fred@cateringcontracts.com
W: www.cateringcontracts.com

Modern Railways RVE Expo
Key Publishing, Units 1-4, Gwash Way Industrial Estate, Ryhall Road, Stamford, Lincolnshire, PE9 1XP
T: 01780 755131
E: events@rve-expo.co.uk
W: www.rve-expo.co.uk/

Mole Solutions
Alconbury, Huntingdon, Cambridgeshire, PE28 4DA
T: 01480 413141
E: info@molesolutions.co.uk
W: www.molesolutions.co.uk/

Mono Design
4 St Andrews House, Vernon Gate, Derby, DE1 1UJ
T: 01332 361616
E: lynne@monodesign.co.uk
W: www.monodesign.co.uk

Moonbuggy Ltd
Solway Ind. Est, Maryport, Cumbria, CA15 8NF
T: 01900 815831
F: 01900 815553
E: r.smith@moonbuggy.com
W: www.moonbuggy.com

Moore Concrete Products Ltd
Caherty House, 41 Woodside Rd, Ballymena, Co. Antrim, BT42 4QH, Northern Ireland
T: 028 2565 2566
F: 028 2565 8480
E: info@moore-concrete.com
W: www.moore-concrete.com

MoreVision ExcelWraps
T: 0113 815 2220
W: www.excelwraps.com/

Morgan Advanced Materials
Upper Fforest Way, Swansea Enterprise Park, Swansea, SA6 8PP
T: 01792 763052
F: 01792 763167
E: meclsales@morganplc.com
W: www.morganelectrical materials.com

Morgan Hunt
5th Floor, 16 Old Bailey, London, EC4M 7EG
T: 020 7419 8968
F: 020 7419 8999
E: rail@morganhunt.com
W: www.morganhunt.com

Morgan Marine Ltd
Llandybie, Ammanford, Carms, SA18 3GY
T: 01269 850437
F: 01269 850656
E: sales@morgan-marine.com
W: www.morgan-marine.com

Morgan Sindall Group
Corporation Street, Rugby, Warwickshire, CV21 2DW
T: 01788 534500
F: 01788 534579
E: info@morgansindall.com
W: https://www.morgansindall.com/

D Morgan plc
New Hey, Chester Road, Great Sutton, Ellesmere Port, CH66 2LS
T: 0151 339 8113
F: 0151 347 1254
E: contact@dmorgan.co.uk
W: www.dmorgan.co.uk/

Mornsun Guangzhou Science & Technology Co Ltd
No 5, Kehui St 1, Kehui Development Centre, Science Avenue, Guangzhou Science City 510660, Luogang District, China
T: 0086 203860 1850 8810
F: 0086 203860 1272
E: info@mornsun.cn
W: www.mornsun-power.com

Morris Lubricants
Castle Foregate, Shrewsbury, Shropshire, SY1 2EL
T: 01743 232200
E: info@morris-lubricants.co.uk
W: www.morrislubricants.co.uk/

Morris Site Machinery
Station Rd, Four Ashes, Wolverhampton, WV10 7DB
T: 0845 409 0280
F: 01902 790355
E: info@morrismachinery.co.uk
W: www.morrismachinery.co.uk

Morrison Utility Services Ltd
Fitzwilliam House, Middle Bank, Doncaster, South Yorkshire, DN4 5NG
T: 01302 898303
E: chris.ford@morrisonus.com
W: www.morrisonus.com

Mors Smitt UK Ltd (A Wabtec Company)
Graycar Business Park, Barton-under-Needwood, Burton upon Trent, Staffordshire, DE13 8EN
T: 01283 357263
F: 01283 722651
E: sales.msuk@wabtec.com
W: www.morssmitt.com

Morson International
Stableford Hall, Monton, Eccles, Manchester, M30 8AP
T: 0161 707 1516
F: 0161 788 8372
E: rail@morson.com
W: www.morson.com

Morson Projects Ltd
Adamson House, Centenary Way, Salford, Manchester, M50 1RD
T: 0161 707 1516
F: 0161 786 2360
E: andy.hassall@morson-projects.co.uk
W: www.morsonprojects.co.uk

Motorail Logistics
Quinton Rail Technology Centre, Station Road, Long Marston, Stratford upon Avon, Warks, CV37 8PL
T: 01789 721995
F: 01789 721396
E: ruth.dunmore@motorail.co.uk
W: www.motorail.co.uk

Mott MacDonald Group
Mott MacDonald House, 8-10 Sydenham Rd, Croydon, Surrey, CR0 2EE
T: 020 8774 2000
F: 020 8681 5706
E: railways@mottmac.com
W: www.mottmac.com

Mouchel
4 Matthew Parker Street, London, SW1H 9NP
T: 020 7227 6800
F: 020 7277 6801
E: consultingsales@mouchel.com
W: www.mouchel.com

Movares
Mireille Ros, Leidseveer 10, 3511 SB Utrecht, Netherlands
T: 0031 30265 3101
F: 0031 30265 3111
E: info@movares.nl
W: www.movares.com

Movement Strategies
31-35 Kirby Street, Farringdon, London, EC1N 8TE
T: 020 3540 8520
E: info@movementstrategies.com
W: www.movementstrategies.com/

Moveright International Ltd
Dunton Park, Dunton Lane, Wishaw, Sutton Coldfield, B76 9QA
T: 01675 475590
F: 01675 475591
E: andrew@moveright international.com
W: www.moverightinternational.com

Moxa Europe GmbH
Einsteinstrasse 7, D-85716 Unterschleissheim, Germany
T: 0049 893700 3940
F: 0049 893700 3999
E: europe@moxa.com
W: www.moxa.com/rail

MPB Structures
4th Floor, Hamilton House, Mabledon Place, London, WC1H 9BB
T: 020 7554 8864
W: www.mpb.co.uk/

MPEC Technology Ltd
Wyvern House, Railway Terrace, Derby, DE1 2RU
T: 01332 363979
F: 08701 363958
E: andrew.whawell@mpec.co.uk
W: www.mpec.co.uk

MPH Construction
Bromfield House, Bromfield Industrial Estate, Queens Lane, Mold, Flintshire, CH7 1XB
T: 01352 755151
F: 01352 758892
E: info@mphconstruction.co.uk
W: mph.futurestudios.net/

MPI Ltd
International House, The Chase, Foxholes Business Park, Hertford, Hertfordshire, SG13 7NN
T: 01992 501111
F: 01992 583384
E: info@mpi.ltd.uk
W: www.mpi.ltd.uk

MR Site Services Ltd
Unit 6, Worcester Trading Estate, Blackpole, Worcester, WR3 8HR
T: 01905 755055
F: 01905 755053
E: welding@mrsiteservices.co.uk
W: www.mrsiteservices.co.uk

MRO Software Now part of IBM UK Ltd
PO Box 41, North Harbour, Portsmouth, PO6 3AU
T: 0870 542 6426
E: maximo@uk.ibm.com
W: www.maximo.com

MRX Technologies Ltd
22 Royal Scot Rd, Pride Park, Derby, DE24 8AJ
T: 01332 381418
F: 01332 381421
E: bww@mrxtech.co.uk
W: www.mrxtech.com

MSc Traction Oy
Alasniitynkatu 30, FIN-33560 Tampere, Finland
T: 358 050 532 1469
E: info@msc.eu
W: www.msc.eu

MSD Construction UK Ltd
Manvers House, Pioneer Close, Wath Upon Dearne, Rotherham, S63 7JZ
T: 01709 878988
F: 01709 878918
E: enquiries@msdconstruction.com
W: www.msdconstruction.com

Mtag Composites
Unit 4A, Cowbridge Business Park, Boston, Lincolnshire, PE22 7DJ
T: 01205 352992
W: www.mtagcomposites.co.uk/

MTM Power Messtechnik Mellenbach GmbH
Zirkel 3, 98744 Schwarzatal, Germany
T: 0049 69154 2628
E: info@mtm-power.com
W: www.mtm-power.com

MTR Corporation
Samuel House, 6 St Alban's Street, London, SW1Y 4SQ
T: 020 7766 3500
F: 020 7839 6217
E: europe@mtr.com.hk
W: www.mtr.com.hk

MTR Elizabeth Line
63 St Mary Axe, London, EC3A 8NH
T: 020 7444 0213
E: enquiries@mtrcrossrail.co.uk
W: www.mtrcrossrail.co.uk

MTR Training Ltd
See HSS Training Ltd

MTU UK Ltd
Unit 29, The Birches Ind. Est, East Grinstead, West Sussex, RH19 1XZ
T: 01342 335450
F: 01342 335470
E: naomi.thornton@mtu-online.com
W: www.mtu-online.com

Multicell
Swannington Rd, Broughton Astley, Leicester, LE9 6TU
T: 01455 283443
F: 01455 284250
E: help@multicell.co.uk
W: www.multicell.co.uk

Multipulse
Units 1-2, Goldsworth Park Trading Est, Kestrel Way, Woking, Surrey, GU21 3BA
T: 01483 713600
F: 01483 729851
E: sales@multipulse.com
W: www.multipulse.com

J Murphy & Sons Ltd
Hiview House, 81 Highgate Rd, London, NW5 1TN
T: 020 7267 4366
F: 020 7428 3107
E: info@murphygroup.co.uk
W: www.murphygroup.co.uk

Murphy Surveys
Head Office UK, 39-41 North Road, London, N7 9DP
T: 020 3598 3775
E: info@murphysurveys.co.uk
W: www.murphysurveys.co.uk

MVA Consultancy
See Systra UK

MWH Treatment Ltd
Biwater Place, Gregge St, Heywood, Lancs, OL10 2DX
T: 01706 626258
F: 01706 626294
E: info@mwhglobal.com
W: www.mwhglobal.com

Nacco (UK) Ltd
Office 3, The Dairy, Crewe Hall Farm, Old Park Rd, Crewe, Cheshire, CW1 5UE
T: 01270 254100
F: 0872 115 0919
E: sales@naccorail.co.uk
W: www.naccorail.com

Napier Turbochargers Limited
Ruston House, PO Box 1, Waterside South, Lincoln, Lincolnshire, LN5 7FD
T: 01522 516666
E: napier_enquiry@wabtec.com
W: www.napier-turbochargers.com

National Car Parks Ltd (NCP)
Saffron Court, 14B St Cross Street, London, EC1N 8XA
T: 0345 050 70 80
E: derek.hulyer@ncp.co.uk
W: www.ncp.co.uk

National College for Advanced Transport & Infrastructure (NCATI)
Faraday Wharf, Innovation Birmingham Campus, Holt Street, Aston, Birmingham, B7 4BB
T: 0330 120 0375
E: enquiries@ncati.ac.uk
W: https://nchsr.ac.uk/

National Composites Centre
Feynman Way Central, Bristol & Bath Science Park, Emersons Green, Bristol, BS16 7FS
T: 0117 370 7600
E: info@nccuk.com
W: www.nccuk.com

National Express East Anglia
See Greater Anglia

National Express Group Plc
75 Davies St, London, W1K 5HT
T: 020 7529 2000
F: 020 7529 2100
E: info@natex.co.uk
W: www.nationalexpressgroup.com

National Infrastructure Commission (NIC)
E: enquiries@infrastructure-commission.gsi.gov.uk
W: www.nic.org.uk/

National Rail Enquiries
T: 08457 484950
W: www.nationalrail.co.uk

National Railway Museum
Leeman Rd, York, YO26 4XJ
T: 0800 047 8124
E: info@railwaymuseum.org.uk
W: www.railwaymuseum.org.uk

National Training Academy for Rail (NTAR)
Unit 5, Heathfield Way, Kings Heath, Northampton, NN5 7QP
T: 01604 594440
E: info@ntar.co.uk
W: www.ntar.co.uk

The Nationwide Accreditation Bureau Ltd
The Olympic Office Centre, 8 Fulton Rd, Wembley, HA9 0NU
T: 08458 902902
F: 08458 903903
E: enquiries@thenab.co.uk
W: www.thenab.co.uk

Nationwide Healthcare Connect
See Healthcare Connections Ltd

Native Land
The Pavilion, 118 Southwark Street, London, SE1 0SW
T: 020 7758 3650
F: 020 7437 4831
E: reception@native-land.com
W: www.native-land.com/

Natural Cement Distribution Ltd
10-11 Fountain Parade, Mapplewell, Barnsley, South Yorkshire, S75 6FW
T: 01226 381133
F: 01226 381177
E: enquiries@naturalcement.co.uk
W: www.naturalcement.co.uk

Navaho Technologies Ltd
8/9 Hayters Court, Grigg Lane, Brockenhurst, Hants, SO42 7PG
T: 02380 000010
F: 02380 988598
E: sales@navaho.co.uk
W: www.navaho.co.uk

Navigant Consulting
5th Floor, Woolgate Exchange, 25 Basinghall Street, London, EC2V 5HA
T: 020 7469 1111
F: 020 7469 1110
E: inquiries@navigant.com
W: www.navigant.com/

Nazeing Glass Works Ltd
Nazeing New Rd, Broxbourne, Herts, EN10 6SU
T: 01992 464485
F: 01992 450966
E: sales@nazeing-glass.co.uk
W: www.nazeing-glass.com

NCH (UK) Ltd - Chemsearch
Landchard House, Victoria St, West Bromwich, B70 8ER
T: 0121 524 7300
F: 0121 500 5386
W: www.chemsearch.co.uk

NCL Installations Ltd
Orchard Rise, 173 Yardley Fields, Yardley, Birmingham, B33 8RP
T: 0121 783 9480
M: 07711 060407
E: nicholas.lane9@gmail.com
W: www.on-train.co.uk

NDC Consultants
Unit 6, Berkeley Business Park, Wainwright Road, Worcester, WR4 9FA
T: 01905 756000
F: 01905 756010
E: info@ndcconsultants.co.uk
W: www.ndcconsultants.co.uk/

Neale Consulting Engineers Ltd
Highfield, Pilcot Hill, Dogmersfield, Fleet, Hants, RG27 8SX
T: 01252 629199
F: 01252 815625
E: ncel@tribology.co.uk
W: www.tribology.co.uk

Neary Rail
9 Coal Pit Lane, Atherton, Manchester, M46 0RY
T: 01942 881470
F: 01942 884147
E: info@neary.co.uk
W: www.neary.co.uk

NedRailways
See Abellio

Nedtrain BV
Kantorencentrum Katereine 9, Stationshal 17, 3511 ED, Utrecht, Netherlands
T: 0031 30 300 4929
F: 0031 30 300 4647
W: www.nedtrain.nl

Nelsons Solicitors
Sterne House, Lodge Lane, Derby, DE1 3WD
T: 01332 372372
E: enquiries@nelsonslaw.co.uk
W: www.nelsonslaw.co.uk

Nemesis Rail Ltd
Burton Rail Depot, Derby Rd, Burton upon Trent, Staffordshire, DE14 1RS
T: 01283 531562
E: enquiries@nemesisrail.com
W: www.nemesisrail.com

Nenta Traintours
Railtour House, 10 Buxton Rd, North Walsham, Norfolk, NR28 0ED
T: 01692 406152
F: 01692 406152
E: ray.davies@nentatraintours.co.uk
W: www.nentatraintours.co.uk

Neon Hire Services Ltd
Unit 27, Icknield Way Farm, Tring Road, Dunstable, Bedfordshire, LU6 2JX
T: 01582 478000
F: 01582 668006
W: www.neonhire.co.uk/

Neopul UK
Beaufort House, 11th Floor, 15 St Botolph Street, Aldgate, London, EC3A 7BB
W: www.neopul.pt

NES Track
Station House, Stamford New Rd, Altrincham, Cheshire, WA14 1EP
T: 0161 942 4016
F: 0161 942 7969
E: nestrack.manchester@nes.co.uk
W: www.nestrack.co.uk

Network Certification Body Ltd
Ground Floor, Caldecotte, The Quadrant, Eldergate, Milton Keynes, MK9 1EN
T: 01908 784002
E: ncbenquiries@networkrail.co.uk
W: www.net-cert.co.uk

Network Construction Services Ltd
Ercall House, Pearson Rd, Central Park, Telford, Shropshire, TF2 9TX
T: 01952 210243
F: 01952 290168
E: sales@ncsjob.co.uk
W: www.ncsjob.co.uk

Network Rail Consulting Ltd
42 Upper Berkeley Street, London, W1H 5PW
T: 020 3356 0454
E: contactnrc@networkrail.co.uk
W: www.networkrailconsulting.co.uk

Network Rail Infrastructure Ltd
1 Eversholt Street, London, NW1 2DN
T: 020 7557 8000
W: www.networkrail.co.uk

Network Rail Property
6 Burrell St, London, SE1 0UN
T: 0800 830840
E: property@networkrail.co.uk
W: property.networkrail.co.uk

Network Storage Systems Ltd
21 Leebrook Place, Woodland Heights, Owlthorpe, Sheffield, S20 6QL
T: 0800 633 5933
E: sales@networkstoragesystems.co.uk
W: www.networkstoragesystems.co.uk

Neway Training Solutions Ltd
Kelvin House, RTC Business Park, London Rd, Derby, DE24 8UP
T: 01332 360033
F: 01332 366367
E: enquiries@neway-training.com
W: www.neway-training.com

DIRECTORY

Nomad Digital Limited
5th Floor, One Trinity, Broad Chare, Newcastle-upon-Tyne, NE1 2HF
T: 020 7096 6966
F: 0191 221 1339
E: experts@nomadrail.com
W: www.nomad-digital.com

Nomix Enviro Ltd - A division of Frontier Agriculture Ltd
The Grain Silos, Weyhill Rd, Andover, Hants, SP10 3NT
T: 01264 388050
F: 01522 866176
E: nomixenviro@frontierag.co.uk
W: www.nomix.co.uk

Nord-Lock Ltd
Kingsgate House, Newbury Road, Andover, Wilts, SP10 4DU
T: 01264 355557
F: 01264 369555
E: enquiries@nord-lock.co.uk
W: www.nord-lock.com

Norgren Ltd
See IMI Precision Engineering

Nortek Global HVAC
Fens Pool Avenue, Brierley Hill, West Midlands, DY5 1QA
T: 01384 489250
E: info.reznor@nortek.com
W: https://www.nortekhvac.com/

North East Railtours
See SRPS Railtours

North Highland Consulting
8th Floor, 120 Holborn, London, EC1N 2TD
T: 020 7812 6460
E: info@northhighland.com
W: www.northhighland.com/

North Star Consultancy Ltd
78 York St, London, W1H 1DP
T: 020 7692 0936
F: 020 7692 0937
E: enquiries@northstarconsultancy.com
W: www.northstarconsultancy.com

Northern
Northern House, 9 Rougier St, York, YO1 6HZ
T: 0333 222 0125
F: 0113 247 9059
E: enquiries@northernrailway.co.uk
W: https://www.northernrailway.co.uk/

Northern Ireland Railways
See Translink NI Railways

Northsouth Communication
129 Main St, Lochgelly, KY5 9AF
T: 01592 782144
E: enquiries@northsouthcommunication.co.uk
W: www.northsouthcommunication.co.uk

Northston Engineering Consultancy Ltd
Northston, School Street, Sulgrave, OX17 2RR
M: 07469 192830
E: graham@northstonengineering.com
W: www.northstonengineering.com

Northwood Railway Eng. Ltd
9 Scot Grove, Pinner, Middx, HA5 4RT
T: 020 8428 9890
E: davidnbradley@btopenworld.com

Norton & Associates
32a High St, Pinner, Middx, HA5 5PW
T: 020 8869 9237
F: 07005 964635
E: mail@nortonweb.co.uk
W: www.nortonweb.co.uk

Norton Rose Fulbright LLP
3 More London, Riverside, London, SE1 2AQ
T: 020 7283 6000
F: 020 7283 6500
E: tim.marsden@nortonrosefulbright.com
W: www.nortonrose.com

Norwest Holst Construction
See Indigo

Nottingham Trams Ltd
NET Depot, Wilkinson St, Nottingham, NG7 7NW
T: 0115 942 7777
E: info@thetram.net
W: www.thetram.net

Novacroft
Lakeside House, 9 The Lakes, Bedford Road, Northampton, NN4 7HD
T: 0845 330 0601
F: 0845 330 0745
E: projects@novacroft.com
W: www.novacroft.com

Novah Ltd
Unit 12, Jensen Court, Astmoor Industrial Estate, Runcorn, Cheshire, WA7 1SQ
T: 01928 242918
F: 01928 567838
E: sales@novah.co.uk
W: www.novah.co.uk

Novus Rail Ltd
Solaris Centre, New South Prom, Blackpool, FY4 1RW
T: 01253 478027
F: 01253 478037
E: mmcm@novusrail.com
W: www.novusrail.com

NR Engineering Ltd
Duckworth Mill, Skipton Road, Colne, Lancs, BB8 0RH
T: 01282 868500
F: 01282 868157
E: sales@nrengineering.co.uk
W: www.nrengineering.co.uk

NRL
Second Floor, Atlas House, Caxton Close, Marus Bridge, Wigan, Lancs, WN3 6XU
T: 01942 326727
F: 01942 829729
E: rail@nrl.co.uk
W: www.nrl.co.uk/rail

NSAR (National Skills Academy for Rail)
11 Carteret Street, London, SW1H 9DJ
T: 0203 021 0575
E: enquiries@nsare.org
W: www.nsar.co.uk

NTM Sales & Marketing Ltd
PO Box 2, Summerbridge, Harrogate, HG3 4XN
T: 01423 781010
F: 01423 593953
E: info@xl-lubricants.com
W: www.xl-lubricants.com

NTRS (Network Training & Resource Solutions)
Unit 3&4, Churchill Way, Chapeltown, Sheffield, S35 2PY
T: 0844 809 9902
F: 0844 809 9903
E: info@ntrs.co.uk
W: www.ntrs.co.uk

Nu Star Material Handling
Lakeside, Ednaston Business Centre, Ednaston, Derby, DE6 3AE
T: 0115 880 0070
F: 0115 880 0071
E: matt@nu-starmhl.com
W: www.nu-starmhl.com

Nucleus VP Group
The Oasts, Charmans Farm, Westerham, Kent, TN16 1QP
T: 0844 775 0000
E: info@nucleusvp.com
W: www.nucleusvp.com

Nufox Rubber Ltd
Unit 1, Bentley Ave, Middleton, Manchester, M24 2GP
T: 0161 655 8800
F: 0161 655 8801
E: info@nufox.com
W: www.nufox.com/

Nusteel Structures
Lympne, Hythe, Kent, CT21 4LR
T: 01303 268112
F: 01303 266098
E: general@nusteelstructures.com
W: www.nusteelstructures.com

Nuttall Finchpalm
See BAM Nuttall

NVR Fleet UK
See Hitachi Capital Vehicle Solutions Ltd

Oakland Consulting
West One, 114 Wellington Street, Leeds, West Yorkshire, LS1 1BA
T: 0113 234 1944
F: 0113 234 1988
E: contactus@oaklandconsulting.com
W: www.oaklandconsulting.com/

Oce UK Ltd
Oce House, Chatham Way, Brentwood, Essex, CM14 4DZ
T: 0870 600 5544
F: 0870 600 1113
E: info@oce.com
W: www.oce.com

Odgers Ray & Berndtson
11 Hanover Square, London, W1S 1JJ
T: 020 7529 1111
F: 020 7529 1000
E: info@rayberndtson.co.uk
W: www.odgers.com

Office of Rail and Road
25 Cabot Square, London, E14 4QZ
T: 020 7282 2000
F: 020 7282 2040
E: contact.cct@orr.gsi.gov.uk
W: www.orr.gov.uk

Ogier Electronics Ltd
Unit 13, Sandridge Park, Porters Wood, St Albans, Herts, AL3 6PH
T: 01727 845547
F: 01727 852186
E: david.sproule@ogierelectronics.com
W: www.ogierelectronics.com

Oil Analysis Services Ltd
Unit 6/7, Blue Chalet Ind. Park, London Rd, West Kingsdown, Kent, TN15 6BQ
T: 01474 854450
F: 01474 854408
E: ihbrown@oas-online.co.uk
W: www.oas-online.co.uk

Oilaway
Wakefield Road, Rothwell Haigh, Leeds, West Yorkshire, LS26 0SB
T: 0113 205 9332
E: info@oilaway.net
W: www.oilaway.net

Oldcastle Enclosure Solutions
IDA Industrial Est., Racecourse Rd, Roscommon, Republic of Ireland
T: 00353 9066 25922
F: 00353 9066 25921
W: www.oldcastleprecast.com/plants/enclosures/pages/default.aspx

Oldham Engineering
Castle Iron Works, Overens Street, Oldham, Lancashire, OL4 1LA
T: 0161 627 5822
F: 0161 626 3500
E: sales@oldham-eng.com
W: https://oldham-eng.com/

Oleo International
Grovelands, Longford Rd, Exhall, Coventry, CV7 9NE
T: 02476 645555
F: 02476 645900
E: sales@oleo.co.uk
W: www.oleo.co.uk

Omega Red Group Ltd
Dabell Ave, Blenheim Ind.Est., Bulwell, Nottingham, NG6 8WA
T: 0115 877 6666
F: 0115 876 7766
E: enquiries@omegaredgroup.com
W: www.omegaredgroup.com

Omnicom Balfour Beatty Ltd
Eboracum Way, Clifton Park Avenue, York, YO30 5PB
T: 01904 778100
F: 01904 778150
E: info@omnicomengineering.co.uk
W: www.omnicomengineering.co.uk

On Track Design Solutions Ltd
1st Floor Suite, 11 Pride Point Drive, Pride Park, Derby, DE24 8BX
T: 01332 204450
F: 01332 204458
E: brianchadwick@ontrackdesign.co.uk
W: www.ontrackdesign.co.uk

On Track Flooring Ltd
Unit E18, Langham Park, Low's Lane, Stanton by Dale, Derbys, DE7 4RJ
T: 0115 932 1691
F: 0115 930 9951
E: info@ontrackflooring.co.uk
W: www.ontrackflooring.co.uk/

ON Train Limited
Orchard Rise, 173 Yardley Fields, Yardley, Birmingham, B33 8RP
T: 0121 783 9480
M: 07527 811700
E: sales@on-train.co.uk
W: www.on-train.co.uk

Onboard Retail Solutions
See Iridium Onboard

One Big Circle
The Engine Shed, Station Approach, Bristol, BS1 6QH
T: 0845 838 7178
E: info@onebigcircle.co.uk
W: onebigcircle.co.uk

One Four Nine Creative
E: info@onefourninecreative.com
W: www.onefourninecreative.com

One Way
26 Basepoint, Andersons Road, Southampton, Hampshire, SO14 5FE
T: 0845 644 8843
W: www.oneway.co.uk/

One-On Ltd
7 Home Farm Courtyard, Meriden Rd, Berkswell, West Midlands, CV7 7SH
T: 0845 505 1955
F: 0845 505 1977
E: info@one-on.co.uk
W: www.one-on.co.uk

OnTrac Ltd
Floor 1, Baltimore House, Baltic Business Quarter, Gateshead, Tyne and Wear, NE8 3DF
T: 0191 477 4951
W: www.on-trac.co.uk/

Open Technology Ltd
1 Woodlands Court, Albert Drive, Burgess Hill, West Sussex, RH15 9TN
T: 0845 680 4004
F: 0845 680 4005
E: info@opentechnologyuk.com
W: www.opentechnologyuk.com

Opentree Ltd
Cabinet House, Ellerbeck Court, Stokesley Business Park, North Yorkshire, TS9 5PT
T: 01642 714471
F: 01642 714451
E: sales@opentree.co.uk
W: www.opentree.co.uk

Opinsta
Suites 35-37, The White House, 111 New Street, Birmingham, B2 4EU
M: 07375 812874
E: info@opinsta.com
W: www.opinsta.com

OptaSense
Building A8, Room 1005, Cody Technology Park, Ively Road, Farnborough, Hampshire, GU14 0LX
T: 01252 392000
W: www.optasense.com/

Optilan Communication Systems
Sibree Rd, Stonebridge Ind. Est, Coventry, CV3 4FD
T: 01926 864999
F: 01926 851818
E: sales@optilan.com
W: www.optilan.com

Newburgh Precision Limited
Bessemer Way, Rotherham, S60 1FB
T: 01709 724260
T: 01709 839312
E: sales@np-ltd.co.uk
W: www.np-ltd.co.uk/

Newbury Data Recording Ltd
T: 0870 224 8110
F: 0870 224 8177
E: ndsales@newburydata.co.uk
W: www.newburydata.co.uk

Newby Foundries Ltd
Smith Road, Wednesbury, West Midlands, WS10 0PB
T: 0044 (0) 121 556 4451
F: 0044 (0) 121 505 3626
E: sales@newbyfoundries.co.uk
W: www.newbyfoundries.co.uk

Newby Foundries Ltd
Steel Castings Division, 1 Cornwall Road, Smethwick, B66 2JT
T: 0044 (0) 121 555 7615
F: 0044 (0) 121 505 3626
E: sales@newbyfoundries.co.uk
W: www.newbyfoundries.co.uk

NewRail Centre for Railway Research
Stephenson Building, Newcastle University, Claremont Rd, Newcastle-upon-Tyne, NE1 7RU
T: 0191 208 8575
F: 0191 208 8600
E: newrail@ncl.ac.uk
W: www.newrail.org

Newton Europe
2 Kingston Business Park, Kingston Bagpuize, Oxon, OX13 5FE
T: 01865 601 300
F: 01865 601 348
E: info@newtoneurope.com
W: www.newtoneurope.com

Nexala Ltd
Suite 34, The Mall, Beacon Court, Sandyford, Dublin 18, Republic of Ireland
T: +353 (0) 1 4800 519
E: rail-lifecycle@trimble.com
W: www.trimble.com/rail-lifecycle

Nexans
Nexans House, Chesney Wold, Bleak Hall, Milton Keynes, MK6 1LF
T: 01908 250840
F: 01908 250841
E: iandi.sales@nexans.com
W: www.nexans.com

Nexus (Tyne & Wear Metro)
Nexus House, 33 St James Blvd, Newcastle upon Tyne, NE1 4AX
T: 0191 203 3333
F: 0191 203 3180
E: contactus@twmetro.co.uk
W: www.nexus.org.uk/metro

Nexus Alpha Group
London House, 7 Prescott Place, Clapham, London, SW4 6BS
T: 020 7652 2051
F: 020 7622 6817
E: commercialdept@nexusalpha.com
W: www.nexusalphagroup.com

Nexus Training
105 Sheffield Rd, Godley, Hyde, Cheshire, SK14 2LT
T: 0161 339 2190
E: info@nexustraining.org.uk
W: www.nexustraining.org.uk

NFM Technologies
5, place Jules Ferry, 69456 LYON Cedex 06, France
T: +33 (0)4 26 84 87 00
F: +33 (0)426 848 710
W: www.nfm-technologies.com/

NG Bailey
Denton Hall, Ilkley, West Yorkshire, LS29 0HH
T: 01943 601 933
E: enquiries@ngbailey.co.uk
W: www.ngbailey.co.uk

Nichols Group Ltd
7-8 Stratford Place, London, W1C 1AY
T: 020 7292 7000
T: 020 7292 5200
E: operations@nichols.uk.com
W: www.nicholsgroup.co.uk

Nigel Nixon Consulting
Suite 1, AD Business Centre, Hithercroft Rd, Wallingford, Oxon, OX10 9EZ
T: 01491 824030
F: 01491 824078
E: nigel@nigelnixon.com
W: www.nigelnixon.com

Nightsearcher Ltd
Unit 4, Applied House, Fitzherbert Spur, Farlington, Portsmouth, PO6 1TT
T: 023 9238 9774
F: 023 9238 9788
E: sales@nightsearcher.co.uk
W: www.nightsearcher.co.uk

Nimble Media
Unit 6, Old Station Yard, Ashwell, Oakham, Rutland, LE15 7SP
T: 01780 432930
E: info@nimblemedia.co.uk
W: www.nimblemedia.co.uk

Nitech Ltd
4-6 Highfield Business Park, Churchfields Ind. Estate, St Leonards on Sea, East Sussex, TN38 9UB
T: 01424 852788
F: 01424 851008
E: sales@nitech.co.uk
W: www.nitech.co.uk

NMB Minebea UK Ltd
Doddington Rd, Lincoln, LN6 3RA
T: 01522 500933
F: 01522 500975
W: www.nmb-minebea.co.uk

No1 Scaffolding Service
Swinbourne Rd, Burnt Mills Ind.Est., Basildon, Essex, SS13 1EF
T: 01268 724793
F: 01268 725606
E: enquiries@no1scaffolders.co.uk
W: www.no1scaffolders.co.uk

IN ASSOCIATION WITH  Nomad Digital

Optimized Systems & Solutions Ltd
SIN D-7, PO Box 31, Derby, DE24 8BJ
T: 01332 771700
F: 01332 770921
W: www.o-sys.com

Optimum Consultancy Ltd
Spencer House, Mill Green Rd, Haywards Heath, West Sussex, RH16 1XQ
T: 020 3694 4100
F: 01444 448071
E: enquiries@optimum.uk.com
W: www.optimum.uk.com

Opus International Consultants Ltd
Yale Business Village, Wrexham Technology Park, Wrexham, LL13 7YL
T: 01978 368100
F: 01978 368101
E: mark.valentine@opusinternational.co.uk
W: www.opusinternational.co.uk

Oracle Recruitment
See Acorn People

Orchard Consulting
See Optimum Consultancy Ltd

Ordnance Survey
Romsey Rd, Southampton, SO16 4GU
T: 02380 305030
F: 02380 792615
E: customerservice@ordnancesurvey.co.uk
W: www.ordnancesurvey.co.uk

Orient Express
T: 020 7921 4028
F: 020 7805 5908
E: oesales.uk@orient-express.com
W: www.orient-express.com

Orion Electrotech
4 Danehill, Lower Earley, Reading, RG6 4UT
T: 0118 923 9239
F: 0118 975 3332
E: rail@orion-group.co.uk
W: www.orionelectrotech.com

Orion High Speed Logistics
T: 01332 343295
E: orion@railopsgroup.co.uk
W: orion.railopsgroup.co.uk/

Orion Rail Services Ltd
30 Hepburn Road, Hillington Park, Glasgow, G52 4RT
T: 0141 892 6666
F: 0141 892 6662
E: sales@orioneng.com
W: www.orionrail.co.uk/

Osborne Clarke
One London Wall, London, EC2Y 5EB
T: 020 7105 7000
E: enquiries@osborneclarke.com
W: www.osborneclarke.com

Osborne Rail
Fonteyn House, 47-49 London Rd, Reigate, Surrey, RH2 2PY
T: 01737 378200
F: 01737 378295
E: enquiries@osborne.co.uk
W: www.osborne.co.uk

OSL Rail
The Railway Exchange, Weston Road, Crewe, Cheshire, CW1 6AA
T: 0845 271 9171
F: 08701 236249
E: enquiries@o-s-l.uk.com
W: oslglobal.com/service/rail/

Otis Ltd
Chiswick Park, Building 5 Ground Floor, 566 Chiswick High Road, London, W4 5YF
T: 020 8495 7750
W: www.otis.com/site/gb/

OTN Systems
Industrielaan 17b B-2250, B-2250 Olen, Belgium
T: 003214252847
F: 003214252023
E: info@otnsystems.com
W: www.otnsystems.com

Overhead Line Engineering Ltd
4B Mallard Way, Pride Park, Derby, DE24 8GX
T: 01332 342122
M: 07501 467095
E: contact@ole-limited.co.uk
W: www.ole-limited.co.uk/

Owen Williams
See Amey

Oxera Consulting
Park Central, 40/41 Park End Street, Oxford, OX1 1JD
T: 01865 253000
E: enquiries@oxera.com
W: www.oxera.com/

Oxford Archaeology
Janus House, Osney Mead, Oxford, OX2 0ES
T: 01865 980700
E: dan.poore@oxfordarch.co.uk
W: oxfordarchaeology.com/

Oxford Economics
Abbey House, 121 St Aldates, Oxford, OX1 1HB
T: 01865 268 900
E: mailbox@oxfordeconomics.com
W: www.oxfordeconomics.com/

Oxford Hydrotechnics Ltd
Suite 2, The Great Barn, Baynards Green, Bicester, Oxon, OX27 7SR
T: 01869 346001
F: 01869 345455
E: info@h2ox.net
W: www.h2ox.net

PA Consulting
123 Buckingham Palace Road, London, SW1W 9SR
T: 020 7333 5865
W: www.paconsulting.com/

Palfinger AG
Lamprechtshausener Bundesstraße 8, 5101 Bergheim, Austria
T: +43 (0)662 2281-0
F: +43 (0)662 2281-81077
E: info@palfinger.com
W: https://www.palfinger.com/en/

Panasonic Computer Products Solutions
Panasonic House, Willoughby Road, Bracknell, Berks, RG12 8FP
T: 01344 853366
W: www.toughbook.eu

Panasonic Electric Works UK Ltd
Sunrise Parkway, Linford Wood, Milton Keynes, MK14 6LF
T: 01908 231555
F: 01908 231599
E: info-uk@eu.pewg.panasonic.com
W: www.panasonic-electric-works.co.uk

Pandrol UK Ltd
63 Station Road, Addlestone, Surrey, KT15 2AR
T: 01932 834500
E: info@pandrol.com
W: www.pandrol.com

Panolin
Ripon Way, Harrogate, N Yorks, HG1 2AU
T: 01423 522911
F: 01423 530043
E: admin@cardev.com
W: www.cardev.com

Pantrak Transportation Ltd
John G. Russell Building WKR, Container Base, Gartsherrie Road, Coatbridge, North Lanarkshire, ML5 2DY
T: 01292 442457
F: 01698 749672
M: 07974 724 173
E: eroser@pantrak.com
W: www.pantrak.com

Parallel Project Training
Davidson House, Forbury Sq, Reading, RG1 3EU
T: 0845 519 2305
F: 0118 900 0501
E: withyoualltheway@parallelprojecttraining.com
W: www.parallelprojecttraining.com

Park Signalling's products and services enable the useful life-extension and enhanced performance of older signalling equipment.

Technology & Products Solutions

Parallel Studios
22 Balmoral Ave, Bedford, MK40 2PT
F: 01234 217200
E: rick@parallelstudios.co.uk
W: ricktks.magix.net/website/about_us.30.html#home

Park Signalling Ltd
3rd Floor, Houldsworth Mill Business Centre, Houldsworth St, Reddish, Stockport, SK5 6DA
T: 0161 219 0161
E: info@park-signalling.co.uk
W: www.park-signalling.co.uk

Parkeon Ltd
10 Willis Way, Fleets Ind Est, Poole, Dorset, BH15 3SS
T: 01202 339339
F: 01202 339369
E: sales_uk@parkeon.com
W: www.parkeon.com

Parker Hannifin (UK) Ltd
Tachbrook Park Drive, Tachbrook Park, Warwick, CV34 6TU
T: 01926 317878
F: 01926 317855
E: filtrationinfo@parker.com
W: www.parker.com

Parker KV Division
Presley Way, Crownhill, Milton Keynes, MK8 0HB
T: 01908 561515
F: 01908 561227
E: saleskv@parker.com
W: www.parker.com

Parry People Movers Ltd
Overend Rd, Cradley Heath, West Midlands, B64 7DD
T: 01384 569553
E: info@parrypeoplemovers.com
W: www.parrypeoplemovers.com

Parsons Brinckerhoff
WSP House, 70 Chancery Lane, London, WC2A 1AF
T: 020 7314 5000
F: 020 7314 5111
E: railandtransit@pbworld.com
W: www.wsp-pb.com/en/

Parsons Transportation Group
Holborn Gate, High Holborn, London, WC1V 7QT
T: 020 8326 5621
F: 020 3102 6906
E: enquiries.pgil@parsons.com
W: www.parsons.com

Partex Marking Systems (UK) Ltd
Unit 61-64, Station Road, Coleshill, Birmingham, B46 1JT
T: 01675 463670
E: sales@partex.co.uk
W: www.partex.co.uk

Partsmaster Ltd (NCH Europe)
NCH House, Springvale Avenue, Bilston, West Midlands, WV14 0QL
T: 01902 510335
E: victoria.summerfield@nch.com
W: www.partsmaster.com

Passcomm Ltd
Unit 24, Tatton Court, Kingsland Garage, Warrington, Cheshire, WA1 4RR
T: 01925 821333
F: 01925 821321
E: info@passcomm.co.uk
W: www.passcomm.co.uk

Passenger Transport Intelligence Services
T: 01729 840756
M: 07972 213486
E: info@passtrans.co.uk
W: www.passtrans.co.uk

Passenger Transport Networks
49 Stonegate, York, YO1 8AW
T: 01904 611187
E: ptn@btconnect.com
W: www.passengertransportnetworks.co.uk

Pathfinder Systems UK PTY Ltd
Unit 6, Bighams Park Farm, Waterend, Hemel Hempstead, HP1 3BN
T: 07711 189366
F: 020 7328 8818
E: cel@pathfindersystems.com.au
W: www.pathfindersystems.com.au

Pathfinder Tours
Stag House, Gydynap Lane, Inchbrook, Woodchester, Glos, GL5 5EZ
T: 01453 835414/834477
F: 01453 834053
E: office@pathfindertours.co.uk
W: www.pathfindertours.co.uk

Pauley Interactive
Bletchley Leys Farm, Whaddon Road, Milton Keynes, MK17 0EG
T: 01908 522532
E: info@pauley.co.uk
W: www.pauley.co.uk

A J Paveley
416 Goldon Hillock Road, Sparkbrook, Birmingham, B11 2QH
T: 01217721739
E: sales@ajpaveley.com
W: www.ajpaveley.com

Paypoint
1 The Boulevard, Shire Park, Welwyn Garden City, Herts, AL7 1EL
T: 08457 600633
E: enquiries@paypoint.com
W: www.paypoint.com

PB – Consult GmbH
Am Plaerrer 12, 90429 Nuremburg, Germany
T: 0049 911 32239 0
F: 0049 911 32239 10
E: info@pbconsult.de
W: www.pbconsult.eu

PB Design & Development
Unit 9/10, Hither Green Ind. Est., Clevedon, Bristol, BS21 6XT
T: 01275 874411
F: 01275 874428
E: sales@pbdesign.co.uk
W: www.pbdesign.co.uk

PBH Rail Ltd
The Old Coach House, 4a Custance Walk, York, YO23 1BX
T: 01904 655666
F: 01904 655667
E: darren.pudsey@pbhrail.com
W: www.pbhrail.com

PBL Training
53 Guildford St, Bagshot, Surrey, GU19 5NG
T: 01276 477499
F: 01276 562726
E: mike@pbl-training.com
W: www.pbl-training.com

PCC.eu
Units 51/52, Llantarnam Ind. Park, Cwmbran, NP44 3AW
T: 01633 214565
F: 01633 864752
E: info@pcc.eu.com
W: www.pcc.eu.com

PD Devices Ltd
Unit 1, Old Station Yard, South Brent, Devon, TQ10 9AL
T: 01364 649248
E: marketing@pddevices.co.uk
W: www.pddevices.co.uk

PDG Helicopters
The Heliport, Dalcross, Inverness, IV2 7XB
T: 01667 462740
F: 01667 462376
E: enquiries@pdghelicopters.com
W: www.pdghelicopters.com/

Peacock Salt Ltd
North Harbour, Ayr, KA8 8AE
T: 01292 292000
F: 01292 292001
E: info@peacocksalt.co.uk
W: www.peacocksalt.co.uk

Pearsons Engineering Services Ltd
17 Ilkeston Road, Heanor, Derbys, DE75 7DR
T: 01773 763508
F: 01773 763508
E: nathan@pearsonsengineeringservices.co.uk
W: www.pearsonsengineeringservices.co.uk

A S Peck Engineering Ltd
116 Whitby Rd, Ruislip, Middx, HA4 9DR
T: 01895 621398
F: 01895 613761
E: mark.jones@aspeckeng.co.uk
W: www.aspeckeng.co.uk

Peeping Ltd
See Tracsis Plc

PEI Genesis UK Ltd
George Curl Way, Southampton, SO18 2RZ
T: 02380 621260
F: 02380 621270
E: peiuk@peigenesis.com
W: www.peigenesis.com

Peli Products (UK) Ltd
Peli House, Peakdale Rd, Brookfield, Glossop, Derbys, SK13 6LQ
T: 01457 869999
F: 01457 869966
E: sales@peliproducts.co.uk
W: www.peliproducts.co.uk

Pell Frischmann
5 Manchester Square, London, W1A 1AU
T: 020 7486 3661
F: 020 7487 4153
E: pflondon@pellfrischmann.com
W: www.pellfrischmann.com

Pelma Services and Autobuild Ltd
Chestnut Tree Cottage, One Pin Lane, Farnham Common, Bucks, SL2 3QY
T: 01753 648484
E: pelma@btconnect.com
W: www.autobuildltd.co.uk

Peninsula Rail Task Force
Cllr Mark Coker (chair), Plymouth City Council, The Council House, Plymouth, PL1 2AA
W: peninsularailtaskforce.co.uk/

Penna plc
5 Fleet Place, London, EC4M 7RD
T: 0800 028 1715
E: corporate@penna.com
W: www.penna.com/

Pennant Consulting Ltd
1 Sopwith Cres., Wickford Business Park, Wickford, Essex, SS11 8YU
T: 01268 493495
E: enquiries@pennant-recruit.com
W: www.pennant-consult.com

Pennant Information Services Ltd
Parkway House, Palatine Rd, Northenden, Manchester, M22 4DB
T: 0161 947 6940
F: 0161 947 6959
E: john.churchman@pennantplc.co.uk
W: www.pennantplc.co.uk

Pennant International Group Plc
Parkway House, Palatine Rd, Northenden, Manchester, M22 4DB
T: 0161 947 6940
F: 0161 947 6959
E: john.churchman@pennantplc.co.uk
W: www.pennantplc.co.uk

Penrillian
Clint Mill (Floors 3 and 4), Cornmarket, Penrith, Cumbria, CA11 7HW
T: 01768 214400
F: 01768 214409
E: enquiries@penrillian.com
W: www.penrillian.com/

Pentair
Postbus 487, 5000 AL Tilburg, Netherlands
T: 0808 234 4670
F: 0808 234 4676
W: www.erico.com/

Pentaxia
40-44 Longbridge Lane, Ascot Business Park, Derby, DE24 8UJ
T: 01332 574 870
F: 01332 573 568
E: enquiries@pentaxia.co.uk
W: www.pentaxia.co.uk

People 1st
Hospitality House, 11-59 High Road, London, N2 8AB
T: 020 3074 1222
E: info@people1st.co.uk
W: www.people1st.co.uk

Perco Engineering Services Ltd
The Old Nurseries, Nottingham Rd, Radcliffe on Trent, Nottingham, NG12 2DU
T: 0115 933 5000
F: 0115 933 4692
E: info@perco.co.uk
W: www.perco.co.uk

Permali Gloucester Ltd
Permali Park, Bristol Rd, Gloucester, GL1 5TT
T: 01452 528282
F: 01452 507409
E: fraser.rankin@permali.co.uk
W: www.permali.co.uk

Permalok Fastening Systems Ltd
Plumtree Industrial Estate, Harworth, Doncaster, S Yorks, DN11 8EW
T: 01302 711308
F: 01302 719823
E: info@permalokfastening.co.uk
W: www.permalokfastening.co.uk

Permanent Way Institution
5 Mount Crescent, Warley, Brentwood, Essex, CM14 5DB
T: 01277 230031
E: info@thepwi.org
W: www.thepwi.org

Permaquip Ltd
Brierley Industrial Park, Stanton Hill, Sutton-in-Ashfield, NG17 3JZ
T: 01623 513349
F: 01623 517742
E: sales@permaquip.co.uk
W: www.permaquip.co.uk

Perpetuum Ltd
Unit 2, Strategic Park, Comines Way, Hedge End, Southampton, SO30 4DA
T: 02380 765888
F: 02380 765889
E: info@perpetuum.com
W: www.perpetuum.com/rail

PESA
Zygmunta Augusta 11, PL-85 082 Bydgoszcz, Poland
T: 0048 52339 1360
E: marketing@pesa.pl
W: www.pesa.pl

Petards Joyce-Loebl Ltd
390 Princesway North, TVTE, Gateshead, Tyne & Wear, NE11 0TU
T: 0191 420 3000
E: rail@petards.com
W: www.petards.com

Peter Brett Associates
Caversham Bridge House, Waterman Place, Reading, RG1 8DN
T: 0118 950 0761
F: 0118 959 7498
E: reading@peterbrett.com
W: peterbrett.com/

Peter Davidson Consultancy
Brownlow House, Ravens Lane, Berkhamsted, Herts, HP4 2DX
T: 01442 891665
F: 01442 879776
E: mail@peter-davidson.com
W: www.peter-davidson.com

Peter Staveley Consulting
247 Davidson Rd, Croydon, CR0 6DQ
T: 07973 168742
E: peter@peterstaveley.co.uk
W: www.peterstaveley.co.uk

Petrotechnics Ltd
Pavilion 3, Craigshaw Business Park, Craigshaw Road, West Tullos, Aberdeen, AB12 3QH
T: 01224 337200
F: 01224 337201
E: info@petrotechnics.com
W: www.petrotechnics.com/

Pfisterer
Unit 9, Ellesmere Business Park, off Swingbridge Rd, Grantham, Lincs, NG31 7XT
T: 01476 578657
F: 01476 568631
E: info.uk@pfisterer.com
W: www.pfisterer.co.uk

Pfleiderer
See RAIL.ONE GmbH

PFS Ltd
Unit 2-3, Wheaton Court, Wheaton Road, Witham, Essex, CM8 3UJ
T: 01376 535260
F: 01376 535268
E: trevor.mason@pfsfueltec.com
W: www.pfsfueltec.com

Phi Group Ltd
Hadley House, Bayshill Road, Cheltenham, Glos, GL50 3AW
T: 01242 707600
F: 0870 333 4127
E: marketing@phigroup.co.uk
W: www.phigroup.co.uk

Phoenix Contact Ltd
Halesfield 13, Telford, Shropshire, TF7 4PG
T: 0845 881 2222
F: 0845 881 2211
E: info@phoenixcontact.co.uk
W: www.phoenixcontact.co.uk

Phoenix Systems UK Ltd
Unit 48, Standard Way, Fareham Industrial Park, Fareham, Hants, PO16 8XQ
T: 0845 658 6111
F: 0845 658 6222
E: neills@phoenixsystemsuk.com
W: www.phoenixsystemsuk.com

PHS Besafe incorporating Hiviz Laundries Ltd
PHS Group, Western Industrial Estate, Caerphilly, CF83 1XH
T: 02920 809120
F: 02920 863288
E: enquiries@phs.co.uk
W: www.phs.co.uk

Pickersgill-Kaye Ltd
Pepper Road, Hunslet, Leeds, West Yorkshire, LS10 2PP
T: 0113 277 5531
F: 0113 276 0221
E: enquiries@pkaye.co.uk
W: www.pkaye.co.uk/

Picow Engineering Group
1 Station House, Lowlands Road, Runcorn, Cheshire, WA7 5TQ
T: 01928 567337
F: 01928 575401
W: www.picow.co.uk/

Pilkington Glass Ltd
Prescot Rd, St Helens, Merseyside, WA10 3TT
T: 01744 28882
F: 01744 692660
E: classics@pilkington.com
W: www.pilkington.com

Pilz Automation Technology
Pilz House, Little Colliers Field, Corby, Northants, NN18 8TJ
T: 01536 460766
F: 01536 460866
E: sales@pilz.co.uk
W: www.pilz.co.uk

Pinsent Masons
City Point, One Ropemaker St, London, EC2Y 9AH
T: 020 7418 7000
F: 020 7418 7050
W: www.pinsentmasons.com

Pipe and Piling Supplies Ltd
Suite 4a, Buko Tower, Dalton Road, Glenrothes, Fife, KY6 2SS
T: 01592 770312
F: 01592 770313
E: enquiries@pipeand pilingsupplies.com
W: www.pipeandpilingsupplies.com/

Pipeline Drillers Ltd
10 Kirkford, Stewarton, Kilmarnock, KA3 5HZ
T: 01560 482021
F: 01560 484809
E: info@pipelinedrillers.co.uk

Pipex PX
Pipex House, 1 Belliver Way, Roborough, Plymouth, Devon, PL6 7BP
T: 01752 581200
F: 01752 581209
E: sales@pipexpx.com
W: www.pipexpx.com

Pirtek (UK) Ltd
199 The Vale, Acton, London, W3 7QS
T: 020 8749 8444
F: 020 8749 8333
E: info@pirtek.co.uk
W: www.pirtek.co.uk/

Pitchmastic PmB Ltd
Panama House, 184 Attercliffe Rd, Sheffield, S4 7WZ
T: 0114 270 0100
F: 0114 276 8782
E: info@pitchmasticpmb.co.uk
W: www.pitchmasticpmb.co.uk

Plan Me Project Management
PO Box 281, Malvern, WR14 9EP
T: 07906 439055
F: 0800 471 5332
E: info@planme.com
W: www.planme.com

Planet Platforms
Brunel Close, Century Park, Wakefield 41 Ind. Est, Wakefield, WF2 0XG
T: 0800 085 4161
F: 01924 267090
E: info@planetplatforms.co.uk
W: www.planetplatforms.co.uk

A Plant
See Ashtead Plant Hire Co Ltd (APlant)

PlasmaTrack
Power Road Studios, 114 Power Road, Chiswick, London, W4 5PY

Plasser Machinery, Parts & Services Ltd
Manor Rd, West Ealing, London, W13 0PP
T: 020 8998 4781
F: 020 8997 8206
E: info@plasser.co.uk
W: www.plasser.co.uk

Platform 5 Publishing
52 Broadfield Road, Sheffield, S8 0XJ
T: 0114 255 2625
F: 0114 255 2471
E: andrew.dyson@platform5.com
W: www.platform5.com/

Platipus Anchors Ltd
Unit Q, Philanthropic Rd, Kingsfield Business Centre, Redhill, Surrey, RH1 4DP
T: 01737 762300
F: 01737 773395
E: info@platipus-anchors.com
W: www.platipus-anchors.com

porterbrook
At the heart of Britain's railway for over 25 years

We provide high quality, digitally-enabled rolling stock to help deliver a safe, reliable and sustainable railway.
www.porterbrook.co.uk

Playle Consultancy Ltd
1579 London Road, Leigh-On-Sea, Essex, SS9 2SG

Plettac Security UK Ltd
Unit 39, Sir Frank Whittle Business Centre, Great Central Way, Rugby, Warks, CV21 3XH
T: 0844 800 1725
F: 01788 544549
E: info@plettac.co.uk
W: www.plettac.co.uk

Plextek
The Plextek Building, London Road, Great Chesterford, Saffron Walden, CB10 1NY
T: 01799 533200
E: hello@plextek.com
W: www.plextek.com

Plexus
Bay 150, Shannon Industrial Estate, Shannon, Co. Clare, Republic of Ireland
T: 353 61 771 500
F: 00 353- (0) 61- 474446
E: mail@itwep.com
W: www.itwplexus.co.uk

Plowman Craven Ltd
2 Lea Business Park, 141 Lower Luton Rd, Harpenden, Herts, AL5 5EQ
T: 01582 765566
F: 01582 765370
E: post@plowmancraven.co.uk
W: www.plowmancraven.co.uk

PM Safety Consultants Ltd
Suite D, 3rd Floor, Saturn Facilities, 101 Lockhurst Lane, Coventry, CV6 5SF
T: 02476 665770
F: 02476 582401
E: info@pmsafety.com
W: www.pmsafety.com

PMA UK Ltd (Thomas & Betts Ltd)
Unit 4, Imperial Court, Magellan Close, Walworth Ind. Est., Andover, Hants, SP10 5NT
T: 01264 333527
F: 01264 333643
E: sales@pma-uk.com
W: www.pma-uk.com

PMProfessional Learning
See Aikona Management Ltd

Pneumatrol
West End Business Park, Blackburn Road, Oswaldtwistle, Accrington, Lancs, BB5 4WZ
T: 01254 872277
F: 01254 390133
E: sales@pneumatrol.com
W: www.pneumatrol.com/

Pochins Ltd
Brookes Lane, Middlewich, Cheshire, CW10 0JQ
T: 01606 833333
F: 01606 833331
W: www.pochins.plc.uk/

Pod-Trak Ltd
Crove House, 14 Aintree Road, Perivale, Middx, UB6 7LA
T: 0845 450 4190
F: 020 998 6901
E: enquiries@pod-trak.com
W: www.pod-trak.com

Poise Group Ltd
Fleet House, 8-12 New Bridge Street, London, EC4V 6AL
T: 020 3086 9400
E: info@poisegroup.uk
W: www.poisegroup.uk/

Polyamp AB
Box 229, Atvidaberg, 597 25, Sweden
T: 0046 120 85410
F: 0046 120 85405
E: info@polyamp.se
W: www.polyamp.com

Polydeck Ltd
Unit 14, Burnett Ind Est, Cox's Green, Wrington, Bristol, Somerset, BS40 5QS
T: 01934 863678
F: 01934 863683
E: sales@gripfast.co.uk
W: www.polydeck.co.uk/

Polyflor Ltd
Transport Flooring Division, PO Box 3, Radcliffe New Rd, Whitefield, Manchester, M45 7NR
T: 0161 767 1111
F: 0161 767 1100
E: transport@polyflor.com
W: www.polyflor.com

Polypipe
Charnwood Business Park, North Rd, Loughborough, Leics, LE11 1LE
T: 01509 615100
F: 01509 610215
E: emma.thompson@polypipe.com
W: www.polypipe.com

Polyrack Tech-Group
Steinbeisstrasse 4, D-75334 Straubenhardt, Germany
T: 0800 7659 7225
E: sales@polyrack.com
W: www.polyrack.com

Polysafe Level Crossings
25 King St. Ind. Est., Langtoft, Peterborough, PE6 9NF
T: 01778 560555
F: 01778 560773
E: sales@polysafe.co.uk
W: www.polysafe.co.uk

Pontoonworks
The Old Glove Factory, Bristol Road, Sherborne, Dorset, DT9 4HP
T: 01935 814950
F: 01935 815131
E: office@pontoonworks.co.uk
W: www.pontoonworks.co.uk

PORR AG
Absberggasse 47, A-1100 Wien, Austria
T: 43 (0)50 626-0
W: www.porr.at/

Portaramp UK Ltd
Units 3&4, Dolphin Business Park, Shadwell, Thetford, Norfolk, IP24 2RY
T: 01953 681799
F: 01953 688153
E: sales@portaramp.co.uk
W: www.portaramp.co.uk

Portastor
New Lane, Huntington, York, YO32 9PR
T: 01904 656869
F: 01904 611760
M: 07710 313301
E: action@portastor.com
W: www.portastor.com

Portec Rail Group
Stamford Street, Sheffield, S9 2TL
T: 0114 256 2225
F: 0114 261 7826
E: uk.sales@portecrail.co.uk
W: www.portecrail.com

Porterbrook Leasing Company Ltd
Ivatt House, 7 The Point, Pinnacle Way, Pride Park, Derby, DE24 8ZS
T: 01332 285050
F: 01332 285051
E: enquiries@porterbrook.co.uk
W: www.porterbrook.co.uk

Portwest Clothing Ltd
Commercial Rd, Goldthorpe Ind. Est., Goldthorpe, S.Yorks, S63 9BL
T: 01709 894575
F: 01709 880830
E: info@portwest.com
W: www.portwest.com

Portwest Construction Ltd
Unit 3, Whitworth Court, Manor Park, Runcorn, Cheshire, WA7 1WA
T: 01928 597818
E: info@portwestconstruction.com
W: www.portwestconstruction.com/

Postfield Systems
53 Ullswater Cres., Coulsdon, Surrey, CR5 2HR
T: 020 8655 6080
F: 020 8655 6082
E: sales@postfield.co.uk
W: www.postfield.co.uk

Potensis Ltd
7th Floor, Froomsgate House, Rupert St, Bristol, BS1 2QJ
T: 0117 910 7999
F: 0117 927 2722
E: office@potensis.com
W: www.potensis.com

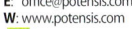

Potter Logistics Ltd
Melmerby Ind. Est. Green Lane, Melmerby, Ripon, North Yorks, HG4 5HP
T: 01353 646703
E: sales@potterlogistics.co.uk
W: www.potterlogistics.co.uk

Powdertech (Corby) Limited
Cockerell Road, Phoenix Parkway, Corby, Northants, NN17 5DU
T: 01536 400890
E: richard.b@powdertech.co.uk
W: www.powdertechcorby.co.uk

Powelectrics
12 Ninian Park, Tamworth, Staffs, B77 5ES
T: 01827 310666
E: dave.oakes@powelectrics.co.uk
W: www.powelectrics.co.uk

Powell Dobson
Suite 1F Building One, Eastern Business Park, Wern Fawr Lane, Old St. Mellons, Cardiff, CF3 5EA
T: 03333 201001
M: 029 2079 1212
W: www.powelldobson.com/en/

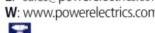

Power 4 from Fox & Cooper
See Stuart Group

Power Electrics Generators Ltd
St. Ivel Way, Warmley, Bristol, BS30 8TY
T: 0117 947 9700
F: 0117 947 9702
E: sales@powerelectrics.com
W: www.powerelectrics.com

Power Electronics (PE Systems Ltd)
Victoria St, Leigh, Lancs, WN7 5SE
T: 01942 260330
F: 01942 261835
E: sales@pe-systems.co.uk
W: www.pe-systems.co.uk

Power Jacks Ltd
Balmacassie Commercial Park, Ellon, Aberdeenshire, AB41 8BX
T: 01358 285100
E: sales@powerjacks.com
W: www.powerjacks.com

Powerbox Group
4/5 Knights Court, Magellan Close, Walworth Ind. Est, Andover, Hants, SP10 5NT
T: 01264 384460
F: 01264 334337
E: warren.venn@powerboxgroup.co.uk
W: www.powerbox.info

Powernetics Systems Ltd
Jason Works, Clarence St, Loughborough, Leics, LE11 1DX
T: 01509 214153 x205
F: 01509 262460
E: jag@powernetics.co.uk
W: www.powernetics.co.uk

Powertron Convertors Ltd
See Martek Power Ltd

Praxis
See Altran UK Ltd

Praybourne Ltd
Unit 2c, Eagle Road, North Moons Moat, Redditch, Worcs, B98 9HF
T: 0844 669 1860
F: 01527 543 752
E: enquiries@praybourne.co.uk
W: www.praybourne.co.uk

PRB Consulting
167 London Rd, Hailsham, E.Sussex, BN27 3AN
T: 0845 557 6814
E: paul.brace@prbconsulting.co.uk
W: www.prbconsulting.co.uk

PRC Rail Consulting
7 Hunters Rise, Kirby Bellars, Melton Mowbray, Leics, LE14 2DT
T: 01664 810118
E: piers.connor@railway-technical.com
W: www.railway-technical.com

Pre Metro Operations Ltd
Regent House, 56 Hagley Road, Stourbridge, West Midlands, DY8 1QD
T: 01384 441325
F: 01384 396587
E: premetro@aol.com
W: www.premetro.co.uk/

Preformed Markings Ltd
Unit 6, Oyster Park, 109 Chertsey Rd, Byfleet, Surrey, KT14 7AX
T: 01932 359270
F: 01932 340936
E: info@preformedmarkings.co.uk
W: www.preformedmarkings.co.uk

Premier Calibration Ltd
Unit 3K/L, Lake Enterprise Park, Sandall Stores Rd, Kirk Sandall, Doncaster, DN3 1QR
T: 01302 888448
F: 01302 881197
E: enquiries.premcal@btconnect.com
W: www.premiercalibration.co.uk/

Premier Pits
Town Drove, Quadring, Spalding, Lincs, PE11 4PU
T: 01775 821222
F: 01775 820914
E: info@premierpits.com
W: www.premierpits.com

Premier Stampings
Station St, Cradley Heath, West Midlands, B64 6AJ
T: 01384 353100
F: 01384 353101
E: ashleyh@premierstampings.co.uk
W: www.premierstampings.co.uk

Premier Train Catering
See Creative Rail Dining

Preserved Traction Technical Services
3 No4 Pembroke Rd, London, N15 4NW
E: markb754@aol.com
W: www.preservedtraction techservice.com

Preston Trampower Ltd
Preston Office, 1 Navigation Way, Preston, Lancashire, PR2 2YP
T: 01772 730290
F: 01772 730291
E: lincoln.shields@trampower.co.uk
W: www.prestontrampower.co.uk

Price Tool Sales Ltd
See Birchwood Price Tools

Price Waterhouse Coopers LLP
1 Embankment Place, London, WC2N 6NN
T: 020 7583 5000
F: 020 7822 4652
E: julian.smith@uk.pwc.com
W: www.pwcglobal.com

PriestmanGoode
150 Great Portland St, London, W1W 6QD
T: 020 7580 3444
M: 07376 286884
E: studio@priestmangoode.com
W: www.priestmangoode.com

Primat Recruitment
Lingfield Point, Darlington, DL1 1RW
T: 01325 744400
W: www.primatrecruitment.com

Prime Rail Solutions Ltd
Dartford Road, March, Cambridgeshire, PE15 8AE
T: 01733 462420
E: peter@primerailsolutions.com
W: www.primerailsolutions.com

Priority Vehicle Hire Ltd
Unit 1, Bestmans Lane Ind. Estate, Bestmans Lane, Kempsey, Worcester, WR5 3PZ
T: 01905 821843
E: enquiries@priorityhire.co.uk
W: www.priorityhire.co.uk/

Pro Style
Unit 7b, Crondal Road, Bayton Road Industrial Estate, Coventry, CV7 9NH
T: 02476 367441
F: 02476 367145
E: info@pro-style.co.uk
W: www.pro-style.co.uk/

ProActive Rail
78 York Street, London, W1H 1DP
T: 020 7993 6049
F: 020 7625 4530
W: www.proactiverail.co.uk/

Product Innovation Ltd
39 St Gabriels Road, London, NW2 4DT
T: 020 8452 3968
F: 020 8452 5665
E: peter.frank@productinnovation.com
W: www.productinnovation.com

Professional Lifting Services (PLS)
Unit 7, Parkview Works, 870 Penistone Road, Sheffield, S6 2DL
T: 0114 285 5488
F: 0114 285 4553
W: www.plsltd.co.uk/

Progress Rail Services
Eastfield, Peterborough, PE1 5NA
T: 01733 583000
E: mcdonald_michael@cat.com
W: www.progressrail.com

Project Leaders Ltd
Sarre House, Canterbury Road, Sarre, Kent, CT7 0JY
T: 01843 847848
F: 01843 842463
W: projectleaders.co.uk/

Project7 Consultancy
Westpoint House, 5 Redwood Place, Peel Park, East Kilbride, G74 5PB
T: 0844 568 6840
F: 0844 568 6850
W: www.project7consultancy.com/

Prolec Ltd
25 Benson Rd, Nuffield Ind. Est., Poole, Dorset, BH17 0GB
T: 01202 681190
F: 01202 677909
E: info@prolec.co.uk
W: www.prolec.co.uk

Pro-Link Europe
Irene House, Five Arches Business Park, Maidstone Rd, Sidcup, Kent, DA14 5AE
T: 020 8309 2700
F: 020 8309 7890
E: enquire@prolink-europe.com
W: www.prolink-europe.com

Prospects College of Advanced Technology (PROCAT)
Basildon Campus, Luckyn Lane Entrance, Basildon, Essex, SS14 3AY
T: 0800 389 3589
E: enquiries@procat.ac.uk
W: www.procat.ac.uk/

Prostaff Rail Recruitment
172 Buckingham Ave, Slough, Bucks, SL1 4RD
T: 01753 575888
W: www.prostaff.com

Prostyle Ltd
Unit 7, Brindley Road, Bayton Road Industrial Estate, Coventry, Warks, CV7 9EP
T: 02476 367441
F: 02476 367145
E: info@pro-style.co.uk
W: www.pro-style.co.uk

Prostyle Ltd
Unit 7, Brindley Road, Bayton Road Industrial Estate, Coventry, Warks, CV7 9EP
T: 02476 367441
F: 02476 367145
E: info@pro-style.co.uk
W: www.pro-style.co.uk

Protec Fire Detection Plc
Protec House, Churchill Way, Nelson, Lancs, BB9 6RT
T: 01282 717171
F: 01282 717273
E: sales@protec.co.uk
W: www.protec.co.uk

Proteq
Head Office, The Pinnacle Works, Station Road, Epworth, Doncaster, DN9 1JU
T: 01427 872572
F: 01427 875094
E: info@proteq.co.uk
W: www.proteq.co.uk

Provertha
21 Tarrant Wharf, Arundel, West Sussex, BN18 9NY
E: service@provertha.com
W: www.provertha.com

PRV Engineering
Pegasus House, Polo Grounds, New Inn, Pontypool, Gwent, NP4 0TW
T: 01495 769697
F: 01495 769776
E: enquiries@prv-engineering.co.uk
W: www.prv-engineering.co.uk

Prysm Rail
See Archer Safety Signs

Prysmian Cables & Systems
Chickenhall Lane, Eastleigh, Hants, SO50 6YU
T: 023 8029 5029
F: 023 8060 8769
E: marketing.telecom@prysmian.com
W: www.prysmiangroup.com

PSV Glass and Glazing Ltd
Hillbottom Rd, High Wycombe, Bucks, HP12 4HJ
T: 01494 533131
F: 01494 462675
E: rail@psvglass.co.uk
W: www.psvglass.com

PTH Group Ltd
See BHSF Occupational Health Ltd

PTM Design Ltd
Unit B2, Sovereign Park Ind Est, Lathkill St, Market Harborough, LE16 9EG
T: 01858 463777
F: 01858 463777
E: sales@ptmdesign.co.uk
W: www.ptmdesign.co.uk/

PTP Associates
The Lodge, 21 Harcourt Rd., Dorney Reach, Berks, SL6 0DT
T: 01628 776059
E: ces@ptpassociates.co.uk
W: www.ptpassociates.co.uk

Publica
10 Clerkenwell Green, London, EC1R 0DP
T: 020 7490 3986
E: mail@publica.co.uk

Pullman Rail
Train Maintenance Depot, Leckwith Rd, Cardiff, CF11 8HP
T: 02920 368850
F: 02920 368874
E: sales@pullmanrail.co.uk
W: www.pullmanrail.co.uk

PULS UK Ltd
Unit 10, Ampthill Business Park, Station Road, Ampthill, Beds, MK45 2QW
T: 01525 841001
E: sales@puls.co.uk
W: www.puls.co.uk

Pulsarail
See Praybourne Ltd

Pulsarail Workwear
108 Manchester Road, Carrington, Manchester, M31 4BD
T: 0161 777 4230
W: www.pulsarailworkwear.co.uk/

Pyeroy Group
Kirkstone House, St Omers Rd, Western Riverside Route, Gateshead, Tyne & Wear, NE11 9EZ
T: 0191 493 2600
F: 0191 493 2601
E: mail@pyeroy.co.uk
W: www.pyeroy.co.uk

Pym & Wildsmith (Metal Finishers) Ltd
Bramshall Ind. Est, Bramshall, Uttoxeter, Staffs, ST14 8TD
T: 01889 565653
F: 01889 567064
E: enquiries@pymandwildsmith.co.uk
W: www.pymandwildsmith.co.uk

Q'Straint
Unit 72-76, John Wilson Business Park, Whitstable, Kent, CT5 3QT
T: 01227 773035
F: 01227 770035
E: info@qstraint.co.uk
W: www.qstraint.com

QA-Aikona Ltd
Rath House, 55-65 Uxbridge Rd, Slough, SL1 1SG
T: 0845 757 3888
E: info@qa.com
W: www.qa.com

QC Data Ltd
Park House, 14 Kirtley Drive, Castle Marina, Nottingham, NG7 1LD
T: 0115 941 5806
F: 0115 947 2901
E: rjohnson@qcdata.com
W: www.qcdata.com

QED Scaffolding
Lock Street, St Helens, Merseyside, WA9 1HS
T: 01744 751117
F: 01744 755779
E: enquiries@qedscaffolding.com
W: www.qedscaffolding.com/

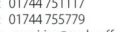

QHi Rail
City Park, Watchmead, Welwyn Garden City, Herts, AL7 1LT
T: 01707 379870
E: info@qhirail.com
W: www.qhirail.com

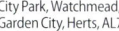

QikServe
Randolph House, 2nd Floor, 4 Charlotte Lane, Edinburgh, EH2 4QZ
E: hello@qikserve.com
W: https://www.qikserve.com/

QinetiQ
Cody Technology Park, Ively Road, Farnborough, Hampshire, GU14 0LX
T: 0117 952 8442
E: railservices@qinetiq.com
W: www.qinetiq.com

Qmatic Ltd
Derwent House, Ground Floor, University Way, Cranfield Technology Park, Bedfordshire, MK43 0AZ
T: 01234 757110
F: 0845 123 0201
E: info.uk@qmatic.com
W: www.qmatic.com/

Qognify
Tallis House, 2 Tallis Street, London, EC4Y 0AB
E: info.emea@qognify.com
W: https://www.qognify.com/

The QSS Group Ltd
2 St Georges House, Vernon Gate, Derby, DE1 1UQ
T: 01332 221400
F: 01332 221401
E: enquiries@theqssgroup.co.uk
W: www.theqssgroup.co.uk

QTS Plant
QTS Group, Rench Farm, Drumclog, Strathaven, S. Lanarks, ML10 6QJ
T: 01357 440222
F: 01357 440364
E: enquiries@qtsgroup.com
W: www.qtsgroup.com

Qualitrain Ltd
Bridge House, 12 Mansfield Rd, Tibshelf, Derbys, DE55 5NF
F: 01773 590671
E: richard.bates@qualitrain.co.uk
W: www.qualitrain.co.uk

Qualter Hall & Co Ltd
PO Box 8, Johnson St, Barnsley, South Yorkshire, S75 2BY
T: 01226 205761
F: 01226 286269
E: admin@qualterhall.co.uk
W: www.qualterhall.co.uk

Quartzelec
Castle Mound Way, Central Park, Rugby, Warwickshire, CV23 0WB
T: 01788 512512
E: info.uk@quartzelec.com
W: www.quartzelec.com/

Quasar Associates
8 Flitcroft St, London, WC2H 8DJ
T: 020 7010 7700
F: 020 7010 7701
E: jonathan@quasarassociates.co.uk
W: www.quasarassociates.co.uk

Quattro Plant Ltd
Greenway Court, Canning Rd, Stratford, London, E15 3ND
T: 020 8519 6165
F: 020 8503 0505
E: sales@quattroplant.co.uk
W: www.quattroplant.co.uk

Qube Global Software
9 King Street, London, EC2V 8EA
T: 020 7726 3200
F: 020 7726 3201
E: info@qubeglobal.com
W: www.qubeglobal.co.uk/

Quest Diagnostics
Unit B1, Parkway West, Cranford Lane, Heston, Middx, TW5 9QA
T: 020 8377 3378
F: 020 8377 3350
E: uksales@questdiagnostics.com
W: www.questdiagnostics.com

Quickbuild (UK) Ltd
Imperial House, 1 Factory Rd, Silvertown, London, E16 2EL
T: 020 7473 2712
F: 020 7476 2713
E: davidbrowne@hiremasters.co.uk
W: www.hiremasters.co.uk/ www.quickbuild.uk.com

Quickway Buildings
Hardy's Yard, London Rd, Riverhead, Sevenoaks, Kent, TN13 2DN
T: 01304 612284
F: 01304 620012
E: sales@quickway-wingham.co.uk
W: www.quickway-wingham.co.uk

QW Rail Leasing
12 Plumtree Court, London, EC4A 4HT

R E Cooke Limited
Brunel Drive, Stretton Business Park, Burton Upon Trent, Staffordshire, DE13 0BY
T: 01283 561671
F: 01283 510960
E: sales@recooke.co.uk
W: www.recooke.co.uk/

R&B Switchgear Services Ltd
Switchgear House, The Courtyard, Green
Lane, Heywood, Lancs, OL10 2EX
T: 01706 369933
F: 01706 364564
E: ian.penswick@rb-power.co.uk
W: www.rbswitch.co.uk

R&I Consulting
29 Marylebone Rd, London, NW1 5JK
T: 020 3598 2479
E: info@raics.co.uk
W: www.raics.co.uk

R&W Rail
Cheriton Mill Offices, Alresford, Hampshire, SO24 0NG
T: 02380 845379
W: https://www.rwcivilengineering.co.uk/what-we-do/rail/

R.S. Clare & Co Ltd
8-14 Stanhope St, Liverpool, L8 5RQ
T: 0151 709 2902
F: 0151 709 0518
E: info@rsclare.co.uk
W: www.rsclare.com

R2P GmbH
Lise-Meitner-Straße 4, DE-24941 Flensburg, Germany
T: 01628 635497
M: 07747 460509
E: uk@r2p.com
W: www.r2p.com/

Ra'alloy Ramps Ltd
A3 Stafford Park 15, Telford, Shropshire, TF3 3BB
T: 01952 291224
E: enquiries@raalloy.co.uk
W: www.raalloy.co.uk/

Racon
2nd Floor, Mercantile Chambers, 53 Bothwell Street, Glasgow, G2 6TS
T: 0141 248 3038
E: info@racon-ms.com
W: www.racon-ms.com/

RAICS
See R&I Consulting

Rail & Road Protec GmbH
Lise-Meitner-Strasse 4, D-24941 Flensburg, Germany
T: 01628 635497
F: 00461 500 33820
E: info@r2protec.com
W: www.r2protec.com

Rail Academy
Newcastle College Rail Academy, William St, Felling, Gateshead, Tyne & Wear, NE10 0JP

Rail Accident Investigation Branch
The Wharf, Stores Rd, Derby, DE21 4BA
T: 01332 253300
F: 01332 253301
E: enquiries@raib.gov.uk
W: www.raib.gov.uk

Rail Alliance
The Control Tower, Quinton Rail Technology Centre, Station Rd, Long Marston, Stratford upon Avon, Warks, CV37 8PL
T: 01789 720026
E: info@railalliance.co.uk
W: www.railalliance.co.uk

Rail Audit & Assurance Services (RAAS)
54 Highfield Rd, Cheadle Hulme, Stockport, SK8 6EP
T: 0161 486 1237
E: stockport@raas.co.uk
W: www.raas.co.uk

Rail Charter Services
Craven House, 16 Northumberland Avenue, London, WC2N 5AP
W: www.railcharterservices.co.uk/

Rail Delivery Group
2nd Floor, 200 Aldersgate Street, London, EC1A 4HD
T: 020 7841 8000
E: info@raildeliverygroup.com
W: www.raildeliverygroup.com

Rail Door Solutions Ltd
Blackhill Drive, Wolverton Mill, Milton Keynes, MK12 5TS
T: 01908 224140
F: 01908 224149
E: info@raildoorsolutions.co.uk
W: www.raildoorsolutions.co.uk

Rail Forum Midlands
Lonsdale House, Quaker Way, Derby, DE1 3HD
T: 01332 593550
E: info@midlandsrail.co.uk
W: www.midlandsrail.co.uk/

Rail Freight Group
7 Bury Place, London, WC1A 2LA
T: 020 3116 0007
F: 020 3116 0008
E: phillippa@rfg.org.uk
W: www.rfg.org.uk

Rail Freight Services
Stone Terminal, Horn Lane, Acton, London, W3 9EH
T: 0208 896 9192
F: 0208 869 6829
E: enquiries@railfreightservices.co.uk
W: www.railfreightservices.co.uk/

Rail Gourmet Group
169 Euston Road, London, NW1 2AE
T: 020 7529 8330
F: 020 7922 6596
E: jfleet@railgourmetuk.com
W: www.railgourmet.com

Rail Images & Rail Images Video
5 Sandhurst Crescent, Leigh on Sea, Essex, SS9 4AL
T: 01702 525059
F: 01702 525059
E: info@railimages.co.uk
W: www.railimages.co.uk

Rail Industry Contractors Association Ltd (RICA)
Gin Gan House, Thropton, Morpeth, Northumberland, NE65 7LT
T: 01669 620569
E: enquiries@rica.uk.com
W: www.rica.uk.com

Rail Industry First Aid Association (RIFAA)
Po Box 1152, Doncaster, DN1 9NL
T: 01302 329 729
F: 01302 320 590
E: bookings@rifaa.com
W: www.rifaa.com

Rail Innovations
M: 07730 303799
E: greg@railinnov.com
W: https://railinnov.com/

Rail Insights Ltd
Highlands, St Andrews Rd, Henley-on-Thames, RG9 1PG
T: 01491 414218
E: info@railinsights.com
W: www.railinsights.com

Rail Manche Finance EEIG
Times House, Bravingtons Walk, Regent Quarter, London, N1 9AW
T: 020 7042 9961
F: 020 7833 3896
E: david.hiscock@rmf.co.uk
W: www.rmf.co.uk

Rail Measurement Ltd
79 River Lane, Cambridge, CB5 8HP
T: 01223 522475
M: 07803 290252
E: stuart.grassie@railmeasurement.com
W: www.railmeasurement.com

Rail North
See Transport for the North (TfN)

Rail Op UK Ltd
Gowers Farm, Tumblers Green, Braintree, Essex, CM77 8AZ
T: 0845 450 5232
F: 01376 388295
E: info@railop.co.uk
W: www.railop.co.uk

Rail Operations Developments Ltd
Electra House, Electra Way, Crewe Business Park, Crewe, CW1 6GL
T: 01270 588500
F: 01270 588500
E: enquiries@rodl.co.uk
W: www.railoperationaldevelopment.co.uk/

Rail Operations Group
6 Snow Hill, London, EC1A 2AY
E: angela.cburch@railopsgroup.co.uk
W: www.railopsgroup.co.uk

Rail Order
Unit 11, Billet Lane, Normanby Enterprise
Park, Scunthorpe, DN15 9YH
T: 01724 292860
F: 01724 292242
E: sales@rail-order.co.uk
W: www.rail-order.co.uk

Rail Personnel Ltd
Level 26, Office Tower, Convention Plaza, 1 Harbour Rd, Wanchai, Hong Kong, China
T: 00 852 2753 5636
F: 00 852 2305 4512
E: info@railpersonnel.com
W: www.railpersonnel.com

Rail Photo Library
F: 0116 259 2068
E: studio@railphotolibrary.com
W: www.railphotolibrary.com

Rail Positive Relations
The Bothy, 18 Holloway Rd, Duffield, Derbys, DE56 4FE
T: 07973950923
E: rupert@railpr.com
W: www.railpr.com

Rail Products UK
Mountcairn, 22 Cairneymount Road, Carluke, ML8 4EN
T: 01555 773027
E: derek@railproducts.uk.com
W: www.railproducts.uk.com

Rail Professional Development
Cranes House, 5 Paycocke Rd, Basildon, Essex, SS14 3DP
T: 01268 822842
F: 01268 822841
E: info@rpd.co.uk
W: www.rpd.co.uk

Rail Research UK Association (RRUKA)
See UK Rail Research and Innovation Network (UKRRIN)

Rail Restorations North East Ltd
8A Hackworth Industrial Park, Shildon, County Durham, DL4 1HF
T: 01388 777138
F: 01388 777138
E: enquiries@rail-restorations-north-east.co.uk
W: www.rail-restorations-north-east.co.uk

Rail Safety Solutions
Unit 27, Royal Scot Rd, Pride Park, Derby, DE24 8AJ
T: 01332 989593
F: 020 3142 5301
E: info@railsafetysolutions.com
W: www.railsafetysolutions.com

Rail Safety Systems BV
See Innovative Railway Safety Ltd

Rail Settlement Plan Ltd
See Rail Delivery Group

Rail Supply Group
E: secretariat@railsupplygroup.org
W: www.railsupplygroup.org

Rail Tech Group (Railway & Signalling Engineering) Ltd
91 Dales Rd, Ipswich, Suffolk, IP1 4JR
T: 01473 242344
F: 01473 242379
W: www.rttrainingsolutions.co.uk/railway-courses/

Rail Technology Ltd
Mill End Lane, Alrewas, Staffs, DE13 7BY
T: 01283 790012
F: 01283 792371
E: info@railtechnologyltd.com
W: www.railtechnologyltd.com

The Rail Technology Unit (RTU) at Manchester Metropolitan University
Rail Technology Unit, Manchester Metropolitan University, John Dalton Building,
Chester St, Manchester, M1 5GD
T: 0161 247 6247
F: 0161 247 6840
E: j.grey@bham.ac.uk
W: www.mmu.ac.uk/business/our-expertise/expertise.php?area=sustainability_and_climate_change&expertise=railway_research_and_consultancy

Rail Training International Ltd
North Suite, Parsonage Offices, Church
Lane, Canterbury, Kent, CT4 7AD
T: 01227 769096
F: 01227 479435
E: rtiuk@rti.co.uk
W: www.rti.co.uk

Rail Vision
2 Cygnus Court, Beverley Rd, Pegasus Business Park, East Midlands Airport, Castle Donnington, Leics, DE74 2UZ
T: 01509 672211
E: enquiries@rail-vision.com
W: www.rail-vision.com

Rail Waiting Structures
Unit 60, Dyffryn Business Park, Llantwit Major Rd, Llandow, Vale of Glamorgan, CF71 7PY
T: 01446 795444
F: 01446 773344
E: rail@shelters.co.uk
W: www.railwaitingstructures.com/

RAIL.ONE GmbH
Ingolstaedter Strasse 51, 92318 Neumarkt, Germany
T: 0049 9181 8952-0
F: 0049 9181 8952-5001
E: info@railone.com
W: www.railone.com

Rail-Ability Ltd
Tilcon Ave, Baswich, Stafford, ST18 0YJ
T: 01785 214747
F: 01785 214717
E: skelly@railability.co.uk
W: www.railability.co.uk

Railcare Ltd
See Knorr-Bremse Rail UK

Railcare Sweden Ltd
Unit 1, Derwent Park, 214-216 London Road, Derby, DE1 2SX
T: 01332 647388
E: info@railcare.co.uk
W: www.railcare.co.uk/

Raileasy
10 Station Parade, High St, Wanstead, London, E11 1QF
T: 0906 2000 500
E: admin@raileasy.co.uk
W: www.raileasy.co.uk

Railex Aluminium Ltd
12/26 Dry Drayton Ind. Est., Dry Drayton, Cambridge, CB3 8AT
T: 0845 612 9555
F: 01954 210352
E: tony@railex.net
W: www.railex.net

Railfuture
24 Chedworth Place, Tattingstone, Suffolk, IP9 2ND
T: 0117 9272954
E: info@railfuture.org.uk
W: www.railfuture.org.uk

RailRoute Ltd
The Business and Innovation Centre, Enterprise
Park East, Sunderland, SR5 2TA
T: 0191 516 6354
E: info@railroute.co.uk
W: www.railroute.co.uk

Railscape Ltd
15 Totman Cresc, Brook Rd Ind Est, Rayleigh, Essex, SS6 7UY
T: 01268 777795
F: 01268 777762
E: info@railscape.com
W: www.railscape.com

Railsite Telecom
10 The Street, West Horsley, Surrey, KT24 6AX
T: 01483 286456
W: https://railsitetelecom.co.uk/

Railtex/Infrarail
See Mack Brooks Exhibitions Ltd

Railtourer Ltd
See West Coast Railway Co.

Railway Approvals Ltd
Derwent House, RTC Business Park, London Rd, Derby, DE24 8UP
T: 01332 483800
F: 01332 483800
E: sales@railwayapprovals.com
W: www.railwayapprovals.co.uk

Railway Benefit Fund (RBF)
1st Floor, Millennium House, 40 Nantwich Road, Crewe, CW2 6AD
T: 0345 241 2885
E: info@railwaybenefitfund.org.uk
W: www.railwaybenefitfund.org.uk

Railway Brake Services Ltd
Unit 2, Sidings Industrial Estate, Wetmore Road, Burton On Trent, Staffordshire, DE14 1SB
T: 01283 440102
F: 01538 340051
E: support@railwaybrakeservices.co.uk
W: www.railwaybrakeservices.co.uk/

Railway Children
1 The Commons, Sandbach, Cheshire, CW11 1EG
T: 01270 757596
E: hello@railwaychildren.org.uk
W: www.railwaychildren.org.uk/

Railway Civil Engineers Association
One Great George St, Westminster, London, SW1P 3AA
T: 020 7665 2238
E: rcea@ice.org.uk
W: www.rcea.org.uk/

The Railway Consultancy Ltd
1st Floor, South Tower, Crystal Palace Station, London, SE19 2AZ
T: 020 8676 0395
F: 020 8778 7439
E: info@railwayconsultancy.com
W: www.railwayconsultancy.com

Railway Convalescent Home (RCH)
Bridge House, 2 Church St, Dawlish, Devon, EX7 9AU
T: 01626 863303
F: 01626 866676
E: sueg@rch.org.uk
W: www.rch.org.uk

Railway Drainage Ltd
The Steadings, Maisemore Court, Maisemore, Glos, GL2 8EY
T: 01452 422666
F: 01452 423516
E: info@rdlonline.co.uk
W: www.rdlonline.co.uk

Railway Employees & Public Transport Association
See REPTA (Railway Employees and Public Transport Association)

Railway Engineering Associates Ltd
125 Boden St, Glasgow, G40 3QF
T: 0141 556 0415
E: henry@rea.uk.com
W: www.rea.uk.com

Railway Engineers Forum (REF)
T: 020 7651 7910
E: lwquinn@bechtel.com
W: www.theref.org.uk

Railway Finance Ltd
Barrow Rd, Wincobank, Sheffield, S9 1JZ
T: 01223 891300
F: 01223 891302
E: nick.preston@railwayfinance.co.uk
W: www.railwayfinance.co.uk

Railway Heritage Trust
1 Eversholt St, London, NW1 2DN
T: 020 7904 7354
E: rht@railwayheritagetrust.co.uk
W: www.railwayheritagetrust.co.uk

Railway Industry Association
22 Headfort Place, London, SW1X 7RY
T: 020 7201 0777
F: 020 7235 5777
E: ria@riagb.org.uk
W: www.riagb.org.uk

The Railway Mission
Rugby Railway Station, Station Approach, Rugby, Warwickshire, CV21 3LA
M: 07718 971919
E: office@railwaymission.org
W: www.railwaymission.org

Railway Study Forum (within CILT)
PO Box 375, Burgess Hill, West Sussex, RH15 5BX
W: https://ciltuk.org.uk/about-us/professional-sectors-forums/forums/rsa-main

Railway Support Services
Montpellier House, Montpellier Drive, Cheltenham, Glos, GL50 1TY
T: 0870 803 4651
F: 0870 803 4652
E: info@railwaysupportservices.co.uk
W: www.railwaysupportservices.co.uk

Railway Systems Engineering & Integration Group
Birmingham Centre for Railway Reasearch & Education College of Engineering Sciences, University of Birmingham, Edgbaston, Birmingham, B15 2TT
T: 0121 414 4342
F: 0121 414 4291
E: j.grey@bham.ac.uk
W: www.eng.bham.ac.uk/civil/study/postgrad/railway.shtml

Railway Touring Company
14a Tuesday Market Place, Kings Lynn, Norfolk, PE30 1JN
T: 01553 661500
F: 01553 661800
E: enquiries@railwaytouring.co.uk
W: www.railwaytouring.co.uk

Railways Pension Scheme
2nd Floor, Camomile Court, 23 Camomile St, London, EC3A 7LL
T: 0800 234 3434
E: csu@rpmi.co.uk
W: www.railwayspensions.co.uk

Railweight
Foundry Lane, Smethwick, Birmingham, B66 2LP
T: 0845 246 6714
F: 0845 246 6715
E: sales@railweight.co.uk
W: www.averyweigh-tronix.com/railweight

Ramboll UK Ltd
240 Blackfriars Road, London, SE1 8NW
M: 07799 864156
E: steve.brown@ramboll.co.uk
W: www.ramboll.co.uk

Rambus Ecebs Ltd
The Torus Building, Rankine Ave, Scottish Enterprise Technology Park, East Kilbride, G75 0QF
T: 01355 272911
F: 01355 272993
E: enquiries@ecebs.com
W: www.ecebs.com

Ramtech Electronics Ltd
Abbeyfield House, Abbeyfield Rd, Nottingham, NG7 2SZ
T: 0115 957 8282
F: 0115 957 8299
E: matt.sadler@ramtech.co.uk
W: www.ramtech.co.uk

Railway Industry Association
The voice of the UK rail supply community
Call us or visit our website to see how we can help grow your business
ria@riagb.org.uk
+44 (0)20 7201 0777
www.riagb.org.uk
@railindustry

Ranstad CPE
Forum 4, Parkway, Solent Business Park, Whiteley, Fareham, PO15 7AD
T: 01489 560000
F: 01489 560001
E: railteam@ranstadcpe.com
W: www.ranstadcpe.com/rail

Raspberry Software Ltd
9 Deben Mill Business Centre, Old Maltings Approach, Melton, Woodbridge, Suffolk, IP12 1BL
T: 01394 387386
F: 01394 387386
E: info@raspberrysoftware.com
W: www.raspberrysoftware.com

Ratcliff Palfinger
Bessemer Rd, Welwyn Garden City, Herts, AL7 1ET
T: 01707 325571
F: 01707 327752
E: info@ratcliffpalfinger.co.uk
W: www.ratcliffpalfinger.com

Rayleigh Instruments
Raytel House, Brook Rd, Rayleigh, Essex, SS6 7XH
T: 01268 749300
F: 01268 749309
E: sales@rayleigh.co.uk
W: www.rayleigh.co.uk

RazorSecure
Suite 10, Innovation Centre, Basing View, Basingstoke, RG21 4HG
E: sales@razorsecure.com
W: www.razorsecure.com

RBC Schaublin
Rue De La Blancherie 9, Delemont, 2800, Switzerland
T: 0041324211300
M: 0041799176809
E: office.d@schaublin.ch
W: www.schaublin.ch

RE: Systems
Systems House, Deepdale Business Park, Bakewell, Derbys, DE45 1GT
T: 01629 813961
F: 01629 813185
E: steve.england@re-systems.co.uk
W: www.re-systems.co.uk

REACT Beyond Cleaning
Stanhope Rd, Swadlincote, Derbys, DE11 9BE
T: 08707 510422
F: 08707 510417
E: info@ractbeyondcleaning.co.uk
W: www.reactbeyondcleaning.co.uk

Reactec
Vantage Point, 3 Cultins Road, Edinburgh, EH11 4DF
T: 0131 221 0920
F: 0131 229 9051
W: www.reactec.com/

Readypower Rail Services
620 Wharfedale Road, Winnersh, Berks, RG41 5TP
T: 01189 774901
E: info@readypower.co.uk
W: www.readypower.co.uk

Real Time Consultants Plc
118-120 Warwick St, Royal Leamington Spa, Warks, CV32 4QY
T: 01926 313133
F: 01926 422165
E: contract@rtc.co.uk
W: www.rtc.co.uk

Realtime Trains
E: tom@swlines.co.uk
W: www.realtimetrains.co.uk

Rebo Systems
Beckeringhstraat 21, NL-3762 EV Soest, Netherlands
T: 0031 0356 016 941
E: info@rebo.nl
W: www.rebosystems.com

Record Electrical Associates Ltd
Unit C1, Longford Trading Est., Thomas St., Stretford, Manchester, M32 0JT
T: 0161 864 3583
F: 0161 864 3603
E: alanj@reauk.com
W: www.record-electrical.co.uk

Recruitrail (Recruit Engineers)
Bank Chambers, 36 Mount Pleasant Rd, Tunbridge Wells, Kent, TN1 1RA
T: 01909 540825
F: 0870 443 0453
W: www.recruitrail.com

Red Lion Controls
The News Building, 3 London Bridge Street, London, SE1 9SG
T: 020 3868 0909
E: euroqe@redlion.net
W: www.redlion.net

Red Plant Ltd
Red House, The Corner, Parkside, Wootton, Canterbury, Kent, CT4 6RR
T: 0845 838 7584
E: info@redplant.co.uk
W: www.redplant.co.uk

Redman Fisher Engineering Ltd
Marsh Road, Middlesbrough, Teesside, TS1 5JS
T: 01952 685110
F: 01952 685117
E: sales@redmanfisher.co.uk
W: www.redmanfisher.co.uk

RedRay LLP
Lantern House, 39-41 High Street, Potters Bar, Hertfordshire, EN6 5AJ
T: 01707 662997
M: 07799 387741
E: enquiries@redray.co.uk
W: www.redray.co.uk/

Redstone Associates
T: 0161 848 9982
E: dave.carter@redstonerail.co.uk
W: www.redstoneassociates.co.uk

Rees Bradley Hepburn (RBH) Ltd
Diddington Farm, Diddington Lane, Meriden, West Midlands, CV7 7HQ
T: 01675 443939
F: 01675 443477
E: info@rbh.co.uk
W: www.rbh.co.uk/

Rehau Ltd
Hill Court, Walford, Ross-on-Wye, Herefordshire, HR9 5QN
T: 01989 762655
F: 01989 762601
E: anthonia.ifeany-okoro@rehau.com
W: www.rehau.co.uk

Reid Lifting Ltd
Unit 1, Severnlink, Newhouse Farm Ind. Est, Chepstow, Monmouthshire, NP16 6UN
T: 01291 620796
F: 01291 626490
E: enquiries@reidlifting.com
W: www.reidlifting.com

Reinforced Earth Company
Innovation House, Euston Way, Telford, Shropshire, TF3 4LT
T: 01952 204357
F: 01952 201753
E: info@reinforcedearth.co.uk
W: www.reinforcedearth.co.uk

Relec Electronics Ltd
Animal House, Justin Bus. Park, Sandford Lane, Wareham, Dorset, BH20 4DY
T: 01929 555700
F: 01929 555701
E: sales@relec.co.uk
W: www.relec.co.uk

Reliable Data Systems
March House, Lime Grove, West Clandon, Guildford, Surrey, GU4 7UH
T: 01483 225604
E: rdsintl@rdsintl.com
W: www.rdsintl.com

Renaissance Trains Ltd
4 Spinneyfield, Ellington, Cambs, PE28 0AT
T: 07767 643360
E: info@renaissancetrains.com
W: www.renaissancetrains.com

Rendel Limited
61 Southwark St, London, SE1 1SA
T: 020 7654 0500
F: 020 7654 0401
E: london@rendel-ltd.com
W: www.rendel-ltd.com

resonate
IMAGINE THE JOURNEY
• TRAFFIC MANAGEMENT
• SIGNALLING CONTROL
• OPERATION MANAGEMENT
• CUSTOMER XPERIENCE
www.resonate.tech
E-mail: hello@resonate.tech
Tel: +44 1332 221 000 for general enquiries

REPTA Est. 1893
Railway Employees & Public Transport Association
Join today!
REPTA: Transport Staff Benefits Organisation.
See our benefits booklet. You can join on line at
www.repta.co.uk
Or send a cheque payable: REPTA £7.00 inc. P&P to:
Colin Rolle, 4 Brackmills Close, Forest Town, Mansfield NG19 0PB t 01623-646789 - *Quote Ref: MR*
Free Love2shop Card & competitive insurances - **JOIN TODAY!**

Rennsteig Werkzeuge GMBH
An der Koppel 1, D-98547 Viernau, Germany
T: 49 0368 474 410
E: info@rennsteig.com
W: www.rennsteig.com

Renown Railway Services
Brookside House, Brookside Business Park, Cold Meece, Staffs, ST15 0RZ
T: 01785 764484
F: 01785 760896
E: enquiries@renownrailway.co.uk
W: www.renownrailway.co.uk

REO (UK) Ltd
Units 2-4, Callow Hill Road, Craven Arms Business Park, Craven Arms, Shropshire, SY7 8NT
T: 01588 673411
F: 01588 672718
E: main@reo.co.uk
W: www.reo.co.uk/

Replin Fabrics
March St Mills, Peebles, EH45 8ER
T: 01721 724311
F: 01721 721893
E: enquiries@replin-fabrics.co.uk
W: www.replin-fabrics.co.uk

REPTA (Railway Employees and Public Transport Association)
c/o 4 Brackmills Close, Forest Town, Mansfield, Notts, NG19 0PB
T: 01623 646789
E: peter@24foxglove.co.uk
W: www.repta.co.uk

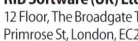

Resonate
Hudson House, 2 Hudson Way, Pride Park, Derby, DE24 8HS
T: 01332 221000
F: 01332 221008
E: hello@resonate.tech
W: www.resonate.tech/

Resourcing Solutions
Vector House, 5 Ruscombe Park, Ruscombe, Berks, RG10 9JW
T: 0118 932 0100
F: 0118 932 1818
E: info@resourcing-solutions.com
W: www.resourcing-solutions.com

Rethinking Transport
E: jon@rethinkingtransport.com
W: www.rethinkingtransport.com

Retro Railtours Ltd
2 Brookfield Grove, Ashton-under-Lyne, Lancashire, OL6 6TL
T: 0161 330 9055
E: info@retrorailtours.co.uk
W: www.retrorailtours.co.uk

Revitaglaze
Unit 2, Swanwick Business Centre, Bridge Road, Southampton, Hants, SO31 7GB
T: 020 3384 0220
F: 01372 200881
E: marketing@revitaglaze.com
W: www.revitaglaze.com

Rexel UK Ltd
Eagle Court 2, Hatchford Brook, Hatchford, Sheldon, Birmingham, B26 3RZ
T: 0121 366 1000
F: 0121 366 1029
E: marc.roberts@rexel.co.uk
W: www.rexel.co.uk

Rexquote Ltd
Broadgauge Business Park, Bishops Lydeard, Taunton, Somerset, TA4 3RU
T: 01823 433398
F: 01823 433378
E: sales@rexquote.co.uk
W: www.rexquote.co.uk

RGS Rail
6 Clarendon St, Nottingham, NG1 5HQ
T: 0115 959 9687
E: enquiries@rgsexecutive.co.uk
W: www.rgsexecutive.co.uk

Rhenus Lupprians (Romac)
Keiler House, Challenge Rd, Ashford, Middx, TW15 1AX
T: 01784 422900
F: 01784 423105
E: sales@lupprians.com
W: www.lupprians.com

Rhomberg Sersa UK Ltd
Unit 2, Sarah Court, Yorkshire Way, Doncaster, DN3 3FD
T: 0300 303 0230
E: info.uk@rhomberg-sersa.com
W: rhomberg-sersa.com/en

RIB Software (UK) Ltd
12 Floor, The Broadgate Tower, 20 Primrose St, London, EC2A 2EW
T: 020 7596 2747
F: 020 7596 2701
W: www.rib-software.co.uk

Ricardo Rail Ltd
Edward Lloyd House, 8 Pinnacle Way, Pride Park, Derby, DE24 8ZS
T: 01332 268700
F: 01332 268799
E: ukrailenquiries@ricardo.com
W: www.ricardo.com

Richmond Interior Supplies Ltd
Units 2 - 4, Chichester Business Centre, Chichester Street, Rochdale, Lancashire, OL16 2AU
T: 01706 525623
E: info@richmonds-ltd.co.uk
W: www.richmonds-ltd.co.uk/

Riello UPS Ltd
Unit 50, Clywedog Rd North, Wrexham Ind.Est., Wrexham, LL13 9XN
T: 01978 729297
F: 01978 729290
E: marketing@riello-ups.co.uk
W: www.riello-ups.co.uk

Riggotts & Co Ltd
Unit X, Lodge Lane Industrial Estate, Tuxford, Newark, Nottinghamshire, NG22 0NL
T: 01777 872525
W: www.riggott.co.uk/

DIRECTORY

Riley & Son (E) Ltd
Baron St, Bury, Lancs, BL9 0TY
T: 0161 764 2892
F: 0161 763 5191
E: rileys@btconnect.com
W: www.rileyandson.co.uk

RINA Consulting Ltd
Cleeve Rd, Leatherhead, Surrey, KT22 7SA
T: 01372 367345
E: infolh@rina.com
W: www.rinaconsulting.org/

RIQC Ltd
2 St Georges House, Vernon Gate, Derby, DE1 1UQ
T: 01332 221421
F: 01332 221401
E: enquiries@riqc.co.uk
W: www.riqc.co.uk

Risk Solutions
Dallam Court, Dallam Lane, Warrington, WA2 7LT
T: 01925 413984
E: enquiries@risksol.co.uk
W: www.risksol.co.uk

Risktec Solutions
Wilderspool Park, Greenalls Ave, Warrington, WA4 6HL
T: 01925 611200
F: 01925 611232
E: enquiries@risktec.co.uk
W: www.risktec.co.uk

Ritelite Systems Ltd
Meadow Park, Bourne Rd, Essendine, Stamford, Lincs, PE9 4LT
T: 01780 765600
F: 01780 765700
E: sales@ritelite.co.uk
W: www.ritelite.co.uk

Rittal Ltd
Braithwell Way, Hellaby Ind Est, Hellaby, Rotherham, South Yorks, S66 8QY
T: 01709 704000
F: 01709 701217
E: information@rittal.co.uk
W: www.rittal.co.uk

Riviera Trains
116 Ladbroke Grove, London, W10 5NE
T: 020 7727 4036
F: 020 7727 2083
E: enquiries@riviera-trains.co.uk
W: www.riviera-trains.co.uk

RJ Power Ltd
Unit 15, Lawson Hunt Ind. Park, Guildford Road, Broadbridge Heath, Horsham, West Sussex, RH12 3JR
T: 0845 034 1480
F: 0845 034 1481
E: info@rjpower.biz
W: www.rjpower.biz

RMD Kwikform UK
Brickyard Road, Aldridge, Walsall, WS9 8BW
T: 01922 743743
F: 01922 743400
E: info@rmdkwikform.com
W: www.rmdkwikform.com/

RMS Locotec locomotive Hire
British American Railway Services, Stanhope Station, Stanhope, Bishop Auckland, DL13 2YS
T: 01388 526203
E: documentcontroller@britamrail.com
W: www.rmslocotec.com

RMS Rail Projects Ltd
2 White House Close, New Road, Laxey, Isle of Man, IM4 7BA
T: 01388 526203
E: mfairburn@britamrail.com
W: www.rmslocotec.com/#/rms-rail-projects/4534062441

RMT
National Union of Rail, Maritime & Transport Workers, Unity House, 39 Chalton St, London, NW1 1JD
T: 020 7387 4771
F: 020 7387 4123
E: info@rmt.org.uk
W: www.rmt.org.uk

RNA Recruitment Ltd
Mere House, Brook St, Knutsford, Cheshire, WA16 8GP
T: 01302 366003
W: www.rnarecruitment.com

Roan Building Solutions
First Floor, Unit 1, Calder Close, Calder Park, Wakefield, WF4 3BA
T: 0845 1211687
M: 07972359917
E: predshaw@roanbuildings.co.uk
W: www.roanbuildings.co.uk

Robel Bahnbaumaschmen GmbH
Industriestrasse 31, D 83395, Freilassing, Germany
T: 0049 8654 6090
F: 0049 8654 609100
E: info@robel.info
W: www.robel.info

Robert West Consulting
Delta House, 175-177 Borough High St, London, SE1 1HR
T: 020 7939 9916
F: 020 7939 9909
E: london@robertwest.co.uk
W: www.robertwest.co.uk

Röchling Composites and Engineering Plastics
Waterwells Business Park, Waterwells Drive, Gloucester, GL2 2AA
T: 01452 727900
F: 01452 728056
E: sales@roechling-plastics.co.uk
W: www.roechling-plastics.co.uk

Rock Rail Holdings Ltd
Capital Tower, 91 Waterloo Road, London, SE1 8RT
T: 020 3170 0870
E: london@rockrail.com
W: www.rockrail.com

ROCOL
Rocol House, Wakefield Rd, Swillington, Leeds, LS26 8BS
T: 0113 232 2600
F: 0113 232 2740
E: customer-service.safety@rocol.com
W: www.rocol.com

Roevin Engineering
4th Floor, Clydesdale Bank House, 33 Lower Regent St, Piccadilly, London, WC1Y 4NB
T: 0845 643 0486
F: 0870 759 8443
E: rail@roevin.co.uk
W: www.roevin.co.uk

Rogers Stirk Harbour + Partners (RSHP)
The Leadenhall Building, 122 Leadenhall Street, London, EC3V 4AB
T: 020 7385 1235
F: 020 7385 8409
E: enquiries@rsh-p.com
W: www.rsh-p.com/

Rollalong Ltd
Woolsbridge Ind. Park, Three Legged Cross, Wimborne, Dorset, BH21 6SF
T: 01202 824541
F: 01202 826525
E: enquiries@rollalong.co.uk
W: www.rollalong.co.uk

Romag
Leadgate Ind. Est., Leadgate, Consett, Co Durham, DH8 7RS
T: 01207 500000
F: 01207 591979
E: tiffany.sott@romag.co.uk
W: www.romag.co.uk

Romic House
A1/M1 Business Centre, Kettering, Northants, NN16 8TD
T: 01536 414244
F: 01536 414245
E: sales@romic.co.uk
W: www.romic.co.uk

Ronfell Ltd
Challenge House, Pagefield industrial Est., Miry Lane, Wigan, WN6 7LA
T: 01942 492200
F: 01942 492233
E: sales@ronfell.com
W: www.ronfell.com

Rose Hill P&OD Ltd
35 Colworth House, Colworth Park, Sharnbrook, Bedfordshire, MK44 1LQ
M: 07771 612321
E: info@rose-hill.co.uk
W: www.rose-hill.co.uk

Rosehill Rail
Spring Bank Mills, Watson Mill Lane, Sowerby Bridge, West Yorks, HX6 3BW
T: 01422 317482
F: 01422 316952
E: stuart.wilson@rosehillrail.com
W: www.rosehillrail.com

Rosemor International Ltd
Rosemor House, OYO Unit F, Moses Winter Way, Wallingford, Oxfordshire, OX10 9FE
T: 01491 838011
F: 01491 832010
E: gerry@rosemor.com
W: www.rosemor.com

Rosenqvist Rail AB
Hyggesvägen 4, 824 34 Hudiksvall, Sweden
T: 0046 650 16505
F: 0046 650 16501
E: info@rosenqvist-group.se
W: www.rosenqvistrail.se

Rothwell Electrical Services
Unit 3, Yorvale Business Park, Hazel Court, James Street, York, YO10 3DR
T: 01904 413172
F: 01904 413174
W: rothwellelect.co.uk/

Roughton Group
A2 Omega Park, Electron Way, Chandlers Ford, Hants, SO53 4SE
T: 023 8027 8600
F: 023 8027 8601
E: hq@roughton.com
W: www.roughton.com

"Rowe Hankins Ltd."
Power House, Parker St, Bury, Lancs, BL9 0RJ
T: 0161 765 3000
F: 0161 705 2900
E: sales@rowehankins.com
W: www.rowehankins.com

Roxtec Ltd
Unit C1, Waterfold Business Park, Bury, Lancs, BL9 7BQ
T: 0161 761 5280
F: 0161 763 6065
E: russell.holmes@uk.roxtec.com
W: www.roxtec.com

Royal British Legion Industries (RBLI)
Royal British Legion Village, Hall Rd, Aylesford, Kent, ME20 7NL
T: 01622 795900
F: 01622 795978
E: sales.office@rbli.co.uk
W: www.rbli.co.uk/manufacturing/services/19/

Royal Haskoning Ltd
Rightwell House, Bretton, Peterborough, PE3 8DW
T: 01733 334455
F: 01733 262243
E: info@rhdhv.com
W: www.royalhaskoning.com

RPS Consulting Services
Sherwood House, Sherwood Avenue, Newark, Nottinghamshire, NG24 1QQ
T: 01636 605700
F: 01636 827309
E: alan.skipper@rpsgroup.com
W: www.rpsgroup.com

RS Components Ltd
Birchington Rd, Corby, Northants, NN17 9RS
T: 0845 602 5226
W: www.rswww.com/purchasing

RSK STATS Health & Safety Ltd
Spring Lodge, 172 Chester Rd, Helsby, Cheshire, WA6 0AR
T: 01928 726006
F: 01928 725633
E: info@rsk.com
W: www.rsk.com

RSK Ltd
18 Frogmore Rd, Hemel Hempstead, Herts, HP3 9RT
T: 01442 437500
F: 01442 437550
E: info@rsk.co.uk
W: www.rsk.co.uk

RSL Cityspace
Unit 3, Fullwood Close, Aldermans Green Industrial Estate, Coventry, Warks, CV2 2SS
T: 02476 587894
E: support@rslcityspace.co.uk
W: www.rslcityspace.co.uk/

RSSB
Block 2, Angel Square, 1 Torrens St, London, EC1V 1NY
T: 020 3142 5300
E: enquirydesk@rssb.co.uk
W: www.rssb.co.uk

RTC Group
The Derby Conference Centre, London Rd, Derby, DE24 8UX
T: 01332 861336
F: 0870 890 0034
E: info@rtcgroupplc.co.uk
W: www.rtcgroupplc.co.uk

RTI UK
35 Old Queen St, London, SW1H 9JD
T: 020 7340 0900
F: 020 7233 3411
E: rtiuk@rti.co.uk
W: www.rti.co.uk

RTS Infrastructure Services Ltd
The Rail Depot, Bridge Rd, Holbeck, Leeds, LS11 9UG
T: 01132 344899
E: info@rtsinfrastructure.com
W: www.rtsinfrastructure.com

RTS Solutions Ltd
Atlantic House, Imperial Way, Reading, RG2 0TD
T: 0118 903 6045
F: 0118 903 6100
E: stuart@rts-solutions.net
W: www.rts-solutions.net

Rubirail
Victoria Buildings, 27 Victoria Rd, Draycott, Derby, DE72 3PS
T: 01332 872483
E: info@rubirail.co.uk
W: www.rubirail.co.uk/

RUGGED MOBILE Systems Ltd
Park View Business Centre, Combermere, Whitchurch, Shropshire, SY13 4AL
T: 0845 652 0816
F: 0845 652 0817
E: info@rm-systems.co.uk
W: www.ruggedmobilesystems.co.uk

Rullion Engineering Personnel
Aldermary House, 10-15 Queen Street, London, EC4N 1TX
T: 0203 201 1217
E: justin.ayling@rullion.co.uk
W: www.rullion.co.uk

RWD Technologies UK Ltd
Furzeground Way, First Floor, Stockley Park, Uxbridge, UB11 1AJ
T: 020 8569 2787
F: 020 8756 3625
E: info@gpstrategies.com
W: www.rwd.com

Rydon Signs
Unit 3, Peek House, Pinhoe Trading Est, Exeter, Devon, EX4 8JN
T: 01392 466653
F: 01392 466671
E: sales@rydonsigns.com
W: www.rydonsigns.com

S H Lighting
Salcmbe Rd, Meadow Lane Ind. Est, Alfreton, Derbys, DE55 7RG
T: 01773 522390
F: 01773 520693
E: sales@shlighting.co.uk
W: www.shlighting.co.uk

S M Consult Ltd
3 High St, Stanford in the Vale, Faringdon, Oxon, SN7 8LH
T: 01367 710152
F: 01367 710152
E: info@smcsolar.co.uk
W: www.smconsult.co.uk

S&T Cover Ltd
Railway Goods Yard, Dutton Lane, Eastleigh, Hampshire, SO50 6AA
T: 023 8072 8830
F: 023 8072 8660
E: enquiries@s-tcover.co.uk
W: www.s-tcover.co.uk/

S.E.T Ltd
Atlas Works, Litchurch Lane, Derby, DE24 8AQ
T: 01332 346035
F: 01332 346494
E: sales@set.gb.com
W: www.set.gb.com

Sabre Rail
Grindon Way, Heighington Lane Business Park, Newton Aycliffe, Co Durham, DL5 6SH
T: 01325 300505
F: 01325 300485
E: sales@sabrerail.com
W: www.sabrerail.com

Safeaid LLP
Signal House, 16 Arnside Rd, Waterlooville, Hants, PO7 7UP
T: 02392 254442
F: 02392 257444
E: sales@safeaidsupplies.com
W: www.safeaidsupplies.com

Safeglass (Europe) Ltd
Nasmyth Building, Nasmyth Ave, East Kilbride, G75 0QR
T: 01355 272438
F: 01355 272788
E: sales@safeglass.co.uk
W: www.safeglass.co.uk

Safeguard Pest Control Ltd
6 Churchill Bus. Park, The Flyers Way, Westerham, Kent, TN16 1BT
T: 0800 195 7766
F: 01959 565888
E: info@safeguardpestcontrol.co.uk
W: www.safeguardpestcontrol.co.uk

Developing and investing in passenger focused rolling stock and rail infrastructure solutions
www.rockrail.com

INVESTOR / DEVELOPER / ASSET MANAGER

ROCK rail

Transforming tomorrow's infrastructure today

Rittal is the world's largest manufacturer of enclosures and associated products for both indoor and outdoor applications with an extensive stock holding in the UK.

A: Rittal Ltd, Braithwell Way
   Hellaby Industrial Estate
   Hellaby, Rotherham
   South Yorkshire S66 8QY

P: +44 (0)1709 704000
F: +44 (0)1709 701217
E: information@rittal.co.uk
W: www.rittal.co.uk

Rowe Hankins Ltd.

Keeping Rail Journeys Moving Since 1985

Rowe Hankins Ltd. specialises in innovative trainborne and wayside products; as well as having service capabilities in engineering and design to overhaul and repair.

Precision... made here

T: +44(0) 161 765 3000
W: www.rowehankins.com
E: sales@rowehankins.com

IN ASSOCIATION WITH Nomad Digital

Safestyle Security Services
Exe. Suite 1, Cardiff International Arena, Mary Ann St, Cardiff, CF10 2EQ
T: 02920 221711
F: 02920 234592
E: office@safestylesecurity.co.uk
W: www.safestylesecurity.co.uk

Safetell Ltd
Unit 46, Fawkes Ave, Dartford Trade Park, Dartford, DA1 1JQ
T: 01322 223233
F: 01322 277751
E: sales@safetell.co.uk
W: www.safetell.co.uk

Safetrack Baavhammar AB
1 Moleberga, S-245 93 Staffanstorp, Sweden
T: 0046 4044 5300
F: 0046 4044 5553
E: sales@safetrack.se
W: www.safetrack.se

Safetykleen UK Ltd
2 Heath Road, Weybridge, Surrey, KT13 8AP
T: 01909 519300
E: skuk@sk-europe.com
W: www.safetykleen.co.uk

SAFT Ltd
1st Floor, Unit 5, Astra Centre, Edinburgh Way, Harlow, CM20 2BN
T: 01279 772550
F: 01279 420909
E: igb.info@saftbatteries.com
W: www.saftbatteries.com

SAFT Power Systems Ltd
See AEG Power Solutions Ltd

Saint Gobain Abrasives Ltd
Doxey Rd, Stafford, ST16 1EA
T: 01785 279550
F: 01785 213487
E: sonia.uppal@saint-gobain.com
W: www.saint-gobain.com

Saira Electronics
75 Chesterwood Road, Kings Heath, Birmingham, B13 0QQ
T: 0039 045 630 4558
E: saira@sairaelectronics.com
W: www.sairaelectronics.com

Saltburn Railtours
16 Bristol Ave, Saltburn, TS12 1BW
T: 01287 626572
E: r.dallara@btinternet.com
W: www.saltburnrailtours.co.uk

Samsung Electronics Hainan Fibreoptics
c/o Go Tel Communications Ltd, 4 Hicks Close, Wroughton, Swindon, SN4 9AY
T: 01793 813600
F: 01793 529380
E: robindash@gtcom.co.uk
W: www.samsungfiberoptics.com

Samuel James Engineering
21 Ashton Close, Beaumont Leys, Leicester, LE4 2BQ
T: 0116 235 0380
E: sales@samuel-james.co.uk
W: samuel-james.co.uk

Samuel Taylor Ltd
Arthur Street, Redditch, Worcs, B98 8JY
T: 01527 504910
F: 01527 500869
E: sales@samueltaylor.co.uk
W: www.samueltaylor.co.uk

Santon Switchgear Ltd
Unit 9, Waterside Court, Newport, NP20 5NT
T: 01633 854111
F: 01633 854999
E: sales@santonswitchgear.co.uk
W: www.santonswitchgear.com

SAP (UK) Ltd
Clockhouse Place, Bedfont Road, Feltham, Middlesex, TW14 8HD
T: 0800 0852 631
W: https://go.sap.com/uk/

Sapa Extrusions
Pantglas Ind. Est., Bedwas, Caerphilly, CF83 8DR
T: 02920 854600
F: 02920 865229
E: sales.haeuk@hydro.com
W: www.sapagroup.com/en/extrusions-uk/

Sartoria Corporatewear
Gosforth Rd, Derby, DE24 8HU
T: 01332 342616
F: 01332 226940
W: www.sartorialtd.co.uk.co.uk

SAS International
31 Suttons Business Park, Reading, Berkshire, RG6 1AZ
T: 0118 929 0900
F: 0118 929 0901
W: sasintgroup.com/

Savigny Oddie Ltd
Wallows Ind. Est, Wallows Rd, Brierley Hill, West Midlands, DY5 1QA
T: 01384 481598
F: 01384 482383
E: keith@oddiefasteners.com
W: www.savigny-oddie.co.uk

SB Rail (Swietelsky Babcock)
Kintail House, 3 Lister Way, Hamilton International Park, Blantyre, G72 0FT
T: 01698 203005
F: 01698 203006
E: shona.jamieson@babcock.co.uk
W: www.babcock.co.uk/rail

SBC Rail Ltd (Stanton Bonna)
Littlewell Lane, Stanton by Dale, Ilkeston, Derbys, DE7 4QW
T: 0115 944 1448
F: 0115 944 1466
E: sbc@stanton-bonna.co.uk
W: www.stanton-bonna.co.uk

Scantec
Spinnaker House, Morpeth Wharf, Twelve Quays, Wirral, CH41 1LF
T: 0151 666 8999
E: info@scantec.co.uk
W: www.scantec.co.uk/

SCCS
Hq1 Building, Phoenix Park, Eaton Socon, St Neots, Cambs, PE19 8EP
T: 01480 404888
F: 01480 404333
E: sales@sccssurvey.co.uk
W: www.sccssurvey.co.uk

SCG Solutions
335 Shepcote Lane, Sheffield, S9 1TG
T: 0114 221 1111
E: sales@scgsolutions.co.uk
W: www.scgsolutions.co.uk

Schaltbau Machine Electrics
335/336 Springvale Industrial Estate, Woodside Way, Cwmbran, NP44 5BR
T: 01633 877555
F: 01633 873366
E: sales@schaltbau-me.com
W: www.schaltbau-me.com

Scheidt & Bachmann (UK) Ltd
7 Silverglade Business Park, Leatherhead Rd, Chessington, Surrey, KT9 2QL
T: 01372 230400
F: 01372 722053
E: info@scheidt-bachmann.de
W: www.scheidt-bachmann.de

Schenck Process UK
Unit 3 Alpha Court, Capitol Park, Thorne, Doncaster, DN8 5TZ
T: 01302 321313
F: 01302 554400
E: enquiries@schenckprocess.co.uk
W: www.schenckprocess.co.uk

Schneider Electric Ltd
Stafford Park 5, Telford, Shropshire, TF3 3BL
T: 01952 209226
F: 01952 292238
E: gb-marcoms@gb.schneider.electric.com
W: www.schneider-electric.co.uk

Schoenemann Design Ltd
Friar Gate Studios, Studio 26, Ford Street, Derby, DE1 1EE
T: 01332 258345
M: 07831 332790
E: andrew@schoenemanndesign.co.uk
W: https://schoenemanndesign.co.uk/

Schofield Lothian Ltd
Temple Chambers, 3-7 Temple Ave, London, EC4Y 0DT
T: 020 7842 0920
F: 020 7842 0921
E: enquiries@schofieldlothian.com
W: www.schofieldlothian.com

Schroff UK Ltd
Maylands Ave, Hemel Hempstead, Herts, HP2 7DE
T: 01442 240471
F: 01442 213508
E: schroff.uk@pentair.com
W: www.schroff.co.uk

Schweerbau GmbH & Co KG
UK Branch Office, 20 Beattyville Gardens, Ilford, IG6 1JN
F: 020 7681 3971
E: verheijen@schweerbau.de
W: www.schweerbau.de

Schweizer Electronic
Peter House, Oxford Street, Manchester, M1 5AN
T: 01827 289996
E: info@schweizer-electronic.co.uk
W: www.schweizer-electronic.co.uk

Schwihag AG
Lebernstrasse 3, CH-8274 Tägerwilen, Switzerland
T: 0041 71 666 8800
F: 0041 71 666 8801
E: info@schwihag.com
W: www.schwihag.com

Scientifics
ESG House, Bretby Business Park, Ashby Rd, Burton upon Trent, DE15 0YZ
T: 0845 603 2112
F: 01283 554401
E: sales@esg.co.uk
W: www.esg.co.uk

Scisys
Methuen Park, Chippenham, Wilts, SN14 0GB
T: 01249 466466
F: 01249 466666
E: marketing@scisys.co.uk
W: www.scisys.co.uk

ScotRail
See Abellio ScotRail

Scott Bader
Wollaston, Wellingborough, Northants, NN29 7RL
T: 01933 663100
E: composites@scottbader.com
W: www.scottbader.com

Scott Brownrigg – Design Research Unit
77 Endell St, London, WC2H 9DZ
T: 020 7240 7766
F: 020 7240 2454
E: enquiries@scottbrownrigg.com
W: www.scottbrownrigg.com

Scott White & Hookins
Fountain House, 26 St Johns St, Bedford, MK42 0AQ
T: 01234 213111
F: 01234 213333
E: info@swh.co.uk
W: www.swh.co.uk

Scott Wilson Railways
See URS

Scotweld Employment Services
See SW Global Resourcing

SCP
Colwyn Chambers, 19 York Street, Manchester, M2 3BA
T: 0161 832 4400
E: info@scptransport.co.uk
W: scptransport.co.uk/

Screwfast Foundations Ltd
1st Floor, 4 Sandridge Park, Porters Wood, St. Albans, Herts, AL3 6PH
T: 01727 821282
F: 01727 828098
E: info@screwfast.com
W: www.screwfast.com

SCT Europe Ltd
See Wabtec Rail Ltd

SEA (Group) Ltd
Building 450, Bristol Business Park, Coldharbour Lane, Bristol, BS16 1EJ
T: 01373 852000
F: 01373 831133
E: info@sea.co.uk
W: www.sea.co.uk

Search Consultancy
198 West George St, Glasgow, G2 2NR
T: 0141 272 7777
F: 0141 272 7788
E: glasgow@search.co.uk
W: www.searchconsultancy.co.uk

Seaton Rail Ltd
Bridlington Business Centre, Enterprise Way, Bridlington, YO16 4SF
T: 01262 608313
F: 01262 604493
E: info@seaton-rail.com
W: www.seaton-rail.com

Secheron SA
Rue de pre-Bouvier 25, Zimeysa 1217 Meyrin, Geneva, Switzerland
T: 0041 22 739 4111
F: 0041 22 739 4811
E: info@secheron.com
W: www.secheron.com

Seetru Ltd
Albion Dockside Works, Bristol, BS1 6UT
T: 0117 930 6100
E: info@seetru.com
W: www.seetru.com/

Sefac UK Ltd
1-6 Barton Rd, Water Eaton, Bletchley, MK2 3HU
T: 01908 821274
F: 01908 821275
E: info@sefac-lift.co.uk
W: www.sefac-lift.co.uk

Sekisui Chemical GmbH
Königsallee 106, 40215 Düsseldorf, Germany
T: +49 211 36977 0
F: +49 211 36977 31
E: contact@sekisui-rail.com
W: www.sekisui-rail.com

Scott Cables
Painter Close, Anchorage Park, Portsmouth, Hampshire, PO3 5RS
T: 02392 652552
F: 02392 655277
E: sales@scottcables.com
W: www.scottcables.com

Selectequip Ltd
Unit 7, Britannia Way, Britannia Enterprise Park, Lichfield, Staffs, WS14 9UY
T: 01543 416641
F: 01543 416083
E: sales@selectequip.co.uk
W: www.selectequip.co.uk

Selectrail (Australia) Pty Ltd
1/11 Trevi Crescent, Tullamarine, VIC 3043, Australia
T: 6103 9335 0600
E: info@selectrail.com
W: www.selectrail.com

Selex ES Ltd
8-10 Great George St, London, SW1P 3AE
F: 0207 340 6199
E: amanda.lachlan@selex-es.com
W: www.selex-es.com

Sella Controls
Carrington Field St, Stockport, Cheshire, SK1 3JN
T: 0161 429 4500
F: 0161 476 3095
E: sales@sellacontrols.com
W: www.sellacontrols.com

Selwood Ltd
Bournemouth Road, Chandler's Ford, Eastleigh, Hampshire, SO53 3ZL
T: 023 8026 6311
F: 023 8026 0906
W: www.selwood.co.uk/

Semikron Ltd
9 Harforde Court, John Tate Rd, Foxholes Business Park, Hertford, SG13 7NW
T: 01992 584677
F: 01992 503837
E: sales.skuk@semikron.com
W: www.semikron.com

Semmco Ltd
9 Kestrel Way, Goldsworth Park Trading Est, Woking, Surrey, GU21 3BA
T: 01483 757200
F: 01483 740795
E: sales@semmco.com
W: www.semmco.co.uk

Semperit Industrial Products
25 Cottesbrooke Park, Heartlands, Daventry, Northants, NN11 8YL
T: 01327 313144
F: 01327 313149
E: ian.rowlinson@semperit.co.uk
W: www.semperit.at

Senator Security Services Ltd
1 The Thorn Tree, Elmhurst Business Park, Lichfield, Staffs, WS13 8EX
T: 01543 411811
F: 01543 411611
E: senatorgroup@senatorsecurity.co.uk
W: www.senatorsecurity.co.uk

Senceive Ltd
Hurlingham Studios, Ranelagh Gardens, London, SW6 3PA
T: 020 7731 8269
E: info@senceive.com
W: www.senceive.com

SENER Group
1st Floor East, Adamson House, 2 Centenary Way, Salford, Manchester, M50 1RD
T: 0161 786 1950
W: www.sener.es/home/en

SenseAir AB
Flottiljgatan 49, SE-721 31, Vasteras, Sweden
T: 0046 21800099
E: mark.hawthorne@senseair.com
W: www.senseair.com/

Serco Caledonian Sleepers Ltd
Basement and Ground Floor, 1-5 Union Street, Inverness, IV1 1PP
T: 0330 060 0500
W: https://www.sleeper.scot/

Serco Transport Services
Serco House, 16 Bartley Wood Bus. Park, Bartley Way, Hook, Hants, RG27 9UY
T: 01256 745900
F: 01256 744111
E: generalenquiries@serco.com
W: www.serco.com/markets/transport

Serco Rail Technical Services
Derwent House, RTC Business Park, London Rd, Derby, DE24 8UP
T: 0330 109 8852
F: 01332 385362
E: enquiries.srts@serco.com
W: www.serco.com/srts

Serfis Construction and Engineering Ltd
9a Church Street, Kidderminster, Worcestershire, DY10 2AD
T: 01562 822082
F: 01562 820813
E: info@serfis.co.uk
W: serfis.co.uk/

SES Security
The Barrows, Roydon Road, Harlow, Essex, CM19 5BL
T: 020 8804 5058
W: www.thesesgroup.co.uk/security/

Setec Ltd
11 Mallard Way, Derby, DE24 8GX
E: craig.king@setecltd.co.uk
W: www.setecltd.co.uk

Severfield
Severs House, Dalton Airfield Industrial Estate, Dalton, Thirsk, North Yorkshire, YO7 3JN
T: 01845 577896
F: 01845 577 411
W: www.severfield.com/

Severn Lamb
Tything Rd, Alcester, B49 6ET
T: 01789 400140
F: 01789 400240
E: sales@severn-lamb.com
W: www.severn-lamb.com

The Severn Partnership Ltd
Lambda House, Hadley Park East, Telford, Shropshire, TF1 6QJ
T: 01952 676775
E: info@severnpartnership.com
W: www.severnpartnership.com

Severn Valley Railway
Number One, Comberton Place, Kidderminster, Worcs, DY10 1QR
T: 01562 757900
E: mktg@svr.co.uk
W: www.svr.co.uk

Seymourpowell
The Factory, 265 Merton Rd, London, SW18 5JS
T: 020 7381 6433
E: lucy.kirby@seymourpowell.com
W: www.seymourpowell.com

SGA (Stuart Gray Associates)
88 Spring Hill, Arley, Works, CV7 8FE
T: 01676 541402
E: info@stuartgrayassociates.co.uk
W: www.stuartgrayassociates.co.uk

SGH Martineau LLP
No.1 Colmore, Birmingham, B4 6AA
T: 0800 763 1000
F: 0800 763 1001
E: andrew.whitehead@sghmartineau.com
W: www.sghmartineau.com

SELLA CONTROLS
An independent company providing innovative communication systems and safety control solutions to the rail industry.
SELLA CONTROLS
Carrington Field Street, Stockport, Cheshire, SK1 3JN, United Kingdom
T: +44 (0) 161 429 4500 F: + (0) 0161 476 3095
E: sales@sellacontrols.com
www.sellacontrols.com

SGS Correl Rail Ltd
Gee House, Holborn Hill, Birmingham, B7 5PA
T: 0121 326 9900
F: 0121 328 5343
E: gary.winstanley@sgs.com
W: www.sgs.com

SGS Engineering (UK) Ltd
Unit 2, West Side Park, Belmore Way, Derby, DE21 7AZ
T: 01332 576850
F: 01332 753068
E: sales@sgs-engineering.com
W: www.sgs-engineering.com

SGS UK Ltd
Inward Way, Rossmore Business Park, Ellesmere Port, CH65 3EN
T: 0151 350 6666
F: 0151 350 6600
W: www.sgs.com

Shannon Rail Services Ltd
Orphanage Road Sidings, Reeds Crescent, Watford, Herts, WD17 1PG
T: 01923 254567
F: 01923 255678
E: info@shannonrail.co.uk
W: www.shannonrail.co.uk

Shay Murtagh Precast Ltd
Raharney, Mullingar, Co Westmeath, Republic of Ireland
T: 0844 202 0263
E: sales@shaymurtagh.co.uk
W: www.shaymurtagh.co.uk

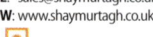

SHB Hire Ltd
18 Premier Way, Abbey Park Industrial Estate, Romsey, Hampshire, SO51 9DQ
T: 01794 511458
E: enquiries@shb.co.uk
W: www.shb.co.uk/

Sheerspeed Shelters Ltd
Unit 3, Diamond House, Reme Drive, Heath Park Ind. Estate, Honiton, Devon, EX14 1SE
T: 01404 46006
F: 01404 45520
E: sales@sheerspeed.com
W: www.sheerspeed.com

Shell UK Oil Products Ltd
Brabazon House, Concord Business Park, Threapwood Rd, Manchester, M22 0RR
T: 08708 500924
F: 0161 499 8930
E: lubesenquiries-uk@shell.com
W: www.shell.co.uk/lubricants

Shere Ltd
See ATOS Origin

Sheridan Maine
Regus House, George Curl Way, Southampton, SO18 2RZ
T: 0871 218 0573
F: 0871 218 0173
E: southampton@sheridanmaine.com
W: www.sheridanmaine.com

SIEMENS

Trusted by our partners we are pioneering transportation, moving people sustainably and seamlessly from the first mile to the last. As a strong UK partner with UK manufacturing and R&D, Siemens Mobility Limited is constantly innovating in our portfolio of rolling stock and service, signalling, control and electrification. With digitalisation we are enabling mobility operators to make trains and infrastructure intelligent, increase value sustainably over the entire lifecycle, enhance passenger experience and guarantee availability.

Siemens Mobility Limited, Euston House, 24 Eversholt Street, London, NW1 1AD
Email: info.mobility.gb@siemens.com
www.siemens.co.uk/rail

Sherwin-Williams Protective & Marine Coatings
Tower Works, Kestor St, Bolton, Lancs, BL2 2AL
T: 01204 521771
F: 01204 382115
E: enquiries.pm.emeas@sherwin.com
W: protectiveemea.sherwin-williams.com/

Shield Batteries
277 Stansted Rd, Bishops Stortford, Herts, CM23 2BT
T: 01279 652067
F: 01279 758041
E: info@shieldbatteries.co.uk
W: www.shieldbatteries.co.uk

Shilcocks
Grosvenor House, 102 Beverley Road, Kingston-upon-Hull, HU3 1YA
T: 01482 221858
F: 01482 322244
E: admin@shilcocks.com
W: www.shilcocks.com/

Shilling Media Services
62 North St, Bourne, Lincs, PE10 9AJ
T: 01778 421550
F: 01778 421550
M: 07736 635916
E: chris@shillingmedia.co.uk
W: www.shillingmedia.co.uk

Shoosmiths
1 St Martin's Le Grand, London, EC1A 4AS
T: 020 7205 7017
M: 07836 720537
E: martin.fleetwood@shoosmiths.co.uk
W: www.shoosmiths.co.uk

Shorterm Rail
The Barn, Philpots Close, Yiewsley, Middx, UB7 7RY
T: 01895 427900
E: info@shortermgroup.co.uk
W: www.shorterm.co.uk

Shotcrete Services Ltd
Old Station Yard, Hawkhurst Rd, Cranbrook, Kent, TN17 2SR
T: 01580 714747
E: stuart.manning@shotcrete.co.uk
W: www.shotcrete.co.uk

SICK (UK) Ltd
Waldkirch House, 39 Hedley Rd, St Albans, Herts, AL1 5BN
T: 01727 831121
F: 01727 856767
E: info@sick.co.uk
W: www.sick.co.uk

Siegrist-Orel Ltd
Pysons Rd Ind. Est., Broadstairs, Kent, CT10 2LQ
T: 01843 865241
F: 01843 867180
E: info@siegrist-orel.co.uk
W: www.siegrist-orel.co.uk

Siemens Mobility Ltd
Euston House, 24 Eversholt St, London, NW1 1AD
T: 020 7227 0722
F: 020 7227 4435
E: info.mobility.gb@siemens.com
W: www.siemens.co.uk/rail

Siemens Rail Automation
Langley Park, Pew Hill, Chippenham, Wiltshire, SN15 1JD
T: 01249 441441
E: info@railautomation.gb@siemens.com
W: www.siemens.co.uk/rail

Siemens RUGGEDCOM UK
Princess Road, Princess Parkway, Manchester, M20 2UR
T: 0161 446 5000
F: 0161 446 5742
E: ianpoulett@ruggedcom.com
W: www.siemens.com/ruggedcom

Sig Cyclone
Unit 16 Gerald House, Sherwood Network Centre, Sherwood Energy Village, Newton Hill, Ollerton, Notts, NG22 9FD
T: 07833 433404
E: liane.launders@sigcyclone.co.uk
W: www.sig-ukgroup.com

SIG plc
Hillsborough Works, Landsett Road, Sheffield, S6 2LW
T: 0114 285 6327
E: sigri@sigplc.co.uk
W: www.sigri.co.uk

SigAssure UK Ltd
Gerald House, Unit 4, Ebor Court, Randall Park Way, Retford, Notts, DN22 7WF
T: 01777 707809
E: info@sigassure-uk.com
W: www.sigassure-group.co.uk

Sigma Coachair Group UK Ltd
Unit 1, Queens Drive, Newhall, Swadlincote, Derbys, DE11 0EG
T: 01283 559140
F: 01283 225253
W: www.sigmacoachair.com

Signal House Ltd
Cherrycourt Way, Stanbridge Rd, Leighton Buzzard, Beds, LU7 4UH
T: 01525 377477
F: 01525 850999
E: sales@signalhouse.co.uk
W: www.signalhousegroup.co.uk

Signalling Construction UK Ltd
Unit 56, Coleshill Industrial Estate, Coleshill, Birmingham, B46 1JT
T: 01675 464746
E: info@sculktd.com
W: www.sculktd.com

Signalling Solutions Ltd
See Alstom Transport

Signature Aromas Ltd
Signature House, 65-67 Gospel End St, Sedgley, West Midlands, DY3 3LR
T: 01902 678822
F: 01902 672888
E: enquiries@signaturearomas.co.uk
W: www.signaturearomas.co.uk

Signet Solutions
Kelvin House, RTC Business Park, London Rd, Derby, DE24 8UP
T: 01332 343585
F: 01332 367132
E: enquiries@signet-solutions.com
W: www.signet-solutions.com

SignPost Solutions
Unit 5, Clarendon Drive, The Parkway, Tipton, West Midlands, DY4 0QA
T: 0121 506 4770
F: 0121 506 4771
E: i.thomas@signfix.co.uk
W: www.signfix.co.uk

Sill Lighting UK
3 Thame Park Bus. Centre, Wenman Rd, Thame, Oxon, OX9 3XA
T: 01844 260006
F: 01844 260760
E: sales@sill-uk.com
W: www.sill-uk.com

Silver Atena
Cedar House, Riverside Business Park, Swindon Rd, Malmesbury, Wilts, SN16 9RS
T: 01666 580000
F: 01666 580001
E: info@silver-atena.com
W: www.silver-atena.com

Silver Fox Ltd
Swallow Court, Swallowfields, Welwyn Garden City, Herts, AL7 1SA
T: 01707 373727
F: 01707 372193
E: marketing@silverfox.co.uk
W: www.silverfox.co.uk

Silver Software
See Silver Atena

SilverRail
The Heal's Building, 22 Torrington Place, London, WC1E 7HJ
T: 0845 834 1069
E: info@silverrailtech.com
W: silverrailtech.com/

Simco External Framing Solutions
Leamore Lane, Bloxwich, Walsall, West Midlands, WS2 7DQ
T: 01922 494900
F: 01922 494982
E: webenquiry@simcoefs.com
W: www.simcoefs.com/

Simmons & Simmons
City Point, One Ropemaker St, London, EC2Y 9SS
T: 020 7628 2020
F: 020 7628 2070
E: juliet.reingold@simmons-simmons.com
W: www.simmons-simmons.com

Simona UK
Telford Drive, Brookmead Ind. Park, Stafford, ST16 3ST
T: 01785 222444
F: 01785 222080
E: mail@simona-uk.com
W: www.simona.de

SIMS
Fourth Floor, Roman Wall House, 1-2 Crutched Friars, London, EC3N 2HT
T: 020 7481 9798
F: 020 7481 9657
E: inbox@sims-uk.com
W: www.simsrail.co.uk

Simulation Systems Ltd
Unit 12, Market Ind.Est, Yatton, Bristol, BS49 4RF
T: 01934 838803
F: 01934 876202
W: www.simulation-systems.co.uk

Sinclair Knight Merz
See Jacobs UK Ltd

John Sisk & Sons Ltd
1 Curo Park, Frogmore, St Albans, Herts, AL2 2DD
T: 01727 875551
F: 01727 875642
W: www.johnsiskandson.com/uk

Site Eye Time-Lapse Films
Unit 8D, Top Lands, County Business Park, Cragg Road, Cragg Vale, Halifax, West Yorkshire, HX7 5RW
T: 01422 884477
E: info@site-eye.co.uk
W: www.site-eye.co.uk

Site Vision Surveys
19 Warwick St, Rugby, Warks, CV21 3DH
T: 01788 575036
F: 01788 576208
E: mail@svsltd.net
W: www.svsltd.net

SITECH UK & Ireland
Morgans Business Park, Norton Canes, Cannock, Staffs, WS11 9UU
T: 0845 600 5669
E: info@sitechukandireland.com
W: www.sitechukandireland.com

Skanska UK
Maple Cross House, Denham Way, Maple Cross, Rickmansworth, Herts, WD3 9SW
T: 01923 423100
F: 01923 423111
W: www.skanska.co.uk/

SKF UK Ltd
Railway Sales Unit, Sundon Park Rd, Luton, LU3 3BL
T: 01582 496490
F: 01582 496327
E: stewart.mclellan@skf.com
W: www.skf.com

Skills4Rail
35 Auckland Rd, Birmingham, B11 1RH
T: 01217714219
E: sales@sills4rail.co.uk
W: www.skills4rail.co.uk

SKM Colin Buchanan
New City Court, 20 St. Thomas Street, London, SE1 9RS
T: 020 7939 6160
E: acassidy@globalskm.com
W: www.skmcolinbuchanan.com

Škoda Transportation
Emila Škody 2922/1, 301 00 Plzeň, Czech Republic
T: +420 378 186 666
F: +420 378 186 455
E: transportation@skoda.cz
W: www.skoda.cz/en

Skymasts Antennas
Unit 2, Clayfield Close, Moulton Park Ind. Est, Northampton, NN3 6QF
T: 01604 494132
F: 01604 494133
E: info@skymasts.com
W: www.skymasts.com

SLC Rail
Suite 203, Guildhall Buildings, Navigation Street, Birmingham, B2 4BT
T: 0121 285 2622
E: enquiries@slcrail.com
W: www.slcrail.co.uk/

Slender Winter Partnership
The Old School, London Rd, Westerham, Kent, TN11 1DN
T: 01959 564777
F: 01959 562802
E: swp@swpltd.co.uk
W: www.swpltd.co.uk

Smart Component Technologies Ltd
3M Buckley Innovation Centre, Firth St, Huddersfield, HD1 3BD
E: r.bromley@hud.ac.uk
W: www.hud.ac.uk

SmartWater Technology Ltd
27 Queen Anne's Gate, London, SW1H 9BU
T: 0333 320 7797
F: 0333 320 7798
E: enquiry@smartwater.com
W: www.smartwater.com

SMC Light & Power
Belchmire Lane, Gosberton, Lincs, PE11 4HG
T: 01775 840020
F: 01775 843063
E: info@smclightandpower.com
W: www.smclightandpower.com

SMC Pneumatics Ltd
Vincent Ave, Crownhill, Milton Keynes, Bucks, MK8 0AN
T: 0845 121 5122
F: 01908 555064
E: sales@smcpneumatics.co.uk
W: www.smcpneumatics.co.uk

SME Ltd
Unit 1, Lloyd St, Parkgate, Rotherham, S62 6JG
T: 08444 930666
F: 08444 930667
W: www.sme-ltd.co.uk

SMI Conferences
SMI Group Ltd, Unit 122, Great Guildford Business Square, 30 Great Guildford St, London, SE1 0HS
T: 020 7827 6000
F: 020 7827 6001
E: info@smi-online.com
W: www.smi-online.co.uk

Smith Bros & Webb Ltd
Britannia House, Arden Forest Ind.Est, Alcester, Warks, B49 6EX
T: 01789 400096
F: 01789 400231
E: sales@sbw-wash.com
W: www.sbw-wash.com

Smith Cooper
Wilmot House, St Helen's House, King St, Derby, DE1 3EE
T: 01332 332021
F: 01332 290439
E: janet.morgan@smithcooper.co.uk
W: www.smithcooper.co.uk

Smiths Connectors
Research, Design & Development Centre, Centennial Park Unit 130, Centennial Avenue, Elstree, Hertfordshire, WD6 3SE
T: 020 8236 2400
F: 020 8208 4114
E: info@smithsconnectors.com
W: www.smithsconnectors.com

Smiths Rail
Stratton Business Park, London road, Biggleswade, Bedfordshire, SG188QB
T: 01767 604706
E: dellerm@smithsrail.com
W: www.smithsmetal.com

SML Resourcing
Unit 3.07, New Loom House, 101 Back Church Lane, London, E1 1LU
T: 020 7423 4390
F: 020 7702 1097
E: jobs@sml-resourcing.com
W: www.sml-resourcing.com

SMP Electronics
Unit 6, Border Farm, Station Rd, Chobham, Woking, Surrey, GU24 8AS
T: 01276 855166
F: 01276 855115
E: sales@smpelectronics.com
W: www.samalite.com

Snap-On Rail Solutions
38A Telford Way, Kettering, Northants, NN16 8SN
T: 01536 413904
F: 01536 413874
E: rail@snapon.com
W: www.snapon.com/industrialuk

SNC-Lavalin
2 Roundhouse Road, Pride Park, Derby, DE24 8JE
T: 01332 223 000
F: 01332 223 001
W: www.snclavalin-railandtransit.com/

Society of Operations Engineers (SOE)
22 Greencoat Place, London, SW1P 1PR
T: 020 7630 1111
F: 020 7630 6677
E: soe@soe.org.uk
W: www.soe.org.uk

Socomec UPS (UK)
Units 7-9, Lakeside Business Park, Broadway Lane, South Cerney, Cirencester, Glos, GL7 5XL
T: 01285 863300
F: 01285 862304
E: rail.ups.uk@socomec.com
W: www.socomec.co.uk/

Softech Global Ltd
Softech House, London Rd, Albourne, West Sussex, BN6 9BN
T: 01273 833844
F: 01273 833044
E: info@softechglobal.com
W: www.softechglobal.com

Sogefi Rejna SpA
Via Nazionale 7, Raffa di Puegnago (BS), I-25080, Italy
T: 39 365 526 213
E: giovannico.dore@sogefigroup.com
W: www.sogefigroup.com

SOLID Applications Ltd
Old Market Place, Market St, Oldbury, B69 4DH
T: 0121 544 1400
E: anton.plackowski@saplm.co.uk
W: www.solidapps.co.uk/

IN ASSOCIATION WITH Nomad Digital

Solo Rail Solutions
Landor St, Saltley, Birmingham, B8 1AE
T: 0121 327 3378
E: robpugh@solorail.com
W: www.solorail.com

Solum Regeneration
6 Cavendish Place, London, W1G 9NB
T: 020 7462 2759
E: info@solumregeneration.co.uk
W: www.solumregeneration.co.uk

Solution Rail
22 Somers Way, Bushey, Herts, WD23 4HR
F: 0871 989 5700
E: enquiries@solutionrail.co.uk
W: www.solutionrail.co.uk

Solvay Speciality Polymers
Baronet Rd, Warrington, WA4 6HA
T: 01925 943546
F: 01925 943548
E: shayel.ahmed@solvay.com
W: www.solvayplastics.com

Sonic Rail Service Ltd (SRS)
Unit 15, Springfield Ind. Est, Springfield Rd, Burnham-on-Crouch, Essex, CM0 8UA
T: 01621 784688
F: 01621 786594
E: stewart.robinson@sonicrail.co.uk
W: www.sonicrail.co.uk

Sonic Windows Ltd
Unit 14/15, Beeching Park Ind.Est., Wainwright Rd, Bexhill on Sea, E Sussex, TN39 3UR
T: 01424 223864
F: 01424 215859
E: enquiries@sonicwindows.co.uk
W: www.sonicwindows.co.uk

Sotera Risk Solutions Ltd
22 Glanville Rd, Bromley, BR2 9LW
T: 01737 551203
F: 01737 551203
M: 07946 638424
E: chris.chapman@sotera.co.uk
W: www.sotera.co.uk

SOUNDEX Solutions
The Old Dairy, Southfield Avenue, Northampton, NN4 8AQ
T: 0800 814 4422
F: 0800 814 4423
E: enquiries@soundexsolutions.com
W: www.soundexsolutions.com

South Western Railway
4th Floor, South Bank Central, 30 Stamford Street, London, SE1 9LQ
T: 0345 6000 650
W: https://www.southwesternrailway.com/

South Yorkshire Passenger Transport Executive
11 Broad St West, Sheffield, S1 2BQ
T: 0114 276 7575
F: 0114 275 9908
E: comments@sypte.co.uk
W: www.sypte.co.uk

Southco Manufacturing Ltd
Touch Point, Wainwright Rd, Warndon, Worcs, WR4 9FA
T: 01905 346722
F: 01905 346723
E: info@southco.com
W: www.southco.com

Southeastern
Floor 2, Four More London Riverside, London, SE1 2AU
T: 020 7620 5000
W: www.southeasternrailway.co.uk

Southern Electric Contracting
55 Vastern Rd, Reading, RG1 8BU
T: 0118 958 0100
F: 0118 953 4755
E: marketing@sec.eu.com
W: www.sec.eu.com

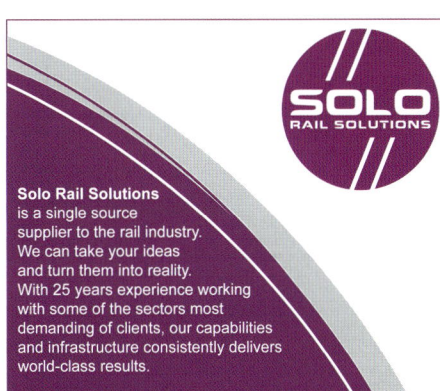

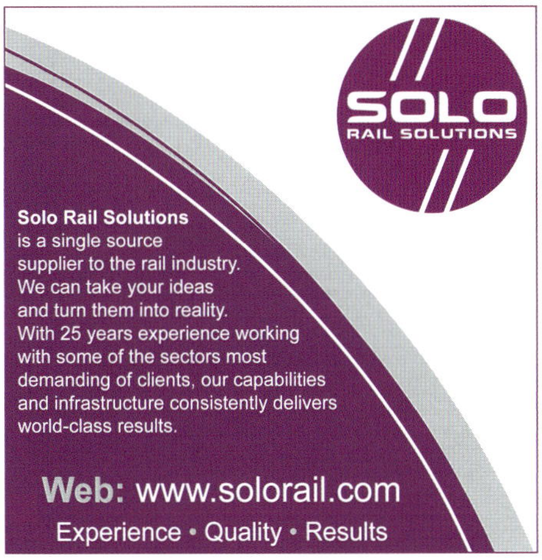

SOLO RAIL SOLUTIONS
Solo Rail Solutions
is a single source
supplier to the rail industry.
We can take your ideas
and turn them into reality.
With 25 years experience working
with some of the sectors most
demanding of clients, our capabilities
and infrastructure consistently delivers
world-class results.
Web: www.solorail.com
Experience • Quality • Results

Sovereign Planned Services On Line Ltd
Unit 9, Galveston Grove, Oldfields Business Park, Fenton, Stoke-on-Trent, Staffs, ST4 3PE
T: 01782 914274
E: sales@sovonline.co.uk
W: www.sovonline.co.uk

SPAL Automotive
Unit 3, Great Western Busisness Park, Worcester, Wr4 9PT
T: 01905 613714
E: matthew@spalautomotive.co.uk
W: www.spalautomotive.co.uk

Spartan Safety Ltd
Unit 3, Waltham Park Way, Walthamstow, London, E17 5DU
T: 020 8527 5888
F: 020 8527 5999
E: ryan@spartansafety.co.uk
W: www.spartansafety.co.uk

Specialist Engineering Services Ltd (SES)
SES House, Harworth Business Park, Blyth Road, Harworth, Doncaster, DN11 8DB
T: 01302 756800
E: info@ses-rail.co.uk
W: www.ses-rail.co.uk/

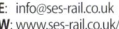

Specialist Plant Associates
Airfield Rd, Hinwick, Wellingborough, Northants, NN29 7JG
T: 01234 781882
F: 01234 781992
E: info@specialistplant.co.uk
W: www.specialistplant.co.uk

Specialist Project Integration Ltd (SPI)
Bowback House, 299 Silbury Boulevard, Milton Keynes, MK9 1NR
T: 01908 671933
E: innovate@thinkspi.co.uk
W: www.thinkspi.com

Spectro
Palace Gate, Odiham, Hampshire, RG29 1NP
T: 01256 704000
F: 01256 704006
E: enquiries@spectro-oil.com
W: www.spectro-oil.com

Spectrum Freight Ltd
PO Box 105, Chesterfield, Derbys, S41 9XY
T: 01246 456677
F: 01246 456688
E: sales@spectrumfreight.co.uk
W: www.spectrumfreight.co.uk

Spectrum Technologies
Western Avenue, Bridgend, Mid Glamorgan, CF31 3RT
T: 01656 655437
F: 01656 655920
E: ehardy@spectrumtech.com
W: www.spectrumtech.com

Speedy Hire Plc
Chase House, 16 The Parks, Newton le Willows, Merseyside, WA12 0JQ
T: 01942 720000
F: 01942 720077
E: admin@speedyhire.co.uk
W: www.speedyhire.co.uk

Spence Ltd
Parcel Deck, Barnby St, Euston Station, London, NW1 2RS
T: 020 7387 1268
F: 020 7380 1255
E: info@spenceltd.co.uk
W: www.spenceltd.co.uk

Spencer Group
One Humber Quays, Wellington Street West, Hull, East Yorkshire, HU1 2BN
T: 01482 766340
F: 01469 532233
E: mailbox@cspencerltd.co.uk
W: www.thespencergroup.co.uk

Speno International SA
Route du Nant-d'Avril 94, Case Postale 1, CH-1217 Meyrin 1, Switzerland
T: 0041 22906 4600
F: 0041 22906 4601
E: info@speno.ch
W: www.speno.ch

Sperry Rail International Ltd
Trent House, RTC Business Park, London Rd, Derby, DE24 8UP
T: 01332 262565
F: 01332 262541
E: jtansley@sperryrail.com
W: www.sperryrail.com

SPI Piling Ltd
See A E Yates Group

Spitfire Tours
PO Box 824, Taunton, TA1 9ET
T: 0870 879 3675
E: info@spitfirerailtours.co.uk
W: www.spitfirerailtours.co.uk

SPL Powerlines UK Ltd
Unit 3A, Hagmill Cres, East Shawhead Enterprise Park, Coatbridge, Lanarkshire, ML5 4NS
T: 01236 424666
F: 01236 426444
E: office@powerlines-group.com
W: www.powerlines-group.com

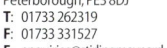

STADLER trains are tailored to customers requirements, represent smart investment and feature state-of-the-art technology. Reliable and safe, they offer maximum comfort for passengers.
www.stadlerrail.com
STADLER

Spring Personnel
1 Canal Arm, Festival Park, Stoke on Trent, ST1 5UR
T: 01782 221500
F: 01782 221600
E: personnel@spring.com
W: www.spring.com

SPX Rail Systems
Unit 7, Thames Gateway Park, Choats Rd, Dagenham, Essex, RM9 6RH
T: 020 8526 7100
F: 020 8526 7151
E: brian.cannon@spx.com
W: www.spx.com/en/spx-rail-systems/

SRPS Railtours
SRPS Office, 17-19 North Street, Bo'ness, West Lothian, EH51 0AQ
T: 0131 202 1033
E: railtours@srps.org.uk
W: www.srpsrailtours.com

SRS Rail System Ltd
Unit 3, Riverside Way, Gateway Business Park, Bolsover, Chesterfield, Derbyshire, S44 6GA
T: 01246 241312
F: 01246 825076
E: info@srsrailuk.com
W: www.srsrailuk.com/

SSDM
See Aura Brand Solutions

SSE Enterprise Rail
Inveralmond House, 200 Dunkeld Road, Perth, PH1 3AQ
W: sse.com/whatwedo/sse-enterprise/rail/

SSP
169 Euston Rd, London, NW1 2AE
T: 020 7543 3300
F: 020 7543 3389
E: clare@templemerepr.co.uk
W: www.foodtravelexperts.com/uk/home/

St Leonards Railway Engineering Ltd
Bridgeway, St Leonards on Sea, E Sussex, TN38 8AP
T: 01233 617001

Stadler Pankow GmbH
Lessingstrasse 102, D-13158 Berlin, Germany
T: 0049 309191 1616
F: 0049 309191 2150
E: stadler.pankow@stadlerrail.de
W: www.stadlerrail.com

Stadler Rail AG
Ernst-Stadler-Strasse 1, 9565 Bussnang, Switzerland
T: +41 (0)71 626 21 20
F: +41 (0)71 626 21 28
E: stadler.rail@stadlerrail.com
W: www.stadlerrail.com/en/

Stagecoach Group
10 Dunkeld Rd, Perth, PH1 5TW
T: 01738 442111
F: 01738 643648
E: info@stagecoachgroup.com
W: www.stagecoachgroup.com

Stagecoach Supertram
Nunnery Depot, Woodbourn Rd, Sheffield, S9 3LS
T: 0114 275 9888
F: 0114 279 8120
E: enquiries@supertram.com
W: www.supertram.com

Stahlwille Tools Ltd
Unit 2D, Albany Park Ind. Est, Frimley Rd, Camberley, Surrey, GU16 7PD
T: 01276 24080
F: 01276 24696
E: scottsheldon@stahlwille.co.uk
W: www.stahlwille.co.uk

Standish Engineering Co Ltd
Mayflower Works, Bradley Lane, Standish, Lancashire, WN6 0XF
T: 01257 422838
F: 01257 422381
E: nick@cnc-machining.co.uk
W: www.standishengineering.co.uk/

Stanley Tools
Sheffield Business Park, Sheffield City Airport, Europa Link, Sheffield, S3 9PD
T: 0114 244 8883
F: 0114 273 9038

Stannah Lifts
Anton Mill, Andover, Hants, SP10 2NX
T: 01264 339090
E: liftsales@stannah.co.uk
W: www.stannahlifts.co.uk

Stansted Express
See Greater Anglia

Stanway Consulting
Aztec West, 2440/2430 The Quadrant, Almondsbury, Bristol, BS32 4AQ
T: 01454 878798
E: info@stanwayconsulting.co.uk
W: stanwayconsulting.com/

Star Fasteners (UK) Ltd
Unit 1, 44 Brookhill Road,, Pinxton, Nottinghamshire, NG16 6RY
T: 0115 932 4939
F: 0115 944 1278
E: sales@starfasteners.co.uk
W: www.starfasteners.co.uk

STARC Ltd
4a Mina Avenue, Slough, Berkshire, SL3 7BY
M: 07940 838842
E: enquiries@starcltd.co.uk
W: starcltd.co.uk/

Statesman Rail Ltd
PO Box 83, St Erth, Hayle, Cornwall, TR27 9AD
T: 0345 310 2458
F: 0115 944 1278
W: www.statesmanrail.com

STATS
See RSK Ltd

Stauff Ltd
500 Carlisle St East, Off Downgate Drive, Sheffield, S4 8BS
T: 01142 518518
F: 01141 518519
E: sales@stauff.co.uk
W: www.stauff.co.uk

Staytite Ltd
Staytite House, Coronation Rd, Cressex Bus. Park, High Wycombe, Bucks, HP12 3RP
T: 01494 462322
F: 01494 464747
E: fasteners@staytite.com
W: www.staytite.com

Steam Dreams
PO Box 169, Albury, Guildford, Surrey, GU5 9YS
T: 01483 209888
F: 01483 209889
M: 07775 735005
E: info@steamdreams.co.uk
W: www.steamdreams.com

Steatite Ltd
Ravensbank Business Park, Acanthus Rd, Redditch, Worcs, B98 9EX
T: 01527 512400
F: 01527 512419
E: sales@steatite.co.uk
W: www.steatite.co.uk

Steconfer
1 St. Peters Square, Manchester, M2 3DE
W: www.steconfer.com/en/

Steelteam Construction (UK) Ltd
46 Goods Station Rd, Tunbridge Wells, Kent, TN1 2DD
T: 01892 533677
F: 01892 511535
E: sales@steelteamconstruction.co.uk
W: www.steelteamconstruction.co.uk

Steelway Rail
Queensgate Works, Bilston Rd, Wolverhampton, West Midlands, WV2 2NJ
T: 01902 834911
F: 01902 452256
E: sales@steelway.co.uk
W: www.steelway.co.uk

Steer
28-32 Upper Ground, London, SE1 9PD
T: 020 7910 5000
F: 020 7910 5001
E: sdginfo@sdgworld.net
W: www.steerdaviesgleave.com

Stego UK Ltd
Unit 12, First Quarter Bus. Park, Blenheim Rd, Epsom, Surrey, KT19 9QN
T: 01372 747250
F: 01372 729854
E: info@stego.co.uk
W: www.stego.co.uk

Stemmer Imaging
The Old Barn, Grange Court, Tongham, Surrey, GU10 1DW
T: 01252 780030
F: 01252 780001
E: admin@stemmer-imaging.co.uk
W: www.stemmer-imaging.co.uk/en/

Stent
See Balfour Beatty Ground Engineering

Step On Safety Ltd
Units 3-4, 122 Station Road, Lawford, Manningtree, Essex, CO11 2LH
T: 01206 396446
E: info@steponsafety.co.uk
W: www.steponsafety.co.uk

Stephenson Harwood LLP
1 Finsbury Circus, London, EC2M 7SH
T: 020 7809 2618
F: 020 7003 8220
E: graeme.mclellan@shlegal.com
W: www.shlegal.com

Sterling Transport Consultancy
19 Aston Chase, Stone, Staffordshire, ST15 8SD
M: 07711 055825
E: lee@sterlingtransportconsultancy.com

Stewart Signs Rail
Trafalgar Close, Chandlers Ford Ind. Est, Eastleigh, Hants, SO53 4BW
T: 023 8025 4781
F: 023 8025 5620
E: sales@stewartsigns.co.uk
W: www.stewartsigns.co.uk

Stirling Maynard
Construction Consultants, Stirling House, Rightwell, Bretton, Peterborough, PE3 8DJ
T: 01733 262319
F: 01733 331527
E: enquiries@stirlingmaynard.com
W: www.stirlingmaynard.com

STM Security
1st Floor, Solar House, 1-9 Romford Road, Stratford, London, E15 4LJ
T: 020 3597 4264
F: 020 8555 8960
E: comms@stmsecurity.com
W: www.stmsecurity.com/

Stobart Rail
Solway Business Centre, Carlisle, Cumbria, CA6 4BY
T: 01228 882300
F: 01228 882301
E: grant.mcnab@stobartrail.com
W: www.stobartrail.co.uk

DIRECTORY

Stock Redler Ltd
See Schenck Process UK

Stocksigns Ltd/ Burnham Signs
43 Ormside Way, Holmethorpe Ind Est, Redhill, Surrey, RH1 2LG
T: 01737 764764
F: 01737 763763
E: jgodden@stocksigns.co.uk
W: www.stocksigns.co.uk

Stockton Engineering Management Ltd
1 Warwick Row, London, SW1E 5ER
T: 020 7808 7808
F: 020 7117 5253
E: info@stocktonlondon.com
W: www.stocktonlondon.com

Stored Energy Technology
See S.E.T. Ltd

Story Contracting
Burgh Rd Ind Est, Carlisle, Cumbria, CA2 7NA
T: 01228 590444
F: 01228 593359
E: feedback@storycontracting.com
W: www.storycontracting.com/

Strabag
Donau-City-Str. 9, 1220 Vienna, Austria
T: 0043 1 22422-0
E: pr@strabag.com
W: www.strabag.com/

STRAIL (UK) Ltd
Room 2, First Floor, 3 Tannery House, Tannery Lane, Send, Woking, Surrey, GU23 7EF
T: 01483 222090
F: 01483 222095
E: richard@srsrailuk.co.uk
W: www.strail.com

Strainstall UK Ltd
Unit 10, City Business Park, Easton Road, Bristol, BS5 0SP
T: 01761 414939
E: enquiries@strainstall.com
W: www.strainstall.co.uk

Strata Geotechnics
Summit Close, Kirkby-in-Ashfield, Nottinghamshire, NG17 8GJ
T: 01773 304056
E: info@stratageo.co.uk
W: www.stratageotechnics.com/

Strataform
See TechnoRail (Technocover)

Stratasys Solutions Ltd
Suite 1, 3rd Floor, 11-12 St James's Square, London, SW1Y 4LB
W: www.stratasys.com

Strategic Team Group Ltd
Strategic Business Centre, Blue Ridge Park, Thunderhead Ridge, Glasshoughton, Castleford, West Yorks, WF10 4UA
T: 01977 555550
F: 01977 555509
E: contact@strategicteamgroup.com
W: www.strategicteamgroup.com

Strathclyde Partnership for Transport
131 St Vincent Street, Glasgow, G2 5JF
T: 0141 332 6811
E: enquiry@spt.co.uk
W: www.spt.co.uk

Street Crane Co. Ltd
Chapel-en-le-Frith, High Peak, Derbys, SK23 0PH
T: 01298 812456
F: 01298 814945
E: sales@streetcrane.co.uk
W: www.streetcrane.co.uk

Streets UK
Suite 411, Baltic Chambers, 50 Wellington Street, Glasgow, G2 6HJ
E: info@streets-uk.com
W: www.streets-uk.com/

Structural Fabrications Limited
2 Castings Road, Sir Francis Ley Industrial Park South, Derby, DE23 8YL
T: 01332 747400
F: 01332 747447
E: sales@structural-fabrications.co.uk
W: structuralfabrications.co.uk/

Strukton Rail
Westkanaaldijk 2, NL-3542 DA Utrecht, Netherlands
T: 31 30 248 66 94
E: info@struktonrail.com
W: www.struktonrail.com

STS Rail
First Floor, 27 Cobham Road, Ferndown Industrial Estate, Wimborne, Dorset, BH21 7PE
T: 01202 950270
E: telecoms@sts-rail.com
W: www.sts-rail.com/

STS Signals
See Mors Smitt UK Ltd (A Wabtec Company)

Stuart Group
Middleplatt Road, Immingham, Lincs, DN40 1AH
T: 01469 551230
F: 01469 551239
E: enquiries@stuartgroup.info
W: www.stuartgroup.ltd.uk

Stuart Maher Ltd (SML)
Unit 3.07, New Loom House, 101 Back Church Lane, London, SE1 1LU
T: 020 7423 4390
F: 07092 810 920
E: nick.stuart@stuart-maher.co.uk
W: www.stuart-maher.co.uk

Studio Egret West
3 Brewhouse Yard, London, EC1V 4JQ
T: 020 7549 1730
E: hello@egretwest.com
W: egretwest.com/

Suez environnement
SITA House, Grenfell Road, Maidenhead, Berkshire, SL6 1ES
T: 01628 513100
W: www.sita.co.uk/

Sulzer Dowding & Mills
193 Camp Hill, Bordesley, Birmingham, B12 0JJ
T: 0121 766 6161
F: 0121 766 7247
E: engineering.birmingham@sulzer.com
W: www.sulzer.com

Superform Aluminium
Cosgrove Close, Worcester, WR3 8UA
T: 01905 874300
F: 01905 874301
E: enquiries@superform.net
W: www.superforming.com

Superjet London
Unit 5, Kennet Rd, Dartford, Kent, DA1 4QN
T: 01322 554595
F: 01322 557773
E: chris@superjet.co.uk
W: www.jetchem.com

Supersine Duramark
See Aura Brand Solutions

Surge Protection Devices Ltd
Unit 1, Ash Royd Farm, Royd Road, Meltham, Holmfirth, West Yorkshire, HD9 4BG
T: 01484 851747
F: 01484 852594
E: info@surgedevices.co.uk
W: www.surgedevices.co.uk

Survey Inspection Systems Ltd (SIS)
Green Lane Ind. Est, Enterprise House, Meadowfield Ave, Spennymoor, Co Durham, DL16 6JF
T: 01388 810308
F: 01388 819260
E: sales@survey-inspection.com
W: www.survey-inspection.com

Survey Systems Ltd
Willow Bank House, Old Road, Handforth, Wilmslow, SK9 3AZ
T: 01625 533444
F: 01625 526815
E: enquiries@survsys.co.uk
W: www.survsys.co.uk/rail

SW Global Resourcing
270 Peters Hill Rd, Glasgow, G21 4AY
T: 0141 557 6133
F: 0141 557 6143
E: admin@sw-gr.com
W: sw-gr.com

Swallow Site Services Ltd
3 Hertford House, Hugo Gryn Way, Shenley, Hertfordshire, WD7 9AB
T: 020 8447 3727
E: john.cronin@swallow-site.biz
W: www.swallow-site.biz/

Sweetnam & Bradley Ltd
Industrial Est, Gloucester Rd, Malmesbury, Wilts, SN16 0DY
T: 01666 823491
F: 01666 826010
E: sales@sweetnam-bradley.com
W: www.sweetnam-bradley.com

Sweett Group
60 Grays Inn Rd, London, W1X 8AQ
T: 020 7061 9000
F: 020 7430 0603
E: eryl.evans@sweettgroup.com
W: www.sweettgroup.com

Swietelsky Babcock
See SB Rail (Swietelsky Babcock)

Swietelsky Construction Company Ltd
7 Clairmont Gardens, Glasgow, G3 7LW
T: 0141 353 1915
E: office@swietelsky.at
W: www.swietelsky.com

Sydac Ltd
Derwent Business Centre, Clarke St, Derby, DE1 2BU
T: 01332 299600
F: 01332 299624
E: sales@sydac.co.uk
W: www.sydac.co.uk

Sylmasta Ltd
Unit 1, Dales Yard, Lewes Rd, Scaynes Hill, W Sussex, RH17 7PG
T: 01444 831459
F: 01444 831971
W: www.sylmasta.co.uk

Synectic Systems Group Ltd
3-4 Broadfield Close, Sheffield, South Yorkshire, S8 0XN
T: 0114 2552509
F: 0114 2582050
E: sales@synx.com
W: www.synecticsystems.com

Synergy Health Plc
Gavenny Court, Brecon Rd, Abergavenny, Monmouthshire, NP7 7RX
T: 01873 856688
F: 01873 585982
E: enquiries@synergyhealthplc.com
W: www.synergyhealthplc.com

Syntax Conultancy
1 College Place, Derby, DE1 3DY
T: 01332 293605
F: 01332 296128
E: marketing@syntaxconsultancy.com
W: www.syntaxconsultancy.com

Systecon (UK) Ltd
PO Box 4612, Weymouth, Dorset, DT4 9YY
T: 0871 641 2202
F: 01305 768480
E: phil.sturgess@systecon.co.uk
W: www.systecon.co.uk

System Store Solutions Ltd
Ham Lane, Lenham, Maidstone, Kent, ME17 2LH
T: 01622 859522
F: 01622 858746
E: sales@systemstoresolutions.com
W: www.system-store.com

Systra UK
Fourth Floor, Dukes Court, Duke St, Woking, Surrey, GU21 5BH
T: 01483 742941
F: 01483 755207
E: sgulyvasz@systra.com
W: www.systra.com

T & R Williamson Ltd
36 Stonebridgegate, Ripon, N Yorks, HG4 1TP
T: 01765 607711
F: 01765 607908
E: info@trwilliamson.co.uk
W: www.trwilliamson.co.uk

T & RS Engineering Ltd
Unit 8, Buccaneer Drive, Fountain Court, Doncaster, DN9 3QP
T: 01302 315011
E: mail@trsengineering.co.uk
W: www.trsengineering.co.uk

TAC Europe
Matrix House, Basing View, Basingstoke, Hants
T: 08700 600822
F: 01256 356371
E: enquiries@taceurope.com
W: www.taceurope.com

Talascend Ltd
First Floor, Broadway Chambers, Hammersmith Broadway, London, W6 7PW
T: 020 8600 1600
F: 020 8741 2001
E: info@talascend.com
W: www.talascend.com

Talentwise
44 Royal Scot Road, Pride Park, Derby, DE24 8AJ
T: 01332 344 443
E: daniel.taylor@fordandstanley.com
W: www.fordandstanley.com/employers/talentwise/

Talgo
Paseo del tren Talgo, 2, 28290 Las Matas, Madrid, Spain
T: (+34) 91 631 38 00
F: (+34) 91 631 38 93
E: marketing@talgo.com
W: https://www.talgo.com/en/

Tanfield Engineering Systems
Tanfield Lea Ind. Est. North, Stanley, Co Durham, DH9 9NX
T: 01207 521111
F: 01207 523355
W: www.tanfieldengineering systems.com/

Tangerine Ltd
Unit 9, Blue Lion Place, 237 Long Lane, London, SE1 4PU
T: 020 7357 0966
F: 020 7357 0784
E: mail@tangerine.net
W: www.tangerine.net

Tasty Plant Sales
Unit 4, Asheridge Business Centre, Asheridge Road, Chesham, Bucks, HP5 2PT
T: 0845 677 4444
E: info@tastyplant.co.uk
W: www.tastyplant.co.uk

TATA Consultancy Services (TCS)
4th Floor, 33 Grosvenor Place, London, SW1X 7HY
T: 020 7245 1800
F: 020 7245 1875
E: uk.info@tcs.com
W: www.tcs.com/

Tata Steel Projects
Meridian House, The Crescent, York, YO24 1AW
T: 01904 454600
F: 01904 454601
E: tatasteelprojects@tatasteel.com
W: www.tatasteelrail.com/en/

Tata Steel Rail
See British Steel

Tate Rail Ltd
Station House, Station Hill, Cookham, Berks, SL6 9BP
T: 0844 381 9956
F: 0844 381 9957
E: info@taterail.com
W: www.taterail.com

Taylor Airey Ltd
2a Charing Cross Road, London, WC2H 0HF
T: 020 8017 4655
E: enquiries@taylorairey.com
W: www.taylorairey.com

Taylor Precision Plastics / Commercial Vehicle Rollers Ltd
Mile Oak Ind. Est, Maesbury Rd, Oswestry, Shropshire, SY10 8GA
T: 01691 679536
F: 01691 670538
E: sales@cvrollers.co.uk
W: www.cvrollers.co.uk

Taylor Technology Systems
Horizon Business Centre, Unit 25, Alder Close, Erith, Kent, DA18 4AJ
T: 020 8320 9944
E: sales@taylortechnology systems.com
W: www.taylortechnology systems.com/

Taylor Woodrow
Astral House, Imperial Way, Watford, Herts, WD24 4WW
T: 01923 233433
F: 01923 800085
E: david.booker@taylorwoodrow.com
W: www.taylorwoodrow.com

Taylormade Fasteners Ltd
Units 4&5, Watery Lane Ind. Est, Willenhall, West Midlands, WV13 3SU
T: 01902 631222
F: 01902 601891
E: mlane@taylormadefasteners.co.uk
W: www.taylormadefasteners.co.uk

Taziker Industrial Ltd t/a TI Protective Coatings
Unit 6, Lodge Bank, Crown Lane, Horwich, Bolton, BL6 5HY
T: 01204 468080
F: 01204 695188
E: sales@ti-uk.com
W: www.ti-uk.com

TBA Protective Technologies
Unit 3, Transpennine Trading Estate, Gorrells Way, Rochdale, OL11 2PX
T: 01706 647422
E: contact.sky@tba-pt.com
W: www.tba-pt.com

TBAT Innovation Limited
Unit 3, Bradley Court, Maple Road, Trent Lane, Castle Donington, Derby, DE74 2UT
T: 01332 819740
E: info@tbat.co.uk
W: www.tbat.co.uk/

TBI Consulting
7 Sunset Avenue, Woodford Green, Essex, IG8 0ST

TBM Consulting Group
Unit 8, H2O Business Complex, Sherwood Business Park, Annesley, Nottingham, NG15 0HT
T: 01623 758298
F: 01623 755941
E: nfletcher@tbmcg.com
W: www.tbmcg.com

TBM Rail
Unit B, The Quantum, Marshfield Bank, Crewe, Cheshire, CW2 8UY
T: 0844 8008577
E: enquiries@tbmrail.com
W: www.tbmrail.com

TCP Ltd
Quayside Industrial Park, Bates Road, Maldon, Essex, CM9 5FA
T: 01621 850777
F: 01621 843330
E: mail@tcp.eu.com
W: www.tcp.eu.com

TDK-Lambda UK
Kingsley Ave, Ilfracombe, Devon, EX34 8ES
T: 01271 856600
F: 01271 856741
E: powersolutions@emea.tdk-lambda.com
W: www.emea.tdk-lambda.com

TE Connectivity
1 rue Paul Martin, F-21220 Gervey-Chambertin, France
T: 33 03 80 58 32 13
E: rail@te.com
W: www.te.com/energy

TEAL Consulting Ltd
Deangate, Tuesley Lane, Godalming, Surrey, GU7 1SG
T: 01483 420550
E: info@tealconsulting.co.uk
W: www.tealconsulting.co.uk

Team Surveys Ltd
Team House, St Austell Bay Business Park, Par Moor Rd, St Austell, PL25 3RF
T: 01726 816069
F: 01726 814611
E: email@teamsurveys.com
W: www.teamsurveys.co.uk

Tecalemit Garage Equipment Co Ltd
Eagle Rd, Langage Business Park, Plymouth, PL7 5JY
T: 01752 219111
F: 01752 219128
E: sales@tecalemit.co.uk
W: www.tecalemit.co.uk

Tecforce
Litchurch Lane, Derby, DE24 8AA
T: 01332 268000
F: 01332 268030
E: sales@tecforce.co.uk
W: www.tecforce.co.uk

Technical Cranes Ltd
Holmes Lock Works, Steel St, Holmes, Rotherham, S61 1DF
T: 01709 561861
F: 01709 556516
E: info@technicalcranes.co.uk
W: www.technicalcranes.co.uk

Technical Cranes Ltd
Holmes Lock Works, Steel St, Holmes, Rotherham, S61 1DF
T: 01709 561861
F: 01709 556516
E: info@technicalcranes.co.uk
W: www.technicalcranes.co.uk

Technical Programme Delivery
10 Station Hill, Henley on Thames, RG9 1AY
T: 01932 228710
F: 01932 228710
E: pac@tpd.uk.com
W: www.tpd.uk.com

Technical Resin Bonders
See TRB Lightweight Structures Ltd

Technical Strategy Leadership Group
4th Floor, The Helicon, 1 South Place, London, EC2M 2RB
T: 020 3142 5300
W: www.rssb.co.uk/groups-and-committees/rssb-board/technical-strategy/technical-strategy-leadership-group

Technocover
See TechnoRail (Technocover)

Technology Project Services Ltd
1 Warwick Row, London, SW1E 5LR
T: 020 7963 1234
F: 020 7963 1299
E: mail@tps.co.uk
W: www.tps.co.uk

Technology Resourcing Ltd
The Technology Centre, Surrey Research Park, Guildford, GU2 7YG
T: 01483 302211
F: 01483 301222
E: railways@tech-res.co.uk
W: www.railwayengineeringjobs.co.uk

TechnoRail (Technocover)
Henfaes Lane, Welshpool, Powys, SY21 7BE
T: 01938 555511
F: 01938 555527
E: admin@technocover.co.uk
W: www.technocover.co.uk

Tecton Ltd
186 Main Road, Fishers Pond, Eastleigh, Hants, SO50 7HG
T: 02380 695858
F: 02380 695702
E: admin@tectononline.com
W: www.tecton.co.uk

Tees Valley Combined Authority
Cavendish House, Teesdale Business Park, Stockton-on-Tees, Tees Valley, TS17 6QY
T: 01642 524400
E: info@teesvalley-ca.gov.uk
W: www.teesvalley-ca.gov.uk/

TEK Personnel Consultants Ltd
Norwich Union House, Irongate, Derby, DE1 3GA
T: 01332 360055
F: 01332 363345
E: derby@tekpersonnel.co.uk
W: www.tekpersonnel.co.uk

Telefonica O2 Ltd
260 Bath Road, Slough, Berkshire, SL1 4DX
W: www.o2.co.uk/

Telemecanique Sensors
T: 0870 608 8608
E: gb-customerservices@schneider-electric.com
W: www.tesensors.com/uk/en/

Telent Technology Services Ltd
Point 3, Haywood Rd, Warwick, CV34 5AH
T: 01926 693564
F: 01926 693023
E: services@telent.com
W: www.telent.com

Telerail Ltd
Royal Scot Suite, Carnforth Station Heritage Centre, Warton Rd, Carnforth, Lancs, LA5 9TR
T: 01524 735774
F: 01524 736386
E: info@telerail.co.uk
W: www.telerail.co.uk

Telerail Networks Ltd
Spaceworks, Benton Park Road, Newcastle Upon Tyne, NE7 7LX

Telespazio VEGA UK
350 Capability Green, Luton, Beds, LU1 3LU
T: 01582 399000
E: info@vegaspace.com
W: www.telespazio-vega.com

Televic Rail
Leo Bakaertlaan 1, B-8870 Izegem, Belgium
T: 0032 5130 3045
E: rail@televic.com
W: www.televic-rail.com

Temple Group Ltd
Devon House, 58-60 St Katharine's Way, London, E1W 1LB
T: 020 7394 3700
F: 020 7394 7871
E: enquiries@templegroup.co.uk
W: www.templegroup.co.uk

Ten 47 Ltd
Unit 2B, Frances Ind. Park, Wemyss Rd, Dysart, Kirkcaldy, KY1 2XZ
T: 01592 655725
F: 01592 651049
E: sales@ten47.com
W: www.ten47.com

TenBroeke Company Ltd
Dorset House, Refent Park, Kingston Rd, Leatherhead, Surrey, KT22 7PL
T: 01372 824722
F: 01372 824332
E: paul.tweedale@tenbroekco.com
W: www.tenbroekeco.com/

TenCate Geosynthetics UK Ltd
PO Box 773, Telford, Shropshire, TF7 9FE
T: 01952 588066
E: service.uk@tencate.com
W: www.tencategeosynthetics.com

Tenconi SA
via della Stazione 50, CH-6780 Airolo, Italy
T: +41 91 873 30 00
F: +41 91 873 30 01
E: tenconi@tenconi.ch
W: www.tenconi.ch/en/

Tenmat Ltd (Railko Ltd)
Ashburton Road West, Trafford Park, Manchester, M17 1RU
T: 0161 872 2181
F: 0161 872 7596
E: info@tenmat.com
W: www.tenmat.com

televic rail

Your global partner for
» Passenger Information
» Condition Based Maintenance

www.televic-rail.com

Tensar International
Cunningham Court, Shadsworth Business Park, Shadsworth, Blackburn, BB1 2QX
T: 01254 262431
F: 01254 266868
E: info@tensar-international.com
W: www.tensar.co.uk

Tension Control Bolts
TCB House, Clywedog Road South, Wrexham Industrial Estate, Wrexham, LL13 9XS
T: 01978 661122
E: info@tcbolts.co.uk
W: www.tcbolts.co.uk

Terram Ltd
Mamhilad Park Estate, Pontypool, Gwent, NP4 0YR
T: 01495 757722
F: 01495 762383
E: info@terram.co.uk
W: www.terram.com

Terrawise Construction Ltd
104 The Court Yard, Radway Green Business Centre, Radway Green, Crewe, Cheshire, CW2 5PR
T: 01270 879011
F: 01270 875079
E: info@terrawise.co.uk
W: www.terrawise.co.uk

TES 2000 Ltd
TES House, Heath Industrial Park, Grange Way, Colchester, CO2 8GU
T: 01206 799111
F: 01206 227910
E: info@tes2000.co.uk
W: www.tes2000.co.uk

Testo Ltd
Newman Lane, Alton, Hants, GU34 2QJ
T: 01420 544433
F: 01420 544434
E: info@testo.co.uk
W: www.testo.co.uk

Tevo Ltd
Maddison House, Thomas Road, Wooburn Green Industrial Park, Wooburn Green, Bucks, HP10 0PE
T: 01628 528034
E: sales@tevo.eu.com
W: www.tevo.eu.com

Tew Engineering Ltd
See LB Foster Europe

Thales UK
The Quadrant, 4 Thomas More Square, 17 Thomas More Street, London, E1W 1YW
T: 020 3300 6000
F: 020 3300 6994
E: uk.enquiries@thalesgroup.com
W: www.thalesgroup.com/transportation

The Rail Logistics Company
John De Mierre House, Bridge Road, Haywards Heath, West Sussex, RH16 1UA
T: 01444 849375
W: theraillogisticscompany.com/

The Technical Strategy Leadership Group (TSLG)
Block 2, 1 Torrens St, Angel Square, London, EC1V 1NY
T: 0203 142 5300
E: innovations@futurerailway.org
W: www.futurerailway.org/leadership/pages

ThermaCom Ltd
Celsius House, Summit Close, Kirkby in Ashfield, Notts, NG17 8GJ
T: 01623 758777
E: sales@thermagroup.com
W: www.thermagroup.com

Thermal Economics Ltd
Thermal House, 8 Cardiff Rd, Luton, Beds, LU1 1PP
T: 01582 450814
F: 01582 429305
E: info@thermal-economics.co.uk
W: www.thermal-economics.co.uk

Thermit Welding (GB) Ltd
87 Ferry Lane, Rainham, Essex, RM13 9YH
T: 01708 522626
F: 01708 553806
E: rsj@thermitwelding.co.uk
W: www.thermit-welding.com/

Thomas & Betts Ltd
See PMA UK Ltd (Thomas & Betts Ltd)

Thomas Vale Construction
Lombard House, Worcester Road, Stourport on Severn, Worcestershire, DY13 9BZ
T: 01299 827770
E: general@thomasvale.com
W: www.thomasvale.com/

Thomson Rail Equipment Ltd
Valley Rd, Cinderford, Glos, GL14 2NZ
T: 01594 826611
F: 01594 825560
E: sales@thomsonrail.com
W: www.thomsonrail.com

Threepwood Consulting
76 King Street, Manchester, M2 4NH
M: 07748 182460
E: ian.naylor@threepwoodconsulting.com
W: www.threepwoodconsulting.com

Threeshires Ltd
Piper Hole Farm, Eastwell Rd, Scalford, Leics, LE14 4SS
T: 01664 444604
F: 01664 444605
E: enquiries@threeshires.com
W: www.threeshires.com

Through Life Support Ltd
Red Lodge, Bends Mill, Stonehouse, Gloucestershire, GL10 3RF
T: 01453 820376
M: 07803 698999
E: david.williams@throughlifesupport.com
W: www.throughlifesupport.com

Thurlow Countryside Management Ltd
2 Charterhouse Trading Est, Sturmer Rd, Haverhill, Suffolk, CB9 7UU
T: 01440 760170
F: 01440 760171
E: info@t-c-m.co.uk
W: www.t-c-m.co.uk

Thurrock Engineering Supplies Ltd
Unit 1, TES House, Motherwell Way, West Thurrock, Essex, RM20 3XD
T: 01708 861178
F: 01708 861158
E: info@thurrockengineering.com
W: www.thurrockengineering.com

TI Protective Coatings
See Taziker Industrial Ltd t/a TI Protective Coatings

TICS Ltd
Oxford House, Robin Hood Airport, Sixth Avenue, Doncaster, DN9 3GG
T: 01302 623074
F: 01302 623075
E: info@tics-ltd.co.uk
W: www.tics-ltd.co.uk

Tidyco Ltd
Unit 2, Pentagon Island, Nottingham Road, Derby, DE21 6BW
T: 01332 851300
E: enquiries@tidyco.co.uk
W: www.tidyco.co.uk

Tiflex Ltd
Tiflex House, Liskeard, Cornwall, PL14 4NB
T: 01579 320808
F: 01579 320802
M: 07967 343256
E: panderson@tiflex.co.uk
W: www.tiflex.co.uk

Time 24 Ltd
19 Victoria Gardens, Burgess Hill, West Sussex, RH15 9NB
T: 01444 257655
F: 01444 259000
E: sales@time24.co.uk
W: www.time24.co.uk

Timeplan Ltd
12 The Pines, Broad St, Guildford, Surrey, GU3 3BH
T: 01483 462340
F: 01483 462349
E: dave@timeplansolutions.com
W: www.timeplansolutions.com

TLT
One Redcliff Street, Bristol, BS1 6TP
T: 0333 006 0000
F: 0333 006 0011
W: www.tltsolicitors.com/

TMP Worldwide
Chancery House, Chancery Lane, London, WC2A 1QS
T: 020 7406 5075
E: contactus@tmpw.co.uk
W: www.tmpw.co.uk

Tolent Construction Ltd
Ravensworth House, 5th Avenue Business Park, Team Valley, Gateshead, Tyne & Wear, NE11 0HF
T: 0191 487 0505
F: 0191 487 2990
E: tyneside@tolent.co.uk
W: www.tolent.co.uk/

Tony Gee and Partners LLP
Hardy House, 140 High St, Esher, Surrey, KT10 9QJ
T: 01372 461600
F: 01372 461601
E: enquiries@tonygee.com
W: www.tonygee.com

Tony Miles Railway Writing and Photography
51 Braemar Avenue, Stretford, Manchester, M32 9WA
T: 0161 864 3396
M: 07973 619915
E: tonymiles61@btinternet.com

TopDeck Parking
Springvale Business & Industrial Park, Bilston, Wolverhampton, WV14 0QL
T: 01902 499400
F: 01902 494080
E: info@topdeckparking.co.uk
W: www.topdeckparking.co.uk

Topdrill
7 Deeping Gate, Stonebridge, Milton Keynes, MK13 0DE
T: 01908 321925
E: info@topdrill.co.uk
W: www.topdrill.co.uk

TenBroeke Co
Transforming Infrastructure Delivery
SPECIALISTS IN PROJECT DELIVERY
INTEGRATION, COORDINATION, COOPERATION
TenBroeke Co
www.tenbroekeco.com

Toray Textiles Europe Ltd
Crown Farm Way, Forest Town, Mansfield, Notts, NG19 0FT
T: 01623 415050
F: 01623 415070
E: sales@ttel.co.uk
W: www.ttel.co.uk

Torrent Trackside Ltd
Network House, Europa Way, Britannia Enterprise Park, Lichfield, Staffs, WS14 9TZ
T: 01543 421900
F: 01543 421931
E: mail@torrent.co.uk
W: www.torrent.co.uk

Total Access (UK) Ltd
Unit 5, Raleigh Hall Ind. Est, Eccleshall, Staffs, ST21 6JL
T: 01785 850333
F: 01785 850339
E: enquiries@totalaccess.co.uk
W: www.totalaccess.co.uk

Total Rail Solutions
Crossway, Stephenson Road, Houndmills, Basingstoke, Hants, RG21 6XR
T: 01962 711642
F: 01962 717330
E: info@totalrailsolutions.co.uk
W: www.totalrailsolutions.co.uk/

TotalKare HDWS Ltd
Block G1, Dandy Bank Road, Pensnett Trading Estate, Kingswinford, DY6 7TD
T: 0121 585 2724
E: sales@totalkare.co.uk
W: www.totalkare.co.uk

Totectors (UK) Ltd
9 Pondwood Close, Moulton Park Ind. Estate, Northampton, NN3 6RT
T: 0870 600 5055
F: 0870 600 5056
E: sales@totectors.net
W: www.totectors.net

Touchstone Renard Ltd
152-160 City Road, London, EC1V 2NX
T: 020 3954 2576
M: 07768 366744
E: paustin@touchstonerenard.com
W: www.touchstonerenard.com

Tower Surveys Ltd
Opus House, 21 Vivian Avenue, Nottingham, NG5 1AF
T: 0115 960 1212
F: 0115 962 1200
E: info@towersurveys.co.uk
W: www.towersurveys.co.uk

TP Matrix Ltd
TP House, Prince Of Wales Industrial Units, Vulcan Street, Oldham, Greater Manchester, OL1 4ER
T: 0161 626 4067
F: 0161 627 1741
E: service@tpmatrix.co.uk
W: www.tpmatrixrail.co.uk/

TPA Portable Roadways Ltd
TPA Head Office, Dukeries Mill, Claylands Industrial Estate, Worksop, Notts, S81 7DJ
T: 0870 240 2381
F: 0870 240 2382
E: enquiries@tpa-ltd.co.uk
W: www.tpa-ltd.co.uk

TPK Consulting Ltd (RPS Group)
Centurion Court, 85, Milton Park, Abingdon, Oxon, OX14 4RY
T: 01235 438151
F: 01235 438188
E: rpsab@rpsgroup.com
W: www.rpsplc.co.uk

TQ Technical and Vocational
Pearson Academy of Vocational Training, Bangrave Road South, Corby, Northants, NN17 1NN
T: 01536 351300
E: technical@tq.com
W: www.tq.com/technical/

TRAC Engineering Ltd
Dovecote Rd, Eurocentral, North Lanarkshire, ML1 4GP
T: 01698 831111
F: 01698 832222
E: engineering@trac.com
W: www.tracengineering.com

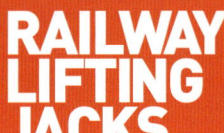

TRaC Global
100 Frobisher Business Park, Leigh Sinton Road, Malvern, Worcs, WR14 1BX
T: 01684 571700
F: 01684 571701
E: quoteme@tracglobal.com
W: www.tracglobal.com

TRAC Training Ltd
5 Dovecote Road, Eurocentral, North Lanarkshire, ML1 4GP
T: 01698 748700
F: 01698 832222
E: training@trac.com
W: www.tractraining.com

Track Access Services Ltd
Unit 4, The Sidings, Station Road, Shepreth, Hertfordshire, SG8 6PZ
T: 01763 261708
E: mail@trackaccess.co.uk
W: www.trackaccess.co.uk

Track IQ, a Wabtec Company
17-19 King William St, Kent Town, South Australia, AUSTRALIA 5067, Australia
T: +61(0)8 7099 4600
E: tiqtrackiqinfo@wabtec.com
W: www.trackiq.com.au/

Track Maintenance Equipment Ltd
Witham Wood, Marley Lane, Haslemere, Surrey, GU27 3PZ
T: 01428 651114
F: 01428 644727
E: info@tmeltd.co.uk
W: www.tmeltd.co.uk

Track Safe Telecom (TST)
See Centregreat Rail Ltd

Tracklink UK Ltd
Unit 5, Miltons Yard, Petworth Rd, Witley, Surrey, GU8 5LH
T: 01428 685124
F: 01428 687788
E: enquiries@tklink.co.uk
W: www.tklink.co.uk

Tracksure
Wheelsure Holdings PLC, 8 Woburn Street, Ampthill, Beds, MK45 2HP
T: 01525 840557
F: 01525 403918
E: sales@wheelsure.co.uk
W: wheelsure.co.uk/tracksure/

Trackwork Ltd
PO Box 139, Kirk Sandall Lane, Kirk Sandall Ind. Est, Doncaster, DN31WX
T: 01302 888666
F: 01302 888777
E: sales@trackwork.co.uk
W: www.trackwork.co.uk

Tracsis Plc
33 Brunel Parkway, Pride Park, Derby, DE24 8HR
T: 01332 226860
E: info@tracsis.com
W: www.tracsisops.com

Tractel UK Ltd
Old Lane, Halfway, Sheffield, S20 3GA
T: 0114 248 2266
F: 0114 247 3350
E: tracteluk.info@tractel.com
W: www.tractel.com

TracTruc Bi-modal
See Truck Train Developments Ltd (and TracTruc Bi-Modal)

Traditional Traction Ltd
100 Swan Street, Sible Hedingham, Essex, CO9 3HP
M: 07787 520449
E: info@traditional-traction.com
W: www.traditional-traction.com

Traffic Management Services Ltd
PO Box 10, Retford, Notts, DN22 7EE
T: 01777 705053
F: 01777 709878
E: info@traffic.org.uk
W: www.traffic.org.uk/

Train Chartering (Luxury Train Club)
Benwell House, Preston, Chippenham, Wilts, SN15 4DX
T: 01249 890176
E: info@luxurytrainclub.com
W: www.luxurytrainclub.com/

Train Fleet (2019) Ltd
Great Minster House, 33 Horseferry Road, London, SW1P 4DR

TrainFX Ltd
4 Newmarket Court, Derby, DE24 8NW
T: 01332 366175
E: jacquit@trainfx.com
W: www.trainfx.com

Train'd Up
Elmbank Mill, Menstrie Business Centre, Menstrie, Clackmannanshire, FK11 7BU
T: 0845 602 9665
F: 0870 850 3397
E: enquiries@traindup.org
W: www.traindup.org

Trainline
Trainline Holdings Ltd, 498 Gorgie Rd, Edinburgh, EH11 3AF
T: 08704 111111
W: www.thetrainline.com

Trainpassenger.com Ltd
Suite 364, 12 South Bridge, Edinburgh, EH1 1DD
T: 0131 235 2358
E: info@trainpassenger.com
W: www.trainpassenger.com

Traka plc
30 Stilebrook Road, Olney, Bucks, MK46 5EA
T: 01234 712345
W: www.traka.com/

Trakside Systems Ltd
See High Voltage Maintenance Services Ltd

Traktionssysteme Austria GmbH (TSA)
Brown-Boveri-Straße 1, 2351 Wiener Neudorf, Austria
T: +43 (0)2236 8118-0
F: +43 (0)2236 8118-237
E: office@traktionssysteme.at
W: www.traktionssysteme.at/en/

TRAM Power Ltd
99 Stanley Rd, Bootle, Merseyside, L20 7DA
T: 0151 547 1425
F: 0151 521 5509
M: 07976 040618
E: lewis.lesley@trampower.co.uk
W: www.trampower.co.uk

Tramlink (Croydon)
See Transport for London

Tranect Ltd
Unit 4, Carraway Rd, Gilmoss Ind. Est, Liverpool, L11 0EE
T: 0151 548 7040
F: 0151 546 6066
E: sales@tranect.co.uk
W: www.tranect.co.uk

Transaction Systems Ltd
See Kiepe Electric Ltd

Transcal Ltd
Firth Rd, Houstoun Ind. Est, Livingston, West Lothian, EH54 5DJ
T: 01506 440111
F: 01506 442333
E: info@transcal.co.uk
W: www.transcal.co.uk

Transdek
Bryans Close, Harworth, Doncaster, DN11 8RY
T: 01302 752276
F: 01302 752434
E: info@transdek.com
W: www.transdek.com/

Translec Ltd
Saddleworth Business Centre, Huddersfield Rd, Delph, Oldham, OL3 5DF
T: 01457 878888
F: 01457 878887
E: mail@translec.co.uk
W: www.translec.co.uk

Translink NI Railways
Central Station, East Bridge St, Belfast, BT1 3PB
T: 02890 666630
F: 02890 899452
E: feedback@translink.co.uk
W: www.translink.co.uk

Transmitton
See Siemens Mobility Ltd

TransPennine Express
Bridgewater House, 60 Whitworth St, Manchester, M1 6LT
T: 0345 600 1671
F: 0161 228 8120
E: tpecustomer.relations@firstgroup.com
W: www.tpexpress.co.uk

Transport & Travel Research Ltd (TTR)
Minster House, Minster Pool Walk, Lichfield, Staffs
T: 01543 416416
F: 01543 416681
E: enquiries@ttr-ltd.com
W: www.ttr-ltd.com

Transport 2000
See Campaign for Better Transport

Transport Benevolent Fund CIO
Suite 2.7, The Loom, 14 Gowers Walk, London, E1 8PY
T: 0300 333 2000 (ETD 00 38571)
F: 0870 831 2882
E: help@tbf.org.uk
W: www.tbf.org.uk

Transport Design International Ltd
Clifford Mill, Clifford Chambers, Stratford upon Avon, Warwickshire, CV37 8HW
T: 01789 205011
W: www.tdi.uk.com/

Transport Focus
Fleetbank House, 2-6 Salisbury Square, London, EC4Y 8JX
T: 0300 123 0860
F: 020 7630 7355
E: info@transportfocus.org.uk
W: www.transportfocus.org.uk

Transport for Edinburgh
55 Annandale Street, Edinburgh, EH7 4AZ
W: transportforedinburgh.com/

Transport for Greater Manchester
2 Piccadilly Place, Manchester, M1 3BG
T: 0161 244 1000
E: customer.relations@tfgm.com
W: www.tfgm.com/

Transport for London
55 Broadway, London, SW1H 0BD
T: 020 7222 5600
E: enquire@tfl.gov.uk
W: www.tfl.gov.uk/rail

Transport for the East Midlands
First Floor Offices, South Annexe, Pera Business Park, Nottingham Road, Melton Mowbray, Leicestershire, LE13 0PB
W: www.emcouncils.gov.uk/transport-for-the-east-midlands-tfem

Transport for the North (TfN)
2nd Floor, 4 Piccadilly Place, Manchester, M1 3BN
T: 0161 244 0888
E: mediarelations@transportforthenorth.com
W: www.transportforthenorth.com

Transport for the South East
County Hall, St Anne's Cresent, Lewes, BN7 1UE
T: 0300 3309474
E: tfse@eastsussex.gov.uk
W: transportforthesoutheast.org.uk/

Transport for Wales
South Gate House, Wood Street, Cardiff, CF10 1EW
T: 0300 200 6565
W: tfw.gov.wales/

Transport for Wales Rail Services
St Mary's House, 47 Penarth Rd, Cardiff, CF10 5DJ
T: 03333 211202
W: https://tfwrail.wales/

Transport for West Midlands (TfWM)
Customer Relations, 16 Summer Lane, Birmingham, B19 3SD
T: 0121 200 2787
E: customerrelations@centro.org.uk
W: www.centro.org.uk

Transport iNet
Loughborough University, Hazlerigg Building, Loughborough, Leicestershire, LE11 3TU
T: 01509 635270
F: 01509 635231
E: info@transport-inet.org.uk
W: www.transport-inet.org.uk/

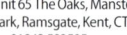

Transport Investigations Ltd
Unit 65 The Oaks, Manston Business Park, Ramsgate, Kent, CT12 5FD
T: 01843 593595
E: info@transportinvestigations.co.uk
W: www.transportinvestigations.co.uk

Transport Scotland
Buchanan House, 58 Port Dundas Rd, Glasgow, G4 0HF
T: 0141 272 7100
E: info@transportscotland.gsi.gov.uk
W: www.transportscotland.gov.uk

Transport Systems Catapult
The Pinnacle, 170 Midsummer Boulevard, Milton Keynes, MK9 1BP
T: 01908 359 999
E: reception@ts.catapult.org.uk
W: https://ts.catapult.org.uk

Transportation Planning International
Crystal Court, Aston Cross, Rocky Lane, Aston, Birmingham, B6 5RH
T: 0121 333 3433
F: 0121 359 3200
E: info@tpi-bham.co.uk
W: www.tpi-world.com

Transsol Ltd
Unit 8, Marley House, Roseberry Place, Dalston, London, E8 3GD
T: 020 7923 4591
F: 0870 052 5838
E: enquiries@transsol.co.uk
W: www.transsol.co.uk/

Trans-Tronic Ltd
Whitting Valley Rd, Old Whittington, Chesterfield, Derbys, S41 9EY
T: 01246 264260
F: 01246 455281
E: sales@trans-tronic.co.uk
W: www.trans-tronic.co.uk

Transurb Technirail
Ravenstein Street 60/18, B-1000 Brussels, Belgium
T: 32 81 25 20 09
E: simulator@transurb.com
W: www.transurb.com/simulation

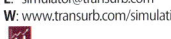

Transys Projects Ltd
See Kiepe Electric Ltd

Trapeze Group Rail Ltd
Jervaulx House, 6 St Mary's Court, Blossom Street, York, YO24 1AH
T: 01904 639091
F: 01904 639092
E: sales.railuk@trapezegroup.com
W: www.trapezegroup.com

Tratos Ltd
10 Eagle Court, Britton St, Farringdon, London, EC1M 5QD
T: 0845 413 9990
F: 020 3553 4815
E: john.light@tratos.co.uk
W: www.tratos.co.uk

Travel Info. Systems
Suite 3, Grand Union House, 20 Kentish Town Rd, London, NW1 9NX
T: 020 7284 8071
F: 020 7267 1133
E: enquiries@travelinfosystems.com
W: www.travelinfosystems.com

Traxsydes Training
Room 11, E.L.O.C, 80-86 St Mary Rd, Walthamstow, London, E17 9RE
T: 020 8223 1257
F: 020 8223 1258
E: bookings@traxsydes.co.uk
W: www.traxsydes.co.uk

TRB Lightweight Structures Ltd
12 Clifton Rd, Huntingdon, Cambs, PE29 7EN
T: 01480 447400
F: 01480 414992
E: sales@trbls.com
W: www.trbls.com

TRE Ltd
See Hitachi Information Control Systems Europe

Treadmaster Flooring
See Tiflex Ltd

Trelleborg Industrial AVS
1 Hoods Close, Leicester, LE4 2BN
T: 0116 267 0300
F: 0116 267 0510
E: rail@trelleborg.com
W: www.trelleborg.com/industrialavs

Tremco Illbruck Limited
Coupland Rd, Hindley Green, Wigan, WN2 4HT
T: 01942 251400
F: 01942 251410
E: uk.info@tremco-illbruck.com
W: www.tremco-illbruck.com

Trenitalia UK Ltd
The Broadgate Tower, Third Floor, 20 Primrose Street, London, EC2A 2RS
W: www.trenitalia.com/

Trent Instruments Ltd
Unit 39, Nottingham South and Wilford Ind. Est, Ruddington Lane, Nottingham, NG11 7EP
T: 0115 969 6188
F: 0115 945 5696
E: phillip@trentinstruments.co.uk
W: www.trentinstruments.co.uk

TRI Control Systems
Colham Green House, Colham Green Road, Uxbridge, Middlesex, UB8 3QQ
T: 01895 257500
W: tricontrols.com/

Tribo Rail
PO Box 676, Bury, BL8 9RR
T: 01298 214980
E: enquiries@triborail.com
W: www.triborail.com

Triforce Security Solutions Ltd
Westmead House, Westmead, Farnborough, Hants, GU14 7LP
T: 01252 373496
E: enquiries@triforcesecurity.co.uk
W: www.triforcesecurity.co.uk

Trimble UK
Trimble House, Meridian Office Park, Osborn Way, Hook, Hants, RG27 9HX
T: 01256 760150
F: 01256 760148
W: www.trimble.com

Triscan Systems Ltd
4 Petre Court, Clayton Business Park, Accrington, Lancs, BB5 5HY
T: 0845 225 3100
E: info@thetriscangroup.com
W: www.thetriscangroup.com

Tritech Rail/Tritech Rail Training
See AECOM

TRL (Transport Research Laboratory)
Crowthorne House, Nine Mile Ride, Wokingham, Berks, RG40 3GA
T: 01344 773131
F: 01344 770356
E: rail@trl.co.uk
W: www.trl.co.uk

Trojan Services Ltd
Curtis House, 34 Third Avenue, Hove, East Sussex, BN3 2PD
T: 0845 074 0407
F: 01243 783654
E: info@trojan-services.com
W: www.trojan-services.com

Trolex Ltd
Newby Rd, Hazel Grove, Stockport, SK7 5DY
T: 0161 483 1435
F: 0161 483 5556
E: sales@trolex.com
W: www.trolex.com

Trough-Tec Systems Ltd (TTS)
Bennetthorpe, Doncaster, DN2 6AA
T: 01302 343633
E: info@ttsrail.co.uk
W: www.ttsrail.co.uk

TRS Staffing Solutions
8th Floor, York House, Kingsway, London, WC2B 6UJ
T: 020 7419 5800
F: 020 7419 5801
E: info-uk@trsstaffing.com
W: www.trsstaffing.com

Truck Train Developments Ltd (and TracTruc Bi-Modal)
4 Elfin Grove, Bognor Regis, W.Sussex, PO21 2RX
T: 01243 869118
M: 07748 550964
E: pmtrucktrain@tiscali.co.uk
W: www.trucktrain.co.uk

TruckTrain Developments Limited
4, Elfin Grove, Bognor Regis, West Sussex, PO21 2RX
T: 01243 869118
E: pmtrucktrain@tiscali.co.uk
W: www.trucktrain.co.uk

Trueform Engineering Ltd
Unit 12, Pasadena Trading Estate, Pasadena Close, Hayes, Middlesex, UB3 3NQ
T: 020 8280 8800
F: 020 8848 1397
E: sales@trueform.co.uk
W: www.trueform.co.uk

Truflame Welding
Truflame House, 56 Newhall Rd, Sheffield, S9 2QL
T: 0114 243 3020
F: 0114 243 5297
E: sales@truflame.co.uk
W: www.truflame.co.uk

TS Components Ltd
Ladywood House, Ladywood Works, Lutterworth, Leics, LE17 4HD
T: 01455 550495
E: info@tscomponents.com
W: www.tscomponents.com

TSL Turton Ltd
PO Box 17, Effingham Street, Sheffield, S4 7YP
T: 0114 270 1577
F: 0114 275 6947
E: sales@tslturton.com
W: www.tslturton.com

TSO
Chemin du Corps de Garde, CS 80035, 77508 Chelles Cedex, France
T: (33) 01 64 72 72 00
F: (33) 01 64 26 30 23
E: info@tso.fr
W: www.tso.fr

TSP Projects
Meridian House, The Crescent, York, YO24 1AW
T: 01904 454600
F: 01904 454601
W: www.tspprojects.co.uk/

TSSA (Transport Salaried Staffs' Association)
Walkden House, 10 Melton St, London, NW1 2EJ
T: 020 7387 2101
F: 0141 3329879
E: enquiries@tssa.org.uk
W: www.tssa.org.uk

TT Electronics plc
Clive House, 12-18 Queens Rd, Weybridge, Surrey, KT13 9XB
T: 01932 825300
F: 01932 836450
E: info@ttelectronics.com
W: www.ttelectronics.com

TTCI UK
13 Fitzroy St, London, W1T 4BQ
T: 020 7755 4080
F: 020 7755 4203
E: michele_johnson@aar.com
W: www.ttc.aar.com

TTG Transportation Technology (Europe) Ltd
The iD Centre, Lathkill House, rtc Business Park, London Rd, Derby, DE24 8UP
T: 01332 258867
F: 01332 258823
E: enquiries@ttgeurope.com
W: www.ttgtransportation technology.com

TTI Inc
Suite S06, Business & Technology Centre, Bessemer Drive, Stevenage, Herts, SG1 2DX
T: 01438 794170
F: 01438 791139
E: kasey.sweetlove@uk.ttiinc.com
W: www.ttieurope.com/page/campbell-collins

TTPP Construction Consultants
1st Floor, Crowne House, 56-58 Southwark Street, London, SE1 1UN
T: 020 7940 6500
F: 020 7378 0136
E: enquiries@ttpp.co.uk
W: www.ttpp.co.uk/

TTR
See Transport & Travel Research Ltd (TTR)

Tube Lines
15 Westferry Circus, Canary Wharf, London, E14 4HD
T: 0845 660 5466
E: enquiries@tubelines.com
W: www.tubelines.com

Tuchschmid Constructa AG
Langdorfstrasse 26, CH-8501, Frauenfeld, Switzerland
T: 0041 52 728 8111
F: 0041 52 728 8100
E: w.luessi@tuchschmid.ch
W: www.intermodallogistics.co.uk

Tufnol Composites Ltd
76 Wellhead Lane, Perry Barr, Birmingham, B42 2TN
T: 0121 356 9351
F: 0121 331 4235
E: sales@tufnol.co.uk
W: www.tufnol.com

Turbex Ltd
Unit 1, Riverwey Ind. Park, Newman Lane, Alton, Hants, GU34 2QL
T: 01420 544909
F: 01420 542264
E: sales@turbex.co.uk
W: www.turbex.co.uk

Turbo Power Systems Ltd
1 Queens Park, Queensway North, Team Valley Trading Est, Gateshead, Tyne & Wear, NE11 0QD
T: 0191 482 9200
F: 0191 482 9201
E: sales@turbopowersystems.com
W: www.turbopowersystems.com

Turkington Precast
James Park, Mahon Rd, Portadown, Co. Armagh, BT62 3EH, Northern Ireland
T: 028 38 332807
F: 028 38 361770
E: gary@turkington-precast.com
W: www.turkington-precast.com

Turnell & Odell Ltd
Sanders Road, Finedon Road Industrial Estate, Wellingborough, Northants, NN8 4NL
T: 01933 222061
E: sales@toengineering.co.uk
W: toengineering.co.uk/

Turner & Townsend
Low Hall, Calverley Lane, Horsforth, Leeds, LS18 4GH
T: 0113 258 4400
F: 0113 258 2911
E: lee@turntown.com
W: www.turnerandtownsend.com

Turner Diesel Ltd
Unit 1A, Dyce Ind. Park, Dyce, Aberdeen, AB21 7EZ
T: 01224 214200
F: 01224 723927
E: diesel.sales@turner.co.uk
W: www.turner-diesel.co.uk

Tusp Ltd
Ground Floor, Unit 7, Highpoint Business Village, Henwood, Ashford, Kent, TN24 8DH
T: 01233 640257
E: enquiries@tusp.co.uk
W: www.tusp.co.uk

TUV Product Service Ltd
Octagon House, Concorde Way, Segensworth, North Fareham, Hants, PO15 5RL
T: 01489 558100
F: 01489 558101
E: info@tuvps.co.uk
W: www.tuvps.co.uk

TUV-SUD Rail GmbH
Westendstrasse 199, 80686, Munich, Germany
T: 0049 89519 03537
F: 0049 89519 02933
W: www.tuv-sud.co.uk

TVS Supply Chain Solutions
Logistics House, Buckshaw Avenue, Chorley, Lancashire, PR6 7AJ
T: 01257 265 531
E: info@tvsscs.com
W: https://www.tvsscs.com/

TXM Plant Ltd
TXM Plant House, Harbour Rd Trading Est, Portishead, Bristol, BS20 7AT
T: 01275 399400
F: 01275 399500
E: info@txmplant.co.uk
W: www.txmplant.co.uk

TXM Projects Ltd
1 St Peters Court, Church Lane, Bickenhill, Solihull, B92 0DN
T: 01675 446830
F: 01675 446839
E: simon.pitt@txmprojects.co.uk
W: www.txmprojects.co.uk

TXM Recruit Ltd
Blackhill Drive, Wolverton Mill, Milton Keynes, Bucks, MK12 5TS
T: 0845 2263454
F: 0845 2262453
E: info@txmrecruit.co.uk

Tyco Fire and Integrated Solutions
Tyco Park, Grimshaw Lane, Newton Heath, Manchester, M40 2WL
T: 0161 455 4400
W: www.tycofis.co.uk/

Tyne & Wear Metro
See Nexus (Tyne & Wear Metro)

Tyrolit
Eldon Close, Crick, Northants, NN6 7UD
T: 01788 824500
E: gborder@tyrolit.com
W: www.tyrolit.co.uk

Tyrone Fabrication Ltd (TFL)
Goland Rd, Ballygawley, Co Tyrone, BT70 2LA
T: 028 8556 7200
F: 028 8556 7089
E: sales@tfl.eu.com
W: www.tfl.eu.com

Tyseley Locomotive Works Limited
670 Warwick Rd, Tyseley, Birmingham, B11 2HL
T: 0121 708 4960
F: 0121 708 4960
E: office@vintagetrains.co.uk

UK Accreditation Service (UKAS)
2 Pine Trees, Chertsey Lane, Staines-upon-Thames, TW18 3HR
T: 01784 429000
E: info@ukas.com
W: https://www.ukas.com/

UK Power Networks Services
Newington House, 237 Southwark Bridge Rd, London, SE1 6NP
T: 0207 397 7695
E: rail@ukpowernetworks.co.uk
W: www.ukpowernetworks.co.uk/internet/en/infrastructure-services/rail/

UK Rail Leasing
Beal Street, Leicester, LE2 0AA
T: 0116 262 2783
E: info@ukrl.co.uk
W: www.ukrl.co.uk

UK Rail Research and Innovation Network (UKRRIN)
UKRRIN Coordinating Hub, Partnerships Team, RSSB The Helicon, One South Place, London, EC2M 2RB
T: 020 3142 5300
E: ukrrin@rssb.co.uk
W: www.ukrrin.org.uk/

UK Railtours
T: 01438 715050
E: john@ukrailtours.com
W: www.ukrailtours.com

UK Trade & Investment - Investment Services
1 Victoria St, London, SW1H 0ET
T: 0845 539 0419/020 7333 5442
E: enquiries@ukti-invest.com
W: www.ukti.gov.uk

UK Ultraspeed
Warksburn House, Wark, Hexham, Northumberland, NE48 3LS
T: 020 7861 2497
F: 020 7861 2497
E: ncameron@bell-pottinger.co.uk
W: www.500kmh.com

UKDN Waterflow
2480 Regents Court, The Crescent, Birmingham Business Park, Solihull, West Midlands, B37 7YE
T: 0121 788 4787
E: solutions@ukdnwaterflow.co.uk
W: ukdnwaterflow.co.uk/

UKRS Projects Ltd
See Bowen Projects Ltd

UKTram
Centro House, 16 Summer Lane, Birmingham, B19 3SD
E: info@uktram.co.uk
W: www.uktram.co.uk/

UKWSL
Alexander House, Cafferata Way, Newark-on-Trent, Nottinghamshire, NG24 2TN
T: 01636 640744
F: 01636 640745
W: www.ukwsl.co.uk/

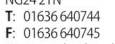

Ultimate Hearing Protection
13 Moorfield Road, Orpington, Kent, BR6 0HG
T: 01689 876885
E: sales@ultimateear.com
W: www.ultimateear.com

Ultra Electronics PMES Ltd
Towers Business Park, Wheelhouse Rd, Rugeley, Staffs, WS15 1UZ
T: 01889 503300
F: 01889 572929
E: enquiries@ultra-pmes.com
W: www.ultra-pmes.com

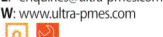

Ultra Electronics-Electrics
Kingsditch Lane, Cheltenham, Glos, GL51 9PG
T: 01242 221166
F: 01242 221167
E: info@ultra-electrics.com
W: www.ultra-electrics.com

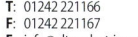

Ultrimax Coatings
Clayfield Industrial Estate, Tickhill Road, Doncaster, Yorkshire, DN4 8QG
T: 01302 856666
F: 01302 571510
E: sales@ultrimaxcoatings.co.uk
W: www.ultrimaxcoatings.co.uk/

Underground Pipeline Services Ltd
See Integrated Water Services Ltd

Unic Cranes Europe
See GGR Group Ltd

UNIFE
Avenue Louise 221, B-1050 Brussels, Belgium
T: 0032 2642 2328
F: 0032 2626 1261
E: judit.sandor@unife.org
W: www.unife.org

Unilathe Ltd
Ford Green Business Park, Ford Green Road, Smallthorne, Stoke-on-Trent, Staffs, ST6 1NG
T: 01782 532000
F: 01782 532013
E: enquiries@unilathe.co.uk
W: www.unilathe.co.uk

Unilite International
The Lab, Moons Moat North Industrial Estate,
Winyates Way, Redditch, B98 9FG
T: 01527 584344
F: 01527 584345
E: sales@unilite.co.uk
W: https://www.uni-lite.com/

Unilokomotive Ltd
Dunmore Rd, Tuam, Co. Galway, Republic of Ireland
T: 00353 93 52150
F: 00353 93 52227
E: omcconn@unilok.ie
W: www.unilok.ie

Unipart Dorman
Wennington Rd, Southport, Merseyside, PR9 7TN
T: 01704 518000
F: 01704 518001
E: dorman.enquiries@unipartdorman.co.uk
W: www.unipartdorman.co.uk

DIRECTORY

Unipart Rail Ltd
Jupiter Building, First Point, Balby Carr Bank, Doncaster, DN4 5JQ
T: 01302 731400
F: 01302 731401
E: enquiries@unipartrail.com
W: www.unipartrail.com

Unite - The Union
Unite House, 128 St Theobald's Road, Holborn, London, WC1X 8TN
T: 020 7611 2500
E: executive.council@unitetheunion.org
W: www.unitetheunion.com

United Kingdom Society for Trenchless Technology
Camden House, Warwick Road, Kenilworth, Warks, CV8 1TH
T: 01926 513773
E: admin@ukstt.org.uk
W: www.ukstt.org.uk

United Springs Ltd
Mandale Park, Norman Road, Rochdale, Lancs, OL11 4HP
T: 01706 644551
F: 01706 630516
E: sales@united-springs.co.uk
W: www.united-springs.com

Universal Boltforgers Ltd
28 Dudley Road West, Tividale, Oldbury, West Midlands, B69 2PJ
T: 0121 522 5950
F: 0121 520 5333
E: office@universal-boltforgers.co.uk
W: www.universalboltforgers.co.uk/

Universal Heat Transfer Ltd
Well Spring Close, Carlyon Rd, Atherstone, Warks, CV9 1HU
T: 01827 722171
F: 01827 722174
E: sales@uhtltd.com
W: www.universalheattransfer.com

The Universal Improvement Company
First Floor, Millennium House, 40 Nantwich Road, Crewe, CW2 6AD
M: 07941 451021
E: info@theuic.com
W: www.theuic.com

Universal Railway Equipment Ltd
Princess Royal Buildings, Whitecroft Rd, Bream, Lydney, Glos, GL15 6LY
T: 01594 560555
E: unirail@btconnect.com
W: www.peeway.co.uk

University of Derby - Faculty of Arts, Design & Technology
Markeaton St, Derby, DE22 3AW
T: 01332 593216
E: adtenquiry@derby.ac.uk
W: www.derby.ac.uk

UP3
Hersham Place Technology Park, Molesey Road, Walton-on-Thames, KT12 4RZ
T: 020 3432 1432
E: hello@up3.co.uk
W: www.up3.co.uk

UR Group
Unit 12, Woodside Road, South Marston Park, Swindon, Wiltshire, SN3 4WA
T: 01793 756980
E: uk@ur-group.com
W: www.ur-group.com/

Urban Hygiene Ltd
Sky Business Park, Robin Hood Airport, Doncaster, South Yorks, DN9 3GN
T: 01302 623193
F: 01302 623167
E: enquiries@urbanhygiene.com
W: www.urbanhygiene.co.uk

Urban Transport Group
Wellington House, 40-50 Wellington Street, Leeds, LS1 2DE
T: 0113 251 7204
E: info@urbantransportgroup.org
W: www.urbantransportgroup.org/

Experts in Supply Chain and Technology & Product Solutions for the Rail Industry.

Supply Chain Solutions

Technology & Products Solutions

We address the challenges of the rail industry across the asset life cycle by working collaboratively with our partners to deliver technology and supply chain solutions that **improve performance**, **reduce risk** and **optimise cost**.

UNIPART RAIL

Urbis Lighting Ltd
See Urbis Schreder Ltd

Urbis Schreder Ltd
Sapphire House, Lime Tree Way, Hampshire International Business Park, Chineham, Basingstoke, Hants, RG24 8GG
T: 01256 354446
F: 01256 841314
E: sales@urbis-schreder.com
W: www.urbis-schreder.com

Uretek UK Ltd
Unit 6, Peel Rd, Skelmersdale, Lancs, WN8 9PT
T: 01695 50525
F: 01695 555212
E: sales@uretek.co.uk
W: www.uretek.co.uk

URS
Scott House, Alencon Link, Basingstoke, Hants, RG21 7PP
T: 01256 310200
F: 01256 310201
E: rail.marketing@scottwilson.com
W: www.urscorp.eu

URS Corporation Ltd
6-8 Greencoat Place, London, SW1P 1PL
T: 0115 907 7086
F: 0115 907 7001
E: railways@scottwilson.com
W: www.urscorp.eu

VA Rail Ltd
Level 37, One Canada Square, Canary Wharf, London, E14 5DY
M: 07802 549727
E: enquiries@varail.co.uk
W: www.varail.co.uk/

VAE UK Ltd
Sir Harry Lauder Rd, Portobello, Edinburgh, EH15 1DJ
T: 0131 550 2297
F: 0131 550 2660
E: jim.gemmell@vae.co.uk
W: www.voestalpine.com/vae

Vaisala Ltd
Elm House, 351 Bristol Rd, Birmingham, B5 7SW
T: 0121 683 1200
F: 0121 683 1299
E: liz.green@vaisala.com
W: www.vaisala.com

Valmont Stainton Ltd
Unit 5, Dukesway, Teesside Industrial Estate, Thornaby, Cleveland, TS17 9LT
T: 01642 766242
F: 01642 765509
E: stainton@valmont.com
W: www.valmont-stainton.com

Van der Vlist UK Ltd
Burma Drive, Kingston upon Hull, HU9 5SD
T: 01482 210100
F: 01482 216222
E: info@vandervlist.co.uk
W: www.vandervlist.com/en/european_offices/uk

Van Elle
Kirkby Lane, Pinxton, Notts, NG16 6JA
T: 01773 580580
F: 01773 862100
E: mark.williams@van-elle.co.uk
W: www.van-elle.co.uk

Vapor Ricon Europe Ltd
Meadow Lane, Loughborough, Leicestershire, LE11 1HS
T: 01509 635920
F: 01509 261939
E: riconuk@wabtec.com
W: www.ricon.eu

Variable Message Signs Ltd (VMS)
Unit 1, Monkton Business Park North, Mill Lane, Hebburn, Tyne & Wear, NE31 2JZ
T: 0191 423 7070
F: 0191 423 7071
E: sales@vmstech.co.uk
W: www.vmslimited.co.uk

Vector Management Ltd
Strathclyde House, Green Man Lane, London Heathrow Airport, Feltham, Middx, TW14 0NZ
T: 020 8844 0444
F: 020 8844 0666
E: ju-liang.trigg@vecman.com
W: www.vecman.com

Vectra Group Ltd
See Arcadis LLP

Veea Systems
Cambridge House, Henry Street, Bath, BA1 1JS
T: 01225 618120
W: www.veea.com

Vendigital Ltd
91 Wimpole Street, London, W1G 0EF
T: 020 3871 2769
E: info@vendigital.com
W: https://vendigital.com/

Veolia
5 Limeharbour Court, Limeharbour, London, E14 9RH
T: 01784 496200
F: 01784 496222
E: carol.taylor@dalkia.co.uk
W: veolia.co.uk

Verint Systems
241 Brooklands Rd, Weybridge, Surrey, KT13 0RH
T: 01932 839500
F: 01932 839501
E: marketing.emea@verint.com
W: www.verint.com

Veritec Sonomatic Ltd
Ashton House, The Village, Birchwood Bus.Park, Warrington, WA3 6FZ
T: 01925 414000
F: 01925 655595
E: jl@vsonomatic.com
W: www.vsonomatic.com/

Versaperm Limited
10 Rawcliffe House, Howarth Road, Maidenhead, Berkshire, SL6 1AP
T: 01628 777668
E: webcontact@versaperm.com
W: www.versaperm.com/

Vertemax Limited
Spinney House, Wilcox Close, Aylesham, Kent, CT3 3EP
T: 01227 711072
E: info@vertemax.com
W: www.vertemax.com

Vertex Systems
See AMCL Systems Engineering Ltd

Vertex Systems Engineering
Soane Point, 6-8 Market Place, Reading, RG1 2EG
T: 0118 925 5462
F: 0118 925 5888
E: enquiries@vertex-se.com
W: www.vertex-se.com

Veryards Opus
See Opus International Consultants Ltd

VGC Group
Cardinal House, Bury St, Ruislip, Middx, HA4 7GD
T: 08456 201201
E: enq@vgcgroup.co.uk
W: www.vgcgroup.co.uk

Vi Distribution
Unit 7, Springvale Business Centre, Millbuck Way, Sandbach, Cheshire, CW11 3HY
T: 01270 750520
F: 01270 750521
E: sales@vidistribution.co.uk
W: www.vidistribution.co.uk

Victa Railfreight Ltd
51 Granville Road, Maidstone, Kent, ME14 2BJ
T: 01622 690978
F: 01622 692096
E: enquiries@victa-railfreight.com
W: www.victa-railfreight.com/

Video 125 Ltd
Glade House, High St, Sunninghill, Berks, SL5 9NP
T: 01344 628565
E: sales@video125.co.uk
W: www.video125.co.uk

VINCI Construction UK Ltd
See Taylor Woodrow

Vintage Trains Ltd
670 Warwick Rd, Tyseley, Birmingham, B11 2HL
T: 0121 708 4960
F: 0121 708 4963
E: vintagetrains@btconnect.com
W: www.vintagetrains.co.uk

Viper Innovations
Unit 3A, Marine View Office Park, 45 Martingale Way, Portishead, Bristol, BS20 7AW
T: 01275 787878
E: enquiries@viperinnovations.com
W: www.viperinnovations.com/

VIP-Polymers
15 Windover Road/, Huntingdon, Cambridgeshire, PE29 7EB
T: 01480 411333
F: 01480 413991
W: www.vip-polymers.com/

Vision Infrastructure Services Ltd
Unit 7, Durham Lane, West Moor Park, Doncaster, DN3 3FE
T: 01302 831730
F: 01302 832671
E: ian@visioninfrastructureservices.com
W: www.visioninfrastructureservices.com

Vistorm Ltd
See HP Information Security

Visual Security Services
1st Floor, Digital House, Stourport Road, Kidderminster, Worcestershire, DY11 7QH
T: 01562 747241
E: enquiries@visualsecurityltd.co.uk
W: www.visualsecurityltd.co.uk/

Visul Systems
Kingston House, 3 Walton Rd, Pattinson North, Washington, Tyne & Wear, NE38 8QA
T: 0191 402 1960
F: 0191 402 1906
E: info@visulsystems.com
W: www.visulsystems.com

Vita Safety Ltd
1 Gillingham Rd, Eccles, Manchester, M30 8NA
T: 0161 789 1400
F: 0161 280 2528
E: ian.hutchings@vitasafety.com
W: www.vitasafety.com

Vital Rail
The Mill, South Hall St, Salford, M5 4TP
T: 0161 836 7000
F: 0161 836 7001
E: info@vital.uk.com
W: www.vital-rail.com

Industry Leading Rail Consultancy

- Making the complex simple
- Industry Strategy
- Brand, Revenue and Market Development
- Operating Excellence
- Engineering Improvement
- Timetable and Resourcing Planning
- Digital Railway and Technology Deployment

t. 07802 549727
enquiries@varail.co.uk
varail.co.uk

VA RAIL

Vitec
3 Cae Gwrydd, Greenmeadow Springs Bus. Park, Cardiff, CF15 7AB
T: 02920 620232
F: 02920 624837
E: cardiff@vitecconsult.com
W: www.vitecwebberlenihan.com

Vitra Ltd
30 Clerkenwell Road, London, EC1M 5PG
T: 020 7608 6200
F: 020 7608 6201
W: www.vitra.com/en-gb/

Vivarail Ltd
Kineton Road Industrial Estate, Westfield Road, Southam, Warks, CV47 0JH
T: 01789 532230
E: info@vivarail.co.uk
W: www.vivarail.co.uk/

Vix Technology
406 Cambridge Science Park, Cambridge, CB4 0WW
T: 01223 728700
E: uk.marketing@vixtechnology.com
W: www.vixtechnology.com/

Viztek Ltd
North East Business & Innovation Centre, Wearfield, Enterprise Park East, Sunderland, SR5 2TA
T: 0191 516 6606
E: info@viztekltd.co.uk
W: www.viztekltd.co.uk

VMS
See Variable Message Signs Ltd (VMS)

Voestalpine UK Ltd
Voestalpine House, Albion Place, Hammersmith, London, W6 0QT
T: 020 8600 5800
E: catherine.crisp@voestalpine.com
W: www.voestalpine.com

Vogelsang Ltd
Crewe Gates Ind. Est, Crewe, Cheshire, CW1 6YY
T: 01270 216600
F: 01270 216699
E: sales@vogelsang.co.uk
W: www.vogelsang.co.uk

Voith Turbo Ltd
Unit 49, Metropolitan Park, Bristol Road, Greenford, Middlesex, UB6 8UP
T: 0208 667 0333
F: 020 8569 1726
E: VTGBRailSales@voith.com
W: www.voith.com

VolkerFitzpatrick Ltd
Hertford Rd, Hoddesdon, Herts, EN11 9BX
T: 01992 305000
F: 01992 305001
E: enquiries@volkerfitzpatrick.co.uk
W: www.volkerfitzpatrick.co.uk

VolkerRail
Units 4 & 6, Carr Hill Road, Doncaster, South Yorks, DN4 8DE
T: 01302 791100
F: 01302 791200
E: marketing@volkerrail.co.uk
W: www.volkerrail.co.uk

IN ASSOCIATION WITH Nomad Digital

vossloh

VOSSLOH COGIFER UK Limited

Manufacturers of all types of Switch and Crossing Systems and ancillary components for the **Heavy Rail, High Speed** and **Light Rail markets.**

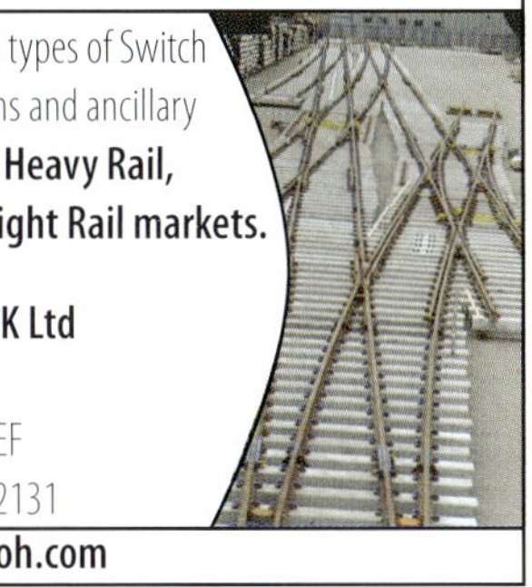

Vossloh Cogifer UK Ltd
80A Scotter Road,
Scunthorpe DN15 8EF
Tel: +44 0 1724 862131
Web: www.vossloh.com

Volo TV & Media Ltd
Departure Side Offices, Platform 1, Paddington Station, Pread St, London, W2 1FT
T: 020 7706 4775
F: 020 7402 2498
E: findoutmore@volo.tv
W: www.volo.tv

Vortex Exhaust Technology
53 Tower Road, Globe Industrial Estate, Grays, Essex, RM17 6ST
T: 01375 372037
E: enq@vortexexhausttechnology.com
W: www.vortexexhausttechnology.com/

Vortok International
Innovation House, 3 Western Wood Way, Langage Science Park, Plymouth, Devon, PL7 5BG
T: 01752 349200
F: 01752 338855
E: gfermie@vortok.co.uk
W: www.vortok.co.uk

Vossloh AG
Vosslohstrasse 4, 58791 Werdohl, Germany
T: 0049 2392 520
F: 0049 2392 520
W: www.vossloh.com

Vossloh Cogifer UK Ltd
80a Scotter Rd, Scunthorpe, North Lincs, DN15 8EF
T: 01724 862131
F: 01724 295243
E: info@vfs.vossloh.com
W: www.vossloh.com

Vossloh Fastening Systems GmbH
Vosslohstrasse 4, D-58791 Werdohl, Germany
T: 0049 2392 52 0
F: 0049 2392 52 375
E: info@vfs.vossloh.com
W: www.vossloh.com

Voyager Leasing (a subsidiary of the Royal Bank Of Scotland)

Vp Group plc
Central House, Beckwith Knowle, Otley Road, Harrogate, North Yorkshire, HG3 1UD
T: 01423 533400
F: 01423 565657
W: www.vpplc.com

VTG Rail UK Ltd
Sir Stanley Clarke House, 7 Ridgeway, Quinton Business Park, Birmingham, B32 1AF
T: 0121 421 9180
F: 0121 421 9192
E: sales@vtg.com
W: www.vtg-rail.co.uk

VTS Track Technology Ltd
See Vossloh Cogifer UK Ltd

Vulcanite UK and Europe
PO Box 456, Newcastle, NE3 9DR
T: 0191 490 6203
M: 07554 447099
E: stuart.ramsay@contitech.uk
W: www.vulcanite.com

Vulcascot Cable Protectors Ltd
Unit 12, Norman-D-Gate, Bedford Rd, Northampton, NN1 5NT
T: 0800 035 2842
F: 01604 632344
E: sales@vulcascot cableprotectors.co.uk
W: www.vulcascotcableprotectors.com

W A Developments Ltd
See Stobart Rail

Wabtec Rail Ltd
PO Box 400, Doncaster Works, Hexthorpe Rd, Doncaster, DN1 1SL
T: 01302 340700
F: 01302 790058
E: wabtecrail@wabtec.com
W: www.wabtecgroup.com

Wabtec Rail Scotland
Caledonia Works, West Langlands Street, Kilmarnock, Ayrshire, KA1 2QD
T: 01563 523573
F: 01563 541076
W: www.wabtecgroup.com

Voith Turbo Limited
Rail Division
Unit 49 Metropolitan Park,
Bristol Road, Greenford,
Middlesex. UB6 8UP
United Kingdom
Tel: +44 20 8667 0333
Email: VTGBRailSales@voith.com

VOITH
Inspiring Technology for Generations

Wacker Neuson (GB) Ltd
Lea Rd, Waltham Cross, Herts, EN9 1AW
T: 01992 707228
F: 01992 707201
E: chris.pearce@eu.wackergroup.com
W: www.wackerneuson.com

WAGO Ltd
Triton Park, Swift Valley Industrial Estate, Rugby, CV21 1SG
T: 01788 568008
E: ukmarketing@wago.com
W: www.wago.com

Wagony Swidnica S.A.
UL. Strzelinska 35, 58-100 Swidnica, Poland
T: 0048 74 856 2000
F: 0048 853 0323
E: secretariat@gbrx.com
W: www.gbrx.com

A N Wallis & Co Ltd
Greasley St, Bulwell, Nottingham, NG6 8NG
T: 0115 927 1721
F: 0115 875 6630
E: mark.rimmington@an-wallis.com
W: www.an-wallis.com

Warwick Manufacturing Group (WMG)
International Manufacturing Centre, University of Warwick, Coventry, CV4 7AL
T: 024 7652 4871
E: wmg@warwick.ac.uk
W: https://warwick.ac.uk/fac/sci/wmg

Washroom Washroom
Units 1-10, Hill Farm, Epping Lane, Abridge, Essex, RM4 1TU
T: 0845 470 3000
F: 0845 470 3001
E: contact@washroom.co.uk
W: www.washroom.co.uk

Washtec UK Ltd
Unit 14A, Oak ind. Park, Great Dunmow, Essex, CM9 1XN
T: 01371 878800
F: 01371 878810
W: www.washtec-uk.com

Waterflow
See UKDN Waterflow

Waterman Infrastructure & Environment Ltd
Pickfords Wharf, Clink St, London, SE1 9DG
T: 020 7928 7888
F: 020 7902 0992
M: 07880 554632
E: paul.worrall@watermangroup.com
W: www.watermangroup.com/

Wath Group
Pump House, Station Road, Wath Upon Dearne, Rotherham, South Yorkshire, S63 7DQ
T: 01709 876900
F: 01709 878863
E: info@wath.co.uk

Waverley Rail Project
See Borders Railway Project

Wavesight Ltd
Unit 13, Dencora Way, Sundon Business Park, Luton, Beds, LU3 3HP
T: 01582 578160
F: 01582 578298
E: sales@wavesight.com
W: www.wavesight.com

WDS Component Parts Ltd
Richardshaw Road, Grangefield Industrial Estate, Pudsey, Leeds, LS28 6LE
T: 0113 290 9852
E: sales@wdsltd.co.uk
W: www.wdsltd.co.uk

Webasto AG
Kraillinger Strasse 5, 82131 Stockdorf, Germany
T: 0049 89 857 948 444
F: 0049 89 899 217 433
E: tac3@webasto.com
W: www.rail.webasto.com

Webro Cable & Connectors Ltd
Vision House, Meadow Brooks Business Park, Meadow Lane, Long Eaton, Nottingham, NG10 2GD
T: 0115 972 4483
F: 0115 946 1230
E: info@webro.com
W: www.webro.com

WEC Group Ltd
Spring Vale House, Spring Vale Rd, Darwen, Lancs, BB3 2ES
T: 01254 773718
F: 01254 771109
E: stevecooke@wecl.co.uk
W: www.welding-eng.com

Weedfree
Holly Tree Farm, Park Lane, Balne, Goole, DN14 0EP
T: 01405 860022
F: 01405 862283
E: sales@weedfree.net
W: www.weedfree.net

Weidmuller Ltd
Klippon House, Centurion Court Office Park, Meridian East, Meridian Business Park, Leicester, LE19 1TP
T: 0116 282 1261
F: 0116 289 3582
E: marketing@weidmuller.co.uk
W: www.weidmuller.co.uk

Weightmans
High Holborn House, 52-54 High Holborn, London, WC1V 6RL
T: 020 7822 1900
F: 020 7822 1901
E: sarah.seddon@weightmans.com
W: www.weightmans.com

Weighwell Engineering Ltd
Weighwell House, Woolley Colliery Road, Darton, Barnsley, South Yorkshire, S75 5JA
T: 0114 269 9955
F: 0114 269 9256
E: sales@weighwell.com
W: www.weighwell.com

Wabtec Faiveley UK

Through the combined resources of Wabtec and Faiveley Transport...

...our organisation is one of the world's largest public rail equipment companies, with a presence in all key freight rail and passenger transit geographies worldwide.

www.wabtec.com

Weir Waste Services Ltd
Fawdry House, 50 Cato Street, Waterlinks, Birmingham, B7 4TS
T: 0121 772 6726
F: 0121 773 1244
E: sales@weirwaste.co.uk
W: www.weirwaste.co.uk/

Weld-A-Rail Ltd
Lockwood Close, Top Valley, Nottingham, NG5 9JN
T: 0115 926 8797
F: 0115 926 4818
E: admin@weldarail.co.uk
W: www.weldarail.co.uk

The Welding Institute
See Institute of Rail Welding

Welfare Cabins UK (WCUK)
See Garic Ltd

A J Wells & Sons Vitreous Enamellers
Bishop's Way, Newport, IOW, PO30 5WS
T: 01983 537766
F: 01983 537788
E: enamel@ajwells.co.uk
W: www.ajwells.com

Wentworth House Rail Systems Ltd
Vale House, Aston Lane North, Preston Brook, Cheshire, WA7 3PE
T: 01270 448405
E: enquiries@railelectrification.com
W: www.railelectrification.com

Werther International SpA
Via F Brunelleschi 12F, 42124-Cadè (RE), Italy
T: 39 0522 9431
E: sales@wertherint.com
W: www.wertherint.com

West Coast Railway Co.
Jesson Way, Carnforth, Lancs, LA5 9UR
T: 01524 732100
F: 01524 735518
E: info@wcrc.co.uk
W: www.wcrc.co.uk

West Midlands Metro
Travel Midland Metro, Metro Centre, Potters Lane, Wednesbury, West Midlands, WS10 0AR
T: 0121 502 2006
F: 0121 556 6299
W: https://westmidlandsmetro.com/

West Midlands PTE
See Transport for West Midlands (TfWM)

West Midlands Rail Executive (WMRE)
16 Summer Lane, Birmingham, B19 3SD
T: 0121 214 7423
E: contact@westmidlandsrail.com
W: www.westmidlandsrail.com/

West Midlands Trains
2nd Floor, 134 Edmund Street, Birmingham, B3 2ES
T: 0121 634 2040
F: 0121 654 1234
W: https://www.wmtrains.co.uk/

West of England Combined Authority (WECA)
3 Rivergate, Temple Way, Bristol, BS1 6ER
T: 0117 428 6210
E: info@westofengland-ca.gov.uk
W: www.westofengland-ca.org.uk/

West Yorkshire Combined Authority
Wellington House, 40-50 Wellington St, Leeds, LS1 2DE
T: 0113 251 7272
E: metroline@westyorks-ca.gov.uk
W: www.westyorks-ca.gov.uk/

Westcode Semiconductors
Langley Park Way, Langley Park, Chippenham, Wilts, SN15 1GE
T: 01249 444524
F: 01249 659448
E: customerservices@westcode.com
W: www.westcode.com

Westcode UK
Porte Marsh Industrial Estate, Carnegie Road, Calne, SN11 9PS
T: 01249 822283
E: enquiries@westcodeuk.com
W: westcodeuk.com

Westermo Data Communications Ltd
Talisman Business Centre, Duncan Rd, Park Gate, Southampton, SO31 7GA
T: 01489 580585
F: 01489 580586
E: sales@westermo.co.uk
W: www.westermo.com

Western Rail Services
Unit 5H, Cricket Street, Wigan, Lancs, WN6 7TP
T: 01942 245599
F: 01942 825544
E: info@railcable.co.uk
W: www.railcable.co.uk

Westinghouse Platform Screen Doors
Knorr-Bremse Rail Systems (UK) Ltd, Westinghouse Way, Hampton Park East, Melksham, Wilts, SN12 6TL
T: 01225 898700
F: 01225 898705
E: wpsd.enquiries@knorr-bremse.com
W: www.platformscreendoors.com

Westinghouse Rail Systems
See Siemens Rail Automation

Westley Engineering Ltd
120 Pritchett St, Aston, Birmingham, B6 4EH
T: 0121 333 1925
F: 0121 333 1926
E: g.dunne@westleyengineering.co.uk
W: www.westleyengineering.co.uk

Weston Williamson
12 Valentine Place, London, SE1 8QH
T: 020 7401 8877
F: 020 7401 8349
E: team@westonwilliamson.com
W: www.westonwilliamson.com

Westquay Trading Co. Ltd
3F Lyncastle Way, Appleton Thorn, Warrington, WA4 4ST
T: 01925 265333
F: 01925 211700
E: enquiries@westquaytrading.co.uk
W: www.westquaytrading.co.uk

Westshield Ltd
Ashcroft House, Bredbury Park Way, Bredbury, Stockport, Cheshire, SK6 2SN
T: 0161 682 6222
F: 0161 682 6333
E: info@westshield.co.uk
W: www.westshield.co.uk

Wettons
Wetton House, 278-280 St James's Rd, London, SE1 5JX
T: 020 7237 2007
F: 020 7252 3277
E: mark.hammerton@wettons.co.uk
W: www.wettons.co.uk

WG Specialist Coatings
Foston Depot, Woodyard Lane, Foston, Derbyshire, DE65 5PY
T: 01283 584806
F: 01283 584805
E: simon.starmer@wgtanker.com
W: www.wgtanker.com/

WH Davis Ltd
Langwith Rd, Langwith Junction, Mansfield, Notts, NG20 9SA
T: 01623 741600
F: 01623 744474
W: www.whdavis.co.uk

Wheelsets (UK) Ltd
Unit 4B, Denby Way, Hellaby Industrial Estate, Rotherham, S66 8NZ
T: 01302 322266
F: 01302 322299
E: martin@wheelsets.co.uk
W: www.wheelsets.co.uk

White & Case LLP
5 Old Broad St, London, EC2N 1DW
T: 020 7532 1000
F: 020 7532 1001
E: cmillersmith@whitecase.com
W: www.whitecase.com

DIRECTORY

White Young Green
See Amey

Whiteley Electronics Ltd
See Gemma Lighting

Whitmore Rail
Whitmore Europe, City Park, Watchmead, Welwyn Garden City, Herts, AL7 1LT
T: 01707 379870
E: info-uk@whitmores.com
W: www.whitmores.com

Whoosh Media
Spoken Ink Ltd, Suite 40-41, The Hop Exchange, 24 Southwark Street, London, SE1 1TY
T: 020 7403 6763
E: info@whooshmedia.co.uk
W: www.whooshmedia.co.uk

Wicek Sosna Architects
Unit 15, 21 Plumbers Row, London, E1 1EQ
T: 020 7655 4430
E: office@sosnaarchitects.co.uk
W: www.sosnaarchitects.co.uk

WiFi Spark
5 Cranmere Court, Lustleigh Close, Matford
Business Park, Exeter, EX2 8PW
T: 0344 848 9555
E: info@wifispark.com
W: www.wifispark.com/

Wilcomatic Ltd
Unit 5, Commerce Park, 19 Commerce Way, Croydon, CR0 4YL
T: 020 8649 5760
F: 020 8680 9791
E: sales@wilcomatic.co.uk
W: www.wilcomatic.co.uk

Wilkinson Star Ltd
Shield Drive, Wardsley Ind Est, Manchester, M28 2WD
T: 0161 793 8127
F: 0161 727 8538
E: steve.ross@wilkinsonstar.com
W: www.wilkinsonstar.com

WilkinsonEyre
33 Bowling Green Lane, London, EC1R 0BJ
T: 020 7608 7900
F: 020 7608 7901
E: info@wilkinsoneyre.com
W: www.wilkinsoneyre.com/

WillB Brand Consultants
Somerset House, The Strand, London, WC2R 1LA
W: www.willbaxter.com

William Bain Fencing Ltd
Lochin Works, 7 Limekilns Rd, Blairlin Ind. Est, Cumbernauld, G67 2RN
T: 01236 457333
F: 01236 451166
E: sales@lochrin-bain.co.uk
W: www.lochrin-bain.co.uk/

William Cook Rail
Cross Green, Leeds, LS9 0SG
T: 0113 249 6363
F: 0113 249 1376
E: castproducts@william-cook.co.uk
W: www.william-cook.co.uk

Williamette Valley Company – WVCO Railroad Division
1075 Arrowsmith St, Eugene, OR 97402, United States
T: 001 541 484 9621
F: 001 541 284 2096
E: sales@wilvaco.co.uk
W: www.wvcorailroad.com

Willie Baker Leadership & Development Ltd
Aggborough Farm, College Rd, Kidderminster, Worcs, DY10 1LU
E: willie@williebaker.co.uk
W: www.williebaker.co.uk

Wilmat Ltd
Wilmat House, 43 Steward Street, Birmingham, B18 7AE
T: 0121 454 7514
F: 0121 456 1792
E: sales@wilmat-handling.co.uk
W: www.wilmat-handling.co.uk/

Winckworth Sherwood
Minerva House, 5 Montague Close, London, SE1 9BB
T: 020 7593 5000
F: 0207 593 5099
E: info@wslaw.co.uk
W: www.wslaw.co.uk

Wind River UK Ltd
Oakwood House, Grove Business Park, White Waltham, Maidenhead, Berks, SL6 3HY
T: 01793 831831
F: 01793 831808
E: sue.woolley@windriver.com
W: www.windriver.com

Windhoff Bahn und Anlagentechnik GmbH
Hovestrasse 10, D-48431 Rheine, Germany
T: 0049 5971 580
F: 0049 5971 58209
E: info@windhoff.de
W: www.windhoff.de

Windsor Link Railway
Suite 1, Unit A1, Tectonic Place, Holyport Road, Maidenhead, Berkshire, SL6 2YE
W: www.windsorlink.co.uk/

Winn & Coales (Denso) Ltd
Denso House, Chapel Rd, London, SE27 0TR
T: 020 8670 7511
F: 020 8761 2456
E: mail@denso.net
W: www.denso.net

Winstanley & Co Ltd
See Transcal Ltd

Winsted Ltd
Units 7/8, Lovett Rd, Hampton Lovett Ind Est, Droitwich, Worcs, WR9 0QG
T: 01905 770276
F: 01905 779791
E: info@winsted.co.uk
W: www.winsted.com

Wintersgill
110 Bolsover St, London, W1W 5NU
T: 020 7580 4499
F: 020 7436 8191
E: info@wintersgill.net
W: www.wintersgill.net

Wireless CCTV Ltd
Mitchell Hey Place, College Road, Rochdale, Lancs, OL12 6AE
T: 01706 631166
E: sales@wcctv.com
W: www.wcctv.com

Witt O'Brien's Ltd
Trent House, RTC Business Park, London Rd, Derby, DE24 8UP
T: 01332 222299
F: 01332 222298
E: info@wittobriens.com
W: www.wittobriens.co.uk

WM Plant Hire Ltd
Manor Farm Lane, Bridgnorth, Shropshire, WV16 5HG
T: 01452 722200
F: 01452 769666
E: info@wmplanthire.com
W: www.wmplanthire.com

WMG Centre HVM Catapult
International Digital Laboratory, The University of Warwick, Coventry, Warks, CV4 7AL
T: 02476 572696
E: wmghvmcatapult@warwick.ac.uk
W: www.wmghvmcatapult.org.uk

Woking Homes
Oriental Rd, Woking, Surrey, GU22 7BE
T: 01483 763558
F: 01483 721048
E: administration@woking-homes.co.uk
W: www.woking-homes.co.uk

Wolfin
Icopal UK, Barton Dock Road, Stretford, Manchester, M32 0YL
T: 0843 224 9690
F: 0843 224 7401
E: sales@wolfin.co.uk
W: www.wolfin.co.uk/

Woma (UK) Ltd
Davenport House, Davenport Gate, Macadam Way, West Portway Industrial Estate, Andover, SP10 3SQ
T: 01264 369828
E: sales@woma.uk.com
W: www.woma.uk.com/

Women in Rail
123 Victoria Street, London, SW1E 6DE
T: 020 7592 0796
E: womeninrail@angeltrains.co.uk
W: www.womeninrail.org

Wood & Douglas Ltd
Lattice House, Baughurst, Tadley, Hants, RG26 5LP
T: 0118 981 1444
F: 0118 981 1567
E: sales@woodanddouglas.co.uk
W: www.woodanddouglas.co.uk

Wood & Wood Signs
Heron Rd, Sowton Estate, Exeter, EX2 7LX
T: 01392 444501
F: 01392 252358
E: info@wwsigns.co.uk
W: www.wwsigns.co.uk

Woodward Diesel Systems
Lancaster Centre, Meteor Business Park, Cheltenham Rd East, Gloucester, GL2 9QL
T: 01452 859940
F: 01452 855758
E: corpinfo@woodward.com
W: www.woodward.com

Workmates Daniel Owen
1st Floor, Genesis House, 17 Godliman St, London, EC4V 5BD
T: 0207 539 1660
W: www.mdo.co.uk/sectors/rail

Workthing
Beaumont House, Kensington Village, Avonmore Rd, London, W14 8TS
T: 0870 898 0022
F: 0870 898 0033
E: info@workthing.com
W: www.workthing.com

Worldline
Triton Square, Regents Place, London, NW1 3HG
T: 020 7830 4447
F: 020 7830 4445
W: www.uk.worldline.com/

Worlifts Rail Division
Guild House, Sandy Lane, Wildmoor, Bromsgrove, Worcs, B61 0QU
T: 0121 460 1113
F: 0121 460 1116
E: rail@worlifts.co.uk
W: www.worlifts.co.uk

WPB Contractors
Unit 1, Heron Business Centre, Henwood, Ashford, Kent, TN24 8DH
T: 01233 664335
E: info@wpbcontractors.co.uk
W: https://www.wpbcontractors.co.uk/

Wrekin Circuits Ltd
29/30 Hortonwood 33, Telford, Shropshire, TF1 7EX
T: 01952 670011
F: 01952 606565
E: sales@wrekin-circuits.co.uk
W: www.wrekin-circuits.co.uk

WRS Cable Ltd
MGB House, Langage Business Park, Plympton, Plymouth, Devon, PL7 5JY
W: www.wrscables.com

The WS Group (Tracksure)
8 Woburn St, Ampthill, Beds, MK45 2HP
T: 01525 840557
F: 01525 403918
E: sales@tracksure.co.uk
W: www.tracksure.co.uk

WSP UK
Mountbatten House, Basing View, Basingstoke, Hants, RG21 4HJ
T: 01256 318802
F: 01256 318700
W: www.wspgroup.com

WVCO Railroad Division of The Williamette Valley Company
1075 Arrowsmith St, PO Box 2280, Eugene, OR 97402, United States
T: 001 541 484 9621
F: 001 541 284 2096
E: sales@wvcorailroad.com
W: www.wvcorailroad.com

WWP Consultants
5-15 Cromer St, London, WC1H 8LS
T: 020 7833 5767
F: 020 7833 5766
W: www.wwp.co.uk

Wynnwith Rail
Wynnwith House, Church St, Woking, Surrey, GU21 6DJ
T: 01483 748206
E: rail@wynnwith.com
W: www.wynnwith.com

Wyse Rail Ltd
Lincoln Road, Cressex Business Park, High Wycombe, Bucks, HP12 3RH
T: 0808 168 1675
F: 0845 873 0965
E: info@wysegroup.co.uk
W: www.wysegroup.co.uk

WyvernRail Plc
Wirksworth Station, Station Rd, Wirksworth, Derbys, DE4 4FB
T: 01629 821828
E: wirksworth_station@wyvernrail.co.uk
W: www.mytesttrack.com

XEIAD
22 Lower Town, Sampford Peverill, Tiverton, Devon, EX16 7BT
T: 01884 822899
E: info@bridgezoneltd.co.uk
W: www.xeiad.com/

Xervon Palmers Ltd
331 Charles St, Glasgow, G21 2QA
T: 0141 553 4040
F: 0141 552 6463
E: info@xervonpalmers.com
W: www.xervonpalmers.com

XiTRACK Ltd
See Dow Hyperlast

XL Lubricants Ltd
See NTM Sales & Marketing Ltd

X-Press Spares Ltd & Co KG
Daimlerstr. 49, 48432 Rheine, Germany
T: +49 5971 - 800155-0
F: +49 5971 - 800155-9
E: info@xpress-spares.de
W: www.xpress-spares.de

XRail Group Limited
30th Floor, 40 Bank Street, Canary Wharf, London, E14 5NR
T: 020 3102 9562
E: enquiries@xrailgroup.com
W: www.xrailgroup.com/

Yardene Engineering 2000 Ltd
Daux Rd, Billingshurst, West Sussex, RH14 9SJ
T: 01403 783558
F: 01403 783104
E: sales@yardene.co.uk
W: www.yardene.co.uk

A E Yates Group
Cranfield Road, Lostock Industrial Estate, Bolton, BL6 4SB
T: 01204 696175
E: tadmin@aeyates.co.uk
W: www.aeyates.co.uk

Yellow Group Limited
Yellow House, Haydock Park Road, Derby, DE24 8HT
T: 01332 470214
F: 01332 258823
E: enquiries@yellow-group.com
W: www.yellow-group.com

Yeltech Ltd
Upper Unstead Farm Cottage, Unstead Lane, Bramley, Guildford, GU5 0BT
T: 0845 052 3860
E: sales@yeltech.co.uk
W: www.yeltech.co.uk

YJL Infrastructure Ltd
39 Cornhill, London, EC3V 3ND
T: 020 7522 3220
F: 020 7522 3261
W: www.yjli.co.uk

Young Rail Professionals (YRP)
E: info@youngrailpro.com
W: www.youngrailpro.com

Zarges (UK) Ltd
Holdom Ave, Saxon Park Ind. Est, Bletchley, Milton Keynes, MK1 1QU
T: 01908 641118
F: 01908 648176
E: sales@zargesuk.co.uk
W: www.zargesuk.co.uk

Zebraware
Chadwick House, Birchwood Park, Cheshire, WA3 6AE
T: 01925 500150
E: contact@zebraware.com
W: zebraware.com

ZEDAS GMBH
A-Hennecke-Strasse 37, D-01968 Senftenberg, Germany
T: 0049 3573 7075 0
E: info@zedas.com
W: www.zedas.com

Zep UK
PO Box 2, Tanhouse Lane, Widnes, Cheshire, WA8 0RD
T: 0151 422 1000
F: 0151 422 1011
E: info@zep.co.uk
W: www.zep.co.uk

Zephir SpA
Via Salvador Allende N.85, I-41122 Modena, Italy
T: 39 059 25 25 54
E: zephir@zephir.eu
W: www.zephir.eu

Zeta Specialist Lighting Ltd
Telford Road, Bicester, OX26 4LB
T: 01869 322500
E: info@thezetagroup.com
W: zetaled.co.uk/

Zetica
Units 15/16, Hanborough Business Park, Long Hanborough, Oxon, OX29 8LH
T: 01993 886682
F: 01993 886683
E: rail@zetica.com
W: www.zeticarail.com

ZF Services UK Ltd
Abbeyfield Rd, Lenton, Nottingham, NG7 2SX
T: 0333 240 1123
F: 0844 257 0666
M: 07803 626420
E: gavin.donoghue@zf.com
W: www.aftermarketzf.com

ZF UK Laser Ltd
9 Avacado Court, Commerce Way, Trafford Park, Manchester, M17 1HW
T: 0161 871 7050
F: 0161 312 5063
E: info@zf-uk.com
W: www.zf-uk.com

Zigma Ground Solutions
Unit 11, M11 Business Link, Parsonage Lane, Stansted, Essex, CM24 8TY
T: 0845 643734
E: amandacc@zigmagroundsolutions.com
W: www.zigmagroundsolutions.com

Zipabout
6 Worcester Street, Oxford, OX1 2BX
T: 01865 242906
E: alex.froom@zipabout.com
W: www.zipabout.com

Zircon Software Ltd
Bellefield House, Hilperton Rd, Trowbridge, Wilts, BA14 7FP
T: 01225 764444
F: 01225 753087
E: info@zirconsoftware.co.uk
W: www.zirconsoftware.co.uk

Zodiac Interconnect UK Ltd
220 Bedford Avenue, Slough, Berks, SL1 4RY
T: 01753 896600
F: 01753 896601
E: cristophebigare@zodiacaerospace.com
W: www.zodiacaerospace.com/en/zodiac-interconnect-uk

Zollner UK Ltd
Clayton Business Ctr, Midland Rd, Leeds, LS10 2RJ
T: 0113 270 3008
E: signal@zoellner.de
W: www.zoellner.de/

Zonegreen
Sir John Brown Building, Davy Ind. Park, Prince of Wales Rd, Sheffield, S9 4EX
T: 0114 230 0822
F: 0871 872 0349
E: info@zonegreen.co.uk
W: www.zonegreen.co.uk

Zoppas Industries Heating Element Technologies
Via Podgora 26, I-31029 Vittorio Veneto (TV), Italy
T: 39 0438 9101
E: rica@zoppas.com
W: www.zoppasindustries.com

Z-Tech Control Systems Ltd
Unit 4 Meridian, Buckingway Business Park, Anderson Rd, Swavesey, Cambridge, CB24 4AE
T: 01223 653500
F: 01223 653501
W: www.z-tech.co.uk/

ZTR Control Systems
8050 Country Rd, 101 East, Shakopee, Minnesota, 55379, United States
T: 001 952 233 4340
F: 001 952 233 4375
E: railinfo@ztr.com
W: www.ztr.com/rail

Zuken
1500 Aztec West, Almondsbury, Bristol, BS32 4RF
T: 01454 207800
E: sales-uk@zuken.com
W: www.zuken.com

Zwicky Track Tools
See Arbil Lifting Gear